THE OXFORD HANDBOOK OF

SYSTEMATIC THEOLOGY

THE OXFORD HANDBOOK OF

SYSTEMATIC THEOLOGY

Edited by

JOHN WEBSTER
KATHRYN TANNER
IAIN TORRANCE

OXFORD UNIVERSITY PRESS

OXFORD
UNIVERSITY PRESS

Great Clarendon Street, Oxford OX2 6DP

Oxford University Press is a department of the University of Oxford.
It furthers the University's objective of excellence in research, scholarship,
and education by publishing worldwide in

Oxford New York

Auckland Cape Town Dar es Salaam Hong Kong Karachi
Kuala Lumpur Madrid Melbourne Mexico City Nairobi
New Delhi Shanghai Taipei Toronto

With offices in

Argentina Austria Brazil Chile Czech Republic France Greece
Guatemala Hungary Italy Japan South Korea Poland Portugal
Singapore Switzerland Thailand Turkey Ukraine Vietnam

Oxford is a registered trade mark of Oxford University Press
in the UK and in certain other countries

Published in the United States
by Oxford University Press Inc., New York

Reprinted 2010

ISBN 978-0-19-956964-9

Printed in the United Kingdom by
Lightning Source UK Ltd., Milton Keynes

Contents

PART II SOURCES

PART III CONVERSATIONS

PART IV PROSPECTS

List of Contributors

William J. Abraham is Albert Cook Outler Professor of Wesley Studies and University Distinguished Teaching Professor in Perkins School of Theology at Southern Methodist University in Dallas, Texas.

Richard Bauckham is Professor Emeritus of New Testament and Bishop Wardlaw Professor Emeritus at the University of St Andrews.

Ellen T. Charry is Margaret W. Harmon Associate Professor of Systematic Theology at Princeton Theological Seminary in Princeton, New Jersey.

Francis X. Clooney, SJ is Parkman Professor of Divinity and Professor of Comparative Theology at Harvard Divinity School in Cambridge, Massachusetts.

Oliver D. Crisp is Reader in Theology at the University of Bristol.

Oliver Davies is Professor of Christian Doctrine at King's College London.

Ralph Del Colle is Associate Professor of Theology at Marquette University in Milwaukee, Wisconsin.

Dawn DeVries is John Newton Thomas Professor of Systematic Theology at Union Theological Seminary and Presbyterian School of Christian Education in Richmond, Virginia.

William A. Dyrness is Professor of Theology and Culture at Fuller Theological Seminary in Pasadena, California.

Michael A. Fahey, SJ is Professor Emeritus of Catholic Theology at Marquette University and Adjunct Professor of Theology at Boston College in Chestnut Hill, Massachusetts.

Douglas Farrow is Associate Professor of Christian Thought at McGill University in Montreal.

David Fergusson is Professor of Divinity and Principal of New College, University of Edinburgh.

Paul S. Fiddes is Professor of Systematic Theology, University of Oxford and Professorial Research Fellow, Regent's Park College, Oxford.

Stephen E. Fowl is Professor of Theology and Chair of the Theology Department at Loyola College in Maryland.

Gordon Graham is Henry Luce III Professor of Philosophy and the Arts at Princeton Theological Seminary in Princeton, New Jersey.

Richard B. Hays is George Washington Ivey Professor of New Testament at Duke University Divinity School in Durham, North Carolina.

Stephen R. Holmes is Senior Lecturer in Theology at St Mary's College, University of St Andrews.

Reinhard Hütter is Professor of Christian Theology at Duke University Divinity School in Durham, North Carolina.

David H. Kelsey is Luther A. Weigle Professor Emeritus of Theology at Yale Divinity School in New Haven, Connecticut.

Duane Stephen Long is Professor of Systematic Theology Marquette University.

Walter Lowe is Professor Emeritus of Systematic Theology at Candler School of Theology, Emory University in Atlanta, Georgia.

Rebecca Lyman is Samuel M. Garrett Professor of Church History at Church Divinity School of the Pacific in Berkeley, California.

Joy Ann McDougall is Associate Professor of Systematic Theology at Candler School of Theology, Emory University in Atlanta, Georgia.

Ian McFarland is Associate Professor of Systematic Theology at Candler School of Theology, Emory University in Atlanta, Georgia.

Ian S. Markham is Dean and President of Virginia Theological Seminary.

Andrew Moore, University of Oxford.

Nancey Murphy is Professor of Christian Philosophy at Fuller Theological Seminary in Pasadena, California.

Ben Quash is Professor of Christianity and the Arts, King's College, London.

C. Kavin Rowe is Assistant Professor of New Testament at Duke University Divinity School in Durham, North Carolina.

Christopher Rowland is Dean Ireland's Professor of the Exegesis of Holy Scripture, University of Oxford.

Fred Sanders is Associate Professor of Theology in the Torrey Honors Institute at Biola University in La Mirada, California.

Katherine Sonderegger is Professor of Systematic Theology at Virginia Theological Seminary in Alexandria, Virginia.

Bryan D. Spinks is Professor of Liturgical Studies at Yale Divinity School in New Haven, Connecticut.

Kathryn Tanner is Dorothy Grant Maclear Professor of Theology at the University of Chicago Divinity School.

Iain Torrance is President and Professor of Patristics at Princeton Theological Seminary in Princeton, New Jersey.

John Webster is Professor of Systematic Theology at the University of Aberdeen.

Michael Welker is Professor of Systematic Theology at Ruprecht-Karls-Universität in Heidelberg.

A. N. Williams is Lecturer in Patristic and Medieval Theology and Fellow of Corpus Christi College, Cambridge.

Charles M. Wood is Lehman Professor of Christian Doctrine and Director of the Graduate Program in Religious Studies at Perkins School of Theology, Southern Methodist University in Dallas, Texas.

Foreword

This handbook is intended as an overall account of the field of systematic theology as it is undertaken by contemporary practitioners. Though it is chiefly interested in current systematics, it is not a survey of modern theological trends; nor does it recommend a particular approach to systematic theology or a particular version of Christian doctrine. Its aim is to take stock of where the discipline lies. Each of the authors has been asked (1) to offer an analysis of the state of the question in their assigned topic; (2) to indicate important issues of contention, whether formal or material, and how they are variously resolved; (3) to make judgements about the ways in which inquiry into a particular topic might more fruitfully be pursued.

The project has been a long time in the making; the editors record their gratitude to the contributors for giving time and energy to the work, and to the staff of the Press who have demonstrated heroic patience in the face of editorial tardiness. Special thanks are also due to Rob Price, who spent many hours preparing the text for publication.

John Webster
Kathryn Tanner
Iain Torrance

INTRODUCTION: SYSTEMATIC THEOLOGY

JOHN WEBSTER

THE theological discipline to which this handbook is devoted is variously identified as Christian doctrine, dogmatics, or systematic theology. There is no firmly established usage of these terms; a preference for one or other of them is often arbitrary. Of the three, 'Christian doctrine' is the most general and descriptive, indicating that the field of inquiry is Christian teaching, but making no prescriptions about what might count as normative Christian teaching or about the form which an account of it might take. 'Dogmatics' is often, though not exclusively, used to denote the rather more determinate study and exposition of dogma, that is, of authorized church teaching; it is somewhat less current in contemporary theology, especially in English. 'Systematic theology', on the other hand, is broader in compass than dogmatics, if the latter is taken to be concerned with teaching which has acquired ecclesial definition and approval, since systematic theology occupies itself more generally with Christian claims about reality. Further, as the adjective suggests, 'systematic' theology is especially interested in the scope, unity, and coherence of Christian teaching. Finally, systematic theology is often a preferred term for those accounts of Christian teaching which are especially concerned to coordinate their subject matter with what is held to be true outside the sphere of Christian faith. However, such clarifications of the terms do not always correspond to their actual deployment by particular theologians; in any specific case, use determines meaning. The choice of 'systematic theology' for the title of this handbook simply reflects its wide contemporary currency and its inclusiveness.

The subject matter which is engaged in systematic theological inquiry is Christian teaching, that is, Christian claims about reality. Systematic theology attempts a conceptual articulation of Christian claims about God and everything else in relation to God, characterized by comprehensiveness and coherence. It seeks to present Christian teaching as a unified whole; even though particular exercises in the genre (such as the chapters of this handbook) may restrict themselves to only one or other element of Christian doctrine, they have an eye for its place in the entire corpus. The shape of a comprehensive and coherent account of Christian claims, as well as the lineaments of the particulars, depend upon judgements reached about the sources, norms, and ends of systematic theology, and about its relation to other spheres of intellectual activity. With respect to *sources*, practitioners of systematic theological work make judgements about where to look for instantiations of or raw material for Christian teaching. Such instantiations would include texts judged to be of enduring substance and authority (scripture, the ecumenical creeds, confessional documents); the theological, liturgical, and spiritual traditions of Christian self-articulation; the practices of whatever are taken to be normative strands of the church; or Christian religious experience. Judgements about sources, however, go hand-in-hand with acceptance of *norms*, that is, criteria by which decisions may be reached about which sources furnish the most authentic, reliable, and persuasive Christian teaching (a norm is a source to which preponderant authority is accorded). Judgements about sources and norms are, in turn, bound up with judgements about the proper *end* of a systematic account of Christian teaching, that is, about the aims and audiences of the undertaking. Is systematic theological work primarily directed internally, to order ecclesial disarray, to reinforce or repudiate some aspect of Christian self-expression, whether theoretical or practical, to promote reappraisal and revision of existing patterns of belief? Or is it primarily directed externally, as defensive, apologetic, or missionary self-explication *contra Gentiles*, seeking to chasten or perhaps entice the cultured despisers of Christian teaching? Judgements about the end or orientation of systematic theology involve decisions about its relation to the work of reason in other fields, especially those which enjoy intellectual prestige or which are considered to be contiguous with Christian theology, such as philosophy or history. Finally, all of these judgements are shaped by, and often shape, a construal of the material content of Christian teaching.

Because the work of systematic theology requires these various discriminations, it is—like any other sphere of intellectual inquiry possessed of historical duration and material depth—characterized by a measure of internal contestation. The contests are generally of two kinds: material, that is, contests about the content of Christian claims to reality which are the matter upon which systematic theology goes to work; and formal, that is, contests about the task, modes, and structure of systematic theology. Our concern in this chapter is with the formal elements of the discipline, leaving later chapters to treat material matters—bearing in mind, however, that separating out material and formal scarcely does justice to their coinherence in what are commonly taken to be the most commanding representative works of systematic theology. Before entering the discussion, however, a skeletal account of the genesis and development of the discipline will help place in context contemporary contests about its nature and tasks.

I. History

Conceptual reconstruction of Christian teaching is a post-apostolic enterprise. The texts of the apostolic period which established themselves as the New Testament canon are not concerned for systematic order or conceptual regularity. Some New Testament materials, notably the Pauline corpus, the Fourth Gospel, and the Letter to the Hebrews, deploy elaborate patterns of conceptual argument in the course of articulating the Christian gospel and its requirements, but even these writings are occasional, serving didactic, paraenetic, or polemical purposes and lacking significant interest in speculative entailments (such as the reconstruction of the doctrine of God required by the confession of a triune pattern in God's saving operations). They do not attempt a comprehensive presentation of Christian teaching, and their unity is that given by common attention to saving events rather than unity at a formal, conceptual level.

Early Christian literature from the period after the apostles does not recognize the distinctions between exegetical, doctrinal, moral, and practical-pastoral theology familiar in modern divisions of theological labour, and to a casual glance the texts of this period in which Christian teaching is expounded present themselves as unschematic and at times random. The impression indicates not so much a lack of intellectual rigour on the part of the authors of these texts as a conception of the nature and genres of Christian doctrine which differs substantially from those which emerged much later in the history of theology. Early post-apostolic explications of doctrine, undertaken primarily for the purposes of edification or combating heresy, generally adopt some variant of the commentarial or expository genre, though not without a measure of thematic organization (even here, however, the exegetical element bears the load, as in Irenaeus' *Against Heresies*). Similarly, Clement of Alexandria's construal of the Christian faith in his *Miscellanies* in terms of the pedagogical work of the divine Logos yields only a very loosely structured set of reflections (Clement himself calls his work 'promiscuously variegated' (*Miscellanies* 6.1, in Roberts and Donaldson 1990: ii. 480)). A firmer thematic ordering emerges in Origen's *On First Principles*, which follows a sequence of God, the world, freedom, and scripture, with other topics such as the soul, angels, incarnation, and eschatology (sometimes awkwardly) inserted. Origen's ordering of the material of Christian teaching was adapted and supplemented in, for example, John of Damascus' *On the Orthodox Faith*, in which topical treatments are fitted into a sequence roughly following the order of God's acts in the economy: creation, redemption, and perfection. For other patristic writers such as Augustine (both in *On Faith and the Creed* and in the *Enchiridion*), the order of the Apostles' Creed offers a basic narrative-topical order for the exposition of Christian teaching.

The more settled organization of Christian teaching into doctrinal topics owes much to Lombard's *Sentences*, which divides the material into a (to moderns) more recognizable sequence: God, creation, humankind, sin, incarnation, salvation, sacraments, eschatology. Something of the same pattern can be found in Bonaventure's *Breviloquium*. Although Aquinas's *Summa theologiae* is rhetorically and argumentatively different from earlier texts because of its use of Aristotelian methods of analysis, and shows much greater interest in the speculative entailments of Christian teaching, its fundamental structure reflects the Christian kerygma's concern for God in relation to creatures. Like the *Sentences*, the summa genre does not necessarily entail complete systematization and the hypertrophy of concepts arrived at by speculative deduction; it may, in fact, be an informal and less ambitious summarization, categorization, and extension of Christian teaching—though these limitations were not always reflected in the traditions of commentary evoked by both Lombard and Aquinas.

In many respects, the doctrinal work of the magisterial reformers recalls earlier modes of expounding Christian teaching, in that it takes the form of extensive biblical commentary or polemical and hortatory works in which doctrine is not so much a discrete interest as an ingredient of practical divinity. Even in more formal presentations of doctrine, there is little attempt at systematic completeness, and a marked hesitancy towards (which sometimes becomes a fierce repudiation of) the speculative accretions which had grown up around the *Sentences* in particular. In this connection, the strict practical minimalism of Melanchthon's *Loci communes*, which in its original 1521 edition does not address apparently speculative topics such as Trinity or incarnation, is characteristic, along with Zwingli's *True and False Religion* (though elsewhere, such as in his handling the doctrine of providence, Zwingli gives evidence of considerable speculative powers). Even in its elaborated 1559 edition, Calvin's *Institutes* is to be set in the same company; its selection of topics, its proportions, and its modes of argument and appeal are shaped not by systematic considerations but by a sense of which aspects of the biblical gospel require highest profile in meeting the demands of Christian nurture and the defence of the church.

Accounts of Christian teaching begin to assume a form more readily recognizable as systematic theology only in the post-Reformation period of doctrinal and confessional consolidation. There are a number of signs of this: increasing attention to theological foundations prior to the exposition of positive doctrine; methods of argumentation seeking to persuade by evidences and proofs, and placing high value on deduction; an ordering of the material in which the historical shape of the divine economy is sometimes eclipsed by topical division; a certain distance from practical divinity. Such moves are not unrelated to the formal separation of dogmatic theology from moral theology and *theologia historica* (that is, the exposition of the faith tied to the narrative sequence of God's dealings with creatures). Nevertheless, this formative phase of the discipline ought not to be belaboured as systematic domestication of the Reformation impulse (Muller 2000: 101–17), any more than the work of Aquinas can be reduced to a set of fine logical discriminations. Keckermann (1571?–1608), usually considered the first to use the term *theologia systematica*, is also the first great representative of the so-called 'analytical' method in which doctrinal exposition is oriented towards practical issues concerning human salvation and destiny rather than speculative questions concerning God and God's decrees.

Schleiermacher's *The Christian Faith*, which dominated Protestant doctrinal theology for a century and beyond, is in some respects a radicalization of the analytical dogmatics of the seventeenth century, transposing the economic-soteriological interest into a focus on the immanent reality of the ecclesial experience of redemption, which furnished both the material and the formal principle for his dogmatics (an obvious result of this is Schleiermacher's drastic minimalism in discussing God *in se*). Schleiermacher's prestige, combined with the rise of historical study of the genesis and growth of doctrine which emphasized the arbitrary character of much classical Christian dogma, pressed for a reconception of systematic theology as a fully historical enterprise focused on the life and activity of the Christian community as the medium of Christian teaching. Mediating theologies (of which the last and greatest representative is the system of Christian doctrine set out by Dorner), which sought a critical integration of positive doctrine with prevailing cultural norms, were largely overtaken by neo-Protestantism, whose dogmatic achievement begins with Ritschl's magisterial *Christian Doctrine of Justification and Reconciliation*. Ritschl's influence was widespread, not only in Germany but also amongst British and American doctrinal thinkers.

Much of the history of twentieth-century systematic theology was shaped by Barth's early repudiation of neo-Protestantism and his attempt to reconceive the systematic theological task. His achievement was immense, in part because he was able to transform an astonished rediscovery of divine aseity into a positive covenantal dogmatics in the analytical tradition, one possessed of seemingly limitless confidence in the interpretative power of classical trinitarian and Christological teaching. This, allied to Barth's very considerable descriptive and dramatic powers and his boldness in redrawing the overall shape of Christian doctrine, makes the *Church Dogmatics* a text with which all contemporary systematic theology must at some point enter into negotiation. Alongside Barth, the concerns of theological liberalism were continued, especially by those who drew on the resources of existential philosophy and phenomenology to interpret Christian teaching—Rahner amongst Roman Catholics, and Tillich amongst the Protestants. Both continue to exert influence, especially in North American theology, in particular by exemplifying a mode of systematic theology concerned for the coordination of Christian teaching and human self-understanding (for representative works, see Macquarrie 1977; Hodgson and King 1983; Fiorenza and Galvin 1991). Even though existentialism no longer enjoys widespread currency, the method of correlation exercises a continuing hold, especially in feminist and liberation theologies (Chopp and Taylor 1994).

Although the study of Christian doctrine continues to engender vigorous debate both in German- and English-language theology (renewed interest in the doctrine of the Trinity in the last twenty years is only the most obvious instance of the liveliness of the discussion), there have been relatively few really authoritative attempts at comprehensive accounts of the field. Beyond the textbook literature, much of the influential material has been presented as essays and monographs on particular *loci* or themes. The overall accounts which have commanded most attention are the systematic theologies of Pannenberg (1991–8) and Jenson (1997–9), both ecumenically minded Lutherans, both attracted to an ecclesiology and sacramental theology centred on divine and creaturely participation, both seeking to chart a fresh direction after Barth. Pannenberg is more cautious, offering a good deal more historical elaboration, and has a strong concern for the relation of systematic theology to non-theological fields of inquiry, most of all philosophy and the history of religion. Jenson is more radical, both materially and formally; the work's ellipses are its doctrines of the Trinity and the church, and its treatment of these themes is characterized by a high degree of conceptual inventiveness which, coupled with a certain maximalism in framing its judgements, makes it markedly innovative.

II. Task

As it has emerged over the course of its history, the task of systematic theology is the explication of Christian doctrine in its full scope and in its integrity. In much classical Christian dogmatics, as well as in some modern systematics, the scope of the discipline requires consideration of both *credenda* and *agenda*, thus prohibiting any separation of doctrine and ethics (although the distancing of morals from dogma in the modern period, entailed by the authority accorded to natural morality as prior to positive religions, makes their coinherence problematic for some practitioners of either field). Systematic theology is a 'positive' science, that is, an inquiry into an antecedent subject matter, and its work is guided by and responsible towards Christian faith and its various forms of self-expression. Very few approach the task in the purely constructive manner proposed by Kaufman (1975); most undertake their work in relation to a range of sources recognized as bearers of authority. In pre-modern Christian theology, these sources were commonly widely distributed amongst liturgical, creedal, and scriptural materials, though the supremacy of the latter was universally acknowledged. In the dogmatics stemming from the Protestant Reformation, scripture furnished the matter of doctrine, reinforced by the teaching of the early Christian centuries (for a modern example, see Torrance 1993). More recently, some have commended the language and practice of worship as a basic source for systematic work (Schlink 1967: 16–84; Pannenberg 1970: 182–210; Wainwright 1980); others emphasize the historical experience of faith as fundamental (Haight 1990). Whatever may be taken to be its sources, however, systematic theology is generally undertaken as a work of *re*construction, referring back to realities (scriptural, practical, existential) which present themselves for systematic consideration. Yet the dividing line between construction and reconstruction is not easy to discern. It is difficult to imagine a systematic account of Christian teaching which simply recorded positive data, for it would lack the abstraction and schematism necessary for a conceptual representation of the material. To make a representation of Christian teaching is to construe it, to commend a version of it which may not be made up but is certainly made. This, in turn, reinforces the need for criteria against which the adequacy of systematic construals can be assessed.

The task of systematic construction has both an internal and an external orientation. In its internal orientation—what might be called the dogmatic-analytic element of the task—systematic theology concerns itself with ordered exposition of Christian claims about reality. In its external orientation—what might be called the apologetic-hermeneutical element of the task—systematic theology concerns itself with the explication and defence of Christian claims about reality in order to bring to light their justification, relevance, and value. Different systematic theologies tend to give priority to one or other element. Barth's *Church Dogmatics* is written out of a conviction that dogmatic description is sufficient to persuade, and that independent apologetics inhibits rather than enables extramural presentation of the substance of Christian faith. Pannenberg, on the other hand, judges this procedure to be introverted, and proposes by contrast that 'systematic theology ascertains the truth of Christian doctrine by investigation and presentation of its coherence as regards both the interrelation of the parts and the relation to other knowledge' (1991–8: i. 21–2). Thus the process of systematic reconstruction in relation to whatever else is taken to be true is intrinsic to the establishment of its truth, which cannot be presupposed. From a different perspective again, the 'revisionist' tradition in North American theology, much influenced by Tillich's method of correlation between 'message' and 'situation', envisages doctrinal construction emerging from the encounter between the content of the Christian tradition and cultural-intellectual or experiential realities (e.g., Gilkey 1979).

These different orientations of systematic theology are rarely found in pure form. One of the most sophisticated recent attempts to combine them is found in the work of the Jesuit systematician Frans Jozef van Beeck. Van Beeck resists the notion that the structures of religion and the structures of culture are discrete entities to be kept mutually isolated or, perhaps, brought into conversation. Rather, they form a continuum, in relation to which the central task of systematic theology is 'the search for new forms of unity between religion and culture' (van Beeck 1989: 42). Undertaking this task involves both 'positive' theological work, presenting Christian belief in its integrity, and 'fundamental' theology, studying the human condition as it harbours the possibility of integration into God's kingdom. The skill required to achieve this combination of description and the demonstration of credibility is 'spiritual discernment', that is, a well-judged sense of the 'discretionary fit' between church and culture in a theological representation of Christianity (van Beeck 1989: 42). The project is, of course, underwritten by a Catholic vision of the realm of cultural forms as ordered towards participation in God.

Verdicts about the task of the discipline have consequences for its content and shape. A comparison of the ground plans of Macquarrie's and Jenson's respective systematics is illuminative here. Macquarrie considers systematic theology to be 'systematic in the sense that it seeks to articulate all the constituent elements of theology in a coherent whole, and that it seeks to articulate this whole itself with the other fields that go to make up the totality of human knowledge, and especially with those disciplines which stand in a specially close relation to theology' (Macquarrie 1977: 39). This generates a tripartite division of the material into philosophical theology (a prolegomenal or natural theological phenomenology of human and divine being, language, revelation, and religion), symbolic theology (covering Trinity, creation, Christ and salvation, the Spirit, and the last things), and applied theology (ecclesiology and ethics). The conception privileges the generic over the symbolic and positive, with the result that the real engine of the account is to be located in its prolegomena; it is here that the most important decisions are taken. This, in turn, is reflected in the distribution of weight: trinitarian theology, for example, receives only a fairly brief treatment, and has little effect either retroactively on the philosophical theology or prospectively on other topics in symbolic and applied theology. Jenson's conception, by contrast, shows a distinct preference for the ecclesial and dramatic. Theology is defined as 'the thinking internal to the task of speaking the gospel' (Jenson 1997–9: i. 5); Jenson accordingly eschews any pre-theological foundations in a more inclusive ontology or epistemology, on the grounds that 'if theological prolegomena lay down conceptual conditions of Christian teaching that are not themselves Christian teaching... the prolegomena sooner or later turn against the *legomena*' (Jenson 1997–9: i. 9). Hence in arranging the material, Jenson does not move *towards* what Macquarrie calls 'symbolic theology' but *from* it (and would resist the term 'symbolic' as suggesting that positive doctrine is reducible to some antecedent philosophical phenomenology). Consequently, trinitarian theology bulks very large, not only in the treatment of the doctrine *per se*, but across the entire corpus of Christian teaching: in one sense, Jenson's systematic theology as a whole is a set of amplifications or extensions of the doctrine of the Trinity.

III. Form and Organization

In reconstructing Christian teaching, systematic theology proceeds by a process of conceptual abstraction and schematization. Both are necessary for rational representation in that they enable the theologian to generate a projection of Christian claims about reality which will display both the core content of those claims and also their overall shape when taken together.

Form

Rational representation requires skilful use of concepts. This is true not only of speculative inquiries but also of a discipline like systematic theology, which has usually been considered to have a strongly practical dimension insofar as it originates in and aims at the understanding and improvement of Christian practice. Concepts are 'abstractions', not in the sense that they discard the practical in favour of the purely speculative, but in the sense that they articulate general perceptions which might otherwise be achieved only by laborious repetition. Systematic theological concepts (Trinity, election, providence, incarnation, regeneration, and so on) function as shorthand which enables more deliberate, reflective apprehension than can be had from the more immediate bearers of Christian claims such as scripture. Of course, scripture is by no means lacking in conceptual vocabulary; but it is more occasional, directed by particular circumstances, and shows less concern for the clarity, consistency, and thoroughness which have to characterize a systematic representation of Christian teaching.

The sources of systematic theological concepts are varied. Some are drawn from scripture, though often their systematic deployment involves a measure of generalization and regularization as concepts are put to work in different contexts and for different purposes than those in which they originally functioned ('justification' is a good example here). Other concepts are borrowed, adapted, or constructed from resources outside the sphere of Christian faith. The generation and use of such concepts usually involves a set of complex negotiations over time, in the course of which what are deemed inappropriate connotations in the original use may be eliminated or minimized, and the concept is reshaped or extended to serve as a more fitting projection of Christian reality claims (the language of 'substance' in the Christian doctrine of God and Christology exemplifies this: see Stead 1977).

The most illuminating systematic theologies are often characterized by (1) conceptual ingenuity, resourcefulness, and suppleness, which enable a projection of Christian claims suitable to draw attention to their richness and complexity; (2) conceptual transparency, which enables a more penetrating understanding of the primary modes of Christian articulation of the gospel; and (3) broad knowledge and sensitive and creative deployment of concepts inherited from the Christian theological tradition. By contrast, systematic theologies are less successful if they are conceptually monotonous or stiff, if concepts threaten to overwhelm or replace that which they are intended to represent, or if the concepts do not have a discernible relation to well-seated theological usage.

The systematic theologies of the last two and a half centuries can be divided into two very rough groups, according to the way in which they understand the relation between systematic theological concepts and the Christian reality claims of which these concepts offer a reflective representation (the groupings are merely heuristic, and ought not to be generalized). In the first group, Christian reality claims are taken to be 'symbolic', non-final though not, of course, unnecessary expressions of something anterior. What lies behind them may be, for example, experiential (such as the experience of redemption or liberation), or social and moral (a common direction of human ethical purpose). In the second group, Christian reality claims are considered irreducible; they are not expressive, and cannot be translated without serious loss, since their content lies on their surface rather than residing behind or beneath them.

The 'symbolic' understanding of Christian reality claims took hold in systematic theology largely as a result of at least two sea changes in western intellectual culture following the period of the great scholastic dogmatic systems in the later sixteenth and seventeenth centuries. One was appeal to natural religion and morality as anterior (and in important ways superior) to positive theological teaching, capable of easing intractable confessional conflict. A second was the development of idealist interpretations of Christian teaching (notably at the hands of Kant), in which the capacity of doctrines to act as incitements to moral performance was considered to be largely independent of their reference to reality.

If Christian reality claims are considered 'symbolic' in this way, then the work of systematic theology can be thought of as their transposition from the realm of *Vorstellung* (representation) to that of *Begriff* (concept)—the terms are Hegel's, but they are widely representative and were reinforced in historical studies of Christian doctrine (such as those of Baur or Harnack) which treated Christian dogma as an arbitrary expression of the essence of Christianity. To conceptualize is to move beyond the immediate in order to penetrate and rearticulate its essence in language more stable and better grounded. Much of the systematic literature of neo-Protestantism in the nineteenth and early twentieth centuries works along these lines. Troeltsch, for example, in Heidelberg lectures from 1912/13 proposed that the systematic task is that of raising 'Christian faith conceptions to the level of dogmatic-systematic form... retrieving that which is essential to these conceptions and giving the most precise conceptual expression to what they instinctively imply' (Troeltsch 1991: 62). This 'essential element' is what Troeltsch calls 'the *Christian principle*' whose purpose is 'to bring the complex of multiple appearances together into a central formula that will express the unifying root and driving force behind the whole'—which in the case of Troeltsch is Christianity as 'a religion of *personality*' (Troeltsch 1991: 63). Systematic concepts push through the multiple phenomenal realm to its underlying moral foundation. In contemporary systematic theology, this approach remains a significant presence in revisionist theologies and in some styles of comparative theology (Ward 1994). In approaching the doctrine of the divine attributes, for example, a sophisticated revisionist theologian such as Farley considers Christian reality claims as 'symbolic bespeakings of God' produced by the 'discursive imaging activity' (Farley 1996: 79) which occurs in the sphere of redemption. The systematic task is not to repeat these symbolizations as if they constituted the end point of theological reflection, but rather to subject them to critical reconceptualization, in order to resist the tendency of mythology to 'finitize the sacred by construing God as a specific entity' (Farley 1996: 82).

This approach to the nature of systematic theological concepts ranges from a modest constructivism to something approaching pure nominalism. Nearly all systematicians (even potent realists like Barth or T. F. Torrance) incorporate some element of it. When it exercises a strong influence, its effect is to encourage the generation of systematic theological concepts which are relatively detached from the immediate language of Christian self-expression, not only rhetorically but also materially, and which exhibit a distinct preference for the general rather than the particular and dramatic. If, on the other hand, Christian reality claims are considered not to be reducible to general moral or religious proposals, systematic theological conceptualization assumes a different role. First, both in rhetoric and in genre it is a good deal less distant from the everyday idiom of Christian teaching. Systematic theological concepts are then considered as a discursive enlargement of Christian teaching but not as an improvement upon it or as a means of access to better-warranted apprehension of the truth. Systematic theology in this mode will often invest heavily in persuasion by citation, commending a construal of Christianity not by appeal to external norms but by building up a portrait of Christian doctrine which commends itself by descriptive cogency. Second, in this approach the role of concepts is to offer a kind of conceptual anatomy (or perhaps 'grammar' (Lindbeck 1984)) of Christian teaching.

Organization

Systematic theology aims at a comprehensive, well-proportioned, and unified conceptual representation of Christian teaching. In conceptualizing Christian doctrine in its full scope, systematic theology treats a relatively stable range of topics, even though individual essays may adjust the proportions or placement of certain elements of the whole, and may judge some topics outside their concern. The common order of the topics emerges from bearing in mind two principles: (1) the theme of Christian teaching is God and everything else in relation to God; (2) Christian teaching about God and everything else is best drawn from the sequence of the divine economy in which God's relation to creatures is enacted, a sequence set out in scripture and confessed in such primary documents as the Apostles' and Nicene Creeds. Attending to these two principles in some form yields an outline in which systematic theology begins with a substantial presentation of the doctrine of God, and especially of God's life in himself, followed by an account of the history of the relations of God and creatures, usually in some combination of episodic and thematic treatment. Here the topics covered include: creation, creatures, sin, the history of the covenant with Israel, the person of the Son and his work as saviour, the Holy Spirit, the church in its nature, calling, and activities, the future of all things. Much else can be built into the framework, such as consideration of the moral-theological entailments of the topics, or matters of particular confessional prominence (the doctrine of election or aspects of ecclesiology, for example). Some doctrines may be used to guide the exposition of others (such as Lutheran identification of the doctrine of justification by faith as 'the article by which the church stands or falls', or Christology in Barth's Reformed dogmatics). Further, prolegomenal matters may often be treated before the presentation of systematic theology proper.

In certain respects, order is a relatively unimportant and arbitrary affair, though the material naturally unfolds itself in certain ways: putting the doctrine of God first secures a sense of divine priority, and the retention of an economic sequence makes it easier to discern the reference of the conceptual material back to more immediate articulations of Christian teaching. Proportion, however, is a rather more significant matter. This is in part because systematic representations of Christian teaching, even the most abstract, are nearly always occasional, directed towards particular contexts. They may, for example, seize upon one or other aspect of Christian doctrine and deploy it to encourage or chasten a development in the teaching of the church. Or they may pay particular attention to a doctrine because it is considered to be under threat from external critique. The demands of pastoral and apologetic occasion, however, place strain on the overall shape of Christian doctrine, and can lead to distortion. Under pressure from such demands, doctrines can expand or contract, or can be made to serve purposes for which they were not intended. Teaching about the person and work of Christ may be expanded in such a way as to eclipse pneumatology; teaching about the church may take over tasks more properly assigned to teaching about the prophetic, priestly, and kingly ministries of the ascended Christ. Accordingly, a major systematic theological task is to register and correct such deformations by requiring that particular elements in the corpus be handled so as not to disturb the coherence and balance of the whole. And, once again, judgements about proportion depend upon material judgements about the substance of Christian teaching.

Matters of order and proportion point towards the decisive issue concerning the organization of systematic theology, namely the degree to which it may legitimately seek to generate a unified *system* of Christian teaching. Any enterprise of rational representation requires some kind of schema as a medium through which its subject matter can be displayed and interpreted. A schema is an ordered projection of the subject matter, generated by the productive work of reason in which human understanding makes use of a set of categories in order to realize knowledge. Because rational representation is 'productive' or 'projective' in this way, much hangs on whether the schemas of which reason makes use are inventive (be the invention innocent or sinister) or receptive, that is, whether they organize inert material by projecting it as a unified whole, or merely discern and follow an antecedent connectedness in the subject matter itself. More simply: how do invention and discovery relate in the work of systematization?

From one point of view, the question of system is 'the question of eschatology, of how far our intellectual constructions may anticipate such eschatological perfection of knowledge as may one day be granted to us' (Gunton 2000: 36). Systematic schematization may neglect the mind's fallibility and the provisionality of its representations, turning *theologia viatorum* into *theologia beatorum* (though it ought to noted that the Protestant scholastics, often thought to be consummate transgressors here, were sharply aware of the imperfection of theological intelligence). From another point of view, systematic representation may mischaracterize the object of Christian teaching, especially when that 'object' is considered to be the personal communicative presence and activity of God. It was for this reason that Barth mistrusted the systematic impulse: a dogmatic system 'loses contact with the event' (Barth 1956: 863), and in a well-ordered dogmatics 'the position usually occupied...by an arbitrarily chosen basic view belongs by right to the Word of God, and the Word of God alone' (Barth 1956: 866). Whatever order there may be must therefore derive from the material centre of Christian teaching, and not from the demands of schematization. Others take a lead from social-philosophical critiques of closed systems, arguing that any systematic presentation must be subject to 'the prophetic objection to a fixed, congealed system' (Ritschl 1987: 94).

All this suggests that, by virtue of its subject matter, no representation of Christian teaching can attain a fully determinate rendering of the topic; aspirations to do so can be fulfilled only by reduction or selection. Highly elaborate systematization inhibits catholicity and demonstrates the wrong sort of confidence in theological systematization.

Such objections are motivated by a concern to ensure fit between the material content of Christian teaching and the forms in which it is presented. Equally, the demand for a comprehensive and coherent presentation can be warranted materially by appeal to the unity of God. 'If God is indeed one, and if that oneness is a *revealed* oneness, thus far there is a case for ordering what we are taught of God into, if not a system, then at least a dogmatics in which (1) who and what kind of being God is and (2) the various relations between God and the world... are held to be related to one another' (Gunton 2000: 37). 'System' ought not to be confused with 'deductive system', fully elaborated *more geometrico* (Tillich 1951–63: i. 58–9). The criteria for appropriate systematic construction might then be as follows: (1) the systematic character of the schema should not be imposed by analytical reason but should emerge from attention to the subject matter's self-unfolding; (2) systems must retain provisionality and openness to revision from sources which cannot be given exhaustive description within the system; (3) systems must be indicative of, not a replacement for, the persons, events, and acts which form the substance of Christian teaching; (4) formal, systematic coordination must serve material scope and coherence. Many systematicians have thought these criteria best met by a combination of economic sequence and topical description; the *loci* method is often judged the most apt formal organization.

In the end, however, the most memorable and consistently stimulating works in systematic theology are not those which have maximally elaborate or coherent ground plans, but those which register the grandeur of Christian truth in their concepts and schematism, and in which material, rather than formal, skills have been paramount.

References

Barth, Karl (1956). *Church Dogmatics* I/2. Edinburgh: T. & T. Clark.

Chopp, Rebecca, and Taylor, Mark (eds.) (1994). *Reconstructing Christian Theology.* Minneapolis: Fortress.

Farley, Edward (1996). *Divine Empathy: A Theology of God.* Minneapolis: Fortress.

Fiorenza, Francis, and Galvin, John (eds.) (1991). *Systematic Theology: Roman Catholic Perspectives.* Minneapolis: Fortress.

Gilkey, Langdon (1979). *Message and Existence.* New York: Seabury.

Gunton, Colin (2000). *Intellect and Action.* Edinburgh: T. & T. Clark.

Haight, Roger (1990). *Dynamics of Theology.* New York: Paulist.

Hodgson, Peter, and King, Robert (eds.) (1983). *Christian Theology: An Introduction to its Traditions and Tasks.* London: SPCK.
Jenson, Robert (1997–9). *Systematic Theology.* 2 vols. Oxford: Oxford University Press.
Kaufman, Gordon (1975). *An Essay on Theological Method.* Missoula: Scholars.
Lindbeck, George (1984). *The Nature of Doctrine.* Philadelphia: Westminster.
Macquarrie, John (1977). *Principles of Christian Theology.* London: SCM.
Muller, Richard (2000). *The Unaccommodated Calvin.* Oxford: Oxford University Press.
Pannenberg, Wolfhart (1970). *Basic Questions in Theology,* i. London: SCM.
—— (1991–8). *Systematic Theology.* 3 vols. Grand Rapids: Eerdmans.
Ritschl, Dietrich (1987). *The Logic of Theology.* Philadelphia: Fortress.
Roberts, A., and Donaldson, J. (eds.) (1990). *Ante-Nicene Fathers: The Writings of the Fathers down to A.D. 325.* Edinburgh: T. & T. Clark.
Schlink, Edmund (1967). *The Coming Christ and the Coming Church.* Edinburgh: Oliver and Boyd.
Stead, Christopher (1977). *Divine Substance.* Oxford: Clarendon.
Tillich, Paul (1951–63). *Systematic Theology.* 3 vols. Chicago: University of Chicago Press.
Torrance, Thomas (1993). *The Trinitarian Faith.* Edinburgh: T. & T. Clark.
Troeltsch, Ernst (1991). *The Christian Faith.* Minneapolis: Fortress.
Van Beeck, Frans Jozef (1989). *God Encountered: A Contemporary Catholic Systematic Theology,* i. *Understanding the Christian Faith.* San Francisco: Harper.
Wainwright, Geoffrey (1980). *Doxology: The Praise of God in Worship, Doctrine, and Life. A Systematic Theology.* New York: Oxford University Press.
Ward, Keith (1994). *Religion and Revelation.* Oxford: Oxford University Press.

Suggested Reading

Barth (1956: 853–84).
Diem, Hermann (1959). *Dogmatics.* Edinburgh: Oliver and Boyd, 303–12.
Ebeling, Gerhard (1979). *The Study of Theology.* London: Collins, 125–38.
Gunton (2000: 19–45).
Jeffner, Anders (1977). *Kriterien christlicher Glaubenslehre.* Uppsala: Almqvist & Wiksell.
Pannenberg, Wolfhart (1976). *Theology and the Philosophy of Science.* London: Darton, Longman and Todd, 404–23.
Ritschl (1987: 78–97).
Schwöbel, Christoph (2002). *Gott in Beziehung.* Tübingen: Mohr Siebeck, 1–24.
Van Beeck (1989: i. 38–93).

PART I

DOCTRINES

CHAPTER 1

THE EXISTENCE OF GOD

WILLIAM J. ABRAHAM

I. Setting Out the Standards of Success

We begin by getting clarity on the subject in hand. In the Christian tradition God is publicly identified and named as the triune God. This trinitarian identity of the Christian God is not a matter of speculation but of communal, historical, and linguistic fact. Christians are baptized in the name of God, Father, Son, and Holy Spirit; they worship God as Father, Son, and Holy Spirit; in their creeds they publicly and officially confess that they believe in the Trinity; in their lives they seek to imitate the Son who has brought them to the Father in the power of the Holy Spirit. Identifying God as the triune God clearly narrows the options. The question before us is this: Why confess and affirm that this God exists?

In the early twentieth century philosophers and theologians would have rejected this way of posing the problem of the existence of God and asked a different question. The question of the existence of God was posed in terms not of the triune God but of the God of generic theism. To claim that God exists was to claim that there exists a bodiless, eternal, omnipotent, omniscient, omnipresent, and all-good creator and sustainer of the universe. Once this was agreed then the discussion could proceed. Assenting to the existence of God in an intellectually responsible manner was thought to have three conditions attached to it. First, one had to show that the concept of God was coherent, that is, that it did not involve any explicit or hidden contradictions. Second, one had to show that there was good evidence for the existence of this God. One was required to have in hand a natural theology that deployed true premisses and valid conclusions. Thirdly, if one desired to enrich the description of God, then one could do so by appeal to special divine revelation, but only if revelation was secured by appropriate credentials (Flew 1966).

It is a mark of how things have changed in the course of a century that the consensus represented by this network of assumptions no longer holds. To be sure, various elements of it linger on, but they are on the way to being historical curiosities. Consider the problems involved in reverse order. It is misleading to think of divine revelation in terms of credentials; divine revelation itself should be considered as evidence for the reality of God. It is epistemologically question-begging to insist that the debate about God's existence be cast essentially in terms of propositional evidence and that such evidence be made a condition of intellectual responsibility. While internal coherence is a condition of all properly formed propositions, the concept of God is too firmly lodged in our linguistic practices and communities to require this kind of initial vetting. Most importantly, the conception of God on offer is an abstraction that does not match the actual conception of God at issue, say, in the Christian tradition. While the concept of God deployed in general theism may still have its uses, it simply does not capture the God identified in the history and practices of the Christian faith.

What is at issue in the end is not the existence of the God of mere theism but the reality of the triune God of the Christian faith. Anything less that this simply fails to reach the subject before us. Posing the issue in this way is not a strategy of evasion, or an arbitrary way of cooking the books in advance, or a way to make life easier. On the contrary, it makes life a lot more difficult; it ensures that the proper epistemological books be consulted; and it avoids the dodging of the real problem that has to be addressed.

Many robust trinitarians have been profoundly uneasy with offering any kind of evidence for the reality of God. The collapse of classical natural theology in the wake of Hume and Kant was certainly one factor behind this unease. Anxiety about relying on reason was reinforced by the hostility to theology that was the hallmark of the analytical tradition in the wake of Russell and Ayer. It did not help that champions of natural theology were often theological minimalists, revisionists, and liberal Protestants for whom the Trinity was an optional extra. More importantly, natural theology simply cannot reach as far as the Trinity. The internal requirements of theology exposed the limitations of reason. The weight therefore fell on the appeal to divine revelation.

In the hands of Barth, revelation was brilliantly deployed as a weapon against natural theology (Barth 1975). Barth made a virtue out of necessity by insisting that the one and only God is made known fully, finally, and exclusively in divine revelation in Jesus Christ. Conceptually the true God of divine revelation is the triune God of the Christian tradition. Belief in God in no way depends on reason; indeed to rely on reason or natural theology is to seek an alien deity, an idol;

common honesty and the logic of belief requires the rejection of natural theology and an exclusive reliance on revelation as the highest ground of truth in theology. Natural theology is not just invalid; it is theologically corrupting. Wedded to a socio-linguistic vision of language derived from Wittgenstein, Barth's vision was ingeniously reworked in the United States so as to secure the internal autonomy of theology from philosophy (Lindbeck 1984). The echo of this synthesis is clearly audible in a new generation of evangelical theologians who have recently bought tickets on the train of narrative theology (Vanhoozer 2005).

The present air of confidence in Christian theology has provided space for theologians to pursue radically new agendas. On the one hand, it has compelled some to enrich the content of theology by drawing on the insights from the oppressed and the marginalized. Liberation theologians and their allies have followed up on the Barthian veto on reason and sought to purify reason of its oppressive dysfunctions and to fill out the vision of God in ways that make theology emancipatory (e.g., Fulkerson 1994; Althaus-Reid 2000; Rieger 2001; Isasi-Díaz 2004). On the edges of this trajectory theology has been set free to explore its pastoral and healing functions within the church and culture. On the other hand, the 'radical orthodoxy' movement launched a frontal attack on all forms of secular reason (Milbank 1990; Milbank et al. 1999; Davis et al. 2005). On this model, God becomes the saviour of reason itself. Here theology moves from the margins into the very heart of the academy. Sensible English dullness transformed into Celtic passion promises to cleanse the metaphysical stables with the broom of Neoplatonic insight. Where once the existence of God was dismissed as a proposition in search of cognitive content, now the reality of God provides meaning and hope to a political and metaphysical universe that is otherwise in ruins. Though theologians have been banished from the public square, their public humiliation has turned into an extraordinary recovery of nerve.

There are important tensions below the surface. While there is a new confidence abroad, there is disagreement on how to proceed in providing warrant for belief in God. In framing the issue in these terms I am deliberately reworking the questions that have been central in debates about the existence of God. Natural theology was not simply a matter of working out the validity and soundness of arguments for the existence of God. It represented an effort to secure the rationality of belief in God. Moreover, it is one thing to challenge the content of a genuine revelation from God; it is quite another to raise probing questions about someone's claim to having received divine revelation. Barth's veto of natural theology has been abundantly fruitful in subsequent theology, but it cannot be sustained. It rested on a narrow construal of natural theology and on a mistaken view of the debate about divine revelation. We cannot shut down debate about the genuine location of divine revelation by claiming that, once we possess it, we have to treat it as ultimate. It is the possession that is at issue, not the logic of commitment. Moreover, when we raise the legitimate issue of whether it is rational to believe in the God identified in Christian revelation and truly celebrated as the Trinity, we are right back at the conceptual foundations of natural theology. Nor can the Barthian veto be sustained by reworking it into the language of being, narrative, grammar, perspective, forms of life, language games, and the like. Important as these concepts may be, they mask strategies of evasion.

The current intellectual and social location of the Christian tradition confirms that the issue of the rationality of belief in God remains as pressing as ever. Christian theologians operate in a radically pluralistic world where rival metaphysical and revelatory claims compete for attention and commitment. To be sure, atheists often conceal the great diversity of options that they offer; it is rare that they offer a positive case for the comprehensive visions and convictions that they recommend for assent. However, they can no longer hide beneath the cloak of theories of meaning or the shawl of epistemological dogma. All is now out in the open, so a robust Christian vision of God is but one ontology on display. Even more importantly, claims to divine revelation are now firmly back on the agenda with the resurgence of Islam. If we have lost the art of adjudicating between rival claims to divine revelation, then we simply have to go back to school and relearn it. Both global and local conditions combine to destroy the insularity that shields the theologian from providing some account of why we should accept the theology on offer. This is not a return to the bad old days of the Enlightenment. The conceptual shortcomings, the narrow dogmatisms, the concealed interests of the European Enlightenments—these are all too visible to the informed student. The questions of what to believe and why to believe, however, cannot be suppressed; they are intrinsically and contextually inescapable.

It is crucial to note how the terrain has been transformed over the last generation. Two variables have changed simultaneously. First, the existence of God is now framed in terms of a robust version of Christian theism. The Barthian revolution has rightly ousted the kind of minimalist theism that was the standard option in the modern period. Second, the categories of evaluation cannot be prejudged in advance. Here again the Barthian revolution is pivotal because it has insisted that factors internal to the Christian tradition be allowed a place at the table. This requirement dovetails aptly with the epistemological changes that have become commonplace within analytical philosophy. The result is an epistemological freedom that creates space for fruitful new options.

II. Trinity and Truth

Bruce Marshall has exploited this freedom in an exceptionally interesting manner. Steeped in the history of theology and writing with the clarity and rigour of the analytical tradition, he has staked out a position which maintains the internal commitments of the post-Barthian consensus without its liabilities. Drawing on the logic of identity, he notes how the Christian doctrine of God is inescapably trinitarian in content. In Christian worship the Christian deity is precisely identified as Father, Son, and Holy Spirit. The three persons of the Trinity are identified by expressions which refer to actions or characteristics unique to each. Such expressions are supplied by the scriptural narratives and liturgical practices of the church. Thus the Father is the one who sent Jesus, the Son; the Son is the one sent by the Father; and the Holy Spirit is the one who unites the faithful to the Son. However, there is more to the identity of the Trinity than this.

> The God identified in the church's invocation—the triune God—the church holds to be the creator, redeemer, and perfecter (or consummator) of the world, and in particular of human life and history. To put the point at the highest level of generality, the church holds the triune God and the actions of that God to be of ultimate and universal significance, and has an open-ended variety of ways to characterize this significance. (Marshall 2000: 43)

What this initially means is that belief in the Trinity is both essential and central to the Christian community. It is essential in that it is necessary to the community's identity and survival; it is central in that it is the least dispensable of the community's overall system of beliefs.

Like all beliefs, Christian beliefs are truth claims. But central beliefs are not merely true; they are such that the Christian community treats them as epistemically primary. Thus if a conflict arises, say, between belief A and B, if A is epistemically primary the community persists in holding A true and rejects or modifies B. Furthermore, in the case of belief in the Trinity, the primacy is unrestricted; it applies across the full range of possible beliefs. This insight furnishes a critical clue as to how the church will decide the truth of beliefs other than belief in the Trinity: it will test their truth by seeing how well they cohere with the beliefs that constitute its identification of the triune God. The truth of the Trinity becomes the critical norm by which all other truths are evaluated.

Marshall's move represents a radical reversal of the standard strategy of theology in the modern period in debates about the existence of God. Rather than check how well belief in God comports with other beliefs, the reverse is the case. Other beliefs must fit with the constitutive beliefs of the church. Marshall is well aware that this appears to undermine any claim to have the right to believe. It looks as if any community can help itself to such a strategy and thus claim victory in the quest for truth. Resolving this dilemma takes Marshall into the deep waters of justification and truth.

For Marshall the notions of meaning, justification, and truth are logically interrelated. He insists that the meaning of sentences cannot be determined independently of decisions about the truth of sentences and beliefs. Following Donald Davidson in his vision of radical interpretation, he rejects the epistemic dualism of scheme and content, according to which a system of beliefs and concepts is called upon to fit some kind of experience or sensation. This leads him in turn to reject both any kind of global scepticism and the foundationalism that seeks to overcome it. Most importantly, it leads him to hold that only beliefs can justify beliefs. Indeed, justification can only be a matter of coherence among beliefs. Given the conceptual connections between meaning, truth, and justification, Marshall can stand by his claim that the Trinity functions as epistemically primary for the Christian community. In the end there is no epistemology without trinitarian theology.

Marshall does not, however, adopt a coherence theory of truth. Here he begins with Tarski's famous T-sentence of the form, *'Grass is green' if and only if grass is green* (Tarski 2001 [1944]), and then enriches it by a sophisticated reading and deployment of trinitarian doctrine. Truth is predicated of sentences and beliefs; but believing a true sentence does not descend as a bolt from the blue. On a trinitarian reading of the world, even our believing as we do happens because of the appropriate joint agency of Father, Son, and Holy Spirit. The only exceptions to this are those sentences which speak of the evil actions of created free agents; in such cases there is nothing in God of which they are the origin and likeness. In the main, however, Marshall can integrate the claim that Jesus is the truth and the claim that we believe the deep things of the gospel by the Spirit with the best account of truth currently available. In the end there is no truth without trinitarian theology. The radical reversal of the standard position is well captured in the following:

> According to our theologically disciplined notion of truth, beliefs justified according to these standards will generally be true in case the triune God—and especially, in his distinctive way, the risen Christ—undertakes his truth-bestowing act (1) with regard to belief in the narratives which identify him, (2) with regard to no belief inconsistent with these narratives, and (3) with regard to beliefs which there is otherwise good reason to hold. Truth will be accessible to belief if we can count on the triune God to do just this—if, when it comes to our own beliefs, his truth-bestowing act is not for the most part inaccessible to us. Presumably God bestows truth on no false beliefs, since true beliefs are all and only those to which he has granted truth. But we need not always be able to tell which beliefs God makes true; it suffices that we can tell for the most part, and especially with regard to those beliefs which are epistemically primary. (Marshall 2000: 278)

The deep interrelation that Marshall develops between justification, truth, and theology does not mean that theology is hidden away in some ghetto where it can ignore objections and alien claims. While theology brings its own explanatory power to the discussion, it must still deal with contemporary understandings, say, of history and science. Thus it may have to change its understanding of some of its beliefs—even central beliefs. Capacity to assimilate novel beliefs and to include alien beliefs is constitutive of epistemic responsibility. Novel and alien beliefs include beliefs that are widely believed in contemporary culture; so there is no isolationism here. What counts as rationality at this point is that we be prepared to give up any particular belief, even the most central. Rationality does not then involve the attainment of some positive prize; it is enough to be ready to meet the challenges presented by our neighbours. There is no need to offer some kind of independent support for the existence of God. On the contrary, belief in the triune God has an epistemically privileged position in our thinking about all truth.

There is a pleasing leanness and austerity to Marshall's project. He has reached for a maximum theological outcome with minimum philosophical outlay. Indeed, he has provided the kind of theological vision of truth that has rarely been seen since the medieval period. It is no accident that he is an exceptionally astute interpreter of Aquinas. Yet he systematically rejects any appeal to natural theology, direct divine revelation, and religious experience. Thus there is a generous updating of the tradition rather than simply a fresh restatement.

III. *Sensus Divinitatis* and Knowledge of God

One way to think of Marshall's project is to see it as underwriting the claim that God alone provides warrant for beliefs about God. A similar strategy is visible in the work of Alvin Plantinga. Working out of very different epistemological resources, Plantinga also rejects the claim that the existence of God rests on evidence that falls outside the terrain of divine agency. Belief in the great things of the gospel—Plantinga's happy codeword for trinitarian theism—depends on the proper functioning of our cognitive capacities. A belief 'has warrant for a person S only if that belief is produced in S by cognitive faculties functioning properly (subject to no dysfunction) in a cognitive environment that is appropriate for S's kind of cognitive faculties, according to a design plan that is successfully aimed at truth'. When a belief meets these conditions and does enjoy warrant, 'the degree of warrant it enjoys depends on the strength of the belief, the firmness with which the belief is held' (Plantinga 2000: 156). Applied to belief in the triune God, proper functioning involves the proper use of our *sensus divinitatis*, that is, a faculty implanted in us by God but deeply impaired by the consequences of sin. As we are exposed to the great truths of the gospel, the Holy Spirit repairs our *sensus divinitatis* and triggers the truth about God in our minds. Generally we rely on such faculties as memory, perception, reason, sympathy, induction, and the like; if Christian belief is true, we are entitled to rely on our repaired *sensus divinitatis*. In this case Plantinga appeals not so much to the doctrine of the Trinity as to a Christian vision of creation, fall, and redemption.

Once again we have a radical reversal. Epistemology is relocated within theology rather than theology having to meet some kind of external yardstick. The existence of God is built, as it were, into the very foundations of epistemology. This does not mean that the theologian can ignore objections. On the contrary, potential defeaters require rebuttals. On this score Plantinga's work on the problem of evil is a model of intellectual rigour. He readily extends his reach to deal with a whole host of objections to Christian belief derived from philosophical, Marxist, and Freudian sources. Moreover, Plantinga can naturally help himself to any and every argument that counts in favour of the existence of God. Belief in God is properly basic rather than epistemically primary. Thus his work on the positive but restricted status of the ontological argument is especially ingenious. However, neither natural theology nor for that matter appeal to special divine revelation are essential for belief in God to be warranted. Belief in God is properly basic; it can be held without any evidence as a particular belief lodged in the foundations of a healthy noetic structure. There are plenty of good arguments for the existence of God, but they are not essential to rationality, as evidentialists once insisted.

IV. Revisionary Natural Theology

It has sometimes been noted that the kind of position developed by Marshall and Plantinga fits snugly with a cultural situation where it is not coming to belief in God that is challenged, but retaining belief in God. Thus they are less interested in bringing unbelievers to faith than in keeping believers from abandoning faith. Moreover, their positions give pride of place to the work of the Holy Spirit in initiating faith. For many in Europe, where unbelief is much more common, such appeal to the Spirit initially comes across as question-begging and even perverse. The locks have been changed without appropriate approval. There has long been a fecund tradition of natural theology in Britain that insists on evidence that is independent of theology but refuses to be restricted to deductive proof or strict probabilistic argument. The core of this tradition is the appeal to cumulative case arguments that, when taken together, underwrite the rationality of belief in God. Richard Swinburne has articulated the most comprehensive development of this tradition. The final goal remains belief in the Trinity; the means of getting there are traditional. Swinburne moves first to establish belief in the God of traditional theism by way of a revision of the classical inductive arguments for theism; with that in place he enriches this theism by special divine revelation to take us all the way to the trinitarian faith of the church.

The hallmark of Swinburne's initial work is the use of Bayes's theorem in order to quantify as far as possible the appeal to contingency, apparent order, teleology, consciousness, and the like. What especially interests Swinburne is the simplicity and explanatory power of theism. Initially he concludes that the existence of God is neither very probable nor very improbable on the evidence taken as a whole minus the evidence of religious experience. 'My conclusion so far has been that the probability of theism is none too close to 1 or 0 on the evidence so far considered.' However, the appeal to religious experience changes the final outcome. When religious experience is factored in, 'theism is more probable that not' (Swinburne 1979: 290–1). Given this background conclusion, we are then free to explore the possibility of special divine revelation in scripture. The appropriate evidence in this case must be supplied by content and by miracle. Thus the content must fit our moral and spiritual needs; while a miracle, like a resurrection, shows God's vindication of the proposed revelation. It might appear that this does not get us to the Trinity. However, Swinburne relocates the divine revelation of scripture within the church and argues that the creed be taken as a preface to scripture. Thus the Trinity is secured by a vision of divine revelation that builds the doctrine of the Trinity into its proper identity and interpretation. Swinburne is also persuaded of the doctrine of the Trinity by way of metaphysical arguments that echo the proposals of the Victorines of the medieval period; thus he can appeal to metaphysical considerations that confirm or strengthen the appeal to divine revelation.

As already noted, the argument from religious experience is central to Swinburne's project. He develops this argument in terms of a very general principle of rationality called the principle of credulity. On this principle, things are as they appear to be unless there is good reason to believe otherwise. Swinburne carefully applies this principle to religious experience, casting the argument in terms of perception of the divine. This is a theme that has been explored with exceptional power and clarity by William Alston. Alston nests his appeal to religious experience in a broader theory of perception that is conceptualized in terms of doxastic practices. All appeals to doxastic practice are circular; any appeal to external support will circle back to trust in our doxastic practices. However, this is not the end of the matter. Doxastic practices work within a complex network of mechanisms and practices that operate to trigger our beliefs. These doxastic practices involve large families of mechanisms rather than single mechanisms. Each family has certain formal features. They are socially established; they are subject to change; they work together even though they are irreducibly plural; they provide *prima facie* justification rather than *ultima facie* justification; they display self-support; and they can be defended in terms of practical rationality, since engaging in them 'is a reasonable thing to do given our aims and situation' (Alston 1991: 180). Each family also has its own unique features. Thus they have their own conceptual scheme suited to the relevant mode of reality; they have appropriate sources and results; they have relevant ways of handling defeaters and overriders; and they have their own presuppositions.

Alston's unique contribution to the discussion is having explored this vision of doxastic practice as it applies to an inclusive range of experiences of God. Experiences of God are contrasted to calling up mental images, entertaining propositions, reasoning, remembering, and the like. Characteristically there is an awareness of God that is self-presenting, whether directly or indirectly; thus the appeal is not by way of explanation. The crux of the argument is that experiences of God should be understood as embedded in a doxastic practice whose implications should be taken as reliable. This is how both ordinary believers and the great saints of the church have naturally construed them. Lodged within the doctrinal commitments of scripture and the church, these experiences should be taken as veridical rather than illusory. They are embedded in what Alston dubs 'Christian mystical perceptual practice', a term intended to capture their epistemic significance (Alston 1991: 193). As Alston sees it, the rejection of this practice as *prima facie* reliable invariably rests either on forms of epistemic imperialism, where the standards of one doxastic practice are taken as normative for all, or on a double standard, where the Christian mystical perceptual practice is condemned for features shared by other practices that are approved. While the weight garnered from religious experience in this schema is modest, its cognitive value is genuine. It lends its own irreducible load to the total evidence that supports the classical faith of the church.

V. Canonical Commitment and Epistemology

An interesting feature of the foregoing landscape is the extraordinary fecundity and freshness of the arguments developed to support the rationality of a robust version of Christian theism. Whole new seams have been discovered and mined as resources for belief in God. At present the seams stand as separate channels; indeed, the walls of division can be thick to the point of impenetrable. Three observations are in order at this point. First, as in the patristic situation, the participants in the debate can all assent to the existence of the same God even while they disagree on the strategy for articulating the rationality of belief in this God. This underlying consensus is easily missed in that epistemologists want to get things right and are quick to seize on problems in the work of colleagues. Second, many of the participants have been driven by challenges to belief in God to develop their own original epistemological theories. Hence the debate about the existence of God has shifted the direction of the debate. Where in much of the modern period there was one-way traffic between philosophy and theology, now the traffic flows in both directions. Theology is no longer the poor relation; she has her own voice and her own insights to contribute to the discussion. Third, much of this new work remains undervalued, if not unknown, both in theology and philosophy. In part this is because of the specialization of the contemporary academy; more generally it stems from deep divisions across the major movements that constitute contemporary theology and philosophy.

In the debate about the reality of God, the tone, the style, and the conclusions have changed radically over the last century. It is no exaggeration to speak of a quiet revolution. The earlier discussion was hostile to faith, the majority voices were self-confident in their scepticism, and it took courage and ingenuity for figures, like Basil Mitchell at Oxford, just to keep the issues on the table (Mitchell 1957). The later discussion is marked by a living commitment to robust forms of faith; the burden of proof has now shifted to the sceptical side; and the wealth of material defies easy delineation. The earlier discussion was public and noisy; philosophers acted like elephants trumpeting their proposals across the room. The later discussion has been stealthy and quiet; philosophers have calmly infested the buildings like termites, and many still remain hidden in the woodwork. It will take time for a new generation to evaluate and assimilate the new data, insights, and arguments that have emerged. There are also very significant tracts of unfinished business.

One issue that demands attention is the place of community in the identification of Christian belief and in the formation of good judgement. Marshall, for example, holds that baptismal and eucharistic practice require commitment not just to belief in the Trinity but also to the claim that the Trinity has epistemological primacy in the internal ordering of Christian belief. If this is offered as a contested unpacking of the implications of Christian belief, then there is surely no problem. However, it is obvious that participation in the liturgical practice of the church does not commit us to such a specific epistemological proposal. More generally we need to distinguish between the canonical or officially adopted commitments of the church and the epistemological strategies that are deployed to explain or defend them. The debate between communities with different official commitments has in fact been exceptionally fruitful in terms of epistemological inquiry. Other consequences of ecclesial division for the life of faith itself have of course been less than salutary. The place of official epistemological commitments in the divided communities of Christianity is clearly a matter for sensitive analysis.

This attention to communal commitments becomes all the more urgent when we reflect on the diversity of positions adopted by theologians and philosophers in the epistemology of theology. Plantinga offers his central proposals in terms of a model whereby we can make sense of warranted belief in God. Basil Mitchell developed his groundbreaking suggestions on cumulative case arguments as a strategy for the defence of the rationality of Christian theism (Mitchell 1974). Furthermore, it is clear that our interpretation of canonical teachers like Thomas Aquinas can shift across the generations. Thus an official commitment to a positive relation between faith and reason, even when cast in terms of the work of Aquinas, can be spelled out in a great variety of ways. To take a very different example, the idea of papal infallibility, a much-neglected theme in epistemology, can be reworked in new contexts in ways that are breathtaking in their diversity.

Such a rich variety of options prompts further reflection on the role of Christian communities in identifying and evaluating epistemological proposals.

The place of community in arriving at an accurate picture of the place of tradition in the formation of good judgement is also worthy of note. Judgement is inescapable in philosophy. The temptation to reduce complex issues to a manageable form that can be settled by some kind of calculus is intense. However, if our epistemological nets are cast too narrowly, then we may miss important insights that are essential in the debate about the existence of God. Happily, general work in virtue epistemology and in social epistemology can help open up the terrain, but we have barely scratched the surface to date.

VI. Revisiting Divine Revelation

An older terrain deserving fresh exploration is the topic of divine revelation. The reasons for the neglect of this crucial epistemological concept are illuminating. Given that general revelation was often confused with natural theology, it was to be expected that this dimension of the topic would be sent into the nether regions when natural theology was rejected. However, there is an obvious distinction between natural theology and general revelation. To believe in general revelation is to believe that God is made manifest in creation; to believe in natural theology is to hold that certain arguments for the existence of God are valid and sound. The first is a claim about perception of the divine in creation; the second is a claim about the legitimacy of various arguments with premisses and conclusions. When philosophers began revisiting the possibility of natural theology, they were tacitly aware of this distinction, and so the topic of divine revelation rightly remained in limbo. This was especially the case with respect to special revelation, that is, to claims to revelation rooted in particular historical events or in scripture. The obvious strategy was to avoid appeal to considerations that were not publicly agreed and accessible.

When the debate about natural theology is relocated in the more general arena of the rationality or justification of religious belief, then the resources for rethinking what is involved in appeals to divine revelation become readily available. We can surely think of the appeal to general revelation as a claim to the perception of divine action in creation rather than, say, inference to the best explanation. The same applies to cases of special revelation. Christians claim to see God revealed in the life, death, and resurrection of Jesus Christ. Thus the extensive work on perception of the divine comes into play immediately. We are no longer confined to the older strategy of working out criteria of special revelation that we then apply to the putative cases on offer. Identifying divine revelation is a matter of discernment first and foremost. To be sure, the initial identification of special revelation can then be confirmed and strengthened by evidence, by signs and miracles, but to turn the latter into some kind of criteria of truth is to misread the content of the discussion and the direction in which it should proceed.

Moreover, it is obvious that the concept of divine revelation is modelled on the idea of personal agents revealing themselves in what they do. This opens up whole new vistas that deserve attention. It is clear that some actions are more revelatory than others. Thus it is important to get beyond generic talk about agency and action and specify the actions through which God is made known. The place of divine speech-actions to particular prophets and apostles takes on special significance. So too does the action of God in the incarnation of Jesus Christ. Here the language of the Word of God becomes vital in highlighting where the heartbeat of revelation is to be located. The place of agency can also highlight the importance of divine hiddenness in any comprehensive account of the rationality of belief in God. There is a radical element of decision on God's part on whether to remain hidden or be revealed. Philosophers who set up their own standards as to how God should be revealed run the risk not just of mistaking their standards but of cognitive idolatry. What, why, and how God reveals cannot be isolated from the wider purposes of God in creation and redemption. Clearly God sets the agenda on these matters, not human agents. Creation and redemption are self-involving concepts that necessarily have profound consequences for our identity, commitments, and action. They reach not just to the head but also to the heart and to the hand; hence there are moral and spiritual dimensions to the epistemological issues that cannot be bracketed out if we are to do justice to what is at stake.

One way to capture the moral and spiritual significance of divine revelation is to note that it calls for unrestrained commitment in the sense that the proper response to divine revelation is that of radical trust in God. However, this is simply the reverse side of a crucial epistemological feature of special revelation in the Christian tradition. If divine revelation is correctly identified, then the believer has access to knowledge; indeed, the believer has access to God's own knowledge. This insight was widely recognized in the medieval period but lost in the modern era. Divine revelation was reduced to scripture, scripture was treated as a form of ancient tradition, appeal to tradition was identified as a way of authority, and ways of authority were rejected in the name of reason. Good historical investigation and greater conceptual rigour can now unravel the pitfalls of this development. Delivered from its captivity, we are free to reconsider the unique role that divine revelation rightly has in claims to knowledge. To have divine revelation is to have access to divine knowledge; we have entrance to the reality of God and to the purposes of God for the world.

Some will worry that heading in this direction will open the door to fanaticism and to an assault on hard-won intellectual virtue. Some claims to divine revelation do indeed tear the fabric of intellectual life. Not all do, however. What is at issue here is the nature of divine revelation as a threshold concept. Once we come to believe in divine revelation, then everything may have to be rethought in the light of the new world that has been opened to view. This rethinking includes fresh reflection on the nature and limits of the very cognitive capacities that brought us to believe in God and in divine revelation in the first place. It is no accident that theologians like Marshall are prepared to develop trinitarian visions of justification and truth. Even though divine revelation does no explicit epistemic work for him, it is clear that divine revelation was critical for some of the medieval figures that are important sources for his reflections. Marshall himself also appeals to scripture; in so doing he appears to be relying on a vision of scripture that sees it as a source of special revelation. If claims to divine revelation can call for the revision of our initial epistemological insights, then we can be sure that they may also make a difference to other epistemological commitments. However, we must proceed with care here; we do not know in advance how things will turn out.

It may appear that the topic of divine revelation is taking us off course and away from reflection on the existence of God. This is not the case. If I am right that we have undergone a revolution, then the parameters of earlier discussion have changed. Once we take divine revelation seriously as an epistemic notion, then we simply have to follow the evidence where it takes us. Indeed, one topic crying out for immediate analysis is whether divine revelation constitutes good evidence for the existence of God. In the case of human agents we come to know of their existence in and through communication with them. It is not that we come to believe that certain people exist and then try to figure out what they may have revealed to us. The reality is coextensive with the revelation; divine existence comes with divine revelation. So divine revelation can be thought of not just as a source of new information about God; it constitutes evidence in its own right for the reality of God. The standard separation of the evidence *for* God from actual divine revelation *from* God clearly needs revisiting at this point.

Divine revelation may also require a revisiting of the standard application of central epistemological concepts. In coming to believe in divine revelation we cross a threshold, but there is a journey up to the threshold and a journey on the other side of it. Thus the process of justifying in this case cannot be thought of in purely synchronic terms, that is, in terms of inspecting singular propositions and checking them in various ways for veracity. There is also a diachronic dimension to justifying many of our beliefs, especially when we are dealing with complex networks of belief such as belief in the triune God. We know historically that monotheism and trinitarian theism arose as a matter of development over time in Jewish and Christian communities. It was never simply a matter of a snapshot of the relevant considerations; it was more like an ongoing journey where crucial considerations only came into play after other considerations had been acknowledged. Justified belief was not just a matter of quick verification but was more an issue of discovery and confirmation over time. Similar considerations are at play in claims to rationality and knowledge in the case of the existence of God; it takes time to gain these much-coveted prizes. Once we recognize this diachronic dimension of epistemology, then we can also readily see the need to explore the place of spiritual direction and religious practice in the confidence and tenacity of mature believers. At this point, spirituality takes on epistemological overtones that can easily remain hidden if we insist on entertaining merely synchronic conceptions of rationality, justification, and knowledge.

The debate about the existence of God has undergone a startling revolution that few expected and no one predicted. The concept of God at stake has been refigured to do justice to the God that Christians actually worship. The debate about natural theology has been relocated in the wider terrain of the epistemology of theology. Theology has rediscovered its own epistemological assets and invented new ones. The resources of epistemology have been enriched to make available a more apt network of concepts, insights, and arguments. Divine revelation has been refigured to make visible a strong undercurrent of reason below the surface. Theologians have long practised the delicate art of turning the water of philosophy into the wine of theology; philosophers have now matched the miracle by turning the water of theology into the wine of philosophy.

References

Alston, William P. (1991). *Perceiving God: The Epistemology of Religious Experience.* Ithaca and London: Cornell University Press.

Althaus-Reid, Marcella (2000). *Indecent Theology: Theological Perversion in Sex, Gender, and Politics.* London: Routledge.

Barth, Karl (1975). *Church Dogmatics* I/1. Edinburgh: T. & T. Clark.

Davis, Creston, Milbank, John, and Zizek, Slavoj (eds.) (2005). *Theology and the Political: The New Debate.* Durham: Duke University Press.

Flew, Anthony (1966). *God and Philosophy.* London: Hutchinson.

Fulkerson, Mary McClintock (1994). *Changing the Subject: Women's Discourse and Feminist Theology.* Minneapolis: Fortress.

Isasi-Díaz, Ada María (2004). *En La Lucha / In the Struggle.* Minneapolis: Fortress Press.

Lindbeck, George (1984). *The Nature of Doctrine: Religion and Theology in a Postliberal Age.* Philadelphia: Westminster.

Marshall, Bruce (2000). *Trinity and Truth.* Cambridge: Cambridge University Press.

Milbank, John (1990). *Theology and Social Theory: Beyond Secular Reason.* Oxford: Blackwell.

—— Pickstock, Catherine, and Ward, Graham (eds.) (1999). *Radical Orthodoxy: A New Theology.* London: Routledge.

Mitchell, Basil (1974). *The Justification of Religious Belief.* New York: Seabury Press.

Mitchell, Basil (ed.) (1957). *Faith and Logic: Oxford Essays in Philosophical Theology.* London: George Allen and Unwin.

Plantinga, Alvin (2000). *Warranted Christian Belief.* New York: Oxford University Press.

Rieger, Joerg (2001). *God and the Excluded: Visions and Blindspots in Contemporary Theology.* Minneapolis: Fortress.

Swinburne, Richard (1979). *The Existence of God.* Oxford: Clarendon.

Tarski, Alfred (2001 [1944]). 'The Semantic Conception of Truth and the Foundations of Semantics'. In Michael P. Lynch (ed.), *The Nature of Truth: Classic and Contemporary Perspectives,* Cambridge: MIT Press, 331–64.

Vanhoozer, Kevin J. (2005). *The Drama of Doctrine: A Canonical-Linguistic Approach to Christian Theology.* Louisville: Westminster John Knox.

Suggested Reading

Abraham, William J. (2006). *Crossing the Threshold of Divine Revelation.* Grand Rapids: Eerdmans.

Alston (1991).

Aquino, Frederick D. (2004). *Communities of Informed Judgment.* Washington, DC: Catholic University of America Press.

David, Caroline Franks (1989). *The Evidential Force of Religious Experience.* Oxford: Clarendon.

Gale, Richard (1991). *On the Nature and Existence of God.* Cambridge: Cambridge University Press.

Griffiths, Paul J., and Hütter, Reinhard (eds.) (2005). *Reason and Reasons of Faith.* New York: T. & T. Clark.

Hauerwas, Stanley (2001). *With the Grain of the Universe.* Grand Rapids: Brazos.

Howard-Snyder, Daniel, and Moser, Paul K. (2002). *Divine Hiddenness: New Essays.* Cambridge: Cambridge University Press.

Mackie, J. L. (1982). *The Miracle of Theism: Arguments For and Against the Existence of God.* Oxford: Clarendon.

Marshall (2000).

Mavrodes, George I. (1988). *Revelation in Religious Belief.* Philadelphia: Temple University Press.

Milbank (1990).

Mitchell (1974).

Plantinga (2000).

Swinburne (1979).

CHAPTER 2

THE TRINITY

FRED SANDERS

I. Introduction: The Task of the Doctrine of the Trinity

THE doctrine of the Trinity stands out as more than a single doctrine within Christian theology. The word Trinity denotes a field within which an extraordinary range of dogmatic material must be comprehended, brought to expression, and integrated. Its most obvious constituent territories are those of Christology and pneumatology, but through these it also determines the comprehensive *loci* of revelation and soteriology, taking up the full scope of salvation history and providing the framework for the confession of God's gracious self-giving in the economy of salvation. Furthermore, the doctrine of the Trinity has as its characteristic feature that it takes up all of this material together, against the horizon of the eternal being of God *in se*, systematically posing the question of how salvation history is to be correlated with the divine being in itself. To characterize the doctrine of the Trinity in this way is already to charge it with its defining task: The task of the doctrine of the Trinity is to describe the connection between God and the economy of salvation.

More concretely, the doctrine of the Trinity asks about how the threefold act of God in history (the Father sending the Son and the Spirit) corresponds to the triune being of God in eternity. Trinitarianism did not originate from asking about this correspondence as if it were an open question, but on the basis of the primal Christian conviction that God is truly present to his people in Christ (Immanuel, God with us) and the Spirit. There is no prior abstract principle in place dictating that God's salvific actions, whatever they might be, must be revelatory of the divine life itself. In the majestic freedom and condescension of God, it simply is the case that he has elected to open this triune divine depth for human knowledge and fellowship, by accomplishing salvation in this threefold way. The correspondence is grounded in God's determination to be our salvation in person, and his accompanying refusal to neglect, delegate, or even merely create human salvation. Positing himself as the source, means, and end of salvation, God makes himself present to us in salvation history in the same way as he exists in the uttermost depths of his own exalted being: as Father, Son, and Holy Spirit. The doctrine of the Trinity is 'the change in the conception of God which followed, as it was necessitated by, the New Testament conception of Christ and His work' (Denney 1895: 70). On the basis of the gospel of God, Christian faith confesses the God of the gospel. When systematic theology takes up the doctrine of the Trinity, it is scrutinizing and conceptually clarifying this simultaneous confession of God and the gospel. The following chapter is a description of the doctrine of the Trinity from this evangelical perspective.

From the primary task of describing the connection between God and the economy of salvation, there is derived a secondary, critical task of the doctrine of the Trinity. The doctrine functions to identify God, or to specify the particular identity of the God who is the referent of all Christian discourse. 'It is the business of the doctrine of the Trinity', Karl Barth said in 1932, 'to answer the question who God is', and to distinguish 'the Christian doctrine of God as Christian... in contrast to all other possible doctrines of God' (Barth 1975: 301). To say with all seriousness that this doctrine identifies God is to treat it as God's proper name, which is the direction in which Robert W. Jenson developed Barth's lead in his influential 1982 book *The Triune Identity*. Thus 'Father, Son, and Holy Spirit' names the Christian God, just as 'Yahweh' and 'Allah' name the divinities of Judaism and Islam (assuming for the moment that 'Yahweh' points to a biblical monotheism disconnected from a constitutive Christology or pneumatology, as opposed to the New Testament construal of Yahweh via Christology and pneumatology) (see Soulen 2002). This critical naming function derives from the task of describing God's connection to the economy of salvation, because it is neither as a set of syllables nor as a conventional label that 'Father, Son, and Holy Spirit' does the work of naming, but as a condensed narrative providing 'identifying descriptions' from God's history with his people. 'Thus the phrase, "Father, Son, and Holy Spirit" is simultaneously a very compressed telling of the total narrative by which Scripture identifies God and a personal name for the God so specified' (Jenson 1997–9: i. 46). The Christian God is specified when Israel's monotheism is elaborated through a Christology and pneumatology so robust as to be constitutive of that monotheism. Where any of these elements are lacking, God-talk has not yet specified its referent well enough to single out the God who has revealed himself in the sending of the Son and the Spirit. Lesslie Newbigin has shrewdly pointed out that the doctrine of the Trinity has usually seemed less urgent in historical periods when Christian theology thought it could take the identity of its God for granted, whereas epochs marked by a greater awareness of cultural diversity and doctrinal pluralism (the fourth, sixteenth, and late twentieth centuries, for example) have considered the identity of God as something that requires deliberate specification (Newbigin 1963).

II. The Place and Field of Trinitarianism

Because the doctrinal territory being surveyed here is a field-encompassing field, it is a locus where basic decisions are made which have ramifications for all of theology. Even the doctrine's proper place within systematic theology is a matter of unusually sharp contention. There was a traditional scholastic sequence, deriving from Aquinas (who in this departed from Lombard), which first established the doctrine of the one God (his existence, essence, attributes, and operations), and then turned to the triunity of that God (processions, persons, missions) (*ST* 1a. 2–26 and 27–43, in Aquinas 1975). A two-part doctrine of God thus preceded the doctrine of creation, at the beginning of the system. Modern theologians like Rahner have complained that the scholastic order brings with it the temptation to develop the doctrine of the one God in a 'quite philosophical and abstract' manner which 'refers hardly at all to salvation history', meanwhile locking the Trinity 'in even more splendid isolation, with the ensuing danger that the religious mind finds it devoid of interest' (Rahner 1970: 17–18). Rahner could also rightly acknowledge, however, that 'if the treatise *De Deo Uno* is to be real theology and not mere metaphysics, it cannot speak of the one God and his nature without speaking of the God of history and of a historical experience of him, of the God of a possible revelation and self-communication. Hence it is already orientated to the treatise *De Deo Trino*, which deals with such a God in salvation-history' (Rahner 1986: 1767).

In Protestant theology, a similar traditional order (Muller 2003) was overturned by Friedrich Schleiermacher, who postponed discrete consideration of the Trinity until an appendix of his carefully structured *Glaubenslehre*, because the doctrine fell outside of the range of things which could be described scientifically within his method of exegeting the Christian consciousness of redemption. Barth somewhat puckishly inverted Schleiermacher's decision and set the doctrine at the very beginning of his *Church Dogmatics*, precisely where a prolegomena might be expected. As Robert W. Jenson observed, 'It was Barth who taught postmodern theology that the doctrine of Trinity is there to be used: that it is not a puzzle but rather the framework within which theological puzzles can be solved. The *Kirchliche*

Dogmatik is a parade of trinitarian solutions to questions that modern theology had answered in unitarian fashion' (Jenson 1997–9: i. 154). For his part, Jenson crafted his own *Systematic Theology* with such an expansive account of the Trinity that it has room for his entire Christology, pneumatology, and atonement theology, reflecting his view that the identity of God is only rendered by the presentation of these economic events by which God identifies himself. On this plan, the doctrines of creation, the church, and eschatology could easily have been developed internal to the doctrine of the Trinity, 'but organizing the work on the plausible principle that finally *all* Christian teaching in one way or another tells God's own story would of course have obliterated the point' (Jenson 1997–9: ii. v).

Since the mere external sequencing of the doctrines is hardly a matter of great importance, consensus at the level of the table of contents is no goal worth seeking. The substantive concerns behind these questions of order, however, can be seen in the tension between two structural principles. On one hand, since systematic theology must presuppose Christology and pneumatology pervasively, it is best to deploy the doctrine of the Trinity immediately in order to allow it to shape the treatment of every doctrine. On the other hand, since the doctrine of the Trinity cannot be elaborated without rather detailed accounts of its subfields, it should be postponed until those doctrines (at the very least, the doctrines of Christ and the Spirit) are in place. All these elements mutually presuppose each other, and while systematic theology must strive to attest 'the *circumincessio* in which all the treatises of dogmatic theology are in the nature of things involved' (Rahner 1986: 1767), it is not possible to say everything at once, at least for those who live and work 'where a word has both a beginning and an ending' ('*ubi verbum et incipitur et finitur*'; Augustine, *Confessions* 9. 10).

Whenever the time comes, in a comprehensive systematic theology, to give an account of the doctrine of the Trinity, the connection between God and the economy of salvation must be described with adequate attention to both poles. In the history of the doctrine, a formidable array of conceptual categories has emerged to this end: mission, procession, person, nature, consubstantiality, relations of origin, perichoresis, psychological and social analogies, etc. Each of these categories continues to be important and illuminating in its proper place, but each has also proven capable of breaking free from its place and becoming an independent centre of interest. Whether the free-floating element is the Cappadocian account of relations, the psychological models from the final books of Augustine's *De trinitate*, or Aquinas's anatomizing of internal processions, there has been a recurring tendency for the conceptual apparatus, helpful in itself, to escape the orbit of the gospel and begin exerting an independent gravitational pull on later theology. For this reason, the history of the doctrine of the Trinity is punctuated by laments about the doctrine's apparent abstractness, irrelevance, and inscrutability—laments which are themselves expressions of the enduring Christian instinct to keep the trinitarian confession transparent to its biblical, experiential, and evangelical basis.

To establish good order among the elements, the doctrine of the Trinity must take its orientation from the dynamics of God's saving act. What vigorous trinitarian theology demands is a flexible and modest conceptual framework which retains enough vestiges of the biblical narrative to situate the conceptual elements. Much contemporary trinitarian theology operates within such a framework, though the framework itself is usually left implicit, and there is considerable difference of opinion about its precise borders. One possible explication of the framework is as follows. The field of the doctrine of the Trinity can be plotted within the coordinates of two intersecting axes which trace the dynamics of God's self-giving. The defining axis runs from the immanent life of God to the outward acts of God in creation. The other axis connects the two trinitarian persons who are revealed by their personal presence in the missions of the economy, and is therefore an axis running between the Son and the Holy Spirit. The resulting field provides the context for situating the traditional conceptual apparatus of trinitarianism, highlighting certain elements while relegating others to the background. For instance, questions about how the three can be one, or about analogical aids to understanding, are temporarily suspended because they can arise meaningfully and concretely only after being situated within the field defined by these axes. More significantly, the suggested field indicates the presence and action of the first person of the Trinity only obliquely. 'The invisible Father' is not mappable on these coordinates because of the unique, mediated way he comes to be present in the economy of salvation. Just as the hypostatic depth of God the Father is what brings forth the Son and Spirit *ad intra*, it is his love which grounds their missions in the economy. The massive attention which patristic authors gave to the Father–Son relationship is represented in modern theology by the immanent-economic axis, which was often the real point at issue in Arian controversies: is the messianic Son also an eternal Son? The other advantages of this framework are that it frustrates the over-neatness of habitual geometries, resists the seductions of the magic number three, keeps the immanent and economic poles from collapsing into each other, draws special attention to the nexus between Christology and pneumatology, and postpones elaborate conceptual definitions long enough to cede priority to the substantial descriptive work which must precede them.

III. Recentring Trinitarianism on the Economy of Salvation

All of what has been said above reflects the widespread consensus in contemporary theology that the doctrine of the Trinity must be developed in a way that is centred on the *oikonomia*, the history of salvation. A classic expression of this commitment emerged from the *Mysterium Salutis* group of Roman Catholic theologians who took up the task of carrying out the theological renewal called for by Vatican II. The subtitle of their multi-volume work, published between 1965 and 1976, was *Grundriss heilsgeschichtlicher Dogmatik*, and the work attempted to recast all of Christian doctrine in terms of the key motif of salvation history, a category which had emerged from the *nouvelle théologie* of the early twentieth century as well as from dialogue with Protestant thought, and which subsequently informed the council. The assignment of setting the doctrine of the Trinity in the framework of the mystery of salvation fell to Karl Rahner, whose chapter for the series was entitled 'The Triune God as the Transcendent Primal Ground of Salvation History' (Feiner and Löhrer 1965–76: ii. 317). This chapter was later published separately as his influential short book *The Trinity* (Rahner 1970). Of all the mysteries of faith, the teaching about God's essential triunity seemed to many theologians, from that mid-century vantage point, to be the least promising for *heilsgeschichtliche* treatment because least engaged with salvation history. As Rahner later reflected, 'Since St Augustine, the "immanent" Trinity has been so much to the fore in theological discussion . . . and the "economic" Trinity has been so obscured in Christology and *De Gratia* by the principle that all actions *ad extra* in God are common to all three persons or belong to God as one, that it is hard to see what Christian existence has to do with the Trinity in actual life' (Rahner 1986: 1765–6). When, in light of the mystery of salvation, Rahner located the Trinity as 'the transcendent primal ground' of salvation history, he was articulating the consensus that marks the twentieth century's renewed interest in the doctrine: a resolute focusing of attention on the economy of salvation as the ground and criterion of all knowledge about the Trinity.

On the whole, this trend to an economic recentring of trinitarian theology has been a beneficial and necessary corrective within the long history of the doctrine. Although the importance of such recentring is often exaggerated by self-congratulatory contemporary theologies, there had indeed been a dangerous tendency in older works to construct the doctrine of the immanent Trinity from speculative or metaphysical arguments. Whenever the doctrine of the Trinity has been presented as a teaching about the inner life of God, and this inner life is filled out conceptually without sustained reference to God's self-revelation and self-giving in salvation history, the doctrine has gone adrift. It is true that God exists eternally as one being in three persons. The danger lies in stating this doctrine in a way that is opaque to its mode of revelation. In more daring versions of speculative theology, this abstraction takes the form of transcendental deductions from the concept of interpersonal love, or the structure of absolute subjectivity, or some other phenomenon sufficiently complex to entertain a threefold dialectic treatment. In conservative theologies of various kinds, a different kind of abstraction threatens to reduce knowledge of the Trinity to a merely verbal transfer of information, as if God transferred a set of propositions about his threefoldness in order to make it known for its own sake. Either way (through speculative expansion or propositional reduction), dislocated from God's saving acts the doctrine of the immanent Trinity becomes distracting, theologically non-functional, and nettlesome. Against such 'exclusive concentration on the immanent Trinity' which has 'brought the doctrine of the Trinity into disrepute among Catholics and Protestants alike, and has often led to its being dropped from the theological curriculum', David Coffey contends, 'The proper study of the Trinity is the study of the economic Trinity' (Coffey 1999: 16).

On the other hand, merely to narrate the events of salvation history, that is, to tell the story of the Father's sending of the Son and Spirit, without allowing the claims of the narrative to push back into the eternal being of God, is to stall out at the level of the economy of salvation without actually saying anything about God himself. Soteriology then exhausts theology proper. However conceptually unstable the position may be, a great deal of trinitarian theology in the late twentieth century took as its starting point a strong interpretation of Karl Rahner's theological *Grundaxiom* that 'the economic Trinity is the immanent Trinity, and vice versa' (Rahner 1970: 22). Taken in its most radical sense, this axiom indicates not merely an epistemological focus on the economy of salvation, but (especially in the direction indicated by the vice versa) a denial that God in himself is triune apart from salvation history. Catherine Mowry LaCugna's *God For Us: The Trinity and Christian Life*, for example, inveighed against 'the non-soteriological doctrine of God' or any version of immanent trinitarian theology which claimed to be 'an analysis of what is "inside" God' rather than 'a way of speaking about the structure or pattern of God's self-expression in salvation history' (LaCugna 1991: 225). Speaking programmatically, for LaCugna 'the fundamental issue in trinitarian theology is not the inner workings of the "immanent" Trinity, but the question of how the trinitarian pattern of salvation history is to be correlated with the eternal being of God' (LaCugna 1991: 6). This way of framing trinitarianism includes both a salutary affirmation and an unfortunately polemical denial. The advent of 'scare quotes' around the 'immanent' Trinity, for example, is symptomatic.

Such reductionistically economic trinitarianism is equivalent to a denial of the immanent Trinity altogether, and leaves theology with nothing beyond structure, pattern, and history, with no way of referring to the God who takes his stand in that history. As Karl Barth had already asked in the 1930s, 'What would "God for us" mean if it were not said against the background of "God in Himself"?' (Barth 1975: 171). Wolfhart Pannenberg's theological system depicts God as very closely engaged with history, but Pannenberg also warns that the priority of the immanent Trinity must be maintained:

It is certainly true that the trinitarian God in the history of salvation is the same God as in His eternal life. But there is also a necessary distinction that maintains the priority of the eternal communion of the triune God over that communion's explication in the history of salvation. Without that distinction, the reality of the one God tends to be dissolved into the process of the world. (Pannenberg 2000: 51)

What Pannenberg describes in somewhat metaphysical terms can be stated more personally: without this distinction, the freedom of God is eclipsed. Paul D. Molnar has argued that 'All Christian theologians realize that the purpose of a doctrine of the immanent Trinity is to recognize, uphold and respect God's freedom' (Molnar 2002: ix), and has shown how the distinction must be not simply asserted, but guarded with vigilance at strategic points such as *creatio ex nihilo*, the pre-existence of Christ as *logos asarkos*, and the distinction between the Holy Spirit and the human spirit.

Notwithstanding the variety of 'post-Rahnerian programmes to collapse the immanent Trinity into the economic' which flourished for a time (Gunton 2003: 71), the twentieth-century recentring of the doctrine of the Trinity on the economy of salvation does not of itself entail denying the immanent Trinity nor assimilating *theologia* to *oikonomia* without remainder. The editors of *Mysterium Salutis* had already recognized this in the period just prior to the ecumenical revival of interest in trinitarian theology:

without the depth dimension of *theologia*, all talk about the *oikonomia* and salvation history becomes admittedly flat and merely foreground. What Barth said of evangelical theology holds also for Catholic: 'The subject of evangelical theology is God in the history of his acts.' (Feiner and Löhrer 1965–76: i, xxx; cf. Barth 1963: 9)

Such easy balance is characteristic of any elaboration of trinitarian theology which recalls that its criterion is the clear articulation of the gospel. Thus Thomas F. Torrance strikes the same equipoise:

the historical manifestations of God as Father, Son, and Holy Spirit have evangelical and theological significance only as they have a transhistorical and transfinite reference beyond to an ultimate ground in God himself. They cannot be Gospel if their reference breaks off at the finite boundaries of this world of space and time, for as such they would be empty of divine validity and saving significance—they would leave us trapped in some kind of historical positivism. The historical manifestations of the Trinity are Gospel, however, if they are grounded beyond history in the eternal personal distinctions between the Father, the Son, and the Holy Spirit inherent in the Godhead, that is, if the Fatherhood of the Father, the Sonship of the Son, and the Communion of the Spirit belong to the inner life of God and constitute his very Being. (Torrance 1996: 6)

If a speculative construction of the immanent Trinity is one possible abstraction from the serious business of trinitarian theology, the opposite abstraction is a speculative deconstruction of the immanent Trinity which reduces trinitarian theology to 'some kind of historical positivism'.

IV. The Economic-Immanent Axis

Epistemic priority may rest with the economic Trinity, but ontic priority resides in the immanent. The two are bound together. Much depends, then, on the direction being followed by any particular theological treatment of the Trinity. Augustine's *De trinitate*, for example, begins with the sendings of the Son and Spirit, asking how sender and sent can be equal in all ways. From here Augustine climbs to the eternal relations of origin revealed by the missions, and ends with an attempt to conceive of the one God's immanent triunity. Aquinas's *Summa Theologiae*, on the other hand, begins with the most fundamental logical distinction, the processions (*ST* 1a. 27, 1: 'Are there processions in God?'), and ends with missions (*ST* 1a. 43, 1: 'Is it suitable for a divine person to be sent?'). In whichever direction it moves, trinitarian theology must make the trip along the axis between God *in se* and God *pro nobis*, tracing God's covenant faithfulness as it is grounded in his character, and thus following what Barth called 'the way of the knowledge of God' (Barth 1957: 179).

Considered as an actual movement of God's grace from above to below, the immanent-economic axis is the occasion for wonder and praise, the one event of divine self-giving than which nothing greater can be thought. Here theology inevitably approximates pure doxology. Considered as a reflective movement of thought from below to above, however, the economic-immanent axis is an intellectual project whose closest analogues are observation, induction, and the formation of conceptual models. Here theology confronts the demand that it be rigorous, consistent, and creative in articulating how the various elements of the biblical witness are to be integrated. It is one thing to assert, with Barth, that 'to the involution and convolution [*Ineinander und Miteinander*] of the three modes of being in the essence of God there corresponds exactly their involution and convolution in his work' (Barth 1975: 374). It is another thing to describe how the particular involution and convolution seen in the economic relations among Jesus Christ, his Father, and their Spirit are to be construed as revealing the very life of God. It is no surprise that the thorniest problems of the doctrine of the Trinity tend to be located precisely here.

The notoriously difficult question of the *filioque*, for example, is mainly an extended discussion about the extent to which the economic missions are revelatory of the immanent processions. The pentecostal Spirit is obviously poured out on all flesh by the Father and the exalted Son; they are the senders behind the advent of the Spirit. If it were axiomatic that every mission is revelatory of a procession, then the Spirit would obviously proceed, within the immanent Trinity, from the Father and also the Son: *filioque*. But there are good reasons to withhold assent from so immediate a deduction, and not simply the monopatrist or anti-filioquist reasons traditionally urged by the eastern churches. More fundamentally, the direct deduction of trinitarian relations from the history of salvation is rendered unworkable by what Gary D. Badcock has called 'the problem of economic diversity', which is a 'diversity, not only of the possible trinitarian *interpretations* to which the economy of salvation is susceptible, but of the actual economic basis of trinitarian theology itself' (Badcock 1997: 213; see 212–29).

Father, Son, and Spirit interact in so many ways in the economy of salvation that we are actually confronted with the material for multiple models that resist harmonizing. In the instance of the *filioque*, while the Word pours out the Spirit, the Spirit also brings about the incarnation of the Word. As Bruce D. Marshall summarizes, 'Thus we can read off from the economy both that the Spirit originates from the Son, and that the Son originates from the Spirit. But these look like contradictories, so one of them has to be false' (Marshall 2004*b*: 197). Why do filioquists ignore the trinitarian implications of the spiritual conception of Christ and of the other triadic configurations? Why do monopatrists refuse to read back along the trajectory of the Son's sending of the Spirit? Without some criterion for deciding which economic relations are revelatory of God's own life, such problems are not resolvable, and divergent conclusions are bound to seem arbitrary.

If the excess of economic configurations seems at first to set a limit to coherent trinitarian constructs, the sheer abundance of relationships may also hold untapped possibilities. There are economic relations among Father, Son, and Spirit which are clearly witnessed in scripture, but which have been underused in developing the doctrine of the immanent Trinity. Relatively early in the development of the doctrine of the Trinity, the Christian tradition gave privileged status to one set of relations as the foundation of trinitarian difference: relations of origin. The *filioque* disagreement is precisely over these primal relations, to the exclusion of the others. For example, it has not normally been considered relevant that John of Damascus described the Holy Spirit as 'the companion of the Word and the revealer of His energy, ... an essential power ... proceeding from the Father and resting in the Word, and showing forth the Word' (*On the Orthodox Faith* 1.7, in Schaff 1980: ix. 5b). Is John mobilizing these verbs and prepositions to describe the *oikonomia*, or does he allude to the Spirit's accompanying, manifesting, and resting on the Word within the immanent Trinity as well? If they are realities within the immanent Trinity, are they any less decisive than the relations of origin? In ecumenical dialogue over the *filioque*, Jürgen Moltmann has proposed distinguishing between two dimensions of God's life: the constitutional level of the processions, and the relational level at which all of these other pluriform and perichoretic relations take place. The two dimensions need not be thought of as temporally sequential nor ontologically ranked, merely as distinct (Moltmann 1981). Pannenberg likewise has argued that there is a 'richly structured nexus of relationships' among the three, and that while the persons are indeed constituted by their relations to each other, 'yet the persons cannot be reduced to individual relations' such as origin. 'None of the other relations is merely incidental to the Son and Spirit in their relation to the Father. All have a place in the distinctiveness and fellowship of the trinitarian persons' (Pannenberg 1991–8: i. 320). Robert W. Jenson, typically, makes the point more clearly but too drastically: 'that the Spirit rests upon the Son is not a phenomenon merely of the economic Trinity—there are in any case no such phenomena' (Jenson 1997–9: i. 143).

The thorough privileging of the relations of origin has put a certain amount of pressure on trinitarianism, forcing the rest of the data to find recognition elsewhere, as for instance in Moltmann's somewhat idiosyncratic constitutive-relational distinction. The same pressure has also found release in established doctrinal traditions like the exploration of the divine energies in Eastern Orthodoxy, or the explication of eternal decrees and an immanent trinitarian covenant in Reformed thought. In their own ways, each of these traditions opens up zones where the manifold relations of the three persons can be confessed without causing confusion over the processions. Whatever their limits, they approach the insight that relational complexity in the *oikonomia* may faithfully enact the richness and multiplicity of the personal relations in the being of the one God. The sudden popularity of a strong version of social trinitarianism in the late twentieth century is probably most charitably understood as another of these attempts to trace the richness of the economic configurations to their transcendent ground in the divine being. Granted such a 'richly structured nexus of relationships' among Father, Son, and Holy Spirit in the history of salvation, the immanent-trinitarian nexus must be equally rich and no less structured, even as we move upward along the axis from economic to immanent. This move alone, however, would not signal what is novel in contemporary social trinitarianism. The characteristic social-trinitarian move is to transpose the conceptual apparatus as well, positing in the immanent Trinity three distinct centres of consciousness, volition, and agency, which stand as persons over against each other with faculties of their own. At issue are some general questions of theological language, such as whether terms like 'person' and 'self' can be employed univocally at both ends of the axis. Equally important is the gap that appears here between an ancient valorizing of essence categories (with person categories relatively understocked), over against a modern elaboration of person categories (with an accompanying emptying out of essence categories). The strength of this recent social trinitarianism is this: Everyone is bound to be a social trinitarian at the economic level. Porting over all of the categories (person, mind, agent, will, faculties, etc.), however, as univocally true of the eternal divine persons, is probably an instinctive attempt to bridge the gap between the richly interpersonal economy (Jesus and his Father) and the sheer austerity of the relations of origin confessed by classic trinitarianism (paternity and filiality). Whatever that 'richly structured nexus of relationships' is among Father, Son, and Spirit, it must be confessed to be love. Wherever relations of origin seem inadequate to bear that description, there will be a need to articulate the other relations in which scripture sets before our eyes the love of the Father and the Son in the Spirit.

Fraught questions such as the *filioque* and the meaning of personhood are rooted, then, in the prior question of what criteria should guide trinitarian theology in interpreting the economy of salvation as revelatory of the divine life. Prior to that question, however, is a fundamental question of why Christian doctrine should regard the *oikonomia* as revelatory of *theologia* proper in the first place. Where does the initial cue come from that lets the interpreter know to start the project? Does the economy itself teach us to read the economy as an image or revelation of God's self? Walter Kasper has warned against behaving as if the Trinity is deducible from the history of salvation 'by a kind of extrapolation'. Reading evidence from the economy back into the immanent Trinity 'was certainly not the path the early church followed in developing the doctrine of the Trinity in the form of confession and dogma' (Kasper 1984: 276). Kasper points away from the welter of events that make up the economy and fixes our attention first on the primal ecclesial act of baptism in the triune name, a practice and formula which developed 'from the risen Lord's commission regarding baptism', that is, the great commission passage, Matthew 28: 19. 'Knowledge of the trinitarian mystery was thus due directly to the revelation of the Word and not to a process of deduction' (Kasper 1984: 276).

Whatever riches of the knowledge of God are revealed in the history of salvation, to approach the history as if it were self-evidently God's self-revelation would run perilously close to positing a general principle about the God–world relationship, a general principle which would itself be underdetermined by revelation. Divine revelation is inalienably linked to intention on the part of the revealer, and 'unfolds through deeds and words bound together by an inner dynamism', to use the words of Vatican II's *Dei Verbum* (§2, in Tanner 1990: ii. 972). Kasper's caution is a good reminder that theology should have a good conscience about behaving as if it were led by scripture, even taking crucial guidance from the inspired text as containing, among other things, revealed propositions. Kasper's own theological work is an instance of a project that is well disposed toward revelation through history and committed to reading the signs of the Trinity in the history of salvation. He admits, however, that theology is in possession of a rudimentary doctrine of the immanent Trinity even before it turns to the task of exegeting salvation history under the guidance of an axiom that the economy is revelatory: 'This axiom presupposes knowledge of the immanent Trinity and is meant to interpret and concretize the immanent Trinity in an appropriate way' (Kasper 1984: 277). Carried out in conjunction with some amount of verbal revelation, reading the economy is not a self-initiated or self-norming project. As Bruce D. Marshall notes, 'if we are to "read" the economic data in a way which yields a coherent set of results regarding the relations of origin among the divine persons, we need guidance which the economic data do not themselves provide—perhaps from some sort of authoritative teaching about what makes each person the unique individual he is' (Marshall 2004*b*: 197). Any such authoritative teaching would of course have to be handled not as a sheer given, but scrutinized to see whether 'an inner dynamism' between word and deed can be discerned. The main lines of the doctrine of the Trinity have been defined by a Christian tradition which at least thinks it does discern such a relation.

What is needed above all is a holistic approach which can assess all of the economic evidence in one massive movement of theological understanding. Because of the uniquely integral character of the doctrine of the Trinity, it cannot be formulated in a fragmentary way, one bit of evidence after another. Specifically, the fragmentary approach cannot of itself underwrite the necessary transposition of the biblical evidence from the salvation-history level to the transcendent, immanent-trinitarian level, a transposition which requires that all the evidence be reinterpreted simultaneously with its structuring patterns intact. Making the jump from economy to Trinity requires a kind of economy-wide gestalt perception, in which the involution and convolution of Father, Son, and Spirit around the life of Jesus are seen as one coherent pattern bearing a discernible, describable, threefold form. This triune form, once recognized, can then be understood as the projection onto human history of the form of God's triune life. Taken in isolation, none of the elements of the economy makes a particularly strong case for being read back into the immanent Trinity: not even the begetting of the Son or the procession of the Spirit. They must be perceived together integrally, together with the structures obtaining among them, in order to motivate and accomplish the jump to the immanent Trinity.

This becomes a more urgent requirement the more trinitarian theology settles into its task of reflection on revelation that is always mediated by the text. Arguments about texts can quite readily degenerate into fragmentary observations and isolated proofs, to the detriment of the larger doctrinal outlines. This tendency has been exacerbated by the rise of a crucial dialogue partner for modern systematic theology: the discipline of historical-critical biblical research. The overall trend of modern biblical scholarship has been toward a severe attenuation of the traditional exegetical arguments by which the doctrine of the Trinity was crafted and by which it has been supported since patristic times. This is true not only of biblical criticism in its most corrosively sceptical expressions, which have often enough been explicitly anti-trinitarian in scope and motivation. Richard A. Muller has argued that what was occurring in the era after the Reformation, and is continuing today, is a massive 'alteration of patterns of interpretation away from the patristic and medieval patterns that had initially yielded the doctrine of the Trinity and given it a vocabulary consistent with traditional philosophical usage' (Muller 2003: 62). To say that this brings us to a crisis is not to lament the contribution of critical biblical research: Who today would want to support the doctrine of the Trinity using the strangely agglomerated testimony of Proverbs 8 (translated, no less, with Wisdom saying, 'God created me at the beginning of his ways'), the *comma johanneum*'s 'three that bear witness in heaven', and an allegorical gloss on the Good Samaritan leaving two coins (the Son and the Spirit) with the innkeeper? The vocabulary and conceptual apparatus of trinitarianism need to be chastened and kept near to scripture, and critical scholarship demands this. But the discipline also tends toward fragmentation and a kind of textual atomism which make the trinitarian construal of scripture impossible. Whatever weaknesses may have hobbled patristic and medieval interpretative practices, and however unusable some of those techniques may be for us, their great virtue was always their grasp of the overall meaning of scripture. The doctrine of the Trinity is a large doctrine, and its formulation and defence have always required a certain ampleness of reflection on the revealed data. The way forward is to admit that, in Colin Gunton's words, 'it must be acknowledged that there is some doubt as to whether Scripture supports the creedal confession directly or without great labour'. For the justification of a crucial trinitarian doctrine like the Son's eternal generation, 'prooftexting is not enough.... [W]e must go beyond any single proof-text or texts and examine the broader context in which it must be understood, that of Scripture as a whole' (Gunton 2003: 63). The doctrine of the Trinity is a conceptual foregrounding of the entire matrix of economic revelation. Only in this comprehensive context can the Christological *monogenesis* of John 1: 18 be combined with the pneumatological *ekporeusis* of John 15: 26 to produce a doctrine of the eternal Trinity. It is senseless to try to retain the result of the early church's holistic interpretation of scripture (the doctrine of the Trinity) without cultivating, in a way appropriate for our own time, the interpretative practice which produced that result. The crucial interpretative practice, which as we have seen must inform both exegesis and doctrinal theology, is attention to the economy of salvation as a coherent whole.

V. Real Presences

The doctrine of the Trinity, centred on the history of salvation and inquiring systematically into the connection between that history and the God who takes his stand therein, is an account of the real, personal presence of the Son and the Spirit among us. The economy of salvation is actuated by the two kairotic missions, the Christological and the pneumatological (Gal. 4: 4–6). These two missions are mutually constitutive, or configured internally toward one another, such that it is hard to know whether it is best to go on describing them as two missions or as a single, twofold mission of the Son and the Spirit. Without the anointing Spirit, there is no *christos*, no anointed one. On the other hand, the Spirit is the 'Spirit of Jesus Christ', the 'Spirit of the Son', and comes decisively into the church through the ascended Christ on the basis of his accomplished work of incarnation, death, and resurrection. The outpouring of the Spirit seems to presuppose the work of Christ and to find its purpose in extending that work or applying it. The incarnation and atonement, on the other hand, seem to be ordered toward making the pentecostal indwelling possible. The Irenaean metaphor of the Father taking hold of the world through his two hands has become increasingly common, and a growing awareness of the interpenetration between Christology and pneumatology has opened new paths for theological exploration (Del Colle 1994). All of this, however, is predicated on the fact that the second and third persons of the Trinity are confessed to have been actually sent out from their inalienable centre in the divine life, to enter our existence in manners appropriate to each of them: hypostatic union on the one hand, and indwelling on the other. These missions, of course, are not categories of creation but of redemption, and we are bypassing the question of personal trinitarian presences in creation to pursue the decisive question of how the persons of the Trinity are present in redemption. To put it another way, we are asking how systematic theology in the various ecumenical traditions has developed the doctrine of grace in trinitarian terms.

By common consent, it was for us and our salvation that God has drawn very near in the Son and the Spirit. But the distinct theological traditions of the Christian churches have explicated this rather alarming nearness in various ways: through doctrines of appropriations, of energies, and of created grace. Each of these doctrines is attended with some ambiguity regarding the nearness which it permits. Appropriation, for example, is the ancient practice of attributing to one person of the Trinity a characteristic or action which is in fact common to the Trinity as a whole. The ancient creed appropriates the creation of heaven and earth to God the Father almighty, but this is not to be understood as proper or exclusive: the Son and Spirit are also the creator, are also the almighty. It is proper to refer creation to the first person of the Trinity because from the first person proceeds everything within the Godhead. The whole point of appropriation is to illuminate or illustrate the distinct features of each person, even in those undivided external acts of the Trinity where no distinct personal action is manifest (Emery 2005). However, the doctrine can easily function the other way, relegating every apparent trinitarian disclosure in history to being a function of the one God causing effects within creation, but sending signals that these effects are to be referred in name or understanding to one particular person of the Trinity. External actions appropriated to a trinitarian person are not real presences in the way incarnation and Pentecost are. A central task embraced by western theology, in fact, is explicating the missions of the Son and Spirit as being proper, not merely appropriated.

The theology of the eastern churches does not use the doctrine of appropriations as thoroughly as western theology, preferring to describe external actions of the Trinity as concerted rather than undivided. Instead, it has employed a conceptual distinction between the ineffable divine essence and the uncreated energies around that essence; the redeemed can participate in the latter but not in the former. The doctrine seems to have been crafted to explain how monks involved in hesychastic prayer were in fact communing with the true God, seeing uncreated light rather than created. Yet this doctrine, designed to underwrite intimate contact with God, can also convert suddenly into its opposite and serve as an explanation of how Christian religious experience does not in fact strike home in the heart of God. In this case, much depends on whether the uncreated energies are thought of in entitative terms, or alternatively as divine actions. The more the energies are described in entitative terms, the more they seem to be buffers between God and the human person. When they are construed more dynamically along the lines of divine actions, it seems clearer that believers are immediately in the hands of God their redeemer.

Roman Catholic theology under the Thomist rubric (and this includes magisterial teachings such as those of Trent and Vatican I) has spoken of God's personal presence to believers in a way that includes the notion of created grace. According to this tradition, God does not directly and personally act on the created person without a created medium, but instead causes effects in the redeemed by the infusion of a gift which is distinct from himself. The point of the doctrine is not to deny God's personal agency, but to account for it in a way that recognizes the form of its reception by a creature and to preserve the kind of room for creaturely freedom which direct divine action on the soul would seem to obliterate. Sympathetically understood, as for instance it has been in dialogue with Eastern Orthodoxy (Williams 1999; Marshall 2004*a*), created grace is not a substitute for uncreated grace (the personal presence of God, particularly of the Holy Spirit), but the means by which uncreated grace causes effects in the soul. On the other hand, once in place the doctrine has acted as an obstacle to a clear confession of differentiated trinitarian presence: the Spirit's indwelling is less proper to the third person and more proper to the Godhead, and the Our Father is addressed to God the Trinity rather than God the Father. This set of questions in Roman Catholic theology is vexed, as interpreters like Yves Congar have freely admitted (Congar 1997: ii. 79–99).

In contrast to this, classical Protestant theology has tended to hold to a direct and apparently naive use of biblical language, taking some biblical statements about the three persons at face value without subjecting them to the sophisticated analysis of the medieval scholastic traditions. From the clear but unelaborated statements of Calvin ('the Holy Spirit is the bond by which Christ effectually unites us to himself'; *Institutes* 3. 1. 1, in Calvin 1960: 538) to the more scholastic works of Owen and Turretin, the indwelling of the Holy Spirit in the believer is described, without nuance or qualification, as a direct personal office proper to the third person of the Trinity distinctly. On the Reformed side of Protestantism, this commitment is strengthened by two things: a notorious lack of squeamishness over the notion that direct divine action can move the human will without obliterating properly human freedom; and a preference for categories of interpersonal fellowship as opposed to categories of ontological participation. It is worth noting, however, that the Wesleyan and Pietist offshoots of Protestantism affirm the Spirit's direct personal presence, either not noticing or not caring that their commitment to libertarian human agency might equally lead them to install created grace as a buffer between God and human action.

The doctrine of the Trinity, as an ancient landmark of consensual Christian belief, has long been the site of great ecumenical convergence (the *filioque* notwithstanding). If the varied theological and confessional traditions have anything in common, it is the ancient doctrine of God, or theology proper. However, with the recent recentring of the doctrine on the economy of salvation, certain latent tensions have come to the surface. Oddly, the more clearly the doctrine of God's triunity is integrated into soteriology (an integration demanded by exigencies internal to both doctrines), the more the Trinity will be elaborated in terms shaped by confessional concerns and disputes regarding soteriology. When Trinity and gospel are closely linked, contentions about the character of the gospel also show up in the doctrine of God. This is something of a paradox in recent developments. The ecumenical centrality of trinitarian confession, however, is no illusion. We should gamble on the possibility that the convergence of the various doctrinal traditions in the doctrine of God might have a greater depth of ingression in the Christian church's web of belief than do the details of the various soteriological elaborations. Greater attention to the connection of Trinity and gospel could then be expected to open new avenues of approach to some deadlocked problems. For example, in the thicket of questions surrounding the direct personal presences of Son and Spirit in the economy of grace, it may be possible to marshal economic-trinitarian resources before undertaking a redescription of the zone between God and man traditionally populated by accounts of appropriations, uncreated energies, and created grace. The economic Trinity itself may contain adequate resources for addressing the concerns that arise here: the enhypostatic Christology of post-Chalcedonian conciliar thought puts the eternal Logos personally into the economy in a way that deserves further exploration, and a proper mission of the Holy Spirit as the agent of divine indwelling is the pneumatological parallel. Between these two hypostatically distinct missions, there may be enough space for a satisfactory account of human freedom (Smail 1988: 66–73). The way forward is a more determined commitment to these two real presences (and decidedly downstream from them, the sacraments). In this way, Christian theology can confess the integral doctrine of the Trinity in a way that acknowledges, with all the saints and also with appropriate conceptual integrity and rigour, 'what is the breadth and length and height and depth, and to know the love of Christ' (Eph. 3: 18).

References

Aquinas, Thomas (1975). *Summa Theologiae.* London: Blackfriars.

Badcock, Gary D. (1997). *Light of Truth and Fire of Love: A Theology of the Holy Spirit.* Grand Rapids: Eerdmans.

Barth, Karl (1957). *Church Dogmatics* II/1. Edinburgh: T. & T. Clark.

—— (1963). *Evangelical Theology: An Introduction.* New York: Holt, Rinehart and Winston.

—— (1975). *Church Dogmatics* I/1. Edinburgh: T. & T. Clark.

Calvin, John (1960). *Institutes of the Christian Religion.* Philadelphia: Westminster.

Coffey, David (1999). *Deus Trinitas: The Doctrine of the Triune God.* New York: Oxford University Press.

Congar, Yves (1997). *I Believe in the Holy Spirit.* 3 vols. New York: Crossroad Herder.

Del Colle, Ralph (1994). *Christ and the Spirit: Spirit-Christology in Trinitarian Perspective.* New York: Oxford University Press.

Denney, James (1895). *Studies in Theology: Lectures Delivered in Chicago Theological Seminary.* London: Hodder and Stoughton.

Emery, Gilles (2005). 'The Personal Mode of Trinitarian Action in Saint Thomas Aquinas', *The Thomist* 69: 31–77.

Feiner, Johannes, and Löhrer, Magnus (1965–76). *Mysterium Salutis: Grundriss Heilsgeschichtlicher Dogmatik.* 5 vols. Einsiedeln: Benziger Verlag.

Gunton, Colin E. (2003). 'And in One Lord Jesus Christ... Begotten not Made'. In id., *Father, Son, and Holy Spirit: Essays toward a Fully Trinitarian Theology.* London: T. & T. Clark, 58–74.

Jenson, Robert W. (1982). *The Triune Identity: God According to the Gospel.* Philadelphia: Fortress.

—— (1997–9). *Systematic Theology.* 2 vols. New York: Oxford University Press.

Kasper, Walter (1984). *The God of Jesus Christ.* New York: Crossroad.

LaCugna, Catherine Mowry (1991). *God For Us: The Trinity and Christian Life.* New York: HarperCollins.

Marshall, Bruce D. (2004*a*). '*Ex Occidente Lux?* Aquinas and Eastern Orthodox Theology'. In Jim Fodor and Frederick Christian Bauerschmidt (eds.), *Aquinas in Dialogue: Thomas for the Twenty-First Century,* Oxford: Blackwell, 19–46.

—— (2004*b*). 'The Trinity'. In Gareth Jones (ed.), *The Blackwell Companion to Modern Theology,* Oxford: Blackwell, 183–203.

Molnar, Paul D. (2002). *Divine Freedom and the Doctrine of the Immanent Trinity: In Dialogue with Karl Barth and Contemporary Theology.* Edinburgh: T. & T. Clark.

Moltmann, Jürgen (1981). 'Theological Proposals towards the Resolution of the *Filioque* Controversy' In Lukas Vischer (ed.), *Spirit of God, Spirit of Christ: Ecumenical Reflections on the* Filioque *Controversy,* World Council of Churches Faith and Order Paper No. 103, London: SPCK, 164–73.

Muller, Richard A. (2003). *Post-Reformation Reformed Dogmatics: The Rise and Development of Reformed Orthodoxy, ca. 1520 to ca. 1725,* iv. *The Triunity of God.* Grand Rapids: Baker Academic.

Newbigin, Lesslie (1963). *Relevance of Trinitarian Doctrine for Today's Mission.* London: Edinburgh House.

Pannenberg, Wolfhart (2000). 'Books in Review: Robert W. Jenson, *Systematic Theology*: Volumes I & II'. *First Things* 103 (May): 49–53.

—— (1991–8). *Systematic Theology.* 3 vols. Grand Rapids: Eerdmans.

Rahner, Karl (1970). *The Trinity.* New York: Herder and Herder.

—— (1986). 'Trinity in Theology'. In id. (ed.), *Encyclopedia of Theology: The Concise Sacramentum Mundi.* New York: Crossroad, 1764–71.

Schaff, Philip (ed.) (1980). *A Select Library of the Nicene and Post-Nicene Fathers of the Christian Church.* 2nd series. Edinburgh: T. & T. Clark.

Smail, Thomas A. (1988). *The Giving Gift: The Holy Spirit in Person.* London: Hodder and Stoughton.

Soulen, R. Kendall (2002). 'The Name of the Holy Trinity: A Triune Name'. *Theology Today* 59/2 (July): 244–61.

Tanner, N. P., SJ (ed.) (1990). *Decrees of the Ecumenical Councils.* 2 vols. Georgetown: Sheed and Ward.

Torrance, Thomas F. (1996). *The Christian Doctrine of God: One Being Three Persons.* Edinburgh: T. & T. Clark.

Williams, A. N. (1999). *The Ground of Union: Deification in Aquinas and Palamas.* Oxford: Oxford University Press.

Suggested Reading

Badcock (1997).

Coffey (1999).

Congar (1997).

Davis, Stephen T., Kendall, Daniel, and O'Colins, Gerald (eds.) (1999). *The Trinity: An Interdisciplinary Symposium on the Trinity.* New York: Oxford University Press.

Jenson (1997–9).

Kasper (1984).

LaCugna (1991).

Molnar (2002).

Pannenberg (1991–8: i. 259–448).

Rahner (1970).

Torrance (1996).

CHAPTER 3

THE ATTRIBUTES OF GOD

STEPHEN R. HOLMES

I. Introduction

Perhaps no doctrine of theology is more ubiquitous than that of the divine attributes or perfections. It is possible to receive, and perhaps, given a liturgy to follow, even to celebrate, the eucharist without any theological understanding of what is being done—although it will hardly be an honouring celebration in the latter case. It is certainly—gloriously—possible to be redeemed without any notion of redemption. At times it has been proposed that Christians should restrict their language to biblical terms and so refuse to engage in Christological or trinitarian theology. (This procedure was seriously proposed as a way through the fourth-century trinitarian controversies, and has occasionally been revived since the Reformation by radical Protestant and Free Church groups wary of any dependence on tradition.) It is, however, impossible to speak about or to God without some commitment concerning the divine attributes. A sentence that begins 'God is . . .', praise that asserts 'Lord, you are . . .', or intercession that pleads some aspect of the character of God ('have mercy, Lord, for you are . . .') all already betray a doctrine of the divine perfections. That a word (e.g., 'good') is held to be a more adequate continuation of each of these statements than other possible words (e.g., 'bad', 'morally indifferent') is a theological commitment.

Abraham pleads the perfections of God over the cities of the plain: 'Shall not the Judge of all the earth do what is just?' (Gen. 18: 25). The highest praises, and the deepest laments, of the psalmists alike turn on recalling before God his attributes: 'Great is the LORD, and greatly to be praised; his greatness is unsearchable.... On the glorious splendour of your majesty... I will meditate.... They shall celebrate the fame of your abundant goodness, and shall sing aloud of your righteousness.... The LORD is gracious and merciful, slow to anger and abounding in steadfast love' (Ps. 145: 3–8); 'Has his steadfast love ceased for ever?... Has God forgotten to be gracious? Has he in anger shut up his compassion?' (Ps. 77: 8–9). In just these few verses it is proclaimed that God is just, righteous, great, majestic, abundantly good, gracious, merciful, steadfast in love, slow to anger, compassionate; the task of a doctrine of God's perfections is to bring some order to such exuberant and heartfelt exclamations.

That the issue is ubiquitous does not make it easy, of course. There are at least five problems in this task:

1. There is an issue of *derivation*. How do we decide which words are appropriate completions of the sentence 'God is...'? 'Good' might seem easy, but terms like 'wrathful' or 'impassible' have generated extended and heated debate in recent decades.
2. There is an issue of *span*. 'God is good' presumably does not say everything Christian theologians would wish to say about God. How many words are necessary before we may claim that the list displays some measure of comprehensiveness? The *Westminster Shorter Catechism* defines God as 'a Spirit, infinite, eternal, and unchangeable, in his being, wisdom, power, holiness, justice, goodness, and truth', which Charles Hodge asserts is 'the best definition of God ever penned by man' (Hodge 1960: i. 367). Is Hodge right? On what criteria might the question be decided?
3. There is a problem of *analogy*. I may well find myself affirming in prayer one morning that 'God is good', and then in conversation soon afterwards affirming of a certain undergraduate student that she is also 'good', and perhaps of a cricketer in the headlines that he is 'very good'. 'Good' in each context carries a discernibly different meaning: the cricketer demonstrates finely honed physical ability and coolness under pressure; the student shows academic promise; and God—what does 'good' mean when applied to God? Clearly something different from the two other uses in the example, but is it something different from every use with a human being as a referent? This seems likely: of which of the saints will it be said 'she is good in exactly the same way that God is good'? But if this is so, how does any meaning attach to the word 'good' when applied to God?
4. There is a philosophical problem of *definition*. Is it appropriate to call God 'good' because there is some external standard of goodness against which we may measure God? If so, does this not suggest that there is something greater than God, which stands in judgement over him? But if not, does 'good' mean anything at all—is it not just an empty cipher we choose to apply to God, when we apparently could have as easily and appropriately chosen 'evil'?

5. There is a *historical* problem concerning the relationship of certain divine attributes to other areas of theology. Briefly stated, there are a class of attributes (including impassibility, simplicity, and immutability) that were until about 1800 held to be necessary to orthodox accounts of the Trinity, the incarnation, and the atonement. Since then, it has been widely assumed and argued by both philosophers and theologians that such attributes are in fact in straight contradiction with trinitarian theology, Christology, and soteriology.

These five issues will give shape to the account of the divine perfections in this chapter.

II. The Question of Derivation

How may we discover words that are adequate to the task of naming God? Here immediately we come face to face with what will be the core problem of this chapter. If we were to ask the historical question, 'prior to 1800, how were such words discovered in Christian theology?' the answer is surprisingly easy. One method dominates, the method of the *viae* (ways), and it is found in embryonic form in the fathers of both East and West, in developed form in the great medieval Catholic summae, and virtually unchanged in the Lutheran and Reformed school dogmatics of the seventeenth century. God, on this account, is utter perfection, the *summum bonum*, or 'the absolute' in more modern language. Therefore to discover what may be truly said about God, one attributes to him every discernable good to the highest possible degree, and denies of him completely every discernable limitation.

The former procedure is the *via eminentiae*, the 'way of eminence'. Potency, the ability to act, is a discernable good in human life, as is knowledge. God, therefore, must be as potent as it is possible to be, 'omnipotent', and as knowing as it is possible to be, 'omniscient'. The latter procedure is the *via negativa*, or 'negative way'. The inevitable ending of human existence is perceived to be a bad thing, which we would be better without. Therefore, God is understood to be 'immortal'. A consideration of spatial limitation, or finitude, might be held to teach us that God is 'infinite'. To these must be added a third 'way', the *via causalitatis*, or 'way of causality', in which it is assumed that effects demonstrate something of their cause, and so a knowledge of creation can lead us to a knowledge of God. As St Thomas Aquinas argued, every change is caused by a prior change, and so tracing the causal chain back one reaches either an infinite regression, which he takes to be impossible, or 'at some first cause of change not itself being changed by anything', which he identifies with God (*ST* 1a. 2, 3, in Aquinas 1975).

I have quoted St Thomas, but St John of Damascus' codification of the tradition of the Greek fathers or Francis Turretin's Reformed polemics would both witness to the same method. As I have indicated, however, around 1800 there is a radical shift in approach to the question. It is difficult to find a theologian (as opposed to a philosopher of religion) in the twentieth century who would accept such a method. For an eloquent and forceful statement of the objections, we might turn to Emil Brunner. In his *Christian Doctrine of God*, he suggests that there is 'an actual contradiction between two ideas of God, which... cannot be combined..., the philosophical and speculative Idea of God on the one hand, and on the other, one which is based upon the thought of God in revelation' (Brunner 1949: 241–2). The God of Abraham and the God of the philosophers are alien, and great harm is done by any attempt to bring them together.

That such an attempt was made, and was so enormously influential, is traced to two causes: the unreflective but disastrous adoption of methods of Greek philosophy by the church fathers and the enormous influence in later centuries of the writings of Pseudo-Dionysius. (This corpus is now fairly universally believed to date from the fifth century; however, the medievals tended to assume it was by the Dionysius who was converted by Paul in Athens (Acts 18), and so had almost apostolic authority.) The task for theology today is to perform or complete the criticism of Greek philosophy and so to purge the Christian account of divine attributes of those claims about God that lack theological warrant. I have followed Brunner in this criticism, but to indicate its ubiquity amongst recent theologians, it may be found in extreme form in Jenson (1997–9: i, esp. 9–11, 112–13, 131–3, 153), Moltmann (1974; 1981), and Gunton (2002); and in measured form in Barth (1957: 329–30) and Pannenberg (1971). This is also, of course, a part of the standard feminist criticism of traditional Christian doctrines of God.

If such criticism can be bracketed for a moment, it may be asked whether the method of the *viae* is retrievable. As I described it above, two problems are evident, but they may provide each other's solution. First, this appears to be a doctrine of God derived quite apart from revelation, an exercise entirely in natural theology. The procedure as described could be practised without difficulty by one who had never opened the biblical text or heard the name of Jesus Christ. This, of course, is not a logical problem (it does not make the position incoherent), and, indeed, in recent years it has been seen as a strength, rendering a doctrine of God that is generally rationally accessible and so open to philosophical investigation without worrying about difficult concepts such as revelation or faith. This philosophical procedure has become known as 'perfect being theology', and has given rise to a number of works exploring the logical coherence of a God who is held to exhibit every human virtue maximally, and to be completely free of every human weakness.

However philosophically attractive such a procedure, it is fair to say that a doctrine of God built without reference to scripture or the gospel is going to appear odd theologically, to say the least, so this remains my first problem. The second lies in the smuggled premiss in each of the three ways: the first two rely on assumptions that we know which aspects of human existence are positive, and which are limitations (Clark Pinnock (2001) makes the point provocatively with a book title, *Most Moved Mover*). The third relies on the assumption that good logical arguments can be made from the nature of effects to their cause.

Given this, might we claim that the smuggled knowledge in the *via eminentiae* and the *via negativa* is precisely the place where accounts of revelation become decisive? That is, we know what is a good, and so must be predicated eminently of God, and what is a limitation, and so must be denied of God, only through a study of scripture, or through a telling of the story of Jesus, or however else we might choose to describe revelation. Consider such attributes as mercy, compassion, or humility: it is not difficult to point to ethical traditions in history or across the world that deny that such things are goods, yet Christian theology has wanted to ascribe each word to God on the basis of what is revealed in the Bible and, in particular, in the gospel story. If the question concerning the influence of Greek philosophy can be adequately answered, this procedure would seem to provide a logically sound and theologically satisfying account of the derivation of the divine attributes.

(The problem with the *via causalitatis* reduces very simply to a set of questions concerning natural theology. If there happen to be well-formed logical arguments that move from details of the created order to facts about the creator, then natural theology is possible and will contribute in part to the doctrine of the divine perfections. I presently believe that there are no such arguments—I think the doctrine of *creatio ex nihilo* necessarily denies their existence—and so tend to the view that the *via causalitatis* is a dead end.)

I will argue by the end of this chapter that the problem concerning Greek philosophy can be solved, but it is perhaps worth pausing to ask about the derivation of the divine perfections if it cannot. The answers provided by the critics are surprisingly unified, differing only in detail. The perfections become in one way or another descriptions of God's relationship to the world, rather than descriptions of God's own life *in se*. The more extreme version of this tends to suggest that God's own life is somehow defined in his relationship to the world (so Jenson or Moltmann); this has the merit of coherence but is an unacceptable move. The more cautious version appears to suggest that God indeed has, or could have had, a life apart from the world, but that this life is not properly described as 'holy' or 'good'. 'In Himself, however, God is not the Almighty, the Omniscient, the Righteous One; this is what He is in relation to the world which he has created' (Brunner 1949: 247; cf. Pannenberg 1991–8: i. 359–70). This is an equally difficult conclusion.

III. The Question of 'Span'

Even if we have adequately answered the question of definition and can demonstrate that 'love' and 'holiness' are words adequate to God, to speak only of God's love with no mention of God's holiness—or, indeed, to speak only of

God's holiness with no mention of God's love—seems still to speak improperly. This is the question of 'span'. If the task is to find language adequate to speak of God, then it is not just that the language chosen must refer adequately, it must also demonstrate some degree of comprehensiveness.

Of course, no one has ever 'comprehended' that light which shines in the darkness (John 1: 5), but the limitations of a doctrine of divine perfections is a matter for the next section. One may meaningfully aim at adequacy, at an account that is at least not obviously lopsided or incomplete and that points towards each facet of the character of God revealed in the biblical witness. One could make two lists of words traditionally attributed to God of the same length, where one was manifestly less adequately comprehensive than the other. Consider, for instance, the two claims, 'God is holy, just, righteous, jealous, and unchanging', and 'God is holy, loving, righteous, merciful, and unchanging'.

An examination of the history of attempts to list the perfections of God, particularly in the Protestant scholastics, suggests that one particular procedure has regularly been adopted by theologians aiming at comprehensiveness: the splitting of the attributes into two classes. In Reformed dogmatics these are generally described as 'communicable' and 'incommunicable' attributes. Quite apart from the echoes of Reformed-Lutheran polemics over the *communicatio idiomatum*, such language is perhaps unhappy in suggesting an inability on God's part. Nonetheless, the intention is right: God has graciously and sovereignly chosen that his creatures will image forth or share certain perfections of his being, whereas others he has sovereignly and graciously chosen to retain as marks of his majesty alone. Thus creatures may love, but no creature is infinite; some creatures are made holy by God, but no creature is immutable. The attributes are thus not 'communicable' and 'incommunicable' so much as 'communicated' and 'uncommunicated'.

It may seem that this distinction relates directly to the distinction between the *via eminentiae* and the *via negativa* described above, but this is not in fact the case. To take only one example, God has chosen to create the angels immortal, at least according to classical Christian dogmatics. (Many writers also assert that angels are spiritual, i.e., unembodied, which would be another example of an attribute derived from the *via negativa* which nonetheless appears to be communicable; this point is disputed in the tradition, however.) Some scholastic writers did in fact use 'positive' and 'negative' attributes as their twofold distinction, thus aligning precisely with the *viae*.

Other language that has been used to describe the two classes includes 'personal' and 'absolute'. While this is superficially attractive, in that words such as 'love' or 'holiness' seem more obviously 'personal' than words like 'eternity' or 'immutability', it seems to me even more unhappy, not least in its echoes of technical trinitarian language. If some perfections of God are labelled 'personal', then there will be an inevitable pressure to align them to the trinitarian persons in ways that the 'impersonal' attributes are not aligned. 'Absolute' and 'relative' has a similar flaw, both echoing 'relation' language in the Trinity and perhaps suggesting that

God is 'eternal' in himself but 'loving' only in relation to the creation. Barth chooses to describe the two classes as 'perfections of God's love' and 'perfections of God's freedom'; this echoes his fundamental definition of God throughout *Church Dogmatics* II/1 as 'the One who loves in freedom' (Barth 1957: 257). Barth offers good reasons for his decision, but the language appears in danger of suggesting that 'love' and 'freedom' are the controlling perfections of God, under which all else must be arranged. The same might be said of Pannenberg's opting for 'infinity' and 'love'—indeed, Pannenberg claims centrality for 'infinity' as an attribute of God (Pannenberg 1991–8: i. 396). As will be seen, there are good dogmatic reasons to refuse to promote any of the perfections above the others.

It will be noted, however, that all these different forms of twofold division have a similar intention, even if at the margins one perfection or another might fall on either side of the line depending which schema we choose. There are those perfections of God for which an analogue may be found in the creature, and those which are utterly beyond anything in our experience. The 'positive' attributes, the 'perfections of God's loving', the 'communicated' perfections, refer to aspects of God's nature that may be hinted at through human stories ('out of pity for him, the lord of that slave released him and forgave him.... And in anger his lord handed him over.... So my heavenly Father will also do to every one of you'; Matt. 18: 23–35). The 'negative' attributes, the 'perfections of God's freedom', the 'uncommunicated' perfections, refer to aspects of God's nature about which we can only speak by denying that certain facets of our common experience can be mapped in any way onto God ('God is not a human being, that he should lie, or a mortal, that he should change his mind'; Num. 23: 19).

The further question of 'span' might appear more linguistic than theological. Assuming that we can argue that God may properly be described as both 'merciful' and 'loving', there is perhaps a question as to whether one needs, in writing a theology of the perfections of God, to include the word 'merciful' alongside the word 'loving', or whether the latter word covers all the semantic ground necessary and so effectively includes the former. This is more than a linguistic issue, however, and in fact gets near to the heart of any doctrine of the divine perfections, in that it asks both what words mean when attributed to God, and how the different attributes of God are in fact related to each other. To these issues I now turn.

IV. The Question of Analogy

Our language—all our language—is inadequate to the task of speaking of God. Even when we refer to those perfections that we call 'positive' or 'communicable' or 'communicated', we are always using language that is doubly difficult. There is a linguistic issue, and there is a further theological issue. The linguistic issue concerns the semantic ranges of words. If we describe God as 'just', we use a word that in English is patient of a variety of different meanings; the extent to which it illuminates or obscures the use of other words such as the Latin *iustus*, the Greek *dikaios*, or the Hebrew *tsaddiq* is a matter of some theological controversy. There is a need, therefore, to specify the precise nuance of meaning intended. This, however, immediately raises a theological issue. It seems theologically necessary to assert the uniqueness of God, that there is no creature that is good or loving in precisely the same way as God, and so such words must be used with a semantic range that is unique. How, though, may such a unique semantic range possibly be identified or specified?

(Returning for a moment to perfect-being theology, the widespread failure to struggle with questions of analogy is one of the weaknesses of the movement. Phrases such as 'whatever else it may mean, omniscience must at least imply...' are very common and suggest a lack of engagement with the serious apophaticism of the very writers—Anselm, Thomas, etc.—that perfect-being theologians generally claim to be expounding.)

The classical answer to such questions has been some form of a doctrine of analogy. The standard discussion is again in St Thomas Aquinas, q. 13 of the *Summa Theologiae*. Thomas insists that human words are used positively and literally of God, and goes on to ask how this is the case. He distinguishes three possible uses of words: the univocal use, in which a word is used in precisely the same sense in two different statements ('the jacket is blue'; 'the trousers are blue'); the equivocal use, in which a word is used in different senses in different statements ('the blues' as a musical form bear no discernable relation to the colour, for example); and the analogical use, in which a word is used in similar but separable senses in different statements ('the blues' as a musical form and 'the blues' as a psychic state, describing a mild depression, would seem to have some similarity of meaning, in that the musical form seems particularly suited to expressing the psychic state). Thomas claims that the words we use to name God are analogous to the same words used of created realities. God is truly, and primarily, 'good' (Thomas insists on the primacy of the divine meaning in *ST* 1a. 13, 6); as such, God is the cause of all goodness in creatures, and so when we speak of a creature being 'good' we are using an analogous term, suggesting that the partial and limited goodness of creatures is similar to, if not the same as, God's primary and infinite goodness.

(Notice that this is not, or at least not yet, an account of how God may be known; it is possible to develop a doctrine of analogy into an account of how God may be known by arguing from effect to cause in a form of the *via eminentiae* discussed above. It is even arguable that Thomas did this. His doctrine of analogy, however, is fundamentally a claim about how words applied to God may be said to have some positive meaning; it applies without distinction to a claim based on straight biblical citation—God is love—and to a claim based on some form of natural theology.)

Generally, the notion that words are used of God and creatures analogously has been accepted; some interesting arguments have arisen over the necessary basis of such analogy, but they do not dispute the general point that words are used analogically. John Duns Scotus, for instance, suggested that analogy necessarily collapses into equivocation unless there exists some underlying univocal concept. He therefore suggested that for any communicated perfection of God—goodness, say—three distinguishable concepts were present: goodness *simpliciter*, which is univocal; divine goodness, which is goodness *simpliciter* held in the most perfect degree; and creaturely goodness, which is goodness *simpliciter* in a limited and imperfect form. Divine goodness and creaturely goodness can then be held to be analogous. Such an account seems in danger of denying the primacy and priority of God's goodness, whatever logical gains are made. Pannenberg agrees with Scotus' critique, insisting that the basic point about analogy relying on an underlying univocity has never been effectively answered, although he notes the influence of recent linguistic theories in this regard. His own procedure, however, merely uses an appeal to the history of concepts and the way language has been used in faith communities to make the same sort of point as Thomas does using analogy (Pannenberg 1991–8: i. 384–96).

Even if we leave to one side such questions and accept the use of analogy, this only solves half the problem, and what is, theologically, the less interesting half: God's goodness is, on Thomas's account, the primary reality of which all creaturely goodness is but a limited, partial, and inexact analogy. Does this help us to specify what is meant by the assertion 'God is good'?

Here an appeal to the particular shape of revelation is necessary. The Bible is not, essentially, composed of propositions such as 'God is good', although it is certainly not without them. Rather, its essential form is narrative, together with a significant number of prayers addressed to God and paraenetic material exploring what life pleasing to God might look like in various contexts. If all we had were a series of assertions that God is good, loving, holy, etc., then it might be difficult to give content to those words. If, however, we can combine a claim that God is good with such narratives, prayers, and commands, then there is a possibility of recognition. In narrative history we can see ways in which this God has acted, ways which resonate with our experiences of human goodness; we can hear prayers that appeal to something we can identify with our own knowledge of what it is to love; we can be confronted by commands that bring to mind accounts of created holiness. Thus we may begin to understand what true goodness, love, and holiness—the goodness, love, and holiness of God of which our experiences are only pale shadows—might look like.

V. The Question of Definition

In his *Euthyphro*, Plato has Socrates asking whether an act is pious because it is loved by the gods, or whether it is loved by the gods because it is pious. Transposed into Christian theology, the question becomes pressing, and gives rise to one of the most controversial areas of the classical doctrine of the perfections of God.

When we say 'God is good', it seems that we must either be claiming that the word 'good' is merely a cipher we choose to apply to God's actions (and 'wicked' would have done just as well), or that we are asserting that there is a standard of goodness somewhere in existence against which we may measure God. In medieval theology, the two sides of the debate became known as 'nominalism' and 'realism': in the first case, 'good' is merely a name (Latin *nomen*); in the second case, 'good' is something real. On the one hand, it seems that God may be capricious, unaccountable (if nominalism were correct, how could Abraham demand, 'Shall not the Judge of all the earth do what is just'?); on the other, it seems that God is subject to something beyond himself. It seems that neither position is acceptable.

There is a relatively straightforward logical solution to this problem, which has recently been the subject of much theological, and indeed philosophical, controversy. It is the assertion that God is simple. 'Simplicity' in this context is the property of being uncompounded and so without parts. If God is simple, then his goodness cannot be meaningfully distinct from his essence (because if it were God would be compound in some sense), and so God's goodness is in fact God himself.

Such a claim has two interesting consequences. First, it suggests that every perfection of God is necessary for God to be who he is: if God's goodness is in some sense identical with God himself, then God cannot be himself without being good. Second, it provides a neat and (to my mind) convincing solution to the *Euthyphro* dilemma: 'goodness' is neither merely a name we apply to God's actions nor a standard beyond God by which he may be judged. Rather, it is God's own character to which he may indeed be held accountable (it is precisely because he is 'Judge of all the earth' that he will do what is just). So far, so good.

The claim also has another apparent consequence, however, and if this does follow, it is completely devastating—hence the recent controversy. It is this: if God is simple, then God is identical to his goodness; and, if God is simple, then God is identical to, say, his omniscience; therefore, by basic logic (if $A = B$ and $A = C$, then $B = C$), God's goodness is identical with God's omniscience. Such a statement appears to be mere nonsense, and such logic has recently led many philosophers to query the coherence of any doctrine of divine simplicity.

Such arguments must be wrong; it is hard to believe that such a trivial objection went unnoticed by almost every Christian (and, incidentally, Jewish and Islamic) theologian or philosopher of the medieval and early modern periods. Indeed, the standard treatments make claims that stand in flat contradiction to the conclusion of this argument. Something else must be going on, something that invalidates the form of such arguments. Thomas, indeed, asks the question 'are all the words predicated of God synonymous' (*ST* 1a. 13, 4), raising precisely this form of argument in the first objection. Nonetheless, on the basis of the biblical use of divine attribution (*sed contra*, 'Jeremiah says, "Most strong, mighty and powerful, the Lord of Armies is thy name"'; Jer. 32: 18), he denies that the conclusion follows. The argument appears to go something like this: although properly God's goodness is primary and creaturely goodness only derived, in our knowing this order is necessarily reversed: we first know derived goodness, and from that begin to understand what it means to call God good. We cannot know God's simple perfection directly, but only through a series of divided and varied 'perfections' of which we observe the derivative forms in creatures. Thus we give God many names (good, loving, omniscient, etc.) which each refer in a partial and imperfect, but nonetheless real, way to the single perfection of God. The sort of logical argument I sketched above fails because 'Synonyms signify the same thing from the same point of view. Words that signify the same thing thought of in different ways do not, properly speaking, signify the same, for words only signify things by way of thoughts' (*ST* 1a. 13, 4 ad 1).

(Again returning to perfect-being theology, questions about the doctrine of simplicity are very widespread there, possibly because, as I have already indicated, this tradition seems to lack any serious account of God's incomprehensibility, and so generally assumes that the meaning of words applied to God is fairly clear. Thus the arguments in the paragraph above are simply missed.)

Thomas thus bases his logical defence on the philosophy of language. Post-structuralist linguistic theories will tend to lend some support to Thomas's case, but there is perhaps another form of argument that can be deployed, one more theologically grounded and so less open to buffeting by the winds of philosophical fashion. Amongst the classical perfections of God is the claim that God is incomprehensible—what God is is unknowable to human minds. Such a claim seems intuitively plausible, and a theological reading of a text such as Exodus 33: 18–22 might establish it. If God is incomprehensible, then it is at least questionable whether we know enough to make arguments respecting his essence. Thomas continually points out that our words signify imperfectly when applied to God; this is a result not just of the nature of language, but also of the nature of God. (As Pannenberg recognizes, Thomas's appeal is more to God's transcendence as the basis of his unknowability than to his infinity; unlike Pannenberg, I regard this as a positive feature of the account, picking up on a clear biblical theme of the otherness of God from the creatures (Pannenberg 1991–8: i. 344).) The apparent logical difficulty I began with, then, is more precisely stated as an argument of the form: the word 'good' imperfectly but really signifies the simple perfection of God; the word 'omniscient' imperfectly but really signifies the simple perfection of God; therefore 'good' and 'omniscient' mean the same thing. This looks much less convincing.

If it is logically possible to assert divine simplicity, however, the theological appropriateness of the doctrine has been severely questioned in recent years. Once again we are back to the fundamental shift in the doctrine of the divine perfections that occurred around the nineteenth century. The core issue becomes the relationship of a doctrine of divine simplicity to trinitarian doctrine. From Gregory of Nyssa's defence of the doctrine of the Trinity for Ablabius in the late fourth century to Francis Turretin's defence against the Socinians in the late seventeenth, there was an assumption on all sides that to believe in divine simplicity was to be an orthodox trinitarian, and to deny simplicity was to attack the doctrine of the Trinity; in the twentieth century it seems that writers virtually universally assume the precise opposite: either one may continue to believe in divine simplicity, or one may believe in the Trinity, but the two are mutually exclusive. Finally, then, this chapter needs to deal with the core historical issue.

VI. The Problem of History

When Walter Smith wrote his hymn 'Immortal, invisible, God only wise' in the mid-nineteenth century, he was celebrating a vision of God that was passing. There is no hymn more regularly condemned in theological conversation or instruction than this one. It celebrates, undergraduates are regularly told, a pagan Greek idea of God that thoroughly infected the Christian church and is only now, thankfully, being driven out. The doctrine of divine perfections is emblematic of this pagan idea in at least three ways, and so of all doctrines is most ripe for radical revision.

First, it is claimed that several standard perfections of God are in fact Greek impositions, theologically unwarranted. God is not impassible, immutable, or eternal, at least not in standard ways. Further, as already noted, one of the necessary logical supports of the whole account of the divine perfections, divine simplicity, is held to be profoundly problematic. Third, the whole doctrine, both in its methods of derivation, and in its relative prominence compared to the 'properly Christian' account of God as Trinity, is fundamentally compromised. If a doctrine of divine perfections is to remain any part of Christian theology, it will be in a subordinate place, in a chastened tone, and in a very different form.

What are the reasons for this change? There are, it seems to me, several. One has already been noted: a historical account of the rise of Christianity that suggests unwarranted Greek influence in formative periods. The classic account of such history is of course in the school of Ritschl and Harnack, but it pre-dates them (Baur's elaborate account of catholic Christianity as the triumphant outcome of a Hegelian synthesis between Jewish and Greek roots is similar in form, although it lacks the negative judgement on the Greek influence.) For scholars such as Ritschl, the scientific study of the historical Jesus had seemingly confirmed that miracles, particularly the resurrection, and a fascination with things both eschatological (including such issues as sin and atonement) and metaphysical were not part of the teaching of the man from Nazareth, but later accretions. Christianity as we know it, with sacrament and liturgy and theology, looks like a Greek mystery cult built on the flimsiest of historical recollection of a simple moral teacher.

Of course, such accounts have been comprehensively discredited by historical study. They introduce a motif, however, which seems to have endured. If we emphasize the differences between 'Jewish' and 'Greek' ways of thinking, and so portray the early history of Christianity as a fundamentally Jewish movement inculturating itself within a Hellenistic milieu, then we make it very easy to argue that this or that feature of later Christianity is Hellenistic, and so non-native, and so an inappropriate accretion that should be removed.

It is not a hard task to list the various problems with the procedure so stated: the notion of uniform and separate cultures is merely ridiculous (one glance at Philo disproves both parts of the thesis, even ignoring the three centuries of Macedonian occupation of Palestine, the varieties of Graeco-Roman culture attested in history, and the varieties of Jewish culture demonstrated by the Gospels); to argue from 'non-native feature' to 'inappropriate accretion', particularly in the case of a process of inculturation, is merely question-begging; and so on. However, such arguments do not prove that every claim of improper Greek influence is false, only that not every such claim is true. There is a need for some hard historical and theological work on the details of the issues, but it seems to me that the legacy of Baur, Ritschl, and Harnack has been to create a presumption in many theologians' minds that the arguments can be settled in one direction relatively easily. Such a presumption needs to be challenged.

(The claimed influence of Pseudo-Dionysius noted above is a particular issue here. Suffice to say that it is not clear that he is treated as any more of an authority than any other church father. Looking at *ST* 1a. 13, for instance, it is the case that Pseudo-Dionysius is cited more than any other father (seven direct references of the sixteen to patristic sources; there are also nine to scripture and four to Aristotle), but since he had written a book entirely on the subject of the question (*The Divine Names*), this might not be surprising. It is notable however that, uniquely amongst the sources cited (apart from an isolated reference to Boethius), he is always cited in the objections—that is, in every case Thomas takes the opposing position on the question to Pseudo-Dionysius. To suggest, as Brunner did, that Thomas uncritically follows the earlier writer seems to fly in the face of the evidence.)

A second reason for the shift would seem to be the influence of Kantian philosophy. I indicated above that, amongst theologians who uphold the 'Hellenizing' criticism concerning the perfections, there is a surprising degree of unanimity on the proposition that the perfections refer not to God *in se*, but to God's action towards the creation. Such an account naturally brings to mind Schleiermacher's careful account of how he understood not just the doctrine of divine perfections but every doctrine: as a precise statement of an aspect of the basic religious experience of humanity (Schleiermacher 1928: 76–8, 125–8). There is little doubt that somewhere behind this particular decision is the challenge of Kant's denial of the possibility of any knowledge of the noumenal. Theologically transposed, Kant's arguments could easily be held to suggest that we cannot have any knowledge of God *in se*, but only of God in relation to us. The continuing influence of Kant's epistemological questioning is a part of the pressure against the classical doctrine of the divine perfections.

For a third reason, let me return to the end of the previous section, and the question of the relationship of the doctrine of the divine perfections to the doctrine of the Trinity. The issue here has been a fundamental change in assumptions about the doctrine of the Trinity, far more than any issue to do with the divine perfections. If one holds, as all pre-Romantic trinitarian doctrine held, that the divine persons are utterly one in being, will, thought, power, action—and indeed in all perfections save only the relations of origin that distinguish them (unbegottenness, begottenness, procession), then it is not difficult to hold Trinity and simplicity together. If one views the three divine persons as separate centres of will, thought, and action, as seems to have become popular in the twentieth century, then it is much more difficult.

The underlying influence here may well be Romanticism. At the heart of the Romantic spirit is a particular emphasis on, and vision of, the notion of personhood, or personality. The essence of personhood is self-determination, and so volition; the expression of personhood is therefore spontaneous reaction, and so emotion; and personhood must be understood as the highest good imaginable. Given all this, there would seem to have been strong cultural pressure both to rewrite the doctrine of the Trinity in ways that make the three persons 'persons' in the full Romantic sense, and to deny those aspects of the traditional perfections of God that seemed to offend against Romantic notions of personhood. Whatever the weaknesses of Barth's proposal to replace 'person' with 'mode of being' in technical trinitarian discourse, it at least defended against this failing.

(On this latter point, consider how much in contemporary rejections of God's eternity, immutability, and impassibility is explicitly motivated by rhetorical claims concerning the supposed inability of an impassible, immutable, eternal God to be passionate, loving, and involved in human suffering. I believe all three points to be demonstrably false, but their prominence might be evidence for the cultural demand that God be appropriately Romantic.)

Thus far I have tried to suggest that there are at least problems with the historical explanation offered for why the classical account of the divine perfections went so wrong, and to suggest that there are good reasons to suppose some of the demands for revision are driven by cultural pressure. Neither of these is yet an argument for truth or falsity, of course; they are attempts to shift the burden of proof slightly.

The basic appeal of most revisionist theology in this area, and the fourth and last reason I can find advanced by writers who want to recast the doctrine of divine perfections, is exegetical. It is claimed that Smith's 'unresting, unhasting, and silent' God is simply alien to the biblical revelation. If this is the case, then regardless of the historical details, the doctrine of divine perfections must be rewritten. Of course, proponents of more traditional views throughout history have read and appealed to the Bible, so, unless there is some decisive shift in biblical interpretation which renders the more modern exegesis more convincing, this must remain a point of dispute which may be argued in either direction.

If Baur or Ritschl were right, of course, and we could find in the New Testament evidence of a later Hellenizing of a simple ethical religion, then there would be a good reason to prefer the more modern approaches. Scientific exegesis would have revealed to us a fact of decisive importance for this discussion which Augustine, Thomas, and Turretin could not have known. Unfortunately for such a line of argument, there are few biblical scholars who would now accept Baur's or Ritschl's reconstructions even in broad outline. It does seem to me, however, that recent methods of exegesis do lend support to the revisionist case in two particulars. First, the development of higher criticism has led to a willingness, unparalleled in theological history, to lay aside certain texts and simply exclude them from influencing theological work. Whilst most practitioners of such critical practices would claim that they are applying objective canons to determine which texts should be dismissed, more recent studies have deconstructed such claims to objectivity to expose the smuggled assumptions which are being reinforced by the results of the process. The scripture principle that theology should employ will remain controverted, but I will proceed on the basis that no text should be excluded from the canon, and so assume that in this there is no reason to prefer the newer ways of constructing a doctrine of the divine perfections.

The second hermeneutical strategy that seems relevant here is the rise of literary critical approaches to the scriptures. When the Old Testament histories, particularly, are read using the tools of literary analysis, God is revealed as a passionate, involved, acting, and reacting character in the narrative, and this is regularly invoked as evidence that the doctrine of divine perfections stands in need of revision. But such a procedure again involves the issue of smuggled premisses: the categories of 'literature' and 'narrative'—even the category of 'character'—are derived from Romantic notions of what makes for good writing. Although medieval exegetes did not theorize so carefully, they read the histories as narratives with Aristotle's *Poetics*—and much technical Greek historiography—in their minds, and thus came to rather different conclusions.

So I suggest that there is no good exegetical reason to presume that more recent exegetical claims concerning the divine perfections are more convincing than older ones. I will end this essay with a sketch of a doctrine of the divine perfections that highlights and addresses some of the core exegetical choices.

VII. The Perfections of God

What God is is indeed unspeakable in human language and unknowable by human minds. The task, however, is to find words adequate to God. Mindful of earlier comments about semantic ranges and the impossibility of giving a definitive list of the divine perfections, rather than insisting on particular words, I shall attempt to give a set of 'classes' of perfections which together will indicate an adequate span for the doctrine. Any such categorization can only be schematic, so some perfections will fit into more than one 'class', indicating places where there is some overlap between them. As an overarching schema for my account, I will use the twofold division above between communicated and uncommunicated perfections. The following claims rest on unrehearsed exegetical decisions; several of them are contentious, but the defence of God's being properly named as 'wrathful', for instance, cannot be attempted here.

'God is love' (1 John 4: 8). For a first 'class' of communicated perfections we may look to what I will call perfections of the divine condescension. God loves, God is merciful, gracious, generous, faithful, and long-suffering. God sovereignly and freely orientates himself towards his creatures, accepting them despite their sin and failure, and pledging his commitment to them. Connected with these biblically would be the claim that God is 'jealous' (a claim made repeatedly in the Torah—three times, for instance, in Deuteronomy 4–6) and even 'wrathful': God's condescension to his creatures implies also a set of attitudes that have as their closest created analogues such negative emotional reactions as jealousy, anger, or hatred, directed towards all that would damage or harm God's creation, or frustrate God's plan for his creation.

'God is a righteous judge' (Ps. 7: 11). A second class of communicated perfections might be described as perfections of the divine governance. God rules over his creation, and so is righteous, just, wise, steadfast, majestic, and sovereign. God graciously and freely reigns as Lord over all that he has made; by his own choice he is enthroned as king and judge, and he exercises these roles perfectly. Because of this, the biblical claims that God is merciful and gracious must also be included in this class of perfections: mercy, too, is an exercise of wise sovereignty. Finally, governance implies insight, and so under this head we may also insist that God is properly named as omniscient, wise, and all-seeing.

'Holy, holy, holy is the Lord of hosts; the whole earth is full of his glory' (Isa. 6: 3). For a final class of communicated perfections, we might choose the title 'perfections of the divine goodness'. God's actions are perfect in ethical and intentional ways as in all other ways, and so God is good, holy, righteous, pure, upright, and faithful. Because God is these things, however, he cannot look on sin (Hab. 1: 13); therefore God is also properly described as implacable, wrathful, terrible, and jealous.

'If I were hungry, I would not tell you, for the world and all that is in it is mine' (Ps. 50: 12). For a first class of uncommunicated perfections, we might choose the title 'perfections of the divine self-sufficiency'. God needs nothing, does not grow or change, and is not damaged or affected by his creation. Amongst the perfections of God, therefore, we may include aseity, impassibility, immutability, eternity, self-sufficiency, omnipotence, freedom, and transcendence. Because God needs nothing from the world, however, he is free to be involved within his creation, therefore God must also be described as loving, gracious, omnipresent, and immanent.

'No one shall see me and live' (Exod. 33: 20). A second class of uncommunicated perfections may be called 'perfections of the divine glory'. The majesty of God is such that it is unbearable to human beings, at least to unredeemed human beings, but the vision of God remains the chief good of humankind and the deepest desire of our hearts. God is, therefore, properly named as beautiful, glorious, terrible, majestic, holy, and awesome.

Such a list cannot be comprehensive. Looking over it, I immediately note that basic biblical assertions concerning the compassion (Jas. 5: 11) or spirituality (John 4: 24) of God are missing. A collection of such words, each filled out by biblical narrative and example, and all held to be not in competition but genuinely separable and also truly united aspects of the one simple inexpressible nature of God, is the final aim of a doctrine of the divine perfections.

References

Aquinas, St Thomas (1975). *Summa Theologiae.* London: Blackfriars.

Barth, Karl (1957). *Church Dogmatics* II/1. Edinburgh: T. & T. Clark.

Brunner, Emil (1949). *The Christian Doctrine of God.* London: Lutterworth.

Gunton, Colin E. (2002). *Act and Being: Towards a Theology of the Divine Attributes.* London: SCM.

Hodge, Charles (1960 [1871–3]). *Systematic Theology.* London: James Clarke and Co.

Jenson, Robert W. (1997–9). *Systematic Theology.* 2 vols. New York: Oxford University Press.

Moltmann, Jürgen (1974). *The Crucified God.* London: SCM.

—— (1981). *The Trinity and the Kingdom of God: The Doctrine of God.* London: SCM.

Pannenberg, Wolfhart (1971). 'The Appropriation of the Philosophical Concept of God as a Dogmatic Problem of Early Christian Theology'. In id., *Basic Questions in Theology,* ii, London: SCM, 119–83.

—— (1991–8). *Systematic Theology.* 3 vols. Grand Rapids: Eerdmans.

Pinnock, Clark H. (2001). *Most Moved Mover.* Carlisle: Paternoster.

Schleiermacher, F. D. E. (1928). *The Christian Faith.* Edinburgh: T. & T. Clark.

Suggested Reading

Aquinas, St Thomas (1975: 1a. 2–13).

Barth, Karl (1957: 256–677).

GUNTON (2002).

PANNENBERG, WOLFHART (1991–8: i. 337–448).

ROGERS, KATHERIN A. (2000). *Perfect Being Theology*. Edinburgh: Edinburgh University Press.

TURRETIN, FRANCIS (1992–7 [1679–85]). *Institutes of Elenctic Theology*. Phillipsberg: Presbyterian and Reformed, i. 183–252.

WEINANDY, THOMAS G. (2000). *Does God Suffer?* Edinburgh: T. & T. Clark.

CHAPTER 4

CREATION

DAVID FERGUSSON

THE doctrine of creation has undergone a resurgence of interest in recent years. Relatively neglected during mid-twentieth-century theological debates, it has attracted wide attention in the last generation. There are several factors contributing to this renewed interest. The ecological crisis has encouraged study of the theology of the natural environment, while also recalling the problematic legacy of earlier church teaching and practice in this field. Physicists have reinvigorated the case for older cosmological and design arguments for the existence of God as creator. Attention to the finely tuned structure of the cosmos in the first moments of its existence has led to strong claims for a divine intention superintending the birth of the universe. At the same time, biblical scholars have rediscovered how pervasive is the theme of creation throughout scripture. Salvation history has a cosmic context that cannot be ignored. Recognition of this biblical integration of creation with other significant themes has in turn promoted a sense of its significance for other articles of faith. This applies particularly to the doctrines of the Trinity, anthropology, and redemption. In the field of comparative theology, study of the doctrine of creation has been undertaken with reference not only to Judaism, Christianity, and Islam but also to the eastern religions. Some discussion of each of these areas will be offered, following an initial account of the doctrine of creation in scripture and the history of the church.

I. The Testimony of Scripture in Modern Theology

The appearance of two creation stories at the opening of the Bible might suggest to the casual reader that a belief in creation precedes other articles of faith. Acting as a preface to a more distinctive revelation in history, the account of creation could be seen as little more than a scene-setting for an ensuing narrative. This is a mistaken assumption. Both creation stories are embedded in wider beliefs about the nature of God, the environment, human beings, animals, and the redemption that awaits the cosmos. Moreover, despite their location in Genesis 1–2, we cannot suppose that these were written or originated in advance of other portions of the Bible.

Genesis 1 famously recounts the story of a creation in six days. The formal structure of the story suggests its use in liturgy, while the emphasis on the sabbath rest is redolent of later Israelite religion. Recent exegesis has pointed out that the climax of the story is not the creation of human beings on the sixth day, but the day of rest that follows. 'The goal of every Jewish and every Christian doctrine of creation must be the doctrine of the sabbath' (Moltmann 1985: 276). On the sabbath, the world and its maker rejoice in the harmony of the good creation. Stressing the cosmic dimension of the day of rest, recent theology has sought to offset the anthropocentrism that has sometimes characterized earlier theologies of creation. The world is not made only for human benefit but for the glory of God, a glory that is attested also by other forms of life. In this criticism of anthropocentrism, strong ecological concerns are clearly at work. The life of the planet and its manifold species belong to God's good creation; these have a divinely appointed place not reducible to the service of human interests.

There are several other significant features of this story. While there are debates about the grammatical structure of its opening phrase—these are mirrored in the different English translations of the text—it is in any case uncertain whether Genesis 1: 1–2 offers a description of creation out of nothing. The formless void and the deep appear already to exist prior to the creative action of God. The divine word initially creates light from darkness and order out of chaos. This textual uncertainty became a point of doctrinal debate in later centuries. What is clear, however, is that for Genesis 1 the creation of the world proceeds serenely by a series of divine commands. There is no temporal interval, let alone conflict, between the speaking of God's word and its execution. God speaks and it is accomplished. In this respect, the Hebrew creation story contrasts with other ancient near eastern creation myths that depict the making of the world as a struggle between rival forces. Although there may linger a residual element of the surd in the references to the formless void and the face of the deep, the act of creation takes place by the effortless and uninterrupted speech of God. Despite hints of struggle elsewhere in the canon, the work of creation is here a free, unconstrained act. A similar testimony is offered in the first article of the Apostles' Creed: 'I believe in God the Father Almighty, maker of heaven and earth.' This is significant, as we shall see, for recent trinitarian constructions of the God–world relationship in which creation is presented as a free act, but one entirely consistent with the divine being.

The interpretation of the six days of creation occasioned much controversy, particularly in the nineteenth century. Were these literal days of twenty-four hours' duration, during which the world as we know it today came into being? If so, then the opening chapter of the Bible seems radically at odds with the world view of much modern science that holds to a gradual evolution of matter and life over many billions of years. This controversy becomes more apparent than real if we can understand the creation narratives as testifying to the origin of the world in the being and act of God. The scientific account of the *how* of creation can thus sit alongside the theological account of its *why.* Since theology and science function at different levels of explanation, these are not competing but complementary accounts of the world. While this does not exclude the prospect of dialogue, it should be sufficient to avoid contesting on religious grounds the overwhelming consensus within the modern scientific community regarding cosmic evolution. Two further considerations lend support to this argument for complementary types of explanation. The genre and symbolism of the two creation stories suggest that we are in the realm of theological and ethical description, rather than the discourses of science and history. Second, the writings of the early church fathers, particularly Augustine, reveal an impressive capacity to interpret these texts in non-literal ways, thus suggesting that symbolic readings are not the invention of modern thinkers intent merely on accommodating scripture to contemporary secular thought.

Recent cultural conflict has been generated, particularly in the USA, by attempts to present Genesis 1–2 as offering an alternative cosmology to that of the modern scientific world view. Instead of galaxies, planets, and life forms emerging from a violent explosion from a point of infinite density around twelve billion years ago, 'creation science' has attempted to maintain a 'young universe' only thousands of years old (Frye 1993). While allowing for some changes that are attributed to the effects of the flood, the world is perceived as created in much the same condition as we observe it today. The intellectual impossibility of this movement is evident from its attempt to challenge not merely biological evolution but the confirmed theories of other well-established scientific disciplines, including cosmology, astronomy, physics, geology, and palaeontology. From the theologian's perspective, it is an unnecessary fight to pick for the reasons outlined above. As Steve Jones, the distinguished geneticist, has often said, the conflict between science and religion resembles a fight between a tiger and a shark. Each will prevail on its own proper territory, but it will be hopelessly defeated by encroaching on the domain of the other.

The creation of human beings in the divine image has provided Christian anthropology with one of its leading concepts. The *imago Dei* has been interpreted in a variety of ways, some of which reflect philosophical presuppositions that could not have been shared by the writers and redactors of Genesis 1. In its Hebraic context, the divine image refers not to the possession of an immortal soul (as in the Greek tradition) but more to the role exercised by human beings in the cosmic order. As those who can hear and obey the divine word, human beings are charged with acting on God's behalf in relation to one another and to the rest of creation. This more functional or relational account of the divine image makes better sense of the succeeding verses that speak of the roles of human beings in the world already made. This recent exegesis favouring relational, rather than substantival, accounts of the *imago Dei* meshes with more holistic anthropologies that stress the essential embodiedness of human beings (Macquarrie 1982; van Huyssteen 2006). The reaction against Cartesian body–mind dualism and the privileging of the intellect in modern philosophy has provoked theology to return to its Hebraic roots in stressing the person as a psychosomatic unity (cf. Kerr 1997). This is further confirmed by the incarnation of the Word of God as an assumption of human flesh. As a human person who is the image of the invisible God, Jesus Christ is not merely a spirit or soul but an embodied human being. This reading of the *imago Dei* has important ethical implications. If it is not a property possessed by human beings but a form of relational life to which we are summoned in Christ, then the diversity and universality of the church becomes an important determinant of how we understand the divine image (McFarland 2005).

Contrary to some later Christian interpretation, Genesis 1: 27 maintains that women and men equally bear the image of God. There is no suggestion of a stratification by which the man more perfectly images God than the woman. However, the divinely authorized dominion by human beings over creation in 1: 28 raises further problems about the ecological impact of the text. In its original pastoral setting, it implies a benign stewardship. At this stage, there is no permission given to eat the flesh of other creatures; this may reflect a vegetarian ideal or eschatological hope. Yet, as we shall see, the language of 'dominion' is problematic and requires careful handling.

Both Genesis 1 and the more anthropologically oriented account in Genesis 2 are narratives of grace. The making of the world in Genesis 1 is a free and unconstrained act of God. There is no sense of divine compulsion or necessity. At the outset, God speaks spontaneously and the world is brought into being. In Genesis 2, Adam is given the garden with its diverse plant and animal life. Eve is created from him to become his lifelong 'helpmate'. Following their disobedience, they do not die as earlier predicted (Gen. 2: 17). Instead they are spared, provision being made for their survival and the propagation of the species. The linkage of creation and salvation history characterizes the maker of the world as also its redeemer. Creation is only the first of God's works. It begins the drama of a covenant relationship that is cosmic in scope. Here recent Christian readings of scripture have been influenced by Jewish exegesis that sees in the creation stories already the commencement of God's work to overcome evil (Levenson 1994). Instead of a world that is merely ordered and conserved in something like its original condition, a more dynamic account emerges in which there is significant change, development, and historical movement. (As we have already seen, this is partially resonant with modern cosmology which understands the physical universe itself to have undergone significant changes over billions of years.) The good creation is not one which is already perfect. It is fit for its purpose and displays the constant love of God for creatures (Berkhof 1986: 174–83). Yet its destiny awaits it in the future. From the beginning, therefore, an eschatological tension emerges in the creation story. The rest on the seventh day is itself an anticipation of that final sabbath when the cosmos comes to its appointed end.

Elsewhere in the Old Testament we find a further integration of creation theology with other central themes in Israelite religion. The Hebrew verb used to denote the creative work of God at the beginning is also a term reserved for the salvific actions of God in history. This linguistic usage connects the past, present, and future activity of God. 'For I am about to create new heavens and a new earth' (Isa. 65: 17). In this context, the making of the world can be seen as the first of God's creative works. The creator's activity continues in nature and history; it reaches its end only with the creation of a new world. Creation and covenant are closely related theological concepts, for example in Hosea 2: 21 and Jeremiah 31: 12. Conversely, threats of disorder and disruption in the life of Israel are also linked to the notion of chaos and the corruption of nature itself. In the Psalms there is a wealth of references to the world as God's creation, yet this is also integrated with other themes of cosmic order, social justice, kingly rule, and the gift of divine law. Psalms 8, 19, and 104 testify to the beauty and order of the world, the providential care of creatures, and the regulation of human conduct by the divine law. Psalms 96–8 celebrate the kingship of God as creator and executor of justice. Creation is again linked to the sovereignty of the Lord and the future redemption of the world. The order of creation is known, affirmed, and represented in the worship of Israel. In singing God's praise, we not only acknowledge but display the divine ordering of the world. God's good work invites responses of human wisdom, ethical obedience, and public celebration.

The notion of 'wisdom' provides further evidence of the integration of creation and salvation in the Old Testament. As the creative agency of God, wisdom is celebrated in the Psalms, Proverbs, Job, and some of the deutero-canonical works. In some places, such as Proverbs 8, wisdom is personified as a divine agent. The divine wisdom by which the world is created is also apparent in the regularity of nature, the divine law, and human affairs. This notion of 'wisdom' is later fused with the Greek concept of 'Logos' and becomes vital for expressing the linking of creation and Christology in the New Testament. In the prologue to John's Gospel the Word (Logos) of God is the one by whom and through whom the world is created. This Word which is made present to Israel becomes incarnate in Jesus Christ. In this cosmic Christology, the significance of Jesus is understood with respect to the origin and purpose of the created order. Already in Paul's writing and elsewhere in the New Testament epistles, we find similar cosmic themes (e.g., 1 Cor. 8: 6, Col. 1: 15–20, Heb. 1: 1–4). By describing creation as Christ-centred, these passages offer two related trajectories of thought. First, the origin and final purpose of the cosmos is disclosed with the coming of Christ into the world and his resurrection from the dead. Second, the significance of Christ is maximally understood by reference to his creative and redeeming power throughout the created universe. Writers at different periods in the history of the church would later use this cosmic Christology to describe the appearance of the incarnate Christ as the crowning moment of history. No longer understood merely as an emergency measure to counteract the effects of sin and evil, the incarnation was the fulfilment of an eternal purpose. The world was made so that Christ might be born. This is captured in Karl Barth's dictum that creation is 'the external basis of the covenant' (Barth 1958: 94).

The rapid development of Christology in the New Testament also provided a further integration of creation and eschatology, along lines already mapped out in the Old Testament. In describing the world that is to come, the New Testament writers again use Christological categories set alongside creation themes. If anyone is in Christ, he or she is a new creation (2 Cor. 5: 17). The world is moving towards the goal that has been promised in Christ (1 Cor. 15: 28). The end of the world will bring about an acknowledgement of 'the name of Jesus . . . in heaven and on earth and under the earth' (Phil. 2: 10). The writer of the Apocalypse transfers to Christ titles ascribed to God in Second Isaiah. He is the first and the last, the beginning and end of all things (Rev. 1: 17; 22: 13). This integration of creation, redemption, and eschatology is also matched by a wealth of pneumatological reference. Both the resurrection of Christ and the life of faith are perceived as the first fruits of a new creation, the produce of the divine Spirit (Rom. 8: 11, 23; 1 Cor. 15: 20).

Several important features emerge from this reading of scripture, all of which are stressed in recent theological debate.

1. The account of creation is not primarily an explanatory hypothesis about how the world got started. Although there are philosophical elements in scripture, particularly in the wisdom literature, the theology of creation is set within the circle of faith. The stories of Genesis 1–2 are as much proclamation as explanation. Their allusions to creation recall us to other vital theological ideas which in turn shape our understanding of the world with reference to God. The world continues always to be dependent upon the will of God. In this sense, creation is a continuous, ongoing action rather than a single event of origination (Schwöbel 1997).

2. The doctrine of creation shapes an account of the God–world relationship. The world is not divine, since it comes into being by the will and word of God rather than any emanation from the divine being itself. This enables the Bible to depict God's transcendence and otherness from creaturely reality, while at the same

time stressing the significance of a relationship that can be characterized by the language of covenant and fellowship. As we shall see in the next section, the ontological distance between God and world is a necessary condition of their particular form of relatedness.

3. In terms of its fitness for its purpose, the goodness of the world is affirmed. The creation narratives of scripture do not allow a denigration of the material world or a dualism that depicts the world as a battleground between rival cosmic powers. Even while it is the arena of decay, suffering, conflict, and sin, this world remains God's good creation. Its goodness is not limited to some past golden age in Eden. The Psalms still testify to the beauty and providential ordering of the cosmos in a post-lapsarian setting. Despite generating intense difficulties in the face of evil, the Bible seems willing to embrace these problems rather than to seek an escape route by diminishing either the goodness or the power of God. In this respect, a theological depth is purchased occasionally at the cost of an easy or simple consistency of ideas.

4. Creation is imperfect in the sense that it is incomplete and unfulfilled. The making of the world is only the first of God's works. As the beginning of a history, it sets in motion a narrative that has a focal point in the coming of Jesus. The ordering of the Christian canon itself suggests a pattern of promise and fulfilment. God's creative work is ongoing throughout the history of Israel and the church. It includes resistance and struggle in its dealing with people and natural forces. It has been said that the Bible offers us not so much a doctrine of creation as a doctrine of the creator. This comment is instructive if it reminds us of the ways in which the description of the world's creation is deeply related to God's other works of redemption. Robert Jenson remarks that what God creates is not so much a 'thing' as a history or a narrative. The loss of this insight, he argues, was 'the great historical calamity of the doctrine of creation' (Jenson 1997–9: ii. 14).

5. The pattern of divine action that unfolds in scripture has a rudimentary trinitarian character. The world is created and ruled by the sovereign God who is confessed as Father. It is informed by the wisdom of God in both its natural harmony and in the gift of law to human beings. Threatened by evil, sin, and death, the world is also the locus for the incarnation of that wisdom or Word through whom it was created and in whom it will finally be recreated. Yet God's action is not confined to creation, incarnation, and eschatological fulfilment. The work of the divine Spirit is persistent, regular, and universal in scope. It indwells all things and acts to bring them to conformity with the divine purpose (Gunton 1998: 170). In modern theology, this understanding of creation as an action of the triune God owes much to Karl Barth, who argued resolutely that the doctrine of creation is a distinctively Christian article and not merely a general theistic preamble that could be established on grounds exterior to revelation. In appropriating creation to God the Father, the creed also directs us to its essential unity with the work of the Son and the Spirit. 'The decisive anchorage of the recognition that creation and

covenant belong to each other is the recognition that God the Creator is the triune God, Father, Son and Holy Spirit' (Barth 1958: 48).

The development of each of these ideas can be traced in recent treatments of the classical idea of creation out of nothing.

II. Creation out of Nothing in Recent Controversy

By the end of the second century, the doctrine of creation out of nothing (*creatio ex nihilo*) had emerged as the standard teaching of the church. The sudden and subsequent unanimity of support for this doctrine is one of the most interesting episodes in the history of dogma. Once argued and defended, it was perceived as the only adequate Christian alternative against Greek views of the eternity of matter and gnostic accounts of emanation.

On the concept of creation out of nothing, scripture is inconclusive, although one can legitimately argue that it is a requisite interpretation of biblical themes (Craig and Copan 2004). The opening verses of Genesis 1 seem to suggest a formless void that preceded the divine act of creation. As disorderly and chaotic, it could not in itself be viewed as the good creation of God. For this reason, rabbinic Judaism did not teach creation out of nothing (Neusner 1991). Other passages in scripture hint at the notion of creation out of nothing (e.g., Rom. 4: 17; Heb. 11: 3), but these may only be metaphorical expressions to describe the power and wisdom of the creator. 2 Maccabees 7: 28 also comes close to the later orthodox notion of creation out of nothing: 'I beg you, my child, to look at the heaven and the earth and see everything that is in them, and recognize that God did not make them out of things that existed.' Yet here again we may simply have a poetic depiction of divine power. In the ancient world, 'what is not' can merely denote that which lacks form and order. It is not until theologians contested the prevailing Greek philosophical assumption about the eternity of matter that the idea of creation out of nothing emerged as a fully articulated concept.

As Gerhard May shows, by about the third quarter of the second century the doctrine of creation out of nothing had become a settled teaching with arguments systematically advanced in its favour (May 1994). Writing to Autolycus, Theophilus of Antioch argues in effect that the eternity of matter would compromise the sovereignty of God. Nothing can be co-eternal with the one God without itself being considered divine. The splendour of God, moreover, is attested by the making of everything *ex nihilo*. 'The power of God is shown in this, that, first of all, He creates out of nothing, according to His will, the things that are made' (*To Autolycus* 2. 13, in Roberts and Donaldson 1990: ii. 99). Here one can begin to detect something like a set of standard arguments for the *ex nihilo* doctrine. Each of these is directed against claims for the eternity of matter. If matter is unoriginate, then God cannot be reckoned the creator of everything. God's nature as the source of everything is thus compromised. Moreover, if both God and matter are unoriginate and coexistent, then matter itself appears in this respect to be divine. As co-eternal, God and matter exist forever alongside one another. This appears to disrupt the transcendence and priority of God in relation to created reality. And, finally, the grandeur and power of God are better represented by a creation out of nothing, rather than a creation out of something.

In their polemics against gnosticism, both Irenaeus and Tertullian reinforce and extend the doctrine of creation out of nothing. It is required not only to contest the assumption about the eternity of matter, but also to maintain the strict ontological distinction between the one God and all created reality. The cosmos does not represent a series of ontological gradations emanating from the divine outwards. There is one God, and everything else exists through the power of the Word of God. Since the Word of God is to be regarded as of the divine essence, it cannot be an intermediate deity that links the one true God with lower levels of reality. On both sides, therefore, the God–world distinction requires the doctrine of creation out of nothing. Neither is the world divine, nor is God divisible and composite like creaturely beings. So we must think of the world as the good creation of the one God from out of nothing. In this respect, 'nothing' simply denotes 'not something'. 'Nothing' is not some shadowy substance suspended between being and non-being. Instead, it refers to what does not exist. In other words, the cosmos is not formed from eternal matter, nor does it emanate from the divine being. One implication of this sharp ontological distinction between creator and creation is that it belongs not to theology but to natural science to discover how the world works. This is a corollary of the Christian refusal to divinize the world, albeit one that has not always been recognized.

A further feature of this contrast with emanationist accounts is the emphasis now given to creation as a free and unconstrained action of God. There is no natural necessity in the creation of the world. Nothing within the divine being requires that the world come into existence or implies that it must possess a particular form. As a free act, creation is gratuitous. God does not need to make the world; its appearance is itself a sheer act of divine grace. Hence emphasis upon the *ex nihilo* doctrine from the late second century entailed a corresponding stress upon creation as a free, unnecessary movement of God *ad extra*.

Already well established by 200, the idea of a creation out of nothing was further reinforced by the Nicene controversy (Pelikan 1971–89: i. 204). In opposition to Arius and his followers, theologians in the fourth century came to affirm a strong distinction between the Father's eternal begetting of the Son (Logos) and the creation of the world. Scripture had taught that all things were made through the Logos in the beginning; however, the Logos was not to be thought of as a creature or half-divinity, an intermediary communicating between the eternal God and the temporal world. This position was not affirmed without protracted struggle and complex debate. These were formally resolved by the affirmation of the Niceno-Constantinopolitan Creed (381) that the Father and the Son were co-eternal and consubstantial. What is significant for the doctrine of creation here is that the ontological difference between God and the world is further accentuated. There is one triune God, three persons in relation to the others fully expressing the divine being. And there is also the world that this God creates and that neither is begotten nor proceeds from out of the divine being.

The recent interest in classical trinitarian theology has been accompanied by a reinvigoration of arguments for creation out of nothing in writers such as T. F. Torrance (1988: 76–109), Wolfhart Pannenberg (1991–8: ii. 1–174), and Colin Gunton (1998). In light of the doctrine that the being of God is constituted by three persons in relation, the God–world distinction is sharpened. The world must be thought of as contingent, since it is not necessitated by the being of God which in itself is complete and self-sufficient. Nor can the world be described as eternal. The life of God is prior to the life of the world, even if this cannot be expressed as a temporal priority. We should not posit the world as co-eternal alongside the triune being. Indeed, despite the difficulties in conceiving God apart from the world, we must think of creation in this respect as something 'new' in the eternal life of God. Nevertheless, the world is always related to God as a created reality; it is endowed with a particular shape and character consistent with the divine life. Sustained in being and possessing a divinely appointed purpose, creation is the locus for ongoing divine action. Hence the ontological differentiating of God and world does not imply a lack of involvement or loss of connectedness between these two. Nor does it imply that an inferior world is at the disposal of a brute divine power. Instead, one should think of the classical difference between creator and creature as enabling and shaping the relationship that obtains between them, a relationship that requires the use of personal categories if it is to be adequately described.

This casting of the God–world relationship in trinitarian terms is partly intended to militate against both deist and pantheist constructions. The relationship between creator and creation is not so remote as to render subsequent divine action and covenant partnership unintelligible. At the same time, an ontological differentiation is maintained that guarantees sufficient distance and otherness for biblical models of personal agency to make sense. Both deism and pantheism in their different ways prevent notions of agency that attach to the work of the triune God. Ironically, they produce the same outcome: God cannot be conceived as acting within the cosmos (Gunton 2002: 12–19).

Although the doctrine of creation out of nothing was uncontested in the Middle Ages and Reformation, it has been heavily criticized in modern theology. In advocating an everlasting creation in which God is always creative, process theology represents a return to something like the earlier idea of creation out of chaos. This alternative construction of the God–world relationship accentuates the divine influence through allurement as opposed to the sheer sovereignty of the *ex nihilo* tradition. Creation is to be understood better as a gradual evolving of patterns of order from chaos (a low-grade physical state or set of events)—patterns which realize values such as consciousness, pleasure, freedom, and love. The deliberate limitation of divine omnipotence is largely presented as a response to the problem of evil. By abridging God's power, a clearer commitment to the goodness of God can be affirmed in the midst of manifold evils. David Griffin, for example, argues that since God and the creation are always coexistent there is a resultant sharing of power (Griffin 2001). Sovereignty is here distributed in a manner that significantly qualifies the *ex nihilo* tradition. Divine power works not through action but through influence and gradual persuasion of creatures. The capacity for this allurement will vary according to the degree of spontaneity and receptiveness of the entity in question. However, while this offers some account of divine presence, it seriously curtails divine action in ways that render vast tracts of scripture and tradition untenable, thus calling into question its adequacy for the faith community. Yet its proposal is relatively innovative in contesting the centuries-long assumption that creation out of nothing is somehow intuitively correct and obviously better than its rivals.

Formidable ethical criticisms of the *ex nihilo* tradition have also been advanced by ecofeminist writers. The stress upon divine will and transcendence militate against anthropological holism, it is claimed. A preference for the intellectual dimension of existence prevails over embodiedness, with disastrous ecological results. The denigration of matter and privileging of mind and will over body lead to a doctrine of creation that does not properly value our material home. Writing in this vein, Sallie McFague has called for a greater stress on the metaphor of the world as God's body (McFague 1987). Against a traditional model that privileges mind over body and male over female, a more holistic account of the God–world relationship is now required. 'The monarchical model encourages attitudes of militarism, dualism, and escapism; it condones control through violence and oppression; it has nothing to say about the nonhuman world. The model of the world as God's body encourages holistic attitudes of responsibility for and care of the vulnerable and oppressed; it is non-hierarchical and acts through persuasion and attraction; it has a great deal to say about the body and nature' (McFague 1987: 78).

It is ironic that the *ex nihilo* tradition should be charged with something resembling a gnostic dualism of mind and matter—the need to avoid such a dualism gave much of the initial stimulus to the doctrine in the writings of Irenaeus and Tertullian. Despite this, it seems that the insistence upon divine transcendence and otherness can lead in some theologies to a disjunction of God and world that undervalues the latter. These have also connected the sovereignty of God to patriarchal rule in ways that are deeply sexist. Yet there are other essential themes in the doctrine of creation including the goodness of the world and its covenantal relation to God that ought to prevent the disjoining perceived in this charge. The tradition may be in need of repair at various points, but it is another matter whether the replacement of the traditional model of creation out of nothing will prove adequate. The order, beauty, and intrinsic goodness of created things are gifted freely by God; these are not produced out of some inner divine need or necessity. The creation of the world with covenant partnership and incarnation in view is hardly the capricious act of a detached despot. Classically conceived, the creation of the world by God's wisdom is not only an act of divine will but one of divine love. In this respect, the traditional doctrine can release us both from notions of creation as a random act of divine force and also from any sense of the world as ontologically unrelated to the being and purpose of its maker (Williams 1999). The castigation of the monarchical model, as above, contains significant elements of caricature, while the alternative model of the world as God's body appears to problematize any personal interaction between creator and creation.

A similar argument is developed by Pannenberg in his relating of the immanent trinity to the act of creation (Pannenberg 1991–8: ii. 20–35). Unlike the relations of origin within the divine being, the creation of the world is not necessary to the identity of God. Without the world, God would remain God in the unity of the three persons. The Father begets the Son, and the Spirit proceeds from the Father 'before all worlds'. Yet the freedom, love, and life within the triune God render the creation of the world an act expressive of the divine identity. It is neither random nor constrained. As the expression *ad extra* of God's life, it can be understood as an act both of divine freedom and love (Pannenberg 1991–8: ii. 19). Eternity and time are thus correlated without being confused or collapsed into one another. Much the same point is made by Eberhard Jüngel when he argues that the character of creation as grace requires a distinction to be made between the eternal relations of the Trinity and the derivation of the world from God. Our dependence on divine grace is recognized by maintaining a clear difference between the Son's coming eternally from the Father and the human creature's coming to be temporally (Jüngel 1983: 384).

As already noted, throughout the Middle Ages the doctrine of creation out of nothing held sway amongst Christian theologians. A fusion of philosophical and theological arguments was advanced in support of the doctrine. Reserved for divine action alone, the concept of creating was sharply distinguished from that of making or changing. Unlike creaturely acts of causation, the divine creating produces a world from out of nothing. This claim was heavily reinforced by cosmological arguments that presented the self-existent God as the necessary explanation of all contingent processes and entities, including matter. Thomas Aquinas, for example, asserts that only God creates and that everything must owe its existence primarily to the creation out of nothing (*ST* 1a. 44, 2, in Aquinas 1975). Aquinas also claimed that this notion was wholly compatible with an everlasting creation, i.e., a world that has no initial temporal boundary. Even a world, such as that supposed by Aristotle, that had no beginning in time would still have to be created by God out of nothing. Nevertheless, Aquinas affirmed a beginning of the world by reference to the teaching of Genesis. It is revealed in scripture that the universe began, thus providing further testimony to the splendour of its creator's work.

In this respect, Christian theology did not experience the tension with philosophy that was present in Islamic thought in the Middle Ages. Al-Ghazali (1058–1111) famously argued that the universe had a beginning in time through the use of the so-called *kalam* cosmological argument. This was rehearsed at a time when Islamic philosophers such as Avicenna had argued for the eternity of the world on the basis of their reading of the classical philosophers. Convinced that the Qur'ān taught that the creation had a beginning, Al-Ghazali argued vigorously against the conclusions of his philosophical predecessors. Yet this friction between philosophical and theological trends was generally not present in the Christian tradition, where the compatibility of reason and revelation was widely accepted.

III. Animals and the Environment: Current Foci

The creation stories in Genesis display a keen sense of human beings as created alongside animals and sharing in their physical existence. Yet much of the tradition has forgotten this vision of a community of creation, instead regarding human beings as exclusively set apart by virtue of their constitution and role in the economy of salvation. This had led to an excessive anthropocentrism in which the importance of other beings has been neglected both in relation to God and to ourselves. In some measure, this is attributable to the way in which the concept of the divine image has been handled. Where it signifies the possession of a non-physical component such as soul, mind, or consciousness, the essential self tends to be defined in contrast to non-rational creatures. This is largely attributable to the influence of the Greek philosophical tradition, especially Platonism, and is quite evident in Augustine and other Christian writers. It reaches its most extreme version in the writing of Descartes, in which animals, on account of their lack of mind, are represented as mere automata rather than as fellow, sentient beings.

Elsewhere in the Christian tradition, animals were only regarded as of ethical significance insofar as they could be considered the property of human beings. For Thomas Aquinas, their moral status was determined by three factors: lack of reason, natural servility, and potential to become human property (*ST* 2a2ae. 64, 1). Yet this hardly reflects the wisdom literature in scripture, which implies that God values animals for their own sakes and not merely for their human usefulness.

The contribution of animals to the narrative of creation is stunningly expressed in Yann Martel's novel, *Life of Pi*. It concludes with the following exchange:

> Which is the better story, the story with animals or the story without animals?
> That's an interesting question . . .
> The story with animals.
> Yes. The story with animals is the better story.
> Thank you. And so it goes with God. (Martel 2002: 317)

More recent theology has recalled the pervasiveness of animals in scripture and suggested that many historical attitudes were seriously disordered (Linzey 1994; Birch and Vischer 1997; Webb 1998). As fellow creatures, animals surround us and accompany us. Their presence may often be unobtrusive, but they are never far away in the teaching and life of Jesus. Our kinship with animals has been further stressed by recent evolutionary science that reveals common ancestral origins and genetic similarities. The bonding of humans with animals has always been a recurrent feature of human life, and not only in rural communities. The growing sense of the divine purpose as intending a community of creation has heightened ethical awareness of animals, whether this be the conditions under which they are housed and slaughtered, or the threat of extinction now posed to many species.

Similar issues arise with respect to the natural environment. A standard charge against Judaeo-Christian attitudes to nature is that these are hierarchical, domineering, and rapacious. The command to exercise dominion over the world (Gen. 1: 26) has sometimes been taken as licence to utilize and exploit natural resources. While the Hebrew verb does indeed seem to connote the notion of mastery, some commentators have argued that in this initial pastoral setting it must be read in terms of a benign stewardship, the exercise of a divinely mandated duty of care for the earth and its inhabitants. Instead of undermining it, the textual tradition can thus be seen as promoting environmental responsibility. In the context of Genesis 1, the gift of 'dominion' must be viewed in terms of responsible representation. However, while this may ease some ecological concerns about the text, other critics have claimed that the role of human beings should not be seen as managing the entire creation on God's behalf. This anthropocentric notion requires to be challenged by the recognition that there are reaches of creation that we should let be as wilderness. The world is not for us alone; it possesses a beauty and value under God's providence that are not dependent upon their instrumental function for human activity. More recent scientific recognition of the age and size of the cosmos tend to reinforce this claim; animals inhabited the earth for hundreds of millions of years prior to the emergence of hominids.

A further concern about overplaying the managerial role of human beings is the need to realize our own dependency upon the natural world and its ecological balance. In this respect, human welfare is a function of a wider harmony of life forms and climatic systems. Without the regularity of seasons, the stability of an eco-structure, the provision of healthy food, and natural resources, our lives become unsustainable. What is required for the well-being of our planet and future generations is a greater wisdom about our relation to the natural world and our dependent status as creatures, as opposed to mere technological knowledge and accumulation of wealth (Northcott 1996; Rasmussen 1996). In articulating our dependent status and place within God's creaturely community, theology has its part to play.

IV. Apologetics

Since at least the early modern period, the doctrine of creation has been closely involved in apologetic responses to developments in the natural sciences. Although the cosmological and design arguments for the existence of God have their roots in classical philosophy, their regular appearance from the seventeenth century is symptomatic of strategies to defend the faith in the face of doubt and criticism.

Karl Barth's vehement attack on natural theology in the twentieth century appeared to declare a moratorium on all such apologetic tactics (Barth 1957: 63–254). These were perceived to defend the faith on neutral territory that conceded too much to forces of unbelief and scepticism. More importantly, apologetics was a displacement of the real locus of theological knowledge—Jesus Christ, the Word of God, in whom alone the divine act and being are revealed to us. Nevertheless, while undermining all evidentialist strategies for asserting the rationality of religious belief, Barth's criticism of natural theology has not altogether banished apologetics even within the tradition that has largely followed him. T. F. Torrance's commitment to theological science and, albeit to a lesser extent, Hans Frei's recognition of '*ad hoc* apologetics' provide scope for showing some consistency of theological knowledge with the natural sciences and philosophy. In any case, the controversy over natural theology should not be confused with the need to develop a theology of nature.

The cosmological argument typically proceeds from the question of why there is a universe at all. In the version expounded by Leibniz, it argues for the existence of a necessary being as the first cause on the grounds that this is the only sufficient explanation for the world. Everything contingent is thus explained if and only if there is a self-existent being. This (non-temporal) version of the cosmological argument differs from the *kalam* proof, which seeks to demonstrate God's existence on the basis that a first self-explanatory cause is necessary to account fully for a temporal sequence of causes (Craig 1979). It functions largely through denying the possibility of actual infinites on the grounds that these are inherently contradictory. Some recent exponents of the cosmological argument have sought support in the scientific consensus for big bang cosmology. According to their reasoning, the universe cannot now be thought of as everlasting. With its otherwise inexplicable commencement at the big bang, the universe requires to be explained by some non-scientific principle. As a proof of God's existence, the difficulty with this argument is that critics can always propose an alternative hypothesis, such as that of a multiverse, or assert bluntly that the universe may be uncaused. Nevertheless, a more modest apologetic strategy can reasonably claim the consistency of big bang cosmology with the classical doctrine of creation out of nothing. As Ernan McMullin has written, 'If the universe began in time through the act of the creator, from our vantage point it would look something like the big bang cosmologists are now talking about' (Kelsey 1985: 190).

Since the eighteenth century, the design argument has been a source of fascination to philosophers and theologians. It argues to the existence of God on the basis of putative marks of design in the observed world. From the time of Newton until Darwin, writers were struck by the majestic regularities of the solar system, the intricate adjustment of biological components in organs such as the eye, and the seemingly providential match of species to their physical environment. Although the most formidable objections to the argument were presented by David Hume in his posthumously published *Dialogues Concerning Natural Religion* (1779), the argument was continually reinvigorated at least until the publication of Darwin's *The Origin of Species* (1859). Here what had been explained by reference to divine providence could now be accounted for on the basis of the principle of natural selection. God had not originally matched species and environment; instead, through a long process of evolution, life forms had changed and adapted according to the ecological niches they occupied. Moreover, the randomness and waste that Darwin perceived seemed to challenge the order and harmony apparently detected by defenders of the design argument.

It would be wrong, however, to suggest that Darwin's theory of evolution terminated the design argument. Other late nineteenth-century writers, some of quite conservative persuasion, perceived in the long process of evolution an emerging beauty and complexity that was consistent with the biblical account of creation. Evolution could thus be perceived as the means by which the creator enabled new patterns of life; indeed, it could be seen as betokening a God continually involved in the history of the world. Instead of a deist creator who merely lights the blue touchpaper, we now have immanent divine involvement in the course of nature and history. Debates about the consistency of evolutionary and theological explanation continue to rage. A range of explanations can be detected. In its most militant form, the neo-Darwinian position, popularized by Richard Dawkins, argues that the pervasive forces of genetic mutation and natural selection are sufficient to render any religious account of the universe redundant (Dawkins 2003: 173–9). Other neo-Darwinists, for example Stephen Jay Gould (1999), appear to suggest that science and religion function at quite different levels of explanation and should not be seen as mutually exclusive, provided each respects the other's domain. Alternatively, the recent work of Simon Conway Morris (2003) suggests that there are significant constraints upon the evolutionary process that make the emergence of complex life forms inevitable, though rare, in the cosmos. This appears to open further possibilities in the contemporary scientific context of a consonance between Darwinian evolution and divine creation. At any rate, it may be a more plausible apologetic strategy than intelligent design theory that too rapidly asserts divine design wherever gaps in current scientific explanation temporarily appear (Dembski and Ruse 2004).

The design argument has also found recent support amongst physicists who claim that the initial conditions governing the universe in its first milliseconds after the big bang are evidence of cosmic fine-tuning. The universe could not have produced stars, planets, and carbon-based life forms had the temperature, the rate of expansion, and the formation of the forces of nature not been precise (Polkinghorne 1988). This series of 'cosmic coincidences' has elicited a sense of wonder and a demand for explanation that is redolent of early forms of the design argument in the scientific community.

Whatever the validity of such arguments, they must fall short of establishing the Christian doctrine of creation. Hume's stricture that the design hypothesis is compatible with a range of theisms should caution against too heavy a reliance upon such strategies. At best, apologetic arguments for a creator based on scientific and philosophical consideration can attempt to show the compossibility of faith with other areas of knowledge. In some respects, this may be redolent of the wisdom literature. But such arguments can neither ground nor exhaust the theology of creation. Deeply connected to other themes derived from scripture and the church's long tradition of reflection upon its witness, the doctrine of creation remains a rich and integral component of Christian theology.

References

Aquinas, St Thomas (1975). *Summa Theologiae.* London: Blackfriars.

Barth, Karl (1957). *Church Dogmatics* II/1. Edinburgh: T. & T. Clark.

—— (1958). *Church Dogmatics* III/1. Edinburgh: T. & T. Clark.

Berkhof, Hendrikus (1986). *Christian Faith.* Grand Rapids: Eerdmans.

Birch, Charles, and Vischer, Lukas (1997). *Living with the Animals: The Community of God's Creatures.* Geneva: World Council of Churches.

Craig, William Lane (1979). *The Kalam Cosmological Argument.* London: Macmillan.

Craig, William Lane, and Copan, Paul (2004). *Creation out of Nothing: A Biblical, Philosophical, and Scientific Exploration.* Leicester: Apollos.

Dawkins, Richard (2003). *A Devil's Chaplain: Selected Essays.* London: Weidenfeld & Nicolson.

Dembski, William, and Ruse, Michael (eds.) (2004). *Debating Design: From Darwin to DNA*. Cambridge: Cambridge University Press.

Frye, Roland (ed.) (1993). *Is God a Creationist?* New York: Scribner's.

Gould, Steven Jay (1999). *Rocks of Ages: Science and Religion in the Fullness of Time*. New York: Ballantine.

Griffin, David Ray (2001). 'Creation out of Nothing, Creation out of Chaos, and the Problem of Evil'. In Stephen Davis (ed.), *Encountering Evil: Live Options in Theodicy*, rev. edn., Louisville: Westminster John Knox, 108–25.

Gunton, Colin (1998). *The Triune Creator: A Historical and Systematic Study*. Edinburgh: Edinburgh University Press.

—— (2002). *The Christian Faith: An Introduction to Christian Doctrine*. Oxford: Blackwell.

Jenson, Robert W. (1997–9). *Systematic Theology*. 2 vols. New York: Oxford University Press.

Jüngel, Eberhard (1983). *God as the Mystery of the World*. Edinburgh: T. & T. Clark.

Kelsey, David (1985). 'The doctrine of creation out of nothing'. In E. McMullin (ed.), *Evolution and Creation*, Notre Dame: University of Notre Dame Press.

Kerr, Fergus (1997). *Theology After Wittgenstein*. 2nd edn. London: SPCK.

Levenson, Jon (1994). *Creation and the Persistence of Evil: The Jewish Drama of Divine Omnipotence*. Princeton: Princeton University Press.

Linzey, Andrew (1994). *Animal Theology*. London: SCM.

Macquarrie, John (1982). *In Search of Humanity: A Theological and Philosophical Approach*. London: SCM.

McFague, Sallie (1987). *Models of God*. Philadelphia: Fortress.

McFarland, Ian A. (2005). *The Divine Image: Envisioning the Invisible God*. Minneapolis: Fortress.

Martel, Yann (2002). *The Life of Pi*. Edinburgh: Canongate.

May, Gerhard (1994). *Creatio ex Nihilo*. Edinburgh: T. & T. Clark.

Moltmann, Jürgen (1985). *God in Creation*. London: SCM.

Morris, Simon Conway (2003). *Life's Solution: Inevitable Humans in a Lonely Universe*. Cambridge: Cambridge University Press.

Neusner, Jacob (1991). *Confronting Creation: How Judaism Reads Genesis: An Anthology of Genesis Rabbah*. Columbia: University of South Carolina Press.

Northcott, Michael (1996). *The Environment and Christian Ethics*. Cambridge: Cambridge University Press.

Pannenberg, Wolfhart (1991–8). *Systematic Theology*. 3 vols. Grand Rapids: Eerdmans.

Pelikan, Jaroslav (1971–89). *The Christian Tradition*. 5 vols. Chicago: University of Chicago Press.

Polkinghorne, John (1988). *Science and Creation*. London: SPCK.

Rasmussen, Larry (1996). *Earth Community, Earth Ethics*. Maryknoll: Orbis.

Roberts, A., and Donaldson, J. (eds.) (1990). *Ante-Nicene Fathers: The Writings of the Fathers down to A.D. 325*. Edinburgh: T. & T. Clark.

Schwöbel, Christoph (1997). 'God, Creation and the Christian Community: The Dogmatic Basis of a Christian Ethic of Createdness'. In Colin Gunton (ed.), *The Doctrine of Creation*, Edinburgh: T. & T. Clark, 149–76.

Torrance, T. F. (1988). *The Trinitarian Faith*. Edinburgh: T. & T. Clark.

van Huyssteen, J. Wentzel (2006). *Alone in the World? Human Uniqueness in Science and Theology*. Grand Rapids: Eerdmans.

Webb, Stephen (1998). *On God and Dogs: A Christian Theology of Compassion for Animals.* New York: Oxford University Press.

Williams, Rowan (1999). 'Good For Nothing? Augustine on Creation'. In Everett Ferguson (ed.), *Doctrinal Diversity: Recent Studies in Early Christianity,* New York: Garland, 31–46.

Suggested Reading

Barth (1958).

Fergusson, David (1998). *The Cosmos and the Creator.* London: SPCK.

Gunton (1998).

McFague (1987).

May (1994).

Moltmann (1985).

Pannenberg (1991–8: ii. 1–174).

Polkinghorne (1988).

Schwarz, Hans (2002). *Creation.* Grand Rapids: Eerdmans.

Tanner, Kathryn (1988). *God and Creation in Christian Theology: Tyranny or Empowerment.* Oxford: Blackwell.

Ward, Keith (1996). *Religion and Creation.* Oxford: Oxford University Press.

Welker, Michael (1999). *Creation and Reality.* Philadelphia: Fortress.

Westermann, Claus (1974). *Creation.* London: SPCK.

CHAPTER 5

PROVIDENCE

CHARLES M. WOOD

I. The Origins of the Doctrine of Providence

How are we to understand events theologically? How, if at all, is God involved in what happens in the course of our lives day to day, in the course of human history, and in the 'natural history' of the world around us? How is God related to what goes on?

For adherents of a genuinely monotheistic faith, questions of this sort are unavoidable. There is no occasion to which God is irrelevant. Even to speak of God's 'absence' or 'hiddenness' is to acknowledge God's relation to the occasion and to our understanding of it. From the beginning, then, Christians have found themselves making claims about God's relation to events—and not only to certain special events, but to all events whatsoever. They have also found themselves reflecting on those claims, and formulating teachings as to what it is proper for Christians to think and to affirm on this subject.

For considerable stretches of time, reflection and teaching generated by this question of God's relation to or involvement in what is going on in the world have formed a distinct doctrinal locus, and the name commonly given to this locus in the theological traditions of the West has been 'providence'. That name, along with a substantial amount of the conceptual resources that have shaped the doctrine of providence, were among the things early Christian thinkers appropriated from their Graeco-Roman environment, and particularly from its Stoic or 'Stoicized' intellectual currents. As the Christian movement began to seek and to gain religious legitimacy, it borrowed heavily from the religious philosophies accepted among the cultured elites of the Roman Empire, and the idea of providence was among the borrowings.

To speak of 'borrowing' here is misleading to some extent, given that this diffused Stoicism helped to shape Christian thinking—and Christian existence—from very early on. It is evident already, for example, in the letters of Paul. Moreover, there are important ways in which Stoicism appears compatible, if not identical, with some key Christian commitments and lends itself readily to Christian uses. For instance, it is an emphatically egalitarian teaching: the path to liberation is open to all, regardless of social status, gender, physical condition, or personal attainments. Further, the liberation that is sought in the Stoic way requires a stringent *ascesis*, a renunciation of worldly concerns, and a thorough conversion. It was natural, and may not even have involved any conscious borrowing, for early Christians to conceptualize the insights and experiential dynamics of the new life in Christ in Stoic terms. As Christianity moved further (and higher) into Graeco-Roman society and culture, the blending became ever more natural, thorough, and subtle.

Along with the formal similarities, however, there are some serious substantive differences between the Stoic and the Christian vision. Where for Stoicism the world from which we seek liberation is ultimately the material world of (for instance) bodies and bodily needs and vulnerabilities, for the Christianity of the New Testament the world in *that* sense is God's good creation; the 'world' (or 'order' of things: *kosmos*) that is to be renounced and opposed is the domination and distortion of that good creation by sin and evil. Where for Stoicism the goal to be reached by *apatheia* is the realization of our true nature, a nature that is (in the words of Boethius) 'self-sufficient, strong, worthy of respect, glorious and joyful' (Boethius 1999: 65), the Christian vision is not one of detachment and invulnerability, but rather one of being 'filled with the energy of love' (to use John Wesley's rendition of *di' agapes energoumene*, Gal. 5: 6), to have 'God's love... poured into our hearts through the Holy Spirit' (Rom. 5: 5), and thus to be subject to a transformation that probably awaits an application of the concept of *perichoresis* for anything like an adequate theological formulation. The deep challenge of this experience to ordinary consciousness is smoothed over in the NRSV of Galatians 2: 20, but is vividly maintained in the language of the Authorized Version: 'I am crucified with Christ: nevertheless I live; yet not I, but Christ liveth in me: and the life which I now live in the flesh, I live by the faith of the Son of God, who loved me, and gave himself for me.' Closely related to these discrepancies, of course, are the differences between the understandings of God which animate these two visions of reality—differences that would not become entirely explicit until the fourth century, and that have still not been fully appreciated.

The implications of these differences for a doctrine of providence are profound. They are responsible for many of the struggles Christians have had with the doctrine through the centuries, and also at least in part responsible for its eventual deconstruction.

II. Providence in Contemporary Theological Reflection

In a remarkably probing article published in 1963, Langdon Gilkey noted the widespread neglect of the doctrine of providence in twentieth-century theology. In the reigning liberal theology of the late nineteenth century, evolutionary optimism had supplanted the more traditional conceptions of divine providence that had been struggling for viability against an accumulation of problems since the late seventeenth century. But when this faith in progress was shattered by the First World War and its aftermath, providence 'was left a rootless, disembodied ghost, flitting from footnote to footnote, but rarely finding secure lodgment in sustained theological discourse' (Gilkey 1963: 171). While the doctrine was explicitly rejected by some authors, standard theological texts for the most part either gave it a brief conventional summary or quietly omitted it. In any case it received little serious examination or constructive restatement. 'It is interesting', Gilkey wrote, 'that of all the major classical doctrines of theology, Providence is the single one which has not been reinterpreted and revitalized by contemporary theology but which has, on the contrary, been generally ignored and in some cases even repudiated' (Gilkey 1963: 174). The situation has not changed markedly since Gilkey wrote. Put plainly, the doctrine has simply been overwhelmed by the challenges it has faced. As Wolf Krötke observes, 'The doctrine of the providence of God stands today as a particularly difficult, perhaps even impossible part of Christian dogmatics' (Krötke 2000: 1190), even though it remains a central, if largely unexamined, element in Christian piety.

The question of God's relation to events did not fade from theology along with the doctrine of providence, however. That question, taking different forms in different settings, has continued to occupy a great deal of theological attention. While for various reasons the terminology of the classical doctrine of providence may not have been conspicuous in these inquiries, they have often been shaped by its problematic legacy. What we might call the question of the doctrine of providence—simply put, how are we to understand theologically what goes on?—has been pursued in recent theology in three major contexts of inquiry, each with its own internal diversity. One has to do with the very intelligibility of the sorts of statements Christians typically make, or might wish to make, concerning God's involvement in events; a second centres on the question of the practical effects of such teachings and beliefs on human lives; and in a third, the leading question is one about the proper sources of a Christian understanding of these matters. These three contexts of inquiry—we might, for convenience, call them the philosophical, the practical, and the historical context—correspond to the three main clusters of problems that have rendered the doctrine of providence such a difficult locus of theological reflection.

The Philosophical Context

How may we conceive of God's relation to events? The *Heidelberg Catechism* informs us that God 'upholds, as it were by his own hand, heaven and earth together with all creatures, and rules in such a way that leaves and grass, rain and drought, fruitful and unfruitful years, food and drink, health and sickness, riches and poverty, and everything else, come to us not by chance but by his fatherly hand' (Miller and Osterhaven 1962: Q. 27). What sense might be given to the notion of God's 'upholding' and 'ruling', or—to use the more common threefold articulation of God's providential action—to God's preservation or sustaining of creaturely reality, God's concurrence or cooperation in creaturely activity, and God's governance or direction of all events toward their proper end? What evidence is there (to put it bluntly) that God is doing anything of the sort? Or, if evidence is somehow beside the point, how are these claims to be taken? Is anything being asserted at all, or does this language have an entirely different function? In an article published only shortly before his examination of the state of the doctrine of providence, Langdon Gilkey pressed the representatives of the then-regnant 'biblical theology movement' to indicate how they, as inhabitants of the modern world and presumably as holders of a modern scientific world view, would have us understand the 'mighty acts of God in history' which scripture attests, and which, in their view, were to be the content of Christian theology and proclamation (Gilkey 1961). Soon, the title of an essay by Frank B. Dilley would extend the challenge: 'Does the "God Who Acts" Really Act?' (1965).

The wide-ranging discussion of this issue, to which systematic theologians, philosophers of religion, historians, and exegetes have all contributed, would be impossible to summarize with any adequacy. The bulk of its publication has taken the form of hundreds of articles in scholarly journals and conference proceedings. (Two among several useful collections might be mentioned: Hebblethwaite and Henderson 1990; Tracy 1994.) The analytic philosophy of action in the latter half of the twentieth century was a rich source of ideas to be extended into theological territory; philosophers of religion and philosophical theologians have appropriated this material, along with earlier philosophical resources, in an effort to address Dilley's question.

In this connection, one important development has been the rise of what David Burrell calls 'tradition-directed inquiry' as a mode of philosophical theology: that is, inquiry into the meaningfulness and meaning of theological concepts that is oriented toward the actual use and theological refinement of these concepts in the religious traditions that have originated or adopted (and adapted) them, rather than, say, toward some abstract 'theism'. In a series of publications, Burrell himself has given considerable attention to tracing out similarities and differences among (and within) the three major Abrahamic traditions in their more philosophically reflective treatments of divine and creaturely power, freedom, knowledge, and agency. The essays collected in Burrell (2004) provide an apt representation of this effort and some hint of its value.

A signal philosophical contribution to Christian reflection on these issues is D. Z. Phillips's recent discussion of the 'problem of evil'. 'Greater damage is often done to religion by those who think of themselves as its philosophical friends, than by those who present themselves as religion's detractors and despisers', he observes (Phillips 2004: p. xi), and he pleads with his fellow philosophers to 'look to the religious contexts in which it has its use' if they are to understand Christian language (Phillips 2004: 6). Taking his own advice, he produces a set of reflections upon God's power and goodness and upon the human struggle with the reality of God that theologians should find powerfully clarifying.

Both Burrell's and Phillips's work illustrate two points vital to the understanding of religious teachings generally, and, under present circumstances, perhaps especially pertinent to the topic at hand. One is the importance of significant experience with the actual language and practice of a specific religious community, and with the normative sources by which these are governed, to an understanding of the key concepts involved. Much philosophical reflection on religious matters has foundered upon the unreflective adoption of *a priori* notions of what (for instance) deity must involve. Burrell and Phillips have taken to heart Wittgenstein's injunction: 'One cannot guess how a word functions. One has to *look at* its use and learn from that' (Wittgenstein 1958: §340). They are redirecting attention to the details of conceptual use. The second, related point also finds support in Wittgenstein's work. Because concepts are basically capacities, to come to understand a new concept is to be able to do something one could not do before. The concepts that play a prominent role in a religious tradition often shape their users' perceptions of themselves and their world, their attitudes and emotions, and their actions in deep and complex ways. They affect the learner, whether the learner is an adherent of the tradition or an 'outsider' seeking to understand. To understand a concept such as 'samsara' or 'grace' or 'providence' involves understanding *with* or *through* the concept. In their attention to these two points concerning religious understanding, Phillips and Burrell are expanding the context of their philosophical inquiry well into the practical and historical contexts to be discussed below, with mutually enriching results. At such places, the ground is being prepared for a new, genuinely systematic-theological approach to the study of the doctrine.

Owing perhaps to the sorts of philosophical resources upon which it has drawn and the ways it has framed and pursued its questions, this voluminous discussion of what sense, if any, might be given to talk about God's involvement in what goes on has been predominantly an Anglo-American affair. The same might be said of two closely related projects in philosophical theology which overlap somewhat with each other and with this one, namely, process theology (in its various forms) and the theological engagement with the natural sciences. There have been some notable exceptions, including an ongoing involvement by German systematic and philosophical theologians attentive to all these developments. Interesting things can happen when these efforts at conceptual analysis are brought into conversation with the traditions of the

Continental Reformation (see, for example, the essays on divine action assembled in Härle and Preul 1987). Perhaps the most comprehensive and exhaustive treatment of this material to date in the context of the doctrine of providence is the Heidelberg *Habilitationsschrift* of Reinhold Bernhardt, *Was heisst 'Handeln Gottes'? Eine Rekonstruktion der Lehre von der Vorsehung* (1999). Bernhardt examines the history of the doctrine of providence since the Reformation, highlighting two major models of divine activity that were particularly prominent in that history. He then explores these models in much more detail, aided by the resources of the contemporary philosophical and systematic-theological discussions, and in light of this re-examination proposes a third model to supplement and interact with the two dominant ones. The reader thereby gains an appreciation of the complexity of the concept of divine activity, particularly within the context of a Christian understanding of God as triune. Bernhardt turns more explicitly to the reconstructive task in the brief final section of his book, proposing (among other things) three very important and closely connected moves: The first is to relocate the doctrine of providence within the context of trinitarian reflection, in order to align it more closely with pneumatology. From early on, providence has been 'appropriated' to the Father; and yet when Christians speak of the presence and activity of God, it is Spirit-language that comes more readily to the fore. The second, a sort of corollary to the first, is to eliminate the traditional separation between God's providential and God's salvific activity so that their deeper coinherence might be realized. The third—offered in agreement with a number of other contemporary writers—is to reconceive the notion of divine power in more radically Christian terms as the 'power of weakness' (1 Cor. 1: 25), and to purge the doctrine of providence of understandings of power which do not befit its character as a Christian doctrine. If taken seriously, these and other related suggestions offered as the fruit of this impressive study might well help create the possibility of a fresh Christian doctrine of providence.

The Practical Context

A second major context of inquiry is primarily concerned not with the philosophical-theological question of the intelligibility of Christian talk about God's relation to the course of events but rather with the practical-theological question of the effects or consequences of that talk. Historically, the Christian doctrine of providence has taught that the way things are is the way God intends them, and that whatever befalls us in life is specifically 'sent' by God for some purpose, even though that purpose may elude our comprehension. Believers are thus to be 'patient in adversity' and 'grateful in the midst of blessing' (as the *Heidelberg Catechism* tells us), trusting that all things are in God's control. In short, the received version of the doctrine of providence has normally functioned to encourage Christians to accept the circumstances of their lives as divinely willed, and to rest content with them, confident that all is for the best.

Seen in this light, the traditional strict distinction between God's providential work and God's saving work seems entirely reasonable. Salvation, in this division of doctrinal labour, has nothing to do with a transformation of our circumstances, e.g., with any movement out of the life station to which God has assigned us, much less with any challenge to the way our society is ordered. We are to work out our salvation *within* those circumstances, and not by seeking to change them. They are as God intends them. As a late seventeenth-century Anglican apologist for providence wrote, 'If we are poor, we must own this to be God's will and appointment that we should be poor; if we be rich, we must consider, that it is God's blessing which maketh rich' (Sherlock 1694: 347).

Half a century later, the pious Samuel Johnson famously observed

> How small, of all that human hearts endure,
> That part which laws or kings can cause or cure!

That part may not be quite as small as Johnson held it to be. There are, to be sure, inevitable sufferings bound up in our creaturely condition, and other sufferings that we willingly accept for the sake of a greater good. But to the extent that the doctrine of providence has led Christians to remain passive, or even to resist change, when suffering might be alleviated, questions are in order. Christians have, on occasion, opposed the use of anaesthesia on the providential grounds that it is wrong to attempt to avoid the pain that God has appointed. Church and civic leaders have, on occasion, appealed to providence to justify keeping the 'working classes' in a state of need and dependence, since this is obviously the state in which God wishes them to exist, presumably for the good of their souls. Christian pastors and neighbours have, for centuries, counselled injured women to bear with patience the abusive treatment they receive from their husbands and to seek whatever good God may be intending for them (or for the abuser) in that situation, rather than removing themselves from it. Christians have, on occasion, opposed the scientific investigation of the causes of floods, for fear that these investigations might lead to proposals for flood control, when clearly the control of floods should be left in the hands of God. Natural disasters are, after all, 'acts of God', and should be allowed to take their intended course—and find their intended victims.

Of course, divine providence has sometimes been invoked on the side of change, in many of these same cases. The God who sends pain, it has been observed, has also sent us the means to alleviate it; the God who sends devastating floods and fires has also given us the intelligence to figure out how to prevent them, or to minimize their harmful effects. Perhaps the situation in which we find ourselves is not, after all, the situation in which God wishes us to remain. However, over the long history of the employment of the doctrine, the counsel of patient acceptance and endurance has far outweighed the counsel of taking action to effect change. Given the Stoic sources of the doctrine, the circumstances of its rise to prominence, and the role of the Christian religion over many centuries as an instrument of social control, this is hardly surprising. The doctrine of providence that early came to be officially sanctioned proved to be an important factor in equipping Christianity to assume the functions of an established religion. It helped the church to address the general human need for assurance and security in the cosmos, and, in the way it did so, to demonstrate its own vital role in promoting political and social stability. The relation between church and empire, and between church and state in the subsequent history of western Christendom, was cemented by providence. 'In effect, the idea of Christian providence constituted a totalising explanation, a kind of theory of everything' (Cameron 1993: 121).

From the standpoint of civil order, frankly, God's generosity can be a problem. So can the idea that things might not be quite as they should be. The notion that God 'makes his sun rise on the evil and on the good, and sends rain on the righteous and on the unrighteous' (Matt. 5: 45), or that hard workers and dutiful children do not necessarily fare any better than latecomers and wastrels, is difficult to square with the conviction that all is right with the world. There must be a reason for these apparent violations of our sense of justice, and the reason must have something to do not merely with general meteorological tendencies but with God's specific and altogether righteous intentions for each recipient of sunshine or rain.

The alliance of the traditional doctrine of providence with the interests of those who benefit from the status quo has not escaped notice. Awareness of this alliance may have had something substantial to do with the long-standing preference of many common folk for the 'heathenish' notion of chance or fortune over the officially sanctioned belief that God has assigned us all to our places and is directing all that occurs—and with the fact that church and civic leaders have sometimes had to work hard to disseminate the doctrine of providence and to monitor its enforcement (Walsham 1999: esp. ch. 1). The alliance has received more critical scrutiny since the rise of historical consciousness with the second phase of the Enlightenment. Consciousness of it had something substantial to do with the rejection of the traditional doctrine of providence by socially concerned church leaders in the nineteenth century (Cashdollar 1978). In contemporary theology it is now under renewed examination by numerous theologians working 'from the underside of history' (Gebara 2002; Gutiérrez 1987; Rankka 1998; Townes 1993; Young 1992).

One of the most important contributions to a Christian understanding of God's providence in the past thirty years is a small book by the Peruvian theologian Gustavo Gutiérrez on the book of Job, *On Job: God-Talk and the Suffering of the Innocent.* With Barth, Gutiérrez sees Job as a type of Jesus Christ, 'the true witness' who speaks rightly of God (Gutiérrez 1987: xviii). That right speaking, in Job's case, accompanies 'two major shifts of viewpoint' (*desplazamientos*) portrayed in the book as Job relates his suffering first to the sufferings of others and then to the gratuitousness of God's love. The first shift is marked by the realization that much human suffering is the result of human injustice, and that, rather than looking to God as its source and the sinfulness of the sufferer as its explanation, we should address the sinfulness of those human agents who are inflicting the suffering. This realization gives rise to a 'language of prophecy' that aims to expose the injustice, address the causes of the sufferings of the poor, and transform the situation.

However, the language of prophecy alone cannot account for all suffering. Samuel Johnson may have been inclined to exaggerate the proportion of human suffering that is outside the sphere of 'laws or kings', but clearly not all suffering can be traced to human injustice. The second *desplazamiento* in the book of Job places suffering into the broader context of creation, and gives rise to a 'language of contemplation'. In the plot of the book, 'Job now understands that the world of justice must be located within the broad but demanding horizon of freedom that is formed by the gratuitousness of God's love' (Gutiérrez 1987: 16). We live in a 'world of grace' transcending justice, and the language of contemplation is an attempt to acknowledge the scope of that grace and at the same time to acknowledge our incapacity to grasp it (Gutiérrez 1987: 88). In the book of Job that broader horizon is symbolized in part by the vastness of creation and by the presence in it of creatures entirely baffling to us, in whose existence God apparently delights.

Gutiérrez does not speak of the suffering that befalls us as being 'sent' specifically by God for some purpose. His theological perspective allows rather for the sheer contingency of much creaturely suffering as a consequence of the freedom generously given to all creatures in and with creation. At the same time, then, there is a sense in which all things do come from God, as the author of creation and of creaturely freedom itself (Gutiérrez 1987: 53–5). To trust in God is to trust in the one from whom all these contingencies proceed, even while faithful response requires a good deal of discrimination so as to avoid 'a resignation to evil and injustice' (Gutiérrez 1987: 54). This need for discrimination, and for maintaining the legitimate and essential 'prophetic' concern within the larger 'contemplative' context, is one of the demanding features of this second *desplazamiento*; but even more demanding (especially for those in privileged circumstances) may be the experience of displacement itself, that is, of realizing what it means to live in a world of grace. Through his account of Job, Gutiérrez describes a process of conversion that may be an essential precondition for a genuinely Christian doctrine of providence: a movement from love of self to love of others, but then beyond both of these to something like what Jonathan Edwards described as 'consent to Being', within which both love of other human beings and love of self are restored, though radically transfigured. In the closing paragraphs of *The Meaning of Revelation*, H. Richard Niebuhr summarized the lesson of such a conversion for our thinking about God's providence in these few words: 'He ministers indeed to all our good but all our good is other than we thought.' In this light, Niebuhr observes, 'we must begin to rethink all our definitions of deity and convert all our worship and our prayers' (Niebuhr 1941: 191, 190). Gutiérrez has confirmed and amplified this insight, anchoring his exposition of Job's truthful witness both in the biblical text and in the experience of the poor of Latin America.

The Historical Context

A third major context of contemporary inquiry in which the legacy of the doctrine of providence is under examination centres on the question of the sources and character of a properly Christian understanding of God's relation to what goes on. What makes a concept or view of 'providence' an authentically *Christian* concept or view? Can there even be a Christian doctrine of providence at all? It has long been recognized that 'providence' and its cognates rarely appear in Christian scripture, especially in a theological context of use, and that the concept was an early import from recognized philosophical sources. Several prominent theologians at various times have recommended against its use on the grounds that it is not merely non-scriptural but also inevitably distorting of Christian witness concerning the reality and character of God. Many others have retained the term, but on the condition that the conceptual content of the doctrine be derived from scripture and purified of alien philosophical influence. Jan Milič Lochman regards the *articulus mixtus* status of the doctrine in post-Reformation Protestant dogmatics as the source of many difficulties: 'The doctrine of providence is therefore directed onto a "theistic track." The traditional predicates of theistic thought—the Godhead as omnipotent, all-knowing, beyond all time and space, and in particular, as having absolute power without the ability to suffer—become dominant' (Lochman 2003: 283). Along with Eberhard Busch (1993), Lochman attempts an exegesis of the relevant passages in the *Heidelberg Catechism* as a biblically grounded alternative to a 'theistic' doctrine, stressing God's companionship with us in our suffering. (The constructive vision of providence sketched in both cases has some kinship with that found in Gutiérrez, and is, I believe, commendable so far as it goes. Whether it can be attributed unproblematically to the *Heidelberg Catechism* is another question, particularly when it comes to the issue of God's deliberate 'sending' of all that happens to us (cf. Busch 2003: 46–7).)

One contemporary attempt to rethink the doctrine of providence on biblical grounds is that of a group of mainly North American evangelical theologians and philosophers whose stance has come to be known as 'open theism' or 'relational theism'. As these names for it may suggest, much of the project has been articulated in a context of philosophical inquiry. It also displays serious pastoral and other practical concerns and considerations. However, the title of a collaborative manifesto by several participants in the project indicates what they view as the authoritative source of the understanding they propose: *The Openness of God: A Biblical Challenge to the Traditional Understanding of God* (Pinnock et al. 1994). They do not hold that theirs is the only understanding that is compatible with scripture, nor that an appeal to scripture is the only relevant appeal; but they do believe that certain philosophical commitments in 'traditional' theism have prevented its adherents from attending as fully to the scriptural evidence as they might. That evidence, as they read it, supports an 'open' view of God's interaction with the world: God does not control all events, but rather responds freely to the free actions of creatures—actions which may or may not be in accord with God's will. Thus the present situation, whatever it may be, cannot be taken simply as God-ordained, and the future is genuinely open. The most comprehensive systematic approach to providence to emerge so far from this movement is John Sanders's *The God Who Risks: A Theology of Providence* (1998). His 'risk' view of providence differs from that of some others in the broader movement as to the extent to which creatures may thwart the divine will indefinitely. The book does not offer a full reformulation of the doctrine of providence, but concentrates on some major points at which the movement as a whole faces firm opposition from other evangelical theologians, some of whom have been emphatic in their condemnation of this explicit departure from the doctrinal norms of Protestant orthodoxy. A more irenic, mediating response to relational theism from a revisionist Calvinist perspective is Terrance Tiessen's *Providence and Prayer: How Does God Work in the World?* (2000). Tiessen's work, like many of the books of the 'open theists' themselves, is written to be accessible to the non-specialist—a recognition, on the part of these theologians, of the fact that the gap between academic discourse and congregational life needs to be bridged if there is to be real doctrinal revitalization on this or any topic. Along with a recent encounter with process thought (cf. Stone and Oord 2001), this evangelical re-examination of the 'logic of sovereignty' that has dominated western doctrines of providence is contributing to the general work of reassessment.

One point at issue in any discussion of the proper sources of a Christian doctrine of providence—as is quite evident from the debates just mentioned—is how scripture is to be read. In this regard, George Lindbeck made an intriguing claim in *The Nature of Doctrine*: 'Whether it will be possible to regain a specifically biblical understanding of providence depends in part on the possibility of theologically reading Scripture once again in literary rather than nonliterary ways' (1984: 119). Lindbeck had in mind the sort of 'postcritical' reading of scripture found in the later work of Karl Barth and both described and exemplified by Lindbeck's colleague Hans Frei.

Karl Barth's exposition of the doctrine of providence, over three hundred pages in length, is found in *Church Dogmatics* III/3. It was published in 1950, more than a decade before Langdon Gilkey's article lamenting the fate of the doctrine. Gilkey was not ignorant of Barth's treatment, but he regarded it as a colossal failure—perhaps the paradigm case of the problem with which his essay dealt. One weakness of Barth's treatment, in Gilkey's view, was its reinforcement of a traditional tendency (cf. Calvin) to regard the rest of creation as only a 'theatre' for the human drama, with no further meaning or purpose; Barth has no language for dealing with God's relation to what goes on in creation as a whole beyond the human realm, and no apparent interest in doing so. But the key weakness, before which even this first one fades into insignificance, is the absence of any treatment of evil in Barth's doctrine of providence. Evil (*das Nichtige*) is given a separate, subsequent section of its own, during which Barth notes that, in light of *das Nichtige*, the doctrine of providence must be entirely rethought. He does not himself provide that rethinking, however, and so his portrayal of God's providence is oddly removed from experienced reality, 'like some economic analysis in which self-interest has casually been omitted' (Gilkey 1963: 189). 'If, then, Providence concerns God's relations to actual, not theoretical, history; if *das Nichtige* is what God does *not* will; and if *das Nichtige* nevertheless distorts if not dominates actual creaturely decisions, what are we to make at this point of God's proclaimed providential sovereignty over this creaturely passage; and what did Barth mean when he said: "Nothing can be done by the creature except the will of God"?' (Gilkey 1963: 190).

As Mike Higton's recent account of Hans Frei's theology indicates, Frei's reading of Barth may shed some further light on the difficulties Gilkey saw in Barth's doctrine of providence. In the early volumes of the *Church Dogmatics*, Barth repeatedly enunciates a principle that creates 'conceptual space' for genuine creaturely freedom within the context of divine freedom. Divine and human freedom are not in competition with one another, and to magnify one is not to diminish the other. In principle, Barth is already a 'theologian of freedom'. Substantively, however, Barth's desire to recover an appreciation for the divine freedom led him to neglect or underplay in his doctrinal expositions the creaturely freedom he was also affirming in theory. The divine agent, rather than activating the freedom of creatures, often appears to be enacting their actions, at the expense of their creaturely identity and integrity. One manifestation of this tension between principle and practice, as Frei saw it, was a relative neglect of 'the contingent details of Jesus' historical life' in Barth's early exegesis (Higton 2004: 58), a problem that is decisively overcome in the fourth volume of the *Dogmatics* where what Lindbeck might call a more fully literary reading of scripture is achieved. Meanwhile, his treatment of providence may be regarded as another manifestation of this tension—another, and particularly unfortunate, instance in which historical contingency and creaturely contingency in general are given less than their due.

'The providential action of God over and in his creation is not that of a mechanical fate to be read off of one occasion. God's work is mysteriously, abidingly mysteriously, coexistent with the contingency of events. The history of his providence is one that must be narrated' (Frei 1975: 163). Whether we are yet capable of such narration remains to be seen.

References

Bernhardt, Reinhold (1999). *Was heisst 'Handeln Gottes'? Eine Rekonstruktion der Lehre von der Vorsehung*. Gütersloh: Chr. Kaiser/Gütersloher Verlagshaus.

Boethius (1999). *The Consolation of Philosophy*. London: Penguin.

Burrell, David B. (2004). *Faith and Freedom: An Interfaith Perspective.* Oxford: Blackwell.

Busch, Eberhard (1993). 'Das der ewig vater unsers herrn Jesus Christ dieselbigen erhelt und regieret ...'. In Jörg Martin et al. (eds.), *'Mit unsrer Macht ist nichts getan ...'*, Frankfurt am Main: Haag und Herchen, 39–54.

Cameron, Averil (1993). 'Divine Providence in Late Antiquity'. In Leo Howe and Alan Wain (eds.), *Predicting the Future*, Cambridge: Cambridge University Press, 118–43.

Cashdollar, Charles D. (1978). 'The Social Implications of the Doctrine of Divine Providence: A Nineteenth-Century Debate in American Theology'. *Harvard Theological Review* 71: 265–84.

Dilley, Frank B. (1965). 'Does the "God Who Acts" Really Act?' *Anglican Theological Review* 47: 66–80.

Frei, Hans W. (1975). *The Identity of Jesus Christ: The Hermeneutical Bases of Dogmatic Theology.* Philadelphia: Fortress.

—— (1991). 'H. Richard Niebuhr on History, Church and Nation'. In Ronald F. Thiemann (ed.), *The Legacy of H. Richard Niebuhr*, Minneapolis: Fortress, 1–23.

Gebara, Ivone (2002). *Out of the Depths: Women's Experience of Evil and Salvation.* Minneapolis: Fortress.

Gilkey, Langdon B. (1961). 'Cosmology, Ontology, and the Travail of Biblical Language'. *Journal of Religion* 41: 194–205.

—— (1963). 'The Concept of Providence in Contemporary Theology'. *Journal of Religion* 43: 171–92.

Gutiérrez, Gustavo (1987). *On Job: God-Talk and the Suffering of the Innocent.* Maryknoll: Orbis.

Härle, Wilfried, and Preul, Rainer (eds.) (1987). *Marburger Jahrbuch Theologie* 1. Marburg: N. G. Elwert Verlag.

Hansson, Mats J. (1991). *Understanding an Act of God.* Uppsala: Acta Universitatis Upsaliensis.

Hebblethwaite, Brian, and Henderson, Edward (eds.) (1990). *Divine Action.* Edinburgh: T. & T. Clark.

Higton, Mike (2004). *Christ, Providence, and History: Hans W. Frei's Public Theology.* London: T. & T. Clark.

Krötke, Wolf (2000). Review of Reinhold Bernhardt, *Was heisst 'Handeln Gottes'? Theologische Literaturzeitung* 125: 1190–3.

Lindbeck, George (1984). *The Nature of Doctrine.* Philadelphia: Westminster.

Lochman, Jan Milič (2003). 'Reconsidering the Doctrine of Providence'. In Wallace M. Alston, Jr. and Michael Welker (eds.), *Reformed Theology: Identity and Ecumenicity*, Grand Rapids: Eerdmans, 281–93.

Miller, Allen O., and Osterhaven, M. Eugene (eds.) (1962). *The Heidelberg Catechism.* Philadelphia: United Church Press.

Niebuhr, H. Richard (1941). *The Meaning of Revelation.* New York: Macmillan.

—— (1996). *Theology, History, and Culture: Major Unpublished Writings.* New Haven: Yale University Press.

Phillips, D. Z. (2004). *The Problem of Evil and the Problem of God.* Minneapolis: Fortress.

Pinnock, Clark H., Rice, Richard, Sanders, John, Hasker, William, and Basinger, David (1994). *The Openness of God: A Biblical Challenge to the Traditional Understanding of God.* Downers Grove: InterVarsity.

Rankka, Kristine M. (1998). *Women and the Value of Suffering: An Aw(e)ful Rowing Toward God.* Collegeville: The Liturgical Press.

Sanders, John (1998). *The God Who Risks: A Theology of Providence.* Downers Grove: InterVarsity.

Sherlock, William (1694). *A Discourse Concerning the Divine Providence.* London: William Rogers.

Stone, Bryan P., and Oord, Thomas Jay (eds.) (2001). *Thy Nature and Thy Name is Love: Wesleyan and Process Theologies in Dialogue.* Nashville: Kingswood.

Tanner, Kathryn (1988). *God and Creation in Christian Theology: Tyranny or Empowerment?* Oxford: Blackwell.

Tiessen, Terrance (2000). *Providence and Prayer: How Does God Work in the World?* Downers Grove: InterVarsity.

Townes, Emilie M. (ed.) (1993). *A Troubling in My Soul: Womanist Perspectives on Evil and Suffering.* Maryknoll: Orbis.

Tracy, Thomas F. (1994). *The God Who Acts: Philosophical and Theological Explorations.* University Park: Pennsylvania State University Press.

Walsham, Alexandra (1999). *Providence in Early Modern England.* Oxford: Oxford University Press.

Wittgenstein, Ludwig (1958). *Philosophical Investigations.* 3rd edn. New York: Macmillan.

Young, Josiah Ulysses (1992). *A Pan-African Theology: Providence and the Legacies of the Ancestors.* Trenton: Africa World Press.

Suggested Reading

Bernhardt (1999).

Billman, Kathleen D., and Migliore, Daniel L. (1999). *Rachel's Cry: Prayer of Lament and Rebirth of Hope.* Cleveland: United Church Press.

Burrell (2004).

Claassens, L. Juliana M. (2004). *The God Who Provides: Biblical Images of Divine Nourishment.* Nashville: Abingdon.

Cowdell, Scott (2000). *A God for This World.* London: Mowbray.

Dietrich, Walter, and Link, Christian (1995–2000). *Die dunklen Seiten Gottes: Willkür und Gewalt.* 2 vols. Neukirchen-Vluyn: Neukirchener Verlag.

Gorringe, Timothy (1991). *God's Theatre: A Theology of Providence.* London: SCM.

Gutiérrez (1987).

Murphy, George L. (2003). *The Cosmos in the Light of the Cross.* Harrisburg: Trinity Press International.

Phillips (2005).

Sanders (1998).

CHAPTER 6

ELECTION

KATHERINE SONDEREGGER

At the heart of the doctrine of election lies the conviction that God *acts*, i.e., chooses or elects, and that such action is characteristic of and essential to the living God. Traditionally, this conviction that God is an acting or self-determining being has led Christian theologians, particularly in the Latin church, to hold that election is an ingredient in a larger doctrine, 'predestination'. Predestination in turn consists of several parts. To begin with, God, an eternal being, wills or 'decrees' both himself and everything creaturely. All creatures are brought into existence and upheld in it through God's decree to create and providentially to sustain what he has created. Even in its bare existence, then, creation cannot be understood apart from the doctrines of election and providence. Human creatures, possessed of rationality and purpose, stand in special relation to the creator: they each and as a whole have a destiny; they are eternally destined, that is, 'predestined', to live with or apart from God. The western tradition has taught that God's decree concerning the world includes a determination of some human lives to salvation: this is election to life or glory. These creatures are 'the elect', the remnant of the faithful, and are received into the heavenly city of God. Paired with this doctrine of election to life is a second determination, understood by some as equal to the first, and by others as decidedly minor to it. The latter argue that God passes over some sinners and permits them to remain in their sins; the former, that God determines or actively wills the rejection or 'reprobation' of some sinners to eternal death, an eternity apart from grace and glory. On either account, these sinners form the 'mass of perdition', the reprobate who never turn from their sins and whose destiny is damnation.

Theologians stress that, in all these decrees, God is entirely just and right: to elect is to set forth God's mercy; to pass over or reprobate, to set forth his justice. Though predestination has been held to determine the eternal end of all human beings, in much of the tradition this doctrine has not been seen as principally concerned with creatures. Rather, election has served as a means to speak about God—the divine holiness, justice, and glory—and about the unique relation of such a God to creatures, the relation of grace. Traditionally, human beings do not initiate grace; rather, God remains the sole and sovereign source and support of grace and of the life with him which this grace effects. The 'grace in which creatures stand' does give rise to a creaturely response: by turns understood as faith, holy living ('sanctification'), or works of selfless love ('merit'). But in the traditional conception of election, such responses do not effect salvation nor do they precede, logically or materially, God's decree. Rather, the tradition teaches that, in predestination, God creates, elects, and determines all creatures to their eternal ends; their life in gracious relation or 'covenant' with God is itself the gracious work of their creator.

In all this, the doctrine of predestination shows the unmistakable influence of St Augustine. Even as Augustine's late work is unthinkable without the letters of the apostle Paul, so the subsequent debates about election within the medieval, Reformation, and modern church in the Latin west are unthinkable without Augustine's teachings concerning the 'cause of grace' and his turbulent, brooding reflections on the sinful will, the creature's fallen state, and the dark mysteries of God's ways with his creatures (Augustine 1980). Thus, in Augustine's shadow, predestination is a doctrine of grace entire, from beginning to end, and God is the proper, sole, and sovereign subject of this decree.

Augustinian convictions have prompted many dogmaticians to treat the doctrine of predestination within the doctrine of God—Karl Barth (1957) is a celebrated modern example—and to show how the act of election resides in, and yet does not alter, the eternal nature of God. To be sure, this doctrine has found several other prominent sites within systematic theology, for example, the doctrine of providence (*ST* 1a. 23, in Aquinas 1975), sanctification (*Institutes* 3. 21–4, in Calvin 1960), and ecclesiology (Schleiermacher 1928: 533–60). And, in our day, new questions have been raised within this doctrine. How is the election of the people Israel to be understood within Christian dogmatics? How do the adherents of other religions stand in relation to election in Jesus Christ? Does God elect or 'preferentially opt' the poor of this world? And in a question inescapably modern, is election universal? Or, perhaps more conceptually framed, is reprobation a necessary element within the doctrine of predestination? These new themes and *loci* will have their day, but it is best to begin with the tradition in the doctrine of God.

I. The Doctrine of Election and the Doctrine of God

God elects. The nature of God is to be an electing being. What do we learn about the doctrine of election when it is considered as constituent of the doctrine of God? We might begin by asking whether God is in fact a being who can act or choose or decide in just such a way. Some theologians, ancient and modern, have held that when we consider the nature of God properly, we see immediately that God does not, indeed cannot, act in this way: it is rankest anthropomorphism to attribute to God the act of choosing or repudiating, ranking or selecting creatures. Paul Tillich appears to have been a member of this camp. His doctrine of God captured an ineffable dimension of depth in symbolic form, an 'ultimate concern' that grounds and sustains being. For Tillich, the doctrine of election expressed in dense, historical symbols the existential struggle for meaning within the polarities of freedom and destiny. But the 'God beyond the God of theism' does not elect in a straightforward, non-symbolic sense (Tillich 1952). Tillich was not alone. Even the young Karl Barth in his commentary on the letter to the Romans derides as 'mythological' the idea of the election of individuals either to life or to destruction (Barth 1968: 324, 358); such derogation of the doctrine of individual election by God is not entirely absent from *Church Dogmatics* II/2 (Barth 1957).

These objections may strike us as peculiarly modern, and perhaps more philosophical than theological in origin; but the problems they raise are far from new. Indeed, Colin Gunton and Robert Jenson have devoted theological careers to exposing the philosophical roots of 'classical theism', an ancestry, they argue, that in the early centuries of the church had already obscured both the triune nature of God and the biblical inheritance of ancient Israel. This is a complex charge, one that reaches deep into the sources of theology and theological argument, but only a fuller exploration of the classical features of the doctrine of God will allow us to assess more exactly how the doctrine of election could properly be seen as an act of such a God.

From the patristic era forward, the nature of God has been held to be both eternal and utterly one. These have led to the teaching that God is simple or, perhaps better said, unique. The conceptual intuition here is that God, in order to be creator, must be not simply first in a sequence of creaturely things—even first both temporally and in dignity. Rather, God must be the radical source of all that is. God must be utterly other than the cosmos made by him, in order that the cosmos may have a true origin and end in God. This intuition is most famously expressed in Thomas Aquinas's designation of God as prime mover, first cause, and necessary being (*ST* 1a. 2). The prophetic texts of Isaiah, long dominant in Christian reading of Israel's scriptures, underscore the radical distinction of God from creatures. This 'prophetic monotheism', combined with a doctrine of the creation of a temporal world, gives rise to a strong doctrine of divine uniqueness and eternity.

Drawing on the language of Greek metaphysics, the early church theologians denoted God as atemporal, without parts, and without motion or change, that is, as eternal, simple, and immutable. Now such a God, if he is to have attributes at all, must hold them uniquely: God must simply *be* his attributes. Although there was some medieval debate over this matter, dogmatic theologians were one in seeing God as radically free from the substance–accident distinction that governs creaturely being. God's relation to the cosmos is unique in turn. Not part of the creaturely realm, not subject to its motion and decay, not waiting on its development or shadows of change, God is himself his own relation to his creation—a doctrine known in turns as God's 'ideal relation' (*ST* 1a. 13, 7; 45, 3 ad 1) or 'spiritual' presence (*ST* 1a. 8, 1 ad 2). Far from denoting divine absence, this spiritual relation allows classical theologians to underscore God's nearness to creation, a closeness that is not external but internal to the creature—movement from within, Thomas says (*ST* 1a. 105, 2 ad 1; 105, 4)—and sustains in being everything that is, directing it to its end in God.

The doctrine of election conforms to the uniqueness and eternity of God. Systematicians in every era have recognized that scripture speaks of God choosing, acting toward, judging, and saving his creatures; the task, then as now, is to reconcile such acts with such a simple and eternal being. A God who is utterly unique, utterly without need stemming from imperfection, utterly free, sovereign, and eternal does not seem to be the same Lord God of Israel who calls, elects, leads, and delivers his people. In other words, can the God of such a nature be coherently conceived of as also the God who acts? How, in such a unique reality, can God's being and God's act be reconciled?

A divine act could be considered merely 'symbolic' or 'mythological'—a term made popular by D. F. Strauss (Strauss 1972: 39–92). Conversely, some say that divine being could be 'liberated' from 'philosophical strictures' to be the living, changing God of the Bible. In the 1930s Karl Barth threw his full weight behind the second of these resolutions: he decried 'natural theology', defending the 'God of Abraham, Isaac and Jacob' against the 'idolatrous' 'God of the philosophers', the God of 'classical theism' (Brunner and Barth 1946). It may well be that a resolution to this dilemma (if such be sought) must be found by looking among these alternatives. Yet one value of the early modern Protestant divines' study of election is their eagerness to find a third way to resolve the dilemma of being and act in God. They were dedicated to a robust and propositional realism in theology: God was truly known by creatures, and theological statements truly expressed God's being and will—but only in a limited way! They appealed to the Aristotelian-Ramist logic, popular among seventeenth-century Reformed divines, which held that all concepts truly predicated of God are themselves simple and timeless, but can be expressed by creatures only dialectically, in complex terms, and in logical rank. Perhaps we might say that doctrines of God and God's acts cannot be fully reconciled without appeal—at least as a first step—to a doctrine of human knowledge of and language about God. Indeed, we might discover here one reason to prefer the Protestant scholastics' appeal to logic and linguistics over other alternatives: in this way they held together the realist, metaphysical aspects of the doctrines of the divine nature and action, yet they also acknowledged the unutterable and inconceivable nature of these doctrines as simply and transcendently true of the God of Christian faith. We will follow this path.

According to classical, pre-modern theists, God is no inert, simple, lifeless immobility. Rather, God is pure act; God's being simply *is* act. God is supremely personal, a pure, unceasing intelligence, a Holy Spirit. Now, if God is Spirit—a claim with resonance from Origen to Hegel—then we must understand God to be intentional. That is, God's life must be understood as thought, or better, as the act of thinking itself. But as there is no thinking without content, so God's very life must intend an object, must reflect within itself on the content of thought. (Augustine's reflection on the *imago Trinitatis* in the human mind springs from considerations like these.) We should say that God *decides* or 'determines himself', in Barth's terms, in that God's thinking, as it is his very nature, conforms entirely to his life and will. The being of God must comprise, in some transcendental fashion, both intellect and will; and, in some simple fashion, these 'faculties' must be one with God's very life and essence. Students of the doctrine of Trinity will recognize where this is headed: the constituents of thought are the persons of the Trinity, the 'incommunicable existence of the triune nature', in Richard of St Victor's phrase (quoted by Thomas Aquinas, *ST* 1a. 29, 3 ad 4). The Logos, reason, or intellect is the personal distinction of the Son; the will, intention, or love, is the personal distinction of the Spirit. These are of one nature with the origin of thought, the Father. Thus, the doctrine of election—the divine act of choosing—is itself a triune act of the divine nature.

Within the traditional idiom of the doctrine of election, this intelligent act of choosing is called the 'eternal decree'. Central to this teaching is the claim that the divine decree is not principally and first a decision about something or someone outside of God. The intentionality of God is not principally directed toward the creaturely realm, to the cosmos the Lord God has made. Rather, God, as living act of thought, intends and elects himself: in the triune life God is his own object, the content of his own thought. For this reason, the scholastics considered the divine decree an 'internal act': to decide or determine is of the essence of God. From this reflection springs Barth's conviction that the doctrine of election belongs to the doctrine of God and even more, to Christology, as the eternal Son is both the electing and the elected God. Only small steps lead the scholastics from this conception of the divine decision to the absolute decree (*decretum absolutum*) of the early modern Reformed dogmaticians.

The divine decree must partake of the necessity, simplicity, and absoluteness of the divine nature; indeed it *is* that nature. Nothing creaturely can determine or alter this decree, nor can the decree depend upon the motion of anything outside of God—anything, that is, *ad extra*. To capture the sovereign uniqueness of the decree, older systematicians spoke of God's election as principally and first to his own glory: God's will is holy and his Spirit is glorious. The justice and mercy of God, refractions of the divine holiness and glory, must also reside in the divine nature and carry the necessity of deity. The plenitude of divine intellectual life is complete in itself, moving, choosing, and determining its own eternal glory and holiness.

What then is the relation of this absolute self-affirmation in God to the cosmos and to creatures which exist outside the divine life? How should we understand the divine decree toward creation (the *decretum ad extra*)? Are there two, separate decrees? Or only one, with two aspects or ends? Could one be transcendent and absolute, the other immanent to and influenced by the creature? Classically, several alternatives have been considered. We might hold that the divine decree *ad extra* just is the internal, absolute decree. Karl Barth's Christological orientation of the doctrine of election falls into this pattern. So too we might consider some process theologians to have identified the internal and external decree in their contention that God 'lures' all life to and into the unfolding divine life, a form of 'panentheism'. Perhaps the Greek predilection for a 'divinization' (*theosis*) model of soteriology reveals a quiet identification of the two aspects of the divine decree. But such positions are rare in Latin doctrines of election. More common is the conviction that some distinction must be drawn between the divine decision in which God intends himself and that in which he orders, governs, and intends the end of all creatures.

One Latin pattern is to consider God to possess or, better, to exhibit a power that escapes all creaturely strictures, an absolute power that is utterly free (*potentia absoluta*). To conceive God properly, it was said, theologians must allow God's essence to determine itself absolutely, apart perhaps from any logical contradiction. Late medieval scholastics used this concept to acknowledge and explore the alternatives which God did not realize in creation. This absolute power acts like a 'limit concept' in that it postulates a distinction in God which cannot be known in itself and whose metaphysical reality we cannot rightly conceive. (It may be that Barth's doctrine of the divine freedom serves as just such a limiting concept in the doctrine of God.) The turn of God toward his creatures is called the 'ordained power' (*potentia ordinata*), which consists in his will for all creatures, his covenant or pact (*pactum*) with creation. Some theologians have considered these covenants to have a history of their own: a covenant of works, followed by one of grace; a covenant of law, then gospel; a 'federalism' first with Adam, and then with Moses, with Christ, and with the church. A danger lurks here, however, a danger terrifyingly alive to Luther. Should these conceptual distinctions be metaphysically 'realized', held to be real 'parts' of God, a sensitive conscience like Luther's could fear that the absolute power is separated entirely from the ordained, and that the absolute power becomes a 'hidden God' who in his sovereign freedom, holiness, and unpredictable judgement is, in the end, the only true God.

A second pattern of relation between the decrees emerged in later Reformed circles and built on Luther's and Calvin's fervent repudiation of the 'hidden' or 'naked' God implied by the concept of *potentia absoluta*. In scholastic idiom we would say that the decree or counsel of God (*consilium Dei*) or the inner act of God's own essence (*opus Dei essentialis ad intra*) is expressed or enacted toward creation in an outer act of

God's own essence (*opus Dei essentialis ad extra*). Notice here that we retain a distinction between the inner and outer aspects of the act of God, yet the external aspect remains an act of the internal being and essence of God. A danger lurks here, too. Now election becomes a doctrine that carries the full weight of the divine uniqueness and eternity and can rest only on the divine glory, his 'good-pleasure' (*eudokia, beneplacitum*)—almost a technical term in classical Reformed dogmatics. There can be no ground to the divine election, just as there is no foundation to God's own being: this constitutes his necessity or self-caused existence. Even Christ cannot be the foundation of election on this understanding of the decrees because the incarnate Word cannot precede the counsel of God but rather only execute it.

A doctrine of election which follows this form takes the Augustinian 'cause of grace' and intensifies it into an internal decree in which the glory and good-pleasure of God affirms itself without taking into account the cause, the merit, or the redemption of creatures. The holiness of God, including his justice and mercy, must be executed: the 'vindicatory justice' of God carries the necessity of the divine being as much as does his mercy. The 'double decree' (*predestinatio gemina*) does not actually develop from a doctrine of sin or the fall, but rather follows from the necessity of the divine being in act. Only those willing to consider the divine decree toward creation to be contingent or fully separate from the internal election of God could allow the divine justice to remain unfulfilled. (We will see this pattern developed by Socinians in the post-Reformation period and by universalists in our own.) What does remain open for debate for the classical, Augustinian dogmaticians of election is the 'order of the decrees'. Is the creaturely goal or range (*scopus*) of the divine good-pleasure the creature as both created and fallen (*creatus et lapsus*)—an 'infra-lapsarian' position—or the creature possibly created and possibly fallen (*creabilis et labilis*)—a 'supra-lapsarian' position? For Reformed dogmaticians, the infra-lapsarian ordering (election 'with a view to the fall') was favoured, becoming the majority position at the Synod of Dordt. But the supra-lapsarian ordering (election 'apart from or before the fall') was not considered church-dividing; it continued to be held by a minority of seventeenth-century divines and was endorsed, on other grounds, by Barth.

A final variant in these highly technical debates in the doctrine of election deserves mention. Lutheran and Roman Catholic dogmaticians after Trent sought an ordering of the decrees which did not, on one hand, entirely sever the divine act of election from the divine nature and its freedom—God's election could not be dependent on creatures and their dispositions—yet which also allowed the decree to be 'conditioned', to encompass the faith or meritorious work foreseen in the graced believer. Systematically, we could say that the doctrine of the divine being in act is coordinated with the doctrine of divine omniscience, such that the doctrine of predestination reports how the creature, created and fallen, is already either the object of grace—through faith or faith alive in works—or eternally passed by. Foreseen faith or merit, each resting on the prevenient or eternal good-pleasure and grace of God, is implied in the doctrine of 'election to the book of life'. As all sides recognized, the danger in this pattern of the doctrine stems from the threat to the divine sovereignty in election in that the act of God could be understood as *grounded* on the human act—a pattern all sides considered Pelagian.

But in all these patterns, we see the divine decree, both internal and external, to carry the necessity and simplicity of the divine nature, making predestination a sovereign and infallible outworking of the divine glory in both justice and mercy. The human objects of election must be chosen or reprobated, and that successfully, eternally, and utterly. Even the 'conditioned decree' of seventeenth-century Lutheranism or the 'middle knowledge' of the Jesuit Molina did not countenance the power of a human creature to undermine, change, or overpower the electing will of God. The logic of the classical doctrine of predestination has struck many Christians, early and late, as ruthless and heartlessly at odds with the God of pity and mercy extolled in scripture. Calvin famously called the doctrine of election an 'awesome decree' (*decretum horribile*) (*Institutes* 3. 23. 7), and so sturdy an orthodox Reformed theologian as Francis Turretin found himself leaning on Paul's poignant hymn to God's mysterious workings (Rom. 11: 33–6) whenever he touched on the decrees (Turretin 1992–7: i. 390). Yet it would be a misreading of the tradition to call it unscriptural, or, indeed, pitiless. All major systematicians of this doctrine appeal constantly and consistently to scripture, especially the 'golden texts' in Romans, Ephesians, and the Gospel of John. Heightened in their piety was the sense of divine holiness and creaturely need and fault, themselves both deep biblical themes. These themes are muted in our day—at least in the academic, systematic theology of our day—yet they cannot fall wholly silent, as the uniqueness and majesty of God are the unshakeable reality confronting every creature.

As we have asked systematically about the relation of being and act in God, and the divine decree *ad intra* and *ad extra*, so here we ask about the relation of the doctrine of election to Christ's person as mediator and to his work as redeemer. More abstractly we might ask, What is the relation of eternity to time, both in incarnation and atonement? Has the incarnate Word brought the eschatological eternity into temporality, such that all creaturely life has already met its end, its *telos*, even as creaturely time unfolds? More concretely we might ask, When do we stand before the great judgement seat of Christ, and where is his throne planted? Again, we begin where the tradition has: with the doctrine of Christ's person, Christology proper.

II. The Doctrine of Election and Christology

Jesus Christ, fully human, fully divine, is the incarnate Word, the Son sent into the world: this is the Chalcedonian doctrine of Christ's person. Now, this person is the redeemer of the world—but is the predicate 'redeemer' the eternal object of the divine decree? Or is redemption the contingent work this eternal person does in the world now fallen from its maker? We might put this another way: Is Christ's person his work; or is his person distinct, logically and eternally, from his work? Could the Son, that is, remain unincarnate? Could the incarnate one not be redeemer? On these questions turned the medieval debate famously associated with Scotus about the necessity of the incarnation and the contingency of the redeeming work of Christ. Regardless of the answer to these questions, all agreed that the gratuity and sovereignty of divine election must be secured: for any pre-modern systematician, creatures and their need could not impel or motivate the divine act. Such considerations led the early dogmaticians, on all sides of this debate, to stipulate that God 'allowed' or 'permitted' the fall, so that creaturely rebellion could not overmaster, incapacitate, or 'surprise' the divine will. Rather, human history, even in its sin, witnessed to and depended upon the eternal knowledge and will of God. Much of the Augustinian conundrum of human free will and the puzzling questions concerning human nature before and after the fall (*ante et post lapsum*) arise from the demand that God remain timelessly sovereign and also that human creatures be temporally responsible for sin. The fall thus serves as a 'limit concept' in the doctrine of the creature much as did the two powers (*absoluta* and *ordinata*) in the doctrine of God. The doctrine of the person of Christ must conform to the systematic decisions made concerning the counsel of God and the fall.

Should the incarnation be a necessary act of God, we would then assimilate the doctrine of election to the doctrine of Trinity. The missions of the persons would be one with their processions: to be begotten as the eternal Son would be identical to his being sent to the world. Just this may be the intent and structure of the often puzzling doctrine in Barth of the eternal, enfleshed Christ (*logos ensarkos*). For the doctrine of election, then, we would affirm here that the triune God eternally wills to be incarnate in the Son, and that this decree comprises within it a temporal execution in first-century Judaea. Election would be the doctrine of God's enfleshed nearness to creation, and the simple necessity of the divine being in act would be expressed in the communion in time of the eternal Word with the world. Redemption or deliverance from sin, in doctrines of this sort, has a rather surprising relation to Christology. The salvation of sinners will be related to the incarnate one either contingently or necessarily. If contingently, then, granted a fallen world, the mission of the eternal Son takes on the task of redeeming sinners. If necessarily, then the incarnate one in his person just *is* communion with God, and this is precisely what redemption means. We might take Duns Scotus' Christology to follow the first pattern, and Friedrich Schleiermacher's the second. In either case, we could find here a systematic ground for a doctrine of universal election to eternal life.

The eternal mission of the Son would be to assume creaturely flesh and live among us as a tabernacle of the divine glory. Or, to borrow Karl Rahner's phrase, there would never be any 'ungraced creation' (Rahner 1978: 142–52). In time, the timeless decree of God to be one with his creatures would insert into human history the eschatological end and *telos* of the creature, to be in harmony with the creator. The original blessing of God's presence with us would be realized in Immanuel regardless of sin or of obedience. This carries the rather odd effect of making Christ himself, in his person, the very election of creaturely reality, its communion with God, or, perhaps, its redemption—all quite apart from human sinners themselves. We would then read 1 Corinthians 1: 30 ('Jesus Christ, who became for us wisdom from God, and righteousness and sanctification and redemption') to be a claim of identity in which our election to life simply *is* the person of the incarnate one. The doctrine of election of individual creatures to life would first be accomplished, completed, and perfected in Christ, and then applied or radiated out to humanity. The purpose of human history would be the patient unfolding of Christ's own election as the incarnate Word to the whole creation.

Such appears to be the form—though not the entire content—of Barth's doctrine of election, in which Christ himself is the elected and electing one, while the election of his community, and the individuals within it, is the secondary outworking of this divine election of the Son. So too we might consider as representative of this understanding of election Rahner's doctrine of the 'supernatural existential' enfleshed in the mediator, the bearer borne by grace. We might also number among these those universalists who take Christ to be the metaphysical and objective mediator of the whole cosmos, the lamb slain from the foundation of the world, such that election is accomplished apart from the recognition or belief of creatures.

Thus far the person of Christ. But how might the doctrine of the work of Christ, the threefold office (*munus triplex*) of prophet, priest, and king, reflect the doctrine of election and bear on the salvation of individual creatures? Here, the picture is considerably more complex as the incarnation is not now viewed as a necessary act of God. The incarnate one now takes on a task, carried out in a particular time and place, leading from stable to cross, in the small villages and lakeside of Galilee and the teeming capital and temple of Jerusalem. This work need not have been assumed by the Son, since his mission is contingent. Yet it is the gracious will of the Father to rescue in the Son. Thus the doctrine of election is both a free act of God and a concrete work of the redeemer. How can such a particular event be the salvation of the world? And how can such a concrete work be the universal deliverance of sinners?

Systematically, we see here the converse side of the Reformed doctrine of the absolute decree: Jesus Christ is neither object nor foundation of election—not necessary to the divine internal decree—but rather the instrument or means by which election is carried out. In this light the details of Christ's earthly ministry and passion begin to do explicit work in the doctrine of election. The moral exhortations of the Sermon on the Mount; the miracles of feeding and healing; the call to bear the cross; the betrayal and desertion of the disciples; the cross, grave, and empty tomb: all these are the means used by the Son of God to redeem the elect. Doctrines of meritorious works, 'condign' or 'congruent' (truly worthy of God or merely treated as such), monastic 'counsels of perfection', and saintly lives of sanctified virtue all spring from the attempt to incorporate and follow the singular pattern of the earthly Redeemer. These particulars, that is, take on something of the 'necessity of the past' or what in Hegelian idiom is termed a 'concrete universal'. Election need not have been realized in just this way, yet it was and so must be. Hence the striking talk of necessity and prophetic prediction in the Gospel passion narratives, at once historical, contingent, and free, and at the same time decreed, necessary, and inexorable. In Barth's terms, the covenant is history, the history of the relation between this king and this people. Jesus Christ is now the object of election in a fresh sense: he is anointed, as are priests, kings, and prophets in ancient Israel, to intercede and sacrifice for a people, to rule and lead them, to proclaim to them the will and truth of God.

The relation between the historical events of the Bible and the eternal disposition of creatures before God has sometimes been referred to as a scandal of particularity. It may be seen as the modern variant of the long-standing Latin teaching about the 'remnant' that will be saved, and the limited, finite number of the elect. Not everyone has been reached by the gospel; not all cultures or eras have been included in the Christian community. Indeed pre-modern dogmaticians were keenly aware of the severely limited scope of the church and the faithful. Does this historical fact become the temporal realization of the eternal decree toward creatures, that only a few be saved? In Christian lands, the widely recognized disparity in individual responses to the faith was taken, on some sides, to be a sign of election: only those whom Christ designated as his own would 'draw near with faith'. Perhaps more striking in the history of the western churches is the conviction, springing from these same roots, that the gospel must be brought to all lands and peoples. On this view, Christian missions are a living and concrete expression of the doctrine of election twinned with the 'scandal of particularity'. Evangelists are the means used by the redeemer to gather into one community the Lord's elect. Thus, history finds its contingent yet necessary end when all the elect have been called: eschatology is the consummation of the doctrine of election.

The contingent and particular character of this dimension of predestination gives rise to a profound indeterminism in the reception of salvation, a problem known by turns as the search for certainty (*certitudo*), or the 'practical syllogism'. The historical presence and visibility of Christian practice renders more, rather than less, acute the epistemic question of individual election. Because singular and concrete, the question is *existential*: Am I, a visible Christian among others, a member of the elect, the faithful remnant? On what grounds may I be sure? Short of universalism in the divine decree, the answer to these questions must take on an existential cast: in myself, my soul and life, I must discern the 'signs' of election. Though sharply divided by teachings on the divine decree, Protestants and Catholics have been united in their practice of introspection for discerning the 'testimony of the Spirit' regarding one's election. Such introspection, Augustinian in character, seeks evidence of the workings of the Holy Spirit in personal, 'saving' faith, in confidence in the divine promises, in holy living, and in confirming, consoling attestations of divine favour and presence.

Modern Questions

In our day, the problem of religious pluralism has on the whole stood in the stead of this pre-modern quest for certainty of election. Here, the singularity and temporal boundedness of Christ's redeeming work makes the doctrine of election troubling for many Christians in a world of other beliefs. Are members of other faiths possibly among the elect? If this is the case, how does Christ's redeeming work reach and apply to them? If not, can reprobation be justly applied to those who have never knowingly rejected the redeemer? Do questions of this sort underwrite Christian missions to adherents of other traditions? Can a world of such diversity in belief and explosiveness in religious conflict tolerate Christian claims to absoluteness in election in Christ? A doctrine of universal salvation strikes many systematicians as attractive when faced with these dilemmas.

Karl Rahner's celebrated doctrine of the 'anonymous Christian' contends that non-Christian belief implicitly reaches out to and lives by the gracious mystery that is made permanent and visible in Jesus Christ (Rahner 1969: 231–49). More Christological still are doctrines such as those of Barth or Hans Urs von Balthasar in which Christ's redeeming work entails Christ becoming the sole and true rejected—the sinless becoming sin for us—such that, in Balthasar's striking image, Christ alone descends in death to hell, indeed, forms and in this way hallows or empties hell itself (Balthasar 1990: 148–88). Less preoccupied by traditional claims of Christian finality, universalists such as John Hick propose a deity of 'noumenal' reality (a reality beyond human knowing), expressed in and recognized by the 'phenomena' (the human experience) of diverse religions—a variant, in contemporary terms, of the Enlightenment distinction between rational and positive religion. Theologians who favour the eschatological dimension of Christian proclamation can make room for final decisions about Christ in the 'eternal future', realized now or after death. Noteworthy in all these positions is the prominent place accorded to the objective moment in the doctrine of election: being chosen by God is accomplished apart from, and is logically distinct from, the conscious confession of Jesus Christ as redeemer. It may well be that the systematic coordination of election with Christology, characteristic of much modern theology, will give way in our day to the earlier coordination with the doctrine of God, so that the absolute decree toward creatures is realized apart from any means, even the believers' confession of this sovereign lordship.

In our day, Jesus Christ goes his way into the world, we might say, as the stranger, an instrument of the Father's working who carries out his Father's business in season and out, but whose name and countenance are known by but a few.

Students of the doctrine of election might ask whether such a portrait of the suffering servant, of an earthly Jesus going his solitary way, deepens our commitment to his cause or distracts us from his risen life and from the commandment to baptize in his name. The doctrine of election in our day is shaped by our answer to this question.

III. The Doctrine of Election and Ecclesiology

Finally, we might ask how the doctrine of election may be systemically articulated with the doctrine of the church proper, ecclesiology, and with theological description of community, nation, and people. Central to modern biblical scholarship has been the conviction that Jesus of Nazareth came to preach the kingdom of God, a realm or community in which God reigned so that justice is done on earth as in heaven. Echoing notes of earlier doctrines of covenant and pact, this emphasis upon the commonwealth of God—to borrow Calvin's term (*Institutes* 4. 20. 8–9)—has raised for the doctrine of election fresh questions about the aim and proper form of the divine decree. Has the tradition rightly focused on the individual creature as human object of the decree? Or, as both Barth and many liberation theologians have asked, is not the community the proper and first object of election, after Jesus Christ himself? *Lumen Gentium*, the Dogmatic Constitution on the Church enunciated by the Second Vatican Council, made prominent the phrase, 'people of God', as the fullest description of the church, folding together distinctions of cleric and lay, visible and invisible, covenants of Old and New Testaments (*Lumen Gentium* §§9–17, in Tanner 1990: ii. 855–62). Standing in the shadow here is the doctrine of the election of Israel, God's chosen, and the relation of Christian doctrines of election to Jews and Judaism, a theme taken up in *Nostra Aetate*, the path-breaking declaration on the church's relation to non-Christian religions (Tanner 1990: ii. 968–71). Scarcely any topic has awakened theologians more to the centrality of the doctrine of election than this theme, the election of Israel, which has proved a deeper and more troubling call to Christian conscience than that of religious pluralism itself.

Modern Questions

If the doctrine of election, in its creaturely aspect, is considered as principally corporate in nature, systematicians would assimilate all other doctrines to this collective purpose and scope. Liberation theologians—here we may take Gustavo Gutiérrez (1983) as exemplary—have demonstrated the thoroughgoing transformation such an assimilation sets in train. In the doctrine of election, the poor in history occupy the place of the remnant within classical doctrine, and the just society, with its radical solidarity, occupies the place of the sanctified community. Again, the formal problems raised by particularity and the seeming caprice of the divine decree make themselves felt in this more immanent, dialectical doctrine of the divine commonwealth or *polis*. The order of the decrees, especially the relation of providence to election, finds its parallel in liberation theology in the conviction that the elect, the oppressed, are found everywhere in the universal, political history of humankind, so that the doctrine of providence is an outworking of the doctrine of election. (In this, liberation theologians agree with Barth, who ordered providence to election by and of Christ.) The poor, agents of God's liberating decree, are the makers of world history, the shapers of the just society that is the eschatological goal of creation. The ringing endorsement by liberation theologians of the 'unitary nature of history' gives rise in new idiom to an old and robust doctrine of the elected community as goal of human history.

But just who belongs by rights to this elect community? The Augustinian 'cause of grace' appears in this collective expression of the doctrine of election with even greater complexity than in pre-modern dogmatics. Augustine's distinction between the earthly and heavenly cities, itself a corporate translation of the parable of wheat and tares (Matt. 13), sets out an ecclesiology in which the elect community resided silently and without marker in the greater community of Christian practice. In practice, however, there was a tension between the Augustinian doctrine of sacraments and the Augustinian doctrine of election. The place or *locus* of forgiving, justifying grace was the baptismal font; the *locus* of the 'medicine of immortality' the Lord's table; the *locus* of renewing, restoring Christian life the confessional or liturgical absolution. In sacramental life, the elect or 'invisible church' appears to be just the 'visible church', baptizing, feeding, and forgiving its members in Christ's name and grace—and this squares uneasily with Augustine's doctrine of election.

So too in contemporary systematics, the doctrine of the elect community stands in tension with the doctrine of the sacraments and with visible Christian practice. In doctrines of universal salvation, the tension is acute: the effective means of grace are sheared off from the public, liturgical acts of the church because the grace that saves need not be found in the earthly church at all. In liberation theologies the matter is more complex. The elect, in one sense, remain a visible community within history: the oppressed and destitute. Yet the formal nature of such an identification allows any number of different classes of people to be defined as the elect, such that election becomes a social construction whose essential nature remains known, if at all, by God alone. So too the sacraments, effective signs of liberating praxis, are on the one hand visible marks of the true, emancipating community; on the other, they are the common property of all just societies and just practices, and thus in essence distinct from the acts of the gathered church. We might also mention the secular version of the doctrine of corporate election, modern nationalism. The influence of Reformed doctrines of election on the apartheid doctrine of South Africa is well known. Race theories, especially in their hidden carriers in 'blood and soil', are a perverse imitation of corporate election. 'Manifest destiny' is a secularizing echo of the church as wayfarer. The hidden yet public character of the sacramental means of grace is mirrored in the contested definitions of true citizenship, true patriotism, and true membership in the superior class and race. The earthly city has its *decretum horribile* too.

In the end, the doctrine of election in our day must return again and again to its roots, the election of the people Israel. The entire vocabulary of the doctrine stems from the biblical depiction of Israel as the beloved child of God, the heir, the chosen, the covenant people dear to its maker. The representative intensification of the elect, from the faithful remnant, to the seven thousand that have not bent the knee, to the anointed king or prophet or judge: all these belong to the history of Israel as the creaturely object of divine election. The typological rehearsal of Jesus as the elect, beloved Son, prominent especially in the birth narratives in Matthew and Luke, distils the history of ancient Israel into the narrative of a single life. Little wonder that Paul's anguish in Romans 9–11 can hardly be contained: the history of Jew amid Gentiles just *is* the unfolding of the divine decree toward the world, the journey of those chosen 'above all the nations of the earth', an election irrevocable and precious in the Lord's sight.

Yet out of these very same sources the Christian tradition has developed a doctrine of corporate election in which the church of Jew and Gentile replaces or 'supersedes' the people Israel as the true, elect people of God. According to this supersessionist view of election, Jews and Judaism belong to the reprobate, cursed for disbelief and rebellion. One is only incorporated into the true, elect community through the laver of baptism, here seen as the conversion away from Judaism. From *Nostra Aetate* forward, many Christian bodies have repudiated supersessionism, especially in the virulent form just presented. Yet the conceptual and structural complexities of the classical doctrine of election, from the eternal and temporal ordering of the decrees to the place of human acts with regard to the divine being in act, remain underdeveloped in Christian doctrines of Israel's election. Future systematic work in the doctrine of election may well take its starting point from the classical problematic of the decree: How can the divine Triunity, absolute and eternal in itself, turn to the creature, such that the history of the covenant from Israel to the church of Jew and Gentile may be understood as an out-working of the complex debates on grace and merit, foreknowledge and predestination, mediation and redemption, reprobation and preterition, all in or through the person and work of Jesus Christ?

The doctrine of election takes its origin from the conviction that God acts, chooses, or elects first and properly himself, and then, secondly and graciously, the creature. Though markedly different in idiom and range in our day from pre-modern doctrines of predestination, still the doctrine of election will remain at the heart of theology's task so long as God is seen as personal, and all his ways as just and true altogether.

References

Aquinas, St Thomas (1975). *Summa Theologiae.* London: Blackfriars.

Augustine (1980). *Anti-Pelagian Writings.* In Philip Schaff (ed.), *A Select Library of the Nicene and Post-Nicene Fathers of the Christian Church,* 1st ser., Edinburgh: T. & T. Clark, vol. v.

Balthasar, Hans Urs von (1990). *Mysterium Paschale: The Mystery of Easter.* Edinburgh: T. & T. Clark.

Barth, Karl (1957). *Church Dogmatics* II/2. Edinburgh: T. & T. Clark.

—— (1968). *The Epistle to the Romans.* Oxford: Oxford University Press.

Brunner Emil, and Barth, Karl (1946). *Natural Theology: Comprising 'Nature and Grace' by Professor Emil Brunner and the reply 'No!' by Dr. Karl Barth.* London: Geoffrey Bles.

Calvin, John (1960). *Institutes of the Christian Religion.* Philadelphia: Westminster.

Gutiérrez, Gustavo (1983). *The Power of the Poor in History.* London: SCM.

Rahner, Karl (1969). *Theological Investigations,* iv. New York: Seabury.

—— (1978). *Foundations of the Christian Faith: An Introduction to the Idea of Christianity.* New York: Seabury.

Schleiermacher, F. D. E. (1928). *The Christian Faith.* Edinburgh: T. & T. Clark.

Strauss, D. F. (1972). *The Life of Jesus Critically Examined.* Philadelphia: Fortress.

Tanner, Norman P., SJ (ed.) (1990). *Decrees of the Ecumenical Councils.* 2 vols. Georgetown: Sheed and Ward.

Tillich, Paul (1952). *The Courage to Be.* New Haven: Yale University Press.

Turretin, Francis (1992–7 [1679–85]). *Institutes of Elenctic Theology.* 3 vols. Phillipsberg: Presbyterian and Reformed.

Suggested Reading

Barth, Karl (1957: 3–506).

Berkouwer, G. C. (1960). *Divine Election.* Grand Rapids: Eerdmans.

Calvin, John (1960: 920–87 (3. 21–4)).

Jewett, P. K. (1985). *Election and Predestination.* Grand Rapids: Eerdmans.

Maury, P. (1960). *Election and Other Papers.* London: SCM.

Pannenberg, W. (1991–8). *Systematic Theology.* 3 vols. Grand Rapids: Eerdmans, iii. 435–526.

CHAPTER 7

THE HUMAN CREATURE

DAVID H. KELSEY

The task of this chapter is to survey the state of the question in Christian theological anthropology at the start of the twenty-first century. Given the variety of questions contemporary theologians take to be central to anthropology, the first challenge is to devise a framework that can both encompass their range and present them fairly. I offer such a framework first, then use it to organize the survey.

I. A Framework

We can distinguish at least three different orders of question about which theologians make a judgement when addressing anthropological topics. They are logically independent of one another. No judgement about any one of them follows necessarily from a judgement about either of the other two.

What is the basic anthropological question raised by Christian practice and belief?

It has traditionally been assumed that the basic anthropological question is, '*What* constitutes us as specifically human beings?' (This is the 'what' question.)

In the more recent history of Christian anthropology two other candidates for the status of basic anthropological question have emerged. By the end of the eighteenth century the power of modern scientific explanation raised questions about traditional Christian assumptions regarding human beings' freedom and responsibility. A basic anthropological question for theology became the 'how' question. It is an existential rather than moral question: '*How* should authentically human beings be oriented to, set into, their social and physical worlds?' By the mid-twentieth century, personal identity became a third candidate for the status of basic anthropological question: 'Theologically speaking, *who* am I? *Who* are we?' (This is the 'who' question.)

A theologian's judgement regarding the relative centrality to theological anthropology of the 'what', 'how', and 'who' questions is not a decision to address one to the exclusion of the others. The questions lead into one another. However, the answers a systematic theologian gives to the other two anthropological questions will tend to be derived from and defined by the answer given to the question judged, however implicitly, to be the properly basic question for theological anthropology.

What is the doctrinal home of theological anthropology?

In the overall systematic network of relations among major Christian doctrines, of which major doctrine is theological anthropology a sub-topic? This is a distinct order of question. It assumes two things that cannot be defended here: that Christian doctrines are roughly systematic, at least in the sense that they are related to one another in a conceptual web such that change in the content of one will ripple across the web to changes in many or all other doctrines; and, secondly, that there is a rough logical hierarchy among Christian doctrines such that some are more basic than others (e.g., God, creation, incarnation, grace and sin, eschatological consummation) and that the non-basic doctrines logically depend non-reciprocally on the more basic ones.

The traditional doctrinal home of theological anthropology has been a doctrine of *creation*. Doctrines of creation traditionally offered both an account of the origin of reality other than God (explaining the claim, God 'created' it) and an account of the general features of the creatureliness of all reality other than God (exploring the implications of its radical ongoing dependence on God, its intelligibility, materiality, finitude, goodness, etc.). Theological anthropological claims were derived by applying the general account of creatureliness to human creatures in particular, qualified by the claim that what distinguishes them as specifically human is that God creates them in the 'image of God'.

The recent history of anthropology involves proposals of novel migrations of the doctrine from one doctrinal home to another. It migrated first to a home in a doctrine of *incarnate grace*. Fundamental to this move is a theological intuition about God's saving grace: It ought not to be explained as the remedy for sin, when 'sin' and 'human nature' have been theologically defined prior to and independently of any explication of grace. Rather, given Jesus' centrality to the Christian good news, 'grace' ought to be explained by reference to its incarnation in the person of Jesus. This intuition is reflected, for example, in Karl Rahner's (1978) and Karl Barth's (1960) shared advocacy of the view that the event of the incarnation of grace is not contingent on the fact of human sin but rather is God's plan, 'before' and independent of humankind's fall into sin ('supra-lapsarianism'), to give himself to creatures. In their judgement, not only sin, but all theological characterizations of human beings (e.g., that they are creatures, fallen, redeemed, destined for eschatological consummation) ought to be elucidated primarily by reference to God's grace, although they explicate 'incarnate grace' in very different ways.

Anthropology migrated next to a home in *eschatology*. This move was prompted by biblical scholarship's stress on the centrality of eschatology to the New Testament's witness to Jesus. Jesus' resurrection is understood as the actualization of his incarnation and the proleptic (ahead-of-time) inauguration of the eschatological kingdom of God. Since that eschatological state has been God's gracious purpose from the beginning, only in it are human beings also fully actualized. Adopting the general principle that, because reality is fully actualized only at the end of a process, it can only be properly understood from that end, Wolfhart Pannenberg (1970) argues that anthropological questions must be answered by reference, not to human beings' origins (doctrine of creation), but to their end (eschatology).

Finally, in the work of still other theologians by the end of the century, influenced especially by John Zizioulas (1985), theological anthropology migrated to a home in the doctrine of the *Trinity*. A root theological intuition behind this move is that Christianity has a unique concept of person first discovered in fourth-century patristic analysis of the doctrine of God as 'one God, three persons'. Unlike modern concepts, 'person' is not defined in moral terms as an autonomous, morally responsible agent, or in existentialist terms as a self-constituting subject, or in psychological terms as a centre of uniquely complex psychodynamics. 'Person' is an ontological concept. Unlike classical Greek ontologies, the church fathers did not define personhood as an essential property that universally qualifies some one kind of substance. A person of the Trinity is a concrete, unique, unrepeatable entity ('hypostasis'). It is constituted by an act of 'absolute' ontological freedom, i.e., not determined or constrained by a fixed nature shared with all other entities of the same kind. Such absolutely free enactment is 'ecstatic'. It consists of an act of giving itself to an other, i.e., an act of love. Persons are constituted by relations that are free acts of self-bestowal (love-relations). The relations constitute persons-in-communion and communion-among-persons. If this concept of person, based in the orthodox doctrine of the Trinity, is theologically normative, then it applies to human persons also, and the basic questions in theological anthropology must be worked out in its terms.

These migrations of theological anthropology from one doctrinal home to another have implications for the way scripture functions as an authority to which anthropological proposals are answerable. These migrations assume that anthropological proposals are logically dependent on and derived from other, more basic doctrines. Those more basic proposals may answer to scriptural authority directly. However, given their derivative status, anthropological proposals accord with scriptural authority only indirectly, through the scriptural basis of the more basic doctrine(s) on which they depend. This way of relating anthropological proposals to scripture is supported by biblical scholarship which identifies both a diversity of anthropological views in scripture and a broad dependence of these views on the anthropological commonplaces of the cultures in which various texts were written. All of this tends to make implausible a contention that there exists a single, 'revealed' anthropology to which theological anthropology is accountable.

What is the proper conceptuality for theological anthropology?

Of the enormous array of anthropological concepts on offer from various physical, social, and human sciences, from quite different philosophical traditions, and from diverse movements in the arts and critical theory, which are most fitted for use in explicating Christian theological anthropological claims? This is yet another distinct order of question. As we shall see, theological anthropologies at the beginning of the twenty-first century emphatically and explicitly disagree about it; we need not review them here.

We can chart major controversies in current theological anthropology by noting how different judgements about the doctrinal home of anthropology and about the most appropriate conceptuality to use in explicating anthropological proposals cut across different judgements about what is the basic question in theological anthropology. Because there currently appear to be no extended anthropological proposals that explicitly take the 'how' question to be basic, our survey has only two main divisions.

II. Survey: Anthropological Proposals in Tension

The 'What' Question

One approach assumes that the basic question of a theological anthropology concerns human nature (the 'what' question). It generates two types of issues, one about the idea of human nature, the other about the intersection of theological anthropology and the several sciences.

The first type turns on whether notions of human nature, theological or otherwise, are constructivist or essentialist. Serene Jones's discussions of feminist anthropologies (1997; 2000) and Edward Farley's *Good and Evil* (1990) are exemplary of the complexity of this controversy.

The early years of feminist theology were marked by tensions between 'constructivist' and 'essentialist' understandings of *what* it is to be a human being. As a type of liberation theology, feminist theology seeks to elucidate the good news of emancipation from the evil that women experience in gender-based oppression. Like most variants of theology focused at the intersection of redemption and evil, it relies on an analysis of what it is to be human to explain how oppression and how liberation are possible for women. The analysis holds that women have been oppressed because dominant anthropologies, both in theology and in patriarchal culture generally, entail that it is *essential* to being a woman to be inferior to males in regard to a broad array of powers and behaviour. That followed from the dominant anthropologies' tacit privileging of men's experience as the index to the powers and behaviours that are essential to being human. Because of their differences from men, women are determined by their *nature* to be weak, dependent, emotional, intuitive, nurturing, etc. Such essentialistic anthropologies warrant oppression of women. The alternative is to develop an anthropology that privileges women's experience as the index to the capacities and powers that define what it is to be human. One feminist response was to develop an alternative account of the essential nature of women's humanity. For example, Mary Daly's 'biological essentialism' (1973) suggests that 'the source of women's revolutionary way of being rests "within them" as part of their embodied distinctiveness' (Jones 2000: 30). Another alternative, now close to a consensus position, urges that *all* concepts of human nature are 'constructed'. Jones points out that even strong versions of this constructivist view, while 'epistemologically sceptical about naturalized claims concerning women's nature', are 'ontologically agnostic', remaining 'uncommitted (but suspicious) on the question of the real status of sexual difference' (Jones 2000: 36).

Jones notes two continuing tensions among constructivist feminist anthropologies. While there has developed a near consensus that 'women' in the phrase 'women's experience' is understood in a constructivist manner, there is no parallel consensus about 'experience' (Jones 1997: 33–4). Some feminist theologians 'employ universalizing and/or ahistorical frames of reference to structure their accounts of human experience' (e.g., phenomenological, process/psychoanalytic, or literary/textual accounts). Others 'opt instead for descriptions of experience which are historically localized and culturally specific', relying on the tools of cultural anthropology to localize experience or on post-structuralist moves to uncover the play of language and power in the construction of identity (Jones 1997: 33–4). Critique by African-American, Latina, and lesbian theologians argues that generalized accounts of 'women's experience' are based on North American straight, middle-class, white women's experience and do not capture the identities of black, Hispanic, and lesbian women. At stake is whether *any* level of generalization about women's identity is appropriate as the subject matter for theological anthropology.

Second, Jones notes that the interest which points to constructivist accounts of women's nature seems to conflict with advocacy of women's agency, another major interest of feminist theology (Jones 2000: 38–42). Because 'agency' is usually understood to have the same meaning for everyone and requires normative claims about what counts as agency, it seems to require an essentializing account. To resolve this tension Jones advocates a 'strategic essentialism' which identifies certain universal features essential to women's nature and experience (e.g., 'agency, embodiment, relationality, and difference') on the basis of pragmatic assessment of what is strategically necessary for women's liberation (Jones 2000: 43–8). Theologically, Jones does not explicitly contextualize that proposal in a doctrine of creation.

Edward Farley (1990) takes pains to avoid those ways in which traditional anthropologies have justified and fostered oppression of women, yet his project might be read as the most fully developed current example of an essentialist account of human nature. Farley shares with feminist anthropologies a primary interest in anthropological issues raised by the intersection of Christian witness to sin and evil and witness to redemption. His book has two parts. Part Two gives 'a theological account of a human condition attested to in religious faiths of the Hebraic and Christian heritage'. It focuses on 'the paradigm or vision of human evil and good (sin and redemption) present in some form in the primary symbols of these faiths' and seeks to discover 'how elements of the paradigm enter and transform' human reality (Farley 1990: xv). Farley holds that it 'is important to distinguish this paradigm of evil and freedom from its narrative and doctrinal expressions' and to set the latter aside (Farley 1990: 139). Part One, of primary interest here, gives an account of 'human reality', i.e., the theologically relevant aspects of an answer to the anthropological 'what' question which would traditionally have been housed in a doctrine of creation. However, although the word 'creature' is often used, no concept of creatureliness as dependence on God surfaces in Part One.

Farley explicitly announces that Continental phenomenology in the fashion of Gabriel Marcel provides the appropriate conceptuality for his project (Farley 1990: xx). He integrates insights from many strands of Continental philosophy and from the biological and social sciences in a 'reflective ontology' of 'human reality'. 'Human reality' is a form of life; it is 'more a species term than an agential term' (Farley 1990: 28). The account is an *ontology* in that it is directed to 'perduring features that constitute the being of something in its region or situation', where 'being' does *not* mean 'a static or timeless essence' but rather a reality's 'characteristic powers or ways of existing' (Farley 1990: xix).

Reflective ontology distinguishes three 'spheres' of human reality: the 'interhuman', the 'social', and the agentially 'personal'. The 'most general feature of our human condition is its tragic character'. 'Tragic' means that 'conditions of well-being require and are interdependent with situations of limitation, frustration, challenge, and suffering' in each of its three spheres. As Part Two goes on to show, human strategies to cope with such suffering, or to avoid it altogether, distort the dynamics of each of the three spheres of human reality and thereby corrupt human reality by inescapably constraining its freedom and creativity. Biblical symbols of 'sin' express experience of such distortion and corruption. Biblical symbols of 'redemption' express experience of the presence of the sacred that 'founds' human reality with both courage to overcome, and reconciliation to heal, distortions and corruptions in all three spheres of human reality. Thus an answer to the 'how' question (courage, reconciliation) is determined by the answer to the 'what' question.

Is Farley's project an instance of that essentializing anthropology which much feminist theology resists? This is unclear for systematic and doctrinal reasons. 'Essence' is equivocal. Feminist critique holds that the internal logic of essentializing anthropologies necessarily predetermines answers to questions about who women are and how they ought to be oriented to their worlds. In its universality, Farley's ontology of human reality looks essentializing. However, he explicitly denies that 'human reality' is a 'static and timeless essence'. It is 'more a species term than an agental term' and specifies the conditions of the possibility of agents having any particular identity and way of being in the world, either corrupted by evil or redeemed, but not 'who' and 'how' anyone actually is. The systematic questions remain: (1) whether proposals regarding any one of the three anthropological questions *necessarily* entail any particular answers to the other two; and (2) whether answers to the anthropological 'what' question can be anything but generalizing.

The doctrinal issue concerns whether human creatureliness is 'good'. Traditional theological accounts of what human beings are, housed in doctrines of creation, entailed that human creatures are good precisely *in* their vulnerability because created by and dependent on God's goodness. It is not clear that answers to the anthropological 'what' question, whether essentialist or constructive, that lack such a theocentric context have a basis on which to affirm creatures' goodness. Rejecting physical and social Manichaeism, Farley stresses that the tragic character of 'human reality' does not entail that it is evil, but neither does it affirm its goodness.

A second type of tension about the anthropological 'what' question turns on whether theological anthropology can be conceptually hospitable to the anthropological implications of several sciences. The theological background of this issue is a consensus that has been growing for several decades that human bodiliness is of major importance to theological anthropology. The consensus has been fostered partly by biblical scholarship, especially of the Old Testament, that has stressed the importance of the body in scripture (e.g., Wolff 1974); partly by historians' recovery of the importance of the body as a subject of theological reflection in the past (e.g., Ashley 1985; Brown 1988; Bynum 1995; Coakley 1997); and partly by feminist reflection on unwarranted and oppressive views of sexuality that have been culturally dominant. To identify living human bodies as an important topic in anthropology is to open the question whether theological claims about the body are coherent with understandings of the human body warranted by the life and human sciences for which it is the central subject of research.

In a programmatic essay Wesley Wildman (1998) argues that a modern secular interpretation of humanity rooted in the findings of the several sciences not only must be incorporated into any theological anthropology concerned about the consistency of truth, but also is normative for some of its claims about *what* bodied human beings are. For example, implications of neurobiology pose challenges to the traditional view that a human being is a composite of a body and a substantial soul that can exist independently of the body. These appear to undercut dualist anthropologies by showing that the mind, i.e., human emotional, intellectual, volitional powers, is bodily based in the brain: No brain, no mind. That tends to undermine the notion that a soul could be the seat of those powers independently of a body. Nancey Murphy (1998), in perhaps the most developed of recent efforts to accept this conclusion and incorporate it in theological anthropology, grants that it is implausible to 'reduce' mental phenomena to epiphenomena of the brain's electrochemistry. 'Mind' has its own 'reality' distinct from, but not separable from, the brain. She argues that human emotional, intellectual, and volitional powers are emergent properties of the brain, having levels of complexity that are greater than the properties of the brain itself, inexplicable as mere aggregates of the brain's properties, but dependent upon the brain. The 'emergence' thesis is controversial among those who otherwise share Murphy's (implicit) agreement with Wildman's programmatic proposal (cf. Gregersen 2000).

On the other side are philosophical theologians, exemplified by John Cooper (1989), who defend classical anthropological dualism partly on philosophical and partly on systematic-theological grounds. Important in Cooper's argument is the systematic point that in theological anthropology claims grounded in a doctrine of creation must include conceptual resources to explain human beings' continuity from creaturely life through death to resurrected life. Since mortal bodies cannot explain such continuity, only dualist anthropologies can provide the needed conceptual resources.

This systematic-theological point is obviously important. Its near absence in theologians' debates about the 'emergence' thesis raises a major issue for that approach. On the other hand, theological defence of dualist anthropologies still lacks elaborated engagement with the anthropological implications of the life sciences. This broad type of dispute about the anthropological 'what' question is in an early stage and has yet to be explicitly and extensively joined.

The 'Who' Question

A second approach supposes that theological anthropology's basic question concerns not our shared human nature (the 'what' question), but our personal identities (the 'who' question). In theological anthropology, 'personal identity' is ambiguous. It might mean the unchanging principle that explains an individual's self-identity through change across time. However, theologians taking 'who' to be the basic anthropological question share the intuition that changes across time are ingredient in 'personal identity', so the latter cannot exclude them. They also share the conviction that accounts of personal identity require 'relational' conceptualities. Further, while they accept the tradition's view that the *imago Dei* lies at the heart of distinctively theological anthropology, they share the judgement that the *imago* has to do first with personal identity ('who' I am) and only on that basis with human nature ('what' I am). Their differences turn on just how to understand 'personal identity'. Stanley Grenz (2001), Alistair McFadyen (1990), Mary McClintock Fulkerson (1997), and Ian McFarland (2001) exemplify different versions of this approach.

For Grenz (2001) the central anthropological task is to recover the 'self' from its loss in postmodern, post-structuralist culture. It requires a theological reconceptualization of the *imago Dei* so that it names, not what constitutes human being, but who human beings are. The loss of 'self' is rooted in the modernist view that 'personal identity emerges . . . primarily as the product of an inward turn' (Grenz 2001: 332). Grenz holds that the proper doctrinal home of anthropology is eschatology. The appropriate conceptuality is 'relational' (Grenz 2001: 304–5).

Doctrinal, exegetical, and historical arguments support these judgements. Doctrinal: The God whose image human beings bear is triune, and each of the three persons is constituted by its relations to the other two (Grenz 2001: 50–1). Human personhood also should be conceived relationally. Given a trinitarian template, human 'relationality' must be understood communally and not in binary I-and-Thou fashion. Historical: Interpretation of the 'image of God' has moved from defining it as an ontological structure constituting human creatures (early and medieval church), to seeing it as a relation to God (Reformers), to seeing it as the divine goal for creation (e.g., Herder, Dorner). Exegetical: In the Old Testament, the content of the 'image of God' is tied to the body by its close association with sexual differentiation (Gen. 1: 27) whose theological significance lies, not in reproduction (Grenz 2001: 277–8), but in its expression of humans' sense of incompleteness (Grenz 2001: 277) and their impulse toward bonding-in-community (Grenz 2001: 279–82). In the New Testament the *imago* is identified with Jesus. Read thus, it becomes clear that the *imago* was not fulfilled at creation but rather is a divinely given eschatological destiny (Grenz 2001: 236–7). This destiny is fulfilled by the eschatological Spirit who, transforming human beings by incorporating them 'in Christ' as one ecclesial body and drawing them into participation in the divine life ('theosis'), reconstructs 'self-in-community' and actualizes the selves' destiny to be *imago Dei.* Only then are we fully 'who' we are. Thus constituted, one's personal identity is no longer the 'product of an inward turn' and no longer focused 'in a static, inward self' vulnerable to loss (Grenz 2001: 336). It is best rendered by narrative, 'making sense out of one's own life, by means of the plot of the Jesus narrative' (Grenz 2001: 329).

This implies answers to the other two anthropological questions. The self-giving love that constitutes the relations among the triune persons typifies 'how' ecclesial human selves ought to be oriented toward their worlds: in love that is a free self-giving to others (Grenz 2001: 312–20). In answer to the 'what' question, Grenz's address to the 'who' question entails an 'ecclesial ontology' (Grenz 2001: 304–66, following Zizioulas) in which the dynamic that constructs 'selves' is the dynamic of the perichoretic *agape* that constitutes the triune persons-in-community (Grenz 2001: 313–20) and 'evokes human love in return' (Grenz 2001: 320). How that evocation happens in humans is unclear; presumably its possibility is the 'impulse' to bonding expressed by their sexuality. Grenz rejects Zizioulas's thesis that 'person', ontologically understood, can be used univocally of divine and human persons. For Grenz the doctrine of the Trinity explains, not *what* it is to be a person, but how the triune God *makes* us 'selves'.

Aside from exegetical disagreements and the brevity of its ontology, Grenz's project focuses important systematic and doctrinal issues. Systematic: Can eschatological consummation be understood simply as the actualization of the 'goal' of creation without the consequence that the movement from 'beginning' to 'end' just *is* God's creative act and that the eschatological state alone is truly 'creation'? If those consequences follow, doctrinal issues follow:

1. Because their creation is incomplete, are creatures not yet 'good creatures' until eschatologically consummated? Then on what grounds are such 'selves' judged to have a dignity that must be respected as an end in itself and never as means?
2. When the *imago Dei* is defined in terms of an eschatological 'ecclesial self', do only those who are in the *ecclesia*, i.e., only 'Christians', bear the *imago* as true 'selves'?
3. In this systematic framework can this conclusion be avoided except by affirmation of soteriological 'universalism'?
4. If the dynamic of the construction of 'selves' by divine love evoking human love is *ontologically* basic to 'selves', can anyone fail to respond in love? If none can fail, how in this scheme can God's evocative love not be an extrinsic violation of the integrity of human creatures?
5. Is it a consequence of the way Grenz relates creation to eschaton that this anthropology opens no conceptual space for inclusion of current knowledge about the (pre-eschaton) development of 'selves'?

McFadyen (1990) also takes the 'who' question to be anthropology's basic question. He too proposes an account of personal identity in terms of God-relatedness, but tries to make the relation intrinsic to avoid violation of personal identities' integrity. He too resists modernity's inward turn in anthropology, not, however, because it leads to postmodernist 'loss of the self', but because by making subjectivity the product of a 'private, internal process' it disconnects personhood from the public realm (McFadyen 1990: 23). He resists both modernity's individualism, insofar as it sees persons as 'self-contained entities cut off from one another and God', and its collectivism, insofar as it makes 'independence from social structures... impossible' (McFadyen 1990: 5). His strategy is to give an account of who we are in terms provided by analysis of *what* personhood is.

McFadyen proposes a dialogical and dialectical understanding of personhood, warranted both by theology and by a philosophical psychology (cf. Harré 1983). He judges that it is best framed in a communications-theory conceptuality (cf. Habermas 1984). Persons are constituted by communicative relations. Communication 'embraces every interaction', not merely linguistic, in which there is exchange of content 'coded or ordered in a way which may produce an effect on those receiving it' (McFadyen 1990: 7). The relevant form of communication is call-and-response dialogue because it is a specifically personal relation, i.e., 'an encounter between two or more partners who are different, [and] have some independence and autonomy in the relation' (McFadyen 1990: 18). The codes shaping communicative relations are inherent in the conventions of some culture, with its arrangements of power and its language, and concretely located in a particular space and time by persons' bodies, which are the medium through which they are present both privately to themselves and publicly to others (McFadyen 1990: 156). A 'personal identity' is 'the communicative form', the stance in relation, 'which a person habitually takes' (McFadyen 1990: 27). Through others' address, intentions, and expectations I receive understandings of what it is to be 'self', and who I in particular am perceived to be as a self, understandings I accept or resist idiosyncratically (cf. McFadyen 1990: 98). Personal identity is 'sedimented' (McFadyen 1990: 113) through this public dialogical history. I acquire a 'sense of self', a 'theory' (McFadyen 1990: 92–3) about myself, and with it the 'capacity to organize oneself in a centred way and act autonomously' and to resist some of others' addresses, intentions, and expectations (cf. McFadyen 1990: 149). Thus personhood is constituted as an ongoing public dialectical process rather than by an asocial, private, interior act. This scheme, which does yield conceptual space for incorporating insights from the several sciences, is a philosophical theory of psycho-social processes.

What makes the project theological is the way McFadyen's theological warrants place all of the above into a larger context of ontological claims: A relational understanding of personhood is warranted by the relational character of traditional theological accounts of creation and re-creation, 'human existence in the image of the triune God and the call of Christ' (McFadyen 1990: 17). God creates persons with autonomy and free responsibility by addressing them dialogically. This dialogue 'determines the structure of human being as response without determining the form or content of that response', i.e., 'it constitutes the ontological structure of human being as relational and responsible' (McFadyen 1990: 22). When persons are distorted by sin, God re-creates them by a new call that consists of the person of Jesus, who is 'the place where divine address and undistorted human response coincide... and is therefore the enacting of the image in its fullness' (McFadyen

1990: 46). Re-created, persons truly image God. Thus personhood is inherently centred outside itself. Since, as created, personhood is already intrinsically related to God, God's relating to re-create does not threaten persons' autonomy and subjectivity. This is a theological answer to the question *what* human persons must be in order to be capable of the dialectical processes analysed by the philosophical warrants. Although the project focuses on the 'who' question and its theological context is the systematic connections between creation and re-creation, the project's doctrinal home finally is creation because 'creation' defines the possibility of 're-creation'.

Response to God's call may take the form of gratitude and openness to God ('vertical image') and openness to other human beings in ways that image the relational 'interpenetrative intersubjectivity' constituting the triune persons ('horizontal image') (McFadyen 1990: 21, 30). Or response may take the form of efforts 'to be a self-constituting and isolated being' (McFadyen 1990: 43), i.e., the form of sin that distorts the image of God both vertically and horizontally. Sin obtains, with the consequence that the entire network of relations that constitute persons is distorted or 'fallen' (McFadyen 1990: 140). Persons are re-created, the image of God restored, when they are conformed to Christ (McFadyen 1990: 47). This is McFadyen's answer to the theological 'how' question. 'In this conformation one's communicational form is established and called out in a directedness out of oneself towards God "for us" in Christ and therefore (because God is "for us" and not just "for me") toward others' (McFadyen 1990: 59). Because Christ's presence is 'relational and therefore also socially determinate', conformation to him is communal (McFadyen 1990: 59). McFadyen also explores the ecclesiological and political implications of these themes (McFadyen 1990: 191–271).

McFadyen's project raises doctrinal and systematic questions.

Doctrinal:

1. How can the concept of dialogue as call and response, used alike of interhuman relations and God–person relations, avoid reducing God to one more voice in a common communicative network? Grenz makes gestures toward a Pannenberg-like panentheistic view of God, which might address this problem, but McFadyen simply affirms a traditional view. If, with the tradition, 'dialogue' is used analogically, what nuancing of '*God* calling' does that require? How much is it then really like 'dialogue'?
2. Given this anthropology, how 'far down' in the dynamics of personhood do the distorting effects of sin go? 'Re-creation' suggests they go so very deep ('bondage of the will'?); redemption involves a new creation. But the possibility of 'response' to God's re-creative 'call' suggests that fallen personhood retains dynamic resources required to be God's dialogue partner. (McFadyen has illuminated persons' 'bondage' in sin in a subsequent book (2000), but it is unclear how its analysis fits his earlier analysis of personhood.)

Systematic:

1. Neither the account of 'what' persons are nor 'who' they are is oriented to illuminating how it is possible for the selfsame persons to be eschatologically glorified.
2. The relations on which McFadyen concentrates are ones that generate response, autonomy, a sense of self, and personal identity. Insofar as they are relations with God, they are said to be ontological relations. However, is it not a systematic confusion to identify genetic relations with ontological relations?
3. McFadyen's answer to the basic anthropological 'who' question systematically depends on a logically prior answer to the 'what' question. Even if it emphasizes the constructivist character of a person's 'sense of self' and 'personal identity', can such a systematic structure escape feminist critiques of essentializing anthropologies?

For Fulkerson (1997), theological accounts of persons' identities as bearers of the *imago Dei* occlude each person's concrete particularity when they are cast as accounts of ways in which persons are the 'same', e.g., as described by a theological ontology (Grenz), or by a philosophical psychology of the dynamics of the creation and re-creation of personal identities (McFadyen), or by a strategic essentialism, no matter how constructivist (Fulkerson 1997: 107). The 'loss of the self' in postmodern post-structuralism is a gift to feminist anthropology, not something to be overcome theologically, because it shows that subject identity does not depend on sameness of substance or body. Rather, 'identity is a function of a position within a system of differences' (Fulkerson 1997: 107). The 'other' is different and difference is binary: insider/outsider, intellectual/emotional, strong/weak, male/female, etc. Post-structuralism helps feminist theology identify the 'outside' case by case, the 'other' that every discourse excludes (including various feminisms, e.g., white, affluent, heterosexual) (cf. Fulkerson 1997: 110). However, post-structuralism does not open a way to describe identity positively. For that, Fulkerson recommends a narrative, rather than theoretical, elucidation of the *imago Dei*: 'A good feminist theological story will be an incomplete story of God-loved creation, a creation for which the only requisite features of imaging God are finitude and dependence' (Fulkerson 1997: 114). Fulkerson warns that the 'implicit universal referent' to the authentic humanity of Jesus 'in the story of the God-loved and dependent *imago Dei* can become a form of hegemony in a number of ways. However, it does not always' (Fulkerson 1997: 115).

McFarland (2001) develops Fulkerson's suggestions into a theological account of who we are that claims 'difference as constitutive of identity' (McFarland 2001: 2). His concern is to warrant claims about persons' equality without excluding the 'different' who are marginalized, as do claims that identity is constituted by 'sameness' (McFarland 2001: 7–10; cf. Fulkerson). Here 'person' is a strictly *theological* term designating who we are in our concrete particularity. It should be 'defined in a purely ostensive manner, as referring to the persons of the Trinity' (McFarland 2001: 127). Because McFarland's central concern is 'who makes us persons', viz., Jesus Christ, God incarnate, 'rather than trying to define what a person is' (McFarland 2001: 9), the doctrinal home that warrants his anthropology is Chalcedonian Christology and the trinitarian understanding of God that it entails (McFarland 2001: 31). The appropriate conceptuality is relational in ways defined and delimited by biblical narratives (cf. Fulkerson) rather than the conceptuality of an ontology (Grenz) or a philosophical psychology (McFadyen).

Trinitarian warrant: Use of the term 'person' in theology is a consequence of 'early Christian reflection on New Testament identification of Jesus with the divine image' (McFarland 2001: 31), the one through whom God's triune life is revealed. Within the trinitarian context 'person' does not designate 'a certain kind of thing..., but simply to be the Father, the Son, or the Holy Spirit' (McFarland 2001: 35), each of whom 'may be supposed to live as a person differently' (McFarland 2001: 70–1). Each is describable only in terms of the particular relationships in which it stands with the others (McFarland 2001: 35). Stories describing Jesus' relations to the Father and the Spirit tell of his mission to represent the Father among estranged human creatures and his call to disciples to represent him in the world, thus calling them to share in his relationship with the Father and Spirit. Human creatures may be called 'persons', not because they replicate the metaphysical dynamic constituting the divine persons (*contra* Zizioulas), but because they are elected by Jesus to participate in the relations that describe him as the concrete particular 'person' he is.

Christological warrant: The Synoptics regularly describe Jesus' own identity by stories highlighting relationships of *difference* from other humans. When they identify him as 'as the one who *was* dead', they render his identity as risen saviour as 'difference *from himself*' (McFarland 2001: 22). 'Because the primary "other" in terms of which Jesus is confessed as risen Lord is none other than Jesus the crucified, the very process that would normally hide this other [according to post-structuralist critique; cf. Fulkerson] brings him into the open' (McFarland 2001: 22). Hence, when the New Testament identifies the risen Christ as the *imago Dei*, in pointing to him it also points to the crucified one who he is not, and therewith points to 'the various reputable and [marginalized] disreputable characters who he is also not, but with whom his narratively rendered identity is irrevocably linked' (McFarland 2001: 22). In relating to his Father, Jesus also represents all these others to the Father also, creating 'the conditions under which we are acknowledged by God as persons in the trinitarian sense that Jesus is'. The traditional name for this is 'justification', but 'in the present context it might as well be termed "personalization"' (McFarland 2001: 44). All human persons are persons *in fact* because, in the particulars of Jesus' story, God concretely relates to them in their relations with others in their differences no matter how they respond (McFarland 2001: 72, 74). We all are equally persons, not by being the 'same' in some respect, but by being different yet equally related-to by Jesus (McFarland 2001: 104).

McFarland distinguishes between the fact and the *form* of personhood (McFarland 2001: 51). This yields answers to the anthropological 'how' question: Grounded in the Spirit, a life may share (though it also may not) 'the basic form of Jesus' life' (McFarland 2001: 52), namely, relating to others in their concrete differences as their neighbour. The context for this is the church, the body of all those to whom, in their interrelatedness, Jesus relates (McFarland 2001: 90). Because the story of Jesus' relating to human 'others' is not yet completed, 'the fullness of Jesus' identity as the Christ has yet to be revealed [i.e., its particular form], even if the fact that Jesus is the Christ has been established by his having been raised to God's right hand' (McFarland 2001: 91). The same eschatological reservation applies to all human 'others'. We cannot know who will ultimately fail to become fully a 'person' in conformity to Christ, so we must treat none now as though they were not 'persons'.

Against the background of this account of the fact and the form of personhood, the anthropological 'what' question must also be addressed because difference cannot be affirmed 'without reference to generic categories of some sort or other' (McFarland 2001: 130). In the doctrine of the Trinity, 'person' is conceptually prior to 'nature'; so too 'insofar as God claims us as persons, what we are takes second place to who we are' (McFarland 2001: 141). McFarland adopts the metaphysical principle that human nature is not constituted by a predetermined, immanent end, but by a God-determined end, the eschaton (McFarland 2001: 142). Nonetheless, what human nature turns out to be eschatologically cannot be totally discontinuous with what it is now. He suggests three persisting principles of human nature: the 'otherness' exhibited in 'dominion' in the mode of self-giving, which entails an obligation to the nonhuman 'other' to be exercised gladly (McFarland 2001: 149, 151); sexuality, which points to the way humans confront 'otherness' among themselves precisely *in* intimate communion (McFarland 2001: 153); and fruitfulness, which is less about procreation than about creating an environment in which children, a third 'other', are welcome (McFarland 2001: 156). These 'symptoms' of human nature are observable in creation, but their significance for human nature is unclear except in the light of Christ (McFarland 2001: 160).

McFarland's project raises doctrinal and systematic issues.

Doctrinal:

1. Despite eschatological reservations about our ability to know who will end up with the proper 'form' of personhood, absent a more developed account of grace (towards 'universalism'?) it is unclear whether the logic of this position entails that only the 'saved' (and thus true members of the church?) are persons. Is it sufficient to affirm that, given the limits of our knowledge, we must treat all human 'others' *as though* they were persons? Or does that set the call to be neighbour to all 'others' on a slippery slope toward an 'as if' ethic whose

ground is not the unqualified moral claim that 'real' persons ineluctably lay on us but our own decision to ascribe personhood to them?

2. Perhaps the obverse of the unclarity about the scope of grace is an unclarity about the deforming and binding dynamics of sin. The reality of human bondage in sin is strongly affirmed (McFarland 2001: 142). However, the anthropological implications of its dynamics are not explored, with the consequence that it is unclear how Jesus' relating to us can avoid being extrinsic.

Systematic:

1. What has the 'form' of being a person to do with the reality, i.e., the 'fact', of being a person? Initially it sounds as though the fact alone constitutes one's reality as person (the 'who' question) and the 'form' has to do with the 'how' question. However, if it is only known eschatologically whether or not one is a person, because only then is the character of its form actualized, then the 'form' seems decisive to the answer of the 'who' question. The systematic question, then, is whether the distinction between the 'fact' and the 'form' of being a person blurs the distinction between two anthropological questions in such a way as to subvert the 'objectivity' of being a person.
2. What is the systematic relation among creation, incarnation, and eschaton in this project? In traditional fashion, they are seen as three moments, beginning, middle, and end, in a single narrative (McFarland 2001: 139). However, it is unclear whether this sequence is understood as an ontological process such that creation is not actual until actualized in an eschatological transformation. In that case, questions about the reality and goodness of creatureliness arise. Sometimes, however, creation seems to be actual only when actualized in the incarnation, by whom we are finally 'personalized' before the eschaton (McFarland 2001: 44). That raises similar questions: Before they encounter Christ, are there no actual persons that lay moral claims on one another? What is the moral status of the human organisms that do exist? The questions remain whether the incarnation is sharply distinguished from the eschaton, equated with the realization of the eschaton, or identified as the still future eschaton proleptically present. On the other hand, sometimes it seems that the eschaton is epistemically, rather than ontologically, decisive: Only then can we know who is an actual person (McFarland 2001: 138).
3. Granted the project explicitly limits itself to a strictly theological account of persons, is the doctrine of creation robust enough to provide conceptual space for engaging the anthropological implications of the several sciences? Can the 'what' question be addressed responsibly in a way that excludes such engagement?

These projects oriented by the anthropological 'who' question are exemplary of two conceptual issues that cut across them all but tend not to be addressed directly by any of them.

1. They share the view that the core anthropological issues focus on the notion of 'personal identity', but they rarely address directly the fact that the phrase is ambiguous. It can be used to name an entity (e.g., Grenz's 'self'), a psychosocial construct that is unique to each individual (e.g., one aspect of McFadyen's project), a psychosocial construct that is unique to a particular group of individuals (e.g., black identity, gay identity, women's identity), and a theologically described status relative to God in which one's identity is 'in Christ' and is best described narratively in the context of Jesus' story (e.g., McFarland's project and part of McFadyen's). There are good theological reasons for using each sense in addressing different issues. But without more explicit clarification the misleading picture is given that all these projects are addressing, and disagreeing about, the same issues.
2. They share the intuition that, however it is understood, 'personal identity' can only be adequately understood 'relationally'. That thesis is subject to serious critique: If relationality is the ontological structure of persons, then 'we are landed with a logical problem of positing relations between relational entities, and so perhaps a never-ending regress of relations.... Persons are ontologically prior to relations' (Harris 1998: 226).

References

Ashley, Benedict M. (1985). *Theologies of the Body: Humanist and Christian.* Braintree: National Catholic Bioethics Center.

Barth, Karl (1960). *Church Dogmatics* III/2. Edinburgh: T. & T. Clark.

Brown, Peter (1988). *The Body and Society: Men, Women and Sexual Renunciation in Early Christianity.* New York: Columbia University Press.

Bynum, Caroline Walker (1995). *The Resurrection of the Body in Western Christianity, 200–1336.* New York: Columbia Universty Press.

Coakley, Sarah (ed.) (1997). *Religion and the Body.* Cambridge: Cambridge University Press.

Cooper, John W. (1989). *Body, Soul and Life Everlasting.* Grand Rapids: Eerdmans.

Daly, Mary (1973). *Beyond God the Father: Toward a Philosophy of Women's Liberation.* Boston: Beacon.

Farley, Edward (1990). *Good and Evil: Interpreting a Human Condition.* Minneapolis: Augsburg.

Fulkerson, Mary McClintock (1997). 'Contesting the Gendered Subject: A Feminist Account of the Imago Dei'. In R. S. Chopp and S. G. Davaney (eds.), *Horizons in Feminist Theology: Identity, Tradition and Norms*, Minneapolis: Fortress.

Gregersen, Nils Hendrik (2000). 'God's Public Traffic: Holist versus Physicalist Supervenience'. In N. H. Gregersen, W. B. Drees, and U. Gorman (eds.), *The Human Person in Science and Theology*, Grand Rapids: Eerdmans.

Grenz, Stanley (2001). *The Social God and the Relational Self.* Louisville: Westminster.

Habermas, Jurgen (1984). *The Theory of Communicative Action*, i. London: Heinemann.

Harré, Rom (1983). *Personal Being*. Oxford: Basil Blackwell.

Harris, Harriet (1998). 'Should We Say that Personhood is Relational?' *Scottish Journal of Theology* 51: 214–34.

Jones, Serene (1997). 'Women's Experience between a Rock and a Hard Place: Feminist, Womanist, and Mujerista Theologies in North America'. In R. S. Chopp and S. G. Davaney (eds.), *Horizons in Feminist Theology: Identity, Tradition, and Norms*, Minneapolis: Fortress.

—— (2000). *Feminist Theory and Christian Theology: Cartographies of Grace*. Minneapolis: Fortress.

McFadyen, Alistair I. (1990). *The Call to Personhood*. Cambridge: Cambridge University Press.

McFarland, Ian (2001). *Difference and Identity*. Cleveland: Pilgrim.

Murphy, Nancey (1998). 'Nonreductive Physicalism: Philosophical Issues'. In Warren Brown, N. Murphy, and H. N. Malony (eds.), *Whatever Happened to the Soul?*, Minneapolis: Fortress, 127–48.

Pannenberg, Wolfhart (1970). *What is Man?* Philadelphia: Fortress.

Rahner, Karl (1978). *Foundations of Christian Faith*. New York: Seabury.

Wildman, Wesley (1998). 'Coordinating Biological, Sociological and Religious Visions of Humanity'. *Zygon* 33: 571–99.

Wolff, H. W. (1974). *Anthropology of the Old Testament*. London: SCM.

Zizioulas, John (1985). 'Personhood and Being'. In *id.*, *Being as Communion: Studies in Personhood and the Church*, Crestwood: St Vladimir's Seminary Press, 27–65.

Suggested Reading

Brown, W., Murphy, N., and Malony, H. N. (eds.) (1998). *Whatever Happened to the Soul?* Minneapolis: Fortress.

Cady, Linell Elizabeth (1997). 'Identity, Feminist Theory and Theology'. In Rebecca Chopp and Sheila Davaney (eds.), *Horizons in Feminist Theology: Identity, Tradition, and Norms*, Minneapolis: Fortress, 17–32.

Coakley, Sarah (2002). *Powers and Submissions: Spirituality, Philosophy and Gender*. Oxford: Blackwell.

Gregersen, N. H., Drees, W. B., and Gorman, U. (eds.) (2000). *The Human Person in Science and Theology*. Grand Rapids: Eerdmans.

Hefner, Philip (1993). *The Human Factor: Evolution, Culture and Religion*. Minneapolis: Fortress.

Hopkins, Dwight N. (2005). *Being Human: Race, Culture and Religion*. Minneapolis: Fortress.

Jeeves, Malcolm (ed.) (2004). *From Cells to Souls—and Beyond: Changing Portraits of Human Nature*. Grand Rapids: Eerdmans.

Jones, Serene, and Lakeland, Paul (eds.) (2005). *Constructive Theology: A Contemporary Approach to Classical Themes*. Minneapolis: Fortress.

Kelsey, D. H. (1997). 'Human Being'. In P. C. Hodgson and R. H. King (eds.), *Christian Theology: An Introduction to its Traditions and Tasks*. Philadelphia: Fortress.

Schwöbel, Christoph (ed.) (1991). *Persons Divine and Human.* Edinburgh: T. & T. Clark.

Thandeka (1997). 'The Self between Feminist Theory and Theology'. In Rebecca Chopp and Sheila Davaney (eds.), *Horizons in Feminist Theology: Identity, Tradition, and Norms*, Minneapolis: Fortress, 79–98.

Vanhoozer, Kevin (1997). 'Human Being, Individual and Social'. In C. Gunton (ed.), *The Cambridge Companion to Christian Doctrine*, Cambridge: Cambridge University Press, 158–88.

CHAPTER 8

THE FALL AND SIN

IAN McFARLAND

WITHIN Christian theology 'the fall' and 'sin' are distinct but closely related concepts. Both refer to the deformation or violation of humanity's relationship to God, but in different registers. Sin is an overarching term for human resistance to or turning away from God. Because God is the source and ground of creaturely existence, this rejection of God leads ultimately to death. The fall, by contrast, refers very specifically to the first sin committed by the first human beings. This primordial sin is understood to have altered the conditions of human existence (rendering it 'fallen') in such a way as to make death the destiny of every human being.

Many of the difficulties associated with Christian teaching on sin ('hamartiology') can be avoided when the concepts of sin and the fall are considered separately. After all, the idea that human beings are capable of and rightly subject to punishment for resistance to a transcendent source of moral value arguably finds a place in most religious traditions. And while the idea of a primordial sin with profound effects on the subsequent condition of human existence is more particular to Christianity and invites questions regarding its historical plausibility, it is conceptually coherent. The Orthodox churches maintain just this kind of relatively clear distinction between present human sinfulness and the primordial sin of the first human beings.[1]

[1] As given dogmatic definition in the sixth decree of the Synod of Jerusalem (1672), Orthodox teaching specifies that human beings inherit the consequences of the first sin, but are not born sinners (though, NB, Decree XVI of the same council commends paedobaptism on the grounds that infants require the remission of original sin). For a contemporary Orthodox interpretation, including points of divergence from western theology, see Ware (1963: 227–30).

In western Christianity, however, these two concepts were combined, such that the consequences of the fall were understood to include not only a weakening of human nature resulting in a natural propensity to sin, but also a deformation of that nature rendering all human beings guilty of sin from birth. Thus, while for the Orthodox the phrase 'original sin' retains the purely historical meaning of 'ancestral sin', among western churches 'original sin' refers both to the first sin of Adam *and* to the congenital sinfulness inherited by Adam's posterity as a consequence of his primordial transgression. As a result, the semantic range of the term 'sin' includes not only particular *acts* that contravene God's will, but also the congenital *state* of opposition to God that subsists apart from and prior to any specific actions a person performs. The conceptual challenges posed by broadening the concept of sin from a specifiable type of human act to the prior and universal condition of all human activity has been the focus of most modern reflection on sin and the fall.

I. The Origins of the Western Doctrine of Original Sin

Christians derive the concept of original sin jointly from the biblical creation story in Genesis 2–3 and its appropriation by Paul in Romans 5. The Genesis account tells how God charges the first human couple to tend the garden of Eden and forbids them to eat the fruit of one of its trees (Gen. 2: 15–17). Subsequently, the serpent entices Adam and Eve to disobey this command (Gen. 3: 1–7). Upon discovering this transgression, God metes out punishment that falls on all subsequent generations of human beings as well as the guilty couple themselves: women are condemned to increased pain in childbirth and subjection to their husbands, and men will have to toil to earn a living from the earth, which is now cursed because of Adam's disobedience (Gen. 3: 9–18).

In spite of God's earlier warning that 'in the day that you eat of [the forbidden tree] you shall die' (Gen. 2: 17), transgression does not bring immediate death. Nevertheless, God's rebuke of Adam includes a forceful affirmation of human mortality: 'you are dust, and to dust you shall return' (Gen. 3: 19); and Adam is expelled from Eden to guard against the possibility that 'he might reach out his hand and take also from the tree of life, and eat, and live for ever' (Gen. 3: 22). In this way, the Genesis narrative seems consistent with Paul's judgement that 'sin came into the world through one man, and death came through sin' (Rom. 5: 12): by creating the conditions in which access to the tree of life was denied, Adam's sin brought death to all humankind.

It is one thing to claim that the first sin brought death into the world, however, and quite another to maintain that it renders all humankind congenitally sinful. Though not unprecedented in the early church,[2] the claim that human beings inherit sinfulness as well as death from Adam was first fully developed by Augustine. In response to the British ascetic Pelagius (whom Augustine understood to teach that human beings could earn salvation by obedience to God's commands) Augustine argued that salvation was a free gift of divine grace. To attribute salvation to human effort seemed to Augustine to render the work of Christ superfluous. Moreover, the confession of Christ as the saviour of all people implied that all needed to be saved—and thus that every human being without exception stood condemned before God as a sinner. Since God's goodness precluded the possibility that human beings had been created sinners, human sinfulness had to be caused by human sinning; and since humanity's sinfulness was *ex hypothesi* universal, Augustine argued that it had to derive from the first human being by propagation rather than (as Pelagius claimed) by imitation.

Critics charged that this position was indistinguishable from fatalism, but Augustine categorically denied that his teaching undermined human responsibility for sinful behaviour. He conceded that original sin meant that the will was enslaved to sin, but denied that human beings sinned by compulsion, arguing instead that all sinful acts were willingly performed and therefore culpable. These claims were defended through an analysis of human willing built on the principles (1) that the will is directed by desire (i.e., that it chooses in accord with what it wants); (2) that it chooses willingly (and therefore responsibly) so long as it is not compelled by an external power; and (3) that its willing is good insofar as its desires are ordered to God as humanity's proper end and sinful insofar as they are not so ordered. Augustine contended that one effect of the fall was to turn human desire away from God, thereby rendering all human deeds sinful, even though they continue to be undertaken willingly (i.e., in accord with desire and not by external compulsion). In this way, human beings remain free in that they *do* whatever they want (indeed, the role of desire in determining action means they cannot do otherwise); but this is of little use for avoiding sin because they cannot *want* whatever they want, and it is what they want—the object of their desire—that determines the character of their actions.

This insistence that sin is unavoidable and yet culpable establishes the conceptual matrix for contemporary reflection on sin and the fall by virtue of the way it ties Christian confession of sin's universality to particular claims regarding its origin, essence, and power. While Augustinian teaching was once dominant in both Catholic and Protestant theology, in the modern period it has been challenged along three fronts: (1) its consistency with the natural history of the human species; (2) its coherence with established notions of moral accountability; and

[2] e.g., Cyprian of Carthage, Epistle 58. 5 in Roberts and Donaldson (1990: v. 354).

(3) its socio-political effects. Assessment of the continued plausibility of the Augustinian position requires an examination of these three issues.

II. Original Sin and Natural History

An obvious objection to the idea of original sin is that it depends on a fallacious account of human history. In both its eastern and western forms, original sin refers to a historical act committed by the first human pair, the effects of which are passed on to all subsequent generations. The plausibility of this claim is undermined by contemporary scientific accounts of human origins, which deviate from that recorded in Genesis. It is now beyond dispute that there was no point where human existence was characterized by immunity from death, absence of labour pains, or an ability to acquire food without toil. Nor are the facts of evolutionary biology consistent with the descent of all human beings from a single ancestral pair (monogenesis).[3] Instead, the best available evidence suggests that modern humans emerged as a splinter population from pre-existing hominid groups within the last quarter of a million years.

The implications of this for theology are substantial. Pre-modern theologians used the idea of the fall to explain natural evil in terms of moral evil,[4] but the geological record makes it clear that natural disasters, disease, suffering, and death long antedate the emergence of the human species. It follows that such phenomena cannot be interpreted as the consequence of human sin. Although the timescale of human evolution vastly exceeds that described in Genesis, the emergence of *Homo sapiens* remains a very recent development in the several-billion-year history of life on earth, and nothing suggests that humanity's advent occasioned any change in the basic conditions of biological existence. Moreover, even if the scope of the fall is limited to the moral sphere, the fact that human beings emerged in a world already infected by disease, death, and disaster would appear to render human sin less inexplicable, if no more excusable.

In light of these difficulties, there has been a strong trend in modern theology to dehistoricize the fall. A particularly influential approach, associated with the twentieth-century theologian Reinhold Niebuhr (who himself drew on the work of

[3] While genetics does establish that all presently living human beings share a common male and female ancestor (the so-called 'Y-chromosomal Adam' and 'mitochondrial Eve'), these two individuals were separated by something in the order of 2,500 generations, and neither can claim the distinction of being the first modern human. See Underhill et al. (2000: 358–61).

[4] In his Bampton Lectures, N. P. Williams argued that the provision of a theodicy was the most significant function of the doctrine of the fall in the early church (Willams 1927: 215).

Søren Kierkegaard), interprets the fall as the inevitable outcome of the tension between the human capacity for self-transcendence on the one hand, and the contingency of spatio-temporal existence on the other: sin follows when human beings try and (inevitably) fail to reconcile their condition of freedom with the constraints of finitude (Niehbur 1941: 194–5, cf. 266–80; cf. Kierkegaard 1980 and Tillich 1957: ii. 39–44). In deriving sin from a constitutive feature of human ontology, however, this line of argument is open to the criticism that it assimilates the fall to creation and thus impugns either the goodness or competence of God as creator.

This difficulty is avoided by those who view original sin as socially mediated, following the lead of the nineteenth-century father of liberal theology, Friedrich Schleiermacher (1928: 282–304).[5] According to this position, it is illegitimate to posit any explanatory precondition of sin distinct from sin itself. Since every individual act of sin thus presupposes an already existing sinfulness, the sinfulness of every individual is attributed to the active sin of all other human beings.[6] More recently, Karl Rahner has developed a similar account of original sin from a specifically Catholic perspective, characterizing original sin as a co-determination of freedom by the guilt of others (Rahner 1990: 110–11). But if this approach succeeds in distancing the fact of sin from divinely created structures of human being, its displacement of the source of sinful behaviour outside the self as sinner weakens the tradition's stress on personal culpability.[7] In the face of these difficulties, some continue to insist that a historical fall is the only possible ground for the twofold claim that all human beings are congenitally sinful and that sin is not rooted in created nature (e.g., Blocher 1997: 58–62).

III. Original Sin and Human Responsibility

As troubling as questions of natural history may be, the most widespread modern objection to the Augustinian doctrine of original sin repeats the ancient, Pelagian

[5] This perspective was developed in an Anglophone context by thinkers like Rauschenbusch (1978). For two very different contemporary attempts to interpret original sin in terms of the combined effects of genetic constitution and social transmission, see Hefner (1993: ch. 8) and Suchocki (1994: chs. 5–7).

[6] Original sin 'operates in every individual through the sin and sinfulness of others', such that 'the congenital sinfulness of one generation is conditioned by the sinfulness of the previous one' (Schleiermacher 1928: §71.2).

[7] It should be noted that at least one interpretation of the communal character of original sin explicitly seeks to avoid this conclusion: 'Adam falls because of Eve, Eve because of Adam. *Not in such a way, however, that the other person immediately takes my burden away but so that he burdens me infinitely with his guilt*' (Bonhoeffer 1959: 77). Cf. ibid. 74–5, where Bonhoeffer distinguishes between 'the series of events preceding an evil deed' and 'making the series ... responsible for the deed'.

argument that the claim that sin that is *both* unavoidable *and* culpable is logically incoherent. This problem is most clearly visible in Augustine's claim that the will is 'bound' in that fallen human beings are unable to direct their desires—and thus their actions—to God as their proper end. Modern western culture is predisposed to reject any notion that a person may be held responsible for dispositional factors that channel or constrain her behaviour. Perhaps still more to the point, the popular equation of freedom with the ability to select any physically possible course of action seems incompatible with being held accountable for failing to will in a way that one is constitutionally incapable of willing. From this perspective, the concept of 'original sin' is an oxymoron, because it combines the idea of human responsibility for action (because the term 'sin' implies free choice) with that of predetermination of action (because the term 'original' implies constraint): to the extent that any aspect of human ontology is declared to be 'original', it cannot coherently be described as 'sin'.[8]

It is largely in response to this kind of criticism that attempts like Niebuhr's to reclaim the Augustinian doctrine of original sin frequently seek to draw a distinction between those constitutive factors of human existence that establish the framework for sinful behaviour on the one hand, and particular sinful acts on the other (cf. Farley 1990). Such approaches seek to depict sin and guilt as ontically inevitable yet not ontologically inherent in human being. Yet on these terms original sin refers only to a tendency of the human will and does not include genuine guilt before God that is prior to (and thus the ground of) any concrete act of willing. A more traditionally Augustinian perspective will be plausible only if personal responsibility can be affirmed even where the capacity for full self-determination is denied, by showing that a sinner can meaningfully be declared guilty while at the same time conceding that her sinfulness is not a product but rather the precondition of her willing.

Recently, Wolfhart Pannenberg has moved in this direction by identifying sin with 'a state of alienation from God' that 'precedes all human acts'. Yet insofar as he immediately adds that sin 'does not come about without our own cooperation and . . . consent', it is ultimately unclear whether his interpretation of the doctrine succeeds in decoupling sinfulness from particular acts (Pannenberg 1991–8: ii. 262; cf. 263). A more consistent position is found in Karl Barth, who shares the modern aversion to the idea of hereditary sin as morally untenable, but is no less critical of the modern tendency to drive a wedge between 'what we are and what we do' (Barth 1956: 403; cf. 500–1). '[Man] sins, but more than that, he is a sinner' (Barth 1956: 495). While Barth has no particular interest in defending the historicity of Adam and insists that each human being is entirely responsible for her own sin, neither does he view the fall in mythic terms. Instead, he argues that humanity's status is

[8] For a classic exposition of this argument in the modern period, see the many works of F. R. Tennant (1902, 1903, 1912).

a matter of God's righteous judgement rather than the ineluctable outworking of some historical or biological dynamic. 'Adam is not a fate which God has suspended over us. Adam is the truth concerning us as it is known to God and told to us' (Barth 1956: 509). In the same way that God imputes to us Christ's righteousness, so God reckons us sinners ('Adam') apart from Christ. Yet though this analogy provides a way of describing humanity's sin as preceding any particular act, it is less successful at providing grounds for the individual's appropriating that sinfulness as her own. After all, since no Christian would claim that her righteousness is her own, it would seem to follow that the sin of Adam is not finally hers either.

IV. Original Sin and Politics

If the first two of modernity's three challenges to the Augustinian doctrine of original sin relate to its compatibility with other dimensions of anthropology, the third has to do with its consequences for Christian practice. From this perspective the doctrine is open to several lines of critique. According to the first, emphasis on sin's universality undermines the possibility of distinguishing between particular instances of sin, leading to the morally questionable claim that newborn infants are no less sinful than fully grown adults. More recently, liberation theologians have developed this objection further, arguing that the tradition's focus on the depravity of the individual tends to obscure the distinction between victims and perpetrators of evil, especially when sin is embedded in social structures that, though sustained by individual actions, are not reducible to the intentionality of individuals.[9] The result is a cultural complacency that fails to address (or even to recognize) some of the most destructive consequences of sin.

A second line of critique works in the opposite direction, arguing that the doctrine of original sin undermines the confession of sin's universality because it is bound up with rhetorical conventions that selectively link sin to particular groups. Within such discourses all people may formally be acknowledged as sinners, but the particular terminology used to describe sin results in certain groups (e.g., inner-city black teenagers, gay and lesbian persons, the chronically unemployed) being marked as especially sinful in a way that differentiates them from the rest of

[9] e.g., the individual sin of racial bigotry (in which one person degrades another because of the colour of her skin) must be distinguished from the social sin of racism (in which persons of a particular skin colour have a disproportionately low access to a society's goods). Both are widely recognized as sins, and it is easy to see how bigotry engenders racism; but the fact that racism may be present even where bigotry is absent means it is not readily identified by analyses of sin that focus on individual attitudes or actions.

the population (Ray 2003; Peters 1994: 156). In brief, while all persons exhibit sin, these groups tend to be seen as instantiating it in a way that both justifies and perpetuates their social marginalization. These patterns of discourse suggest that certain persons are inherently defective with respect to some fundamental dimension of their humanity, and the resulting localization of sinfulness in a particular segment of the population effectively undermines the claim that all persons stand equally condemned before God. The point is not that such classifications necessarily misidentify particular instances of sinful behaviour, but rather that the rhetorical framework in terms of which sin is identified reflects wider, culturally entrenched patterns of inclusion and exclusion. As a result, the church has blind spots in its perception of sin, and its ability to speak truthfully either about or to those classified as especially sinful (as well as to those who are not) is correspondingly weakened.

Still a third problem has been identified by feminist theologians, who have argued that serious harm results from broad characterizations of original sin that fail to take into account differences in social location and thereby establish a false hierarchy of sins that selectively disadvantages particular groups. Thus, accounts that identify original sin with a particular vice (e.g., pride) can have the effect of reinforcing destructive patterns of behaviour by interpreting what is in fact resistance to sin on the part of certain classes of persons as itself a particularly objectionable manifestation of sin (e.g., the 'bitchy' woman or the 'uppity' black). In these circumstances the (in itself theologically valid) conviction that the fall renders all human action inherently sinful becomes the basis for the very different claim that certain attempts to challenge existing conditions—however sinful these may be—are inherently illegitimate because they are themselves manifestations of the primal sin. In this way, too, the doctrine of original sin can undermine the ability to distinguish between and respond appropriately to concrete instances of sin (Saiving 1960; Daly 1974; Plaskow 1980).

V. Original Sin as the Matrix for a Christian Doctrine of Sin

Before assessing the continued plausibility of the Augustinian doctrine of original sin in light of these three objections, it is first necessary to clarify its place in the broader context of Christian theology. As already noted, Augustine posited his understanding of original sin as a corollary of the soteriological principle that human beings were saved by the free gift of God's grace rather than by their own merit. If Christ is truly saviour, then it follows that all need to be saved by him and (therefore) lack the resources to save themselves. In short, the claim that human beings are born sinners (i.e., actually guilty of sin and not just predisposed to sin) derives from and depends logically on the more fundamental conviction that the ultimate vindication of particular human lives before God is pure gift.

This soteriological framework affects Christian claims about what makes human beings human. If humanity's ultimate destiny as human before God is a matter of gift, it follows that the source and guarantor of human identity is located outside the self in God. This perspective is inconsistent with the penchant of most modern thinkers to see the (free) exercise of the will as the source of human identity. In other words, it is a corollary of the Augustinian doctrine of original sin that human identity is rooted in a reality that is prior to human willing. This reality is either the grace of Christ, which leads to eternal life, or the stain of original sin, which leads to death and damnation.

This way of thinking has the further effect of transforming sin from a moral category defined in terms of discreet acts of the will to an ontological one that describes the conditions under which willing takes place. The will is directed by desire, which is in itself not under the control of the will. Again, the will does whatever it wants, but it cannot want whatever it wants. Because in the aftermath of the fall human desire is turned away from God, the will is constitutionally sinful prior to any act of the will (i.e., prior to any concrete thought or deed that could be subjected to moral assessment). It follows that in the same way that grace and salvation are not at bottom matters of personal virtue, neither are sin and damnation fundamentally matters of personal vice. To be sure, the gift of grace naturally issues in virtuous acts (since it orients desire to God), and sin manifests itself in vice (since the sinner's desire is turned away from God and thus necessarily subverts creaturely flourishing); but sin refers in the first instance to the underlying condition of human willing and not to its products. In short, while a sinner is one who commits sins, from an Augustinian perspective it is the fact of being a sinner that leads to concrete acts of sinning and not the other way round.

Understood in this way, the doctrine of original sin serves as the matrix for the Christian doctrine of sin as a whole. While original sin does name a particular historical sin, its primary referent is to the state of sinfulness in which all human beings find themselves by virtue of that sin. A person's status as sinner is thus primarily a function of who she is—someone whose desire is constitutionally turned away from God—and only secondarily of what she does as a consequence of this basic orientation. This perspective rules out the possibility that one's ultimate vindication before God might be based in any property or capacity intrinsic to human being. Because, apart from Christ, one is a sinner and guilty before God, one's salvation in Christ is entirely a matter of grace. Correspondingly, sin is a condition before it is an act and thus is not properly identified by reference to particular misdeeds. Though it remains possible to define sin as a transgression of divine will, in Augustinian perspective such transgression must be understood as a turning from God that inheres in the very structure of fallen humanity. It is the absolute priority of this orientation that guarantees that every particular human act will be sinful.

In summary, the Augustinian doctrine of original sin insists on the pervasiveness of sin both extensively across the human species and intensively within each human being. Its point is to affirm the absolutely free and gracious character of human salvation in Christ. Were the reign of sin any less complete, Christ's role would be correspondingly less ultimate; at best, he would be but one factor among others in determining a person's ultimate destiny, and that would render him something less than Lord. The question remains, however, whether this Augustinian insistence that one's status as sinner is prior to intentionality is tenable. Can sin still be sin if it precedes our every thought and deed, if it is a congenital feature of our existence as fallen human beings? The ability to give an affirmative answer to this question depends on a more detailed examination of moral accountability.

VI. The Nature and Origin of the Fallen Will

Modern unease with the doctrine of original sin is rooted in a conviction that it undercuts the integrity of human beings as moral agents. The assumption underlying this unease is that responsibility for action presupposes that the will is free, in the specific sense of having the ability either to sin or not to sin (generally referred to as 'freedom of indifference' (or *liberum arbitrium indifferentiae*). Nor is this concern simply a preoccupation of the modern period. Early Christians saw in the affirmation of the freedom of the will a crucial counter to pagan and gnostic fatalism (e.g., Justin Martyr, *First Apology* 43–4; Irenaeus of Lyons, *Against Heresies* 4. 37; and Clement of Alexandria, *Stromata* 1. 17; in Roberts and Donaldson 1990), and this conviction has remained a permanent feature of subsequent Christian reflection.[10] From an Augustinian perspective, this strictly moral understanding of sin leads to significant theological problems. Most obviously, it undermines human solidarity in sin, the universality of which becomes fundamentally accidental and, in principle, subject to quantitative variation (i.e., some people turn out to need redemption more than others). One consequence of this qualification of human solidarity in sin is a weakening of the import of the gospel message. For even if it is conceded that no individual person turns out to be free from sin, it remains the

[10] It remains characteristic of Orthodox thought to the present day, and even in the premodern West it has had its champions, including humanists like Erasmus.

case that it is an act of the individual will rather than the grace of Christ that becomes the ground of one's status before God.

By contrast, the Augustinian position denies that the will either is or can be the source of human identity. Yet if from an Augustinian perspective a human being's status before God is determined prior to any act of the will, it is not realized apart from such acts. Although it is grace that turns desire to God, it is in and through the exercise of the will that the individual enacts those desires; likewise, if the fallen will is bound to sin, it nevertheless sins willingly by pursuing the aims of its perverted desires. In short, while the will is not the source of our identity as saint or sinner (i.e., it does not determine *what* we are), it is through our willing that we enact and live out our identities as saints or sinners (i.e., it is that *by which* we are what we are).

This last point is crucial to reconciling the idea of original sin with the concept of personal responsibility. In brief, though Augustine denies that the will is the *source* of human identity (as though fallen human beings were free to direct their desires so as to secure by their own effort their identity as saint or sinner), it remains that identity's *locus*. In the light of the gospel, I recognize that apart from grace my will is inherently sinful, such that all my acts are necessarily sinful (or, in Augustine's language, that I am unable not to sin). Yet this does not mean that I am not responsible for my sins, since the acts of my will are ineluctably *my* acts: that is, insofar as I recognize them *as* my acts (rather than the product of an external act of compulsion in which my will was bypassed), I must acknowledge that they were done willingly, since the will, as the locus of my identity as an agent, is that by reference to which I identify actions as mine.

The situation is much the same when considering how the will is transformed by grace. Here, too, I recognize that the love of God that now motivates my (now virtuous) acts is a gift that my will was in itself powerless to obtain; but the love and the acts that follow from this gift are nevertheless my own. Indeed, the experience of love and hate provides perhaps the most apt illustration of Augustine's understanding of the relationship between the will and personal identity: one does not choose one's loves or hates, but that does not make them any less one's own; on the contrary, those feelings are arguably experienced as more profoundly determinative of one's identity than those actions that are a matter of choice. My love for my wife is far more central to my sense of who I am than the clothes I wear, though the latter is a matter of choice in a way the former is not.

Yet this preliminary resolution to the moral problem of the bound will seems to be vulnerable to the same objection that was raised earlier in relation to Barth's account of original sin. As noted, the saint will see the turning of her will to God as a gift, for which she may claim no credit or reward, even though it remains an object of her willing acceptance (cf. 1 Cor. 15: 10); but the character of the fallen will is different. Here, too, the claim is made that the bondage of the will precedes any choice it makes (cf. Rom. 7: 15–20), but there is no corresponding denial of responsibility. In other words, there is a fundamental disanalogy in that grace (as that which precedes any act of will) is not a matter of personal merit, but sin (though equally prior to any act of will) remains a matter of personal demerit. The obvious question is why such a disanalogy should obtain. Should not the blame for sin be placed with God in the same way that thanks for grace is?

The basis for the disanalogy is that sin is understood to be intrinsic (or 'original') to the fallen person's identity in a way that grace is not. But this observation relieves God of responsibility for sin only if it is possible to show how sin can be held a constitutive feature of human nature without thereby impugning the goodness of God as creator. The doctrine of the fall serves as a means of squaring this circle by allowing the inherent sinfulness of human beings to be affirmed without implicating God in sin.

To see how this is possible, it is first necessary to distinguish two different senses in which sin may be said to be 'natural' to the will. The will cannot be said to be naturally sinful if 'natural' is equated with a 'a constitutive feature of my being for which I am not responsible' (as in, e.g., speaking of someone's natural hair colour). This is because the will is precisely that feature of my being by reference to which I claim responsibility for who I am. In this respect, to argue that the sinfulness of the will is 'natural'—and thus not a matter of personal responsibility—is indeed to undermine the possibility of claiming any action as mine. Yet to systematically deny responsibility for my actions in this way is simply inconsistent with the experience of willing: even if I regard my will as inherently sinful, I cannot coherently evade responsibility for what I will, since any putative denial of responsibility is itself an act of the will that *eo ipso* affirms the very fact of responsibility that it purports to deny. There is just no experientially self-consistent way of positing a condition of the will for which the self is not responsible: because the will is the locus of self identity, there can be no separation of an 'innocent' self from a 'naturally guilty' will. The condition of the will, however acquired, defines the state of the self.

At the same time, the Augustinian position affirms that the sinfulness of the human will is universal, and thus that it *is* 'natural' in the sense of 'inborn'. To make this claim, however, is not to imply any particular theory of sin's transmission, but only to affirm its congenital character. In analogous fashion we may be said to inherit our mortality, though the latter is not transmitted in the same way as blue eyes, fingernails, or the capacity for language. The difference, of course, is that, unlike mortality, original sin is held to include culpability. Once again, however, this feature derives from the peculiar character of the will as that inherent (and thus in an ontological sense 'natural') feature of human being by reference to which I identify myself as a responsible agent (and so distinguish my life from 'nature').[11] Moreover, since any hominid without a fallen will would not need redemption and thus would by definition not be one of those for whom the Word took flesh, it

[11] It is important to note here that to affirm that sinfulness is inherited is not the same as to say that guilt is inherited (an idea that is clearly inconsistent with biblical teaching: cf. 2 Kings 14: 6; Jer. 31: 29–30;

follows that original sin must by definition be traced back to the first human being as the source of 'fallenness'. In this way, soteriological considerations demand that the fall be counted a historical event, though they provide no basis for any description of its psychological presuppositions or dynamics. 'It is not the purpose of the Bible to give information about the origin of evil but to witness to its character as guilt and as the infinite burden of man' (Bonhoeffer 1959: 65).

VII. The Work of the Fallen Will: Sin as Cause and Effect

From an Augustinian perspective the fallen will and original sin are corollaries of what are taken to be the fundamental Christian convictions that (1) all human beings without exception stand equally in need of salvation; and (2) this salvation is mediated exclusively through Jesus Christ.[12] In other words, original sin is not an immediate object of human experience, but is known only indirectly, as that which has been healed and forgiven in Christ: I do not know myself as a sinner until that identity has been fundamentally altered by that grace thanks to which my identity is no longer simply that of a sinner.

Needless to say, this transformation of underlying identity does not mean that Christians cease to resist God in thought, word, and deed any more than it implies that non-Christians lack moral sensibility. It is simply to underline the point that original sin is an ontological category and therefore allows no correlation between confessional status and moral integrity (cf. Rom. 2: 14–16). Original sin is the cause of those concrete acts that violate God's will ('actual sins'), but as such is itself prior to any decision of the will. For this reason it is not empirically verifiable either by reference to the quantity of vice in the world or through psychological analysis of people's motives. Precisely because it puts the will—the locus of the individual's sense of self—in bondage, original sin cannot be isolated by any act of the will. Once again, it is known only as it is forgiven.[13]

Ezek. 18: 20). The individual's guilt is a product of her own sinfulness, so that while the latter may be said to be inherited, the former may not: my guilt is a consequence of my sinfulness, not Adam's.

[12] It is important to note that belief that salvation is mediated through Jesus does not necessarily imply that only Christians are saved; it merely reflects what may be taken to be the founding Christian conviction that salvation is to be defined precisely as life in communion with him as Lord (e.g., John 17: 3; 2 Cor. 5: 6–8; Phil. 1: 23).

[13] If this perspective seems inconsistent with Paul's self-analysis in Romans 7, it may be noted that elsewhere in his correspondence Paul gives no indication that he was in any way troubled by his own sinfulness prior to his experience on the Damascus road (Gal. 1: 14; Phil. 3: 6; cf. Acts 22: 3).

This point has important implications for the practical effects of the doctrine on Christian faith and practice. Against the charge that the idea of original sin promotes an inappropriate levelling that implausibly ascribes sinfulness to newborn infants and, still more catastrophically, makes it difficult to draw any meaningful distinction between the perpetrators and victims of horrendous evils, it is necessary to stress once again that original sin is an ontological rather than a moral category. Thus, to say that neonates are sinful is not to claim that they are worthy of blame or punishment, but only to insist that they are in need of redemption. To maintain (as the tradition does) that such a condition of congenital sinfulness is properly equated with guilt is simply to insist that human beings are congenitally agents and therefore—and quite apart from any abilities they may or may not be thought to possess—are always rightly viewed and treated as subjects.[14]

Though the idea of guilt without blame may seem self-contradictory, the experience of those working with victims of rape, childhood sexual abuse, and other survivors of profound personal violation suggests that the distinction is far from specious. Feminist scholars in particular have argued that while the ascription of blame to survivors of such trauma is completely inappropriate, victims' sense of guilt should not be dismissed on the same terms. While recognizing the importance of treading carefully here (since it is important to check feelings of guilt that derive from victims' often inaccurate perceptions of personal power in or control over a given situation), these scholars have argued that to reject feelings of guilt only serves to further diminish victims' integrity by failing to take them seriously as subjects (Driver and Droisen 1989).[15]

Importantly, this insistence on the agency of survivors of abuse need not blur the distinction between agents and victims of evil. In order to see how this is the case, it is helpful to invoke the traditional distinction between original sin and actual sin. Because it is a deduction from the Christian doctrine of salvation, original sin escapes empirical isolation as a directly observable fact of human existence. As a comprehensive ontological condition that is prior to any concrete act of will, it cannot be measured on an axiological scale that allows for comparative judgements of more and less: all stand equally guilty. By contrast, actual sins refer to products

[14] To argue otherwise (say, by correlating subjecthood with some measurable level of cognitive ability) would seem to leave few resources for objecting to practices like infanticide or the routinized killing of adult persons with severely reduced cognitive function. In the same context, the practice of infant baptism is best viewed not as insurance against the threat of hellfire, but rather as the community's affirmation that the child's status as a subject—one who has been called by God to live in and with the community—is not dependent on the demonstration of any inherent capacities.

[15] McFadyen (2000) offers a careful appropriation of clinical materials in defence of a basically Augustinian understanding of original sin. By contrast, Andrew Sung Park's strict correlation of volition with the perpetrators of oppression leaves him unable to ascribe agency to sin's victims (Park 1993: esp. ch. 4).

of volition, particular instances of resistance to God's will.[16] They are, correspondingly, properly viewed in moral rather than ontological terms and, as such, allow for the kind of distinctions between perpetrator and victim on the one hand, and between greater and lesser offences on the other, that are inapplicable in the case of original sin. It follows that there is nothing about the doctrine of original sin in itself that leads to an inappropriate homogenization of human sinfulness, so long as the ontological and axiological dimensions of hamartiology are kept distinct.[17]

The importance of maintaining this distinction is particularly evident when it comes to correcting ways of talking about original sin that so correlate human sinfulness with a particular set of identifiable behaviours as to underwrite existing patterns of social marginalization and exclusion. If original sin is understood as that which conditions all acts of will rather than being identified with such acts themselves, then there is no theological basis for identifying any one form of actual sin as more fundamental than any other. Any discourse about sin that has this effect must itself be seen as a manifestation of sin, insofar as it implicitly establishes differences in rank according to which certain groups of people turn out to be more guilty before God (and thus more in need of redemption through Christ) than others.

By affirming that humanity is one in its fallenness, the doctrine of original sin establishes a theological framework within which any practices that attempt to exploit particular examples of sin as a means of establishing explicit or implicit hierarchies of sinfulness stand condemned in advance. Original sin means that no one is innocent. At the same time, it does not mean that concrete instances of sinful behaviour lack theological significance. On the contrary, actual sins, as symptoms of original sin, provide an important mechanism for ensuring that the formal confession of sin's universality is not belied by practices that identify sin with the other to the benefit of oneself. Because the depth of sin is known only in its healing, the one who by grace has learned how great her sin is will recognize the ongoing need to confront in herself its always unsuspected depths, precisely as a means of honouring that healing as an ever-renewed gift rather than a possession. As Paul recognized, appeal to one's own conscience is not sufficient here, because the power of sin is deeper than one's own capacity for self-knowledge (1 Cor. 4: 4; cf. Phil. 3: 6).

[16] One might introduce here the category of 'crime' to name that subset of actual sins that so undermine the conditions of social existence as to be rightly subject to some sort of punitive sanction. Needless to say, defining such offences is a matter of human political negotiation and is correspondingly fallible. There is thus no guarantee that in any particular society acts identified as crimes are actually sins (e.g., laws against interracial marriage). Similarly, the (perhaps quite proper) judgement that a given action does not constitute a crime does not imply that it is any less serious a sin (e.g., adultery).

[17] Niebuhr's attempt to make this point by distinguishing between equality of sin and inequality of guilt operates from within an entirely axiological framework and thus invariably slights either one or the other side of the equation (Niebuhr 1941: 233–42). His framework is more productively seen as pointing to the difference between sin and crime described in the previous footnote.

The insight of other persons is required. It is necessary to listen to those whose experience of pain, humiliation, exclusion, and exploitation testify to the presence of sin in the world and provide the empirical basis for identifying and repenting of one's participation in it (Ray 2003: 133–4). In this way, original sin provides a spur for a continued probing of the pervasiveness of sin that is essential to challenging concrete instances of behaviour that violates God's will for the creation.

VIII. Conclusion: Sin-Talk and Christian Faith

Sin and the fall refer respectively to the character and origin of human resistance to God. In the Augustinian tradition the doctrine of original sin functions as a means of bringing these two concepts together by viewing the present fact of sin as the universal outworking of a primordial fall. To confess oneself as fallen is to see sin as a congenital feature of human existence rather than something we acquire over time. In this way, sin is at bottom less something we do (though it is, of course, also that) than an aspect of our fallen existence that shapes all our doing. This means, in turn, that in spite of what we might wish, we are not the masters of our fate or the captains of our souls; rather, our essential character as fallen precedes and shapes our every act of putative self-determination.

This reading of the doctrine raises the question of its function within the wider context of Christian faith and practice. Individual doctrines are not simply free-floating claims. They arise in particular ecclesial settings and have definite implications for other dimensions of Christian faith and practice. If, as the previous paragraphs suggest, the consequence of the Christian doctrine of original sin is the displacement of sin-talk from the realm of morality to that of ontology, what is the effect of this move on the shape of Christian life and work? What, in short, does this doctrine do?

The Augustinian doctrine of original sin arose out of a particular polemical context. Against the contention that salvation, understood as the realization of life in communion with God, is at bottom a matter of human achievement, Augustine countered that it is properly conceived as utter gift. The idea of congenital sinfulness emerges as a corollary to this fundamental conviction: if all human beings stand in need of salvation that they cannot secure themselves, then it follows that they are marked by a congenital resistance to God and God's work. This is original sin. 'The man who is saved in the person of another, and can be saved only in that way, is obviously in himself a lost man' (Barth 1956: 413).

Thus the most basic theological function of the doctrine of original sin is *to magnify divine grace* by stressing the utter impotence of human beings to guarantee their own existence before God. At the same time, it would be quite wrong to conclude that the effect of the doctrine is to undermine the integrity of human beings as subjects. As noted above, the doctrine of original sin does not render the will impotent: whether for good or ill, human beings do what they will. The doctrine of original sin does, however, remind us that what human beings will is not itself a matter of the will's choice. The will's basic orientation toward or away from God is not itself within the compass of the will, any more than any instance of love or hatred is—and yet all love and hatred, whether for creator or creature, remains no less the will's very own. A second function of the doctrine of original sin is therefore *to circumscribe the will as the locus, but not the source, of personal identity*; that is, while I am who I am only through my willing, my willing is ineluctably shaped by a fundamental orientation toward or away from God that is prior to and conditions its every concrete act.

The affirmation of sin as a universal feature of fallen humanity that is antecedent to and independent of the acquisition of any merit or demerit means that a third function of the doctrine of original sin is *to establish a fundamental human solidarity before God*. All people stand equally in need of God's grace; no human being can claim any advantage before God with respect to others. Nor is this situation any different for the believer, who is not distinguished from the non-believer by any personal merit that would provide grounds for condescension (cf. Rom. 4: 4–8). On the contrary, Christians' awareness that they live by grace alone should prompt compassion for others in recognition that no one stands or falls by her own effort. 'This doctrine teaches us to think no worse of others, than of ourselves: it teaches us that we are *all*, as we are by nature, *companions* in a miserable helpless condition; which, under a revelation of the divine mercy, tends to promote mutual *compassion*' (Edwards 1970: 424). It is, correspondingly, incumbent upon Christians to monitor the rhetoric of the faith to avoid the suggestion that any one group of people stands in greater degree of alienation from God than another.

At the same time, however, the confession of human solidarity in sin does not render talk of differences among actual sins superfluous or render attention to their particular forms theologically irrelevant. On the contrary, a fourth and crucial function of the doctrine of original sin is *to provide a framework for enlarging the category of actual sin* to include practices that may previously have been viewed as morally neutral (e.g., slavery) or even virtuous (e.g., the systematic subordination of women). To affirm the doctrine of original sin is to confess that one's own sinfulness conditions one's every act. It is therefore not directly perceptible, but is known only in its being overcome. This side of glory, however, this overcoming remains in process and is never definitive, which means that the Christian must ever confess herself a sinner (1 John 1: 8, 10). If this confession is not to be a mere formality, it must be shaped by a commitment to find out the hidden depths of one's own sin in ongoing dialogue with those whose suffering provides the necessary reference point both for naming sin and for correcting one's participation in it.

The doctrine of original sin is thus revealed in two complementary dimensions. On the one hand, it demands that sin be reconceived as an ontological as well as a moral category: though sin is certainly something people do, it is more fundamentally a disorder that inescapably conditions all our doing—and thereby reminds us that our hope properly rests in God's doing rather than our own. On the other hand, as much as talk of original sin relativizes the significance of actual sins in the face of the universal need of humankind for redemption, it also serves as a constant reminder that the confession of one's sin is not a single event. Sin's very pervasiveness requires a dedication in seeking it out that is inseparable from attention to particular instances of its destructiveness. Just as the resurrection reveals that the final victory has been won without in any way undermining the church's ongoing struggle with worldly powers, so a robust doctrine of original sin is possible only in light of sin's defeat, and yet it commits the believer to the ongoing process of realizing this victory over sin in her own life. In this way, theologically informed sin-talk promotes neither complacency nor pessimism in the face of human depravity, but incites believers to claim God's grace as a power that enables the naming and vanquishing of sin both in themselves and in the world around them.

References

Barth, Karl (1956). *Church Dogmatics* IV/1. Edinburgh: T. & T. Clark.

Blocher, Henri (1997). *Original Sin: Illuminating the Riddle.* Grand Rapids: Eerdmans.

Bonhoeffer, Dietrich (1959). *Creation and Fall: A Theological Interpretation of Genesis 1–3.* London: SCM.

Daly, Mary (1974). *Beyond God the Father: Towards a Philosophy of Women's Liberation.* Boston: Beacon.

Driver, Emily, and Droisen, Audrey (1989). *Childhood Sexual Abuse: Feminist Perspectives.* Basingstoke: Macmillan.

Edwards, Jonathan (1970). *Original Sin.* New Haven: Yale University Press.

Farley, Edward (1990). *Good and Evil: Interpreting a Human Condition.* Minneapolis: Fortress.

Hefner, Philip (1993). *The Human Factor: Evolution, Culture, Religion.* Minneapolis: Fortress.

Kierkegaard, Søren (1980). *The Concept of Anxiety: A Simple Psychologically Orienting Deliberation on the Dogmatic Issue of Hereditary Sin.* Princeton: Princeton University Press.

McFadyen, Alistair (2000). *Bound to Sin: Abuse, Holocaust and the Christian Doctrine of Sin.* Cambridge: Cambridge University Press.

NIEBUHR, REINHOLD (1941). *The Nature and Destiny of Man: A Christian Interpretation*, i. *Human Nature*. London: Nisbet.

PANNENBERG, WOLFHART (1991–8). *Systematic Theology*. 3 vols. Grand Rapids: Eerdmans.

PARK, ANDREW SUNG (1993). *The Wounded Hart of God: The Asian Concept of Han and the Christian Doctrine of Sin*. Nashville: Abingdon.

PETERS, TED (1994). *Sin: Radical Evil in Soul and Society*. Grand Rapids: Eerdmans.

PLASKOW, JUDITH (1980). *Sex, Sin and Grace: Women's Experience and the Theologies of Reinhold Niebuhr and Paul Tillich*. Lanham: University Press of America.

RAHNER, KARL (1990). *Foundations of the Christian Faith: An Introduction to the Idea of Christianity*. New York: Crossroad.

RAUSCHENBUSCH, WALTER (1978 [1917]). *A Theology for the Social Gospel*. Nashville: Abingdon.

RAY, STEPHEN G., JR. (2003). *Do No Harm: Social Sin and Christian Responsibility*. Minneapolis: Fortress.

ROBERTS, A., and DONALDSON, J. (eds.) (1990). *Ante-Nicene Fathers: The Writings of the Fathers down to A.D. 325*. Edinburgh: T. & T. Clark.

SAIVING, VALERIE (1960). 'The Human Situation: A Feminist View'. *Journal of Religion* 40: 100–12.

SCHLEIERMACHER, FRIEDRICH (1928 [1830]). *The Christian Faith*. Edinburgh: T. & T. Clark.

SUCHOCKI, MARJORIE HEWITT (1994). *The Fall to Violence: Original Sin in Relational Theology*. New York: Continuum.

TENNANT, F. R. (1902). *The Origin and Propagation of Sin*. Cambridge: University of Cambridge Press.

—— (1903). *The Sources of the Doctrine of the Fall and Original Sin*. Cambridge: University of Cambridge Press.

—— (1912). *The Concept of Sin*. Cambridge: University of Cambridge Press.

TILLICH, PAUL (1957). *Systematic Theology*. 3 vols. Chicago: University of Chicago Press.

UNDERHILL, PETER A., SHEN, PEIDONG, LIN, ALICE A., et al. (2000). 'Y Chromosome Sequence Variation and the History of Human Populations'. *Nature Genetics* 26/3: 358–61.

WARE, TIMOTHY (1963). *The Orthodox Church*. Harmondsworth: Penguin.

WETZEL, JAMES (1992). *Augustine and the Limits of Virtue*. Cambridge: Cambridge University Press.

WILLIAMS, N. P. (1927). *The Ideas of the Fall and Original Sin*. London: Longmans, Green & Co.

SUGGESTED READING

ALISON, JAMES (1998). *The Joy of Being Wrong: Original Sin through Easter Eyes*. New York: Crossroad.

AUGUSTINE (1980). *Anti-Pelagian Writings*. In Philip Schaff (ed.), *A Select Library of the Nicene and Post-Nicene Fathers of the Christian Church*. 1st ser. Edinburgh: T. & T. Clark, vol. v.

BARTH (1956: 358–513).

—— (1958). *Church Dogmatics* IV/2. Edinburgh: T. & T. Clark, 378–498.

—— (1961). *Church Dogmatics* IV/3.1. Edinburgh: T. & T. Clark, 368–478.
Bonhoeffer (1959).
McFadyen (2000).
Niebuhr (1941).
Plaskow (1980).
Ray (2003).
Suchocki (1994).
Wetzel (1992).

CHAPTER 9

INCARNATION

OLIVER D. CRISP

I. Approaching the Doctrine

The incarnation is the central and defining event of Christian theology. The doctrine that the second person of the Trinity assumes human nature, becoming a man, in order to bring about the salvation of fallen human beings lies at the heart of the traditional teaching of the church (Webster 2001: 113–50). This doctrine can be found in several places in the New Testament, but is most dramatically heralded in the Prologue to the Fourth Gospel: 'And the Word became flesh and lived among us, and we have seen his glory, the glory as of a father's only son, full of grace and truth' (John 1: 14; cf. Rom. 1: 3–4; Gal. 4: 4–5; Phil. 2: 5–8; Col. 2: 9; 1 Tim. 2: 5; 3: 16; Heb. 2: 14). The perennial task of systematic theology, as Donald Baillie pointed out in the mid-twentieth century, is to make sense of this doctrine as reported to us in scripture, which is the 'Christian conviction that God was incarnate in Jesus, that Jesus is God and Man' (Baillie 1961: 83). Yet in the modern period it has been subjected to the corrosives of historical biblical criticism (Wright 1996: 3–144); the scepticism of thinkers of the Enlightenment tradition of Hume, Kant, and Hegel (Macquarrie 1990: 175–335); and, more recently, the denial of or 'incredulity towards' metanarratives associated with postmodernism (cf. Tanner 1997).

This is not to suggest that there have been no defenders of a creedally orthodox account of the incarnation in the same period; arguably the most creative theologian in this regard is Karl Barth (1975), although there are others, e.g., Emil Brunner (1934). And although concern for a creedally orthodox Christology has not always been of paramount importance to recent theologians, in the past quarter-century there has arisen a renewed interest in what we might call constructive and creedally orthodox accounts of the incarnation and, more broadly, the person of Christ. The present chapter will not explore why this is the case—a matter for historians—but will focus instead on the dogmatic content of this recent resurgence of creedally orthodox Christology.

A creedally orthodox account of the incarnation is any approach to the doctrine that takes as its point of departure the high Christology of the great catholic creeds, culminating in the 'definition' of the person of Christ worked out at the Council of Chalcedon in AD 451. During this historically creative period of Christology, the theologians of the church, under the guidance of the Holy Spirit, sought to comprehend what scripture teaches concerning the person of Christ. The resulting synthesis is largely an exposition of the dogmatic proposition that 'Jesus Christ is fully God and fully man', and includes (but is not exhausted by) the following tenets:

1. Christ is of one substance (*homoousios*) with the Father.
2. Christ is eternally begotten of the Father according to his divinity and temporally begotten of the Virgin Mary according to his humanity.
3. Christ is one theanthropic (divine–human) person (*hypostasis*) subsisting in two natures (*phuseis*), which are held together in a personal union (Grillmeier 1965: 544).
4. Christ's two natures remain intact in the personal union, without being confused or mingled together to form some sort of hybrid entity or *tertium* quid.
5. Christ's two natures are a fully divine nature and a fully human nature, respectively, his human nature consisting of a human body and 'rational' soul.

All orthodox theologians upheld this dogmatic synthesis. To give just one example, Thomas Aquinas in his *Summa Contra Gentiles* says:

> It is clear that according to the tradition of the Catholic faith we must say that in Christ there is a perfect divine nature and a perfect human nature, constituted by a rational soul and human flesh; and that these two natures are united in Christ not by indwelling only, nor in an accidental mode, as a man is united to his garments, nor in a personal relation and property only, but in one hypostasis [entity] and one supposit [fundamental substance]. (Aquinas 1975: 189)

We shall return to the dogmatic importance of these issues presently. But before doing so, a few words are in order by way of theological reflection on historical discussions of the early Christological debates.

It has become something of a historical truism to say that the shaping of classical Christology was precipitated by the controversies within the church, inaugurated by thinkers like Arius, Apollinaris, and Nestorius, whose views (or purported views) were eventually anathematized, and by Athanasius, Cyril of Alexandria, and Maximus the Confessor, to name but three prominent thinkers amongst the orthodox (Kelly 1977; Meyendorff 1975). But even if we grant this truism, it has no bearing on the veracity of the Christological formulae the church eventually settled upon. To put it another way: *how* the content of the creeds was arrived at, particularly the Chalcedonian settlement, is a separate issue from *what* the content of those creeds consist in. Historians of dogma sometimes overlook this point. The result is a conflation of the historical vicissitudes that led to the Christological consensus in the fifth century AD with the doctrine of the consensus. On reading some modern historians of dogma one gets the sense that *because* the Chalcedonian definition was reached after protracted political and theological wrangling, the dogmatic content of the definition must be treated as one would treat any such compromise document: as a partially unsuccessful attempt at marrying quite different positions in order to preserve some political and theological unity within the church—or, more cynically, to buttress an emerging ecclesiastical-political hegemony.

In one important respect, such a story about the Christological controversies that precipitated the great ecumenical councils of the church is correct. There was real, often vituperative dispute between theologians aligned with one or the other of the theological parties of the time. The debate between 'Antiochene' and 'Alexandrian' Christology is an example of this (Weber 1983: 111–19). And the Chalcedonian definition is, amongst other things, a theological attempt at bringing aspects of the thinking of these different parties into one unified document. But if this is thought to tell against the theological truth of the consensus position reached at Chalcedon, then this is far from a settled matter. Such a conclusion is in fact an instance of the genetic fallacy, whereby the origin of a particular doctrine is mistakenly thought to tell against its truthfulness. Such a view also seems to betray a certain methodological naturalism with respect to the formation of the ecumenical creeds of the church. That is, such a view treats individual theologians, synods, and councils as if they were the efficient causes of catholic doctrine, not, as traditionally believed, the instrumental causes by which the Holy Spirit brought the church to a greater understanding of the gospel. But there are very good dogmatic reasons for denying methodological naturalism a foothold of this sort in theological accounts of the formation of Christian doctrine. One such dogmatic reason has to do with acknowledging the providential work of the Holy Spirit in leading the church to a right knowledge of the truth even through such circumstances as fuelled the early Christological controversies. But this is just what a purely political or naturalistic reading of the formation of Christian doctrine cannot, or will not, allow.

To be sure, all parties did not endorse the Christology of the consensus, and controversy continued for some time afterwards (there are still ecclesiastical bodies who deny the consensus today). The Third Council of Constantinople in AD 680–1 may be said to be the creedal *terminus ad quem* of this discussion. At that council, it was resolved, amongst other things, that the hypostatic union of Christ's two natures should be understood to mean that he possesses a human will (and centre of operation) in addition to his divine will (and centre of operation). This view was dubbed *dyothelitism* ('two-wills-ism') against the *monothelites* who claimed that Christ had only one will. Some remained implacably opposed to dyothelitism. But this extrapolation of a Chalcedonian Christology remained the orthodox position for the vast majority of both East and West thereafter, and only began to come under sustained theological criticism in the early modern period.

There is a long tradition in theology of regarding the catholic creeds as, if not statements of apophaticism, at least doctrines that 'fence' the mystery of the incarnation. On this way of thinking, the Chalcedonian definition is a way of stating as much as we are able on the basis of what holy scripture teaches. Those who advocate such an apophatic approach to Chalcedon usually think that Chalcedonian Christology is internally consistent, but that the resources of human reason are limited in any attempt to articulate this most central of Christian doctrines. On this approach the Chalcedonian definition is a sort of dogmatic boundary beyond which we may not venture, on pain of unwarranted theological speculation—'unwarranted' and 'speculative' because it is beyond what holy writ allows (cf. Coakley 2002).

But someone might ask, 'Why should the ecumenical creeds play such an important role in Christology? Why not simply return to scripture?' One might as well ask, 'Why should the body of legal opinion that informs our legislature play such an important role in jurisprudence? Why not simply return to a pure, undefiled notion of natural justice?' It is impossible to get behind the tradition to a 'dogmatically pure' New Testament notion of Christology. The ecumenical creeds were produced to explicate and defend the orthodox faith delivered to the saints by the apostles and prophets which was being misrepresented by those who, like Arius or Apollinaris, sought to defend their own unorthodox views on the basis of scripture. This is not to say that the creeds possess an authority equal to that of scripture. But it is to suggest that the creeds—and for present purposes, the Chalcedonian definition in particular—are an important elucidation of the teaching of scripture that all catholic Christians are bound by, unless some creedal statement can be shown to be inconsistent with the teaching of scripture.

Renewed interest in the creedal doctrine of the incarnation in recent theology has come from more than one quarter. There have been philosophers whose work in this area has made considerable strides towards overcoming the scepticism associated with, say, the so-called 'myth of God incarnate' school of Christology, exemplified by thinkers like John Hick and Don Cupitt (Hick 1977). Chief amongst these is the work of Thomas Morris (1986) and his account of 'two-minds' Christology, which seeks to rehabilitate a broadly Chalcedonian account of the incarnation by way of analogy with modern notions of mind: Christ is fully God and fully man because he is one person with two minds, one human and one divine. Christ's human mind is surrounded by the divine mind, but in such an intimate fashion that the divine mind has immediate access to the thoughts of Christ's human mind, whereas his human mind does not necessarily have access to everything his divine mind does. In short, there is, says Morris, an 'asymmetric accessing relation' between these two minds: the divine mind has immediate access to the content of Christ's human mind, but not conversely (Morris 1986: 159). Morris's account of the incarnation is not a defence of the traditional doctrine of the hypostatic union so much as an attempt to show that it is not logically incoherent to claim that one person is both fully God and fully man. This account has been subjected to a number of criticisms and has not convinced everyone. But it has proved difficult to get around. Although it is not the only recent philosophical work of merit on the incarnation, it is perhaps the most influential, and has in many respects set the agenda for subsequent discussion by philosophical theologians (Swinburne 1994; Crisp 2007). (For recent, fruitful work on medieval Christology, see Leftow 2002 and Cross 2002.)

Aside from such philosophical-theological work, there has also been a considerable amount of systematic-theological work. And here there has been less agreement as to the central issues facing the doctrine today, due in part to the complex of problems resulting from the post-Enlightenment history of the doctrine that systematic theologians feel the need to address (Gunton 1997). These include the legacy of post-Kantian theology, particularly the epistemological problem concerning whether we can know anything about Christ's divine nature and therefore whether Jesus of Nazareth is able to reveal to us anything of the divine nature. There is also the problem, neatly captured by Lessing's picture of an 'ugly, broad ditch' between the contingent matter of history and the necessary truths of reason (Lessing 1957: 55). Applied to the incarnation, the problem is how the New Testament accounts of the life and work of a particular Palestinian peasant-prophet can give us necessary truths about the content of theology, even if these accounts are reliable—which many biblical critics think is doubtful. There is also the related problem concerning the wedge that has been driven between the Jesus of history (roughly, the Palestinian Rabbi as reconstructed from the extant documentation of his pre-resurrection dealings) and the Christ of faith (the picture of the resurrected Jesus recorded in the New Testament and expounded in the early church).

II. The Language of Incarnation

We come to the question of the terminology used in discussion of the incarnation. Some theologians find the metaphysical idiom of classical Christology too restrictive, believing that it fails to capture the ethical and religious dimensions that should lie at the heart of Christology. Such theologians often prefer a so-called 'functionalist' Christology, one supposedly pursued in the absence of ontological commitments. However, one cannot escape ontology so easily. The statement 'Christology is not about ontology' is ontological, even if it implies that ontology is something that does not legitimately apply to Christology. Further, Christology is intimately bound up with commitment to at least the ontological claim that, in Christ, God is reconciling the world to himself. So a purely functionalist Christology, where this is taken to mean a Christology without commitment to a particular metaphysical thesis about the person and work of Christ, is simply untenable. One cannot place the incarnation in parentheses in order to speak only of the functions Christ performs as a moral and religious teacher. Not only does such a method in Christology do violence to the gospel (as if one can speak *theologically* of Christ absent his being God incarnate). It also has the theological cart before the horse: Christian theology proclaims that Christ *as* God incarnate teaches us how we should live.

Christology is inherently metaphysical. But not all theologians agree on which metaphysics is appropriate to the incarnation. For instance, Christ's human nature is thought of in different ways in the tradition, and there is more than one way of making sense of Christ's human nature that is consistent with creedal orthodoxy. It is perhaps best to view Christ's human nature as fundamentally a concrete particular—that is, a human body and soul assumed by the Word at the moment of incarnation—an idea common in the patristic and medieval periods (Crisp 2007: ch. 2). But it could be argued that Christ's human nature is fundamentally a property of the Word of God, rather like a human being has the property of 'being rational'. That which is theologically non-negotiable concerns the fact that Christ is both fully human and fully divine, being of one substance with the Father. Orthodox belief requires us to say that Christ has the *same* substance (*homoousios*) as the Father, not merely a *similar* substance to the Father (*homoiousios*), just as water does not have a *similar* chemical composition to H_2O; it has the *same* chemical composition. Orthodoxy also requires us to affirm that Christ is a divine person with a human nature, not a human person with a divine nature, nor a human person and a divine person coexisting. Having said that, however, one could hold a robustly Chalcedonian Christology, affirm all the foregoing, and still be agnostic about whether or not Chalcedonian Christology is the truth of the matter: one could be a metaphysical realist and an epistemological fallibilist about the dogmatic terminology of orthodox Christology.

The distinction between Christology 'from above' and 'from below', which has to do with where one begins one's reflection on the person of Christ, is also prevalent in much contemporary discussion of the incarnation. Theology from above, that is, Christology that begins from the premiss that Christ is God incarnate and works from there outwards, is sometimes said to have been superseded since the Enlightenment by Christology from below, which begins from the premiss that

Christ is the man, Jesus, who is also said to be divine, and works from there (Pannenberg 1968: 33–7; Gunton 1983: 10–55). It is certainly true that there has been much more interest in questions pertaining to the humanity of Christ in this period, not least because of the interest shown in the putative 'Jesus of history' by historical biblical critics. But there is no reason to think it inevitable that someone who begins with a Christology 'from below' will end up with a correspondingly low Christology, where Christ is thought of as merely a man or as theologically important merely in his identifying with us as a man. Presumably, the early church began with a Christology from 'below' in this sense: the apostles thought of Christ as the Messiah when they were his disciples but only understood that Christ was God incarnate at some later date after his resurrection. But the Christology of the apostles, as we have it in the New Testament, is anything but low.

Having said that, Barth is right to begin with a Christology 'from above' which speaks of the incarnation as the event by which God reveals himself to us—for that is what is given in scripture. Thus Barth can say, 'He acts as God when he acts as a human being, and as a human being when he acts as God' (Barth 1958: 115). One does not have to agree with Barth in other respects to find this central insight convincing. The same cannot be said of the historicizing tendency in Pannenberg's early work, which speaks of Christology 'from above' as standing in the place of God himself in order to 'follow the way of God's Son in the world' (Pannenberg 1968: 35). It is difficult to see why Pannenberg thinks Christology 'from above' falls foul of this God's-eye-view objection. Once again, one could hold that in Christ God is revealing something of himself, and that our comprehension of this is fallible.

There are other sorts of terminological issues in Christology, to do with the language inherited from the early Christological debates. Discussions about 'person', 'substance', '*homoiousion*' v. '*homoousion*', 'natures' (divine and human), and so forth, seem endless. Instead of wading into the discussion here, I shall restrict myself to offering some remarks about the dogmatic content such metaphysical disputes must be cognizant of, which are intended to be indicative, not exhaustive.

III. Some Central Dogmatic Issues in the Incarnation

While every theological locus from creation to eschatology has some connection with or implication for a doctrine of the incarnation, three particular issues stand out as dogmatically central. The first issue is the identity of the one who is incarnate. This touches upon what we might call the pre-history of the incarnation. In the Prologue to the Fourth Gospel, we read:

In the beginning was the Word.... He was in the beginning with God. All things came in to being through him, and without him not one thing came into being.... And the Word became flesh and lived among us. (John 1: 1–3, 14)

If it is thought that Christ is 'the Word made flesh', then this raises a question concerning the nature of Christ's existence prior to the incarnation. The second issue has to do with the mode or manner of incarnation. Paul tells us that Christ was 'born of a woman, born under the law' (Gal. 4: 4; cf. Luke 1: 26–38). But this need not imply a virgin birth (putting to one side for the present the birth narratives of Matthew and Luke). So we might ask, 'Was Christ born of a virgin, as the creeds suggest, or is this a mythological accretion that is an irrelevance or a distraction from the central matters of the incarnation?' Thirdly, there are issues to do with the nature of the incarnation itself—in particular, although not exclusively, the personal union between Christ's two natures (cf. 1 Tim. 3: 16).

Let us consider each of these issues in turn, in the context of modern and contemporary theological discussion. The pre-history of the incarnation, particularly the idea that Christ pre-exists his incarnation, has been the subject of some discussion in contemporary theology. One of the most interesting accounts has come from the Lutheran theologian Robert Jenson. He claims that Christ's pre-existence is tied up with what we make of divine eternity. His most recent discussion of Christ's pre-existence is one of the most difficult areas of his stimulating *Systematic Theology*; while he may not be entirely successful on this count, what he does say is characteristically bold and provocative.

Jenson is clear that a doctrine of the incarnation depends upon metaphysical ideas. There are three issues in particular that he believes are critical to a right understanding of the doctrine. First, according to Jenson the Bible shows that it is Christ (i.e., Jesus of Nazareth) who pre-exists the incarnation, and not merely a divine entity who has yet to become incarnate (i.e., the second person of the Trinity). Secondly, Jenson argues that Christ is never *asarkos* (without flesh), but always *ensarkos* (enfleshed). Jenson construes this to mean that the pre-existent Christ is somehow (a part of?) the 'narrative pattern' of the history of Israel. Thirdly, Jenson speaks of the eschatological dimension to the incarnation. Christ's sonship, according to Jenson, comes 'from' his resurrection. In fact, for Jenson, all of God's life comes from the future: 'God's eternity is the infinity of a life. For what obtains in *life* always comes from a future; the difference between God and us is that he, as the Spirit, is his own future and so is *unboundedly* lively' (1997–9: i. 143).

This is difficult to make sense of, and is certainly an untraditional account of the pre-existence of Christ in several respects. Regarding Jenson's claim that Jesus of Nazareth pre-exists the incarnation, it is true that the tradition speaks of Christ pre-existing. But Christ is understood to pre-exist the incarnation according to his divine nature, not as a human being. Indeed, it is hard to see what a human pre-existence could mean. This difficulty is compounded by Jenson's insistence that Christ's *ensarkos* pre-existence means he is somehow (part of) the history of

Israel. (Christ pre-exists as Jesus of Nazareth *and* as the 'narrative pattern' of the history of Israel?) Thirdly, Jenson's comments about the futurity of Christ (and God) constituting his sonship (and, somehow, God's being), means that God is only God because of what he will be, and Christ is only the Son because of what happened at some time after his incarnation. But both of these statements sit rather awkwardly with ideas of God ordaining that his Son will become incarnate (from eternity), and God existing timelessly. But, to be fair to Jenson, part of his argument is directed against the traditional 'Hellenized' notion of divine eternity and its relation to Christ's pre-existence. Since this is an important constituent of the doctrine of the incarnation, it is worthwhile pausing to consider the central tenets of the more traditional approach to this matter.

Classical Christology affirms that the second person of the Trinity is the subject of the incarnation, the one who is incarnate (who assumes human nature), as John's Prologue makes clear. In fact, the Chalcedonian definition speaks of a 'double generation'. Christ is eternally begotten of the Father according to his divine nature, and conceived and born of a virgin according to his human nature. This makes the traditional doctrine clearer, but not entirely clear. It is still difficult to make sense of the classical theological notion that the timeless Word of God assumes a temporal human nature.

Perhaps the best we can do is say that at a particular moment in time Christ's human nature began to exist. This, of course, does not imply that there was a time at which the divine nature of Christ began to be incarnate. Strictly speaking, the divine nature of Christ is incarnate but never wholly *located* in a particular human body. This might be one application of the scholastic notion that *finitum non capax infiniti* ('the finite cannot contain the infinite').

Moreover, if God is timelessly eternal, then there can be no *time* at which the Word of God can be said to do or become anything. Some may see in such reasoning the spectre of Nestorianism, the view that Christ is composed of two persons, one divine, the other human. 'You speak of a timeless divine person that does not have any temporal relation to his human nature,' such an objector may say, 'yet, in Christ is *one theanthropic person*?' But this does not entail Nestorianism (it does not imply the presence of two *persons* in Christ), and has been the view of the vast majority of the theologians of the church, who detected no unorthodoxy in it.

Some classical theologians, like Anselm of Canterbury, argued that 'one who correctly understands the Son's incarnation believes that the Son assumed human being into the unity of his person and not into the unity of his substance'. He goes on, 'God did not assume human being in such a way that the divine and human natures are one and the same, but in such a way that the divine and human person is one and the same. And this can only be in one divine person' (Anselm 1998: 249–50). This touches on several important matters in the incarnation, including the notion that the Son personalized the human nature he assumed in the moment of incarnation, making it his own (the so-called *enhypostatos phusis*). But, for present purposes, it also illustrates that classical theologians were not unaware of the problems associated with claiming the timeless Son assumed temporal human nature. One strategy for preserving the integrity of the hypostatic union, on this model, is to side with Anselm and claim that the Son assumes his human nature into his divine person, not the divine nature, which is shared with the other persons of the Trinity. Although this strategy is not unproblematic, it does indicate how such a view can avoid Nestorianism.

Divine timelessness has fallen on hard times. Theologians like Jenson, finding the traditional metaphysics of the incarnation unpalatable (or unworkable), have opted instead to build their understanding of Christ's pre-existence from the ground up—in the teeth of classical metaphysics. His is a bold manoeuvre, but it raises several considerable problems for the matter of who it is that pre-exists the incarnation. There are problems with the classical view, too. But it, or something very like it, offers the prospect of a more satisfying approach to this Christological conundrum.

The second issue, concerning the mode or manner of the incarnation has also been subjected to various lines of criticism. Emil Brunner speaks for many when he says that the traditional dogmatic claim that Christ was born of a virgin is a legendary accretion that appears late in the New Testament (in the birth narratives of Matthew and Luke, respectively) and for which there is little textual support. 'Everything goes to prove that this doctrine arose rather late, thus that it arose for dogmatic reasons and not out of historical knowledge' (Brunner 1934: 324; cf. Pannenberg 1968: 141–50). Some feminist theologians have even gone as far as suggesting that the idea that Christ was born of a virgin somehow denigrates the birth process—as if Christ could not be sullied by the normal course of procreation. While there might be some truth to these claims, it is perfectly possible for God to have ordained a different mode of incarnation from the one he did choose. There is nothing inherently sinful in procreation, and there is no insuperable theological impediment to Christ being born of a normal physical union between Joseph the Nazarene carpenter and Mary *Theotokos* ('Godbearer'). For such a union could have yielded the human nature that the Word of God assumed, just as he did assume human nature in the 'canonical' incarnation. It might be pointed out that such a union would have yielded a fallen human being. But even if this is granted, there is no reason to think that God could not, by the interposition of the Holy Spirit, cleanse such a human nature in the Son's assumption of it. Although it is a minority report in the tradition, some theologians have defended a view not unlike this one (Shedd 2003: 633–7).

However, the creedal affirmation that Christ was born of a virgin need not be abandoned. It is within God's power to do this, and, as Anselm points out, there is a certain 'fittingness' to this mode of incarnation, even if it was not the only means available (Anselm 1998: 376). The traditional doctrine of the virginal conception and birth of Christ does not denigrate normal human procreation. Theologians in the western tradition since Augustine have tended to think that original sin is inherited or imputed from one generation to the next. Even if there was no reason why God could not have prevented Christ from inheriting original sin through normal human procreation, the fact that Christ was conceived in an abnormal manner makes clear that this person is not a sinner and is therefore in a position to act on behalf of sinners. (This also raises important issues for Christian ethics, particularly concerning human personhood, e.g., when a human embryo 'becomes' a human person. See Jones 2004.)

We turn, more briefly, to the matter of the apparently 'late' appearance of the few scattered references to the virginal conception and birth of Christ in the New Testament. Suppose that Brunner is right and the birth narratives in Matthew and Luke (the only truly unambiguous statements of the virginal conception and birth of Christ in the New Testament documents) were appended to these two Gospels after they were already in circulation. What of dogmatic import follows from this claim? Nothing whatsoever. The fact that these narratives were appended to existing documents (if indeed they were, which is hardly indubitable) does not necessarily have any bearing on their dogmatic status. The idea that the birth narratives of Matthew and Luke have the appearance of legends or miraculous stories like those associated with the conception of certain Greek gods is not especially problematic either (despite claims like those in Warner 1976). When one compares the two sorts of stories (the Gospel accounts with classical stories of miraculous births) the similarities appear rather superficial. In any case, as has already been pointed out, there are good theological reasons for thinking these stories are veridical—reasons to do with their place in the canon.

The hypostatic union, a source of some embarrassment for certain theologians in the second half of the twentieth century, remains a topic of serious theological reflection. There is still disagreement over the legacy of Chalcedon, with some theologians distancing themselves from what they perceive to be an unhelpful or misleading account of the person of Christ (Hick 1993). But there are also theologians from a broad confessional cross-section willing to defend this view with some care (O'Collins 2002; Jenson 1997–9: vol. i; Macquarrie 1990; Gunton 1997).

The hypostatic union raises a cluster of issues. We can only touch upon several of these. First, there is the issue of Christological perichoresis, advocated amongst others by the sublime John of Damascus in *On the Orthodox Faith* (Schaff 1980: ix. 1b–101b). This is the idea that the divine nature of Christ somehow penetrates his human nature, but not conversely, and without compromising the integrity of either of the natures in Christ's theanthropic person. This is a difficult doctrine, and has remained largely, but not entirely, undeveloped in dogmatic theology since the Damascene's synthetic work.

A related but distinct notion has to do with the communication of attributes between Christ's two natures (*communicatio idiomatum*). In post-Reformation theology this was a matter of dispute between the Reformed and the Lutherans. Whereas the Lutherans affirmed that Christ's human nature shared the ubiquity of his divine nature, the Reformed rejected this strong account for something much weaker: there is no real exchange of properties between the natures, but something more like the imputation of some of the properties of one nature to the other, in the theanthropic person of Christ. In this vein Huldrych Zwingli spoke of a Christological application for *alloeosis*, a linguistic device by means of which we can speak of the person of Christ as having done a thing, when we really mean that he had done a thing according to his human or his divine nature, respectively (Stephens 1986: 112–17).

The problem the Reformed detected in the Lutheran account is that if Christ's human nature is everywhere present then every physical object is somehow interpenetrated by Christ's human nature. This does appear to be a consequence of some construals of the Lutheran doctrine (specifically, the *genus maiestaticum*). But one could argue that Christ's human body has the property of being capable of location at more than one place simultaneously. This would be sufficient for the eucharistic purposes of Lutheranism since the body of Christ could be simultaneously present 'in, with, and under' the elements in many different places, without being everywhere present. But it still begs the question about the physical integrity of Christ's body. It certainly seems very strange to think a human body can be located in more than one place *simultaneously* (Holmes 2005; Pieper 1951).

In the nineteenth and early twentieth centuries there was a group of largely German and (latterly) English theologians who took the hypostatic union seriously, but who felt that it was not possible for the Word of God to be contracted to the span of a human being. They took their point of departure in the great Christ-hymn of Philippians 2, where Christ is said to have 'emptied himself [*ekenōsen*]' in order to take 'the form of a slave . . . in human likeness' (Phil. 2: 7). For these *kenotic* Christologies the incarnation could only take place if the Word of God either withheld exercising certain divine prerogatives during his incarnation, or temporarily relinquished them. The scope of this divine 'withholding' or 'forgetting' was disputed. Some kenoticists insisted that only certain divine attributes were affected (omnipotence and omniscience being most popular), whilst others, like Wolfgang Gess (1856), thought that in becoming incarnate the Word of God abdicated almost all his divine prerequisites.

Kenotic Christology was in suspended animation in the mid-twentieth century (Macquarrie 1990: 250). But it has been resuscitated. Today there is a small but robust literature in contemporary Anglo-American (largely philosophical) theology defending modest versions of the doctrine, where Christ is said either to abdicate only those divine attributes thought to be incompatible with being human (e.g., omniscience), or to withhold the exercise of these attributes (Davis 1983; Evans 2002, 2006; Plantinga and Feenstra 1989; Brown 1985). The strong version of the doctrine as found in Gess has disappeared. Alongside this philosophical-theological interest in the doctrine has been a theological interest in the implications of the concept of kenosis for other areas of theology, for example, the doctrine of creation (Polkinghorne 2001). It seems that there are still Christian thinkers who believe it is important to hold on to a robust doctrine of the incarnation, but who also maintain that classical Christology is in tension with the divine attributes (traditionally construed) and think kenotic Christology offers the best way of reconciling these apparently competing theological commitments.

In defence of Chalcedonian Christology, however, it should be pointed out that the incarnation is not a matter of *relinquishing* certain divine attributes, but of taking on a human nature *in addition* to the divine nature the Word of God already possesses. Thus the English Puritan theologian John Owen can say,

> This Word was made flesh, not by any change of his own nature or essence, not by a transubstantiation of the divine nature into the human, not by ceasing to be what he was, but by becoming what he was not, in taking our nature to his own, to be his own, whereby he dwelt among us. (Owen 1965: 46)

Seen in this light, classical Christology may have more to commend itself than contemporary kenoticists think.

IV. An Alternative to Incarnation

There are other approaches to the incarnation we have not touched upon that have been the subject of theological reflection in the modern period. The most important of these has been non-incarnational Christology. This sort of Christology, once common amongst liberal theologians, has a contemporary defender in John Hick, whose theology will serve as a paradigm of this approach (Hick 1993).

Incarnational Christology is clearly a stumbling block to the sort of religious 'pluralism' Hick envisages: roughly, the idea that many of the world's religions, but not all, offer a path to salvation. Much of the impetus for Hick's Christology must be seen in this light. His attempt to detach Christology from the language of incarnation is nothing less than the remaking of Christian doctrine on the procrustean bed of his pluralist hypothesis. So, Hick emphasizes the 'inspiration Christology' of others before him. (Although it should be noted that 'inspiration Christology' is not a synonym for non-incarnational Christology. These two issues are distinct.) According to Hick, Christ is inspired by the Holy Spirit in a remarkable fashion, in a way similar to other great religious teachers, e.g., Gautama Buddha, Muhammad, or Moses. His heightened spiritual state gives him clarity of moral insight and religious authority that less 'inspired' humans cannot emulate. But Christ's awareness of the presence of

God is only different in *degree*, not in *kind*, from our own. (We might, to borrow a phrase from Schleiermacher—one of Hick's theological forebears in some respects—speak of Christ's 'God consciousness' or sense of 'absolute dependence' on God, in this regard.) There is, according to Hick, no qualitative difference between Christ's experience of, and communion with, God, and ours. Christ has just achieved a certain intimacy with the divine that most human beings lack, even though they are capable of it.

Seen in this light, Christ is a moral example to follow and a great religious teacher whose sayings (such as we have) may form the basis of a moral life worth living. Theologians in the incarnational tradition of Christology will have no objection to speaking of Christ as a great moral example or religious teacher. However, Hick and other non-incarnationalists refuse to allow more to be said. Hick's Christ is *fully* but *merely* a man; and when set alongside classical doctrine, this can only yield a very meagre Christology. Although the pluralist presuppositions driving Hick's adoption of a non-incarnational Christology are commendable—particularly his irenic desire to forge a theology of religions, not of a particular religion—his specific, doctrinal conclusions cannot be taken seriously as *Christian* dogmatic theology. For the Christ of non-incarnational Christology cannot save anyone; he can only show how salvation may be attained, which is quite another matter. It is the difference between a lifeguard able to save the drowning man, and a non-swimmer who can only throw the drowning man a buoyancy aid so that he can save himself. The same could be said for other theologians in the last two centuries who have reached similar conclusions about the incarnation—although often for different reasons. Non-incarnational Christology is, as far as Christian dogmatics goes, a theological cul-de-sac.

References

Anselm of Canterbury (1998). *The Major Works*. Oxford: Oxford University Press.

Aquinas, St Thomas (1975). *Summa Contra Gentiles. Book Four: Salvation*. Notre Dame: University of Notre Dame Press.

Baillie, D. M. (1961). *God Was in Christ: An Essay on Incarnation and Atonement*. London: Faber & Faber.

Barth, Karl (1958). *Church Dogmatics* IV/2. Edinburgh: T. & T. Clark.

—— (1975). *Church Dogmatics* I/1. Edinburgh: T. & T. Clark.

Brown, David (1985). *The Divine Trinity*. London: Duckworth.

Brunner, Emil (1934). *The Mediator: A Study of The Central Doctrine of The Christian Faith*. London: Lutterworth.

Coakley, Sarah (2002). 'What Does Chalcedon Solve and What Does it Not? Some Reflection on the Status and Meaning of the Chalcedonian "Definition"'. In Davis, Kendall, and O'Collins (2002).

Crisp, Oliver D. (2007). *Divinity and Humanity: The Incarnation Reconsidered*. Cambridge: Cambridge University Press.

Cross, Richard (2002). *The Metaphysics of The Incarnation*. Oxford: Oxford University Press.

Davis, Stephen T. (1983). *Logic and the Nature of God*. London: Macmillan.

Davis, Stephen T., Kendall, Daniel, and O'Collins, Gerald (eds.) (2002). *The Incarnation: An Interdisciplinary Symposium on the Incarnation of the Son of God*. Oxford: Oxford University Press.

Evans, C. Stephen (2002). 'The Self-Emptying of Love: Some Thoughts on Kerotic Christology'. In Davis, Kendall, and O'Collins (2002).

Evans, C. Stephen (ed.) (2006). *Exploring Kenotic Christology: The Self-Emptying of God*. Oxford: Oxford University Press.

Gess, Wolfgang Freidrich (1856). *Die Lehre von der Person Christi, entwickelt aus dem Selbstbewusstsein Christi und aus dem Zeugniss der Apostel*. Basel: Bahnmaiers Buchhandlung.

Grillmeier, Aloys, SJ (1965). *Christ in Christian Tradition*, i. *From the Apostolic Age to Chalcedon (A.D. 451)*. London: Mowbrays.

Gunton, Colin E. (1997). *Yesterday and Today: A Study of Continuities in Christology*. 2nd edn. London: SPCK.

Hick, John (1993). *The Metaphor of God Incarnate*. London: SCM.

Hick, John (ed.) (1977). *The Myth of God Incarnate*. London: SCM.

Holmes, Stephen R. (2005). 'Some Reformed Varieties of the *Communicatio Idiomatum*'. In Murray Rae and Stephen R. Holmes (eds.), *The Person of Christ*, London: Continuum.

Jenson, Robert W. (1997–9). *Systematic Theology*. 2 vols. New York: Oxford University Press.

Jones, David Albert (2004). *The Soul of the Embryo: An Enquiry into the Status of the Human Embryo in the Christian Tradition*. London: Continuum.

Kelly, J. N. D. (1977). *Early Christian Doctrines*. London: Adam and Charles Black.

Leftow, Brian (2002). 'A Timeless God Incarnate'. In Davis, Kendall, and O'Collins (2002).

Lessing, Gotthold Ephraim (1957). 'On the Proof of the Spirit and of Power'. In Henry Chadwick (ed.), *Lessing's Theological Writings*. Stanford: Stanford University Press.

Macquarrie, John (1990). *Jesus Christ in Modern Thought*. London: SCM.

Meyendorff, John (1975). *Christ in Eastern Christian Thought*. Crestwood: St Vladimir's.

Morris, Thomas V. (1986). *The Logic of God Incarnate*. Ithaca: Cornell University Press.

O'Collins, Gerald (2002). *Incarnation*. London: Continuum.

Owen, John (1965 [1680]). *Christologia; or, A Declaration of the Glorious Mystery of the Person of Christ*. In *The Works of John Owen*. Edinburgh: Banner of Truth, vol. i.

Pannenberg, Wolfhart (1968). *Jesus—God and Man*. London: SCM.

Pieper, Francis (1951). *Christian Dogmatics*, ii. St Louis: Concordia Publishing House.

Plantinga, Cornelius, Jr. and Feenstra, Ronald J. (eds.) (1989). *Trinity, Incarnation, and Atonement: Philosophical and Theological Essays*. Notre Dame: University of Notre Dame Press.

Polkinghorne, John (ed.) (2001). *The Work of Love: Creation as Kenosis*. Grand Rapids: Eerdmans.

Schaff, Philip (ed.) (1980). *A Select Library of the Nicene and Post-Nicene Fathers of the Christian Church*. 2nd ser. Edinburgh: T. & T. Clark.

Shedd, W. G. T. (2003). *Dogmatic Theology*. Phillipsberg: Presbyterian and Reformed.

STEPHENS W. P. (1986). *The Theology of Huldrych Zwingli.* Oxford: Oxford University Press.

SWINBURNE, RICHARD (1994). *The Christian God.* Oxford: Oxford University Press.

TANNER, KATHRYN (1997). 'Jesus Christ'. In Colin E. Gunton (ed.), *The Cambridge Companion to Christian Doctrine*, Cambridge: Cambridge University Press.

WARNER, MARINA (1976). *Alone of All Her Sex: The Myth and Cult of The Virgin Mary.* London: Picador/Pan.

WEBER, OTTO (1983). *Foundations of Dogmatics*, ii. Grand Rapids: Eerdmans.

WEBSTER, JOHN (2001). *Word and Church: Essays in Christian Dogmatics.* Edinburgh: T. & T. Clark.

WILES, MAURICE (1974). *The Remaking of Christian Doctrine.* London: SCM.

WRIGHT, N. T. (1996). *Jesus and the Victory of God.* London: SPCK.

SUGGESTED READING

CALVIN, JOHN (1960). *Institutes of The Christian Religion.* Philadelphia: Westminster, 464–93.

Cyril of Alexandria (2000). *On the Unity of Christ.* Crestwood: St Vladimir's.

DAVIS, KENDALL, and O'COLLINS (2002).

KASPER, WALTER (1976). *Jesus the Christ.* London: Burns & Oates.

MACLEOD, DONALD (1998). *The Person of Christ.* Leicester: InterVarsity.

MCGRATH, ALISTER E. (1986). *The Making of Modern German Christology.* Oxford: Blackwell.

MOLTMANN, JÜRGEN (1990). *The Way of Jesus Christ.* London: SCM.

O'COLLINS (2002).

PANNENBERG (1968).

RAE, MURRAY, and HOLMES, STEPHEN R. (eds.) (2005). *The Person of Christ.* London: Continuum.

CHAPTER 10

SALVATION

PAUL S. FIDDES

I. Salvation and Atonement

'Salvation' is a concept of the widest scope, which is universally comprehensible. It assumes that the life of human beings and that of the wider natural world is distorted, self-destructive, or failing to reach its true potential. Against this background, 'salvation' denotes the healing or making whole of individuals and social groups, and the conserving of a natural environment which is ravaged and polluted by human greed.

A Christian account of salvation is distinctive in several ways. In the first place, the salvation of humankind is understood as a progressive transformation into a more perfect image of God, a process which is rooted in certain decisive events in the past, which continues in the present, and which will come to fulfilment in the future, in a new creation. Salvation in the New Testament thus appears as a happening in three tenses: we 'have been saved', we are 'being saved', and we 'shall be saved'. The goal of salvation is 'divinization' (*theōsis*), a concept which in the past has been more familiar in eastern than western theology (Lossky 1974: 103–10; Staniloae 2000: 191–200), but which is increasingly taking a central place in all modern systematic theology. It is no longer true, if it ever was, that western theology is only interested in a forensic view of salvation, or the acquittal of human beings in a divine law court. *Theōsis* is not, of course, a 'becoming God', but being made into the 'likeness' of God, which means being drawn much more deeply into the relationships in which God exists as a Trinity of love. As Hans Urs von Balthasar puts it, salvation is a 'coming closer to God' or an 'ever intensifying relationship' (Balthasar 1994: 373–83).

The idea of transformation does not just involve the individual, but always places the person in relationship. David Ford aptly speaks of salvation as a 'flourishing' of life, and (drawing on the thought of Emmanuel Levinas) insists that such an abundant life happens 'before the face of the other', in joyfully responding to the ethical demands made upon the self by others (Ford 1999: 4–10, 37–44). Eschatology, as a concept of future salvation, and ecclesiology, as a concept of a transformed human community, thus belong together in the New Testament. A new people is being formed for a new creation. Hope for this new creation can only be announced in symbol and metaphor because it escapes the categories of the old creation in which we live; but expectation of future salvation has a creative effect here and now, making us discontent with the status quo and challenging oppressive structures of human power (Moltmann 1979: 55–7). A doctrine of salvation cannot therefore be separated from political engagement.

Another distinctive note in the Christian understanding of salvation is its diagnosis of the nature of the predicament in which human beings find themselves. Salvation is both 'from' and 'to' something: it is *to* divinization, and *from* sin. Theology has often borrowed from contemporary culture in describing the situation of disorder which runs deeply in human life. An important category here is alienation or estrangement, which appears in both existentialist and Marxist analyses of human life. Human beings are perceived as being alienated from themselves and the world, either because they are caught in the tensions of existence (and especially the tension between freedom and limitations), or because they have been estranged from the objects of their labour through the class struggle (Lash 1981: 169–86). Another category which appears in late modern thinking is that of fragmentation, both of personality and of social relations. This is traced to the attempts of the human self, with its rational consciousness, to control the world rather than recognizing and respecting the 'otherness' of people and nature. The Christian understanding of salvation insists, however, on the religious concept of 'sin' which is woven through this phenomenological analysis, and which points to a breach between the creator and the created.

In the face of the tensions of life, existential and social, we have become anxious and failed to trust in God (Macquarrie 1977: 71–3). We have 'turned away from the infinite ground of our being' (Tillich 1957: 51–6); instead of opening ourselves to the gift of grace which is offered in the midst of the tensions, we have tried to create our own solutions by making some object or person within the world our absolute security. Here Reinhold Niebuhr draws attention to the ancient lure of idolatry, in which a person 'lifts some finite element of existence into the eminence of the divine', using it as 'the ultimate principle of coherence and meaning' (Niebuhr 1941: 176–98). So we make idols for ourselves and place our trust in them. A career, money, a work of art, an organization, or an ideology becomes our 'ultimate concern', and then because we must have it, begins to become 'demonic' in the sense of dominating us (Macquarrie 1977: 260–3). Sin thus takes both an individual and a structural, social form, and ancient images of salvation as victory over hostile powers take on a modern significance.

In this context of the human predicament, perhaps the most distinctive feature of the Christian understanding of salvation is 'atonement'. If 'salvation' is the widest possible concept, reaching into the desirable future, 'atonement' offers a focus of particularity. The idea of 'atonement' insists that salvation depends upon the restoring of relationships between human beings and God, who are estranged from each other. The English word 'at-one-ment' spells out a 'making at one', and in his early English version of the New Testament (1526), William Tyndale was the first to apply it to the Greek word meaning 'reconciliation' (*katallagē*). In succeeding translations the word 'atonement' was widely used for the Hebrew word in the Old Testament which expresses the reconciling effect of sacrifice (*kipper*). Thus the term can designate one particular model of salvation—sacrifice, with associated ideas of purification and expiation of sins—but it also implies, beyond this narrow semantic field, that the divine–human relationship can be repaired only through a specific act or event. In ancient Israel the critical act was the ritual of sacrifice, and for Christian believers atonement happens because of the death of Jesus in a Roman execution one Friday afternoon.

The Christian view of salvation thus moves, in what may seem a scandalous manner, away from general truths about the nature of existence to a very particular moment within it. Salvation, or the healing of life, issues from atonement, and this in turn has its basis in the crucifixion of Christ. All roads lead, not to Rome, but to a mound of earth outside the walls of a Middle Eastern town in a remote corner of the Roman Empire. For some theologians, that particular event simply expresses and reveals in the clearest possible way the self-giving, reconciling love of God which is always available (Tillich 1957: 174–82). However, many—perhaps most—modern theologians find that atonement *depends* in some way upon that moment (Jenson 1997–9: i. 185–9). While affirming a continuous salvific activity of God, they see the cross as not only a disclosure of the process, but as a point which is somehow decisive for salvation, and from which all else stems. Both views, we notice, give a particular significance to the event of the cross of Jesus, and neither of them locks atonement into one place in time and space, sealing it into the past. But it is the second approach, based on a link between a decisive past event and the experience of salvation in the present, that is being explored in this chapter.

If salvation is a continuous process then it happens here and now. It is in the present that God acts to heal and reconcile, entering at great cost into the disruption of human lives, in order to share our predicament and release us from it. Among the reasons we may advance for this perception is the nature of salvation as the healing of broken relationships. Relationships must be re-created through a personal encounter in which those who have broken them are actively involved; we cannot simply pick up the benefits of a transaction that has been completed in the past. A vivid example of this dynamic is the act of forgiveness, which cannot be content simply with the issuing of a legal pardon but which aims at reconciliation, personally painful though this might be. Another reason is the unity between creation and salvation; in the Jewish and Christian vision of creation there is a continual transforming and renewing of what is made by God (Daly 1988: 30–3), as expressed for instance in the Old Testament image of the overcoming of the chaos and wilderness elements of the world. Finally, the belief that God suffers with created beings, always entering with sympathy into situations of pain or desolation, supports the idea that salvation is a present reality.

At this point we need to refer to the technical theological terms 'subjective' and 'objective'. First, an interpretation of atonement may be said to be 'subjective' when it describes salvation as a process in present human experience. It is 'objective' when it locates salvation in a past event, outside our experience and feelings. Obviously then, no theory of atonement can be entirely subjective or objective, but there will be a shifting balance between the two elements in different understandings of atonement.

A second set of 'subjective' and 'objective' elements is often simply, and misleadingly, equated with the balance between past event and present process. This is the polarity of act and response. If the first contrast between objective and subjective puts the past and the present in tension, the second relates the divine and the human. Objectively, salvation is an act of God; since human beings are trapped in a predicament from which they cannot extricate themselves, God must take the initiative in providing a release. Subjectively, salvation must include the human response, for as we have seen, it needs two to make a meeting. We must take care, however, not simply to identify the past event of salvation with the *divine* act, and the present process with the *human* response. The God who has acted in the past event of the cross goes on acting in the process of salvation, taking the initiative in entering the lives of human beings and luring them into response. On the other hand, at the heart of the past event is the human response of Jesus, in open obedience to God his Father, fulfilling human destiny where other human beings have failed.

The movement between action and response leads us to a third, and even more profound polarity between objectivity and subjectivity in salvation. Traditional, strongly 'objective' doctrines of atonement have proposed some kind of change in God resulting from the atoning work of Christ. More 'subjective' accounts have laid the stress upon the power of the cross to produce a change in human attitudes and emotions. While theories that tip the balance towards objectivity stress that there is no reluctance on God's part to forgive and accept, they suggest that something in God requires to be satisfied before forgiving love can be put into effect: Anselm proposes this to be God's honour (*Cur Deus Homo* 1. 10–14, in Anselm 1998: 279–88) and Calvin maintains it is also God's law (*Institutes* 2. 16. 2–5, in Calvin 1960: 504–10). Because human beings are guilty sinners, it is presumed that a debt has to be paid to justice before they can be forgiven. Highly 'objective' views of atonement, and notably 'penal substitution', have thus conceived of a change in God in the sense that a righteous wrath is satisfied through some kind of propitiating act. More 'subjective' views of atonement insist that the only problem lies in human hearts and minds, where attitudes of pride, fear, and anxiety create blockages between God and humankind. While God is always willing to accept created persons, the problem is how to remove the hindrances to acceptance in *them,* and how to persuade people to respond to God's offer of forgiveness.

In a later section it will be argued that any view of a barrier of justice in God's nature is misconceived, though it points to important aspects of justice in the human and divine situation. However, the notion that God is changed by events in the world ought not to be quickly dismissed as 'too objective'. Some theologians, of course, deny that worldly events or human actions, including the death of Christ, can have any causative impact on God at all (Rahner 1978: 211, 255). They suppose that to affirm God as 'pure act' rules out any passivity or unfulfilled potentiality. Others think that God, in divine freedom, is open to being affected and conditioned by the world (Barth 1957: 303), and so can have 'new experiences' during the course of human history. Those who think in this way are themselves divided as to whether this effect on God should be called 'change'. Some urge that change is coherent with the idea of divine suffering, since suffering love is always a movement from one state of being to another, although there is no question of a change in the *character* of God (Williams 1968: 117; Fiddes 1988: 49–56). Others maintain that if God is open 'in advance' to receiving the impact of human sinning then there is no question of change in the strict sense; God is, as it were, immutably ready to receive new experiences, even the experience of estrangement and desolation (Balthasar 1990: ix). In either case, if God can be affected by the kind of response created beings make to God's love, we begin to see how one particular moment could be more intense and critical than others. If God did enter into the human predicament in a decisive way in the cross of Jesus then there would have been an exposure to something 'new' in the divine experience of the world and even of God's own self, a factor that is rightly called 'objective'.

II. Models of Atonement

We must admit that no understanding of the atoning work of Christ is going to integrate subjective and objective dimensions in a completely satisfying way. Theories of atonement are, after all, conceptual tools with which we try to grasp a mystery in the divine–human relationship. The Christian church has never made a single theory definitive for the meaning of atonement, and has rather relied upon a series of metaphors for understanding the work of Christ, derived from different social contexts. 'Sacrifice', associated with expiation and cleansing through blood, stems from the temple cult. 'Redemption' derives initially from the buying of freedom for slaves, but in biblical usage recalls God's rescuing of Israel from the particular slavery of Egypt, and so is associated with victory and liberation. 'Justification' refers to acts of justice in the law court, putting the accused person in the right. The 'kindling' of love in the human heart by a demonstration of divine love, an image popularized by Abelard (*Commentary on the Epistle to the Romans*, in Fairweather 1956: 283), has its setting in social relations, and especially in the intimate context of the family. Colin Gunton has rightly pointed out that a metaphor 'opens windows on reality' in a way that mere rational argument cannot. All our knowledge of the world, let alone our awareness of God's activity in the world, is bound to be indirect, mediated through signs of one sort or another, and so metaphor as indirect speech is a highly appropriate way of making reference to it (Gunton 1988: 40–7).

Now, these models of atonement have tended to shift from an objective to a more subjective colouring in recent years. Earlier theories of atonement—with the partial exception of Abelard's picture of persuasive love—tended to begin at the objective end of the spectrum with some kind of transaction, and then to add a subjective appendix. Modern ideas have tipped the balance the other way; they tend to begin at the subjective end with the present human response to God, and then to affirm an objective 'focus' for response (Macquarrie 1977: 300–3, 324–7). In our culture, the insights of the human sciences into the nature of relationships and personality are bound to exert some influence here; we will understand reconciliation by analogy with the process of healing rather than by analogy with a legal or commercial transaction (Dillistone 1968: 349–52). Using traditional terms, this might be called 'subjective', but such an approach works hard at understanding the 'objective focus' of God's activity, both in past and present events. Essentially this means understanding the cross of Jesus as an event which has a unique degree of power to evoke and create human response to the forgiving love of God.

An objectivity like this takes history seriously, in all its contingency. The relation between history and faith, between the 'Jesus of history' and the Christ of the kerygmatic proclamation, has been much debated during the past two centuries of Christian theology. There has been a growing acceptance that if we affirm that God has acted in human history, then investigation of the life and death of Jesus using the tools of historical method will have at least *some* relevance for the convictions of faith (Pannenberg 1991–8: i. 230–4, 250–7; Dunn 1980: 24–33). Even if there is no exact correspondence between the results of historical research and the Christ confessed by the Christian community, there will be coherence. History, while not validating or creating faith, can shape its *content*. This is especially evident with doctrines of atonement, where history can set some parameters for interpretation.

Liberation theologians, for example, have protested against the development of models for atonement which have ignored the historical evidence that Jesus was executed by Roman imperial authorities as a political disturber, and as a threat to what the human powers of the time considered to be orderly rule. Taking this historical situation seriously means that models of atonement must be relevant for the situation of those who are victims of social, political, and economic oppression in the present day (Boff 1980: 105–13, 288–93; Sobrino 1978: 201–17). A saving God must be seen to be active, then and now, on behalf of the poor and oppressed. Again, while recent research has undermined the view of an absolute conflict between Jesus and the Jewish religious authorities of his day (Sanders 1985: 274–81), it has rendered probable that Jesus was creating a new climate of understanding about the way that God deals with human beings, outside strict demands of law. A historical picture of Jesus as offering entrance to God's kingdom to the outcasts and marginalized in society will shape models of atonement in which the controlling aspect is acceptance and forgiveness, and where it seems inappropriate for a transaction to be based on the satisfaction of a remorseless divine law.

If we give significance to the contingencies of history in shaping models and metaphors of atonement, we are bound to consider the historical status of the resurrection of Jesus. The particularity of salvation, in the Christian view, centres not only on the death of Jesus but also on his life and resurrection. The resurrection is a sign of divine vindication of the whole ministry of Jesus, showing that Jesus was right in his view of how God deals with human beings, offering salvation freely and generously (Pannenberg 1968: 67). It also the sign that sin and death have been overcome through the exposure of Jesus to death: God has taken these enemies to human existence up into the divine life and absorbed them by love (Jüngel 1983: 218–20). It is, finally, the promise of the future renewal of the whole of creation: the transformation of the person of Jesus is a foretaste and assurance that all created beings will be raised to a new level of life. The symbol of 'resurrection of the body' points to the transforming of the whole of the human person, in which every aspect—body, mind, personality—will be taken up into new life in relation with others. This is a hope for corporate and not just individual salvation, in a 'new commonwealth of free responsible beings united in love' which is indicated by the phrase 'body of Christ' (Macquarrie 1977: 360).

Christian theologians generally accept that, since the resurrection of Jesus is an event belonging to the promised new creation, it cannot be *verified* by the tools of historical investigation which are part of the present created order. However, many theologians affirm that the resurrection of Jesus is nevertheless an event 'in history', and can only be interpreted in the context of traditions of belief about resurrection and divine judgement which *can* be explored by historical method (Pannenberg 1968: 88–105). To insist that the resurrection happened 'in history' is paradoxical, but keeps alive the challenge which God's new order always offers to present reality. The 'objective focus' for subjective human response to salvation is thus the coupling of cross and resurrection. As the apostle Paul puts it, salvation is the experience of dying and rising with Christ (Rom. 6: 1–4).

III. The Final Sacrifice

Sacrifice was probably the first image by which the Christian community interpreted its experience of salvation. The death of Christ was understood to be 'the final sacrifice', and the resurrection to be the means by which the benefits of this sacrifice were disseminated to all. The affirmation in the earliest preaching that the death of Christ was 'for us' (*huper hēmōn*) was understood, in the light of the temple cult of Judaism, as an expiation of sins 'for us' (*peri hēmōn*) (Hengel 1981: 50–1). Theologians who think that the image of sacrifice is still a relevant one in our day urge this association with worship, as a Christian practice which is prior to the creation both of stories about the acts of God and of doctrinal concepts (Sykes 1991: 281–8). Salvation happens in the orientation of the self to God in worship, and the image of sacrifice expresses this well.

This modern perception depends upon a priority being given to the idea of sacrifice as a 'sacrifice of praise and thanksgiving'. This echoes the dimension of gift-offering, and perhaps also communion-offering, within the ancient Israelite ritual of sacrifice, which made it possible to spiritualize sacrifice as a matter of inner intentions, as a 'broken and a contrite heart' (Ps. 51). Already seen as necessary to the efficacy of the external act of sacrifice by the prophets of ancient Israel, this spiritualization became essential to Rabbinic Judaism after the loss of the temple in AD 70. In continuity with Judaism, the spiritual sacrifice, or gift-offering of the Christian believer, can thus be envisaged as being made in response to the self-giving of Christ. A subjective sacrifice in us is created by the objective focus of the death of Christ (Young 1975: 111–15, 136–8).

The same link between the subjective and the objective can be extended to the dimension of sin-offering within sacrifice, which became prominent in Israel in the period following the exile. Most Old Testament scholars are agreed that the sin-offering in ancient Israelite religion was not understood as propitiatory, an act satisfying the anger of God, but as expiatory, an act which God provides to 'cover' (*kipper*) or cleanse away sin. While there is no proper theory in the Hebrew Bible as to how sacrifice was thought to remove sin and guilt from the community, there is a hint in Leviticus 17: 11 ('the life of the animal is in the blood; I give it for you') that God was believed to purify people from uncleanness by the pouring out of fresh life to replace tainted life. It is true that a propitiatory element seems to have entered

Israelite religion in the inter-testamental period, particularly in reference to the sacrificial death of the martyrs, but New Testament references to the death of Christ as a sacrifice can be best understood as expiatory, which makes sense of the pervasive imagery of cleansing in the Letter to the Hebrews. The cultic term *hilastērion* as applied to the cross of Christ in Romans 3: 25—which Paul uses alongside metaphors of redemption and justification—is thus to be translated neutrally as 'place of atonement' (Fee 2004: 58); the *meaning* of atonement must be supplied from the wider perspective of Paul's thought, which suggests that God is always to be envisaged as the subject of the atoning act and not the object, which is sin (Dunn 1991: 48–52).

From this perspective the death of Christ may be symbolized as a sin-offering as much as a gift-offering; those who trust in Christ make their self-offering in response to the self-giving of Christ, which is a sacrifice in every sense. It may be seen as an expiatory sin-offering in the sense that a change of attitude towards God in human persons *is* a wiping out of sin. Sin cannot be some kind of independent entity, but is always the orientation and acts of sinners. If the death of Christ has the power to enable the response of worship and trust in God in those who see it, then it is the means of expiating sin and creating fresh life (Fiddes 1989: 75–82).

This perception has relevance for the ongoing discussion as to whether the death of Christ is 'substitutionary' as well as 'representative'. Some thinkers have linked substitution, or what early theologians called a 'wonderful exchange' (*admirabile commercium*), with the propitiation of a wrathful God, and so have discarded it in favour of representation. In representation, the representative acts on behalf of others with whom he or she stands in solidarity, and so 'holds a place open' for them (Kasper 1976: 222; Sölle 1967: 107–12, 130–6). The image of sacrifice, however, has the potential to cut across the two categories. As sacrificial victim, Christ dies as a substitute in so far as other human beings do not need to die as he died, in total alienation, and because 'he does for us what we cannot do for ourselves' (Gunton 1988: 165). Substitution does not have to be associated with propitiation, or what has come to be called 'penal substitution'. The 'exchange' is essentially not a transfer of penalty, but the assuming of human life by God so that human beings can share the divine life. At the same time, this is what Hans Urs von Balthasar calls 'inclusive substitution', a representative function in which the substitute draws others into his own attitude (Balthasar 1994: 350–1).

In recent thought, however, there has been objection to the use of the image of sacrifice for atonement, arising especially from the quarters of both gender studies and social studies. Feminist theologians have protested that concentration on sacrifice has imposed a self-denying role of victim on women, who have generally been expected to be the sacrificers in family and society. Mary Grey, for example, asks the provocative question, 'can women actually be redeemed?' meaning that redemption as usually understood means a step of dying with Christ, and yet women have *always* been expected to be impaled on the cross (Grey 1989: 11). To be redeemed they need to move beyond the victim role and not further into it. Grey thus wishes to replace the images of sacrifice and death with a new image of redemptive suffering, that of *birthing*. This is the kind of pain that leads to change for all, to altered relationships because of the new life produced. No relations are the same again after the birth of a child. In birthing there is a letting go of self, a sense of being torn apart, and yet also a new connectedness. She urges that we need to move away from patriarchal notions of expiation through death to female ideas of new integration through a falling apart (Grey 1989: 142–52).

On the other hand, objection to the association of the death of Christ with sacrifice has been increased by the social theory of René Girard. Girard detects a 'myth of sacred violence', in which the conflict between the desires of those who make up any society is resolved through making a sacrifice. A 'scapegoat' will be identified, an individual or a group of people who will be blamed for failure to achieve what is desired; killing or at least hating the scapegoat will release tensions in society, and this sacrifice will become ritualized in a religion (Girard 1988: 95–103). Girard argues that the death of Jesus cannot be regarded objectively as a sacrifice like this, since the story is told uniquely from the viewpoint of the victim rather than those who hold power, and so exposes the myth for what it is. It is when we hear the story and identify ourselves as the persecutors that we find liberation from the cycle of violence that scapegoats others (Girard 1986: 100–24; Schwager 2000: 225–6).

While in ancient Israelite religion the ritual of the scapegoat was not strictly a sacrifice, like sacrifice it seems to have been viewed as a means of excluding sin from the community. If sin could not be cleansed away (atoned), it could be expelled into the wilderness on the back of the goat (Lev. 16). There was obviously a danger that such rituals could be transferred to the collective persecution and exclusion of human beings. Violence, argues Miroslav Volf, is fed by the images of substitution and sacrifice, which need to be replaced by those of compassion and inclusion (Volf 1996). On these grounds, argue some theologians, the image of sacrifice should either be scrapped (Käsemann 1970: 114) or recognized to be unnecessary (Dalferth 1991: 302). Other theologians argue for the retention and significance of the image of sacrifice, but separated from ideas of propitiation through a victim (O'Collins 2004: 10–13; Sykes 1997: 18; Goldingay 1995: 6–7; Schwager 2000: 199–206).

Despite thoughtful protests, the image of sacrifice seems to be deeply rooted in human consciousness, and indispensable for understanding salvation. But we must take care that it really does lead to the new relations and 'connectedness' for which Mary Grey argues with her image of 'birthing'. Here forgiveness is a significant controlling idea; if this is the context for sacrifice, then sacrifice is the costly entering of another's experience to wipe out or expiate blockages to relationship. Indeed, forgiveness is a kind of birth, a journey from the womb of self-enclosure into the daylight of mutual awareness (Fiddes 1989: 173–5).

IV. Justice and Victory

In attempting to express the belief that Christ has died and risen again 'for us and for our salvation', Christian thinkers have drawn not only on the language of the cult but of the law court. Paul employs the language of 'justification'—of being 'put in right relation' to God and the human community. Images of justice are rooted deeply in the history that surrounds the story of Jesus: somehow, because Jesus was condemned as a criminal in a human trial—both Jewish and Roman—human beings have been declared innocent in God's sight. But in that 'somehow', there is vast room for mystery and misunderstanding.

Recent theology has emphasized that no direct equation can be made between the human condemnation of Jesus and his standing before God. As we have seen, the belief that God raised Jesus from the dead was a belief that God had declared Jesus to be innocent, not guilty, in his conflict with the institutions of law. In this light, the language of 'justification' overturns the system and logic of legalism. Belonging to the ethos of a Hebrew law court, 'justification' signifies the receiving of an accused person back into the community bound together by covenant, and the giving of justice to the righteous poor. There is an extraordinary act of God celebrated in this image, since it is the guilty and the unrighteous who are declared to be justified, due to the death of Christ. Legal language is being employed to deconstruct law. Justification is thus, as Paul Tillich suggests, equivalent to 'acceptance' (Tillich 1962: 160–1).

The image of justification in itself, then, does not describe a mechanism of atonement, such as a transfer of penalty. However, associated with this legal metaphor in Paul, and henceforth in the thinking of the church, are other expressions implying that Christ dies under the condemnation of God, or suffers the 'wrath' of God; notably, Paul writes that in sending his own son in the likeness of sinful flesh, God 'condemned sin in the flesh' (Rom. 8: 3), that God 'made him to be sin' (2 Cor. 5: 21) and that Christ 'became a curse for us' (Gal. 3: 13). In the summary statement of Karl Barth, 'the judge is judged in our place' (Barth 1956: 211, 236–8). The inference is that somehow, through this suffering of judgement, sinners are 'justified'. Some Christian thinkers discount this whole range of ideas as painting an unworthy picture of a God who needs to be 'satisfied' by inflicting a penalty for human sin. However, it is not necessary to proceed so quickly to notions of propitiation, which might be seen as a mistaken conflation of legal language with a certain view of sacrifice, powerfully systematized as it was by John Calvin. Instead we might explore Paul's expressions in the light of ideas of solidarity, identification, and participation. The condemnation of Jesus in a human law court and his subsequent execution can be seen as the *occasion* for Jesus to share in the human predicament of alienation and broken relationships.

In the first place, Christ may be seen as suffering the impact of human sinning. Human beings 'lay their sins on Christ' in the sense of making Christ suffer unjustly. There is a transfer of sins to Christ by human beings, which can be understood in a socio-psychological way in line with Girard's theory of the scapegoat (Schwager 2000). But, with other theologians, we may go further to see the cross as the occasion for Jesus to endure the experience of estrangement from God as well (Pannenberg 1968: 260–3). By entering a situation where he dies as an outcast, under human judgement, Jesus is in a position to undergo a death of total estrangement from both human companionship and from God. This makes it possible for Christ to endure the same penalty against sin that human beings experience, dying under the 'no' that God speaks against a human life which is characterized by rebellion against the divine purpose. Such a view does not envisage God as directly inflicting a penalty on Christ; rather Christ participates in the human situation of being under divine judgement, which might be called exposure to the divine 'wrath' against sin, or the personal opposition of God to sin (Balthasar 1994: 334–9).

This approach affirms that the judgement and wrath of God is never a punishment imposed from outside, but is God's active and personal consent to the inner working out of sin into its inevitable consequences. In accord with the biblical language of God's 'letting his people go' their own way, or 'turning his face away', or 'giving them up', it is what Paul Tillich has called the 'structural justice' in the universe which God's righteousness and human responsibility demands (Tillich 1957: 201). As Karl Barth puts it, 'my turning away from God is followed by God's annihilating turning from me'. Christ treads the dark path to meet the death that sinners have inflicted upon themselves, and to which God consents. The sting of this death is the 'nothingness' whose power and aggressive vitality sinners themselves have fostered and 'towards which they relentlessly hasten' (Barth 1956: 253). Barth also emphasizes that the 'yes' of God to human beings is always hidden under God's 'no', and that wrath is always being overtaken by the will of God to save.

This total identification of Christ with human life can be seen as focused in the cry of dereliction: 'My God, why have you forsaken me?' While some theologians continue the tradition of both Athanasius and Schleiermacher in asserting that Christ could never actually have been or felt forsaken, others have seen this cry as a disclosure of the impact that human sin makes on the inner life of the Trinity. A brokenness and disruption enters into the eternal relations of love, as the Son loses the sense of presence of the Father. While Moltmann follows Luther in graphically calling this a situation of 'God against God' or 'God abandoning God' (Moltmann 1974: 152, 191), Balthasar finds that the separation here is grounded in the infinite differences between the triune persons and their eternal self-emptying. If the life of relations in the Trinity already has this gulf of love at its heart, we can begin to understand how God allows death itself to enter that space. In free will, God allows God's own *otherness* to become a painful *alienation* (Balthasar 1994: 324–8).

If Christ stands under the judgement of God in this way, the question is how this achieves the justification, or right-relating, of all. What is the point of this deep, empathetic identification? One answer would be 'penal substitution' in the strict sense, that is, the satisfaction or propitiation of God's wrathful justice by transferring human punishment to Christ (e.g., Brunner 1952: 284, 296). Among the problems this theory presents is that a principle of law seems to be set above the freedom of God. Further, it tips the balance too far towards objectivity as human beings are not involved in the actual event of reconciliation, but only afterwards. Further still, it assumes a view of 'inflicted penalty', rather than 'structural justice', and this drives too large a wedge between the Father and the Son (Gunton 1988: 65). Nor is sin taken seriously, as is often claimed, since the satisfaction supposedly provided does not cope with the actual brokenness of human lives through sin.

Another answer is that through the participation of Christ in the human predicament, God overcomes and absorbs *sin*. According to Romans 8: 3, it is *sin* and not Christ which is condemned (Wright 2004: 89). In judgement, Barth affirms, Christ stands in the dark place where the road taken runs into death, and there sin is 'killed' (Barth 1956: 254). For Balthasar, when the anger of God strikes Christ, sin is separated from sinners and is overwhelmed by wounded love. Balthasar also approves the view of Sergei Bulgakov that through Christ's experience of sin, he 'destroys' the reality of sin that human beings have created (Balthasar 1994: 314, 345–50). This kind of answer overlaps with the imagery of sacrifice where God expiates sin, but puts it in a quite different context of judgement. It also merges with the metaphor of victory, since sin is being conquered. We must ask, however, *how* sin can be 'destroyed', and here any emphasis on separating the sin from the sinner seems less than helpful. As we saw in considering the model of sacrifice, sin is always a matter of attitudes towards God and others, and so it cannot be detached abstractly from the persons of sinners themselves.

Following the track of the language of justice, we might then say that the suffering of a penalty by Christ transforms the sinner. It prompts us to *penitence* (Moberly 1924: 80). Christ, the obedient Son, comes under judgement, and confesses that God his Father is right in his 'no' to sinful human life. The death of Christ objectively 'upholds the justice of the universe' since there the justice of God is being declared (Forsyth 1938: 150; Gunton 1988: 112). In this way Christ creates penitence within us, moving us and enabling us to confess that God is indeed right. This 'destroys' sin because it changes us, the sinners. It replaces an attitude of sinful rebellion with an attitude of homecoming. If we are to use the language of 'satisfaction' developed by Anselm, we may say that God is satisfied by the return of prodigal sons and daughters; in contrast to Anselm's view, after repentance there is no more debt which needs to be paid. As with sacrifice, the objectivity of the divine act lies in its power to create response in us.

A similar dynamic can be seen to be at work in the image of victory or liberation, which also comes into view with the idea of 'destroying sin'. In recent thinking, the key ideas here—as already mentioned—are 'idolatry' and 'the hostile powers'. In this way, ancient images of the devil and demons are given an existential meaning, as they are in the thought of the apostle Paul, where the major enemies are law, sin, and death, and where 'principalities and powers' are not only cosmic forces but have their human face in the ruling authorities of the state (Caird 1956: 22–6). As we read the Gospel accounts, we find that Christ has, for the first time in human history, broken all the idols that confront humankind. We make idols because, in our anxiety, we fail to trust in God and instead we seek our security elsewhere. Whether personal possessions, or an ideology which controls the state, the idols take a demonic hold upon us. Jesus smashes them through his unfaltering obedience to the Father and trust in him (Tillich 1953: 148–50). He also confronts the powers by breaking the roles that have been thrust upon the outcasts and rejects of society, accepting them freely into the kingdom of God. He breaks the idol of sin itself through unremitting obedience to the Father and finally breaks the idol of self by offering himself to death. One's own self is the last idol, and to give oneself unreservedly is to have vanquished the last demon. So the sacrifice of Christ is his victory, and since God gives God's very self in this event, it is also the victory of God himself.

The church, then, is a community which lives by the justification of God and which shares in God's making of justice. In this community the idols are broken, and so the oppressed, the poor, the marginalized, and the disabled are given full worth and value. This community breaks all barriers, and this is both the result of atonement and the context in which atonement is experienced. The ethical task of the community of the church, says Colin Gunton, is 'to live the justice of God made real by Jesus' bearing of the consequences of human injustice'. This again is a dimension of forgiveness, since God's justice challenges human concepts of 'natural justice'; the cycle of offence and retribution can be broken only by something quite different—by forgiveness in which 'the offence of others is borne rather than avenged' (Gunton 1988: 190–1). In this community, those who have received the benefits of substitution learn to substitute themselves for others (Ford 1999: 68).

V. Forgiveness and Suffering

Forgiveness, as has been stressed several times, is at the heart of a Christian understanding of salvation. Unfortunately, this has often been understood in a transactional or forensic way as a mere issuing of pardon. Following Anselm's theory, it has often been associated with payment of debt and the satisfying of divine honour; what can drop out of sight is that forgiveness is about the healing of interpersonal relations, which Anselm himself wanted to express. The idea of forgiveness, rightly understood in its relational sense, is in fact a process of creative transformation. A key image for this process was offered by H. R. Mackintosh, who wrote that 'the forgiver must set out on voyages of anguish! It is an experience of sacrificial pain, of vicarious suffering' (Mackintosh 1927: 191). Forgiveness involves a painful 'voyage' or journey into the experience of another person because forgiveness, unlike a mere pardon, seeks to win the offender back into relationship (Fiddes 1989: 173–9).

If we think about forgiveness in human relationships, we see that reconciliation is a costly process because there are resistances to it in the attitude of the person who has offended, often manifesting a blend of anxiety and hostility. The one who sets out to forgive must aim to remove those blockages and restore the relationship. So the forgiver sets out on a journey of discovery into the life of the other, bringing the injury done to her back to memory, and living again through the pain of it. This is a voyage of empathy which must go far, to the very point of thinking herself into the mind of the offender, feeling with the guilty person, standing in his shoes, and making a deep effort to understand why he said or did what he did. Only when the forgiver has made this costly journey of sympathy into the experience of the other can she say 'I forgive you'. If, as is likely, the reaction is one of aggression, the forgiver must embark upon a further phase of the journey, which is one of endurance, bearing with and absorbing the hostility of the other. Correspondingly, if there is to be reconciliation, the offender must make his own voyage of discovery; he has been shaken into awareness of what he has done, and there can be no healing unless it is faced up to and sorrowed over in repentance.

Through initiating this mutual journey of awareness, the forgiver is actually discovering how to win the offender back into relationship. Through identification with the feelings of the other, she is learning how to enable the other to accept her forgiveness, since we all need to gain 'the courage to accept that we are accepted' (Tillich 1962: 159–71). The offender will only be enticed to accept forgiveness if he experiences the forgiver as a certain kind of person, not as a harsh critic or judge of his actions, but someone who has truly drawn alongside him and feels with him. Forgiveness, then, is a creative act, 'calling a fresh situation into being' (Mackintosh 1927: 211).

The Lord's prayer bids us to forgive others as we have been forgiven, and the experience of forgiveness in human relationships helps us to interpret *God's* great offer of forgiveness to human beings, creating a new situation universally. The *voyage* of forgiveness points to atonement as having the power that flows from God's participation in the lives of created beings. For Christian believers the life and death of Christ focuses God's journey of forgiveness. While God has always been voyaging into the world to share human life, nowhere does God penetrate more deeply into the creation than here, on a journey of discovery and endurance, awakening an awareness of evil and absorbing its effects. As we have already seen in exploring other models of atonement, the event of the cross is a moment of utter identification with the human situation of alienation and estrangement. An entrance into the human predicament creates a healing response to God by created beings, and the journey of forgiveness exemplifies this clearly.

The Gospel stories of the ministry of Jesus seem to show his taking an initiative which is characteristic of forgiveness, offering acceptance even *before* there is a sign of sorrow in the offender, in the hope that repentance will be provoked. The sympathetic journey into the experience of the other is an enabling act. This interpretation of the nature of forgiveness has, however, been contested. Richard Swinburne, for instance, urges that not only repentance but some kind of reparation should precede all acts of forgiveness, human and divine. He argues, following Aquinas, that reparation is not logically *necessary* in order for God to forgive us, but that it is morally *appropriate.* It is good for our growth in moral character that we should make reparation and 'pay our debts'. Swinburne concludes that since we cannot ourselves make reparation to God or do sufficient penance for the great offence we have committed against him, God himself provides the supreme offering of the life and death of Jesus to plead before him as a means of reparation (Swinburne 1989: 148–52, 160–2). Through our own repentance, acts of penance, and the use of the reparation God has made available, we can enter the realm of forgiveness.

Forgiveness, in this view, is a performative act which accepts the gifts of reparation. But the image of a journey suggests that a simple sequence 'from reparation to forgiveness' may be too neat when we consider the complexity of personal relationships. The initiative of forgiveness breaks through any such sequence with a creative act, *enabling* reparation to be made. This is not 'cheap grace', since forgiveness is only completed in reconciliation, which does require repentance.

The process of forgiveness alerts us to the fact that the suffering of the forgiver has a creative effect. *Only* a suffering participation can alter the situation. This throws light on one objection often advanced against divine passibility, that a God who suffers would not be powerful enough to overcome evil. The dynamic of forgiveness suggests that *only* a suffering God would have the power to overcome evil, by transforming those who do evil. Suffering means being affected, conditioned, and even afflicted by another; while some theologians continue the tradition of the church that God suffers like this only in the human nature of Christ (Weinandy 2000: 172–3), we might argue that it is appropriate for the divine nature if it is rooted in God's own free will and desire for partnership with created beings (Barth 1957: 303; Fiddes 1988: 61–76).

This perception links atonement with theodicy. To claim convincingly that there is a good God in a world of suffering requires God finally to be able to overcome the forces of evil which spoil creation. The cross as an event of atonement and as a theodicy cannot in fact be driven apart, as the cross focuses both the suffering of humankind and the suffering of God. As Jürgen Moltmann has emphasized, the cross of Jesus offers what has been called a 'practical theodicy'—not so much a theoretical explanation of evil and suffering but a means of facing suffering with courage and overcoming its causes. The belief that God is to be found in the crucified Jesus assures us of the presence of God in all suffering. That Jesus suffered forsakenness, even from God his Father, assures us that God is the God of all the forsaken. Moreover, a 'crucified God' does not impose suffering on others but protests against it, motivating us to protest against all individuals, structures, and ideologies that inflict suffering on human beings (Moltmann 1974: 153, 192, 253–4). The metaphor of atonement as victorious liberation (*Christus Victor*) fits especially well here as an event that enables us to oppose, in our turn, the hostile powers in our socicty.

But there is also an element of a theoretical theodicy in the doctrine of atonement. If we trace the emergence of moral evil to the free choices of created beings (the so-called 'free-will defence'), the cross of Christ not only shows us the destructive impact of that human freedom on Christ; it shows us that God takes responsibility for the situation by sharing in the human suffering that results. Moreover, a 'practical' theodicy is at the same time a thoroughly doctrinal understanding of the cross, since the concepts of sacrifice, justification, and redemption point to the overcoming of evil and the nurturing of a life in which created beings can flourish.

VI. Salvation Past and Present

We have been exploring the way that a particular series of events can foster the transformation in human lives that we call salvation. There is, we have seen, a whole range of ways in which we can begin to comprehend the objective, creative power of the death of Jesus in the context of his life and resurrection. From an existential viewpoint, for instance, we can think of the power of a disclosure of something new in human experience, which prompts those who observe it to repeat it in their own lives (Macquarrie 1977: 324–5). So we can 'make the cross of Christ our own', bringing dimensions of victory, sacrifice, and justice into human society. The ability of this event to *create* repetition points us not just to an 'example', but to the self-revelation of God within it.

From a viewpoint of narrative theory we can begin to appreciate the power of a story to create meaning within the hearer or reader. The story of Christ becomes a framework which brings out the significance of our own stories (Dalferth 1991: 314). Moreover, the diversity of human stories means that the primary story of God's saving act in Christ must itself be told in different ways, drawing on a multiplicity of images which in themselves are condensed narratives (Sykes 1997: 20–5). Liberation theologians add that we shall only find the *meaning* of the cross by entering into its experience, which means entering into the stories of those who are poor and who suffer injustice, and engaging ourselves practically in their cause (Sobrino 1978: 227).

The community in which we live also connects the past with the present. From a viewpoint of social dynamics we can begin to see the effect upon us of a community which has lived through the ages under the cross and which links us now with the earliest discipleship. In particular, its practice of the sacraments forms and shapes those who participate in them, enabling them to die and rise with Christ in baptism and to share in the brokenness of Christ for the world in the eucharist. The 'yes' of human beings to God, including the special 'yes' spoken by Mary, is also mediated through the church and enables us to make our response (Balthasar 1994: 357–61). Moreover, we should be open imaginatively to the ways in which these responses influence the whole human community, while remembering that all such mediations are dependent on the response of Christ to God, embodying both God's self-communication to us and a total human openness to the self-offer of God (Rahner 1978: 201; 1972: 176–82).

Here the Chalcedonian confession of the perfect union of God with humanity in Christ points to the heart of the matter. Salvation is possible because Jesus is uniquely one with God, his response as a human son exactly fitting into that eternal movement of relation within God which is like a son relating to a father. So, above all, it is God who links our present existence with the atoning event of the past. The world here and now is held in the embrace of the triune God, in the centre of whose life is the experience of the cross and the resurrection, shaping all the divine relations of giving and receiving in love. In encountering this God, in hearing God's story, and by living in God's community we are enabled to recognize the offer of grace and mercy, and then to respond to it.

References

Anselm of Canterbury (1998). *The Major Works*. Oxford: Oxford University Press.

Balthasar, Hans Urs von (1990). *Mysterium Paschale*. Edinburgh: T. & T. Clark.

—— (1994). *Theo-Drama: Theological Dramatic Theory*, iv. *The Action*. San Francisco: Ignatius.

Barth, Karl (1956). *Church Dogmatics* IV/1. Edinburgh: T. & T. Clark.

—— (1957). *Church Dogmatics* II/1. Edinburgh: T. & T. Clark.

Boff, Leonardo (1980). *Jesus Christ Liberator: A Critical Christology of our Time.* London: SPCK.

Brunner, Emil (1952). *The Christian Doctrine of Creation and Redemption.* Philadelphia: Westminster.

Caird, G. B. (1956). *Principalities and Powers.* Oxford: Clarendon.

Calvin, J. (1960). *Institutes of the Christian Religion.* Philadelphia: Westminster.

Dalferth, I. U. (1991). 'Christ Died for Us: Reflections on the Sacrificial Language of Salvation'. In Stephen W. Sykes (ed.), *Sacrifice and Redemption*, Cambridge: Cambridge University Press, 299–325.

Daly, Gabriel (1988). *Creation and Redemption.* Dublin: Gill and Macmillan.

Dillistone, F. W. (1968). *The Christian Understanding of Atonement.* Welwyn: Nisbet.

Dunn, J. D. G. (1980). *Christology in the Making. An Enquiry into the Origins of the Doctrine of the Incarnation.* London: SCM.

—— (1991). 'Paul's Understanding of the Death of Jesus as Sacrifice'. In Stephen W. Sykes (ed.), *Sacrifice and Redemption*, Cambridge: Cambridge University Press, 35–56.

Fairweather, Eugene R. (ed.) (1956). *A Scholastic Miscellany: Anselm to Ockam.* The Library of Christian Classics, vol. x. London: SCM.

Fee, Gordon D. (2004). 'Paul and the Metaphors for Salvation: Some Reflections on Pauline Soteriology'. In Stephen T. Davis, Daniel Kendall, and Gerald O'Collins (eds.), *The Redemption. An Interdisciplinary Symposium on Christ as Redeemer*, Oxford: Oxford University Press, 43–68.

Fiddes, Paul S. (1988), *The Creative Suffering of God.* Oxford: Oxford University Press.

—— (1989). *Past Event and Present Salvation: The Christian Idea of Atonement.* London: Darton, Longman and Todd.

Ford, David F. (1999). *Self and Salvation: Being Transformed.* Cambridge: Cambridge University Press.

Forsyth, P. T. (1938). *The Work of Christ.* London: Independent.

Girard, René (1986). *The Scapegoat.* London: Athlone.

—— (1988). *Violence and the Sacred.* London: Athlone.

Goldingay, John (1995). 'Old Testament Sacrifice and the Death of Christ'. In id. (ed.), *Atonement Today*, London: SPCK, 3–20.

Grey, Mary (1989). *Redeeming the Dream: Feminism, Redemption and Christian Tradition.* London: SPCK.

Gunton, Colin (1988). *The Actuality of Atonement.* Edinburgh: T. & T. Clark.

Hengel, Martin (1981). *The Atonement: The Origins of the Doctrine in the New Testament.* Philadelphia: Fortress Press.

Jenson, Robert W. (1997–9). *Systematic Theology.* 2 vols. New York: Oxford University Press.

Jüngel, Eberhard (1983). *God as the Mystery of the World.* Edinburgh: T. & T. Clark.

Käsemann, Ernst (1970). *Jesus Means Freedom.* Philadelphia: Fortress.

Kasper, Walter (1976). *Jesus the Christ.* London: Burns & Oates.

Lash, Nicholas (1981). *A Matter of Hope. A Theologian's Reflections on the Thought of Karl Marx.* London: Darton, Longman and Todd.

Lossky, Vladimir (1974). *In the Image and Likeness of God.* London: Mowbrays.

Mackintosh, H. R. (1927). *The Christian Experience of Forgiveness.* London: Nisbet.

Macquarrie, John (1977). *Principles of Christian Theology.* London: SCM.

Moberly, R. C. (1924). *Atonement and Personality.* London: Murray.

Moltmann, Jürgen (1974). *The Crucified God.* London: SCM.
—— (1979). *The Future of Creation.* London: SCM.
Niehbuhr, Reinhard (1941). *The Nature and Destiny of Man,* i. *Human Nature.* London: Nisbet.
O'Collins, Gerald (2004). 'Redemption: Some Crucial Issues'. In Stephen T. Davis, Daniel Kendall, and Gerald O'Collins (eds.), *The Redemption: An Interdisciplinary Symposium on Christ as Redeemer,* Oxford: Oxford University Press, 1–24.
Pannenberg, Wolfhart (1968). *Jesus—God and Man.* London: SCM.
—— (1991–8). *Systematic Theology.* 3 vols. Grand Rapids: Eerdmans.
Rahner, Karl (1972). *Theological Investigations,* ix. London: Darton, Longman and Todd.
—— (1978). *Foundations of Christian Faith: An Introduction to the Idea of Christianity.* London: Darton, Longman and Todd.
Sanders, E. P. (1985). *Jesus and Judaism.* Philadelphia: Fortress.
Schwager, Raymund (2000). *Must there be Scapegoats? Violence and Redemption in the Bible.* Leominster: Gracewing and New York: Crossroad.
Sobrino, Jon (1978). *Christology at the Crossroads: A Latin American View.* London: SCM.
Sölle, Dorothee (1967). *Christ the Representative: An Essay in Theeology after the 'Death of God'.* London: SCM.
Staniloae, Dumitru (2000). *The Experience of God: Orthodox Dogmatic Theology,* ii. *The World: Creation and Deification.* Brookline: Holy Cross.
Swinburne, Richard (1989). *Responsibility and Atonement.* Oxford: Clarendon.
Sykes, Stephen W. (1991). 'Outline of a Theory of Sacrifice'. In id. (ed.), *Sacrifice and Redemption: Durham Essays in Theology,* Cambridge: Cambridge University Press, 282–98.
—— (1997). *The Story of Atonement.* London: Darton, Longman and Todd.
Tillich, Paul (1953). *Systematic Theology,* i. Chicago: University of Chicago Press.
—— (1957). *Systematic Theology,* ii. Chicago: University of Chicago Press.
—— (1962). *The Courage to Be.* London: Fontana.
Volf, Miroslav (1996). *Exclusion and Embrace: A Theological Exploration of Identity, Otherness and Reconciliation.* Nashville: Abingdon.
Weinandy, Thomas G. (2000). *Does God Suffer?* Edinburgh: T. & T. Clark.
Williams, Daniel Day (1968). *The Spirit and the Forms of Love.* Welwyn: Nisbet.
Wright, N. T. (2004). 'Redemption from a New Perspective? Towards a Multi-Layered Pauline Theology of the Cross'. In Stephen T. Davis, Daniel Kendall, and Gerald O'Collins (eds.), *The Redemption: An Interdisciplinary Symposium on Christ as Redeemer,* Oxford: Oxford University Press, 69–100.
Young, Frances M. (1975). *Sacrifice and the Death of Christ.* London: SPCK.

Suggested Reading

Balthasar (1994).
Barth (1956).
Davis, Stephen T., Kendall, Daniel, and O'Collins, Gerald (eds.) (2004). *The Redemption: An Interdisciplinary Symposium on Christ as Redeemer.* Oxford: Oxford University Press.

Dillistone (1968).
Gunton (1988).
Fiddes (1989).
Ford (1999).
Grey (1989).
Jenson (1997–9: i. 165–206).
Macquarrie (1977: ch. 13).
Rahner (1978: chs. 5–6).
Sherry, Patrick (2003). *Images of Redemption: Art, Literature and Salvation.* London: T. & T. Clark.
Sykes, Stephen W. (ed.) (1991). *Sacrifice and Redemption: Durham Essays in Theology.* Cambridge: Cambridge University Press.

CHAPTER 11

JUSTIFICATION

DAWN DeVRIES

In an oft-quoted passage, Paul Tillich maintained that although Protestantism was born from the struggle for the doctrine of justification by faith, the idea had become strange. 'Indeed', he said, 'it is so strange to the modern man that there is scarcely any way of making it intelligible to him.... We have here a breaking-down of tradition that has few parallels. And we should not imagine that it will be possible in some simple fashion to leap over this gulf and resume our connection with the Reformation again' (Tillich 1957: 196). The dogmatic language of the Reformation and of Protestant orthodoxy no longer seemed to resonate with the lives and experiences of people in the modern western world. About a decade and a half after Tillich first published these words, in 1963, the Lutheran World Federation held its fourth assembly in Helsinki. The task before the assembly was to reinterpret the doctrine of justification by faith for the present day, in terms that would be both understandable and compelling. But when the assembly ended, they had failed to produce a document that could be distributed to the member churches. One of the papers presented to the assembly argued:

> [I]t is... an open secret that today neither the church nor the world knows what to do with this doctrine of justification. For the fathers it was the foundation and the rule of faith and life. For the church today it is clearly an embarrassment. Modern man looks upon this doctrine as little more than a form that has come down to him from the past and has lost its meaning. It does not appeal to him. He does not ask about its importance. He neither warms up to it, nor does he contradict it. (Lutheran World Federation 1964: 5)

One might have predicted on the basis of such statements that there would be little future discussion of the doctrine of justification. Yet by the end of the twentieth century, a flurry of publications began to appear, and the earlier pronouncements regarding the irrelevance of justification to modern people suddenly seemed overstated. What factors led to such a shift in perspective? The first section of this chapter will consider four developments in theological scholarship in the last third of the twentieth century that led to renewed vitality in the discussion of justification.

I. Fresh Developments in Scholarship on Justification

In 1957, Hans Küng published what was to become a landmark book: *Justification: The Doctrine of Karl Barth and a Catholic Reflection.* In it he offered a detailed interpretation of Barth's doctrine of justification on its own terms, as well as an attempt, out of his own dogmatic tradition, to answer Barth's questions about the Roman Catholic understanding of justification. Küng believed that the whole of Barth's critique of Catholicism could be reduced to a single question: 'Does the Catholic theology of justification take justification seriously as the sovereign act of God's grace?' (Küng 2004: 92). Barth worried, as had the Reformers and Protestant orthodox divines before him, that the Roman Catholic theology of grace divided the work of salvation between God and human beings, thus making humans responsible, at least in part, for their own salvation. Küng devoted two-thirds of his book to a careful presentation of Roman Catholic dogma concerning salvation, grace, and justification. In the end he was able to discover a broad agreement between Barth's doctrine and the Roman Catholic position, provided each was read sympathetically. For example, on the question of whether justification is purely forensic in nature (involving a declaration regarding the status of the person being justified), as orthodox Protestantism had asserted, or whether it is also ontological (involving a change in the very being of the person being justified), as Catholic orthodoxy maintained, Küng claimed that each side was merely emphasizing one pole of what was necessarily a *double* grace. On this point, he concluded, 'Protestants speak of a declaration of justice and Catholics of a making just. But Protestants speak of a declaring just which includes a making just; and Catholics of a making just which supposes a declaring just. Is it not time to stop arguing about imaginary differences?' (Küng 2004: 221). Similarly, Küng argued that the two sides often misunderstood each other because they used different technical terms to name the same events in the *ordo salutis.* Consequently, when the terms themselves were compared and found to have different meanings, it was not so much that there were fundamental disagreements about the actual process of salvation, but rather that this was an instance of that variety of misinterpretation often called 'comparing apples and oranges' (Küng 2004: 232–5).

Küng concluded his study with a bold assertion: '[O]n the whole there is fundamental agreement between the theology of Barth and that of the Catholic Church. Within this area of discussion Barth has no valid reason for a separation from the ancient Church.... It is without any doubt, then, significant that today there is a fundamental agreement between Catholic and Protestant theology, precisely in the theology of justification—the point at which Reformation theology took its departure. Despite all the difficulties, have we not, after these 400 years, come closer to a meeting of minds, and this in a way which is theologically decisive?' (Küng 2004: 282, 284). The influence of Küng's work was profound, especially in the realm of ecumenical theology. It set in motion a process of dialogue between Lutheran churches worldwide and the Roman Catholic Church that ultimately resulted in the 1999 *Joint Declaration on the Doctrine of Justification.*

Barth himself responded to Küng's book with gentle irony. *If* this actually is the teaching of the Catholic Church, he said, then he would admit he agreed with it, but only because it sounded so much like his own theology. He wondered whether Küng could have found what he did in the Council of Trent if he hadn't read Barth first (Küng 2004: lxvii–lxx). Nonetheless, Barth acknowledged that his own doctrine of justification had been correctly expounded in Küng's book. From the Catholic side, there was little opposition to Küng's thesis. What his book achieved, then, was a reopening of the question of justification as something that was not settled and written in stone as a church-dividing doctrine. The effect was to breathe new life into questions that had begun to seem nothing more than scholastic exercises carried over from another era.

The second relevant development in scholarship is not in the field of systematic theology but rather in biblical studies. It is no secret that the doctrine of justification by faith has everything to do with how Luther (and Augustine before him) read key passages in the writings of St Paul. So it should come as no surprise that fresh discoveries about the Pauline epistles might spark new thinking about the doctrine of justification. By the end of the twentieth century, a school of interpretation had emerged that billed itself as the 'New Perspective on Paul'. The earliest beginnings of this new perspective go at least as far back as Albert Schweitzer's *The Mysticism of Paul the Apostle*, which first appeared in German in 1930. He argued that central to Paul's soteriology was not the doctrine of justification by faith, but rather belief in the mystical existence of believers 'in Christ'. The idea of righteousness by faith, he claimed, when it does appear in Paul's writings, as in Galatians and Romans, is a mere fragment broken off from a larger quasi-physical redemption doctrine that Schweitzer called 'being-in-Christ mysticism'. In fact, he claimed, 'By taking the doctrine of righteousness by faith as the starting-point, the understanding of the Pauline world of thought was made impossible. The interpreters modernized it unconsciously' (Schweitzer 1931: 220).

Thirty years later, in another widely influential essay entitled 'The Apostle Paul and the Introspective Conscience of the West', Krister Stendahl argued that virtually the entire history of western Christian theology had misread Paul's arguments about justification by faith by importing into them the problems of the introspective guilty conscience. 'Where Paul was concerned about the possibility for Gentiles to be included in the messianic community, his statements are now read as answers to the quest for assurance about man's salvation out of a common human predicament' (Stendahl 1976: 86; cf. Käsemann 1971: 60–78). Multiple interpretative errors result from such a pre-understanding of the text, he argued, including a misconstruction of Paul's argument about the law as a general condemnation of legalism applicable to all people. Stendahl agreed with Schweitzer that justification was not the main thing for Paul, but he further added that what highly influential theologians like Augustine and Luther took to be the meaning of Paul's concept was seriously mistaken.

This sets the stage for the book that most people would credit as the actual instigator for the 'new perspective'—E. P. Sanders's *Paul and Palestinian Judaism* (1977). Sanders's work took off from then recent scholarship on Second Temple Judaism (some of it made possible by newly available texts from Qumran), which suggested that earlier presuppositions about Jews and the law that had been used in interpreting Paul were off target. Specifically, this newer reading of rabbinic texts from 200 BC to AD 200 showed explicitly that the Judaism of Paul's time was a religion of grace—a pattern of 'covenantal nomism'—grounded in God's election of a people who are assured of eschatological salvation through their membership in the covenant. The law was given as a form of obedience and submission to life in the covenant, not as the means to earn salvation, and no Jew of the time would have thought of it in that way. Salvation comes from God's free grace, and when a person in the covenant and under Torah sins, God has provided the means of restoration in the rituals of atonement (Sanders 1977: 84–110, 147–82).

Sanders argued that earlier scholars erred by failing to see that Paul did not disagree with the basic soteriological scheme of covenantal nomism he had learned as a Pharisee. Paul's argument was that in the messianic age the means of entrance into the covenant community had changed and that the righteousness conferred on the people of God is a different righteousness—namely, the righteousness one receives through union with Christ in faith (Sanders 1977: 543–56). In other words, Paul's thinking about justification by faith is really not about a different way of being saved, but about a new understanding of the scope of the covenant, the sign of inclusion, and the obligations it laid upon the chosen people. Paul was certainly not worried about Jews who were trying to save themselves through their own works, because such a notion simply was not part of his religious world.

Sanders's book inspired many other scholars to take a fresh look at Paul, and the books are too numerous to consider in the limits of this chapter (Dunn 1996; Dunn and Suggate 1993; Wright 1992 and 2006; Carson, O'Brien, and Seifrid

2001–4; Thielman 1989 and 1994). The scholars of the 'new perspective' school do not agree about all the details in their interpretations of Paul's letters. But we can draw out several conclusions that seem to be shared by them. First, the Judaism of Paul's time was not a form of legalism but a religion of grace, which formed the basis of God's covenant with Israel. The law was given not as a means of salvation (which they believed would come to everyone who belonged to the people of God), but as a means of maintaining the relationship with God in obedience. Thus Paul's problem with 'works of the law' could not have been with some persons trying to earn salvation on the basis of their works, because this was not a known possibility in the Judaism of Paul's day. Second, the 'works of the law' that Paul refers to are not improper attempts to secure God's favour through one's own actions, but rather are a kind of ethnic marker for the Jewish people by which they distinguished themselves from the Gentiles and claimed exclusive right to the covenant. Third, the idea of justification by faith is only a subordinate theme within Paul's understanding of the gospel or salvation history. Fourth, justification is a legal metaphor and should be understood in the context of the Jewish courtroom of Paul's day. The judge declares either for the plaintiff or for the defendant, and the verdict simply states how that person stands with respect to the court. It changes the status of the accused or the accuser. But the term 'righteousness of God [*dikaiosunē theou*]' that Luther discovered in Romans 1: 17 and took to mean the 'righteousness by which God justifies the ungodly' cannot possibly have this meaning. In the context of Second Temple Judaism, this phrase would be read to mean God's own faithfulness in keeping covenant with his people. So fifth, justification is actually about who is included in the covenant people and how one can know it. It is, in short, about ecclesiology rather than soteriology.

A third development in recent scholarship—this time in Luther studies—has contributed fresh enthusiasm to discussions of justification by faith. In the context of ecumenical dialogue with the Eastern Orthodox Church, Finnish theologians began to discover in Luther things that had been forgotten or not emphasized in the orthodox Lutheran dogmatic tradition. The so-called 'new Finnish interpretation of Luther' is chiefly associated with the work of Tuomo Mannermaa. He argues that the orthodox Lutheran doctrine of justification with its emphasis on the forensic character of justification and the imputation of righteousness fails to understand the extent to which Luther himself related forensic justification to ontological justification achieved through mystical union with God in Christ. Faith is the means through which believers are united with Christ and then become 'participants in the divine nature' (2 Pet. 1: 4). According to Mannermaa, the sharp distinction between justification and sanctification that developed in later Lutheran orthodoxy is not present in Luther himself. Rather, Luther sees the two graces as constantly emerging from the centre that unites them: the Christ who is present to faith. In their union with Christ, believers are both forgiven for their sins and enabled to grow in holiness (Mannermaa 2005; see also Braaten and Jenson 1998 and Gerrish 1982: 69–89).

The ecumenical possibilities that Mannermaa's reading of Luther opened up were exciting to many theologians, disturbing to others. The Luther he presented could talk meaningfully to Orthodox theologians about *theosis* as the path of the Christian life. Further, his Luther is much closer to orthodox Catholic teaching on grace. The reason to quarrel with Augustine's understanding of justification is not the idea that faith needs to be 'completed' in something else (Augustine says it must be formed by love). Rather, according to Mannermaa, the argument is only over what it is that justification requires for completion. Luther believed that Augustine got the formula wrong, and that the Christian's faith needs to be formed by Christ (Mannermaa 2005: 26–30).

This leads directly to the last development that has created new excitement over the doctrine of justification, namely, the *Joint Declaration on the Doctrine of Justification* (*JDDJ*) (2000), an ecumenical document that emerged out of decades of dialogue between the Roman Catholic Church and the Lutheran churches and was 'confirmed' by representatives from the Roman Catholic Church's Pontifical Council for Promoting Christian Unity and the President and General Secretary of the Lutheran World Federation in Augsburg on 31 October 1999. In the 'Official Common Statement' section of the document, the Lutheran World Federation and the Roman Catholic Church declare,

> The understanding of the doctrine of justification set forth in this *Declaration* shows that a consensus in basic truths of the doctrine of justification exists between Lutherans and Catholics.... On the basis of this consensus the Lutheran World Federation and the Catholic Church declare together: 'The teaching of the Lutheran Churches presented in this *Declaration* does not fall under the condemnations of the Council of Trent. The condemnations in the Lutheran Confessions do not apply to the teaching of the Roman Catholic Church presented in this *Declaration*.' (*JDDJ* §41)

The occasion was hailed as a watershed moment in ecumenical history, and many have high hopes for what such an agreement can still achieve. But the *Joint Declaration* has not been without its critics. Hans Küng noted that immediately after the Augsburg celebration, 'the Vatican... announced a new jubilee indulgence for the year 2000. As if Luther hadn't propagated his theses on justification by faith alone, specifically without such pious works, on the occasion of that scandalous jubilee indulgence for the new St Peter's!' (Küng 2004: xi).

What are some of the points of agreement in the *Joint Declaration*? First, that justification is the work of the triune God, and that therefore it is 'by grace alone, in faith in Christ's saving work and not because of any merit on our part [that] we are accepted by God and receive the Holy Spirit, who renews our hearts while equipping and calling us to good works' (*JDDJ* §15). Second, that faith itself is the gift of God. Third, that the doctrine of justification has a special place within the system of Christian doctrine. Insofar as it gets to the heart of the gospel in its talk about sin, God's saving action through Jesus Christ, and the renewal of life in the Holy

Spirit, the doctrine of justification 'stands in an essential relation to all truths of the faith' and it is 'an indispensable criterion' for orienting the teaching and practice of the church to Christ (*JDDJ* §16). As the *Joint Declaration* explicates these rather simple and broad points of agreement, it is clear that each side has stretched to accommodate and hear the position of the other side in the dialogue to a remarkable degree. One sees this on several points. For example, on the old division over the question of the cooperation of the human will with divine grace in the work of salvation, the Catholics give a reading of cooperation that emphasizes the absolute priority of grace, while the Lutherans give a reading of the impossibility of cooperation that emphasizes the necessity of the person to be 'involved' in his or her salvation nonetheless (*JDDJ* §17). In a similar fashion the *Joint Declaration* reinterprets from both sides what were previously held to be firm differences on issues such as forensic versus essential righteousness, the phrase *sola fide* (which was explicitly rejected by the Council of Trent), the idea that a justified person can be *simul iustus et peccator* (righteous and a sinner at the same time, a phrase also explicitly condemned by the Council of Trent), the use of the law in the life of a justified person, the possibility of assurance of salvation, and whether the good works of the justified can be considered meritorious (*JDDJ* §§18–25).

The *Joint Declaration* has received a good deal of attention in recent publications, with responses from particular confessional traditions or theological perspectives such as evangelicalism, and assessments of its importance for the future of ecumenical theology in general. It is beyond the scope of this chapter to consider this literature in any detail (see Husbands and Treier 2004; Jüngel 2001; Lane 2002; Malloy 2005; Mattes 2004; Rusch 2003; Stumme 2006). What is important to note at this point is simply the fact that the *Joint Declaration* seems to have revived enthusiasm in a particularly effective fashion for a doctrine that may not so long ago have seemed passé. Whether given theologians agree or disagree with the particulars of the statement itself, it has served as a catalyst for widespread discussion of the significance of the doctrine of justification for Christian faith among both Protestants and Roman Catholics.

II. Contested Issues in the Doctrine of Justification

Now that we have some notion of what has shaped the current discussion of the doctrine of justification, it is time to look conceptually at the issues that are being debated among theologians at the present time and to think about how one might discriminate among the diverse points of view.

One whole set of issues might look at first glance as if it has to do with the sheer 'mechanics' of justification—that is to say, with the processes or procedures by which the person moves from the state of sinfulness to the state of righteousness before God. Protestants and Catholics typically hold distinct views, with some exceptions on both sides, on whether justification involves a divine declaration about a person or whether it involves a divine infusion of a new righteous character (*habitus*) into a person.

Of course, these are the old, classical Reformation-era debates, but they continue to be revisited by theologians in the literature today (e.g., Lane 2002: 158–67). In the terms of the old debate, Protestants would argue that justification, understood as the infusion of grace, goes along with a theology that requires human cooperation in the work of salvation and hence gives up on the doctrine of faith alone. Catholics, on the other hand, would argue that justification, understood as a mere declaration of forgiveness that did not really transform the person being justified, could not really save. The vigorous dialogue of the last fifty years has helped both Protestants and Catholics to see the limitations of these traditional positions and to recognize the rightness in the objections of the other side. In addition, the dialogue has helped Protestants and Catholics alike to recognize that often what are identified as weaknesses or gaps in the position of the other side are in fact addressed by the other side but under another rubric in the *ordo salutis*.

Yet a difference remains that accounts for the metaphors that each side uses to describe the action of justification. The Protestant forensic or declarative concept pictures salvation primarily in terms of personal relationship. The whole point of being saved is to be reoriented to God in a new kind of relationship. This is not something of which one can have more or less. One simply has it, or one does not. The Catholic notion of infused righteousness pictures salvation primarily in terms of a medicine that heals and transforms the person, making her fit for heavenly life. But growing to health and strength is a gradual thing, and certainly one can have more or less of it. We know from experience that a person on the mend can also take a turn for the worse. The basic distinction, then, is between seeing God's grace as a kind of loving acceptance of the sinful person and seeing God's grace as an effective power to release and transform the sinful person (Jüngel 2001: 182–96). Tony Lane is right in commenting that '[t]hese two approaches will inevitably give birth to different spiritualities' (Lane 2002: 163–4).

A second, related matter has to do with the location of the righteousness that justifies the sinner. Most theologians would agree that in Paul's usage, justification is a forensic concept—a courtroom metaphor. It pictures the divine judge declaring on behalf of the sinful person, 'You are in the right'. According both to older Augustinian/Thomistic readings of these texts and to Luther's as well, in order for God to be a righteous judge, he could pronounce that judgement only because there was a righteousness available that covered the person on whom the verdict was pronounced. In Augustine's view, in the reception of the grace of justification the love of God is infused in the believer's heart by the Holy Spirit, enabling him or her to do works of love pleasing to God (*On the Spirit and the Letter* 1–4, 15, in Augustine 1997: 150–3, 158–9). Thus, when God sees the believer and says, 'You are righteous', he is describing what was in fact true about that person by virtue of faith formed by love, and the non-imputation of the sins still adhering to the believer. Lutheranism, on the contrary, emphasizes that the sinner is declared just by virtue of the imputed righteousness of Christ. True, he or she is made to participate in the righteousness of Christ through mystical union with him. But the righteousness of Christ never becomes a possession of the person who is justified. It is always an *alien* righteousness.

Why would this matter one way or another? This question is very much related to the two different metaphors for salvation that we have spoken of already. In the one, salvation is pictured as a personal relationship restored through forgiveness and unconditional love. In the other, salvation is pictured as restoration to the original state of the human being, able to grow towards participation in the heavenly kingdom. It makes perfect sense if you are working with the second metaphor, that you would want to have the righteousness of justification be something that is intrinsic to the person—something that she really possesses. Otherwise, how could you count on your ability to summon it into action in a difficult situation? Righteousness should be something that is a constant, if imperfect feature of one's character (or *habitus* in classical Thomistic terms). If, on the other hand, you are working with the other way of understanding salvation—as restored personal relationship—in a sense it simply gets in the way to become too focused on what one can bring to God as evidence of one's righteousness. That seems almost to be an affront to God's grace. And the idea of a righteousness that *takes you out of yourself* seems to correspond very well with the notion of a transformation of the self in relationship. One is given a new identity that makes a new relationship possible, but this identity is not one that can be heroically created by oneself—it is a gift (Jüngel 2001: 212–14).

A third issue that is always on the edges of the discussion of justification is the role of good works in the Christian life. In other words, what is the relation between justification and sanctification? One general problem with the idea of sanctification is that, with a few exceptions among Wesleyans and evangelicals, it seems that there are almost no theologians who choose to talk about this doctrine any more (cf. Webster 2003). In North America, perhaps, this is because the Puritans and our 'puritanical' tendencies are targets of much undue reproach. But it probably has deeper roots in modern western culture's psychotherapeutic idea of self-examination, the purpose of which is arrival at a greater degree of self-acceptance. This modern attitude, however, would not provide fertile soil for the spiritual practices, such as prayer and confession, which have historically been held to lead to sanctification. In the older tradition, the purpose of introspection and self-examination was precisely *not* to arrive at self-acceptance or satisfaction with the status quo.

In the debates between Lutherans and Catholics the questions about good works cluster around several issues: the role of the Ten Commandments in the life of believers, whether it is right to call the justified person *simul iustus et peccator*, whether good works can be said to earn merit, and whether assurance of salvation is available to believers.

It is unfortunate that John Calvin could not enter this dialogue, because on just these points he might have provided an interesting middle way. This would be especially true of his insistence that 'Christ was given to us by God's generosity, to be grasped and possessed by us in faith. By partaking of him, we principally receive a double grace: namely, that being reconciled to God through Christ's blamelessness, we may have in heaven instead of a Judge a gracious Father; and secondly, that sanctified by Christ's spirit we may cultivate blamelessness and purity of life' (*Institutes* 3. 11. 1, in Calvin 1960: 725). What Calvin argues is that the saving grace of God has two parts that are distinguishable but not separable: justification and sanctification. They need to be distinguished, because they operate in different ways. Justification is *iterative*, and even though the word of forgiveness needs to be said again and again because a human is never free from sin in this life, it is the kind of word that is *total* (at least in Calvin's view)—one cannot have more or less of it. Sanctification, on the other hand, is *cumulative*. It is a grace that accrues over a lifetime, and one can definitely measure progress (and regress) on the road of sanctification. What was unimaginable for Calvin, however, was that there could be justification without sanctification or vice versa. That was simply impossible.

Returning to debates about good works between Lutherans and Catholics, with respect to the Ten Commandments Catholics tend to emphasize the need to keep them, while the old Lutheran battle cry was to 'rightly distinguish law and gospel'. The phrase 'righteous and sinner at the same time' sounds dangerously reckless to Catholic ears, while anything less than this sounds like works-righteousness to Lutheran ears. Merit seems a biblical concept to Catholics, a dangerously self-congratulatory one to Lutherans. And Catholics tend to discourage too easy an assurance of salvation, while Lutherans insist upon bold reliance on the mercy of God. In the *Joint Declaration*, representatives of the two traditions managed to coax these differences in temperament into what looked like basic agreement. But again, there may be different metaphors of salvation and hence different spiritualities at work here, and Calvin's double grace would embrace them both (Gerrish 1982: 82–5, 306–10).

The Catholic understanding of justification as the beginning of the transformation of the person for eternal salvation goes with an understanding of grace as medicine that is infused and that comes to inhere in the person. From this perspective, what the person does or does not do is either praiseworthy or culpable before God strictly on its own terms. It is appropriate, then, to see our good works as rewarded with merits because they are truly ours. Salvation comes about by God's grace, but by God's grace the person is enabled to participate in her own salvation by obeying God's law. In Luther's reading of Paul, the law does nothing except to drive the sinner to despair, because she cannot keep it. Therefore, justification is a sheer gift that never rests on anything in the person receiving it. And since salvation is always a gift of God's grace, the sinner can be assured that nothing she does will take it away from her. It would be a mistake to bring back the law after justification, because the gospel sets sinners free from the law. For Calvin, through the grace of justification the sinner gains the confidence to live the life of faith with boldness, attempting to keep the commandments but knowing that God will accept even imperfect works from her because God acts as a loving parent. On the issue of justification and sanctification, then, there are positions that range from a sharp distinction, almost to the point of separation, to a softer distinction that sees an organic connection between the two graces, to a virtual blurring of the distinction in which sanctification is taken as the completion of justification. Apart from taking sides through confessional loyalty, how can we navigate among the various positions? And are the right questions being debated, or are there others that should be considered as well?

III. Sizing Up the Arguments

Theologians make their decisions about what constitute good or poor theological arguments on the basis of explicit or implicit norms or criteria. These could be rules that determine what will be considered or not considered. They could also be principles or methods that will be applied in interpreting what makes its way into a theological argument. One of the difficulties about theology in our day is that there are so many theologians doing theology according to a great diversity of norms and criteria. Sometimes the different rules by which different groups play seem to amount to separate languages that prevent communication across the boundaries.

According to Schubert Ogden's criteria for assessing theological arguments, a good piece of theology must be both *appropriate* to the original Christian witness and *credible* in that it meets the relevant conditions of truth, universally established with human existence (Ogden 1986: 4–7). These two norms are not competing with each other, as if the credibility norm were some kind of apologetic aim that would corrupt the purity of the gospel. What Ogden says—and I agree—is that the Christian faith makes a truth claim, and it intends to make that truth claim, against other truth claims, under the scrutiny of anyone who takes an interest in the truth. Therefore, a theologian cannot afford to be simply oblivious to the credibility of her language.

If I make my judgements on the basis of these criteria, then, where do we stand with regard to the doctrine of justification by faith? Let us begin with the norm of *appropriateness*. Ogden himself has a historicist way of understanding this: it refers for him to the 'earliest apostolic witness' and to that alone. We have a right and a duty, according to him, to criticize anything in later Christianity that departed from the earliest witness. I myself have a broader understanding of appropriateness. It would include the whole canonical scripture, the development of doctrine, and for me, as a Reformed theologian, especially the Reformed confessions. On the doctrine of justification, there is a mixed report, I think, with respect to the criterion of appropriateness. On the one hand, the kind of painstaking efforts at comparative symbolics that went into the making of Hans Küng's famous book and the dialogues leading to the *Joint Declaration* have taken extremely seriously the need to understand and to maintain faithful continuity with the church's theological wisdom from the past. Where this has led to new possibilities of mutual respect and recognition, we can rejoice.

On the other hand, it is this very intense interest in the canonical and dogmatic tradition of the churches that has led to what I would call a failure with respect to the norm of appropriateness. Not all systematic accounts of justification have come to terms with the new biblical scholarship on Paul and its doctrinal implications. If earliest Christianity and its understanding of what faith and salvation mean a normative criterion for theology, we cannot avoid this task, even though in important respects it may undermine the soteriological tradition of Latin Christian theology, Catholic and Protestant, from Augustine until the twentieth century. That is an intimidating tradition to overturn. Nonetheless, if we are to believe certain biblical scholars, the apostle Paul knew nothing about plagued guilty consciences, fruitless struggles to prove his goodness by keeping the law, and the freedom of conscience granted to an individual in the individual verdict pronounced about him by the divine Judge (Stendahl 1976: 92–5).

What would happen if someone were to try to reconstruct the doctrine of justification and sanctification based on the new reading of the Pauline epistles? Such a reconstruction would yield several things that could be really useful and good correctives for present-day theology. First, it would have to get away from the relentless and thoroughgoing individualism that has always been part of the Protestant way of understanding salvation, and which has become especially acute in recent decades. For Paul, salvation was always about the covenant people of God—it was a collective term. Individuals were saved only as part of the people. Second, it would draw out the importance of ecclesiology, which is often undervalued by many Protestants. Paul understands justification by faith as the marker for membership in the new eschatological people of God. But his overall concern is precisely with that *group*—the people of God, the body of Christ. Third, it would show that there is a natural connection between justice and justification, and that individual salvation does not come apart from justice in the world (Dunn and Suggate 1993: 31–42). Paul's argument against 'works of the law' was not a rejection of the law altogether or a denial of the goodness of the law as a way of expressing God's righteousness in relationships among human beings.

What about the other criterion, *credibility*? For Ogden, this criterion could involve complex arguments in philosophical theology to demonstrate the plausibility of particular claims. Although there is a need for such arguments in their place, there is another, simpler kind of credibility required of Christian doctrine: Does a particular form of theological language have the ability to make a believer's faith more accessible to her, more understandable to her? How does the doctrine of justification by faith stand according to this criterion? An influential American textbook of theology published in 2005 lacks a chapter treating justification and sanctification, and has only a brief definition of the word 'justified' in the concluding glossary (Jones and Lakeland 2005: 296; cf. Chopp and Taylor 1994). This indicates that Tillich's judgement about the doctrine of justification is not off target, in spite of all the recent publications. The majority of contemporary theologians do not find a reason to talk about it, not because contemporary theologians are no longer interested in sin and grace, but because the language and the metaphors of the fourth century and the twelfth century and the sixteenth and seventeenth centuries do not work so well for twenty-first-century men and women.

It is an immense task to begin to think through new language and metaphors for grace, forgiveness, transformation, and new life. Of course, in order to maintain our criterion of appropriateness, we can never completely let go of the word 'justification', which is one that Paul uses repeatedly. But it is not the only word he uses, or even the most important, and that frees the contemporary theologian from slavish bondage to it.

We have covered a lot of territory in this chapter. There has been something of a renaissance of interest in the doctrine of justification at the turn of the twenty-first century. Many of the contested issues are simply new attempts to grapple with the old church-dividing questions. Insofar as theologians are unwilling to move behind or beyond the language of the sixteenth-century debates, it is unlikely that this renewed interest in justification will spread far beyond those who are already engaging in the conversation. If justification really is the article by which the church stands or falls, then it must be able to be interpreted in a way that makes it live for people today. Maybe the first small step toward that would be to try to do for our own day what Luther did so well for his: to hear the gospel as it was taught by Paul and to speak it for the men and women of our own time.

References

Augustine (1997). *The Works of St Augustine: A Translation for the 21st Century*, pt. I, vol. xxiii. Hyde Park: New City Press.

Barton, Stephen C. (ed.) (2003). *Holiness Past and Present*. London: T. & T. Clark.

Bayer, Oswald (2003). *Living By Faith: Justification and Sanctification*. Grand Rapids: Eerdmans.

Braaten, Carl E., and Jenson, Robert W. (eds.) (1998). *Union with Christ: The New Finnish Interpretation of Luther.* Grand Rapids: Eerdmans.

Burgess, Joseph A., and Kolden, Marc (eds.) (2004). *By Faith Alone: Essays on Justification in Honor of Gerhard O. Forde.* Grand Rapids: Eerdmans.

Calvin, John (1960). *Institutes of the Christian Religion.* Philadelphia: Westminster.

Carson, D. A., O'Brien, Peter T., and Seifrid, Mark (eds.) (2001–4). *Justification and Variegated Nomism.* 2 vols. Grand Rapids: Baker Academic.

Chopp, Rebecca S., and Taylor, Mark Lewis (eds.) (1994). *Reconstructing Christian Theology.* Minneapolis: Fortress.

Dunn, James D. G., and Suggate, Alan M. (1993). *The Justice of God: A Fresh Look at the Old Doctrine of Justification by Faith.* Grand Rapids: Eerdmans.

Dunn, James D. G. (ed.) (1996). *Paul and the Mosaic Law: The Third Durham-Tübingen Symposium on Earliest Christianity and Judaism (Durham, September, 1994).* Tübingen: J. C. B. Mohr (Paul Siebeck).

Gerrish, B. A. (1982). *The Old Protestantism and the New: Essays on the Reformation Heritage.* Chicago: University of Chicago Press.

Husbands, Mark, and Treier, Daniel J. (eds.) (2004). *Justification: What's at Stake in the Current Debates.* Downers Grove: InterVarsity.

Joint Declaration on the Doctrine of Justification (2000). The Lutheran World Federation and the Roman Catholic Church. Grand Rapids: Eerdmans.

Jones, Serene, and Lakeland, Paul (eds.) (2005). *Constructive Theology: A Contemporary Approach to Classical Themes.* Minneapolis: Fortress.

Jüngel, Eberhard (2001). *Justification: The Heart of the Christian Faith. A Theological Study with an Ecumenical Purpose.* Edinburgh: T. & T. Clark.

Kärkkäinen, Veli-Matti (2004). *One with God: Salvation as Deification and Justification.* Collegeville: Liturgical.

Käsemann, Ernst (1980). *Commentary on Romans.* Grand Rapids: Eerdmans.

—— (1971). *Perspectives on Paul.* Philadelphia: Fortress.

Küng, Hans (2004). *Justification: The Doctrine of Karl Barth and a Catholic Reflection.* 40th anniversary edn. Louisville: Westminster John Knox.

Lane, Anthony N. S. (2002). *Justification by Faith in Catholic-Protestant Dialogue: An Evangelical Assessment.* London: T. & T. Clark.

Lutheran World Federation (1964). *Messages of the Helsinki Assembly.* Minneapolis: Augsburg.

McGrath, Alister E. (2005). *Iustitia Dei: A History of the Christian Doctrine of Justification.* 3rd edn. Cambridge: Cambridge University Press.

Malloy, Christopher J. (2005). *Engrafted into Christ: A Critique of the Joint Declaration.* New York: Peter Lang.

Mannermaa, Tuomo (2005). *Christ Present in Faith: Luther's View of Justification.* Minneapolis: Fortress.

Mattes, Mark C. (2004). *The Role of Justification in Contemporary Theology.* Grand Rapids: Eerdmans.

Ogden, Schubert M. (1986). *On Theology.* San Francisco: Harper and Row.

Opočenský, Milan, and Rémonn, Páraic (eds.) (1999). *Justification and Sanctification in the Traditions of the Reformation.* Studies from the World Alliance of Reformed Churches 42. Geneva: World Alliance of Reformed Churches.

Pannenberg, Wolfhart (1991–8). *Systematic Theology.* 3 vols. Grand Rapids: Eerdmans.

Rusch, William G. (ed.) (2003). *Justification and the Future of the Ecumenical Movement: The Joint Declaration on the Doctrine of Justification.* Collegeville: Liturgical.

Sanders, E. P. (1977). *Paul and Palestinian Judaism: A Comparison of Patterns of Religion.* Philadelphia: Fortress.

Schweitzer, Albert (1931). *The Mysticism of Paul the Apostle.* London: A. & C. Black.

Stendahl, Krister (1976). *Paul among the Jews and Gentiles.* Philadelphia: Fortress.

Stumme, Wayne C. (ed.) (2006). *The Gospel of Justification in Christ: Where Does the Church Stand Today?* Grand Rapids: Eerdmans.

Thielman, Frank (1989). *From Plight to Solution: A Jewish Framework to Understanding Paul's View of the Law in Galatians and Romans.* Leiden: E. J. Brill.

—— (1994). *Paul & the Law: A Contextual Approach.* Downers Grove: InterVarsity.

Tillich, Paul (1957). *The Protestant Era.* Abridged edn. Chicago: University of Chicago Press.

Webster, John (2003). *Holiness.* Grand Rapids: Eerdmans.

Wright, N. T. (1992). *The Climax of the Covenant: Christ and the Law in Pauline Theology.* Minneapolis: Fortress.

—— (2006). *Paul in Fresh Perspective.* Minneapolis: Fortress.

Suggested Reading

Bayer (2003).

Joint Declaration on the Doctrine of Justification (2000).

Jüngel (2001).

Küng (2004).

McGrath (2005).

Mannermaa (2005).

Pannenberg (1991–8: iii. 211–36).

Tillich, Paul (1948). *The Shaking of the Foundations.* New York: Charles Scribner's Sons, 153–63.

—— (1957: 192–205).

Wright(2006).

CHAPTER 12

RESURRECTION AND IMMORTALITY

DOUGLAS FARROW

Then it is as certain as anything can be, Cebes, that soul is immortal and imperishable, and that our souls will really exist in the next world.

Well, Socrates, said Cebes, for my part I have no criticism, and no doubt about the truth of your argument. But if Simmias here or anyone else has any criticism to make, he had better not keep it to himself, because if anyone wants to say or hear more about this subject, I don't see to what other occasion he is to defer it.

As a matter of fact, said Simmias, I have no doubts myself either now, in view of what you have just been saying. All the same, the subject is so vast, and I have such a poor opinion of our weak human nature, that I can't help feeling some misgivings.

Plato, *Phaedo* 107a

One needs no great sublimity of soul to realize that in this life there is no true and solid satisfaction, that all our pleasures are mere vanity, that our afflictions are infinite, and finally that death which threatens us at every moment must in a few years infallibly face us with the inescapable and appalling alternative of being annihilated or wretched throughout eternity.

Nothing could be more real, or more dreadful than that. Let us put on as bold a face as we like: that is the end facing the world's most illustrious life. Let us ponder these things, and then say whether it is not beyond

> doubt that the only good thing in this life is the hope of another life, that we become happy only as we come nearer to it, and that, just as no more unhappiness awaits those who have been quite certain of eternity, so there is no happiness for those who have no inkling of it.
>
> Pascal, *Pensées* iii. 427

> This grace was given to us in Christ Jesus before the ages began, but it has now been revealed through the appearing of our Saviour Christ Jesus, who abolished death and brought life and immortality to light through the gospel.
>
> 2 Tim. 1: 9–10

I. Introduction to the Christian Tradition

It is Christianity's bold claim to have settled the question of immortality—or rather to announce that the question has been settled—once and for all. Life and immortality have been brought to light through one who has abolished death. Now to abolish death as the means of bringing life and immortality to light is not at all the same thing as to conduct an argument such as Plato's or Pascal's. It is to perform an act, a miracle on a par with the miracle of creation (Athenagoras, *Res.* 3; Justin, *Apol.* 1. 67; in Roberts and Donaldson 1990: ii. 150 and i. 186), and to invite belief, not in the afterlife of the soul, but in 'the resurrection of the body and the life of the world to come' (Apostles' Creed; cf. Stendahl 1965: 9–53).

Belief in this miracle is both foundational to and correlative with belief in the incarnation. One who is both the subject (John 2: 19) and the object (Acts 2: 32) of the miracle of resurrection does not merely stand vindicated *before* God and man but is somehow implicated *in* God and man: in God, because it is to God alone that such power belongs (John 20: 28); in man, because only thus is image-bearing humanity finally achieved (1 Cor. 15: 45). In other words, neither God as creator nor man as creature is fully revealed until life and immortality are brought to light. The claim that they have indeed been brought to light is Christianity's defining feature.

Objections to this claim arose immediately in Judaism and were recrafted by Graeco-Roman opponents of Christianity such as Celsus. They were further refined in the Enlightenment, which sought to bolster them by appeal to a mechanistic and miracle-free universe. The claim has nonetheless stood firmly at the centre of the Christian witness both to Jews and Muslims, who hope for a future resurrection, and to Greeks ancient and modern, who do not. To the latter it is said that death is really abolished; to the former that it is abolished through Jesus Christ.

Arguments with Jews turned mainly on readings of the Old Testament respecting the Messiah's mission and sufferings rather than on his resurrection. If it could be shown that Jesus' sufferings and death were truly messianic, then his resurrection would be less problematic, albeit raising many questions about changes in the mission and status of the chosen people, some of which could be answered only by further miraculous deeds. The New Testament is largely occupied with these arguments and deeds. To date, the most thorough historical work on the subject has been done by N. T. Wright (2003), who shows that Paul and the other apostolic authors occupied a quite definite point on the spectrum of Jewish belief about the resurrection, namely, belief in re-embodiment or 'life *after* "life after death"' (Wright 2003: 31). In the striking words of Isaiah 26: 19, which in inter-testamental times was read with Isaiah 25: 7–8, Hosea 6: 1–2, Hosea 13: 14, Psalm 16: 9–11, Daniel 12: 2, and even the more symbolic Ezekiel 37: 12:

> your dead shall live,
> their bodies shall rise.
> You who dwell in the dust,
> wake up and shout for joy!
> Your dew is like the dew of the morning,
> the earth will give birth to her dead. (NIV)

This position they made more precise, says Wright, in view of their experience of the resurrected Jesus, by thinking in terms of 'transformed re-embodiment'. Wright effectively counters suggestions that 'the resurrection accounts in the Gospels are back-projections of Christian belief from the middle or late first century' and that Paul held a more 'spiritualized' view than either his Pharisaic co-religionists or second-generation Christians (Wright 2003: 718; cf. Schillebeeckx 1979: 329–404). He also distinguishes and integrates, in a manner useful to systematic theology, three ways in which the resurrection of Jesus taught early Christians to think of him as 'son of God', namely: as the Messiah who defeats death, the last enemy, and so inaugurates the eschaton; as the world ruler who challenges the imperium of Caesar, the earthly tyrant who, like the devil, rules through fear of death; and, in a proto-trinitarian sense, as the personal expression of the living God who has full authority over life and death (Wright 2003: 723–31; cf. Heb. 1: 2–3; 6: 1–2).

Arguments with Gentiles could not ignore any of this, but turned especially on the question of salvation for the body, engaging both the radical dualism of gnostics and the moderate dualism of Platonists. To read Athanasius' *On the Incarnation of the Word*, written in the lull between the battle with gnosticism and the great Nicene controversy, is to see just how central to patristic theology was the notion of a Messiah who abolishes death as the means of bringing life and immortality to light. 'The Lord was especially concerned for the resurrection of the body which He was set to accomplish. For what He was to do was to manifest it as a monument of victory over death, and to assure all of His having effected the blotting out of corruption, and of the incorruption of their bodies from thenceforward; as a gauge of which and a proof of the resurrection in store for all, He has preserved His own body incorrupt' (*On the Incarnation of the Word* 22, in Schaff 1980*b*: iv. 48). The Lord 'who banished death from us and made us anew' (*Incarnation* 16) is indeed the central theme of this little theological handbook *cum* missionary tract, and the courage of the martyrs is its imprimatur: 'Now if by the sign of the Cross, and by faith in Christ, death is trampled down, it must be evident before the tribunal of truth that it is none other than Christ Himself that has displayed trophies and triumphs over death, and made him lose all his strength' (*Incarnation* 29).

The fathers thought it impossible to maintain the biblical unity of creation and redemption, or the true character of Christian hope, or the gospel story itself, without maintaining the resurrection of the body. But the task was not easy, for it opened up many questions in anthropology and cosmology. 'Don't you know', asks Gregory of Nyssa in *On the Soul and the Resurrection*, 'how great a swarm of objections our opponents bring forward against this hope?' (Roth 2002: 104). These opponents were raising anew the 'how' question—and with it the vexatious problem of continuity and discontinuity, identity and difference—that Paul faced in 1 Corinthians 15, which became the touchstone for all future treatments of the subject (cf. Hollemann 1996). Appealing to Paul, Gregory argues that 'the resurrection is nothing other than the return of our nature to its original state', a state of perfection from which we have wandered through the dissipation of sin (Roth 2002 1993: 118). His short answer to the objections is that this return makes irrelevant the problems of discontinuity or non-identity that are produced in a world of decay. Our return, by the power of God, to the original perfection is the undoing of the conditions under which such objections are relevant.

Gregory and Paul, then, were at one in overruling such objections. Paul, however, did not see the resurrection as a return, nor did he understand the beginning (our natural state) as Gregory understood it. Gregory's Adam, unlike Paul's, is not a man of the earth but a solitary instantiation on earth of a heavenly archetype. He is a passion-free man, whose multiplication, but for the fall, would have been spiritual rather than sexual. The general resurrection, which will occur when the perfect complement of humans has appeared by the imperfect process of sexual reproduction, will make of each one (Gregory was a universalist) a replica of Adam. Each will have an ethereal and passionless body, though in many cases a long and painful purification of soul will be required before the bodily form is filled with heavenly glory. When all have reached this end, the whole communion—the *totus Christus* that is the eschatological man of God's original design—will enjoy the unceasing gifts of God for eternity.

In this innovation Gregory is following Origen, who also tried to bend Paul to Plato and Plato to Paul. That Origen is closer to Paul than to Plato has more than once been argued, and the same can be said of Gregory. Both believe in a resurrection, and hold after a fashion to the re-embodiment of the soul. Both see in the end something more than what is to be found in the beginning. But both also draw the doctrine of the resurrection into the orbit of the philosophical or cosmological problem of the one and the many, and take Paul's statement that 'flesh and blood cannot inherit the kingdom of God' (1 Cor. 15: 50) rather more literally than Paul seems to have intended. Paul did not mean to exclude flesh and blood from the kingdom (a most un-Jewish idea) but rather to make clear to Jews, and Gentiles too, that access to the kingdom does not come by human strength, or by ethnic identity, or by any means available to mortal man. This is the discontinuity Paul had in view: that the old man must be displaced by the new, 'in the twinkling of an eye', through a transformation already determined for him in Jesus Christ. And this is the continuity: that what is transformed is the whole man; the perishable is clothed with the imperishable, 'the mortal with immortality' (1 Cor. 15: 52–3 NIV). Then is realized the new thing that God had in mind from the beginning, as Gregory would agree (Hart 2003: 410).

Gregory's combination of a sudden change for the body and a gradual change for the soul may make him less consistent than Origen, whose gradualism applies equally to body and soul, but it keeps him nearer to Paul, who himself understood the scriptures 'in a sort of Jewish sense' (*pace* Origen, *On First Principles* 2. 11. 2, in Roberts and Donaldson 1990: iv. 297). Much nearer yet is Irenaeus: 'As therefore the bride cannot be said to wed, but to be wedded, when the bridegroom comes and takes her, so also the flesh cannot by itself possess the kingdom of God by inheritance; but it can be taken *for* an inheritance'—that is, by 'the Spirit of the Father, who purifies man, and raises him up to the life of God' (*Against Heresies* 5. 9. 4, 2, in Roberts and Donaldson 1990: i. 535). And Tertullian also: 'Be not disquieted, O flesh and blood, with any care; in Christ you have acquired both heaven and the kingdom of God' (*On the Resurrection of the Flesh* 51, in Roberts and Donaldson 1990: iii. 584). Irenaeus had the advantage here, since (like the old man by the sea who converted Justin) he did not believe in the native immortality of the soul but only in the deifying gift of the Holy Spirit, on which depends the hope of soul and body alike. His famous maxim, 'Where the Spirit of the Father is, there is a living man' (*Heresies* 5. 9. 3), occurs in the context of his discussion of the words, 'flesh and blood cannot inherit the kingdom of God'. Both Irenaeus and Tertullian, however, in confronting the challenge of gnosticism on which systematic theology cut its teeth, share the assumption that 'man is as much body as he is soul' (*Resurrection* 32) and recognize in the doctrine of bodily resurrection the major test of commitment to the unity of creation and redemption.

Tertullian's treatise on the resurrection rewards close attention. It is not simply an apology for a dogma to which the pagan mind is ill-disposed. It is a defence of the body, without which there can be no defence of either man or God as revealed in Jesus Christ, nor any exposition of eternal life. The resurrection, he thinks, must be so conceived as to lay bare the novelty of redemption without overlooking the selfsameness of that which receives redemption. If the new creation is something other than the old, then 'Christ' is someone other than Jesus, and 'God' someone other than YHWH, as the gnostics taught. In an authentic doctrine of resurrection, then, neither continuity nor discontinuity can be denied, whether of body or of soul. Tertullian makes the martyrs his clients in the case for bodily continuity. 'Changes, conversions, and reformations will necessarily take place to bring about the resurrection', he says, 'but the substance will still be preserved safe' (*Resurrection* 55). These changes are so decisive as to seem almost 'a complete destruction of the former self'; but they introduce a radical discontinuity into 'our condition, not our nature'.

For how absurd, and in truth how unjust, and in both respects how unworthy of God, for one substance to do the work, and another to reap the reward: that this flesh of ours should be torn by martyrdom, and another wear the crown; or, on the other hand, that this flesh of ours should wallow in uncleanness, and another receive the condemnation! Is it not better to renounce all faith at once in the hope of the resurrection, than to trifle with the wisdom and justice of God? Better that Marcion should rise again than Valentinus. For it cannot be believed that the mind, or the memory, or the conscience of existing man is abolished by putting on that change of raiment which immortality and incorruption supplies; for in that case all the gain and fruit of the resurrection, and the permanent effect of God's judgement on soul and body, would certainly fall to the ground. If I remember not that it is I who have served him, how shall I ascribe glory to God? How sing to him 'the new song', if I am ignorant that it is I who owe him thanks? (*Resurrection* 56)

So even the flesh will be preserved, or rather (in the case of the righteous, for the unrighteous too shall rise bodily for judgement) be transformed, since it belongs to the 'I' in question.

Tertullian does not shy from paradox here. The transformed body will be at the same time both passible and impassible, both useless and useful, there being no idleness in the presence of God (*Resurrection* 57, 60). Several principles prevent him from making the mistakes of the heretics, however, who in their blindness continually 'impale themselves on the point of the old and the new man' (*Resurrection* 45). First, Tertullian knows that the scriptures give an affirmative answer to the question 'whether the Lord, when he ordains salvation for man, intends it for his flesh' (*Resurrection* 60). Second, he knows that the heretics' negative answer is bound up with an open or secret hatred of the flesh, and the hatred of the flesh with a repudiation of its creator (*Resurrection* 63). Third, he knows that the God who created the world *ex nihilo* is able to resolve the paradox of continuity and discontinuity: 'For if God produced all things whatever out of nothing, he will be able to draw forth from nothing even the flesh which had fallen into nothing' (*Resurrection* 11). Fourth, he knows that Christ himself is the guarantee of this. 'And so the flesh shall rise again, wholly in every man, in its own identity, in its absolute integrity. Wherever it may be, it is in safe keeping in God's presence, through that most faithful "mediator between God and man, Jesus Christ," who shall reconcile both God to man, and man to God; the spirit to the flesh and the flesh to the spirit' (*Resurrection* 63).

Neither Irenaeus nor Tertullian would have been happy with the view of Origen that 'flesh and blood will perish indeed' (Edwards 2002: 114) as the corporeal nature evolves or reverts with the soul into something spiritual. For them, as for Paul, the perishing of 'flesh and blood' signified the end of human self-dependence; the arrival of something spiritual was not related to the dismissal of flesh-and-blood physicality, but rather was the investiture of the whole person, compounded of body and soul, with the Holy Spirit. This was linked by Irenaeus, who understood the ecclesiological implications better than Tertullian, to the invocation of the Spirit in the eucharistic prayer, and to the mysterious transformation of bread and wine into the body and blood of Christ, which he understood to be an eschatological event grounded in the resurrection (*Heresies* 5. 2. 3, 5. 10). It was the path indicated by Irenaeus and Tertullian and Athanasius that the church followed, rather than that of Origen or Gregory (cf. Bynum 1995).

Augustine, who at first seemed inclined toward a compromise like Gregory's, also trod that path without embarrassment. He restated the Christological principle: 'Christ rose again in the flesh, and showed the immortality of the resurrection in his own body, which he promised unto us in the end of this world, or in the beginning of the next' (*The City of God* 22. 10, in Augustine 1610: ii. 347). He appealed to the martyrs and, more particularly, to the miracles worked in their name as confirmation of 'that faith which professes the resurrection of the flesh unto all eternity' (*City* 22. 9). He dealt with the usual objections about the unsuitability of the flesh for the heavenly realms, and with such supposed difficulties as abortion or cannibalism. 'The sudden and strange power of God' shall give to each the fullness of its potential, and set at nought the defeats of this life. Defects and deformities will be removed, except those (especially the tokens of martyrdom) that enhance the glory of the resurrected and their love for one another. Necessities shall cease, and the unpleasantries of our corruptible bodies; but beauty shall endure. 'These things being duly considered, this is the sum of all, that in the resurrection every man [and woman, for womanhood is no defect, he insists] shall arise with the same body that he had, or would have had in his fullest growth, in all comeliness, and without deformity of any the least member' (*City* 22. 20; cf. 22. 17). This body shall be 'no more natural but spiritual'—that is, wholly subject to the spirit, which shall be wholly subject to God—hence no longer a burden: 'light' not cumbersome, having 'the substance of the flesh, quite exempt from all fleshly corruption' (*City* 13. 19–20, 13. 23, 22. 24; *Enchiridion* 91, in Schaff 1980*a*: iii. 265–6). The man who will live in the resurrection and see God, will live and see God at work in a world good and beautiful, wonderful both in its variety and in its peace, in its motion and in its rest. He will not advance in the praises of God by leaving the world, or by returning to some pre-lapsarian nakedness before he wore his present 'garment of skin' (in the language of Origen and Gregory), but by loving God in freedom in a world made eternally new. 'Flourishing in that incorruptible state', as Irenaeus put it, he shall always hold 'fresh converse with God' in the city of God, and so forget to die (*Heresies* 5. 35–6).

Augustine playfully suggested that the Greeks might approximate the Christian doctrine of the resurrection if they could put together Plato's notion of a return to the body, Porphyry's insistence that the just would never again suffer the evils of the body, and Varro's talk of certain souls returning to their own bodies (*City* 22. 28). But with entire seriousness he challenged the fundamentals of the Platonist tradition by pointing out that the pursuit of happiness requires bodily resurrection and that reason alone can arrive at no real certitude concerning this. This puts in doubt the purpose of the rational life, and the social life as well, unless it is restored by faith in the resurrected Christ (*The Trinity* 13, in Augustine 1991: 342–69; cf. *City* 19. 5–24). Platonist speculation about the native immortality of the soul cannot sustain reason and the pursuit of happiness, or the task of living and dying well, in the way that Christianity can. Neither, of course, can it reckon with the concreteness of the divine judgement on living and dying well. But God has 'fixed a day on which he will have the world judged in righteousness by a man whom he has appointed, and of this he has given assurance to all by raising him from the dead' (Acts 17: 31).

The doctrine of the resurrection did not take shape merely through controversy or the apologetic enterprise, however. Like other doctrines it was (and is) elaborated also by way of the regular conversation with scripture entailed in the liturgical life of the church, as the sermons of Augustine remind us. We may summarize Christian thinking about the resurrection, taking account of its homiletic aspect, under four rubrics.

The resurrection is understood first of all as a *human* event, an event for the man Jesus, whose passionate prayer to YHWH does not go unanswered. From the cross Jesus cries, 'My God, my God, why have you forsaken me?' (Mark 15: 34). He is quoting Psalm 22: 'Why are you so far from helping me, from the words of my groaning? . . . Do not be far from me, for trouble is near and there is no one to help. . . . Save me from the mouth of the lion!' The resurrection is the answer he is given. It is the proof he requires that there is indeed one to deliver him, like Daniel, from the lion's maw and 'the power of the dog'. The resurrection is a human event because it is the event of a man's acknowledgement by God. 'For [God] did not despise or abhor the affliction of the afflicted; he did not hide his face from me, but heard when I cried to him' (Ps. 22: 24; cf. Ps. 88). Without this saving event—the reclamation of body and soul from the power of death—the prayer of Jesus, the despised and rejected one, is itself despised and rejected. But heard and honoured, it becomes the foundation for the belief that even death must yield up its prey to the divine love, which will restore the one who prays to the community of love and life from which he or she has been cut off. It also becomes the basis for a Christian theology of prayer in the name of Jesus, for 'the things which save are the name of our Lord Jesus Christ and the Spirit of our God' (Irenaeus, *Heresies* 5. 11. 1; cf. John Paul II, *Dives in Misericordia* §8).

Second, and by extension, the resurrection is understood as a *political* event. 'We have no king but Caesar', said Jesus' opponents (John 19: 15 NIV); otherwise put, 'We do not want this man to rule over us' (Luke 19: 14). This political judgement God overruled in the resurrection. Jesus was put to death because, in his curious and unacceptable way, he claimed to be the Son of God, the king of Israel (John 1: 49; 19: 7). But he was 'declared to be Son of God with power according to the Spirit of holiness by resurrection from the dead' (Rom. 1: 4). If faithful Jews expected the righteous to rise at the end of the age in order to enter the kingdom of God, by raising Jesus alone, ahead of the rest, God made plain who would have the pre-eminence and authority in that kingdom. He put Jesus forward as Lord. In the ascension Jesus took up his authority and began to exercise it, Pentecost being the first display of his power. 'You have taken your great power and begun to reign' (Rev. 11: 17; cf. Acts. 2: 33–4). Here it should be noted that if the resurrection is not bodily it can have no political meaning, since political authority *is* authority over the body. But if the resurrection is bodily, then no social or political sphere is exempt from the judgement passed by God. The modern notion of the secular as a sphere unconstrained by the gospel is thus a notion foreign to the Christian tradition. The confession, 'Jesus is Lord', is something more than a claim about his power to deliver individuals from sin, death, and the devil. It is a public confession of the scope of his rule, rightly perceived to be in conflict with its alternative, 'Caesar is Lord' (O'Donovan 1996: 146–57; cf. Pagels 1989: 6–7, who prefers to think that the doctrine of bodily resurrection was adopted by the church in order to prop up the hierarchy).

Third, the resurrection is understood as a *cosmic* event, since it marks the appearance of the true *imago Dei* and hence the beginning of God's ultimate purposes for creation: 'The creation waits with eager longing for the revealing of the children of God.... We know that the whole creation has been groaning in labour pains until now; and not only the creation, but we ourselves, who have the first fruits of the Spirit, groan inwardly while we wait for adoption, the redemption of our bodies' (Rom. 8: 19–23). Resurrection hope, in patristic and scholastic elaboration, anticipates life in bodies that are both sentient and impassible (knowing pleasure without pain), agile and subtle (fully responsive to the soul), glorious and spiritual (participant with the soul in the life of the Holy Spirit). It also looks forward to 'the renewal of all things' (Matt. 19: 28; Rev. 21–2), which will involve a widening or extending of creaturely capacities and responsibilities through unhindered communion with God. The appearance of the church is already evidence of this widening or extending (Eph. 2–3; cf. Irenaeus, *Heresies* 4–5). Resurrection hope is not directed away from the created order, then, but towards its restoration and consummation in the unity of man with God. It is therefore the ground also of the moral life, which is a faithful participation in the created order (O'Donovan 1986: 13–15, 76–97).

Fourth, the resurrection is understood as a *divine* event. Only God can abolish death, with all its antecedents and consequences; only God can establish the conditions for perpetual peace. In the resurrection, in which Jesus Christ is made to live anew for God, God lives anew for man, in complete sovereignty. He remains faithful to his covenant and so shows himself to be God. More specifically, he remains faithful to his Son and so declares himself, in time as in the divine eternity, the Son's loving Father. He blesses the Son anew, in his dead humanity, with the Holy Spirit, and so with eternal life. At the same time, the Son, participating with the Father in his own resurrection, shows the indestructibility of his human life through the exercise of his divine power (Heb. 7: 16; cf. *ST* 3a. 53, 4, in Aquinas 1948). In both ways the groundwork is laid for our deification, not in the sense of Lessing or Hegel or Schleiermacher, who would later translate the doctrine of the resurrection of Jesus into a doctrine about the transformation of human consciousness—the revelation to man of his own divinity—but rather in the sense of Irenaeus: that man cannot live without God, and here God chooses not to live without man. The resurrection is the victory of God, not only over 'our weak human nature', but over the 'monstrous' fact of the corruption and disappearance of man (Athanasius, *Incarnation* 6). It is God's refusal to allow the divine image to be defined by sin or by death. It is God bringing life and immortality to light, and so bringing himself to light as he truly is: 'He is immortal and powerful to such a degree as to confer immortality upon what is mortal, and eternity upon what is temporal' (Irenaeus, *Heresies* 3. 20. 2).

II. The Christian Tradition in Modern Debate

'There is no article of the Christian faith which has encountered such contradiction as that of the resurrection of the flesh', observed Augustine (*Expositions on the Book of Psalms* 89.32, in Schaff 1980*a*: viii. 437). We may choose to look no further for an explanation of that fact than Peter Martyr Vermigli's acknowledgment that this doctrine, though it 'involves many chief points of Christian faith necessary for salvation', is 'something far removed from human reason' (*Resurrection* 1, in McLelland 1996: 47). But Vermigli knows better than that. He offers a definition that highlights, not only the efficient cause of the resurrection, but its final cause. The resurrection of the dead 'is a new union of the soul with the body by the force or power of God, so that whole persons may stand before the last judgement and may receive rewards or punishments on the basis of their previous life' (*Resurrection* 12). The scandal of the resurrection, in other words, is the scandal to sinful man of the resurrection of the crucified before it is the scandal to human reason of the resurrection of the flesh. This is worth noticing before entering the world of modern debate on the resurrection, which has been so heavily influenced by objections to the doctrine's rationality.

These objections are rarely new, though attempts to respond to them have generated new insights as well as reproduced old heresies. We may take as our point of departure Hume's contention that 'a miracle can never be proved so as to be the foundation of a system of religion' (*An Enquiry Concerning Human Understanding* 10. 2, in Hume 2000: 97). From here we can trace one arc of modern criticism, which appears already in Lessing's *On the Proof of the Spirit and of Power*: 'If on historical grounds I have no objection to the statement that this Christ himself rose from the dead, must I therefore accept it as true that this risen Christ was the Son of God', in some ontological sense that requires me to 'form all my metaphysical and moral ideas accordingly'? (Chadwick 1956: 54–5). The answer is no, and Lessing makes it plain that the prodosis is granted only for the sake of the argument. The resurrection reports may at least be worthy of deliberation and doubt, but for the purposes of establishing sound metaphysics and morals they can be ignored with the same impunity as 'the old pious legend that the hand which scatters the seed must wash in snail's blood seven times for each throw'. Lessing proceeds, in his *Education of the Human Race*, to substitute reincarnation for resurrection (Chadwick 1956: 97–8).

The other arc can be traced through attacks on the credibility of those who wrote the reports, that is, on the prodosis itself. Critics from Reimarus to Lüdemann have spilt much ink on the Gospels, while not a few theologians have embraced the sceptical results with evident relief (e.g., Carnley 1987; cf. Torrance 1976: 1–26; Wright 2003: 5–6). The resurrection, like all miracles, seemed out of place in a Newtonian universe, and the eventual transcending of Newtonian science and of Kantian philosophy did little to rehabilitate the miraculous. By then the notion was deeply entrenched that faith and reason are compatible only if faith confines itself to the territory between these arcs—to the ellipse of the non-metaphysical and the non-empirical. Faith was privatized, in other words, and articles of faith such as the resurrection were allowed only a subjective significance. Luther had declared reason incompetent in matters of religion; religion was now declared incompetent in matters of public reason. Troeltsch later stated the condition for readmission: If theologians wish to recover a role 'in the formation of ethical and religious ideas for the present', they must confront 'one great fact', viz., that the task in question is to clarify the transformation from medieval to modern presuppositions (Troeltsch 1907: col. 199). One of those presuppositions is the essential similarity of all historical events; which is to say, the impossibility of making any room in a rational account of history for supernatural events. Troeltsch thought that the real point of dispute was not the resurrection but the fall, to which the resurrection was remedy; but he took care to quarantine the whole of salvation history (Morgan and Pye 1990: 192–3, 202). He also chose to ignore the fact that modern resistance to the resurrection looked very much like pre-modern resistance. The Ptolemaic world-view, after all, had put up its own cosmological objections and brought forward its own literary criticism of the Gospels (cf. Augustine, *City* 22. 4 ff.).

More positively, both arcs of modern criticism served to rebuke the extrinsicism that had begun to characterize treatments of the resurrection in Catholic and Protestant apologetics, where it was and sometimes still is argued (Swinburne 2003) that the resurrection can be proven, or at least shown to be probable, on historical or philosophical grounds, with the intention of thereby justifying the Christian religion. That way of thinking tended to detach the doctrine of the resurrection from Christology, much as Christology itself had become detached from theology (cf. Fiorenza 1984; Buckley 1987). Critics reminded these apologists that their case rested finally on an appeal to human authority, which Aquinas had identified as the weakest form of argument. Unfortunately, under the conditions of such theological dismemberment, neither the apologists nor their critics were able to recollect or to follow the logic of Augustine's claim that 'there is nothing more wholesome in the Catholic Church than using authority before argument' (*On the Morals of the Catholic Church* 25. 47, in Schaff 1980*a*: iv. 55). Not until the opening lines of the second edition of Barth's *Römerbrief* would that note be sounded again with any force.

Meanwhile, Friedrich Schleiermacher, who hoped to restore some internal integrity to Protestant theology, could only achieve that by setting traditional eschatology aside (Schleiermacher 1928: 696–722). Rejecting miracles in principle, including perforce the resurrection of Jesus, he politely declared much of Christian eschatology to be what thoughtful gnostics had always supposed it to be, namely, a graphic representation of the life of the soul—psychology, not history. That, of course, did not eliminate altogether the old problem of continuity and discontinuity, which Schleiermacher maintained was insoluble, since no attempt to coordinate the perfecting of the individual soul and the consummation of the church could hope to be successful. Neither goal can be reached in this world, he agreed, but the next world must be perceived in one of two contradictory ways: from the perspective of the church triumphant, it must be a wholly new world, subsequent to the final judgement and exclusive of every sinful or imperfect element (thus Augustine); from the perspective of the soul, however, it must be the home of further development, a development that requires the church but cannot at the outset admit of perfection (thus Gregory). Hence, concluded Schleiermacher, the conviction of a future consummation does not lead to any coherent conception of it. For we cannot easily conceive of the soul's immediate perfection, since such discontinuity would destroy its self-identity, nor yet of its ongoing progress, since such continuity must cut it off from the church and put in doubt the very idea of perfection. Even without the doctrine of bodily resurrection, Christian eschatology cannot give a rational account of itself.

Protestant theology after Schleiermacher had to choose whether or not to be content as religious psychology and/or social ethics (Ritschl's preference), neither of which provided much room for the doctrine of the resurrection or for the interventionist ideas about history and judgement to which it is linked. Barth, who learned from the Blumhardts that psychology was not enough, and from Overbeck and the Great War that ethics was not enough, made the doctrine of the resurrection his starting point in a new attempt at theology. Like Schleiermacher, he wanted a Christianity that was properly Christological; however, he insisted that if it were not wholly eschatological it had nothing to do with Christ (Barth 1968: 314). That led him to consider afresh both the epistemological and the ontological implications of the resurrection, and its political implications too.

Epistemologically, Schleiermacher might well have agreed with Barth that knowledge of the resurrection is 'knowledge that the reconciliation which took place in Jesus Christ is not some casual story, but that in this work of God's grace we have to do with the word of God's omnipotence, that here an ultimate and supreme thing comes into action, behind which there is no other reality' (Barth 1949: 126). But for Schleiermacher that knowledge *is* the resurrection, whereas for Barth it is an *effect* of the resurrection. Barth eventually came to believe that, unless we take the resurrection to be a real event for Jesus, an event with definite coordinates within our common history, theology cannot escape the toils of religious psychology. It cannot really be about God as a man, but only about man as God (cf. Barth 1960: 442; Bonhoeffer 1978: 44). And this will have its own effect on history and politics, as the dead Christ is raised up symbolically into history to support this or that movement or ideology—Nazism, for example, which Barth resisted in the name of the living Christ.

Ontologically, Barth attempted in the massive fourth volume of his *Church Dogmatics* to translate the Chalcedonian dogma, of which Schleiermacher was suspicious, into a more dynamic form. The resurrection of Jesus renders eternal the unity of the God-man, whose personal existence comprises the simultaneous descent of God and ascent of man already fulfilled in the mystery of his earthly life. His resurrection is both the confirmation of this unity and the ground of his lordship over space and time and all its inhabitants. It is the beginning of his *parousia*, his universal revelation. In Barth's approach all extrinsicism is repudiated. The resurrection of Jesus, an event in time that transforms time, is not the historical proof of the validity of the Christian religion or of Christian hope in the kingdom of God. Rather, the resurrected one is himself the kingdom in person and the power of that kingdom. Whatever the Christian legitimately believes in and hopes for, is believed in and hoped for in connection with Jesus, in his activity in the Spirit as the resurrected Lord (Barth 1960: 490).

About the same time, Künneth was also attempting to rethink theology from the standpoint of the doctrine of the resurrection (Barth's dialectical *The Resurrection of the Dead* appeared in 1924, Künneth's more systematic *The Theology of the Resurrection* in 1933), an enterprise pursued further by Torrance, Moltmann, Pannenberg, Jenson, and others. Theologians of this stripe reject Troeltsch's preconditions for public theology, just as they reject any attempt to subject the resurrection to standards of proof incommensurate with its own character. As a miraculous act of re-creation, the resurrection is a unique historical event that must, in the last analysis, be self-verifying. It is not finally a matter of the probable or even of the possible; by its very nature the resurrection posits a *new* history, and therewith the grounds on which it is to be believed and interpreted (Torrance 1976: 26). Hence confession of the resurrected Lord, though quintessentially a public act, can be made only in the Spirit, who brings the new creation to bear on the old (1 Cor. 12: 3). The task taken up by these theologians is to understand the Christological, epistemological, and soteriological implications of the resurrection as well as its bearing on time, history, nature, ecology, politics, ecclesiology, the Trinity, and being as such. 'To be is to rise from the dead', Jenson provocatively proclaims (1982: 182).

In stark contrast, Bultmann, Tillich, Ebeling, and others opted instead for a kerygmatic existentialism that intends to preserve the eschatological urgency of New Testament proclamation while acknowledging with Weiss and Schweitzer its failure as a reading of events in the real world. Talk of an empty tomb, as Hegel had suggested, refers to no place or occasion in human history other than the birth or rebirth of faith in Jesus. In short, the resurrection is a symbol of belief in the crucified one as a symbol of God, or of the divine potential in man (Hegel 1988: 468; Bultmann 1953: 10–11, 41–2; cf. Farrow 1999: 186–91). Variations on this theme are common today, especially among liberal Protestants, but critics respond that all attempts to produce a *theologia crucis* without a *theologia resurrectionis* suffer a major shortcoming: Whatever may be supposed about the 'real' world, from the standpoint of the New Testament the whole procedure is simply unthinkable (Künneth 1965: 152; Barth 1958: 354–5). It cannot deliver the decisive 'Fear not!' that is the gospel's motive force; nor is it obvious how it can support the Christian virtues of faith, hope, and love since it does not find in the resurrection the vindication of divine justice or the consummation of human salvation (cf. Aquinas, *ST* 3a. 53, 1; John Paul II, *Evangelium Vitae* §§29, 38, 67, 105). Arguably, it leaves the entire Christian mission unsupported (Seitz 2001: 117) and nullifies the logic of the martyrs, for the martyrs bear their cross by believing the resurrection and believe the resurrection by bearing their cross.

The defence is offered that in fact it leaves room in the modern world for faith. The charge levelled by Irenaeus against certain second-century teachers—that they spoke as if acquaintance with their own doctrine *were* the resurrection—is nevertheless repeated within contemporary Protestantism. Balthasar may be a little optimistic in stating that 'the tragic opposition between "Barth" and "Bultmann" (taking these names as representatives of two tendencies) does not exist in the Catholic world' (Balthasar 1990: 217; cf. Barth 1956: ix), but the magisterium does insist on adherence to a literal reading of the creed's 'on the third day he rose again in accordance with the scriptures' (*Catechism of the Catholic Church* §§638–55). The symbolist readings of various liberationist and modernist theologians are disavowed (e.g., Haight 1999: 125), as are the gnosticizing speculations of evolutionary mythologists such as Teilhard. Christ does not rise into history or the noosphere or even *simpliciter* into the church (Balthasar 1990: 215; cf. Koch 1965). He rises in his own flesh. Jesus' corporeal humanity is a permanent feature of creation, and his resurrection is the beginning of the world's transfiguration, not of its folding up or dissolution. If Christians are materialists, allows Rahner, they are crass materialists, for they believe that matter 'will last forever, and be glorified forever' (Rahner 1961–92: iv. 351 ff.; cf. vii. 177 ff. and xvii. 16 ff.). Otherwise put: If the church is obliged by God to speak about the resurrection of both body and soul, it cannot speak instead of a liberation of soul from body, or of body from flesh, 'for as it is God truly who raises up man, so also does man truly rise from the dead, and not allegorically' (Irenaeus, *Heresies* 5. 35. 2).

From that perspective, the opposition between 'Barth' and 'Bultmann' does seem to touch on 'the division between faith and non-faith' that passes through the middle of theological science, 'or more precisely put, right though the middle of its concern with those data on which it is built' (Balthasar 1990: 227). Objectivity or exteriority does not preclude subjectivity or interiority, nor does it reduce to apologetics; but it does preclude subjectivity or interiority as a satisfactory starting point. The difference is not successfully negotiated by regarding the resurrection as a real symbol and object of faith that 'historically manifests the permanence for which human beings hope', or by marginalizing the resurrection appearances in favour of existential analysis, as even Rahner tends to do (Fiorenza 1984: 16; cf. Rahner 1978: 238 ff.). Nor is it overcome by way of Schillebeeckx's notion of a Christ who, on the basis of his disciples' Easter conversion experiences (understood as strictly interior encounters), can be spoken of variously as resurrected, exalted, or enthroned without any particular commitment to the bodily nature of the resurrection. That leaves open the question that the New Testament intends to answer, viz., the identity of the risen and returning Lord with the Jesus who was crucified. (See further Fiorenza 1984: 18–46. Not everyone finds this problematic, of course: cf. Allison 2005: 209–12 on Rudolph Pesch, and Allison's own remarks at 331–44; Hall 1996: 387–94.)

Protestant theology, stimulated by its deeper struggle with this opposition and division, has generated the more interesting attempts to refit the doctrine of the resurrection for today. Torrance's important work, *Space, Time and Resurrection*, was informed by his labours in ecclesiology and eschatology and at the interface between theology and the philosophy of science. 'The resurrection of Jesus is an event that happens in history in continuity with the living event of the whole historical existence of Jesus, yet as an event of fulfilled redemption the resurrection issues in a new creation beyond the corruptible processes of this world, on the other side of decay and death, and on the other side of judgement, in the fullness of a new world and of a new order of things' (Torrance 1976: 86). In his attempt to answer the question as to how these things can be thought together, Torrance appealed to the concept of recapitulation and, like Irenaeus, tried to work out a view of creaturely reality capable of accommodating it. If this made the whole historical life of Jesus 'resurrection from beginning to end' (Torrance 1976: 94), it did not obliterate the distinction between pre- and post-Easter forms of existence. Following Calvin and William Milligan, Torrance was careful to distinguish the doctrines of resurrection and ascension and to develop both. His focus on Christ's heavenly priesthood helped to counteract the tendency in Barth, as in some patristic thought, to emphasize the revelation of Christ's divinity at the expense of his reconstituted humanity (cf. Gunton 2003: 67–91; Burgess 2004; Dawson 2004) and drew attention to the problem of the presence and the absence, that is, to the eschatological tension generated by the departure of Jesus (cf. Seitz 2001: 133–48; Marion 2002: 124–52). It also left more room, at least in principle, for coordination of the messianic and the pneumatological dimensions of resurrection theology.

That task was taken up independently by Moltmann (1990: 151–283 and 1996: 47–128), who integrated it with ecological and theodical concerns. Moltmann observes that, of the two main images of hope in the face of death—the immortality of the soul or the resurrection of the body—only the latter does not individualize eschatology or break the solidarity between humans and the earth. But what of the solidarity between God and creation? Moltmann was also seeking an account of history that would double as theodicy. His was a very different account than that offered by Hegel, who tried to move directly from the Passion to Pentecost. 'The Christian belief in the resurrection does not proclaim world-historical tendencies or anthropological hopes', insists Moltmann, 'but the nucleus of a new righteousness in a world where dead and living cry out for righteousness' (Moltmann 1974: 177). The life of the Spirit does not flow directly from Jesus' cross, in other words, but from his resurrection. Redemption comes *to* history rather than *through* history—it is a *novum*, a new creation, albeit *ex vetere* rather than *ex nihilo*. Moltmann's ecological theodicy, however, has curious effects. He regards the cross as the protest of divine love against all creaturely suffering and sees the resurrected one as the beginning of a universal *apokatastasis*. What has been will be again; every creature in its own space–time configuration will enter into eternal life. According to Moltmann, resurrection hope should not be reduced to the expectation of life after death (or of life after life after death). Resurrection is diachronic. It embraces the whole configuration or gestalt, indeed 'the whole life history', not merely some inner kernel or the body that goes to the grave. And just as the resurrection of Jesus entails the resurrection of all persons, not merely for judgement but for salvation, so personal resurrection entails the regeneration of all things whatsoever, sentient and non-sentient.

Pannenberg, who is not a universalist even in the narrower sense, is more consistent with scripture and tradition and a more astute commentator on the modern debate. Strauss quipped in his *Glaubenslehre* (1840–1: ii. 739) that belief in another world, especially a future world, is 'the last enemy that speculative criticism has to fight and, if possible, to overcome' for the sake of the human race. Pannenberg replies that Christianity's resurrection faith is a more humane force just because it does not subordinate the individual to the race. Biblical eschatology, notes Pannenberg (1991–8: iii. 527–646), begins with promises that address the corporate expectations of the covenant people—a theme stripped in the Enlightenment of its covenantal particularity—but adds assurances respecting the fate of the righteous person. The doctrine of bodily resurrection is what holds these hopes together, though it also raises a number of difficult questions about 'the unity of our individual and social destiny' (Pannenberg 1991–8: iii. 549).

Pace Cullmann (1958), Pannenberg does not think that the church was Hellenizing when it eventually embraced the immortality of the soul, since it continued to deny the soul's native divinity. The immortality of the soul is a function of the irrevocable call to communion with God that is graciously confirmed in Christ, a call that can be answered fully only conjointly and by way of bodily resurrection (Pannenberg 1991–8: iii. 570–3; cf. Irenaeus, *Heresies* 2. 34, 4. 38, 5. 1–2; Augustine, *City* 10. 31, 13. 19, 13. 24; see also Ratzinger 1988: 150–61 and Schwarz 2000: 285). Medieval debates about the soul's interim state, however, highlight the problem of continuity and discontinuity, with which Schleiermacher and other moderns also wrestled. The 'inner problematic of the idea of resurrection' lies in the difficulty of conceiving identity while asserting transformation (Pannenberg 1991–8: iii. 573–80). Pannenberg joins Origen in questioning material restoration as the basis of identity and approves of the alternative that the soul contains the ground plan of the body, an approach adopted by Aquinas without the spiritualizing tendency of Origen. But we must not ignore the fact 'that our life history is constitutive for our individuality'. A new or further history of the soul after death would mean a new and different identity. On the other hand, if we turn (with Gilbert Greshake) to resurrection at death, are we not in danger of breaking the relation between the individual and the common destiny? History requires an end, an end in which everyone participates.

Since Pannenberg does not regard death as a defining element of creatureliness, the logic here is not fully transparent. But the crucial challenge for eschatology is to reach an understanding of the relation of time and eternity, and of the end of time to eternal life, while the specific challenge respecting the resurrection is that of maintaining identity. The difficulty in linking the end of time with life disappears only if we see *God* as the end of time, that is, as the future of the world. Likewise, the difficulty in maintaining identity disappears only if we understand that all things already derive their time from the final future that is God. When God, with whom all things exist simultaneously in the totality of their existence, is kept in view, it is no longer necessary to think of identity in terms of an uninterrupted history. God is the guarantor of identity. 'In this light the resurrection of the dead and the renewal of creation may be seen as the act by which God through his Spirit restores to the creatures' existence ... the form of being-for-themselves. Herein the identity of creatures needs no continuity on the time line but is ensured by the fact that their existence is not lost in God's eternal present' (Pannenberg 1991–8: iii. 606; cf. iii. 638–9 and Hick 1976: 224). Men and women go into eternity at death but only at the end of history do they receive back 'the being-for-self of the totality of their existence that is preserved in God, and thus live with all others before God' (Pannenberg 1991–8: iii. 629–30).

Pannenberg thus follows the pattern of Tertullian, who criticized his opponents for conducting their discussion in a disorderly manner, beginning with doubts about the resurrection in order to disparage the creator instead of beginning with the creator himself. Moreover, he is at one with tradition, not only in denying the naturalness of death, but in regarding the resurrection of the just as creating a new time and space for human living. How we are to think about this new time and space, however—whether for Jesus, who is resurrected alone at the beginning of the end of the ages, or for Mary, who follows first of all, or for the rest of the righteous dead—is less than clear. The problem can be traced back to Boethius' concept of God's eternity as pure duration or simultaneity, of which Pannenberg is insufficiently critical. The tendency of this concept is to smother creaturely time by insisting on presenting it whole or all at once. The result, visible variously in Barth (cf. Farrow 1999: 245–54), Moltmann (1990: 267–8; 1996: 294–5), Jenson (1997–9: i. 194–206, ii. 338–52), and Pannenberg (1991–8: iii. 561–2, 573–80), is to obscure the doctrine of bodily resurrection by making it sound more like the resurrection of a history than of a person. Though Pannenberg provides one of the best available maps to theological debate about the resurrection, a map that points us in the right direction, in this regard he succeeds rather at heightening than resolving the difficulty of the doctrine's inner problematic.

III. A Procedural Comment

It is not hard to say why attempts to probe the relation between time and eternity, or between creaturely eternity and divine eternity, regularly go astray: the former relation can be understood rightly only by the resurrected, the latter only by God.

Resurrection theology contains more than a few 'conjuring tricks with time and eternity' (Newbigin 1998: 152) to captivate those who are not content to 'fall short of an explanation' (Peters et al. 2002: 321). That said, to avoid such probing altogether is hardly possible. For the miracle of the resurrection is at once an act that restores order and generates order, the novel order of the Spirit who perfects the Trinity's love for humanity (Pannenberg 1991–98: iii. 630–46; cf. Bulgakov 2002: 417–526, though his universalist construct, like Gregory's and Moltmann's, is as problematic as it is fascinating). Together with the ascension, it invites us to wrestle not only with the transformation of bodies and souls but with the transformation of time and space and of the whole provisional *schēma tou kosmou* (1 Cor. 7: 31) which was 'formed temporary' until the human relation to God should be settled in Christ (Irenaeus, *Heresies* 5. 36. 1; cf. Gen. 3: 22). Failure to do so must also lead to error, and to forgetfulness of the fact that it is impossible, as Newbigin somewhere remarks, to make the resurrection of Jesus fit any world-view except that of which it is the basis. At the very least, this failure will falsely restrict our theological options (e.g., Cooper 1989: 191–4).

What we ought not to do, however—if we allow that the doctrine of the resurrection is grounded not in an argument but in one who has brought life and immortality to light—is to proceed with such probing within a doctrine of creation that is not already informed by the resurrection. Tertullian himself makes this clarification, whereas Schleiermacher, for example, does not. Therein lies one of the main differences between the patristic and the Enlightenment traditions, and between their respective representatives today, on which a brief comment in conclusion.

Schleiermacher is surely right, speaking from the latter tradition, that there is nothing in our religious consciousness, however stimulated by the symbol of the resurrection, to provide us with a clear conception of the Christian hope. But Schleiermacher only speaks that way because he has no other way to speak (Schleiermacher 1928: 697–8; cf. O'Collins 1995: 89–90). He has already rejected the bodily resurrection of Jesus because his understanding of the God–world relation leaves no room for it. Such an event would collapse the polarities on which his world-view depends. And without that event the problem of continuity and discontinuity, as posed by Christian eschatology, becomes insoluble. Tertullian's insistence on beginning with the doctrine of creation might well have led to a similar impasse, were it not for his willingness to think about that doctrine in the light of the resurrection, thus completing the hermeneutical circle. A rather curious remark in *Resurrection* 59 (cf. Irenaeus, *Heresies* 5. 29. 1) provides a clue to his procedure as well as a reply to the likes of Schleiermacher: 'But, you object, the world to come bears the character of a different dispensation, even an eternal one; and therefore you maintain that the non-eternal substance of this life is incapable of possessing a state of such different features. This would be true enough, if man were made for the future dispensation, and not the dispensation for man.' Tertullian seems to be saying that if we attempt to work out the problem of continuity and discontinuity by beginning abstractly with a set of contrasting categories (time and eternity, mortality and immortality, flesh and spirit, the individual and the church, etc.) we are doomed to failure. God, however, has arranged the very nature of things so as to make them serve those whom he has determined not only to create but also to redeem.

From this it follows that the relation between the world as made and the world as perfected, between the man who became a living creature and the man who is made alive forever, may be outwardly incomprehensible to us without being inwardly incoherent. More can be said than that, however. The passage to which Tertullian alludes—'the Sabbath was made for man, not man for the Sabbath'—adds that 'the Son of Man is Lord even of the Sabbath' (Mark 2: 27–8 NIV). Tertullian knows *who the man is* for whom the future dispensation is made. He is, in the first instance, the resurrected and returning Jesus. It is from Jesus that we are to take our cues about continuity and discontinuity. Here, of course, Schleiermacher cannot follow. On his view, doctrines such as the resurrection and ascension do not speak of things that happened to Jesus, but of things that happen in us; that is, they articulate in various ways our recognition of Jesus' 'peculiar dignity' and our longing to be united with him in his perfect God-consciousness. The Easter and post-Easter events 'cannot be laid down as properly constituent parts of the doctrine of his person' (Schleiermacher 1928: 417–24). We are therefore cast back, like Simmias, upon our own negligible resources where eschatology is concerned.

Schleiermacher's reasoning is the very inverse of Tertullian's, in other words. The church's belief in the 'survival of personality' rests on Jesus' endorsement of that notion, but if in fact Jesus has immortality he has just the sort of immortality that is native to the rest of us (Schleiermacher 1928: 698–703; cf. Allison 2005: 225–6). Indeed, he has the sort of immortality that, being native to man, is itself the precondition for the incarnation of God in him. Whereas, for Tertullian, Jesus himself is the precondition for every claim to be made about human immortality, and the judgement that God will exercise through Jesus is the cause of the resurrection and the precondition for the new creation (*Resurrection* 14). Thus also Aquinas, who confirms the Christological principle that guided patristic thought: 'Through seeing Christ, who is our head, rise again, we hope that we likewise shall rise again' (*ST* 3a. 53, 1). And again: 'Christ's resurrection has instrumentally an effective power not only with regard to the resurrection of bodies, but also with respect to the resurrection of souls...; even in our souls we must be conformed with the rising Christ' (*ST* 3a. 56, 2).

Now if we opt for the procedure of Tertullian and Aquinas the difficulties raised earlier by Schleiermacher begin to fall away. The resurrection poses no threat to the personal identity of Jesus. Nor is there any conflict in him between perfection and increase, for it is his nature to be ever more fruitful. The church he calls into being is for the mutual receiving and bearing of the Holy Spirit, a receptacle for the inexhaustible gifts of God. If it now exists as a communion of 'the spirits of just men made perfect' (Heb. 12: 23 RSV) and those still struggling to throw off entangling sin, in the consummation it will not suffer from that limitation; there will be increase without decrease (cf. Farrow 1999: 49–52). As for the sinner's continuity of identity while passing through death and the forge of final judgement, which will remove from body and soul every impediment to life, for this problem too there is the beginning of an answer. Even in that incomprehensible conversion his identity is mediated by Jesus Christ, who is both the judge and the judgement. 'Therefore, if anyone is in Christ, he is a new creation; the old has gone, the new has come' (2 Cor. 5: 17 NIV; cf. Bonhoeffer 1978: 60).

It is in faithfulness to this answer that the church has always insisted on resurrection to righteousness of soul as well as to perfection of body, to the freedom of *non posse peccare* (Augustine, *City* 22. 30) as well as *non posse mori*—the one as dependent on Christ as the other. The doctrine of purgatory, which seeks to articulate the need for righteousness without jeopardizing continuity, may appear to undermine the Christological point. But it need not do so if properly anchored in baptism and the eucharist. For what Schleiermacher pulls apart—the wholly new and that which has a history, the perfect and that which enjoys progress, judgement and salvation—these the sacraments hold together. The grace they extend, and the promise they confirm, is not merely the survival of personality but a recapitulation of the whole person in Christ, and of Christ in the whole person (cf. *City* 13. 23, 22. 22). They do not require time and space *from* us, so much as they make time and space *for* us. They are sacraments of the sudden grace of the resurrection, which is the beginning of true advance: 'Fear not! I am the first and the last, and the living one; I died, and behold I am alive for evermore, and I have the keys of Death and Hades' (Rev. 1: 17–18 RSV).

References

All encyclicals may be found at the Vatican website at http://www.vatican.va/holy_father/john_paul_ii/encyclicals/index.htm or in printed editions from various publishers.

Allison, Dale (2005). *Resurrecting Jesus.* T. & T. Clark.

Aquinas, St Thomas (1948). *Summa Theologica.* Notre Dame: Ave Maria.

Augustine (1610). *The City of God.* 2 vols. London: Griffith Farran Okeden & Welsh.

—— (1991). *The Trinity.* Brooklyn: New City.

Balthasar, H. U. von (1990). *Mysterium Paschale.* T. & T. Clark.

Barth, Karl (1933 [1924]). *The Resurrection of the Dead.* London: Hodder and Stoughton.

—— (1949). *Dogmatics in Outline.* London: SCM.

—— (1956). *Church Dogmatics* IV/1. Edinburgh: T. & T. Clark.

—— (1958). *Church Dogmatics* IV/2. Edinburgh: T. & T. Clark.

—— (1960). *Church Dogmatics* III/2. Edinburgh: T. & T. Clark.

—— (1968). *The Epistle to the Romans*. Oxford: Oxford University Press.
Bonhoeffer, Dietrich (1978). *Christ the Center*. San Francisco: Harper & Row.
Buckley, Michael (1987). *At the Origins of Modern Atheism*. Yale: Yale University Press.
Bulgakov, Sergius (2002). *The Bride of the Lamb*. Grand Rapids: Eerdmans.
Bultmann, Rudolf (1953). *Kerygma and Myth*, i. London: SPCK.
Burgess, Andrew (2004). *The Ascension in Karl Barth*. Aldershot: Ashgate.
Bynum, Caroline Walker (1995). *The Resurrection of the Body in Western Christianity, 200–1366*. New York: Columbia University Press.
Carnley, Peter (1987). *The Structure of Resurrection Belief*. Oxford: Clarendon.
Catechism of the Catholic Church (1994). Vatican City: Libreria Editrice Vaticana.
Chadwick, Henry (1956). *Lessing's Theological Writings*. London: A. & C. Black.
Cooper, John (1989). *Body, Soul and Life Everlasting*. Grand Rapids: Eerdmans.
Cullmann, Oscar (1958). *Immortality of the Soul or Resurrection of the Dead? The Witness of the New Testament*. London: Epworth.
Dawson, Gerrit (2004). *Jesus Ascended: The Meaning of Christ's Continuing Incarnation*. London: T. & T. Clark.
Edwards, Mark (2002). *Origen Against Plato*. Aldershot: Ashgate.
Farrow, Douglas (1999). *Ascension and Ecclesia*. Edinburgh: T. & T. Clark.
Fiorenza, Francis Schüssler (1984). *Foundational Theology: Jesus and the Church*. New York: Crossroad.
Gunton, Colin (ed.) (2003). *The Theology of Reconciliation*. T. & T. Clark.
Haight, Roger (1999). *Jesus: Symbol of God*. Maryknoll: Orbis.
Hall, Douglas (1996). *Professing the Faith: Christian Theology in a North American Context*. Minneapolis: Fortress.
Hart, David (2003). *The Beauty of the Infinite*. Grand Rapids: Eerdmans.
Hegel, G. W. F. (1988). *Lectures on the Philosophy of Religion: The Lectures of 1827*. Berkeley and Los Angeles: University of California Press.
Hick, John (1976). *Death and Eternal Life*. London: Collins.
Holleman, Joost (1996). *Resurrection and Parousia*. Leiden: Brill.
Hume, David (2000). *An Enquiry Concerning Human Understanding*. New York: Oxford University Press.
Jenson, Robert (1982). *The Triune Identity*. Minneapolis: Fortress.
—— (1997–9). *Systematic Theology*. 2 vols. Oxford: Oxford University Press.
Koch, Gerhard (1965). *Die Auferstehung Jesu Christi*. Tübingen: Mohr.
Künneth, Walter (1965). *The Theology of the Resurrection*. London: SCM.
Lüdemann, Gerd (1994). *The Resurrection of Jesus*. London: SCM.
McLelland, Joseph C. (1996). *Philosophical Works: On the Relation of Philosophy to Theology*. Peter Martyr Vermigli Library, ser. 1, vol. iv. Sixteenth Century Essays and Studies, vol. 39. Kirksville: Sixteenth Century Journal Publishers.
Marion, Jean-Luc (2002). *Prolegomena to Charity*. New York: Fordham University Press.
Moltmann, Jürgen (1974). *The Crucified God*. London: SCM.
—— (1990). *The Way of Jesus Christ*. London: SCM.
—— (1996). *The Coming of God: Christian Eschatology*. Minneapolis: Fortress.
Morgan, Robert, and Pye, Michael (eds.) (1990). *Ernst Troeltsch: Writings on Theology and Religion*. Louisville: Westminster/John Knox.
Newbigin, Lesslie (1998). *The Household of God*. Carlisle: Paternoster.

O'Collins, Gerald (1987) *Jesus Risen: An Historical, Fundamental and Systematic Examination of Christ's Resurrection.* New York: Paulist.
—— (1995). *Christology: A Biblical, Historical and Systematic Study of Jesus Christ.* Oxford: Oxford University Press.
O'Donovan, Oliver (1986). *Resurrection and Moral Order: An Outline for Evangelical Ethics.* Grand Rapids: Eerdmans.
—— (1996). *The Desire of the Nations: Rediscovering the Roots of Political Theology.* Cambridge: Cambridge University Press.
Pagels, Elaine (1989). *The Gnostic Gospels.* New York: Vintage.
Pannenberg, Wolfhart (1991–8). *Systematic Theology.* 3 vols. Grand Rapids: Eerdmans.
Pascal, Blaise (1966). *Pensées.* New York: Penguin.
Peters, Ted, Russell, Robert John, and Welker, Michael (eds.) (2002). *Resurrection.* Grand Rapids: Eerdmans.
Plato (1989). *The Collected Dialogues of Plato.* Princeton: Princeton University Press.
Rahner, Karl (1961–92). *Theological Investigations.* 23 vols. London: Darton, Longman & Todd.
—— (1978). *Foundations of the Christian Faith.* London: Darton, Longman & Todd.
Ratzinger, Joseph (1988). *Eschatology.* Washington, DC: Catholic University of America Press.
Roberts, A., and Donaldson, J. (eds.) (1990). *Ante-Nicene Fathers: The Writings of the Fathers down to A.D. 325.* Edinburgh: T. & T. Clark.
Roth, Catherine (2002). *St Gregory of Nyssa: On the Soul and the Resurrection.* Crestwood: St Vladimir's Seminary Press.
Schaff, P. (ed.) (1980*a*). *A Select Library of the Nicene and Post-Nicene Fathers of the Christian Church.* 1st ser. Edinburgh: T. & T. Clark.
—— (ed.) (1980*b*). *A Select Library of the Nicene and Post-Nicene Fathers of the Christian Church.* 2nd ser. Edinburgh: T. & T. Clark.
Schillebeeckx, Edward (1979). *Jesus: An Experiment in Christology.* New York: Seabury.
Schleiermacher, F. D. E. (1928). *The Christian Faith.* Edinburgh: T. & T. Clark.
Schwarz, Hans (2000). *Eschatology.* Grand Rapids: Eerdmans.
Seitz, Christopher (ed.) (2001). *Nicene Christianity: The Future for a New Ecumenism.* Grand Rapids: Brazos.
Stendahl, Krister (ed.) (1965). *Immortality and Resurrection.* New York: Macmillan.
Strauss, D. F. (1840–1). *Die christliche Glaubenslehre in ihrer geschlichtlichen Entwicklung und im Kampfe mit der modernen Wissenschaft.* 2 vols. Tübingen: C. F. Osiander; Stuttgart: F. H. Kohler.
Swinburne, Richard (2003). *The Resurrection of God Incarnate.* Oxford: Clarendon.
Torrance, T. F. (1976). *Space, Time and Resurrection.* Grand Rapids: Eerdmans.
Troeltsch, Ernst (1907). 'Autonomie und Rationalismus in der modernen Welt'. *Internationale Wochenschrift für Wissenschaft, Kunst und Technik* 1: 199–210.
Wright, N. T. (2003). *The Resurrection of the Son of God.* Philadelphia: Fortress.

Suggested Reading

Farrow (1999).
Fiorenza (1984: 1–55).
Künneth (1965).
Moltmann (1990).
Pannenberg (1991–8: iii. 527–646).
Torrance (1976).
Wright (2003).

CHAPTER 13

THE HOLY SPIRIT

MICHAEL WELKER

The doctrine of the Spirit was generally on the margins of earlier twentieth-century systematic theology. In the last half-century, it has acquired renewed significance, not only as a discrete topic but as a dimension of all Christian teaching. Accordingly, the reinvigoration of pneumatology is felt across the systematic corpus: in the doctrine of the Trinity, where the doctrine of the Spirit is often appealed to as a corrective against apparently monistic doctrines of God which lack a sense of the differentiation of the divine persons; in Christology, where the pneumatological dimensions of the person and work of Christ have complemented incarnational teaching; or in ecclesiology and the theology of mission, where pneumatology expands and corrects theologies of the church structured around office and institution. This chapter reflects on the biblical basis and on some of the fruits of these various theologies of the Spirit, especially in the areas of the nature of human community, the personhood of the Spirit, and the relation of the Spirit to ecstatic experience.

I. The Workings of the Holy Spirit

Beginning with the Old Testament witnesses, 'the Spirit' is always associated with deep experiences, experiences of an awesome power (Dunn 2006). This power can 'overcome' individual persons, it can 'rest' upon a single bearer of the Spirit, and it can be 'poured out' upon many human beings. Although it is an awesome power, the Spirit is not a numinous entity. The biblical narratives exhibit the complex but clear forms and structures of its activity.

The Overcoming Spirit

It is in the time of the judges of Israel, within the context of charismatic leadership, that we first encounter a 'fixed, clearly defined, and abundantly attested use' of the word *ruach*, 'spirit' (Westermann 1981: 225). Several texts report similar stories about the descent of God's Spirit (e.g., Judg. 3: 7–11; 6: 34–5; 11: 29; 1 Sam. 11: 6–7). This Spirit enables the people of Israel to regain their capacity for action after having fallen away from Yahweh and placed themselves into desperate situations. When the people are in seemingly unavoidable and dire straits and acknowledge themselves to be so, a person 'over whom the Spirit of God fell' or 'came' rescues the people of Israel or rather enables them to overcome this most dangerous, life-threatening situation. The charismatic person leads Israel out of a situation of fear, lament, and despairing paralysis. He restores solidarity, loyalty, and the capacity for common action among the people. The activity of the Spirit is not yet, as in the third article of the Apostles' Creed, connected with 'the communion of saints, the forgiveness of sins, the resurrection of the body, and the life everlasting'. It is, however, related in an analogous way to the people of God, to rescue from the power of sin and (self-)endangerment, to the restoration of the capacity to act, and to a long phase of life in peace.

The Resting Spirit

The messianic stories about the 'resting of the Spirit' on the 'servant of God' or on the one whom God 'elected' also speak of saving and freeing interventions (Isa. 11; 42: 1–9, 61). Compared with the war stories associated with the early charismatics, these activities do not arouse ambivalent feelings. The 'bearer of the Spirit', frequently identified with Jesus Christ by the New Testament traditions (e.g., Matt. 12: 15–21; Luke 3: 22; John 1: 32–34), will bring justice, mercy, and the universal knowledge of God in Israel and among the Gentiles. This was one of the main intentions of the 'law of God'. From the 'book of the covenant' (Exod. 20: 22–23:33) to the New Testament remark about the 'weightier matters of the law', namely 'justice and mercy and faith' (Matt. 23: 23), we see the interdependencies between these normative regulations in the law of Israel. The bearer of the Spirit is both in continuity and discontinuity with these traditions. In Jesus' teaching and proclamation, in the coming of the reign of God and in the activity of the Spirit, the main intentions of the law are kept; specific regulations, however, are relativized. The bearer of the Spirit brings justice and mercy, and above all he enables the

Gentiles to identify the Israelites as 'ministers of our God' (Isa. 61: 6). Further, this revolution takes place when the bearer of the Spirit, 'who had been inspired by the Spirit', becomes 'a dispenser of the Spirit' (Dunn 1970, 1996).

The Spirit Poured Out

To articulate that Jesus Christ is the dispenser of the Spirit, the New Testament uses the powerful metaphor of the 'pouring out of the Spirit' found in the prophecy of Joel 2: 28–32 but also in Isaiah 32: 15 and Zechariah 12: 10. The Pentecost account quotes Joel extensively (Acts 2: 17–21) and adds that it is the resurrected and exalted Jesus who, 'having received from the Father the promise of the Holy Spirit,... has poured out this that you both see and hear' (Acts 2: 33). The 'pouring out of the Spirit' is clearly connected to a new knowledge of God and a renewal of spiritual insight and proclamation.

The insistence that male and female, young and old, masters and slaves, as well as people of different nations, languages, and cultures will be endowed with prophetic insight and power (Joel 2: 28–32; cf. Welker 1994: 134–58, 230–9) is revolutionary. It occurs in a patriarchal context in which the aged were favoured and slave-holding was common. The Spirit grants prophetic powers not only to those to whom society normally listens and who determine what is normal, reasonable, and can be realistically expected. It also enables women, the young, and even slaves of both sexes to disclose the future which God intends. They do so with each other and for each other. Likewise, the event of Pentecost gives expression to God's intentions towards all human beings. Those who are filled with the Spirit become capable of speaking in a way that can be understood in all the languages of that day. Without eliminating the differences of languages and traditions, everybody is able to understand 'the mighty works of God'.

The presence of God's Spirit is thus not mediated by only one group of people, one nation, or one culture, nor is it only by the ruling party or, for that matter, the oppressed. How can this insight be reconciled with the New Testament assertions that the Spirit is One and a definitely uniting power (1 Cor. 12)? All associations of the Spirit with uniformity and homogeneity have to be corrected, associations which might be evoked by some 'oneness statements' such as 1 Corinthians 12: 13, 'For in the one Spirit we were all baptized into one body'; or Philippians 1: 27, 'you are standing firm in one spirit'; or Philippians 2: 1–2, according to which we have the 'same mind' and 'the same love' by virtue of participating in the Spirit. The Spirit establishes a complex and rich community in which faith, love, and hope are shared and thrive (Rom. 8; 1 Cor. 13; Gal. 5: 5–6). It constitutes a community which continually aims at the establishment and improvement of justice, mercy, and the knowledge of God. Under the guidance of the Spirit, the search for God and the love of God become concrete (Macchia 2006). It is thus not sufficient to understand 'baptism in the Spirit' as an operation with just two 'points of reference', namely God and the human person (Barth 1969).

The Spirit Constituting a Differentiated Community and Personality

The Spirit of God relativizes and abolishes unjust differences and distortions and even natural and cultural differences where these are connected with injustice, coldness, and despair. This does not mean that the Spirit eliminates differences as such; rather it constitutes a differentiated community in which the different gifts of the Spirit interact with and mutually strengthen each other. The unity established and sustained by the Spirit is expressed by the metaphor of a body with different members (1 Cor. 12). The 'body of Christ', constituted by the Spirit, has Jesus Christ as its head; in itself and apart from Christ's lordship it has no monohierarchical structure. This is perfectly compatible with the assurance in 2 Corinthians 3: 17; 'Now the Lord is the Spirit, and where the Spirit of the Lord is, there is freedom.'

The intrinsic richness of the Spirit is acknowledged when its definite givenness to human beings is expressed in terms of the 'pouring out' of the Spirit and 'filling' with the Spirit. The Spirit enables people to gain an immediacy, and even a unity, not only with one another, but above all with Christ himself (1 Cor. 6: 17; Rom. 8: 9). This unity becomes manifest in intimate address to God. Galatians 4: 6: 'God has sent the Spirit of his Son into our hearts, crying, "Abba! Father!"'. On the other hand, this unity, intimacy, and immediacy do not mean uniformity. Persons rich in faith and a complex and lively community are constituted by the Holy Spirit. The Spirit gives humans the power to host in themselves the fullness of Christ and the creativity of God (Zizioulas 1997).

The ability to host the Spirit even in our bodies, and to unite with God in Christ 'in the Spirit' is a breathtaking elevation, an extension of real human existence. The ability to be present 'in the spirit' even when we cannot be bodily present (1 Cor. 5: 3; Col. 2: 5) mirrors this anthropologically and realistically. Visions, experiences of theophany and revelation, and the power to proclaim the gospel in a convincing way are related to the activity of the Spirit. Various New Testaments texts emphasize access to eschatological realities experienced by people who 'have tasted the heavenly gift, and have shared in the Holy Spirit' (Heb. 6: 4). These realities include participation in the resurrection, entrance into the reign of God, and a share in eternal life (Gal. 6: 8) (Berkhof 1965: 21–9). Paul even speaks of salvific repercussions for bodily existence and for the whole creation which allow those 'who have the first fruits of the Spirit' to 'wait for adoption, the redemption of our bodies' (Rom. 8: 23).

The Spirit Freeing from the Power of Sin and Ennobling

Why does the unity of the Spirit have such a complex form? The Apostles' Creed, which connects belief in the Holy Spirit with belief in the communion of saints and the forgiveness of sins, offers an answer to this question. It is not only the Spirit's passion for freedom which works against uniformity and monohierarchical structures, but also for the awareness that the power of sin can corrupt even the search for justice, mercy, and knowledge of God, a search encouraged and guided by the law of God. Through the revelation in Jesus Christ and by the power of the Spirit, God engages the sinful and very complex human conspiracy against life. This conspiracy employed all available means of power to silence and bring about the disappearance of the one who proclaimed God's coming reign and who brought concrete deliverance from sickness and need to many people. In the name of religion, in the name of Jewish and Roman law, in the name of the dominant politics and public opinion of the moment, Jesus of Nazareth was nailed to the cross. The powers which are supposed to serve to maintain a life which is good, pleasing to God, and beneficent to human beings here collaborate against the bearer of the power of life. The Spirit works against this situation in, with, and through the constitution of the body of Christ (Tillich 1963).

The powers of God which counter evil and the forces of sin, freeing creation from self-jeopardy and self-destruction, are often manifest in astoundingly modest ways. This is clear with respect to the spiritual reality of the 'coming reign of God'. According to Jesus' parables, this reign does not come like a violent storm, but like green leaves from a branch or like grass from the ground. While these manifestations are invisible to some, for others they predict a good harvest. God's reign comes like the early morning light which some see as the beginning day while others still call it night and darkness. Jesus' parables speak of this emergent reality brought forth in numerous experiences of mercy, of forgiveness, and of free and unexpected deeds of justice and love.

Similar observations can be made regarding the resurrection of Christ and his presence in 'Spirit and faith'. The resurrection happens in a much less triumphalistic mode than often depicted. Through Jesus' many different appearances and revelations—and despite so much uncertainty and doubt—the insight emerges that Jesus has risen from the dead. Out of a multitude of witnesses, mingled with voices of scepticism and uncertainty, the post-Easter body of Christ grows, bearing Christ's new presence (Turner 1994). It is this complex spiritual reality which overcomes the powers of death and destruction, a reality which guides the search for truth, justice, and salvation in the midst of the powers of sin which generate uncertainty and doubt, a sense of helplessness and despair.

The work of the Spirit against the power of sin is not only a saving and rescuing operation, but also an ennobling one. Most fascinating in the constitution of the post-Easter body of Christ is the fact that the Spirit does not simply get humans back on track, so to speak, but that God rescues human creatures by ennobling them, elevating them, taking them into the divine life. By the power of the Spirit and through their response of faith, humans become members of the body of Christ, of the new creation. They gain a share in the divine life. In the sacraments, Christians celebrate this grace of God in a particularly powerful way.

The Discernment of the Spirits and Truth-Seeking Communities

The biblical traditions know about good and evil spirits, salvific and demonic powers. The New Testament traditions identify the divine Spirit, the Holy Spirit, as the Spirit of the merciful creator and the Spirit of Jesus Christ. This is the living and loving divine power which unites the self-revealing God and connects God and creation in sustaining, saving, and ennobling ways. Every age, however, is haunted by deceiving spirits, by individual and shared certainties which prove to be wrong, misleading, and distorted, by devastating forms of consensus breeding dangerous ideologies or stale theories that block insight over the ages. Thus the 'discernment of the spirits' is a most important task in all fields of experience, knowledge, and conviction (Dunn 1979). The Holy Spirit is not only identified in its differentiated relation to the basic good intentions of the law of God to bring about justice, mercy, and the knowledge of God, and it is not only identified by its relation to Jesus Christ, whose differentiated post-Easter body is constituted by its power. The Holy Spirit is also identified as the 'Spirit of truth' (John 14: 17).

The messianic traditions of the Old Testament declare that the bearer of the Spirit will bring not only justice and mercy to Jews and Gentiles but also a universal knowledge and cognition of God (Isa. 11: 1–9; 42: 6–7; 61: 6). Throughout the New Testament traditions we find an affiliation of the Spirit and truth. Paul says that the Spirit interprets 'spiritual things to those who are spiritual' (1 Cor. 2: 13), and he connects sanctification by the Spirit with belief in truth (2 Thess. 2: 13). John declares concerning God that 'those who worship him must worship in spirit and truth' (John 4: 24). 1 John 5: 6 says that 'the Spirit is the one that testifies, for the Spirit is the truth', and 2 Timothy 1: 14 (RSV) refers to 'the truth that has been entrusted to you by the Holy Spirit who dwells within us'.

Although the New Testament traditions insist that the insight and proclamation in the power of the Spirit are stronger than mere human words and wisdom (1 Thess. 1: 5; 1 Cor. 2: 4; Rom. 15: 19), they clearly emphasize the revelatory and enlightening power of the Spirit in the lives and minds of human beings. 1 Corinthians 2: 10 speaks of God's revelation through the Spirit and says that 'the Spirit searches everything, even the depths of God'. The Spirit provides a depth of insight and circumspection that leads to Paul's claim (1 Cor. 2: 15), 'Those who are spiritual discern all things, and they are themselves subject to no one else's scrutiny.'

It is in truth-seeking communities—in both academic and religious contexts—that the excitement resulting from the experience of the Spirit has to be complemented by the discernment of the spirits. What is it which guides progress in truth-seeking communities and encourages us to make truth claims, even though full evidence is still lacking? How can we be so bold as to speak of true knowledge, when we have to admit that all our important insights are fragmentary? It is the Spirit of God seen as the guiding and encouraging power at work, giving both the boldness and the patience in the individual and common search for truth (Welker 2006).

Truth-seeking communities are not groups of people who look around somehow to find some kind of truth. Nor do they claim to possess the full truth and speak it with the expectation that everybody else must simply listen, agree, and obey. Truth-seeking communities are willing to formulate truth claims and to express an utmost certainty similar to that of the famous words of Luther before the Diet of Worms: 'Unless I am convinced by the testimony of the Scriptures or by clear reason..., I am bound by the Scriptures I have quoted and my conscience is captive to the Word of God' (Luther 1957–86: xxxii. 112). In formulating truth claims, truth-seeking communities not only express utmost certainty, but also topical insight. In addition, they develop standards of argumentation for the challenge of their truth claims and certainties and for the improvement of their insights (Polkinghorne and Welker 2001: 132–48).

II. The Personhood of the Holy Spirit

The Self-Referential Personhood of the Aristotelian Spirit

In his *Metaphysics*, Aristotle proposed a notion of 'the divine' or 'the divinity' and 'the spirit' which was adopted by western elites within and outside of religious communities. This notion of 'the spirit' was used in religious and anthropological theories, in epistemologies, and in theories of cultures. It provided a key concept to orient religious and cultural developments. Although Aristotle's term *nous* has been translated not only as 'spirit', but also as 'reason', 'thought', and 'mind', the activity described by the philosopher appeared to many thinkers to be a convincing candidate for 'the ultimate' and even 'the divine'.

Aristotle describes spirit as a creative and living power of thought which takes part in and becomes a part of what is being thought. 'Spirit becomes itself an object of thought by grasping and thinking that which is thought, so that spirit and that which is thought are identical' (*Metaphysics* 1072^{b}, in Aristotle 1928). The thinking spirit can deal with more or less important contents. What is it that allows us to rank the contents and the activities of the spirit? For Aristotle it is the fuller and stronger self-awareness in the activity of thinking that distinguishes 'higher' activities of the spirit from lower ones. 'Intellectual contemplation (philosophic thought) is what is most pleasant and best. If, then, the Divinity is always doing as well as we sometimes (are), this compels our wonder. If the Divinity is doing still better, this compels our wonder still more. And the Divinity indeed is doing better' (*Metaphysics* 1072^{b}).

This remark of Aristotle's with respect to 'the Divinity' which enjoys 'eternal life' in its self-referential spiritual activity is not a pious gloss. It identifies a problem of human aspiration towards higher and higher 'spiritual' activities. According to Aristotle and to those inspired by him, the stronger the self-actualization and self-awareness, the closer the human spirit gets to the divine. This notion of spirit and its self-referential 'personality' has shaped thinking in epistemology, anthropology, and cultural and social theories. It has also shaped religious thought and guided attempts to understand the 'personhood' of the spirit. This understanding, however, is fundamentally different from that of the Holy Spirit in Jewish and Christian religious thinking. The philosophical spirit is self-referential and a spirit of certainty. The Spirit of the biblical traditions, the 'Spirit of truth', bears witness to Christ and to God the creator and 'does not speak on his own authority' (John 15: 26 RSV). This difference has far-reaching consequences (Welker 1994: 279–341; 2006).

The Context-Sensitive Holy Spirit of the Biblical Traditions

How is the 'personality' of the Holy Spirit to be understood, if it has to be distinguished from the Aristotelian spirit and if self-referentiality is not characteristic of it? The most convincing answer views its personality as connected with its context-sensitivity and encounter-sensitivity (Polkinghorne 2001; 2006). The Holy Spirit is not a power that acts and operates in each and every context in the same way. 1 Corinthians 12: 11 speaks of 'one and the same Spirit, who allots to each one individually just as the Spirit chooses', and Hebrews 2: 4 says that God acts 'by signs and wonders and various miracles, and by gifts of the Holy Spirit, distributed according to his will'.

Although the Spirit is not self-referential in itself, it gains a complex trinitarian self-referentiality in the dual relation to God the creator and to the lordship of Jesus Christ. 2 Corinthians 3: 18 says that it is by 'the Lord who is the Spirit' that we 'are being changed into his likeness from one degree of glory to another'. The text oscillates between the lordship of the Spirit and that of Christ. The Spirit can be understood as the field of Christ's resonance, who provides the self-referential personal structure in the unity with the Spirit. This explains why the Spirit could be described both in personal categories and in field categories (Pannenberg 1991–8: i. 382–4), why one could suggest understanding the Spirit in a complementary way as both a complex public person and the dynamic 'force field [*Kraftfeld*]' of the divinity. In these complementary perspectives a confusion of the Spirit's personhood with human personhood and the notion of a ubiquitous spirit without intentional structure can be avoided. The Spirit becomes present 'where it wills'—and also when we view it as a field of power (Oberdorfer 2006).

The context-sensitivity and encounter-sensitivity of the Spirit is also correlated with its vulnerability. Statements such as 1 Thessalonians 5: 19, 'Do not quench the Spirit'; Ephesians 4: 30, 'Do not grieve the Holy Spirit of God, with which you were marked with a seal for the day of redemption'; the warning of Acts 5: 9 not to test 'the Spirit of the Lord'; and Hebrews 10: 29 about having 'outraged the Spirit of grace' would be impossible if the Spirit were an irresistible force. The power of the Spirit and the subtlety and sensitivity of its activity are not contradictory.

The Hidden Working of the Spirit in Creation

The observation of this texture and dwelling of the Spirit allows an appreciation of its gradual working in ordinary life. We see the Spirit at work not only in dramatic and ecstatic events, but also in patient processes and institutionalized forms, not only in strong and overwhelming personal experiences but also in historical processes and in the mediation of quiet transformations in public life and general insight (Tanner 2006). Here the Spirit comes into view not only as patient 'sustainer', but also as patient 'teacher', guiding the community into a shared recognition of truth.

This is not to be confused with a pantheistic or panentheistic view which sees the Spirit at work in every aspect of creation (Moltmann 2001). The fact that the Spirit 'has filled the world' and 'holds all things together' (Wis. 1: 7; cf. Isa. 34: 16) is not to be confused with an abstract 'ubiquity' of the Spirit. The same texts say that the Spirit 'will flee from deceit, and will leave foolish thoughts behind' (Wis. 1: 5). The hidden working of the Spirit in the world's unfolding history merely through the input of pure information 'would constitute a pneumatological account of continuous creation, divine participation in the evolving fruitfulness of the world, exercised with covert reticence within the open grain of nature' (Polkinghorne 2006; Lossky 1957).

III. The Holy Spirit and the Challenge of and to the Pentecostal and Charismatic Movements

With the notion of the exalted Jesus Christ 'baptizing with the Spirit', the New Testament coined a fresh image that strengthened hope for 'a richer experience of God's vitalizing presence and activity' on earth (Dunn 2006). The early church witnessed to the fulfilment of this hope in its growth and mission within and beyond the realm of Judaism. Real spiritual experiences paved the way for the life and the expansion of the church. Real transformation into the image of Jesus Christ, becoming a member of the body of Christ, was an experience of faith, and the resurrection of a 'spiritual body' enlivened by the Holy Spirit became a focus of Christian hope. Both discontinuity and continuity between the pre-Easter Jesus and the resurrected Christ remained most important. With this orientation the early church was able to 'discern the spirits' in the midst of ecstatic experiences.

The 'crisis experience called the "baptism in the Holy Spirit"' became the hallmark of the Pentecostal and Charismatic movement of the twentieth century; with 500 million members, it is the largest spiritual movement in human history (Macchia 2006; Hollenweger 1988). How this experience is interpreted, however, differs between the different strands of this movement. This has created dynamics which challenge Pentecostals to develop and expand their own understanding of Spirit-baptism and at the same time contribute to an ecumenical pneumatology which could be seminal for other church communities. The experience of empowerment for witness takes on different forms, while the new beginnings of Christian life are seen in more and less spectacular and dramatic ways. In a growing ecumenical consensus it becomes clear that concentration on this charismatic event should not blur, much less dismiss, the Spirit's sanctifying and soteriological work within human lives, which cannot be separated from God's self-disclosure in Jesus Christ, the Spirit-Baptizer (Macchia 2006; Dayton 1988).

The renewed awareness of the personhood of the Spirit and the nature of truth-seeking communities gained at the beginning of the twenty-first century could be of great help in this development towards ecumenical understanding and peace. However the Spirit's relation to truth is to be understood, it is crucial to notice that self-referentiality is not its basis. John 16: 13 says: 'When the Spirit of truth comes, he will guide you into all the truth; for he will not speak on his own, but will speak whatever he hears, and he will declare to you the things that are to come.' The Spirit of truth will bear witness to Christ, not to its own authority (John 15: 26).

The interpretation of the image of 'Spirit-baptism' in the framework of the richly variegated dwelling of the Spirit might open a way to mediate between the insistence on dramatic and sensational individual experiences as 'initiation-events' of faith, and the insistence that the Spirit of truth is characterized by its connection to Jesus Christ and to a wisdom which operates in astounding but not necessarily spectacular ways.

An understanding of the activity of the Spirit as a truth-revealing power is required in both academic and religious contexts. This understanding has to acknowledge the Spirit's empathetic and context-sensitive presence as well as the great variety in its working. So-called emergent processes have to be grasped in order to appreciate the Spirit's working. In emergent processes, new qualities arise out of various interplays between the components of the process or between the members involved in it. The new qualities cannot be derived from the properties of the components but consist only in the interplay between them. While the change perceptible in emergent processes may appear surprising, it is actually to be traced back to the fact that, by means of a new interplay among certain parts or members of the process, an across-the-board change in the interplay of all parts or members has occurred. In emergent processes generated by the Spirit, excitement and awe different from that generated by individual and bodily mediated 'spectacular' experiences come into view, which necessarily goes hand-in-hand with the need to discern the spirits. Although the ancient images of 'pouring' and 'Spirit-baptism' adequately express the power envisioned in the Spirit's activity, a new awareness of the hiddenness of the Spirit in creation and of its patient activity as a comforting, guiding, teaching, and truth-revealing power can and should be raised.

The multicontextual and variegated presence of the Spirit explains the connection between various, quite different phenomena addressed by the biblical traditions. The canonical coherence of the biblical traditions is provided by the Spirit who speaks as the one voice in and through the different voices of the canon (Mark 12: 36; Acts 1: 16; cf. Welker 1994: 264–78). The fact that different modes of access are possible for Jews and Gentiles is related to the activity of the Christ as the messianic bearer and dispenser of the Spirit (Rom. 15: 16; Eph. 2: 18; Isa. 11: 1–9; cf. Welker 1994: 1–49, 303–15). There is thus a full confidence that the Spirit is present in different contexts of trial and danger and that it gives voice to the persecuted and oppressed (Mark 13: 11).

The multicontextual and polyphonic presence of the Spirit challenges simple one-to-one relations and monohierarchical forms of social interaction, questioning their ability to express basic religious experiences and interactions. Theories of emergence have to be used to explain this character and working of the Spirit. The pouring out of the Spirit brings about a pluralistic striving for God's righteousness and truth. The complex unity brought forth by the Spirit is not a postmodern invention, but an act of the divine power by which God works through frail and finite human creatures against the powers of sin and distortion. The Spirit works in emergent ways that alter a complex constellation with a multiplicity of internal relations by reconfiguring these internal relations and clusters of relations, whether gradually or at once. The new relations and constellations not only modify each other but also have unforeseen effects and joint-effects on the whole constellation.

Deep, ecstatic experiences of an awesome power are characteristic of the experience of the Spirit. This holds true for the biblical witnesses and for Pentecostal and Charismatic theologies. This is also the case for philosophical and scientific processes of discovery in which the most amazing truths are found and the most astonishing truth-claims encouraged in the midst of uncertainties and open questions. This finally holds true for breakthroughs in the fight for justice, healing, and peace. The power which conditions these experiences both in natural reality and in human minds is identified as 'the Spirit'. The Spirit has the dual character of a personal, context-sensitive, and intentional event and of a structuring force field which operates in a rich variety of forms. The notion of the 'pouring out' of the Spirit seems to combine both characters and modes.

References

Aristotle (1928). *The Works*, viii. *Metaphysica*. Oxford: Clarendon.

Barth, K. (1969). *Church Dogmatics* IV/4. Edinburgh: T. & T. Clark.

Berkhof, H. (1965). *The Doctrine of the Holy Spirit*. London: Epworth.

Congar, Y. (1983). *I Believe in the Holy Spirit*. New York: Seabury.

Dayton, D. W. (1988). *Theological Roots of Pentecostalism*. Grand Rapids: Zondervan.

Dunn, J. D. G. (1970). *The Baptism in the Holy Spirit: A Re-Examination of the New Testament Teaching on the Gift of the Spirit in Relation to Pentecostalism Today*. London: SCM.

—— (1979). 'Discernment of Spirits: A Neglected Gift'. In W. Harrington (ed.), *Witness to the Spirit: Essays on Revelation, Spirit, Redemption*, Dublin: Irish Bible Association, 79–96.

—— (1996). 'Spirit, Holy Spirit'. In D. R. W. Wood (ed.), *New Bible Dictionary*, 3rd edn., Leicester: InterVarsity, 1125–7.

—— (2006). 'Towards the Spirit of Christ: The Emergence of the Distinctive Features of Christian Pneumatology'. In Welker (2006).

Hollenweger, W. (1988). *The Pentecostals*, 2nd edn. Peabody: Hendrickson.

Lossky, V. (1957). *The Mystical Theology of the Eastern Church*. Cambridge: James Clarke.

Luther, M. (1957–86). *Luther's Works*. 55 vols. St Louis: Concordia.

Macchia, F. D. (2006). *Baptized in the Spirit*. Grand Rapids: Zondervan.

Moltmann, J. (2001). *The Spirit of Life: A Universal Affirmation*. Minneapolis: Fortress.

Oberdorfer, B. (2006). 'The Holy Spirit: A Person? Reflections on the Spirit's Trinitarian Identity'. In Welker (2006).

Pannenberg, W. (1991–8). *Systematic Theology*. 3 vols. Grand Rapids: Eerdmans.

Polkinghorne, J. (2001). 'Faith in the Holy Spirit'. In Polkinghorne and Welker (2001).

—— (2006). 'The Hidden Spirit and the Cosmos'. In Welker (2006).

Polkinghorne, J., and Welker, M. (eds.) (2001) *Faith in the Living God: A Dialogue.* London: SPCK and Philadelphia: Fortress.

Tanner, K. (2006). 'Workings of the Spirit: Simplicity or Complexity?' In Welker (2006).

Tillich, P. (1963). *Systematic Theology*, iii. Chicago: University of Chicago Press.

Turner, M. (1994). 'The Spirit of Christ and "Divine" Christology'. In J. B. Green and M. Turner (eds.), *Jesus of Nazareth, Lord and Christ: Essays on the Historical Jesus and New Testament Christology*, Grand Rapids: Eerdmans, 413–36.

Welker, M. (1994). *God the Spirit.* Philadelphia: Fortress.

Welker, M. (ed.) (2006). *The Work of the Spirit: Pneumatology and Pentecostalism.* Grand Rapids: Eerdmans.

Westermann, C. (1981). 'Geist im Alten Testament'. *Evangelische Theologie* 41 (1981): 223–30.

Zizioulas, J. D. (1997). *Being as Communion.* Crestwood: St Vladimir's Seminary Press.

Suggested Reading

Berkhof (1965).

Congar (1983).

Hendry, G. S. (1956). *The Holy Spirit in Christian Theology.* Philadelphia: Westminster.

Heron, A. (1983). *The Holy Spirit in the Bible, the History of Christian Thought, and Recent Theology.* London: Marshall, Morgan, and Scott.

Lampe, G. W. H. (1977). *God as Spirit.* Oxford: Clarendon.

Macchia (2006).

Moltmann, J. (2001).

Moule, C. F. D. (1978). *The Holy Spirit.* Oxford: Mowbray.

Rogers, Eugene F., Jr. (2005). *After the Spirit: A Constructive Pneumatology from Resources Outside the Modern West.* Grand Rapids: Eerdmans.

Welker (1994).

CHAPTER 14

THE CHURCH

RALPH DEL COLLE

I. The Historical and Theological Reality of the Church

The doctrine of the church, more than most other doctrines, bears witness to the confessional differences that have marked the history of Christianity. Certainly the historical and persistent divisions that fracture the church reflect the many doctrinal and theological divergences professed by these communities. In fact, various and sundry doctrines have been instrumental in the genesis, formation, and continued separation of the Christian churches. Nevertheless, ecclesiology proper—the theological understanding of the church—whether implicit or held explicitly as a matter of doctrine, contributes in no small way to the present state of Christian ecclesial existence and the prospects for its future.

The doctrine of the church ensures the fidelity of the church to the gospel. In the articulation of its identity and mission the doctrine accounts for the church's visible representation and mediation of the gospel such that *coram Deo* the church might indeed be the church. Ecclesiology, therefore, cannot afford to be distracted by digressions that subvert its theological integrity. The sociological reality of the church or churches, that is, the church as a material object, is accessible to any number of analyses that may contribute to understanding the social and corporate nature of Christianity. Clearly these need not be theological. There is no doubt that in the life of actually existing churches and ecclesiastical organizations a good deal of thought and activity proceeds from a self-understanding that has its sources in important, non-theological readings of human social life as religiously enacted.

Add to this the import for ecclesiastical life of the polity and identity of diverse and multiple denominational entities, and theological considerations that should be at the core of ecclesiological reflection can be easily marginalized.

These remarks are not an opening polemical overture in favour of strictly classical theological interests. Contextual ecclesiologies, the utilization of social and cultural analyses, as well as pastoral, practical, and missiological perspectives that might employ insights from the social sciences all have their place. These and other interests, however, often only complicate a situation that is profoundly tragic and even sinful. The churches in their separation and divisions are a countersign to the one church that the economy of salvation portends as a witness to the truth of the gospel (John 17: 20–1). One must squarely face the fact that too often the politics of the church (*politia ecclesiastica*)—within and between churches as well as in the interstices of church, culture, and society—often overshadows and sometimes entirely subsumes the doctrine of the church (*doctrina de ecclesia*). The adage of a strictly praxis-oriented ecumenism, 'doctrine divides, service unites', as an alternative to this dilemma is not sufficiently theological to arrive at Christian unity, much less the meaning of the church. Christian doctrine, including the doctrine of the church, whatever the overt and covert influences of the politics of the church, is still determinative for present ecclesial divisions and for the future possibilities of reconciliation and a united ecclesial witness.

Having said that, the doctrine of the church can no more elide over the church as material object, its historical and sociological reality, than Christology can diminish the importance of the Jesus of history. For the latter, what is at stake is the truth of the incarnation, which theologically considered is not identical with the quest for the historical Jesus (a quest which is important, or not, depending on how Jesus is theologically construed). For ecclesiology the historical actuality of the church is embedded in its theological meaning, something that cannot be captured by the sociological categories of institution and charism (or something comparable), tempting as that might be. This is not to deny that the relationship between structure and life possesses theological weight. The problem is how to conceive it. Traditionally ecclesiology has accounted for this distinction by adverting to the visibility and invisibility of the church, itself a subject of confessional differences over the nature of the church.

II. Faith, Visibility, and the Necessity of the Church

It is better to account for the scandal of division and other ecclesial anomalies in more Pauline terms. Hugo Rahner once countered ecclesiastical triumphalism by reference to 2 Corinthians 12: 9: 'Power is made perfect in weakness'. Power and weakness form a consistent theme for Paul in the Corinthian correspondence (1 Cor. 1: 18–31; 2 Cor. 4: 7–11), one that resonates throughout the New Testament. Only by the simultaneity of *dunamis* and *astheneia*, the power of God and the weakness of the church, can one understand the birth of the church from the mystery of the cross (H. Rahner 1963: 5). This is consistent with the essence of faith in the life of the church, more often than not a test of faith, but revelatory of the grace proceeding from the crucified and risen Lord. Thus Rahner can boast: 'This weak Church is the joy of our faith. Not only despite her weakness, but rather because she is weak' (H. Rahner 1963: 10–11). It is not out of place to be instructed by such sentiments, since as much as they may commend a worthy piety, more importantly they clearly identify the only adequate theological foundations for ecclesial existence and evaluation.

The New Testament, consistent with the entire biblical witness regarding the people of God, neither diminishes the church's high calling nor dismisses its weakness. The church founded upon Jesus Christ ('no one can lay any foundation other than the one that has been laid'; 1 Cor. 3: 11) is the same church that is the object of the admonition, 'Has Christ been divided?' (1 Cor. 1: 13). The church through which 'the wisdom of God in its rich variety might *now* be made known to the rulers and authorities in the heavenly places' (Eph. 3: 10) is also exhorted to 'no longer be children, tossed to and fro and blown about by every wind of doctrine, by people's trickery, by their craftiness in deceitful scheming' (Eph. 4: 14). If Paul's apostolic ministry exemplifies what it means to contend for the true life of the church, 'until Christ is formed in you' (Gal. 4: 19), then the doctrine of the church must account not only for its eschatological consummation in the 'kingdom of Christ and of God' (Eph. 5: 5)—a church 'without a spot or wrinkle' (Eph. 5: 27)—but also for that time '*until* all of us come to the unity of the faith and of the knowledge of the Son of God' (Eph. 4: 13). In other words, the doctrine of the church must speak to the church in such manner that the exhortation rings true: 'Be strong in the Lord and in the strength of his power' (Eph. 6: 10).

If anything, this New Testament posture toward the church is one of faith, as confessed by the later church in the *credo ecclesiam* of the Apostles' and Niceno-Constantinopolitan Creeds. Precisely how the church is an object of faith is of no small import. Although theological opinion has long distinguished between believing *in* the church and believing *the church*, it is well to take a cue from official church teaching. The *Catechism of the Catholic Church* (*CCC*), in commenting on the creedal formulations, states: 'we profess "one Holy Church" (*Credo... Ecclesiam*)'; we do not, however, profess 'to believe *in* the Church, so as not to confuse God with his works and to attribute clearly to God's goodness *all* the gifts he has bestowed on his Church' (*CCC* §750). Thomas Aquinas was even more specific. Faith 'is directed to the Holy Ghost, Who sanctifies the Church; so that the sense is: "I believe in the Holy Ghost sanctifying the Church"' (*ST* 2a2ae. 1, 9 ad 5, in Aquinas 1948). This lays the theological foundation of the church and keeps in perspective the relationship between theological faith created and engendered by the divine Word and the community of faith, the church, itself the mother of faith. If John Calvin can allude approvingly to Cyprian's adage, 'You cannot have God for your Father unless you have the Church for your mother' (*Institutes* 4. 1. 1, in Calvin 1960), it is clearly more a matter of parsing the nature of the church's mediation of faith, not rejecting it.

Staying with Calvin, to profess to believe the church (not *in* the church) 'refers not only to the visible Church... but also to all God's elect, in whose number are also included the dead' (*Institutes*, 4. 1. 2). While this implies a distinction between the visible and invisible church, elsewhere explicitly taught by Calvin, the instrumentality of the visible church is also clearly affirmed. Any doctrine of the church must begin with the theological necessity of the church in order to be ecumenically viable. This is not to suggest that, for so-called 'low-church' ecclesial sensibilities, ecclesiology is an afterthought. The centrality of the church for Christian life and mission is not identical with the theology underlying the mediation of grace in and through the church, especially as this may be associated with order and sacraments. Differences over this matter clearly inform, for example, Schleiermacher's axiomatic distinction between Protestantism and Catholicism: 'the former makes the individual's relation to the Church dependent on his relation to Christ, while the latter contrariwise makes the individual's relation to Christ dependent on his relation to the Church' (Schleiermacher 1928: 103). However, even the Protestant side of this axiom does not undermine the theological necessity of the church.

Historically, this was borne out in the disputes during the Reformation between magisterial Reformers and radicals (Anabaptists, Spirituals, etc.). Disagreements over paedobaptism, for example, came down to very different ecclesial visions in the interest of a pure or a purer church. Similar ecclesial interests continued in the free-church and believers'-church traditions, whether they were separatist, pietistic, or restorationist in orientation. Polemics over ecclesiality, over what constitutes the church proper—the true church and the false church at its most serious, when the ecclesial existence of the other body was denied—were the product of disagreements over ecclesial configurations regarding the necessity of the church. To the heirs of such a history, the doctrine of the church in the present ecumenical context must be articulated in response to the dominical imperative of evangelical mission (Matt. 28: 19–20) and ecclesial unity (John 17: 20–3).

To believe the church, the *credo ecclesiam*, situates the church in the divine economy, the revelation of which is accessible only to faith. As with all matters of divine revelation God's words and deeds constitute the realization of God's presence and self-manifestation in history. Revelation cannot be divorced from its creaturely mediations, this being even more true for that supreme revelation: the Word made flesh in the mystery of the incarnation. Consideration of the church in faith therefore proceeds from the contours of revelation and the modality of grace offered and received. The trinitarian configuration of the divine economy and the particular theology of grace that shapes an ecclesial tradition are determinative for the varieties of ecclesiologies that inform the doctrine of the church.

In fact, the explicit thematization of the church in a trinitarian register would await the significant ecumenical developments of the twentieth century, a century that has resulted in a near consensus that the nature of church life and order is a matter of *communio* or *koinonia*. However, before directly focusing on this development and its importance for ecclesiology, we must first note its direct and indirect provenance in the theological tradition. This is not necessarily tied to the appearance during the late Middle Ages in the West of separate tractates on the church, *De Ecclesia*, which, as Wolfhart Pannenberg notes, should give one pause before assuming as 'self-evident that the concept of the Church should be a separate dogmatic theme' (Pannenberg 1991–8: iii. 21). With the Reformation, and even before with the rise of conciliarism and the event of the Great Schism, this somewhat independent focus on the church could no longer be avoided. Ecclesiological motifs are certainly present prior to the Schism and are not without significance for contemporary theologies of the church. Two examples suffice to illustrate the point with their notable effects upon the present ecclesiological discussion.

J.-M.-R. Tillard, one of the most significant Catholic contributors to a 'communion ecclesiology', made the claim in the spirit of *ressourcement* that this ecclesiology, 'sacramental and mystical before becoming juridical and sociological', was the one held by the undivided church of antiquity, with Augustine, John Chrysostom, and Cyril as fifth-century witnesses respectively from the West, Antioch, and Alexandria (Tillard 2001: 33). Communion bespeaks the relationship between Christ and the church, a '*circumincessio* ("a true mutual inhabiting") between [Christ's] sacramental body and ecclesial body', which is not without a strong pneumatological character (Tillard 2001: 46). Augustine in this regard may be taken as typical.

> Believers know that this is the body of Christ if they do not neglect to be the body of Christ. That they become the body of Christ if they want to live by the Spirit of Christ. No one lives by the Spirit of Christ except the body of Christ. (Augustine, *Homilies on the Gospel of John* 26. 13–14, in Tillard 2001: 46)

The eucharistic overtones are also consistent with the ante-Nicene perspectives of Ignatius of Antioch and Irenaeus of Lyons. Ignatius wrote, 'Wherever the bishop appears, there let the meeting be, just as wherever Jesus Christ is, there is the catholic church' (*Smyrnaeans* 8. 2, in Hinson 1986: 27). Likewise Irenaeus: 'For where the Church is, there is the Spirit of God; and where the Spirit of God is, there is the Church and every gift; and the Spirit is truth' (*Against Heresies* 3. 24. 1, in Hinson 1986: 42). Ecclesiological motifs, embracing also sacramental modalities, cannot be divorced from Christological and pneumatological trajectories. Nor will these ecclesiological interests neglect issues of order in favour of life—a concern of the medieval scholastics as well.

Yves Congar directly addressed the significance of the late appearance of the tractate *De Ecclesia* in a brief study of the ecclesiology of Thomas Aquinas. Whether one agrees with his opinion that Thomas intentionally did not write a separate treatise on the church, it is clear that Thomas and other scholastics did not suffer from an ecclesiological vacuum in their work (Congar 1960: 102). Congar distils ecclesiological themes from various articles in the *Summa Theologiae*, including 'the Trinity, the Divine *Missiones*, anthropology and ethics, christology and soteriology, sacraments and hierarchic ministry' (Congar 1960: 117). The implicit suffusion of his work by ecclesiological interests turns out in Congar's judgement to be determinative, and one that also informs his own theological *ressourcement*. Tillard's explicit 'communion ecclesiology' is the fruit of Congar's efforts and was intended to recover the living centre out of which the distinct doctrine of the church should properly emerge. So for Thomas—and Congar's claim extends to the ecclesiology of the fathers as well—a vital and dynamic ecclesiology takes precedence over the juridical concerns that typify later scholastic treatises on the church. Congar waxes eloquent in his summation of a prospective ecclesiology that attempts to be faithful to Thomas.

> The Church is contemplated as a Spirit-moved, Spirit-known and Spirit-defined reality, as the Body whose living Soul is the Spirit of Life. The Church is contemplated in Christ, as Christ is contemplated in the Church. And the inward Church is not separated from the outward Church, which is its sacramental veil and vehicle. (Congar 1960: 117)

Congar's words are useful because they underscore two major issues that must figure in the doctrine of the church. These are often highlighted by contemporary communion ecclesiologies. First, the church must be situated within the divine economy of the trinitarian missions of the Son and the Spirit. Second, there can be no separation between this rich theological foundation and the 'outward church'.

One might well query whether it was ever the case that the inner life of the church was entirely lost to view. Although the interests of James of Viterbo's *On Christian Government* (*De regimine Christiano*), one of the first tractates on the church (*c.* 1302) are more directed to the defence of ecclesiastical authority in the secular realm, it could speak of the formal and efficient causes of the church's unity as residing respectively in the theological virtues of faith, hope, and charity and in the holy Trinity (James of Viterbo 1995: 16). Indeed, for all its brevity, this text suggests that the confessional differences that ensued as a consequence of the Reformation affected the inner theological reality of the church as much as they did the church's outer sacramental and hierarchical structure. This construal is still significant for 'communion ecclesiology' and shapes the horizon of ecclesiology in its implicit mediation by the theology of grace, suggested no doubt by where the church is mentioned in its creedal confessions. Pneumatology is at the very least implicit in the theology of grace, in how God works salvifically in the lives of believers as, for example, in the *ordo salutis* of justification and sanctification, and by extension in how God works in the church. In some ecclesiologies it is through the church that God acts, and this seems to follow from the creedal confession of the Holy Spirit.

The *credo ecclesiam*, situated as it is between the *credo in Spiritum Sanctum* and the confession of the last things, reflects the *regnum Christi* in the life of the church. For Vatican II this provides a preliminary definition of the church. 'The church, as the kingdom of Christ already present in mystery, grows visibly in the world through the power of God' (*Lumen Gentium* §3, in Tanner 1990: ii. 850). Such a statement must be attended simultaneously by due caution as well as by evangelical boldness regarding the profound truth it attests. At stake is the essence of ecclesiality. The church is an eschatological community, convoked by God in service of the kingdom, itself not to be identified with the kingdom. Yet the shape of the kingdom eschatologically consummated is demonstrative of its ecclesial witness between Pentecost and the *parousia*. In other words, the reign of God is most explicit in the life of the church, signified by word, sacrament, and the way of discipleship, even before its final consummation at the second coming. None of this should be lost in attempts to exploit the eschatological dynamic that informs the church and its mission as if this demanded an either/or choice between so-called ecclesiocentric or regnocentric paradigms for mission, the former concentrating on the church itself as a sign of the kingdom and the latter seeking the likeness of the kingdom in the transformation of society and culture. As Carl Braaten has warned, the temptation to 'de-eschatologize Christianity' by absorbing eschatology into ecclesiology (without remainder) can certainly lead to a dangerous ecclesiocentrism (Braaten 1983: 47). Likewise, to conceive mission solely in terms of the promotion of justice in the secular realm as paradigmatic of the kingdom apart from the proclamation of Christ in evangelization and edification yields a reductive account of the faith. Ecclesiology and eschatology each bear on the other, with the church existing in the 'powers of the age to come' (Heb. 6: 5) and the kingdom reflecting the unity of the divine and human that already constitutes both the inner life of the church and its outward expression.

Although one can assume an ecumenical consensus in situating the church within a dynamic eschatological framework, this does not mean that all confessional differences are overcome or that developments with ecumenical potential within a particular communion immediately lend themselves to the consensus necessary for the restoration of Christian unity. The present consensus has embraced this eschatological vitality as well as a more robustly trinitarian foundation for ecclesial life. Specifically, the church exists within the missions of the Son and the Spirit, the divine economy of the incarnation of the Son and the outpouring of the Holy Spirit. Nicely put by the Catholic/Methodist Dialogue (the Vatican Secretariat for Promoting Christian Unity and the World Methodist

Council), their 1986 *Towards a Statement on the Church* can serve as a marker in this regard.

> Because God so loved the world, he sent his Son and the Holy Spirit to draw us into communion with himself. This sharing in God's life, which resulted from the mission of the Son and the Holy Spirit, found expression in a visible *koinonia* of Christ's disciples, the church. (Rusch and Gros 1998: 237)

Before examination of the maturation of this theme in communion ecclesiology we first turn to developments within one ecclesial tradition to illustrate the point of confessional identity and how it might bear on ecumenism.

III. Confessional Influences: A Case Study in Catholic Developments

Our point of departure is the 1943 encyclical *Mystici Corporis* of Pope Pius XII. This encyclical reflects the juridical concerns of post-Tridentine Catholic ecclesiology—made famous by Robert Bellarmine's definition of the church from his *De ecclesia militante*: 'the society of human beings which is linked by the profession of the same Christian faith under the rule of the legitimate pastors, above all the one vicar of Christ on earth, the Roman pontiff' (Auer 1993: 53). The encyclical also combines such concerns with the theme of the mystical body of Christ and the inner working of grace as developed by Augustine and Aquinas. This latter theme was further developed both in the nineteenth century by Matthias Scheeben (1946: 539–57) and Johan Adam Möhler (1997: 255–76) and more proximately, between the world wars, by the Belgian theologian Emile Mersch (1951). In his encyclical, Pius XII does not by any means neglect the visibility of the church established through its juridical and social bonds of hierarchy and sacrament. Christ as head of the church governs the ecclesial community visibly and invisibly, by reason of hierarchical office and by 'the interior inspiration and impulse of the Holy Spirit in our minds and hearts' (*Mystici Corporis* §68, in Pius XII 1943). Such 'inspiration and impulse' is a 'higher, interior, and wholly sublime communication' through which the church lives the supernatural life of its risen Lord, permeated by his divine power and manifesting this power in 'every gift and created grace' and in the theological virtues of faith, hope, and charity (*Mystici Corporis* §§55–6, 70–3). The theological virtues express what is most distinctive in the Catholic theology of grace that informs its ecclesiology. Quoting the encyclical *Divinum Illud Munus* of Leo XIII (who relied on St Augustine), Pius summarizes, 'Let it suffice to say that, as Christ is the Head of the Church, so is the Holy Spirit her soul.' Ecclesial life rests on an integrated Christological and pneumatological foundation (*Mystici Corporis* §§56–8).

Lumen Gentium, Vatican II's Dogmatic Constitution on the Church, represents a considerable development in Catholic ecclesiology, one not confined to the question of the relationship between the 'one church of Christ' and the Catholic Church—specifically, the claim that the one church of Christ 'subsists in the Catholic Church' (*Lumen Gentium* §8). While continuing to affirm that the church is the mystical body of Christ, *Lumen Gentium* also utilizes other biblical symbols and maintains a more concentrated trinitarian focus. Auxiliary metaphors or images of the church, such as sheepfold, tillage of God, building, family, temple, and spouse are used. It is the church as mystery and sacrament, however, that predominates, linked as it is with the biblical images of the people of God, the body of Christ, and the temple of the Holy Spirit, which taken together underscore the trinitarian dimension of ecclesial life by their allusion to the divine persons.

Both *Mystici Corporis* and *Lumen Gentium* preserve the unity between the invisible and visible dimensions of the church and are rooted in the Christological and pneumatological foundations of ecclesiality. Like *Mystici Corporis*, *Lumen Gentium* utilizes the hypostatic union of the incarnate Son as an analogy for the relationship between the inner life of the church and its outward expression. It is worth quoting in full.

> Christ, the one mediator, set up his holy church here on earth as a visible structure, a community of faith, hope and love; and he sustains it unceasingly and through it he pours out grace and truth on everyone. This society, however, equipped with hierarchical structures, and the mystical body of Christ, a visible assembly and a spiritual community, an earthly church and a church enriched with heavenly gifts, must not be considered as two things, but as forming one complex reality comprising a human and a divine element. It is therefore by no mean analogy that it is likened to the mystery of the incarnate Word. For just as the assumed nature serves the divine Word as a living instrument of salvation inseparably joined with him, in a similar way the social structure of the church serves the Spirit of Christ who vivifies the church towards the growth of the body. (*Lumen Gentium* §8)

Lest one assume that this sets up a strictly incarnational model for ecclesiality, as if the church is a continuation of the Son's incarnation, it should be noted that the transition described by this important paragraph moves from the Son to the Spirit in the analogy suggested. Although not a 'mean' or weak analogy—many Protestants prefer a weak or weaker analogy—the intent is to delineate the relationship between the divine and the human in the church. The relationship between Christology and ecclesiology, mediated by the theology of grace, is at issue, as is also the understanding of Christ's theandric agency.

Within the horizon of the conceptuality and metaphysics of scholastic Christology, Christ's human nature is understood as the instrumental cause of salvation. Efficacious in itself by virtue of the hypostatic union, it manifests and communicates the supernatural life of grace. Christ acts theandrically, the divine person of the Word acting in and through his human nature because of the grace of union. This grace is unique to Christ, his humanity created and assumed (simultaneously as no other) by the eternal Son from the moment of his conception in the womb of the Virgin Mary. Conceived by the power of the Holy Spirit, Christ is also filled with the Holy Spirit, his own personal grace and gifts. From such grace the church is born. Thus Aquinas does not formally distinguish between Christ's capital grace as head of the church (and all creation) and his personal or habitual grace. 'Hence the personal grace, whereby the soul of Christ is justified, is essentially the same as His grace, as He is the Head of the Church, and justifies others; but there is a distinction of reason between them' (*ST* 3a. 8, 5).

This accounting of the grace of Christ, in his person and actions, is consistent with the language of the New Testament. The Johannine prologue identifies the extravagant reception of grace, 'grace upon grace' (John 1: 16), as proceeding from Christ's fullness, the one 'full of grace and truth' (John 1: 14). Paul designates Christ as the last Adam, as he who has become 'a life-giving spirit' (1 Cor. 15: 45). The Spirit in and upon Christ and flowing forth from him as the risen Lord bespeaks the integration of the Christological and pneumatological missions for the life of the church. The *Catechism of the Catholic Church* prefers to speak of the 'joint mission of the Son and the Spirit' (*CCC* §689), thus preventing any artificial separation between the two missions. Jesus, the Spirit-bearer, 'gives the Spirit without measure' (John 3: 34); he sends forth the Spirit as the risen one (John 20: 22).

While debates over the intentionality of the Jesus of history and the social form of his movement abound—debates as to whether Jesus understood his mission as having been sent to the 'house of Israel' (Matt. 15: 24) and so intended to found a church out of his incipient community of disciples—it is to the Christological foundations of the church that we must turn to establish ecclesiality. The risen Lord is at the source of the church's life. The church as the mystical body of Christ as enunciated in *Mystici Corporis* along with the Augustinian notion of the *Christus totus* certainly gives pause if understood as implying the identity of Christ and the church. Statements such as that of Johann Adam Möhler seem to suggest such a notion.

> Thus, the visible Church, from the point of view here taken, is the Son of God himself, everlastingly manifesting himself among men in a human form, perpetually renovated, and eternally young—the permanent incarnation of the same, as in Holy Writ, even the faithful are called 'the Body of Christ'. (Möhler 1997: 259)

When considered within the ambit of both the Christological and pneumatological missions, however, the relation between Christ and his body (as suggested by its Pauline roots: 1 Cor. 12: 12–13) is more nuanced than one of absolute identity.

The risen Christ, as head of the church, indeed permeates the church with his theandric life through the gift of the Holy Spirit. The analogy utilized by *Lumen*

Gentium is between Christ's human nature (including his corporeity) and the divine Son on the one hand, and between the visible structures of the church and the Holy Spirit on the other. Noting this analogy, a document of the International Theological Commission of the Roman Curia comments that the 'continuity between Jesus Christ and the church is therefore not direct but "mediate"... assured by the Holy Spirit, who, being the Spirit of Jesus, acts in order to bring about in the Church the Lordship of Jesus Christ' (Sharkey 1989: 274–5). This also qualifies the analogy of the Holy Spirit as the soul of the church. The indwelling of the Holy Spirit in the church and its members embraces the various graces and gifts given by the Spirit—including both 'hierarchical and charismatic' gifts, the latter embracing 'very outstanding or simpler and more widely diffused' gifts (*Lumen Gentium* §§4, 12). Even so, this does not establish any hypostatic union of the Holy Spirit with the church.

The church, understood as the mystical body of Christ, while deriving its heuristic intelligibility from predominantly Catholic ecclesiological interests, nevertheless poses significant questions for any doctrine of the church, whether this is construed in light of a particular confessional horizon or with direct ecumenical intentionality. It gathers the theological correlates of faith, grace, and visibility into a *status quaestionis* regarding the nature of the church. It lends itself, as the International Theological Commission document notes, to a similar type of dogmatic inquiry about the nature of the divine–human relation that informs Christology. Commenting on *Lumen Gentium* §8 (quoted above), the Commission states:

> The analogy drawn here with the Word incarnate enables us to affirm that the church as 'organ of salvation' must be understood in such a way as not to fall foul of either of those two heretical excesses in Christology known to antiquity. Thus we shall avoid, on the one hand, an ecclesial 'Nestorianism' that would recognize no subsistent relationship between the divine and human elements in the Church's life. On the other hand, we must be equally vigilant against an ecclesial 'monophysitism', for which everything in the Church is 'divinized', leaving no space for the defects and faults of the Church's organization, the sad harvest of the sins and ignorance of men. (Sharkey 1989: 287–8)

Exception may be taken to the application of Chalcedonian norms beyond the realm of Christology proper. Perhaps this is the very problem, suggesting that the church in the *Christus totus* model possesses the same relationship between the divine and the human as does the person of Christ. As presented by the Commission, the issue is how to articulate the relationship between the divine and human elements in the church—their language is 'subsistence'—while excluding the so-called 'monophysite' temptation that so divinizes the human elements of the church that any 'defects and faults' are ignored. The modality of how human words and acts are taken up by God in ecclesial life and praxis, thus constituting the church, is the core concern.

The same document also employs the categories of remembrance and expectation to delineate the identity and difference between Christ and the church—certainly to many Protestants a more hospitable way of putting things. Taking up the dominant metaphor of the church in *Lumen Gentium*, the people of God, these categories underscore the total dependence of the church on Jesus Christ (Sharkey 1989: 276). Combined with the overarching Vatican II themes of the church as mystery and sacrament, this development in Catholic teaching keeps two ecclesiological emphases in focus. First, as mystery the church is always exceeded by the presence of Christ and the Spirit that calls the church into existence, sustains it, and is present in and mediated by it. Second, dependent as the church is on the Christological and pneumatological missions, that is, the single, joint mission of Son and Spirit, the church is also the sacrament of those missions. Analogously again, as with the sacraments themselves, the church is sign and instrument of the presence and salutary agency of God in Christ through the outpouring of the Holy Spirit. As do the sacraments, the church effects what it signifies.

Thus far the variations presented are within the realm of Catholic ecclesiology, noting nuanced but significant developments that have taken place between popes (Leo XIII, Pius XII) and council (Vatican II). By and large the theological symbol of the church as the mystical body of Christ—the dominant symbol between Vatican I and Vatican II—has yielded to the symbol of the church as mystery, sacrament, and people of God, while still holding to the truth of the former. One could also argue that the theological symbol of the church as the mystical body of Christ succeeded that of the church as a juridical and hierarchical society that was dominant in the post-Tridentine era, while at the same time incorporating the structural dimensions of ecclesial life as we have seen. In tracing this development, it is clear that neither Pius XII nor the Second Vatican Council asserts an absolute identity between Christ and the church, even in the *Christus totus* model. Christ is after all the head of the church and, when taken with the spousal image, the distinction between bridegroom and bride is intrinsic to its meaning and intent. Christ cleanses and sanctifies the church, his bride, whom he calls to union with himself in strongly eschatological overtones.

> While... here on earth the church is on pilgrimage from the Lord, it is like an exile who seeks and savours the things that are above, where Christ is seated at the right hand of God, where the life of the church is hidden with Christ in God until it appears in glory with its spouse. (*Lumen Gentium* §6)

Whether this foundational ecclesiology can be taken up with ecumenical intentionality remains to be seen, although the likelihood is not great even though it has had significant influence on the communion ecclesiology that now dominates the field. As a matter of theological analysis and for the sake of future ecumenical prospects, we must take seriously objections to this 'catholicizing' model, many of which have to do with the theologies of grace that inform both its advocates and critics. John Webster is a good example of one who seriously contends for an alternative model from the perspective of an emergent evangelical ecclesiology (even if his remarks are more directed to the communion ecclesiology that we shall shortly come to). His critique is sharp and to the point:

> Barth warned Roman Catholics around the time of Vatican II to beware lest they became liberal Protestants; my worry is that evangelicals will become catholicized Protestants who make the mistake of thinking that the only ecclesiological improvement upon individualism and 'soul liberty' is a rather ill-digested theology of the *totus Christus*. (Webster 2005: 112)

IV. Communion Ecclesiology: An Ecumenical Option

As a measure of the arrival of communion ecclesiology as the dominant model for ecumenism we turn to the World Council of Churches. Its Commission on Faith and Order published *The Nature and Purpose of the Church: A Stage on the Way to a Common Statement* in 1998, a document that has set the agenda for the ecumenical movement. The subsequent process of reception led in 2005 to the publication of a sequel paper by Faith and Order entitled *The Nature and Mission of the Church: A Stage on the Way to a Common Statement.* In light of Webster's comment, it is significant that both documents consign the notion of the 'church as sacrament'—the real basis for catholicizing tendencies—to an explanatory box in which the different positions on its use are acknowledged. However, this also implicitly admits its lack of ecumenical consensus, thereby prohibiting its use in the body of the text (cf. World Council of Churches 1998: 23; 2005: 28–9).

Faith and Order prefers to speak of the church as 'sign and instrument of God's design' (World Council of Churches 1998: 21), or 'sign and instrument of God's intention and plan for the world' (World Council of Churches 2005: 27), language similar to the 'sacramental' terminology utilized by Catholic theologians and magisterial documents. In effect, Faith and Order attempts to say what the 'sacramental model' intends short of the theology of grace that informs the latter. For example, Faith and Order is consistent in identifying the church as 'a divine and human reality' (World Council of Churches 1998: 10; cf. 2005: 15) that already participates in the love, life, and communion of God. As such it is an instrument that makes present throughout history the mercy of God, the earlier document even stating that 'the Church is the instrument through which God wants to bring about what is signified by it' (World Council of Churches 1998: 21; cf. 2005: 27). Compare this, however, to the language of the *Catechism of the Catholic Church.* Although maintaining the analogical sense of the church as sacrament—after all, *Lumen*

Gentium §1 actually states, 'the church is in Christ as a sacrament or instrumental sign of intimate union with God and of the unity of all humanity'—it indeed teaches that the 'Church ... both contains and communicates the invisible grace she signifies' (*CCC* §74). 'Contains' and 'communicates' overstep the limits of the nature of the church, and it is this that so exercises critics of the formula.

Interestingly, *The Nature and Purpose of the Church*, in its summary of the reasons given for and against the formula, ignores the theology of grace. The theological rationale of churches that advocate its use has to do with the 'Church ... as a pointer to what God wants for the world, namely the communion of all together and with him, the happiness for which he created the world' (World Council of Churches 1998: 23). This was strengthened in *The Nature and Mission of the Church* to read as follows: 'those churches who use the expression "Church as Sacrament" do so because they understand the Church as an effective sign of what God wishes for the world: namely, the communion of all together and with the Triune God' (World Council of Churches 2005: 29). Clearly, the notion of the church's sacramentality was clarified for those who support the notion. Those who decline the formula, however, are concerned with the lack of distinction in both documents between the church and sacraments, with the tendency to obscure the sinfulness of the 'communion of Christians', and most importantly with the claim that 'sacraments ... are means of salvation through which Christ sustains the Church, not actions by which the Church realizes or actualizes itself' (World Council of Churches 1998: 23; cf. 2005: 29). It is perhaps this final reason that strikes most directly at the concern of those who believe that the formula confuses Christ and the church. If such is the case with the sacramental model of the church, would such a confusion not be guaranteed if the reference were to the church as the mystical body of Christ? In other words, are we at an unbridgeable confessional divide despite the ecumenical progress of the last century?

A statement by Wolfhart Pannenberg can help to identify clearly the parameters and substance of the dispute, since it utilizes words similar to those employed by *Catechism of the Catholic Church*, yet in critique of the sacramental model.

> The Church is not in and of itself the saving mystery of the rule of God either in its social constitution or in its historical form. It is so only in Christ, therefore only in the event of participation in Jesus Christ as this takes place in its liturgical life. (Pannenberg 1991–8: iii. 42)

To counter the notion that the church 'in and of itself' could be this saving mystery (Is this the same as the *Catechism*'s phrase that the church both 'contains and communicates the invisible grace she signifies'?), Eberhard Jüngel offers clear and yet irenic theses on how Protestants may integrate the notion of sacramentality into the doctrine of the church, even as he cautions against *Lumen Gentium*'s affirmation that the 'divine mystery of salvation is ... continued in the Church' (Jüngel 1989: 206). For Jüngel, the church is a 'sacramental sign' corresponding to the sacramental being of Jesus Christ. The church in its own way represents Christ without equating itself with the work of Christ or its representation of Christ with the continuation of that work. The 'church understands Jesus Christ as the analogue and itself as the analogate', with ecclesial actions of word and sacrament understood as 'testifying to, celebrating and living from' Jesus Christ who himself (not the church) is 'the *opus operatum dei* (the divine work performed)' (Jüngel 1989: 212–13).

No doubt Catholic theologians have distinguished between the sacramental being of Christ and that of the church. One typical example is the distinction that Karl Rahner makes between Christ as the primordial sacrament and the church as the fundamental sacrament (K. Rahner 1963: 18). But this does not necessarily allay the concerns on the other side of the Reformation. It may indeed be the case that the World Council of Churches Faith and Order papers *The Nature and Purpose of the Church* and *The Nature and Mission of the Church* have reached the limits of ecumenical consensus, although their reception by various churches remains in process. As with the Catholic/Lutheran *Joint Declaration on the Doctrine of Justification*, one may also hope that the remaining differences in a common faith are not church-dividing, although in ecclesiology the difficulties increase simply because the establishment of full communion requires positive agreement on fundamental ecclesiological issues.

In fact, the matter has been broached in at least one international bilateral ecumenical dialogue. The Catholic/Reformed Dialogue (the Pontifical Council for Promoting Christian Unity and the World Alliance of Reformed Churches), in its 1990 report *Towards a Common Understanding of the Church*, characterized each communion's understanding of the church with one overarching conception, respectively the Reformed *creatura verbi* and the Catholic *sacramentum gratiae*. The report expressed its hopes as follows.

> The two conceptions, 'the creation of the word' and 'sacrament of grace', can in fact be seen as expressing the same instrumental reality under different aspects, as complementary to each other or as two sides of the same coin. They can also become the poles of a creative tension between our churches. (Gros, Meyer, and Rusch 2000: 805)

In effect, *The Nature and Purpose of the Church* fulfils these expectations on a multilateral ecumenical scale by opting for the *creatura verbi* conception while adverting to the contending understandings of the sacramentality of the church. By establishing the former on both Christological and pneumatological foundations (*creatura Verbi et creatura Spiritus*), it is able to arrive at a *koinonia/communio* ecclesiology that is ecumenically acceptable to a number of ecclesial traditions. Consider its opening definition of the nature of the church: 'The Church belongs to God. It is the creation of God's Word and Holy Spirit. It cannot exist by and for itself' (World Council of Churches 1998: 9; cf. 2005: 13). Such a definition ensures the transition to a communion ecclesiology that is at least comparable to a Catholic communion ecclesiology, proceeding as the latter does from the sacramental ecclesiological model that is built on the conception of the church as the mystical body of Christ.

In sum, the paths to an ecumenical communion ecclesiology are confessionally diverse and not insignificant in light of both the prospects they offer for Christian unity and the differences that remain. The Catholic trajectory traced here is intended to focus those issues that require theological adjudication if we are to arrive at a common understanding of the nature of the church. Even within this Catholic trajectory diverse ecclesiological visions have emerged since the Second Vatican Council concerning both the relationship of the ecclesiology of *Lumen Gentium* to *Mystici Corporis* and the configuration of the communion ecclesiology that is advocated. So even if one interpreted the symbol of the church as the people of God as a displacement (rather than an integral development) of the church as the mystical body of Christ, the latter a mere hierarchology (Comblin 2004: 17–37), one still has to negotiate the theology of grace that underlies magisterial ecclesiology and, for that matter, actual Catholic ecclesial life.

Communion ecclesiology is now semi-officially the ecclesiology of ecumenism. *The Nature and Purpose of the Church* declares that 'the notion of *koinonia* (communion) has become fundamental for revitalizing a common understanding of the nature of the Church and its visible unity' (World Council of Churches 1998: 24; cf. 2005: 21). This was preceded by a similar bold statement by the 1985 Extraordinary Synod of Bishops in the Catholic Church upon the twentieth anniversary of the close of the Second Vatican Council: the 'ecclesiology of communion is the central and fundamental idea of the Council's documents' (Extraordinary Synod 1985: 53). Yet, communion ecclesiology can be as diverse as the theological trajectories that inform it. The sacramental dimension of the church which by necessity figures greatly in Catholic and Orthodox communion ecclesiologies possesses much less resonance, as we have seen, in the proposed ecumenical ecclesiology of the Faith and Order papers, as it would also in most free-church ecclesiologies.

One example is very instructive. Miroslav Volf constructs a free-church communion ecclesiology, one that is conversation with, but very distinct from, the Catholic and Orthodox versions represented respectively by Joseph Ratzinger (now Benedict XVI) and John Zizioulas. Instead of prioritizing the universal church over the local church as does the former, or making the local church dependent upon its eucharistic and therefore episcopal constitution as does the latter (both entailing Christological and pneumatological dimensions), Volf argues that the constitution of the church is based upon 'Christ's unmediated, direct presence in the entire local church as well as in every believer' (Volf 1998: 134). Like more sacramentally oriented proposals, it is derived from the life of the Trinity *ad extra* in the missions of the Son and the Spirit. Although this radical free-church affirmation might sound dissonant to the ears of Catholics and Orthodox, it is one that is fully intelligible within the framework of the theology of grace that informs it. 'Where two or three are gathered in Christ's name, not only is Christ present among them, but a Christian church is there as well' (Volf 1998: 136).

In conclusion, the diversity noted does not necessarily undermine the basic affirmation that '[f]undamentally it is matter of communion with God through Jesus Christ, in the Holy Spirit' (Extraordinary Synod 1985: 53). It is this affirmation that captures the reality of the church. The particulars of ecclesiology remain. Understanding of the traditional four marks of the church—unity, holiness, catholicity, and apostolicity—is enriched as are notions of the church's order and of the relationship between universality and particularity, between the universal church and local churches. The church is indeed a communion of local churches. This communion is actualized in both Word and sacrament. Order in the form of ministerial oversight (*episkopē*) is necessary, and ideally it should be communal, personal, and collegial (World Council of Churches 1998: 45; cf. 2005: 52). The church is *in via*. Therefore however one construes the church's sinfulness, none dispute that the people of God are called to be holy by fidelity to apostolic faith and praxis as the full gospel is proclaimed to all (catholicity). Even if this does not specify what is proper to ecclesiality—which ecclesial elements are necessary and which are not, such as episcopacy—it at least ensures that the visibility of Christian life for a pilgrim people is no small matter.

References

Aquinas, St Thomas (1948). *Summa Theologica*. Notre Dame: Ave Maria.

Auer, Johann (1993). The *Church: The Universal Sacrament of Salvation*. Washington, DC: Catholic University of America Press.

Braaten, Carl (1983). *Principles of Lutheran Theology*. Philadelphia: Fortress.

Calvin, John (1960). *Institutes of the Christian Religion*. Philadelphia: Westminster Press.

Catechism of the Catholic Church (1997). New York: Doubleday.

Comblin, José (2004). *People of God*. Maryknoll: Orbis.

Congar, Yves (1960). *The Mystery of the Church*. Baltimore: Helicon.

The Extraordinary Synod (1985). *Message to the People of God*. Boston: Daughters of St Paul.

Gros, Jeffrey, Meyer, Harding, and Rusch, William G. (eds.) (2000). *Growth in Agreement II: Reports and Agreed Statement of Ecumenical Conversations on a World Level 1982–1998*. Geneva: WCC Publications and Grand Rapids: Eerdmans.

Hinson, E. Glenn (ed.) (1986). *Understandings of the Church*. Philadelphia: Fortress.

James of Viterbo (1995). *On Christian Government*. Woodbridge: Boydell.

Jüngel, Eberhard (1989). 'Church as Sacrament'. In id., *Theological Essays*, Edinburgh: T. & T. Clark.

Mersch, Emile (1951). *The Theology of the Mystical Body*. St Louis: Herder.

Möhler, Johann Adam (1997). *Symbolism: Exposition of the Doctrinal Differences between Catholics and Protestants as Evidenced by their Symbolical Writings*. New York: Crossroad.

Pannenberg, Wolfhart (1991–8). *Systematic Theology*. 3 vols. Grand Rapids: Eerdmans.

Pius XII (1943). *Encyclical Letter of His Holiness Pius XII on The Mystical Body of Christ and Our Union in it with Christ: Mystici Corporis.* Boston: St Paul Editions.

Rahner, Hugo (1963). 'The Church, God's Strength in Human Weakness'. In Albert La Pierre (ed.), *The Church: Readings in Theology*, New York: P. J. Kennedy & Sons.

Rahner, Karl (1963). *The Church and the Sacraments.* New York: Herder and Herder.

Rusch, William G., and Gros, Jeffrey (eds.) (1998). *Deepening Communion: International Ecumenical Documents with Roman Catholic Participation.* Washington, DC: United States Catholic Conference.

Scheeben, Matthias Joseph (1946). *The Mysteries of Christianity.* St Louis: Herder.

Schleiermacher, F. D. E. (1928). *The Christian Faith.* Edinburgh: T. & T. Clark.

Sharkey, Michael (1989). 'Select Themes of Ecclesiology on the Occasion of the Eighth Anniversary of the Closing of the Second Vatican Council'. In id. (ed.), *International Theological Commission: Texts and Documents 1969–1985*, San Francisco: Ignatius.

Tanner, Norman P., SJ (ed.) (1990). *Decrees of the Ecumenical Councils.* 2 vols. Georgetown: Sheed and Ward.

Tillard, J.-M.-R. (2001). *Flesh of the Church, Flesh of Christ: At the Source of the Ecclesiology of Communion.* Collegeville: Liturgical.

Volf, Miroslav (1998). *After Our Likeness: The Church as the Image of the Trinity.* Grand Rapids: Eerdmans.

Webster, John (2005). 'The Visible attests the Invisible'. In Husbands and Treier (eds.), *The Community of the Word: Toward and Evangelical Ecclesiology*, Downers Grove: InterVarsity.

World Council of Churches Faith and Order (1998). *The Nature and Purpose of the Church: A Stage on the Way to a Common Statement.* Faith and Order Paper No. 181. Geneva: World Council of Churches/Faith and Order.

—— (2005). *The Nature and Mission of the Church: A Stage on the Way to a Common Statement.* Faith and Order Paper No. 198. Geneva: World Council of Churches/Faith and Order.

Suggested Reading

Auer (1993).

Comblin (2004).

Congar (1960).

Doyle, Dennis M. (2000). *Communion Ecclesiology: Visions and Versions.* Maryknoll: Orbis.

Journet, Charles Cardinal (2004). *The Theology of the Church.* San Francisco: Ignatius.

Jüngel (1989).

Mersch (1951).

Pannenberg (1991–8: iii. 1–434).

Rahner (1963).

Tillard (2001).

Volf (1998).

Webster (2005).

World Council of Churches (1998).

CHAPTER 15

SACRAMENTS

MICHAEL A. FAHEY, SJ

I. The Shifting Context

The Christian understanding of sacraments as expressed in systematic theology has undergone notable developments since the 1950s. These paradigm shifts began in western Europe partly because of the emergence of the so-called 'new theology' or the return to the early sources (*ressourcement*) that placed renewed stress on biblical hermeneutics, patristic theology, and liturgical studies. At the same time, thanks to both the establishment of the World Council of Churches after the Second World War and the stimulus of the Second Vatican Council, a new willingness emerged among churches to engage in ecumenical discussions on topics including baptism, the eucharist, and ordained ministry. Long-standing issues disputed since the Protestant Reformation were finally being addressed. Catholic bishops in their conciliar document on the liturgy, *Sacrosanctum concilium*, confessed the need for renewal in how their churches were celebrating the sacraments (Tanner 1990: ii. 820–43). Through academic meetings of scholars such as the Societas Liturgica, a cross-section of churches and universities held serious discussions at regular intervals to critique outdated practices and to outline new rituals. And, as a follow-up to its pioneering Lima Document, *Baptism, Eucharist, and Ministry* (World Council of Churches 1982), the Faith and Order Commission further promoted these kinds of explorations by its study *The Nature and Mission of the Church*, promulgated and submitted to the member churches at Porto Alegre, Brazil, in February 2006 (World Council of Churches 2005). Illustrative of the extent to which ecumenical dialogue has contributed to a comprehensive and irenic sacramental theology are two works by Robert W. Jenson, *Visible Words: The Interpretation and Practice of Christian Sacraments* (1978) and *Systematic Theology* (1997–9). Jenson's Lutheran convictions remain solid but are contextualized within international ecumenical consensus and even the decrees of the Second Vatican Council.

A number of churches have formulated their commitment to renewal of their liturgical rituals. These reforms relating especially to the eucharist—how the Lord's Supper is commemorated—have led to new insights about how one should understand the functions of ordained ministry in the various churches. It was recognized that the churches of the West had often neglected the role of the Holy Spirit in their public prayer. Specialized historical studies drew attention to the fact that medieval and post-Reformation sacramental theology had been heavily influenced by the juridical considerations of canon law and even moral theology. It came to be seen that, although medieval scholasticism had brought order to the way the chief ritual celebrations of the church were understood, the decision to combine the sacraments into a single doctrinal treatise *de sacramentis in genere* had obscured the uniqueness of each individual rite. How sacraments differed from one another, it was concluded, was more notable than what they shared in common. This realization promoted new emphasis on each sacrament in its particularity rather than on what was common to all. Modern ecumenical consensus statements, with rare exceptions, have not concentrated on 'the sacraments' but instead explored, for example, unity through baptism, complementary understandings of the eucharistic memorial, as well as other practices that illustrate the 'incarnational principle' operative in the worldwide Christian communities.

It is significant that the major twentieth-century ecumenical agreement, the Lima Document, does not address the theology of sacraments in general, but treats baptism, the eucharist, and ministry as separate entities. The text emphasizes signs as integral to each sacrament but in unique ways. The text also describes the inseparability of God's gift and the personal response in faith. In the practice of infant baptism, it stresses the importance of the faith of the gathered community as well as the need for other Christians to nurture the faith of the neophyte.

Without denying the contributions of late medieval sacramental theology, modern theology came to recognize that discussions about how the sacraments 'caused' grace, or about specific concepts such as the minister of the sacraments, the recipient, one's intention, the number and efficacy of sacraments, or validity, legitimacy, matter, and form, all failed to address sacraments as communal worship or liturgy. To understand sacraments, it was realized, one needed to understand liturgy. Also, as scriptural lectionaries in churches were expanded, and the ministry of the word through biblical preaching and homilies was enhanced, the question was raised whether the oft-asserted distinction between Reformation churches as churches of the word, and Catholic and Orthodox churches as churches of the sacraments, did, in fact, correspond to a real distinction. As recently as the 1960s, Gerhard Ebeling argued that the difference between Reformation and Catholic worship was the difference between a *worthafte Existenz* and a *sakramentale Existenz.* But recently theologians have come to perceive the inseparable unity between word and sacrament. The celebration of the Lord's Supper, for instance, is described as proclamation of the word, enriched with ritual sacramental gestures. Catholics, on the basis of renewed Christology, have also come to describe the proclamation of the word as the Church's essential function, and each sacrament is recognized as a richly compressed form of the Church's gospel word.

In the process of ecumenical dialogue, many of the official consultations began with the sacrament of baptism, which seemed, in the hierarchy of truths, the least contentious. From there, the ecumenical dialogues focused on the Lord's Supper, the eucharist, especially to explore the nature of the long-disputed concept of sacrifice. This in turn led to a discussion of the ordained minister and of the roles of the presbyterate and the episcopate. More, and more insightful, theological elaborations on the sacraments emerged from ecumenical consensus statements than from the writings of individual theologians. For example, the international consensus statement *Facing Unity* drew attention to the interrelatedness of sacrament, proclaimed word, and faith, and it praised a comprehensive view of the sacramental life of the church that gave precedence, over an isolated approach to individual sacraments, to an understanding of the church as the universal sacrament of salvation and unity (Roman Catholic/Lutheran Joint Commission 1985). The sacraments were described as accenting the corporeality, the personal character, and the community dimension of liturgical worship.

In recent decades, the study of Christology has been enriched by drawing it into closer relationship with soteriology. Greater attention has been given to the resurrection of Jesus Christ as the culminating point of salvific activities. With stress on the humanity of Jesus and reflection on the implications of his assuming a material body, the churches have come to appreciate better how Christ, throughout his earthly life and since, channels saving grace through material realities, whether his body or even the human activities that he engaged in. This theology of 'earthly realities'—to use the expression of Belgian theologian Gustave Thils in the title of his study, *La Théologie des réalités terrestres* (1947)—affords a new way of appreciating how material things such as words, water, bread, wine, and oil, gestures like imposition of hands, expressions of reconciliation, and physical signs of love, can somehow 'bear' grace. Of themselves, these parts of the material world are not capable of bestowing God's favour, but by divine will they become a link between the temporal, earthly realm and the eternal, heavenly realm.

This sacramental or incarnational principle is at the heart of Christian convictions about how material creation (pre-eminently the humanity of Jesus) serves as a conveyor, a sign, or a symbol of divine grace and presence. In the sacraments, material objects, even the spoken word, serve as media for divine outpouring into the welcoming human recipient. In the late 1940s, Edward Schillebeeckx developed the idea that the humanity of Jesus Christ, the theandric embodiment of the Logos, is a 'sacrament' of God's encounter (*rencontre, ontmoeting*) with the human race (Schillebeeckx 1963). His writings expanded what theologians such as Otto Semmelroth had developed about the notion of the church itself as the *Ursakrament*, the primordial sign of grace dwelling in our midst, the church as a mediating principle (Semmelroth 1953). God is described as using created realities to offer a sacramental encounter; the church itself is a mediating principle. Sacraments are both acts of Christ and acts of the church.

It had long been recognized that the gestures and attitudes of the incarnate Word during his earthly life are important indications about how his followers should act in the future even when Christ had not issued specific instructions or commands as he had in the case of performing baptisms ('make disciples of all nations, baptizing them', Matt. 28: 19), celebrating the Lord's Supper ('do this in remembrance of me', 1 Cor. 11: 24–5), or expressing forgiveness ('if you forgive the sins of any, they are forgiven', John 20: 23). In its writings and art works, the pre-Reformation church of the West identified seven principal rituals that by then had come to be identified as sacraments. The fact that there are no specific commands of Jesus about all these rituals recorded in scripture did not lessen the church's conviction that these rituals had developed because of the inspiration of the Holy Spirit during the formative years of the church, the period known loosely as 'the apostolic age'. How many of these ecclesial rituals existed was not important, since there were numerous actions that could broadly speaking be considered sacraments, including the consecration of a Christian king, the distribution of ashes, the sprinkling of holy water, and the rite of Christian burial. Eventually the number seven identified specific rites, and the remaining church practices were described as pious customs or sacramentals.

A growing trinitarian thrust is notable in recent descriptions of the sacraments, as for instance the observation by the Groupe des Dombes, a productive, French-language dialogue partnership between Catholics and members of the Église Réformée:

> The Spirit is present and given in the ministry of the sacraments which carry out what the Word proclaims. A sacrament is not solely a figurative rite; it is primarily the celebration of the Christ-event among a number of people who come together to open up their lives to his paschal presence. This common celebration always consists of symbolic words and actions, in harmony with the basic structure of speaking and acting in human life, and is in profound accord with the Church's faith in the Word made flesh. As acts of Christ whom the Father has sent into the world with the power of the Spirit, the sacraments bring people into the fellowship of the Father, Son and Spirit from whom they receive their efficacy (Groupe des Dombes 1980: §§97–8).

This helps to clarify why sacramental acts are performed 'in the name of the Father, and of the Son, and of the Holy Spirit'.

In recent times there has also been a growing awareness that it is in the church that each of the sacraments is celebrated. Especially the eucharist relies upon the power of the Holy Spirit to transform the matter and form of the sacrament into the presence of the risen Christ, whose mystical body is the church. The prayer recited over the elements at the Lord's Supper is known as the *epiklesis* and accounts for the transforming presence of the Holy Spirit.

The new emphases relating to the sacraments allow for the fact that, while it is Christ himself who is properly minister of sacraments, it is legitimate to describe as their 'celebrant', in a certain sense, the entire community of those present, the whole worshipping community, whereas the bishop or presbyter serves not as a 'celebrant' but rather as the 'presider' over the prayer of the celebrating community. Karl Rahner often wrote eloquently on the active role of the attending persons in the sacramental event.

II. Sign, Symbol, or Both?

A great deal of attention has been given to rethinking the word 'sign' in connection with the sacraments and to replacing it with the concept of 'symbol'. In some ecclesiastical quarters, however, the term symbol has met with reluctance, since it appears to imply something less than real. This may be due to an ambiguity in the term 'symbolic' that can suggest something empty, with no basis in reality. But a symbolic gesture can also connote not simply a sign which has a superficial or natural meaning but one with a deeper and supernatural significance accessible only to faith. This concept of symbol carries a more comprehensive sense than a simple sign because it intends to describe a real means of communication between God and humanity under the aspect of a sign. It implies a commingling of a human, this-worldly aspect and a divine component. To be sure, not every sign is a symbol, but every symbol is a sign. This symbolic possibility of a sacrament having a divine component is a consequence of the incarnation. Hence a sacrament relies on an incarnational principle. Religious symbols, to be sure, are not restricted to the sacraments but include all celebrations in which God is worshipped. Because our knowledge originates in our senses, encounter with the divine for us is possible only through sensible signs. As the German theologian and colleague of the late Karl Rahner, Herbert Vorgrimler, has written, 'The sacrament is a symbolic action in which human beings are engaged as believers, as those who celebrate liturgy, as narrators, as persons who act symbolically; but the divine Spirit uses this human action as a means and a way by which to make Jesus Christ, with his historically unique saving activity, memorially, really, and actually present' (Vorgrimler 1992: 71).

Augustine is sometimes identified as the founder of sacramental theology for the West, since he distinguished how the Church performs a visible rite to express an invisible effect. The 'visible sacrament' is a 'sacred symbol' (*sacrum signum*) (*City of*

God 10. 5, in Augustine 1998: 397; Migne 1844–65: 41. 282), and the rite's effect is termed *res sacramenti* (cf. *Letter* 138. 7, in Schaff 1980: i. 483; Migne 1844–65: 33. 527). Hugh of St Victor wrote an important treatise *De sacramentis* which came to influence scholasticism. In his treatment he did not restrict sacraments to the seven principal liturgical rites of the first millennium but included many more signs, including holy water, the cross of ashes on one's forehead, monastic consecration, and the rite of burial (*De sacramentis* 1. 9, 12, in Migne 1844–65: 176. 318–28, 347–64).

Because sacramental celebrations are complex realities, requiring not only external rituals but also interior dispositions, long-lasting effects, and gestures with clarifying words, medieval theology developed a number of distinctions which, at first sight, seem elusive or overly refined. But they are in fact necessary distinctions to explain how a religious ritual could be performed and yet not achieve its intended end. By the advent of scholasticism in the twelfth and thirteenth centuries, the terms involved three distinct but related concepts. The *sacramentum tantum* consists in the sign alone, the external rite (such as pouring of water) in which the minister, using the matter and form of the rite and a particular spoken formula, meets the recipient. This coming together brings about the first effect, the character or symbolic reality termed the *res et sacramentum*. But the ultimate goal of the sacrament requires the recipient to receive the *res sacramenti* (or *res tantum*), namely the religious effect of the sacrament, the actual bestowal of grace, the ultimate reality intended to be conferred by the sacrament.

III. Grace and God's Role

One of the theological distinctions that contributed to a faulty understanding of baptism and eucharist in the late medieval period was the distinction between something achieved *ex opere operato* or *ex opere operantis*. The first term was originally intended to underscore the fact that sacraments achieve their end *ex opere operato Christi*, 'by the power of the completed ritual designed by Christ'. This meant that human beings' role in the sacrament is not the cause but the condition for the effective application of divine grace offered in the sacrament. Unfortunately, in the late medieval period, the formula gave rise popularly to the incorrect notion that sacraments achieve their end automatically, simply by being celebrated, and independently of the faith of the recipient. However widespread this misconceived automatism might have been, this perception was far from orthodox teaching. The Reformers' objections to the way sacraments were often being regarded by the faithful and the clergy singled out this expression. If, according to Catholic belief, the sacraments mediate divine grace and do so 'by the power of the completed ritual' (*ex opere operato*), this conviction needs to be protected against a variety of possible misinterpretations. Obviously, the function of faith is central in the realization of the celebration and for a fruitful reception of the sacraments. Personal faith and proper intention of the church are needed to have the sacraments achieve their end *ex opere operantis* [*ecclesiae*]—through the power of the church's intercessory prayer—implying that the one 'receiving' also has a role to play, albeit far less powerful that the divine role.

The vehemence with which the Reformers objected to this faulty doctrine is understandable in light of their insistence on *sola gratia, sola fide*, and *sola scriptura*. The Reformers perceived that the late medieval mass was deficient, since the scriptural word was not proclaimed in the vernacular. For the Reformers, the mass in its format at that time encouraged a harmful passivity and encouraged superstition. Luther's critique of the medieval sacramental system, *The Babylonian Captivity of the Church* (1520), was not a rejection of all the sacraments as such but was a stinging indictment of false understandings of their workings. It is unfortunate that the Council of Trent, convoked, albeit tardily, to respond to the teachings of the Reformers, adopted such a defensive tone in its written texts and not only did not directly address specific points of critique but expressed its own teaching in a harsh and unforgiving tone. From the numerous conciliar sessions, namely from sessions 7–24 (1547–63) devoted mostly to the sacraments, it is informative to read today the unbending and stern declaration of session 7 (Tanner 1990: ii. 684–9). The contrast between that condemnatory language and the irenic ecumenical consensus statements of today is stunning.

One of the clearest indications of a new age among Reformation theologians in regard to the sacraments is the extensive discussion by Wolfhart Pannenberg in his *Systematic Theology*. In describing the messianic community and individuals, Pannenberg devotes 200 pages to the sacraments under the heading, 'the significatory form of the presence of Christ's salvation in the life of the church' (Pannenberg 1991–8: iii. 237–434). Under this heading he contextualizes baptism, the Lord's Supper, marriage, and ordained ministry. His masterful overview will surely come to be regarded as a classic articulation.

IV. Baptism and Chrismation

In discussing the sacraments of faith, baptism is ordinarily treated first, since it is the sacrament of initiation. One of the more comprehensive descriptions of the effects of baptism is in the opening section of the Lima Document,

Baptism, Eucharist, and Ministry (*BEM*), which draws richly upon the scriptural sources:

Baptism is the sign of new life through Jesus Christ. It unites the one baptized with Christ and with his people. The New Testament scriptures and the liturgy of the Church unfold the meaning of baptism in various images which express the riches of Christ and the gifts of his salvation. These images are sometimes linked with the symbolic uses of water in the Old Testament. Baptism is participation in Christ's death and resurrection (Rom 6: 3–5; Col 2: 12); a washing away of sin (1 Cor 6: 11); a new birth (Jn 3: 5); an enlightenment by Christ (Eph 5: 14); a reclothing in Christ (Gal 3: 27); a renewal by the Spirit (Titus 3: 5); the experience of salvation from the flood (1 Pet 3: 20–21); an exodus from bondage (1 Cor 10: 1–2); and a liberation into a new humanity in which barriers of division whether of sex or race or social status are transcended (Gal 3: 27–28; 1 Cor 12: 13). The images are many but the reality is one. (*BEM* Baptism 2)

Because this sacrament is usually administered to infants, the question naturally arises how a baby can express a personal act of faith. The response proffered is that the Apostles' Creed is recited on behalf of the baby by representatives of the believing community with the fervent prayer that as the child grows up he or she will personally ratify the faith commitment formulated in anticipation on his or her behalf. The dialectic between gift, gratuitously given by God in Christ through the Holy Spirit, and personal response of faith by the individual is reflected in each of the sacraments. It is a dialectic that must be carefully balanced so as to avoid automaticity or Pelagianism.

The most important Protestant theologian of the twentieth century, Karl Barth, in his extensive doctrinal writings did not formally address sacramental theology as such, but as early as *The Teaching of the Church regarding Baptism* (1948), and later in *Church Dogmatics* IV/4 (1969), he strongly opposed the churches' practice of infant baptism—a conviction that generated much debate in the 1960s among theologians such as Eberhard Jüngel and Kurt Aland. Barth's purpose was to bring to bear on the issue of sacramental praxis the light of his neo-Reformation vision of the centrality of the word of God. His conviction was that baptism is a form of the word of God, an acting out of the same word that is preached. The word is operative as it is preached, and thereby constitutes the church. But the recipient of a word cannot be an infant, nor can the word be heard by proxy.

Reformed theologian Thomas F. Torrance has argued convincingly that, in the tradition of Calvin, the sacraments are vehicles of testimony that impart the risen Christ whom they preach (Torrance 1975: 82–138). This is opposed to the view of Barth, who saw sacraments ethically as a grateful human response to a prior divine grace that is neither mediated by the church nor set forth by the sacraments themselves. Torrance views baptism as a modality of God's word which establishes and renews the church in its union with Christ. Baptism proclaims what God has already done in Christ and through his Spirit. The Christian's role in a sacrament consists in receiving divine beneficence, inasmuch as one cannot add to Christ's completed work.

In the history of the church there has long been some variance concerning the age for conferring baptism. Although the documentation for the apostolic church is not conclusive, it is likely that at least some very young children were baptized together with their parents and with their parents' slaves as part of the household's conversion. Where paedobaptism (baptism of infants) is practised rather than believer's baptism, the church explains that the sacramental ritual is more than a rite of several minutes, but rather the beginning of a lengthy assimilation by personal faith extending over years. Parents and fellow parishioners are urged to oversee the development of the baptized child so that it may be brought to the stage of making a personal act of belief, thereby achieving personal adherence to the Christian faith. In order to remind baptized persons of their need to respond personally throughout their entire lives to the gift of baptism, some churches include in their liturgies on various feast days a renewal of baptismal vows and a rededication to what was promised (by proxy) at baptism.

One of the factors that favoured the practice of infant baptism in the Latin church was the prominence of the doctrine of original sin. According to this, the inherited effects of the sin of Adam and Eve so influenced the soul of every newborn that, should it die before the cleansing of original sin through baptism, it would be consigned eternally to limbo, a place of ongoing happiness but without the supernatural gift of the beatific vision. Now that the existence of limbo is held by many to be tenuous, and since other theories have been formulated which would allow infants to choose God freely by a 'final option' in the transitory passage from earthly to eternal life, the pressing urgency of baptism for the removal of original sin and for bestowing the promise of supernatural glory has faded.

During the fourth century, catechumens did not always petition baptism promptly but often postponed their baptism until the approach of death (as was the case even with Constantine). Some saints of the early church, such as Gregory of Nazianzus and Basil of Caesarea, although they considered themselves Christians during their lengthy studies in Athens, were not baptized until their late twenties when they returned home to become monks.

In the early church there emerged a variety of methods for baptizing: total immersion, pouring, even sprinkling in the case of the sick and incapacitated. All were permitted. Much discussed was the issue whether or not to rebaptize one who had received the ritual from a lapsed Christian, a heretic, or even a believer guilty of a grave sin. Rebaptism was rejected in most churches, provided that it could be established that the sinful or unorthodox minister of baptism had intended 'to do what the church intended' in conferring the sacrament. Until modern times, if there was some doubt about the validity of one's baptism, a convert would be baptized 'conditionally' ('If you are not baptized, then I baptize you...').

Throughout the early centuries, the ritual of Christian initiation was ordinarily administered (as is still the case in Eastern Orthodox churches) in one ceremony consisting of three parts: baptism, chrismation (or confirmation), and eucharistic reception. The churches of the West very early on separated confirmation from baptism so that it could be administered by the local bishop and not simply by the presbyter. Today, in western churches that administer confirmation as a distinct rite, confirmation is considered a prolongation of baptism, an opportunity for the young Christian to ratify personally his or her baptismal initiation and so to enter more fully into the mission already conferred by the Holy Spirit. There exist variant practices regarding the age for conferring confirmation on youths. Some churches especially in the Anglican Communion will not distribute first communion to someone who has not yet been confirmed, thereby following the order used in the early church. In the Catholic church of the Roman rite, communion is not offered to children before they have attained the 'age of reason', typically around the seventh year.

In mystagogical catechesis as practised by churches associated with John Chrysostom, Theodore of Mopsuestia, Cyril of Alexandria, and even Ambrose of Milan, catechumens baptized at the Easter Vigil liturgy were not provided in advance with all the details of the Christian faith. Certain prayers and teachings belonging to the 'arcane' tradition were shared only in the days subsequent to baptism, thereby assuring that the holy realities of Christianity would be protected from enemies who might blaspheme or ridicule sacred traditions.

V. Eucharist or Lord's Supper: The Reception of Communion

Because the eucharist is not only a sacrament but also a major ritual of 're-presenting' the benefits of Christ's salvific death, it is not easy to treat it comprehensively in a short space. The Faith and Order Commission, after an extended period of some fifty years, summarized the sacrament as follows:

> The eucharist is essentially the sacrament of the gift which God makes to us in Christ through the power of the Holy Spirit. Every Christian receives this gift of salvation through communion in the body and blood of Christ. In the eucharistic meal, in the eating and drinking of the bread and wine, Christ grants communion with himself. God himself acts, giving life to the body of Christ and renewing each member. In accordance with Christ's promise, each baptized member of the body of Christ receives in the eucharist the assurance of the forgiveness of sins (Mt 26: 28) and the pledge of eternal life (Jn 6: 51–58). Although the eucharist is essentially one complete act, it will be considered here under the following

aspects: thanksgiving to the Father, memorial of Christ, invocation of the Spirit, communion of the faithful, meal of the Kingdom. (*BEM* Eucharist 2)

The Eucharist is a re-enactment, sacramentally, of the sacrifice of Christ on the cross. Misunderstandings of the notion of sacrifice among both Catholics and Reformers created the climate for vehement controversy and mutual recrimination. It is wise to recall, in discussing the disagreements of Christians about the eucharist, that proper instruction in the faith was often weak, especially for the unschooled, and that a variety of superstitions and questionable practices had sprung up around the mass in certain locations. For example, some held that, even without receiving communion, beneficial physical rewards could be obtained merely by looking at the consecrated bread during the elevation of the host. Further, since reception of communion had become infrequent due to an exaggerated sense of reverence, the desire to see the body and blood of Christ became more intense, and 'ocular communion' increased in importance. This prompted the Anglicans, for instance, to state, 'Sacraments were not ordained of Christ to be gazed upon, or to be carried about, but that we should duly use them' (*Thirty-Nine Articles of Religion*, Art. XXV).

Among ordinary Christians the 'real' presence of Christ in the eucharist was sometimes understood in a literalistic sense. Accounts of seeing in the host the crucified Christ or the Christ child proliferated and were occasionally even commemorated in later medieval and Renaissance paintings. The stress on the 'real' presence could obscure the fact that this was a 'sacramental' presence. Because the mass was celebrated in Latin for the western church it was difficult for the faithful to understand what was going on. Some of the language used to describe the meaning of the mass was problematic: it gave the impression that the sacrifice of Calvary had been incomplete, inadequate, and needed to be 'repeated'. Only in more recent times, with the stress on the term 're-presentation', was the mass understood as a covenant renewal.

Frequent reception of communion is a relatively recent phenomenon, having declined until more recent times. Catholicism stands practically alone with its daily celebration of the eucharist. The eastern churches do not practise daily eucharistic celebrations and the number of weekly communicants is often small, perhaps because of fasting and abstinence regulations from food and sexual intercourse. Some Reformation churches celebrate the eucharist infrequently, some on a monthly basis, others weekly. Protestant worship characteristically emphasizes the reading and preaching of scripture, and sometimes gives little prominence to the sacrament.

The ecumenical consensus statements are one in sharing a view of baptism as entry into the *koinonia* or communion of the churches. But, despite this shared fellowship, some churches are reluctant to permit intercommunion or what is more appropriately called eucharistic hospitality or sharing. This unwillingness is based on the fact that, despite a basic sharing of faith, there are still some areas where the churches are not in full visible communion about doctrinal matters. The Decree on Ecumenism of Vatican II said of the Orthodox churches, 'These churches, though separated from us, yet possess true sacraments, above all, by apostolic succession, the priesthood and the eucharist, whereby they are still linked with us in closest intimacy. Therefore some worship in common (*communicatio in sacris*), given suitable circumstances and the approval of church authority, is not merely possible but to be encouraged' (*Unitatis Redintegratio* §15, in Tanner 1990: ii. 917). In regard to other churches, e.g., the churches of the Reformation, while this 'worship in common' or sharing in the sacraments is 'not to be considered as a means to be used indiscriminately for the restoration of Christian unity', nevertheless, 'grace to be had from it sometimes commends this practice' (*Unitatis Redintegratio* §8). This statement illustrates the fact that Catholic teaching is not inexorably opposed to eucharistic hospitality but shows itself to be cautious in its practice.

In connection with the eucharist, Catholics have incorporated a variety of pious devotions that continue to remain foreign to or antipathetic to Reformation Christians. Among these is a prominent display of a tabernacle ostensibly intended to reserve communion for the sick as viaticum, but which also serves as a place for the 'adoration of the Blessed Sacrament'. Exposition of the Blessed Sacrament in a monstrance during a particular period of devotion, or for a procession, is also practised. These devotions cause unease among Reformation Christians who find them remote from the eating and drinking associated with the Lord's Supper. They are also convinced that the presence associated with the tabernacle detracts from the many other forms of the presence of Christ, in the praying community, for example, or in the poor and the destitute. Other eucharistic practices such as the acceptance of stipends for masses, specific 'intentions' applied to the celebration of masses, and the occasional celebration of a 'private mass' (by the priest alone without even one person representing a congregation) are all considered highly suspect by Reformation Christians.

VI. Seven Sacraments, or Two and a Variety of Ordinances?

The preference of the Reformation churches is generally to restrict the word 'sacrament' to baptism and eucharist (since these are clearly New Testament rituals 'instituted' by Jesus) and to describe as ordinances the other rituals in use since the time of the undivided church: marriage, holy orders, confession/penance/

reconciliation, anointing of the sick/extreme unction, and confirmation. The latter can be regarded as legitimate prayers or rites.

Marriage ceremonies for practising Christians are typically performed nowadays in churches according to rituals that vary in length. The wedding ritual is considered by Orthodox and Catholics as a sacrament, although the direct involvement of the church in marriages developed at a later stage. There is a difference between Orthodox and Catholic teaching regarding who may serve as minister(s) of the sacrament of marriage. The Orthodox consider the presiding priest to be the minister of the sacrament, whereas Catholics consider the bride and groom to be the ministers of the sacrament at which the authorized priest presides and provides a nuptial blessing. The Catholic church, however, considers marriage a sacrament only when it takes place between two baptized persons. A *ratum et consummatum* sacramental marriage entered into freely and without constraint is considered by the Catholic church as indissoluble; only in the event of some defect in consent does the church consider itself authorized to declare a marriage null and void. When one or both of the bridal couple possess a dormant faith and go through the ecclesiastical marriage ritual *pro forma*, with little or no religious conviction, it is difficult to see how the *res sacramenti* comes into being.

Holy orders, especially but not exclusively in those churches that have bishops, is regarded as a liturgical rite and involves laying on of hands by the authorized prelate and an invocation of the Holy Spirit to bless the ordained ministry of the candidates. Some Reformation churches have the assembled presbyters impose hands. In the Orthodox and Catholic communities holy orders is seen to be a sacramental liturgy conferred separately according to three levels or degrees: diaconate, presbyterate, and episcopate. A thorny ecumenical question that is far from resolved at the present time is the question of the mutual recognition of holy orders by separated churches. If one were to apply strictly the view that no one can be validly ordained except by a legitimate bishop in apostolic succession within the church, one would be led to consider the ordinations of other churches to be 'absolutely null and utterly void'—to use the terminology of Pope Leo XIII in his 1896 apostolic letter *Apostolicae Curae* in regard to Anglican orders (Denzinger and Schönmetzer 1967: §1966). Several recent historical studies have tried to contextualize this papal judgement and to indicate that it may not in fact embody a definitive teaching of the Catholic church. If one raises the question regarding the status of holy orders in another church not in terms of 'validity' or 'invalidity' but rather in terms of authenticity versus inauthenticity according to the criteria of the church in question, then there may be room for reconsideration of this judgement.

Another much-discussed doctrinal question related to the status of the ordained person is how the priest or bishop presides at sacramental liturgies, especially the eucharist. It has been argued that the ordained person acts *in persona Christi*. This term indicates that the ordained person is delegated by Christ to act as his 'deputy' or a 'vicar'. This idea has even been used by particular churches to argue (although not convincingly) against the ordination of women. Others have argued that, in addition to the priest's role *in persona Christi*, he also serves *in persona ecclesiae*, representing or embodying the prayer of the gathered community (at least half of whom are women).

Confession is the disclosure of one's sins to an ordained person in order to request and obtain reconciliation with the church and from God. It can be either auricular (personal avowal to a priest acting as representative of Christ and the church) or communal (collective admission of sin, with or without private confession, followed by 'sacramental absolution'). It is not practised outside the Orthodox, Roman Catholic, and certain Anglican and Lutheran churches. Even among Catholics there has been a dramatic drop-off in the practice of this sacrament since the 1960s for reasons that are not entirely clear despite both the updating of the ritual and the possibility of 'face-to-face' encounter with the priest. Those churches that practise 'sacramental' confession of sins believe that God, by sending his Son to take on our flesh, encourages the believer to encounter forgiveness through a direct contact that passes through the signs and language of our human condition, specifically through an authorized minister of the church. This is not to imply, however, that this is the only way whereby one can obtain forgiveness of sin and reconciliation from God.

Anointing of the sick (formerly known as **extreme unction**) was typically conferred on a person near death and included a final reception of the eucharist or 'viaticum' (food for the journey into eternity). This ritual is now conferred on persons who have some form of illness but are not necessarily in danger of death. The oil of the sick is used for the ritual, having been blessed by the local bishop during Holy Week (together with the oil of catechumens and chrism for holy orders or confirmation). Instead of being conferred in a hospital or at one's death bed, anointing of the sick is now typically administered at a communal worship service in church. The fears associated with 'last rites' as a harbinger of death have been allayed, and the ritual is now seen as a communal prayer for healing and comfort. Churches which do not regard this ceremony as a sacrament still provide care for and accompaniment of the sick and dying through prayer, reading of scripture, and spiritual direction, but do not typically anoint with blessed oil.

VII. The Domestic Church

One of the new emphases associated with sacramental theology is the idea of family as the domestic church. Vatican II's Dogmatic Constitution on the Church speaks of the 'domestic church in which the parents must be for their children, by word and by example, the first preachers of the faith' (*Lumen Gentium* §11, in Tanner 1990: ii. 858). It is difficult to know how the shortage of ordained ministers and the need to initiate the believing community into a deeper understanding of the meaning of the sacraments will shift the location for the celebration of the sacraments. Is it possible that in decades to come the believing community will meet in smaller groups in house churches and that the head of the family will serve the functions of administering the sacraments currently restricted to the ordained ministry as we presently know it? This issue is obviously connected to the size of the ordained ministry in the specific churches. If the number of ordained ministry is not increased by ordaining married men and also women (both single and married), the heads of households or other members of the faithful might conceivably be called upon to serve the administration of sacraments.

VIII. Conclusion

Christians are convinced that by divine institution the church has received baptism and the eucharist as outward signs of inward grace consisting of words and actions by which God encounters those called to faith. These symbols are recognized as sacraments. It is also believed that the church has authority to institute other rites and ordinances which are valued as sacred signs of God's redeeming love in Christ. Some of these rituals the Orthodox and the Roman Catholic Church recognize also as sacraments, since they see them as derived ultimately from the will of Christ. These sacraments are effective signs by which God bestows grace through faith. Their efficacy should not be considered in any way as merely mechanical or automatic. God works through his Spirit in a mysterious way beyond human comprehension, but he invites a full and free human response. The mysterious and incomprehensible character of sacraments is highlighted in Orthodox theology that respects the apophatic character of what can be grasped by human understanding. The Christian West, in its kataphatic tendencies to categorize and explain the inexplicable, has sometimes lost sight of this aspect of mystery. One of the pioneering theologians and liturgists of the West who warned against this tendency was the Benedictine monk of Maria Laach, Odo Casel, whose two major works, *Die Liturgie als Mysterienfeier* (1922) and *The Mystery of Christian Worship* (1962 [1932]), helped promote this fascination with mystery.

It would be temerarious to attempt to predict what new emphases will arise from theological reflection on the sacraments in the future, or to suggest how central sacramental practices will be celebrated in the churches of coming decades. The decreasing frequency of celebration of the sacraments for individuals and churches cannot be blamed solely on the rise of secularism. The churches themselves have not been sufficiently solicitous of catechesis and preaching the centrality of these rituals. Baptism, confirmation, and church weddings can easily be reduced in the minds of nominal Christians to routine ceremonies devoid of profound significance. The fact that so many Christian marriages end in separation and divorce raises questions about the efficacy of grace. Personal confession of sin to an authorized representative of the church has already experienced a dramatic decline. Some may come to regard anointing of the sick as a ritual similar to the distribution of ashes or of palms or to an intercessory bidding prayer. In the case of ordination, the defection of even a small number of presbyters and bishops is sufficient to undermine credence in the transforming power of grace. Reception of holy communion within the context of a lively worship service with the preached word and the anamnesis or remembering of Christ's sacrificial death has the best chance of remaining a vigorous sacramental practice, albeit one ever prone to the perfunctory. Promoting committed and reverent participation in the sacraments remains a challenge to religious educators and preachers. Theological articulation of sacramental life has too long been dominated by male writers. The pioneering writings of women theologians such as Monika Hellwig's *The Meaning of the Sacraments* (1972) and Susan A. Ross's *Extravagant Affections* (1998) need to be further supplemented.

References

Augustine (1998). *The City of God against the Pagans.* Cambridge: Cambridge University Press.

Barth, K. (1948). *The Teaching of the Church regarding Baptism.* London: SCM.

—— (1969). *Church Dogmatics IV/4: The Christian Life (Fragment). Baptism as the Foundation of the Christian Life.* Edinburgh: T. & T. Clark.

Casel, O. (1922). *Die Liturgie als Mysterienfeier.* Freiburg im Breisgau: Herder.

—— (1962 [1932]). *The Mystery of Christian Worship and Other Writings.* London: Darton, Longman and Todd.

Denzinger, H., and Schönmetzer, A. (eds.) (1967). *Enchiridion symbolorum, definitionum et declarationum de rebus fidei et morum,* 34th edn. Freiburg: Herder.

Finkenzeller, J. (1980). *Handbuch der Dogmengeschichte,* iv/1a. *Die Lehre von den Sakramenten im allgemeinen, von der Schrift bis zur Scholastik.* Freiburg: Herder.

Groupe des Dombes (1980). 'The Holy Spirit, the Church and the Sacraments'. *One in Christ* 16: 234–64.

Hellwig, M. (1972). *The Meaning of the Sacraments.* Dayton: Pflaum/Standard.

Hotz, R. (1979). *Sakramente im Wechselspiel zwischen Ost und West.* Zurich: Benziger.

Jenson, R. W. (1978). *Visible Words: The Interpretation and Practice of Christian Sacraments.* Philadelphia: Fortress.

—— (1997–9). *Systematic Theology.* 2 vols. New York: Oxford University Press.

Lies, L. (1990). *Sakramententheologie: Eine personale Sicht.* Graz: Styria.

MIGNE, J.-P. (1844–65). *Patrologia Latina.* Paris.

PANNENBERG, W. (1991–8). *Systematic Theology.* 3 vols. Grand Rapids: Eerdmans.

PESCH, O. H. (1982). 'Das katholische Sakramentenverständnis im Urteil gegenwärtiger evangelischer Theologen'. In Eberhard Jüngel et al. (eds.), *Verifikationen: Festschrift für Gerhard Ebeling zum 70. Geburtstag,* Tübingen: Mohr, 315–40.

RAHNER, K. (1963). *The Church and the Sacraments,* Quaestiones Disputatae 9. New York: Herder and Herder.

ROMAN CATHOLIC/LUTHERAN JOINT COMMISSION (1985). *Facing Unity: Models, Forms and Phases of Catholic-Lutheran Church Fellowship.* Geneva: Lutheran World Federation.

ROSS, S. A. (1998). *Extravagant Affections: A Feminist Sacramental Theology.* New York: Continuum.

SCHAFF, P. (ed.) (1980). *A Select Library of the Nicene and Post-Nicene Fathers of the Christian Church.* 1st ser. Edinburgh: T. & T. Clark.

SCHILLEBEECKX, E. (1963). *Christ, the Sacrament of the Encounter with God.* New York: Sheed and Ward.

SEMMELROTH, O. (1953). *Die Kirche als Ursakrament.* Frankfurt: J. Knecht.

—— (1965). *Church and Sacrament.* Notre Dame: Fides Press.

TANNER, N. P., SJ (ed.) (1990). *Decrees of the Ecumenical Councils.* 2 vols. Georgetown: Sheed and Ward.

THILS, G. (1947). *La Théologie des réalités terrestres.* 2 vols. Bruges: Desclée de Brouwer.

TORRANCE, T. F. (1975). *Theology in Reconciliation.* London: Chapman.

VORGRIMLER, H. (1992). *Sacramental Theology.* Collegeville: Liturgical.

WENZ, G. (1998). 'Sakramente: II. Systematisch-theologisch'. In *Theologische Realenzyklopädie.* Berlin: Walter de Gruyter, 29. 685–95.

WORLD COUNCIL OF CHURCHES (1982). *Baptism, Eucharist, and Ministry.* Geneva: World Council of Churches.

—— (2005). *The Nature And Mission of the Church: A Stage on the Way to a Common Statement.* Geneva: World Council of Churches.

SUGGESTED READING

CHAUVET, L. M. (1979). *Du symbolique au symbole: Essai sur les sacrements.* Paris: Cerf.

—— (1995). *Symbol and Sacrament: A Sacramental Reinterpretation of Christian Existence.* Collegeville: Liturgical.

GANOCZY, A. (1984). *An Introduction to Catholic Sacramental Theology.* New York: Paulist.

HÄRING, B. (1976). *Sacraments in a Secular Age.* Slough: St Paul.

KILMARTIN, E. J. (1988). *Christian Liturgy: Theology and Practice,* i. *Systematic Theology of Liturgy.* Kansas City: Sheed and Ward.

—— (1987). 'A Theology of the Sacraments: Toward a New Understanding of the Chief Rites of the Church of Jesus Christ'. In Regis A. Duffy (ed.), *Alternative Futures for Worship,* i. *General Introduction,* Collegeville: Liturgical, 123–75.

OSBORNE, K. (1988). *Sacramental Theology* New York: Paulist.

PANNENBERG (1991–8: iii. 237–434).

Power, D. N. (1999). *Sacrament: The Language of God's Giving.* New York: Crossroad.
Richter, K. (1990). *The Meaning of the Sacramental Symbols.* Collegeville: Liturgical.
Schmemann, A. (1973). *For the Life of the World: Sacraments and Orthodox.* Crestwood: St Vladimir's Seminary Press.
White, J. F. (1999). *The Sacraments in Protestant Practice and Faith.* Nashville: Abingdon.

CHAPTER 16

THE CHRISTIAN LIFE

REINHARD HÜTTER

I. Introduction

THE Christian life, in its essence, is life with the triune God made possible by the life, death, and resurrection of Jesus Christ—a life of faith, hope, and charity, exercised in prayer, worship, and discipleship. This basic description of the Christian life reflects the consensus of most contemporary Christian theologians across the spectrum of Catholicism, Orthodoxy, and Protestantism. The consensus ends rather abruptly, however, as soon as the description is expanded. There are fundamental differences within and among the divided Christian communions as to how to conceive a variety of the Christian life's salient aspects: divine and human cooperation, the importance of the theological and cardinal virtues, the constitutive or contingent role of the church in general and of the sacraments in particular, and the precise nature of the Christian life's fundamentally eschatological character. And there are other controversial issues as well: whether the Christian life is primarily, or even exclusively, an 'inner' life, an interiority absorbed in the contemplation of God, or primarily, or even exclusively, an 'outer' life, an exteriority absorbed in service to the neighbour and the world, or properly always a combination of both; whether the Christian life is afflicted or even endangered by the ongoing reality of sin; and whether it remains in some way under God's law.

In short, to account for the current theological debate on the Christian life is a daunting task, because all the central theological tenets of the Christian faith and hence all the ensuing theological differences—several of them of a church-dividing kind—bear upon the theological construal of the Christian life: the doctrine of the Trinity, and especially of the Holy Spirit, creation, sin, redemption, church, and sacraments. Hence any theological account of the Christian life is necessarily ancillary to antecedent dogmatic considerations and definitions. It is for this very reason that a *theology* of the Christian life differs categorically from theological utterances that arise out of the contingent particularities of an individual's Christian life with God (Maritain 1959: 310–83; Thérèse de Lisieux 1958). In contrast to the latter's utter concreteness, a theology of the Christian life remains an exercise of dogmatic, that is, normative theological reflection. Instead of reporting a dialogue between God and the soul, a theology of the Christian life identifies that life's constituents, obstacles, and inner dynamics.

In the following, I will focus upon the most salient controversial issues that continue to shape the various contemporary theological accounts of the Christian life and hence constitute the fundamental options for future theological reflection. Moreover, while the Christian life is the ground from which Christian ethics arises, I will refrain from entering the wide field of Christian moral theology proper. A separate handbook offers a useful introduction to the present state of discussion in this field (Meilaender and Werpehowski 2005). Because there exists no fundamental disciplinary difference between Christian theology and Christian ethics (Hauerwas 1998: 19–36), the Christian life has traditionally been treated as a topic of dogmatic theology (cf. Thomas Aquinas, *Summa Theologiae* 1a2ae, 2a2ae, in Aquinas 1975; Barth 1956; 1957; 1961; 1969). In the subsequent discussion, I intend to follow this venerable tradition. Moreover, in light of the way this handbook is conceived, I will treat the Christian life as the focus of the multiple controversies that have shaped Christian theology since the Reformation—controversies pertaining to sin, perfection, and the role of the law; to salvation, human cooperation, the church, the sacraments, and the relationship between faith and love for the very constitution of the Christian life.

II. The Christian Life in Pneumatological Perspective

There exists a broad agreement across the range of traditions and theologians that the Christian life must first and foremost be interpreted in a pneumatological perspective. The Holy Spirit initiates, accompanies, and brings to fulfilment the Christian life. However, this consensus coexists with significant ongoing disagreement about the specific nature of the Holy Spirit's work.

Spirit and New Creation

The pouring out of the Spirit on all creation is an eschatological event, God's renewing of his creation, giving it a new heart, bringing forth a new heaven and a new earth. 'New creation' is the notion signifying this new reality, ushered in by the Spirit. And there is a broad consensus across the theological spectrum that the Christian life is where this new creation takes hold. But how is it to be interpreted theologically? How does the 'new' creation relate to creation *per se*?

Catholic theology for a long time followed the tradition of the Thomist commentators. In this tradition, the new creation is interpreted in a precise, analogical way as a graced reality into which the human being is drawn by supernatural elevation. In this elevation the human being's substantial form remains in its proper created integrity but is actualized to a degree and proportion that categorically transcends its own capacity of actualization, namely, to the love of, friendship with, and ultimately direct vision of God (Garrigou-Lagrange 1937; Cessario 1996). In what amounted to the most significant theological debate in pre-Vatican II Catholic theology, Henri de Lubac challenged this understanding with an alternative reading of Thomas Aquinas, mainly informed by a reading of the patristic tradition (de Lubac 1946; 1967; 1969). His account built on the notion of humans' creation in the image of God, with an innate desire for the vision of God, which allows him to prioritize the new creation as the overarching end, dynamically and eschatologically integrating created reality. This relationship between nature and grace has found broad support in post-Vatican II Catholic theology, especially among the students of Hans Urs von Balthasar, as well as among Protestant theologians (see most recently Hauerwas 2001 and Milbank 2005). Still, the debate continues (Cottier 2002; Feingold 2001). Does a dynamic integration of creation and new creation not ultimately stand in danger of obfuscating the proper and necessary distinction between God's creative and redemptive agency?

In order to attend to the same phenomenon, Eastern Orthodox theologians sometimes employ the concept of 'transformation' or 'transfiguration' to point out the increasing translucence of the Christian life with the energies of the Holy Trinity. Roman Catholic theologians at points have criticized too radical a notion of transformation, because on a strict conceptual basis it becomes unclear how a genuine transformation (implying a change in substantial form) could secure the identity of the one who is thus transformed. Rather, identity and transformation seem to be mutually exclusive.

As long as it is assumed that 'new creation' has a clear conceptual purchase, the above are crucial matters of theological dispute and inquiry. In much of modern Protestant theology, this has not been the case. Here the tendency to understand 'new creation' as an image for a tangible but ultimately unfathomable reality prevails (Tillich 1955: 15–24; Bultmann 1957). The new creation is understood to be visible primarily as promise, effecting what is promised in the believer and thus giving rise to hope (Barth 1993). According to this notion, the eschatological reality of the 'new creation' is fully present in the word as promise, but in the present world still hidden as its own future. And because this reality is essentially inaccessible outside the word of promise, the notion of 'new creation' is appropriately regarded as a metaphor, carrying over from and gesturing toward an unfathomable future reality.

Hence, one way to characterize the central issue at stake between Catholic and Orthodox theologies on the one hand and most of Protestantism on the other is what kind of reality the Spirit's agency effects in the Christian life. Arguably, in most of Protestant theology faith leads to hope that is exercised in prayer and deeds of love: prayer and action are seen as the earnest of the Spirit in the Christian life, reflecting the promise of the new creation. For Catholic and Orthodox theology, it seems to be central that the Spirit's agency affects the human being tangibly, first and foremost by way of the sacraments, in ways that become part of creaturely reality (infused habits) and that constitute a journey toward the goal of perfect union in charity with the blessed Trinity. Here, 'new creation' functions as a precise description of the created effects of the Holy Spirit's agency.

Spirit and Sin

The question whether the Holy Spirit tangibly affects and renews the Christian life becomes paramount when applied to the doctrine of sin and its varying interpretations. According to Catholic doctrine, sinful acts—be they internal or external—arise from disordered inclinations, turn the person away from God to some inferior good, and offend God. Always involving some degree of intelligent willing, sin 'has been defined as "an utterance, a deed, or a desire contrary to the eternal law"' (*Catechism of the Catholic Church* 1997: §1849; Aquinas, *S T* 1a2ae. 71, 6). There is a strong consensus among Catholic and mainline Protestant theologians that the Christian life is continuously exposed to the power of sin (*Joint Declaration on the Doctrine of Justification* (*JDDJ*) 2000: §28). Of ongoing theological controversy, however, is whether original sin constitutes in the baptized believer a mere potency (*JDDJ* 2000: §30) or an active reality to be ended and overcome only with the person's death.

If, for the baptized believer, sin becomes a sheer potentiality toward concrete sinful acts (be they internal or external), then, with the help of God's sanctifying and preserving grace, the horizon of perfection is opened up. If, on the other hand, original sin remains an active reality—albeit not reigning, but under the reign of Christ (*peccatum non regnans sed regnatum*; *JDDJ* 2000: §29)—then there is an ongoing need for forgiveness irrespective of whether an actual sin has been committed (expressed in the classical Lutheran axiom *simul iustus et peccator*); despite constant growth in faith, Christian perfection in this life is inherently impossible.

This difference, however, does not obtain in a clear-cut way between Catholic and Orthodox accounts on the one hand and Protestant accounts on the other. There are indisputable moments of convergence between a long Catholic tradition spanning from Gregory of Nyssa, Augustine, and Thomas Aquinas to post-Tridentine Roman Catholic theology and the Wesleyan teaching of Christian perfection in love or charity (Wainwright 2003). Indeed, it is noteworthy that for both Catholics and Wesleyans, the essence of perfection is love. The central dogmatic disagreement regards in particular whether baptismal regeneration obtains, and in general whether all of the sacraments together serve as instrumental causes for the Spirit's sanctifying agency, or whether such a sacramental mediation of a definitive creaturely change is *per se* out of the question. But beneath this disagreement is another essential point of convergence between strands of Roman Catholic and Reformation theology—the centrality of the cross for the Christian life, albeit quite differently conceived. The Christian life is marked by external adversity and suffering as well as interior temptations and tribulations, and hence its true nature and character remains presently hidden with Christ in God (Forde 1997; Stein 2002).

Spirit and Law—Spirit and Freedom

Another fundamental dispute regarding the shape of the Christian life concerns the ongoing role of God's law. This dispute intersects with the question of what kind of freedom constitutes the Christian life, 'freedom' being understood distinctly as a positive freedom (contrary to the negative freedom of procedural liberalism; Taylor 1985)—the freedom of a life with God.

One position currently widespread among liberal Protestant theologians, though rather rarely defended in an explicit way, is antinomianism (classically, Fletcher 1997), in which God's law (in any of its normative manifestations, be it as natural or revealed) is held to be irrelevant for the Christian life in its proper sense. Strict antinomianism regards the law as surpassed and abolished by Christ, so that the Christian life is shaped exclusively by the spontaneity of love for the neighbour. Originally, antinomian theologians were eager to ban the law completely from the church's proclamation and teaching (Wengert 1997). A milder but more widespread form, well established in Lutheran theology to this day, holds that the law has a solely negative and extrinsic function in the Christian life: first, curbing sin (the first, or political, use of the law) and second, convicting the sinner and thus preparing the sinner for the gospel of Christ (the second, or theological, use of the law). And since, according to Lutheranism, sin always remains in the baptized believer, the law in its theological use plays an ongoing role in the church's preaching. However, the law remains fundamentally extrinsic to the Christian's freedom (Forde 1984).

The Calvinist tradition, joined by most Evangelical theologians—but also by Lutheran theologians who draw primarily upon Luther's treatise *On Good Works* (1520)—promotes a spiritual interpretation of the Decalogue as the blueprint for good works engendered by faith active in love. For this reason, the Decalogue can be interpreted as the concrete form of genuine Christian freedom (Lochman 1979; Hütter 2004: 111–81). The most significant but also most controversial proposal of twentieth-century Protestant theology was Karl Barth's integral unification of gospel and law as content and form, respectively, of the one Word of God (Barth 1957).

The Roman Catholic account of the Spirit's relationship to the law has traditionally been deeply shaped by the theologies of Augustine and Thomas Aquinas (see especially and most recently the encyclical *Veritatis Splendor*, in John Paul II 1993). The Decalogue displays the way of life according to God's mandates and, as incipient freedom, constitutes the path of liberation from sin toward a life with God in holiness (John Paul II 1993: §17). Most decisive, however, is the new law of the gospel (John Paul II 1993: §18, §24). Citing Thomas Aquinas, *Veritatis Splendor* instructs that this law 'can be called law in two ways. First the law of the spirit is the Holy Spirit... who, dwelling in the soul, not only teaches what is necessary to do by enlightening the intellect on the things to be done, but also inclines the affections to act with uprightness.... Second, the law of the spirit can be called the proper effect of the Holy Spirit, and thus faith working through love (cf. Gal 5: 6), which teaches inwardly about the things to be done... and inclines the affections to act' (John Paul II 1993: §45; cf. Thomas Aquinas, *In Epistulam ad Romanos*, c. VIII, lect. 1, in Aquinas 1929: i. 105).

These variant accounts of the relationship between Spirit and law, and consequently of what constitutes genuine Christian freedom, have their root in two normative issues: first, a salvation-historical reading of scripture that allows for a Christological, or spiritual, interpretation of the revealed law, and especially the Decalogue, versus the strict hermeneutical 'fundamental distinction' between a grammar of command and demand (law) and one of promise and gift (gospel); and second, the fundamental question of how divine and human causalities are related in the Christian life, the issue to which we turn next.

III. Agency, Practice, and *Telos*: Three Fundamental Issues in Controversy

Agency: Divine and Human Causality

The first topic we must address is the one buried deepest under the various conflicting ways of conceiving the Christian life. Failure to account for this fundamental issue up front results in a subsequent failure to understand the theological differences among communions on a whole range of issues pertaining to the Christian life. The first and most fundamental issue is that of the relationship between divine, creative causality and human, created causality, or, differently put, the relationship between divine and human freedom, first and foremost in the very act that constitutes the Christian life—faith. The varied ways of construing this relationship have an immediate impact on how the question of who is the subject of the Christian life is answered. The issue at stake for the Christian life, however, is not primarily the philosophical question of how the human free will is to be accounted for in relation to natural causality (Kant 1997: 535–46), a discussion framed currently by the opposing accounts of compatibilism and incompatiblism, or libertarianism (Kane 2002). The issue at stake, rather, is the theological account of the specific relationship of two causalities to each other—the triune God, creator and redeemer, and the human being, created in the image of God and existing under the condition of sin.

In the western theological tradition, this question has been irreversibly shaped by the paradigmatic controversy between Pelagius and Augustine over the question whether, under the condition of sin, the human being can freely, that is, on his or her own initiative and choice, turn toward God, or whether God, indeed, has to turn the human being first to himself. How are divine and human causality related in this turning, which is the very beginning—and hence is constitutive—of the Christian life itself? All contemporary accounts of this relationship fall into three principal kinds of construals.

Competitive Agency

The construal in many ways most attractive to modern sensibilities grants the most to human spontaneity. God has endowed the human being with the gift of freedom, that is, the gift of spontaneous self-movement, a gift that God could override only at the price of destroying what is most genuinely human about the human being. The unfathomable spontaneity of human freedom is the reason for genuine contingency in the world. God's knowledge of human agency is not a causative knowledge—God knowing what God brings about—but rather the knowledge of future contingents. Since God, in his omniscience, knows all future contingents in all possible worlds, God anticipates free human agency and creates conditions by which the contingency of free human agency falls securely under the purview of divine providence. In the western theological tradition, the Baroque Jesuit philosophers and theologians Luis Molina and Francisco Suarez offered highly developed accounts of God's foreknowledge of future contingents (Craig 1988: 169–233; Flint 1998). The Christian life according to this account is in all its aspects deeply dialogical and dramatic, implying genuine risk. The scope and depth of the risk, however, is a matter of debate among various proponents of this construal. The relationship between God and humans is one of cooperation, or synergism. While human freedom is neither total nor infinite (contrary to some modern construals of human freedom), it is—in its created, finite condition—the freedom of genuine spontaneous self-movement. It remains a disputed question whether this self-movement is diminished by human sin such that it needs antecedently to be restored by grace in order to function properly in relation to God (the Molinist and Suarezian positions)—or whether even under the condition of sin it remains essentially unharmed in relation to God (the Pelagian and semi-Pelagian positions).

This construal can be studied most instructively in the profound work of Sergius Bulgakov in the Eastern Orthodoxy tradition (2002); in a recent version of Molinist congruism articulated most usefully in Gleason (1966); in its adoption among Evangelical philosophers (Craig 1987); in its Protestant Arminian version in the Wesleyan tradition (Runyon 1998); in its adaptation to feminist and process theology (Case-Winters 1990; Cobb 1995); and most recently in the current movement of 'openness theology' especially prominent in American post-Calvinist Evangelical circles (Pinnock 1994; Sanders 1998; Boyd 2000).

The limitation of this construal consists in its failure to distinguish categorically between the ontological levels of divine, creative sovereignty and the created, contingent causality of freedom—in other words, to distinguish clearly between God on the one hand and everything else, including created freedom, on the other. Insisting on the fundamental incompatibility between divine, creative freedom and the freedom of spontaneity with which the human being is endowed amounts to a failure to appreciate the fact that divine, sovereign causality categorically transcends every aspect of creation, including the created reality of the freedom of the creature. According to this approach, divine and human freedom fall under the same overarching concept of freedom; that is, while quantitatively of infinite difference, they are qualitatively of the same kind. Hence, divine and human agency and freedom end up in a competitive relationship.

Exclusive Agency

The second construal, and for modern sensibilities the most offensive, is the classical Reformation account along the lines of Luther (Forde 2005) and Calvin (Sproul 1997). Constitutive for the Reformation account is the sharp distinction between the 'vertical' and 'horizontal' dimensions of the Christian life. In the relationship between God and fallen humanity—the vertical dimension—everything is effected solely by God. God is not merely the first cause of justification but its sole cause. There is no cooperation from the side of the human whatsoever, only a suffering of God's irresistible electing and saving agency. And since for Luther (contrary to Melanchthon and Calvin) justification is an inherently dynamic and comprehensive event (Mannermaa 2005), in the accounts of Luther and strict Lutheranism, God in Christ remains the true subject also of that aspect of the Christian life that Melanchthon and Calvin would term 'sanctification'. Hence, for

Luther and Lutheranism of the strict observance the genuine subject and agent of the Christian life is and remains Christ himself. In all matters pertaining to the constitution of the Christian life, the Christian remains passive and a recipient, even and especially in agency, where Christ acts through him or her. Justification and sanctification (as growth in faith) is a radical suffering; the human form of operation involved in it (faith) is in no way an efficient agency but merely the appropriate form passivity takes in the kind of being the human is (Forde 1984).

The horizontal dimension in this account pertains to the way God sustains creation by way of secondary causality. Here humans are indeed mandated to cooperate with God's own activity in all matters external—matters pertaining to the body, the neighbour, and all political, economic, and religious structures and institutions. In these matters, the human being retains free will under the condition of sin and is capable of cooperating with God's activity of sustaining creation (Seils 1962; Bayer 1995: 116–46; Ulrich 2005). The relationship to God is one of profound passivity; the relationship to body, neighbour, and world is one of incessant activity. The 'crossing' of the two dimensions is the Christian life, the instantiation of Christian freedom, the freedom acquired through faith alone, by which the Christian person is extrinsically constituted through Christ's agency (Joest 1967) and thus liberated for ceaseless service in and to the world (Jüngel 1988). In genuinely Lutheran accounts of the Christian life, there occurs no conceptual intergration of *passio* and *cooperatio*, between the believer suffering the Spirit's ongoing salvific agency at the very centre of the Christian life on the one hand and the human mandated to cooperate with God's sustaining agency as creator on the other. Rather, these aspects remain sharply distinguished from each other and are related merely by the dynamic dialectic of flesh and spirit, that is, the Spirit's sanctifying agency in a person still affected all the way down by sin (Forde 1984).

This account rightly focuses on the *primacy* and *causal agency* of God in justifying faith and salvation. Its emphasis on the utter passivity of the human being in matters of faith and salvation is the result of the legitimate concern that the human being—especially under the condition of sin—cannot be a free agent in relationship to God. However, its unrelenting emphasis on God's exclusive agency and the human being's utter passivity even after the initial conversion by God betrays a univocal, competitive account of divine and human agential causality and hence a failure to appreciate the genuine transcendence of divine causality in the matter of salvation.

Transcendent Agency

A third construal represents arguably a superior synthesis of the former two. It was first intimated in the late works of Augustine, fully developed in the mature theology of Thomas Aquinas, supported in the tradition of Thomist commentators, recovered and crisply reconstrued in the last century by Bernard Lonergan

(2000) and his students (Burrell 1993), and more recently—by way of Karl Barth's theology—also considered by Protestant theologians (Tanner 1988; Webster 1995). According to this account, God's causality is genuinely transcendent: there can in principle never be a competitive relationship between divine and human causality. Rather, divine, creative causality, that is, providence and predestination, operates also by way of free human causality. Because the whole matrix of secondary causality (including the genuine contingency of free human causality) relates instrumentally to the divine transcendent cause, human causality is infallibly directed by divine providence. Moreover, and more importantly, God as the ultimate good, acting by way of final causality, can draw the creature infallibly to himself without diminishing, curbing, or destroying the human being's free will. What is most significant about this third construal of divine and human causality is that it allows for a profound and constant impact of the Holy Spirit upon the Christian life without undercutting a coherent account of human agency. The human being remains the agent of all genuine theological acts, while the dispositions for these acts are the created effects of the Holy Spirit's agency (Cessario 1996). With the exception of the beginning of faith—the *initium fidei*, where the human being is moved and not moving—humans remain free agents in all respects of the Christian life, according to the order of secondary causality, while the Holy Spirit remains the divine transcendental cause of the Christian life.

Significantly, only this third construal allows for an account of infused virtues, that is, a full conceptual acknowledgement that faith, hope, and love are genuinely God's contingent supernatural gifts to the human being and, at the same time, are genuinely activated and enacted by the human being. The infusion of a habit does not compete with or undercut human free agency at all; rather, it constitutes a new set of operative qualities, habits to be actualized by the human agent. It is because of its competitive logic that the first construal must understand all habits as natural outgrowths of human agency, such that if faith, hope, and love are indeed regarded as virtues, that is, positive habits, at all, they constitute thoroughly natural habits—enticed by God's prompting through the Spirit, to be sure, but resulting from natural capacities. The second construal, equally competitive in its logic of divine and human causality, must vehemently reject this possibility. Because of the possible Pelagian, or at least semi-Pelagian, dangers inherent in the first construal, the second denies any anthropological rooting of the Christian life: in its salvific essence, the Christian life is not the enactment of a supernaturally infused gift of the Holy Spirit, which would make it a created reality. Rather, the Christian person, and hence the Christian life, is constituted in the externality of the promissory address of the gospel, which undercuts any notion of a received set of habits intrinsic to the believer's person. Consequently, not only is an account of infused virtues superfluous; such an account, more importantly, would introduce human agency in a domain where it would actively come to compete with God's exclusive salvific agency.

Implications for Faith

Consider the immediate implications of these three construals for the beginning and most central component of the Christian life—faith. According to the first construal, faith is a free human act of intellectual assent and emotive trust, an act that God invites and desires and in relationship to which God can remove obstacles and create incentives yet under no circumstance bring about directly. The potential of faith is an integral component of human nature; more specifically, it comes along as a natural potential of the human faculties of intellect and will. This potential is opened up and concretely addressed by the encounter with God's Word, yet it is actualized solely by the human person. Hence, while its specific object is supernatural, faith itself is a natural capacity. If faith is regarded as an interior principle of activity, that is, a good habit or virtue, it constitutes a thoroughly natural virtue. This approach does safeguard human agency and freedom in the act of faith, but it undercuts the fact that as a theological virtue faith is a divine gift and not merely a grace-initiated actualization of a natural capacity.

According to the second construal, faith is exclusively God's act. God alone brings about the beginning and growth of faith. The human being surely assents and trusts, but God is the sole agent of the will moving the believer to assent and to trust. And only because faith is solely caused by God does it carry the assurance of salvation. In this account, any attempt to construe faith along the lines of habit or virtue would create a competition with the divine causality and thus a presumptuous elevation of the human being. Hence the deep suspicion of any account of the theological virtues in classical Lutheran and Calvinist theology.

Only on the basis of the non-competitive account of divine and human causality—the third construal—is it possible to conceive of faith as an infused operative habit, directly received into the faculties of intellect and will (Cessario 1996). In this third construal, divine causality impacts the very constitution of human causality by way of various operative habits, either acquired or infused—while at the same time categorically transcending human causality. Hence, while the beginning and principle of faith are brought about by God alone (Lonergan 2000)—and in this fundamental sense faith always is God's gift—faith is simultaneously a genuine human act, genuinely activated by properly human causality. The latter is possible because, of these three construals, only the third distinguishes clearly between efficient and final causality and prioritizes final causality. Conversion, or the beginning of faith, occurs by way of God's acting as a final end on the person's intellect and will, turning the person to God as the ultimate specific good to be desired and loved for its own sake, whereby the human person operates in relationship to this final end according to the proper efficient causality of his or her created freedom. Transcendent divine causality and its mode of operation in relation to human agential causality will be fully recovered only after the final causality itself has been recovered as a proper, and the most crucial, causality among intentional agents—and that is, first of all, God (Garrigou-Lagrange 1932; Spaemann and Löw 2005).

We find an important version of the third construal in the theology of the twentieth century's most eminent Protestant theologian, Karl Barth. Barth consistently insists on the non-competitive relationship between divine and human agency in the Christian life: God does all and the human being does all as well. In his late doctrine of baptism (1969), he describes this double agency most explicitly by way of invoking an analogy to the Chalcedonian two-natures logic (Hunsinger 1991: 185–224; Hütter 1993: 101–5), which allows him to account for divine transcendental agential causality and establish a moral ontology that arguably permeates the whole *Church Dogmatics* (Webster 1995). Divine and human agency stand in a differentiated, dialectical unity of infinite qualitative difference: two comprehensive, mutually non-exclusive and non-competitive causal agencies. However, Barth neither offers an integrated account of the two agential causalities nor draws upon the notion of operative qualities, that is, accounts of acquired or infused virtues (Hauerwas 1985: 129–78).

Since all three construals can appeal in various ways to the witness of scripture, their difference remains indeterminable on the grounds of scripture alone. Rather, the fundamental difference between these three construals calls for close attention to the underlying metaphysical assumptions entertained by all parties (including the tacit working assumptions of those who deny any particular metaphysical commitments). The underlying central issue is the theological as well as metaphysical interpretation of the nature of contingency and hence freedom in the constitutive act of the Christian life, faith, and in all its subsequent aspects. The most promising way forward in relating the two causalities is non-competitive, so that divine causality is understood as genuinely transcendent, and human causality as framed by the distinct conditions of the created world such that the very contingency of free human causality not only continues to fall under the purview of divine providence but also remains, qua created, in a fundamentally instrumental relationship to divine causality.

Practice: The Shape of the Christian Life

One of the most noticeable recent developments in English-speaking Protestant theology is the focus on particular practices that constitute or shape the Christian life. The reasons for this trend are manifold: a recovery of Aristotelian practical philosophy, mainly through the works of Alasdair MacIntyre (1984); a re-emergence of the never completely extinguished interest in the practical aspect of the Christian faith in the Wesleyan, Holiness, and Pentecostal strands of American theology (Langford 1983; Wacker 2001); and an overall renewal of interest in various forms of pragmatism after the alleged demise of metaphysical thinking. The so-called 'postmodern condition' led many theologians to abandon theology as the intellectual contemplation, defence, and exposition of revealed truth by interpreting scripture, dogma, and confessional claims and thereby guiding the church's preaching and teaching vocation. With this loss of theology's classical place between metaphysics and scripture, theologians were eager to turn to a subject matter that would allow theology to continue to be of relevance to the church and the wider community, making a tangible difference in human lives. While liberation and feminist theologies together with a renaissance of practical theology had cleared the way several decades earlier with neo-Marxist analysis and the sociology of action (Certeau 1984; Bourdieu 1990), it was a fusion of motifs from Barth, Yoder, and MacIntyre (Hauerwas 2001) that created a critical mass for a sustained turn to Christian practices as a primary subject matter for theology (Volf and Bass 2002). We can currently distinguish three types of theological appropriation of the notion of 'practice' in the Christian life.

The strong ethical aspect of Karl Barth's ecclesiology—the church's vocation to be the witness of God's self-revelation in its structure, practices, and action—offered a welcome point of reception for two theologians deeply influenced by Barth's theology, while never Barthian in the strict sense: John H. Yoder (1992) and Stanley Hauerwas (Hütter 1993; Rasmusson 1995). Yoder and Hauerwas give radical interpretations of the Christian life as being identical with a range of practices: practices *are* the Christian life and vice versa, analogous to the Wittgensteinian insistence that our language *is* our thinking and vice versa. They reject any strong notion of interiority in the Christian life that can be meaningfully abstracted from the practices that are the Christian life.

In stark contrast to the arguably Barthian approach of Yoder and Hauerwas, another group of contemporary theologians works at recovering natural, everyday practices of human life, practices that are conducive to individual as well as communal flourishing, such as honouring the body, hospitality, forgiveness, telling the truth, and dying well (Bass 1997). The task of theologians is to interpret such practices theologically by uncovering their theological implications for non-believers as well as by disclosing them for Christians as loci for meaningful Christian life, action, and interaction, especially also with non-Christians (Tanner 1997; Volf and Bass 2002: 13–32, 51–77, 94–184, 228–42).

While these approaches differ radically in that the first takes its lead completely from the economy of salvation and the second exclusively from the economy of creation, they are remarkably similar in their lack of interest in or outright postmetaphysical rejection of an account of Christian interiority.

Fundamentally different from these two approaches remain theologies that insist on the primacy of the Holy Spirit in the church's agency in general and in the Christian life in particular. In most of these accounts, prioritizing pneumatology results in a clear distinction between, on the one hand, sacraments (first and foremost baptism and the eucharist), along with constitutive as well as essential practices (worship, prayer, catechesis, forgiveness, and reconciliation), and, on the other hand, the unfathomable interiority of the Christian life that is sustained by the sacraments and the various practices but never identical with them (Volf and Bass 2002: 78–93, 185–227; Hütter 2000: 115–46; Wannenwetsch 2004).

In traditional Catholic and Orthodox theology, it is by way of sacramental grace that an interior life is constituted, a life in which the triune God encounters the soul immediately in order to draw it increasingly into the triune life of love. The Christian life is essentially a spiritual life, the end of which is personal union with God, and every Christian is called to such a union (Garrigou-Lagrange 1937; Lossky 1974: 97–111; 1976: 196–235). The unfathomable depth of this life always transcends in principle the range and depth of any of the Christian practices.

Theologians with a basically non-sacramental, congregationalist ecclesiology will tend to favour either practices of witness or natural, everyday practices, depending on whether they prioritize, along the Barthian lines, the economy of salvation with its proper and unique practices of witness or, along liberal Protestant lines, the economy of creation with those practices that sustain human flourishing. For theologians who are committed to substantive and normative notions of apostolicity, catholicity, and sacramentality, however, neither of the two alternatives is acceptable. For them, the concept of practices always takes second place—albeit possibly an important second place—to the primacy of word, sacrament, apostolicity, and dogma on the one hand and the interiority of the Christian life constituted by the Holy Spirit's activity and shaped by the infused virtues of faith, hope, and love on the other. Hence, the deeply differing ways in which theologians currently focus on practices—as a primary or secondary object of a theology of the Christian life—reflect the deep and ongoing doctrinal differences about the nature of the church that continue to divide Christian communions. Is the Christian life constituted by central ecclesial practices, such that they are essential to it, and if so, which ones? Or is the Christian life a life of witness and activity to which these practices only tangentially relate? Any hope for theological agreement on the role and function of practices in the Christian life depends upon a substantive dogmatic rapprochement in matters of ecclesiology.

Telos: The Directedness of the Christian Life

The third fundamental issue pertaining to the Christian life is the question of its end, or *telos*. Is the Christian life fundamentally directed toward God and communion with God (divinization, theosis) or toward the neighbour and the world ('humanization of the human'), or are the two somehow integrally related? This question is most often addressed through interpretation of the double love-commandment, either integrating the second commandment into the first or maintaining a strict disjunction between the two.

The Catholic and Orthodox traditions understand the double love-commandment overwhelmingly in an integral way (Cessario 1996; Sherwin 2005). Hence, in the Christian life, the love of God comprises and shapes all other loves such that the more the Christian life is assimilated to God's love (divinization), the deeper is the dedication to serving the neighbour and the world (*Compendium of the Social Doctrine of the Church* 2004). Christian life is life with God toward God; it is determined completely by its *telos*, which is the final cause of its very existence.

Karl Barth's interpretation of the double love-commandment in *Church Dogmatics* I/2 (1956: 371–456) represents the Protestant alternative to the Catholic and Orthodox understanding. Barth makes a sharp distinction between the two commandments such that the first commandment, the relationship to God, is constituted by the reality of faith—letting God act upon the human and accepting this agency—and by God's love for us, while the second commandment has its own, completely distinct horizontal domain. Because humans are justified by faith alone and remain in relation to God in utter passivity—and acknowledging this is the fulfilling of the first part of the double love-commandment—humans are turned toward the world for a love that is informed by this faith. This precise distinction between the vertical and horizontal dimensions has its normative origin for Protestants in Luther's renowned treatise *The Freedom of a Christian* (1520). This work had a profound and lasting impact on the Protestant interpretation of the double love-commandment and the double directedness of the Christian life, namely, in faith toward God and love toward the neighbour (Käsemann 1969; Jüngel 1988), such that faith is active in love and hence forms it, and not vice versa, as the charge is brought against Catholic theology (Wannenwetsch 2000).

In the integrative understanding, God remains always the sole *telos* of the Christian life, while the love of the neighbour is fully coordinated with the relationship with God as an essential component of the Christian journey toward union with God. The love of God, received and returned in grace, is the activating form of faith in relation to God as well as in relation to the neighbour. In the disjunctive understanding, the humanization of the world becomes a distinct (pen)ultimate end of the Christian life. God, who is the sole cause of faith, comes to stand 'behind' the Christian's existence, which is turned toward the world in order to meet the neighbour's needs. The Christian life is fundamentally a life for others. In Protestant theology, mixed forms can be found wherever there exists a strong emphasis on the inner life of faith exercised by way of prayer, study of scripture, practices of introspection, and communal support and correction (Lutheran and Wesleyan Pietism, Evangelicalism, Pentecostalism). In post-Vatican II Roman Catholicism, mixed forms can be encountered wherever social activism and the struggle for peace and justice become estranged or even completely severed from the church's sacramental life.

This difference gives rise to two fundamentally different types of 'spirituality': the one is always first and last directed toward God, such that it finds everything, including the neighbour and the whole world, in God, while the other has God 'behind' it and is turned toward the world, such that the Christian life in its horizontal dimension is one of radical secular solidarity, a life for the other. Consequently, the role of the sacraments and ecclesial practices such as prayer and worship are seen in fundamentally different ways: for the one they are the path of the Spirit through Christ to the Father, a path on which everything else is found; for the other, because God is antecedently and sufficiently found in justifying faith, they constitute the motivational and spiritual source that continually energizes the Christian life in its fundamental directedness and complete dedication to the ongoing Christian and generally human struggle for the world's humanization.

The undeniable common root of both spiritualities, however, is Christian baptism. It is the initiation into the Christian life, and the regenerative sacramental seal of its eschatological character. The pneumatological constitution of the Christian life, that is, its indelibly Christian character, arises from baptism. Hence, every ecumenical step toward full agreement about the nature of baptism entails an increasing convergence on the nature of the Christian life (Root and Saarinen 1998).

IV. Conclusion

Because theological reflection on the Christian life depends upon antecedent doctrinal decisions, many of the differences addressed above cannot be resolved within the parameters of a theology of the Christian life. Criteria for the assessment of the variant doctrinal claims are the canonical witness of scripture, the dogmatic pronouncements of ecumenical councils and synods, magisterial decisions, deep hermeneutical presuppositions about the witness of scripture as determined by various antecedent theological axioms, differing assessments and articulations of the metaphysical claims entailed in the dogmatic formulations of the councils, and the implicit and constitutive normativity of individual theologians in the various Christian communions arising from the Reformation. And, despite the fact that all theologically relevant sides grant that the canonical witness of scripture as God's word holds overarching priority, there is no obvious *a priori* way to order and to prioritize these criteria, that is, no way antecedent to or abstracted from an already traditioned hierarchy of norms and criteria in relation to scripture.

This situation is both a boon and a bane: while the theology of the Christian life always remains vulnerable to conflicting doctrinal positions, the Christian life *per se*, as it is lived, will always give rise to real instead of notional knowledge (Newman 1985: 12–15), and hence will offer sufficient occasion to recognize across the spectrum of divided communions and in the midst of sin and failure examples of holy living, moments of genuine witness to Christ, intimations of faith, hope, and love, works of charity, justice, and reconciliation—in short, abandonment to God as well as dedication to the neighbour. The praxis of the Christian life allows an anticipatory embrace in love where matters of truth continue to divide. Hence the Christian life holds an ecumenical potential of the greatest intensity and scope. Indeed, the witness to a life of truth and holiness, dedicated to the love of God and neighbour, transcends the divided communions and points to the full and realized communion of saints, as the encyclical letter *Ut Unum Sint* states (John Paul II 1995: §84): 'Albeit in an invisible way, the communion between our Communities, even if still incomplete, is truly and solidly grounded in the full communion of the Saints—those who, at the end of a life faithful to grace, are in communion with Christ in glory. These *Saints* come from all the churches and Ecclesial Communities which gave them entrance into the communion of salvation.'

References

Aquinas, St Thomas (1929). *In Omnes S. Pauli Apostoli Epistolas Commentaria.* 7th edn. Turin: Marietti.

—— (1975). *Summa Theologiae.* London: Blackfriars.

Barth, K. (1956). *Church Dogmatics* I/2. Edinburgh: T. & T. Clark.

—— (1957). *Church Dogmatics* II/2. Edinburgh: T. & T. Clark.

—— (1961). *Church Dogmatics* III/4. Edinburgh: T. & T. Clark.

—— (1969). *Church Dogmatics IV/4: The Christian Life (Fragment). Baptism as the Foundation of the Christian Life.* Edinburgh: T. & T. Clark.

—— (1993). *The Holy Spirit and the Christian Life: The Theological Basis of Ethics.* Louisville: Westminster/John Knox.

Bass, D. C. (ed.) (1997). *Practicing Our Faith: A Way of Life for a Searching People.* San Francisco: Jossey-Bass.

Bayer, O. (1995). *Freiheit als Antwort: Zur theologischen Ethik.* Tübingen: J. C. B. Mohr / Paul Siebeck.

Bourdieu, P. (1990). *The Logic of Practice.* Stanford: Stanford University Press.

Boyd, G. A. (2000). *The God of the Possible: A Biblical Introduction to the Open View of God.* Grand Rapids: Baker.

Bulgakov, S. (2002). *The Bride of the Lamb.* Grand Rapids: Eerdmans.

Bultmann, R. (1957). *The Presence of Eternity: History and Eschatology.* New York: Harper.

Burrell, D. B., CSC (1993). *Freedom and Creation in Three Traditions.* Notre Dame: University of Notre Dame Press.

Case-Winters, A. (1990). *God's Power: Traditional Understandings and Contemporary Challenges.* Louisville: Westminster/John Knox.

Catechism of the Catholic Church (1997). Second Edition, revised in accordance with the official Latin text promulgated by Pope John Paul II. Città del Vaticano: Libreria Editrice Vaticana.

CERTEAU, M. de (1984). *The Practice of Everyday Life.* Berkeley and Los Angeles: University of California Press.

CESSARIO, R., OP (1996). *Christian Faith and the Theological Life.* Washington, DC: Catholic University of America Press.

COBB, J. B. (1995). *Grace and Responsibility: A Wesleyan Theology for Today.* Nashville: Abingdon.

Compendium of the Social Doctrine of the Church (2004). Pontifical Council for Justice and Peace. Città del Vaticano: Libreria Editrice Vaticana.

COTTIER, G. (2002). *Le Désir de Dieu: Sur les traces de saint Thomas.* Paris: Éditions Parole et Silence.

CRAIG, W. L. (1987). *The Only Wise God: The Compatibility of Divine Foreknowledge and Human Freedom.* Grand Rapids: Baker.

—— (1988). *The Problem of Divine Foreknowledge and Future Contingents from Aristotle to Suarez.* Leiden: Brill.

DE LUBAC, H., SJ (1946). *Surnaturel: Études historiques.* Paris: Éditions Aubier-Montaigne.

—— (1967). *The Mystery of the Supernatural.* New York: Herder and Herder.

—— (1969). *Augustinianism and Modern Theology.* New York: Herder and Herder.

FEINGOLD, L. (2001). *The Natural Desire to See God According to St Thomas Aquinas and His Interpreters.* Rome: Apollinare Studi.

FLETCHER, J. F. (1997). *Situation Ethics: The New Morality.* Louisville: Westminster/John Knox.

FLINT, T. P. (1998). *Divine Providence: The Molinist Account.* Ithaca: Cornell University Press.

FORDE, G. (1984). 'The Christian Life'. In C. E. Braaten and R. W. Jenson (eds.), *Christian Dogmatics*, ii, Philadelphia: Fortress, 391–469.

—— (1997). *On Being a Theologian of the Cross: Reflections on Luther's Heidelberg Disputation, 1518.* Grand Rapids: Eerdmans.

—— (2005). *The Captivation of the Will: Luther vs. Erasmus on Freedom and Bondage.* Grand Rapids: Eerdmans.

GARRIGOU-LAGRANGE, R., OP (1932). *Le Réalisme du principe de finalité.* Paris: Desclée de Brouwer.

—— (1937). *Christian Perfection and Contemplation According to St Thomas Aquinas and St John of the Cross.* London: Herder.

GLEASON, R. W., SJ (1966). *The Indwelling Spirit.* Staten Island: Alba House.

HAUERWAS, S. (1985). *Character and the Christian Life: A Study in Theological Ethics.* San Antonio: Trinity University Press.

—— (1998). *Sanctify Them in the Truth: Holiness Exemplified.* Nashville: Abingdon.

—— (2001). *With the Grain of the Universe: The Church's Witness and Natural Theology.* Grand Rapids: Brazos.

HUNSINGER, G. (1991). *How to Read Karl Barth: The Shape of his Theology.* Oxford: Oxford University Press.

HÜTTER, R. (1993). *Evangelische Ethik als kirchliches Zeugnis: Interpretationen zu Schlüsselfragen theologischer Ethik in der Gegenwart.* Neukirchen-Vluyn: Neukirchener Verlag.

—— (2000). *Suffering Divine Things: Theology as Church Practice.* Grand Rapids: Eerdmans.

—— (2004). *Bound to Be Free: Evangelical Catholic Engagements in Ecclesiology, Ethics, and Ecumenism.* Grand Rapids: Eerdmans.

Joest, W. (1967). *Ontologie der Person bei Luther.* Göttingen: Vandenhoeck and Ruprecht.
John Paul II (1993). *Veritatis Splendor/The Splendor of Truth.* Boston: Pauline.
—— (1995). *Ut Unum Sint/On Commitment to Ecumenism.* Boston: Pauline.
Joint Declaration on the Doctrine of Justification (2000). The Lutheran World Federation and the Roman Catholic Church. English-language edn. Grand Rapids: Eerdmans.
Jüngel, E. (1988). *The Freedom of a Christian: Luther's Significance for Contemporary Theology.* Minneapolis: Augsburg.
Kane, R. (ed.) (2002). *The Oxford Handbook of Free Will.* Oxford: Oxford University Press.
Kant, I. (1997 [1781]). *Critique of Pure Reason.* Cambridge: Cambridge University Press.
Käsemann, E. (1969). 'Worship in Everyday Life: A Note on Romans 12'. In id., *New Testament Questions of Today,* London: SCM, 188–95.
Langford, T. A. (1983). *Practical Divinity: Theology in the Wesleyan Tradition.* Nashville: Abingdon.
Lochman, J. M. (1979). *Wegweisung der Freiheit: Abriß der Ethik in der Perspektive des Dekalogs.* Gütersloh: Gütersloher Verlagshaus Gerd Mohn.
Lonergan, B. (2000). *Grace and Freedom: Operative Grace in the Thought of St Thomas Aquinas.* Toronto: University of Toronto Press.
Lossky, V. (1974). *In the Image and Likeness of God.* Crestwood: St Vladimir's Seminary Press.
—— (1976). *The Mystical Theology of the Eastern Church.* Crestwood: St Vladimir's Seminary Press.
MacIntyre, A. C. (1984). *After Virtue: A Study in Moral Theory.* Notre Dame: University of Notre Dame Press.
Mannermaa, T. (2005). *Christ Present in Faith: Luther's View of Justification.* Minneapolis: Fortress.
Maritain, J. (1959). *The Degrees of Knowledge.* New York: Charles Scribner's Sons.
Meilaender, G., and Werpehowski, W. (eds.) (2005). *The Oxford Handbook of Theological Ethics.* Oxford: Oxford University Press.
Milbank, J. (2005). *The Suspended Middle: Henri de Lubac and the Debate concerning the Supernatural.* Grand Rapids: Eerdmans.
Newman, J. H. (1985 [1870]). *An Essay in Aid of a Grammar of Assent.* Oxford: Oxford University Press.
Pinnock, C. (1994). *The Openness of God: A Biblical Challenge to the Traditional Understanding of God.* Downers Grove: InterVarsity.
Rasmusson, A. (1995). *The Church as Polis: From Political Theology to Theological Politics as Exemplified by Jürgen Moltmann and Stanley Hauerwas.* Notre Dame: University of Notre Dame Press.
Root, M., and Saarinen, R. (eds.) (1998). *Baptism and the Unity of the Church.* Grand Rapids: Eerdmans and Geneva: WCC Publications.
Runyon, T. (1998). *The New Creation: John Wesley's Theology Today.* Nashville: Abingdon.
Sanders, J. (1998). *The God Who Risks: A Theology of Providence.* Downers Grove: InterVarsity .
Seils, M. (1962). *Der Gedanke vom Zusammenwirken Gottes und des Menschen in Luthers Theologie.* Gütersloh: G. Mohn.
Sherwin, M. S., OP (2005). *By Knowledge & By Love: Charity and Knowledge in the Moral Theology of St Thomas Aquinas.* Washington, DC: Catholic University of America Press.

Spaemann, R., and Löw, R. (2005). *Natürliche Ziele: Geschichte und Wiederentdeckung teleologischen Denkens.* Stuttgart: Klett-Cotta.

Sproul, R. C. (1997). *Willing to Believe: The Controversy over Free Will.* Grand Rapids: Baker.

Stein, E. [St Teresa Benedicta a Cruce] (2002). *The Science of the Cross.* Washington, DC: ICS.

Tanner, K. (1988). *God and Creation in Christian Theology: Tyranny or Empowerment.* Oxford: Basil Blackwell.

—— (1997). *Theories of Culture: A New Agenda for Theology.* Minneapolis: Fortress.

Taylor, C. (1985). 'What's Wrong with Negative Liberty?' In *id. Philosophy and the Human Sciences: Philosophical Papers*, ii, Cambridge: Cambridge University Press, 211–29.

Thérèse de Lisieux (1958). *Autobiography: The Complete and Authorized Text of* L'Histoire d'une âme. New York: Kenedy.

Tillich, P. (1955). *The New Being.* New York: Charles Scribner's Sons.

Ulrich, H. G. (2005). *Wie Geschöpfe leben: Konturen evangelischer Ethik.* Münster: LIT Verlag.

Volf, M., and Bass, D. C. (eds.) (2002). *Practicing Theology: Beliefs and Practices in Christian Life.* Grand Rapids: Eerdmans.

Wacker, G. (2001). *Heaven Below: Early Pentecostals and American Culture.* Cambridge: Harvard University Press.

Wainwright, G. (2003). 'Vollkommenheit'. In *Theologische Realenzyklopädie*, vol. 35, Berlin: Walter de Gruyter, 35. 273–85.

Wannenwetsch, B. (2000). '*Caritas Fide Formata*: "Herz und Affekte" als Schlüssel zum Verhältnis von "Glaube und Liebe"'. *Kerygma und Dogma* 46: 205–24.

—— (2004). *Political Worship: Ethics for Christian Citizens.* Oxford: Oxford University Press.

Webster, J. (1995). *Barth's Ethics of Reconciliation.* Cambridge: Cambridge University Press.

Wengert, T. J. (1997). *Law and Gospel: Philip Melanchthon's Debate with John Agricola of Eisleben over Poenitentia.* Carlisle: Paternoster and Grand Rapids: Baker.

Yoder, J. H. (1992). *Body Politics: Five Practices of the Christian Community before the Watching World.* Nashville: Discipleship Resources.

Suggested Reading

Bayer, O. (2003). *Living in Faith: Justification and Sanctification.* Grand Rapids: Eerdmans.

Balthasar, H. U. von (1983). *The Christian State of Life.* San Francisco: Ignatius.

—— (2003). *The Laity and the Life of the Counsels: The Church's Mission in the World.* San Francisco: Ignatius.

Barth (1993).

—— (1969).

Benne, R. (2003). *Ordinary Saints: An Introduction to the Christian Life*, 2nd edn. Minneapolis: Augsburg Fortress.

Cessario (1996).

DiNoia, J. A., OP and Cessario, R., OP (1999). *Veritatis Splendor and the Renewal of Moral Theology.* Princeton: Scepter.

Forde (1984 ii. 391–469).

Gutiérrez, G. (1985). *We Drink from Our Own Wells: The Spiritual Journey of a People*, 4th edn. Maryknoll: Orbis.

Hauerwas (1985).

Jones, L. G. (1995). *Embodying Forgiveness: A Theological Analysis.* Grand Rapids: Eerdmans.

Meilaender, G. (2005). *Love Taking Shape: Sermons on the Christian Life.* Grand Rapids: Eerdmans.

Merton, T. (1948). *The Seven Storey Mountain: An Autobiography of Faith.* New York: Harcourt, Brace.

Newman, J. H. (1987). *Parochial and Plain Sermons.* San Francisco: Ignatius.

Plekon, M. (2002). *Living Icons: Persons of Faith in the Eastern Church.* Notre Dame: University of Notre Dame Press.

Stylianopoulos, T. G. (2002). *The Way of Christ: Gospel, Spirituality, and Renewal in Orthodoxy.* Brookline: Holy Cross Orthodox Press.

Thérèse de Lisieux (1958).

Wadell, P. J. (1989). *Friendship and the Moral Life.* Notre Dame: University of Notre Dame Press.

Yoder, J. H. (1972). *The Politics of Jesus: Vicit Agnus Noster.* Grand Rapids: Eerdmans.

CHAPTER 17

ESCHATOLOGY

RICHARD BAUCKHAM

I. Eschatology as the Direction of Christian Theology

Traditionally, eschatology comprised the 'four last things' that Christian faith expects to be the destiny of humans at the end of time: resurrection, last judgement, heaven, and hell. They formed the last section of a dogmatics or a systematic theology, a position they still usually occupy. But in the twentieth century, eschatology ceased to be merely one doctrinal topic among others to be treated after the others; it became something more like a dimension of the whole subject matter of theology. Karl Barth famously claimed in 1921, 'If Christianity be not altogether thoroughgoing eschatology, there remains in it no relationship whatever with Christ' (Barth 1968: 314; cf. 1957: 634–5). While the content given to the term 'eschatology' has varied considerably over the subsequent period, in which Barth's claim has become a favourite quotation in discussions of eschatology (e.g., Moltmann 1967: 39; Pannenberg 1991–8: iii. 532), the indispensable role it attributes to eschatology has been widely endorsed. Moltmann writes, 'From first to last, and not merely in the epilogue, Christianity is eschatology. . . . The eschatological is not one element *of* Christianity, but it is the medium of Christian faith as such, the key in which everything is set, the glow that suffuses everything here in the dawn of an expected new day' (Moltmann 1967: 16).

In the first place it was the study of the New Testament that promoted eschatology to this key significance for theology. Early in the last century, Johannes Weiss (1971 [1892]) and Albert Schweitzer (1954 [1906]) convinced many that the kingdom of God which Jesus preached was not an ethical ideal to be realized progressively in human history, as nineteenth-century liberal theologians had supposed, but the transcendent act of God breaking into history to effect his final purpose for his creation. Both the preaching of Jesus and the theology of Paul came to be seen as thoroughly eschatological in the sense that they focused on the imminent arrival of God's kingdom. Everything else, such as the ethics of Jesus or the pneumatology of Paul, could be understood only in relation to this dominant eschatological focus. This discovery of the centrality and determining character of eschatology within the New Testament could not be ignored by theologians, but it was far from easy to appropriate in a culture dominated by the intellectual legacy of the Enlightenment.

The matter was complicated by a continuing debate among New Testament scholars about the character of eschatology in the New Testament. The so-called 'consistent' (i.e., thoroughgoing) eschatology of Schweitzer and Martin Werner (1957), according to which the eschatology of Jesus and the early Christians referred always to the future, albeit the imminent future, was countered by C. H. Dodd's proposal that 'realized eschatology' was the real message of Jesus and the New Testament writers (1935; 1936). He claimed that they turned the future hope of Jewish expectation into the realized experience of God in the present. Dodd's rather Platonic view of the kingdom as the eternal absolute impinging on human experience was not so different from the appropriation of biblical eschatology in the dialectical theology of the early Barth or the existentialist theology of the mature Rudolf Bultmann (1957). In all of these, the meaning of New Testament eschatology lay in its sense of disruptive transcendence breaking into the present as a moment of confrontation with the eternal. Reference to the temporal future of the world, though acknowledged to be present in the New Testament, was treated as dispensable. For Dodd it was a marginal survival of Jewish ideas; for Bultmann part of the mythological world-view of the first century, from which the gospel itself must be disentangled for its meaning to be communicated to modern people.

In New Testament scholarship a broad consensus emerged that the eschatology of the New Testament writers lies somewhere between 'consistent' and 'realized' eschatology, a position sometimes labelled 'inaugurated' eschatology. There is a tension between the 'already' of experience and the 'not yet' of eschatological fulfilment. The realization of God's final purpose for the world has already decisively begun in the ministry, death, and resurrection of Jesus, but its completion is still awaited. Believers live in the overlap of the old and new ages, between the resurrection of Jesus understood as an eschatological event and their own bodily resurrection at the future *parousia* of Jesus, participating through the Spirit in the new life of the age to come but in the context of the as yet unredeemed world. The emphasis varies in different New Testament authors—for example, between the strong emphasis on the 'already' in the Gospel of John and the strong emphasis on the 'not yet' in the book of Revelation—but most scholars see some element of each throughout.

This consensus by no means fully resolves the relationship between the 'already' and the 'not yet'. Is it that the coming kingdom is anticipated, ahead of its time, in the present, or that eschatological salvation, already in principle achieved, has yet to be fully manifested? Is it a matter of the impact of the future on the past and the present or of the impact of the past on the present and the future? However, in either case, New Testament interpretation hardly encourages a theological claim that the essence of the eschatological message of the New Testament is non-temporal. (As a claim only about the message of the historical Jesus, such a claim is currently popular among members of the Jesus Seminar in the USA who continue to advocate a 'non-eschatological' Jesus.) What is indisputable is that the New Testament in some way or in varying ways treats the 'already' and the 'not yet' of eschatology as necessarily connected. Each entails the other. It is this that makes it unsatisfactory to treat eschatology as only the doctrine of 'the last things'. The coming completion of God's purposes for his creation must set a determinative direction for the understanding of all other topics in theology.

The early twentieth-century discovery of the dominance of eschatology in New Testament theology was the first of two turning points in the theological treatment of eschatology in the modern period. The second came in the 1960s, when a number of German theologians, including Jürgen Moltmann, Wolfhart Pannenberg, Gerhard Sauter (1965) and Johann-Baptist Metz (1969), more or less simultaneously reconnected eschatology with the temporal future of the world. They did not, as has sometimes been supposed, merely create a theological version of modern utopian progressivism (on which see below), because they did not regard the coming kingdom of God or new creation as simply the outcome of the process of history itself. It is God who will finally establish his rule over the world. But, because that rule of God is the final future of the world, promises and anticipations of it occur already in history, and the church's mission in the world has this future of the world in view. This retrieval of a properly future eschatology has enabled systematic theology to reckon with both the 'already' and the 'not yet' of New Testament eschatology and to relate history and eschatology without collapsing eschatology into history.

II. The Christological Basis of Eschatology

The Christian eschatological expectation is founded on the promise of God. It is not the result of extrapolation from the trends of history or the present, nor is it based on scientific predictions of the future. It is the hope aroused and sustained by the promises of the God who created the world and who promises the redemption and completion of his creation. The future of the divine promise is not limited by the potentialities of this world but comes from the transcendent possibilities of the God who created this world with all its potentialities.

While Christian eschatology should not treat the Old Testament promises of God as superseded and irrelevant, it must also recognize that all the promises of God have been ratified in Jesus Christ (2 Cor. 1: 19–20). His ministry, death, and resurrection constitute God's definitive promise for the eschatological future of all things. They could not be understood as such without the Old Testament promises as their interpretative matrix, but they also go beyond the Old Testament promises in that the resurrection of Jesus is in some sense itself already an event belonging to the eschatological future. It is promise in the form of concrete anticipation. What has happened to Jesus is what will happen to the whole creation.

In this way Moltmann is right when he claims, 'Christian eschatology does not speak of the future as such. It sets out from a definite reality in history and announces the future of that reality, its future possibilities and its power over the future. Christian eschatology speaks of Jesus Christ and *his* future' (Moltmann 1967: 17). The resurrection of the crucified Christ is the foundation of Christian eschatological hope and therefore it is also the criterion of such hope: 'the question whether all statements about the future are grounded in the person and history of Jesus Christ provides it with the touchstone by which to distinguish the spirit of eschatology from that of utopia' (Moltmann 1967: 17). This Christological basis and criterion for Christian hope, especially when understood within the wider context of scripture, means that Christian hope cannot be a mere openness to the future without specific content.

While Moltmann and others spoke predominantly of the history of Jesus as the promise of God, Pannenberg has preferred the category of prolepsis or anticipation of the end of history (Pannenberg 1991–8: iii. 537–45). This appeals to the sense in which the kingdom of God was not merely announced by Jesus but actually already present in his ministry, and to the fact that, since resurrection of the dead was the Jewish expectation only for the end of the age, the resurrection of Jesus must be understood as a kind of anticipatory occurrence of the end. But the two concepts are not really far apart or irreconcilable when they are used Christologically. On the one hand, the resurrection of Jesus is *enacted* promise, promise in the form of anticipation. On the other hand, as anticipation of the end, the resurrection of Jesus is promise, precisely because it is *only* a proleptic appearance of the end, not the coming of the kingdom universally. What is important is that the resurrection of the crucified Jesus *entails* the future coming of the kingdom he proclaimed. Its relationship to the eschatological future is constitutive of its meaning for Christian faith. Neither Jesus nor his resurrection can be understood in non-eschatological terms.

The Christological foundation and criterion of eschatology must be distinguished from theological tendencies to collapse eschatology into what has already happened in the history of Jesus. In Karl Barth's mature theology, for example, what is still awaited for the future appears to be no more than the unveiling of what has already happened. But this scarcely does justice to the biblical tension between the 'already' and the 'not yet', that is, to the sense in which the world is still unredeemed and believers themselves await the completion of their salvation in being raised like Jesus. Rather, the resurrection of the crucified Jesus is the basis for expecting from God what has not yet happened in a future still open to the new creation of all things. What has perhaps been underplayed in the use of both the concepts of promise and anticipation is the sense in which the eschatological future depends not only on the past history of Jesus, but also the present and future of Jesus himself. Jesus lives now as the exalted and heavenly Lord who exercises the hidden rule of God in anticipation of its future coming in power and glory, and that future coming of the kingdom will also be the coming, the *parousia*, of Jesus himself. Thus Jesus himself in his own personal identification with God's rule spans the 'already' and the 'not yet' of Christian hope.

The resurrection of the crucified Jesus provides not only a promise but also, as enacted promise, the paradigm case of what the future general resurrection and the new creation of all things must involve. This relates quite closely to the issue of continuity and discontinuity in eschatology, and also to that of immanence and transcendence. While the same Jesus both died and was raised to eternal life, this identity was sustained, by the divine act that raised him, through the contradictions of death and new life, mortality and undying life, suffering and glory, condemnation and vindication. Just such a continuity in discontinuity must also be the case for all of the reality that God will renew at the eschaton. The combination of continuity and discontinuity reflects the faithfulness of God to his creation, which he will neither abandon nor abolish but will take, redeemed and transfigured, into his own eternal life.

Moreover, it is clear that Jesus' resurrection from death was not a potentiality of his human nature. It was not survival of death through some kind of natural immortality. It was the creative act of God who brought new life out of death just as he brought creation itself out of nothing. The eschatological expectation that is founded on the death and resurrection of Jesus therefore depends not on the immanent potential of this world for eschatological fulfilment, but on the creative resources of the God who transcends this world. Genuine transcendence is a touchstone for adequate eschatological thinking.

For a fully trinitarian eschatology, the Christological foundation of Christian hope must be supplemented by the work of the Holy Spirit in Christian experience. The Spirit shares the risen life of Jesus Christ with his people and, just as the resurrection of Jesus is proleptic, anticipating the end, so are the fruit and the gifts of the Spirit in the Christian community. They are the first fruits of the eschatological harvest to come. Here too we must think of divine presence and activity that can surpass the expected and predictable potential of this world, although, as with the coming new creation, the Spirit does not leave aside but fulfils and enhances creaturely abilities and potential. The effect may or may not be 'miraculous', but it is certainly eschatological and orients the whole of Christian experience towards the *parousia* and the new creation.

III. Eschatology in Cultural Contexts

In every age and society Christian theology must engage with the hopes, expectations, and dreads of the future that are cherished in its cultural context. In the patristic period this meant especially Platonism, with its strongly disjunctive view of human nature. For Platonism the mind or soul is the real person and partakes of the immortality of the unchanging world of being, while the body, during earthly life, encumbers the mind with ties to this material world of change and flux. The Platonic hope was therefore for the disembodied life of the mind. The Christian hope of bodily resurrection was deeply repugnant to Platonic thinking, and it was especially by maintaining this hope that the fathers, often much influenced by Platonism, held the line against a thoroughgoing Platonizing of Christian eschatology. The influence that Platonism did have can be seen in the ancient and medieval periods in the kind of other-worldly asceticism that practises detachment from all material things in anticipation of the coming escape of the soul from both its body and the material world. However, although the immortality of the soul was axiomatic in the mainstream theological tradition, so was bodily resurrection. Individuals at death enter on their eternal destiny only in a provisional way, awaiting the resurrection of the body and the renewal of the cosmos.

In the modern period Cartesian dualism has had a similar effect to Platonism in the past and has converged with Platonism's continuing legacy in the tradition. Popular Christian belief in the modern period has tended to envisage the survival of the soul with little reference to the resurrection of the body or the new creation of the material world. To some extent this reflects a failure to take the transcendence of God and his creative potentialities seriously in eschatology. Spiritual immortality can be understood as an inherent property of human nature, whereas bodily resurrection cannot. This suggests that recovery of a holistic eschatology, embracing spirit and body, individual and community, as well as the non-human creation, must go hand-in-hand with an unashamedly transcendent eschatology. It is notable that the loss of transcendence, in favour of a purely immanent divinity, in some nineteenth-century religious thought coincided with intense interest in empirical evidence of post-mortem survival through seances and the like.

However, in the modern period in the West the main dialogue-partner for Christian eschatology has been the idea of progress. The whole of the western culture that stems from the Enlightenment has been characterized by a turn to the temporal future unparalleled in other cultures. Until very recently all eschatology in the western Christian tradition has existed within this modern turn to the future and cannot be understood without recognition of this context. The relationship is complex partly because there is a sense in which this modern progressivism grew out of theological eschatology. Staking everything on a better future, as the modern West has done, would probably never have been conceivable had Christianity not taught people to place hope in the future on the basis of the promises of God. But, on the other hand, the Enlightenment hope of a utopian future for history was a secularization of Christian hope. Most significantly it abandoned transcendence, trusting instead the immanent possibilities of the historical process itself.

In a certain sense it could be said that what the modern idea of progress did was to replace the transcendence of God 'above' with the transcendence of the future 'ahead'. Human hopes and dreams of liberation from the evils of the world were directed to a future that would come about through the power of human reason to reshape the world, with science, technology, and education as the main instruments of this utopian purpose. Progress even became a kind of secular theodicy, in that the justification of history would be its final result. The struggles and the sacrifices of the present were worthwhile because of the result that future generations would enjoy. It should not be missed that, despite the loss of truly divine transcendence, modern progressivism retained from its religious roots human aspirations to salvation that were religious in their dimensions and in their confidence. Some kind of teleological principle immanent in the historical process was supposed to make progress inevitable. History itself was a kind of self-transcending progress from which a qualitatively new future could be expected. In retrospect we can see that, even in its most pretentiously 'scientific' forms, such as Marxism and Darwinism, this was an attempt at a secular inheritance of religion that freighted history and reason with a religious weight they have proved unable to bear. Probably only in the postmodern critique of progressivism (which we shall consider below), with its disillusioned rejection of historical teleology and its suspicious unmasking of Enlightenment reason as an instrument of oppression, has modern western thought finally shaken off its inheritance from Christian eschatology.

The history of Christian eschatology in the nineteenth and twentieth centuries can be understood in large part as the attempts of theologians to position Christian hope for the world somewhere between the two poles of alignment with Enlightenment progressivism and distinction from it. It is not difficult to see, for example, how nineteenth-century liberal theologians could assimilate the immanent teleology of progressivism to God's providential guidance of history to its future in his kingdom. But with the loss of truly divine transcendence went also a loss of the wholeness of the Christian hope. Enlightenment progressivism offered no redemption of the past and no hope for the dead. These could only be left behind. In theology that retained hope for the dead this had to be a wholly other-worldly expectation unrelated to hope for the historical future of the world. Only by taking transcendence in eschatology seriously can Christian hope envisage the past as redeemed, not just left behind, and integrate the future of the individual, body and soul, with the future of the world, historical and cosmological.

Progressivist hope, grounded in grasping the process of history rationally and extrapolating from past to future, was always very vulnerable to historical contradictions of hope. Hence it lost much of its credibility in the twentieth century, though more in Europe than in the USA. The idea of progress, shaken initially by the First World War, was discredited for many by the horrors of Nazism and Stalinism. Instead of either steady or revolutionary approximation to utopia, the century turned out to be, as George Steiner called it, 'the most bestial in human history' (Steiner 1997: 103). The Holocaust, after all, was not just atrocious but, in its technology and its organizational efficiency, a specifically modern kind of atrocity. It posed, for religious believers, the question of theodicy in terms that made progressivism a hopelessly shallow response to the realities of modern human experience. There followed the post-war period of nuclear terror, the abject failure of the Marxist project, and the growing realization that ecological disaster was the unintended result of the modern technological project, with its naive hopes of subjecting the world for human benefit. The Enlightenment sense of human mastery over nature now contends with a sense that human effects on the world have spiralled out of rational control.

Postmodernism has been centrally an attempt at a final break with Enlightenment rationalist progressivism. To the obvious failings of modernity it adds its own radical critique of Enlightenment reason itself, focusing on its drive to universality—another eschatological feature. Enlightenment reason was assumed to be universally valid and its values universally applicable. Postmodernism claims to expose this as an ideology of oppression, by which imperialist exploitation of others could be cloaked in the rhetoric of progress. From this point of view the continuing western drive to universalize its values and institutions looks rather different from how it looks to progressivists. Christian eschatology can certainly learn from the postmodernist critique of progressivism, even though it must also dissent from the extreme relativism of postmodern epistemology.

Such a critical engagement with the postmodern critique of modernity requires Christian eschatology to distinguish itself clearly from modern progressivism. When Jean François Lyotard famously defined the postmodern as 'incredulity towards grand narratives' or metanarratives (Lyotard 1984: xxiv), he had in mind the many variations on the idea of progress that tell an explanatory narrative about the course of history and thereby aspire to rational control over the course of history. It is now common to speak of a Christian metanarrative whose future conclusion is described by eschatology. This Christian metanarrative is better understood as a 'non-modern' metanarrative (Bauckham 2003: 45–53). It does not claim rational understanding of the course of history, and it does not seek history's goal within history as the product of historical trends. The 'not yet' of truly eschatological hope is the divinely given fulfilment of history, which may be anticipated within history but cannot be realized within history. Utopian projects to overcome history, its radical unpredictability, its irreducible plurality, and its vulnerability to evil, are a form of over-realized eschatology. They seem to lead characteristically to violence and totalitarian tyranny. Christian eschatology purged of its alliance with such projects offers instead a hope sustained in the contradictions of history by its expectation of God's kingdom. It can inspire appropriately realistic and flexible anticipations of the kingdom within the concrete conditions of historical life. Its vision of the kingdom offers direction but not a utopian programme.

Postmodernism notwithstanding, the continuing influence of the idea of progress should not be underestimated. It flourishes still in two major forms: a predominantly economic one (the neo-liberal ideology of free-market economic globalization), and a predominantly scientific-technological one. The former, especially in its American version, retains something of the quasi-religious character of the idea of progress: its supposed inevitability, its promise of freedom, and the messianic role in which it casts the United States. Similar qualities belong to the idea of scientific-technological progress espoused by many scientists. Of special interest for Christian eschatology, however, is the way in which the goal of scientific advance is changing from a humanist to a post-humanist one. Either through drastic technological modification of humans or by huge advances in artificial intelligence, which will supersede humans, the future is seen as inevitably post-human. Technological visionaries are committed no longer to the progress of humanity but to the progress of intelligence. From the perspective of a Christian eschatology founded on the resurrection of Jesus, this appears yet another version of the modern attempt to make immanent reality what Christians expect from the transcendent power of God, in this case, the glorified humanity of the exalted Christ and those who will be like him in resurrection.

Finally, an important intellectual player on the contemporary eschatological field is scientific cosmology insofar as it attempts to predict the far future of the universe. Such predictions are the subject of much debate, and different versions may be more or less congenial to Christian eschatological expectations. But, once again, a Christian hope that is founded on the resurrection of Jesus and takes transcendence seriously has no need to suppose that the future of the universe will be what science predicts, not because the predictions are wrong but because they are based on the universe as we know it. The Christian hope for new creation is for a radical transformation of the universe by the God who created it. The scientific predictions are for what will happen to the universe if this transcendent transformation does not occur, just as science would correctly have predicted the decay of the dead Jesus in the tomb had his resurrection not occurred. While it may not be impossible that the scientific concept of emergence, according to which the universe can itself generate the radically new, could accommodate the hope of new creation in some form, it is hard to see that it could account either for the resurrection of Jesus or for the resurrection of the dead and the redemption of the past that Christian eschatology expects.

IV. Holistic Eschatology

Christian hope that reflects the world-view of the Bible is hope for the whole of created reality. It does not divide creation into the immortal and the perishable, that which can transcend the mortality of this world and that which cannot. All too often, however, eschatology, influenced by Platonic or Cartesian dualism, has made precisely such distinctions, promising eternal life for the spirit but not the body, for the individual but not human society, for the personal but not the historical, for humanity but not the non-human creation, for the enduring but not the ephemeral. There are several reasons for resisting such eschatological reduction. One is that scientific insights into the psychosomatic wholeness of human nature (which arguably can include a certain sort of dualism, but hardly a Platonic or Cartesian one), our biological kinship with other animals, and the interconnectedness of all creatures in a web of life on earth make it easier to see how a holistic eschatology does better justice to how the world is than a reductive one. The destiny of the non-human creation—whether humans are to be saved with it or from it—has become a freshly significant issue through the ecological crisis.

Theologically a holistic eschatology is based especially on the bodily resurrection of Jesus. It was not that Jesus' spirit survived his death, but that his whole bodily person was raised by God out of death. The human body signifies interrelationship with other humans and continuity with the whole material world. Jesus' resurrection was in solidarity with the whole of this material, mortal, and transient reality and is therefore the promise that everything of value in the present creation will be taken by God into his eternal life.

In distinction from any kind of immanent utopianism, a holistic Christian eschatology expects an eschatological future for the past. What God through new creation takes into eternity is not simply what creation will be at the end of the temporal process, but all that it has ever been. Nothing of value will be lost. In relation to individual humans, resurrection surely implies not merely that they will continue to live beyond death, but also that the whole of the life they have lived up to death will be gathered, redeemed, and transfigured into their eschatological identity. This need not mean, as some theologians suppose, that there will be no further development for them, but only their endlessly fuller understanding, within the life of God, of the meaning of the lives they lived up to death (Jenson 1997–9:

ii. 346, 348). That seems to presuppose a completeness of mortal lives that is clearly not the case. The issue relates closely to the nature of the 'time' of the new creation. It is possible to imagine a time in which the new can occur but cannot be lost as it is in this transient world.

God's eschatological goal for the world is not only restoration or redemption but also fulfilment and completion. The world as it is is both marred by evil and also, even in its goodness, not yet what it is destined to be. In biblical and traditional imagery, the new creation is more than a return to Eden, a restoration of the originally unblemished state of things; it is a perfecting of that original state, in which humans were innocent rather than maturely good, in which they might not have died but could die, and in which nature, while not yet suffering from human abuse, was in itself transient. The vision of the New Jerusalem in Revelation 21–2 incorporates Eden (22: 1–2) but is also more than Eden: a city into which the kings of the earth bring their glory (21: 24). Nature and human culture are finally reconciled, all that is good in the world and its history is purged of evil and gathered into eternity, and all is transfigured by the indwelling presence of God. It is finally God who gives creation the wholeness it lacks in itself.

The modern age has been dominated by the idea that history has a utopian goal that the process of history, directed by humans, will itself produce. Often the goal has been defined by western culture and, as postmodern critics complain, imposed imperialistically as a universal good for all. Modernity has difficulty with pluralism, but so has Christianity had whenever it has sought impatiently to realize the kingdom of God by force and violence. For this reason it is important to insist that anticipations of the kingdom within history, desirable though they are, are not the coming of the kingdom itself, and that the goal of history lies beyond itself in the final redemption and completion of God's creation that God himself will give. Holistic eschatology cannot be content with the mere fragmentation of reality that a postmodern approach promotes, but can value plurality and difference as penultimate goods that will find their fulfilment, in ways we need not be able to predict, within the fullness and wholeness of the new creation.

V. Eschatological Language

Probably more than any other aspect of theology, other than the doctrine of God, eschatology deals in the symbolic and the imaginative. Like God, eschatological salvation transcends all our concepts. It can speak only of what we have not yet experienced by analogy with what we have. Even a general concept such as 'eternal life' eludes literal understanding: it refers to something analogous to the mortal life we know, differing from the latter in that it is not transient. The difference—what it is to have eternal, rather than mortal, life—can in the end be understood only negatively, and we can appreciate the appropriateness of this especially if we add that eternal life is a creaturely participation in the eternal life of God. Like the doctrine of God and because it speaks of a kind of participation in God that is not presently available to us, eschatological thought and language have an inescapably apophatic character (Isa. 64: 4; 1 Cor. 2: 9; 1 John 3: 2).

In the light of both the nature of eschatology and the ways of actual speaking of eschatological reality in scripture and tradition, we can speak of 'the primacy of imagination in eschatological thought' (Bauckham and Hart 1999: 110). This presupposes a view of the imagination that can distinguish it from free-floating fantasy. The *imaginative* is not necessarily the *imaginary*. Nor should it be seen as an alternative to revelation. Rather, the revelatory promise of God in Christ and scripture appeals to the human imagination, seizes, transforms, and expands it, and makes it the locus and vehicle of human reception of God's promise. It is this Christian imagination that can envision the coming kingdom sufficiently for it to empower Christian living without reducing the kingdom to a reality that can be all too easily perfected already.

Much eschatological language works either by negation or by hyperbole. The hopeful imagination transcends the given either by negating the negatives of present experience or by amplifying the positives, in both cases to an extent that goes beyond the ordinary possibilities of this world. A good example of the first is Revelation 21: 4: God 'will wipe away every tear from their eyes. Death will be no more; mourning and crying and pain will be no more, for the first things have passed away'. In the category of eschatological hyperbole, consider Isaiah 9: 7 ('there shall be endless peace') or Isaiah 11: 9b ('the earth will be full of the knowledge of the LORD as the waters cover the sea'). Eschatological hyperbole can take the form of typology: eschatological salvation will be a new and greater exodus, the Messiah will be a new and greater David. Hyperbole also informs descriptions of the final crescendo of evil in history immediately before the end.

Hopeful imagining is protected from mere speculation in that it is grounded in the promises of God and resourced by the images of scripture. As we have argued, it is especially the resurrection of the crucified Jesus that, as God's definitive promise, acts as the criterion of eschatological hope. We can also be guided by a series of major images or symbols of the eschatological future that feature centrally in the Bible and the Christian tradition, including Antichrist, *parousia* (the coming of Jesus Christ), resurrection, new creation, millennium, last judgement, New Jerusalem, paradise restored, marriage feast, sabbath rest, kingdom of God, vision of God, eternal life (Bauckham and Hart 1999: 109–73). Such symbols serve to stimulate, order, and direct imaginative thought. Several of the most important are the subjects of the following sections of this essay.

Finally, there is a criterion of relevance. Eschatology does not attempt to satisfy mere curiosity, but to order Christian life and mission in the direction of God's coming kingdom. Yet this criterion should not be taken in too narrowly pragmatic a sense. For example, eschatological hope enables us to live with the problem of theodicy, it gives coherence to the rest of Christian belief, and it inspires doxology.

VI. The *Parousia*

The 'coming' (Greek: *parousia*) of Jesus Christ at the end of the history of this world (often known in Christian tradition as the 'second coming') is the focal image in New Testament eschatology. The biblical story of God's renewal and redemption of creation focuses on Jesus, not only centrally—in his life and death and resurrection—but also finally in his *parousia*. Christian theology in the modern period, whether in Christology or in eschatology, has rarely done justice to this focal importance of Jesus himself, the divine and human person, in the completion of world history. It requires not simply that the future of the world depends on the past history of Jesus, but that Jesus himself has a future with the world that is both his own future and the future of the world. He himself as the coming saviour and judge of all determines the final future of all things.

The problem in the modern period has been partly that of the imagery with which the *parousia* is depicted in the New Testament. What we have already said about eschatological language implies that this language should be read for its significance rather than as literal prediction. The *parousia* will not be an event within history, but the event that brings history to an end. Yet, we have no way of talking or thinking about such an event other than as an occurrence in time and space like other events. However, the symbolic nature of the biblical portrayals of the *parousia* does not mean that we can treat Jesus himself as merely part of the imagery. The images refer as genuinely to Jesus' own future as they do to the future of the world and of all humans.

It is because Jesus is forever the one who is uniquely identified with both God and all humanity that he will be the focus of the completion of God's purpose for this world. The biblical imagery of the *parousia* associates it closely with the full and final achievement of God's rule over creation and also with the unveiling of the full and final truth of all things. It is to Jesus as the one who occupies God's throne that all must finally bow the knee (Phil. 2: 10–11), and it is before the judgement seat of Jesus that all must face the truth of their lives (Acts 10: 42). We could say that it is finally in their relatedness to Jesus, who is both God's humanity and humanity's God, that all must reach their final destiny.

VII. The Last Judgement and the Question of Universal Salvation

The notion of eschatological judgement is conveyed by two different biblical images: judgement by military victory and judgement in a court of law. The Christian tradition has treated the latter as the controlling image, picturing the last judgement as a great assize where, following resurrection, all the living and the dead stand before Jesus the judge, who consigns the damned to hell and the redeemed to paradise. However, the alternation and combination of the two images in the New Testament (e.g., Rev. 19: 11–21; 20: 11–15) reminds us that both are images, giving imaginative form to the hope that God must finally remove all evil from his world before it can be the new creation. We have earlier in this essay stressed the holistic character of the eschatological future, when God will take into permanent union with his own eternal life the whole of his creation, both the cosmos and humans in their full, bodily being. Nothing that is good in this world and its history will be lost. But evil—the incomprehensible forces that ravage and destroy God's good creation—cannot survive God's perfecting of that creation. When the truth of all history is finally laid bare before the judgement of God, evil, as evil, must perish. This is not in contradiction to but is required by God's loving and salvific will for all his creatures. They must be delivered from evil.

The mystery of evil in its non-human aspect is impenetrable to us, but it stands for something that is simply evil and has nothing about it that is capable of redemption. Humans are a different matter. Their hope of salvation rests on God's desire and ability to redeem them from evil. An aspect of the significance of seeing Jesus Christ as the final judge is that he is the same as the Christ who enacted and communicated God's love for all humanity, bearing on the cross the judgement on our sin so that we need not. Can this same Christ who died for all condemn some to final judgement? Whereas nearly the whole of the Christian tradition before modern times has answered this question affirmatively, in the modern period many have found the nature of God's love and the universal character of his work of salvation in Christ a basis for expecting the final salvation of each and every human person. As well as a dogmatic conviction of universal salvation, there are also forms of undogmatic hope, such as Karl Barth's refusal to limit the freedom of God (Barth 1961: 477–8) or Hans Urs von Balthasar's statement that, while scripture and the church require us to believe that there is hell, they do not oblige us to claim that it must have inhabitants (Balthasar 1988).

Most theologians in the modern period who maintain the traditional expectation that some will or may receive final condemnation and exclusion from eschatological salvation do so on the basis of human freedom. For Christian theology it must be clear that, when the truth of all human lives comes to light under the scrutiny of God, no one can be saved except by the mercy of God. The judgement is not some kind of arithmetical reckoning of good and bad deeds. If it is discriminatory it must be a discernment of the fundamental alignment of a person's self towards God and towards the good or, conversely, of a fundamental rejection of God and the good. Not even God's mercy can save those who voluntarily make a final choice for evil: they must perish along with evil itself. Such a final choice for evil would be possible if human freedom can persist in rejecting God's love in a way that God knows amounts to an irreversible choice. The mystery of final condemnation relates to the mystery of evil and the mystery of human freedom, and brings us very close to the limits of theological inquiry.

VIII. The Kingdom of God, the Vision of God, and Eternal Participation in God

These are probably the three most important symbols of human destiny in eternity. The kingdom of God, the subject of much of Jesus' preaching, offers a political and social image of the perfection of human society in full accord with the will of God. It may well be the most potent category with which to characterize the continuity between the eschatological future and the present. The fullness of eschatological salvation is already anticipated in all kinds of flourishing in human community inspired by the Spirit of God, especially when priority is given to the poor and the marginalized, with whom Jesus especially identified the kingdom of God.

The vision of God, often called the 'beatific vision', offers a symbol of human destiny that highlights its theocentricity. It combines a sense of being in the immediate presence of God with the idea of knowing God in his true identity, as it were 'face to face'. It has sometimes been understood in a rather intellectualized and individualized way, but need not be. It is the whole person that is engaged in immediate relationship with God, and this can be interpreted in a way that includes all things in the vision of God. Whereas in this world it can be necessary to turn away from other objects of attention in order to focus on God, in eternity all creation, redeemed and perfected, will reflect the glory of God. The vision of God will include seeing God in all things, participating in the transparently and joyously theocentric world of creation indwelt by God.

God himself is the final goal and home of his creation, human and non-human. The common scriptural image of 'eternal life' refers to a kind of participation by creatures in the eternal life of God. Such participation cannot be in all that it means for God to be eternal, but it is an appropriately creaturely way of living from the divine fullness of life and the way in which creatures can transcend the transience and mortality of this world's life. The eastern Christian tradition in particular has used the term 'divinization' (*theōsis*) as the description of the fullness of human destiny. It should not be taken to mean that creatures literally become God, but that they are included as creatures within the divine life, within the eternal perichoresis of the three divine persons. Another term with a similar significance is eschatological panentheism, meaning that God will be in the world and the world will be in God, in the closest union possible for God and creation.

References

Balthasar, Hans Urs von (1988). *Dare We Hope 'That All Men Be Saved'? with A Short Discourse on Hell.* San Francisco: Ignatius.

Barth, Karl (1957). *Church Dogmatics* II/1. Edinburgh: T. & T. Clark.

—— (1961). *Church Dogmatics* IV/3.1. Edinburgh: T. & T. Clark.

—— (1968). *The Epistle to the Romans.* Oxford: Oxford University Press.

Bauckham, Richard (2003). 'Reading Scripture as a Coherent Story'. In Ellen F. Davis and Richard Hays (eds.), *The Art of Reading Scripture*, Grand Rapids: Eerdmans, 38–53.

Bauckham, Richard, and Hart, Trevor (1999). *Hope Against Hope: Christian Eschatology in Contemporary Context.* London: Darton, Longman & Todd.

Bultmann, Rudolph (1957). *History and Eschatology: The Gifford Lectures 1955.* Edinburgh: Edinburgh University Press.

Dodd, C. H. (1935). *The Parables of the Kingdom.* London: Nisbet.

—— (1936). *The Apostolic Preaching and its Developments: Three Lectures with an Appendix on Eschatology and History.* London: Hodder and Stoughton.

Jenson, Robert W. (1997–9). *Systematic Theology.* 2 vols. Oxford: Oxford University Press.

Lyotard, Jean-François (1984). *The Postmodern Condition.* Minneapolis: University of Minnesota Press.

Metz, Johann-Baptist (1969). *Theology of the World.* New York: Herder and Herder.

Moltmann, Jürgen (1967). *Theology of Hope.* London: SCM.

Pannenberg, Wolfhart (1991–8). *Systematic Theology.* 3 vols. Grand Rapids: Eerdmans.

Sauter, Gerhard (1965). *Zukunft und Verheissung: Das Problem der Zukunft in der gegenwärtigen theologischen und philosophischen Diskussion.* Zurich: Zwingli Verlag.

Schweitzer, Albert (1954 [1906]). *The Quest of the Historical Jesus.* London: A. & C. Black.

Steiner, George (1997). *Errata: An Examined Life.* London: Weidenfeld & Nicolson.

Weiss, Johannes (1971 [1892]). *Jesus' Proclamation of the Kingdom of God.* London: SCM.

Werner, Martin (1957). *The Formation of Christian Dogma: An Historical Study of its Problem.* London: A. & C. Black.

Suggested Reading

Bauckham, Richard (2001). 'The Future of Jesus Christ'. In Markus Bockmuehl (ed.), *The Cambridge Companion to Jesus*, Cambridge: Cambridge University Press, 265–80.

Bauckham and Hart (1999).

Bauckham, Richard (ed.) (1999). *God Will Be All in All: The Eschatology of Jürgen Moltmann.* Edinburgh: T. & T. Clark; Minneapolis: Fortress Press.

Ellis, George F. R. (2002). *The Far-Future Universe: Eschatology from a Cosmic Perspective.* Philadelphia/London: Templeton Foundation.

Fergusson, David, and Sarot, Marcel (eds.) (2000). *The Future as God's Gift: Explorations in Christian Eschatology.* Edinburgh: T. & T. Clark.

Moltmann, Jürgen (1996). *The Coming of God: Christian Eschatology.* London: SCM.

Polkinghorne, John C. (2002). *The God of Hope and the End of the World.* London: SPCK.

Schwartz, Hans (2000). *Eschatology.* Grand Rapids: Eerdmans.

Walls, Jerry L. (ed.) (2007). *The Oxford Handbook of Eschatology.* New York: Oxford University Press.

PART II

SOURCES

CHAPTER 18

REVELATION

BEN QUASH

I. Introduction

How is it possible to give appropriate expression to the being of God, who is transcendent, incomprehensible, and hidden? How is it possible even to *refer* to this God without delusion or projection? The doctrine of revelation is how Christian theology explores these questions. This essay will aim to investigate both the legitimacy and sharpness of the questions, and the necessary complexity of the answers, with particular attention to the work of contemporary and recent theologians.

But first, an art-historical illustration, which I hope will offer a way into the topic. Caravaggio's *Calling of St Matthew* (1599–1600) is a painting that seeks to indicate the presence of the divine, and the manifestation of grace, in a particular moment of time. It provokes us to think with it about *how grace appears* in human situations—in the social, historical, and material circumstances of human life. The call of Levi (as St Matthew was then called) is, after all, a supremely gracious moment: one of the most dramatic instances of conversion in the Gospels, in which a tax collector recognizes a new lordship in the person of Jesus Christ, meets an irresistible summons to follow him, and leaves everything (including the failures and corruptions of his past life) to do so.

Against a monotonously plain, dark wall with a grubby, oilskin-covered window set high in it, the painting shows a table with various men seated around or stooping over it. The left end of the table is in shadow; the right end is nearer to the light, a light that comes from a mysterious source we cannot see, but which, in slanting diagonally down from the top right-hand corner of the picture, becomes associated with the outstretched arm of Christ, whose pointing finger follows its line. Christ stands at the extreme right of the picture, in the shadowy space beneath the shaft of light. He is very far from being centre stage, and is certainly one of the last figures one's eye is drawn to. The light cuts across the picture making strong contrasts between the features, expressions, and objects it highlights and the dark ground of the painting as a whole. Levi's face in particular is illumined by the light as he turns towards it,[1] while many of the other figures remain enveloped in shadow, especially the youth at the end of the table furthest from the light, with his head bowed and his fingers playing with coins—suggesting, perhaps, unredeemed humanity and the inability to respond to Christ.[2] Other figures seem poised between light and darkness: they could go either way.

With its chiaroscuro effects and its concentration on an unidealized depiction of its figures (however dramatic), this painting is very typical of Caravaggio's work—especially his later work. And here, as elsewhere, Caravaggio proves himself notably reluctant to depict grace or divine agency in *obvious* ways, unlike many of his artistic predecessors and a good number of his contemporaries. Divine agency in his paintings does not normally arrive in a well-signposted manner by being somehow 'extra' to what the world already contains; we do not usually encounter it in the form of a 'supernatural' agent like an angel, or a celestial window onto heaven, or the visible transfiguration or ascent of saints. The discernment of the divine is thus not made an easy business in Caravaggio's hands. There is no paean to the unmistakeability of divine action in human life. God's self-disclosure—his saving power and action—does not take a form that can clearly be differentiated from other objects and actions and pointed to in straightforward distinction from them. It has to be discerned in the irreducible interactions of people with each other and with their material environment.

Other artists in both pre-modern and modern times have their own way of dealing with the unrepresentability of God—which might mean also, as the early iconoclasts liked to point out, the unrepresentability of Christ's divine nature (however much his human nature lent itself to depiction). Now an uncharitable critic of Caravaggio might say that a shaft of light risks reducing divine realities to the humanly imaginable every bit as much as does a choir of angels sitting literalistically on clouds: it makes the light a representation of the divine. But I think that Caravaggio's eschewal of 'supernatural' divine agents in favour of light shows a caution and discretion that are impressive. What he honours in his approach is something of which Christian theologians down the ages have been acutely aware, and which will be explored at greater length during the course of this essay: God is not just one more thing in the universe. He cannot be described in relation to and

[1] Assuming Levi is the bearded figure seated at the middle of the table, as seems most likely.

[2] A minority of interpreters think that this youth is actually meant to be Levi.

distinction from other creaturely realities as if he were one such reality himself. As Susannah Ticciati writes:

> God is nothing *in particular*; God does not *have* qualities in the way that creaturely realities do, which might be predicated of him. One cannot say, God is *this* and not *that*; for God is not a thing to be distinguished from other things. (Ticciati 2007: 161)

So to avoid showing us anything 'extra' than the normal run of creaturely realities, as Caravaggio avoids it, is to ensure that God is not distinguished from creatures in the way that creatures are distinguished from one another. He leaves the light as itself, whilst opening a possibility that it may simultaneously mean more than itself.

The doctrine of revelation then, as most theologians of the past century have realized just as acutely as their patristic, medieval, and Reformation precursors, is concerned with something very peculiar indeed—what Christoph Schwöbel calls 'conceivable testimonies of the inconceivable' (Schwöbel 2000: 21). The ordinary perceptions of human beings do not 'show' them God in any straightforward sense. Our knowledge of God does not seem to be set in any kind of obvious relation with our ordinary knowing, 'neither one of consummation nor of contradiction' (Davies 2004: 5). The material facts of the world looked on by the Christian believer are no different from those looked on by the atheist. It is not within the power of our ordinary perceptions to tell us, for example, that the material world we inhabit is a *creation* (I assert this despite the claims of certain kinds of natural theology, which have a number of modern forms, and whose claims we will touch on in the next section). So we may say that believer and atheist see the same things, but they see them differently. The believer does not have more information than the atheist—and this, incidentally, is one of the virtues of Caravaggio's general eschewal of supernatural agents and other non-worldly phenomena in the composition of his religious paintings: there is nothing *more* to be seen than what is there anyway. What matters is *how* it is seen. It might be argued that this is exactly what makes painting in some way instructive (by analogy) for a doctrine of revelation, for painters are generally quite aware that they need not concern themselves with what isn't there; their concern is to depict what *is* there in a *new way*, so that we see what we thought was familiar with *new eyes*.

In revelation, Christian theologians tend to argue, it is *God* who enables this depiction of what is there in a *new way*. It is not the product of human initiative; it has nothing to do with our conceptual rigour or linguistic prowess. In revelation, 'God himself becomes our teacher' (Davies 2004: 36). Because he is transcendent, incomprehensible, and hidden, God can only be known when he makes himself known; God ensures his own knowability where nothing else can ensure it. So revelation is essentially divinely given and not humanly found.

This essay will trace various ways in which this insight is being responded to and elaborated—and sometimes questioned—in modern theology.

II. Two Broad Positions on the Doctrine of Revelation

In this section, we will look at two broad positions that represent the characteristic approaches to revelation in the modern period. They help set the agenda for today's debate about the doctrine.

'Reductionist'

I said earlier that twentieth-century theologians have been as acutely aware of the difficulties of giving expression to the being of God as their patristic, medieval, and Reformed precursors were. But that is to pass over the very influential attempts to do so which came to a head in the nineteenth century—attempts which downplayed the peculiarity of revelation either by questioning the need for it, or (which amounts to nearly the same thing) by aligning it closely with what it was felt could be ascertained by human minds on the basis of rational argument, historical enquiry, analysis of the structures of human perception or moral motivation, or any combination of these. It was an ambitious aim, the pursuit of which is often summed up as the characteristic project of nineteenth-century 'liberal Protestantism'. That project's large-scale rejection in the early twentieth century by Karl Barth and others still requires us to take account of it, for it remains influential even by the critiques which it continues to generate.

Trevor Hart writes,

> By the late nineteenth century the most significant streams of Christian theological reflection had either quietly pushed the category [of revelation] aside and substituted for it some other (more 'natural') basis for their endeavour, or else had refashioned the concept in ways which served effectively (if not intentionally) to relocate it within the sphere of human (natural) rather than divine (supranatural) possibilities. (Hart 2000: 38)

How did this happen? In a number of ways. The Ritschlian school, as Hart points out, had argued that the content of revelation was indistinguishable from the teaching and the moral and spiritual example of Jesus during the course of his earthly life. These were by their very nature historical phenomena, accessible with the tools of historical criticism in the same way as any other historical phenomena. So this content was in principle available to anyone with the right tools and methods at his or her disposal. There was no room for the idea that theology's source must be a God who utterly transcends, in his being and activity, the sphere of the human.

Friedrich Schleiermacher, meanwhile, had developed a subtle and distinctive variant on the idea that the structures and workings of human *subjectivity* could be looked to for evidence of the divine. For him it was not the transcendental regulative categories of reason or morality that pointed to a divine source—though this was an influential view in a certain Kantian school of thought at the time—but rather a fundamental intuitive orientation of human beings towards (divine) infinity, at a 'depth' level of consciousness that exceeded cognition but still maintained some relation to experience. He calls it, variously, 'God-consciousness', the 'sense and taste of the Infinite', and the 'feeling of absolute dependence' and locates it at those levels of our being which 'transcend and embrace our more restricted rational experience' (Gunton 2001: 221; Schleiermacher 1988: 77–140 and 1999: 5–31). This enabled Schleiermacher to say that God is immediately present to the human subject, but not isolatable as an object of direct thought.[3] Rather, God is 'co-given' with our experience of the world and ourselves. Any theological statements we might make are *post facto* rationalizations of such co-givenness in experience, because what is co-given remains essentially beyond or above reason.

What unites the various strands of the liberal Protestant project—whether historically, rationally, or experientially based claims to discern God's being and truth—is the conviction that access to the divine is in one way or another a natural phenomenon. Even in the case of Schleiermacher, who is insistent that 'in the Christian religion this general human capacity is decisively modified through contact with the personality of Jesus and his redemptive work', his approach does not accommodate the model of revelation as 'a particular... manifestation which is in some sense additional to, inexplicable in terms of, and even an interruption of, the ordinary ("natural") sources and patterns of our knowing' (Hart 2000: 39–40).

I have called this family of approaches 'reductionist' in their treatment of revelation, not in order to suggest that they lack nuance or sophistication (Schleiermacher's in particular does not), but for the simple reason that they have often been charged with reducing revelation to the terms and conditions of creaturely possibility; they assimilate it to human capacities. One key effect of such approaches is the loss of transcendence—or at any rate that genuine transcendence that 'may not be reconfigured as something merely about human consciousness or a world mystery' (Janz 2004: 213). It might be objected that Schleiermacher with his appeal to a sense of the infinite is indeed gesturing towards some sort of transcendent 'beyond', but it remains a *beyond of experience.* In other words, so it might be argued, this sort of transcendence tells us more about human subjectivity and its functions than it does about God. God's transcendence, on the other hand, is *something about God.* If reference to the transcendent is made something achievable by autonomous human beings as they reflect on the workings of their consciousness, then it is in the end made non-transcendent.

[3] It is important to note that despite his use of the language of 'feeling', he was not claiming that experience of God was empirically available—identifiable, perhaps, with some individual psychological state in the believer.

The Schleiermacherian school, moreover, unlike the Ritschlian, has continued to have important proponents in both Protestant and Catholic theology. Paul Tillich's notion of 'ultimate concern' as a fundamental constitutive characteristic of the human subject means that his theology continues Schleiermacher's project of looking to consciousness for signs of what we might call 'Godwardness'. Karl Rahner sees a way of uniting the broadly idealist tradition in which Schleiermacher operated with the Augustinian/Thomist view that all creatures are naturally teleologically oriented to their fulfillment in God (specifically, in the case of human beings, to the beatific vision). Rahner was fascinated all his life by what it was that makes possible the reception of revelation by human beings. It is in response to just this question that he develops his 'transcendental method'. On this account, there is a pre-thematic orientation on the part of all human beings towards an awareness of the transcendent, which he equates with God. As Karen Kilby puts it, 'transcendental experience is the experience of going beyond all the things we know and choose and love, even as we are knowing and choosing and loving them—and when we go beyond all particular things, what we go towards is, on Rahner's account, God' (Kilby 2005: 99; Rahner 1978: 24–175). There is never any question of leaving behind the concrete, the particular, and the finite in the attainment of this transcendental experience; transcendental experience is always given in and with experience of the concrete. What happens in such experience, though, is that we are opened to a reception of God's communication of himself as the ground of our being, by being opened to the fact that he is simultaneously the ground of all other beings' being too. This is for Rahner the basic form of revelation. Though there are many subtle distinctions that could be drawn, the structural similarities with Schleiermacher's approach are striking. And, like Schleiermacher, Rahner's thought is often accused by its critics of confusing the transcendence of God with the transcendence of the human mind.

There is, of course, a real danger of caricaturing these positions as lacking any sense that revelation describes the unbidden arrival of something from beyond the human self, and, more specifically, as assuming that revealed truth is really always in some sense *known in advance*. This would be unfair. Rahner is clear that the openness of the human spirit to the divine communication is not the divine gift itself; the gift remains gracious—in the same way that for Schleiermacher there is something irreducibly 'not of our making' about our sense of the divine at the root of our consciousness. Indeed, Schleiermacher can be read as a strong defender of *sola gratia* inasmuch as what he seeks ultimately to teach is that our existence belongs altogether to the realm of receptivity—a receptivity to (or dependence on) one who cannot be reduced to any single worldly influence upon the individual, nor even to the sum of such influences (Lash 1988: 123–4). And even Tillich (whose theism is perhaps weakest of the three) is anxious to retain a language of receptivity when he talks of how the ground of our life's meaning is revealed to us. It is a miracle in the sense that we are grasped by 'some particular concrete object, event, or person that functions as a sign-event or religious symbol *through which* the ground of meaning in life makes itself present to persons' (Kelsey 2005: 67; Tillich 1953: 120–46). The key point of concern in assessing these approaches, however, is not so much that they deny some extra-human giver or gift in their doctrines of revelation, but that they suppose the discovery of this gift to be 'an inherent human possibility or capacity which simply needs to be realized and embraced, fertilized and nurtured, or tweaked and reconfigured' (Hart 2000: 43).

There are two further significant forms of reductionist approach which demand to be touched on. The first is the work of a school of Christian philosophers of religion (whose main representative in the UK is Richard Swinburne) who use the methods of analytical philosophy to argue for the reasonableness and plausibility of Christian truth. Having first argued for the rational defensibility of believing that an all-powerful and all-good God exists, Swinburne asks whether it is reasonable to suppose that such a God would give human beings information to help them to understand and relate to him, and concludes that it is. Thus he and the analytic school would contest the claim that the believer has no more information at his disposal than the atheist: revelation is not just revelation *of* God, but revelation *by* God of a set of propositional truths. This school does not claim that such information will always be glaringly obvious even to a careful mind, but it does assume that such information will in principle be available to any thinking person willing to attend intelligently to the words and actions of Jesus as witnessed to in the Bible, the creeds, and the church. The plausibility of revelation will largely be judgeable by 'independent criteria' (Swinburne 1992: 86) and is 'backed by a powerful divine miracle' (Swinburne 1992: 210), namely, the resurrection, whose probability Swinburne asserts by a combination of appeal to historical evidence and argument from premisses about the goodness of God. That this school is properly placed under the reductionist category is shown by its strong focus on revelation as accessible by the rational activity of *weighing and analysing evidence* and by its assertion that this evidence-based approach 'is no different in principle, only in scale, from what it is in science and history' (Swinburne 1992: 219).

The second approach is the ancient tradition of natural theology, which found classical definition in Aquinas's work but has held a distinguished place throughout the history of Christian thought. What Schleiermacher expects to discern from his observation of the nature of the human capacity for experience, this long-standing tradition of theological argument claims to perceive from its observation of the nature of the created order. Bonaventure, for example, held that created things—even though imperfect, material, and changeable—'allow us to discern the existence of what is perfect, spiritual and eternal' (Davies 2004: 37). Aquinas himself held that metaphysics (the inquiry into being) permitted us at least in a formal way to identify existence as the effect of a divine cause: 'What is known as the way of causality achieves a limited knowledge of the kind of being that God is by ascending through a knowledge of the created world which is understood as his effect' (Gunton 2001: 220). In its cruder forms, natural theology is vulnerable to many of the objections that can be lined up against liberal Protestantism (and which could as easily be levelled at Swinburne and the analytical school)—above all, the objection that the content of revelation is somehow capable of being 'found out' by the particularly active or penetrating mind. In fact, Aquinas and other representatives of this approach are typically highly alert to the limited character of such knowledge. Aquinas emphasizes that we cannot know the way in which our theological language applies to God (*ST* 1a. 13, in Aquinas 1975). He asserts that for God to be present to creation as creator is at the same time irreducibly a form of absence, for (as creator of *all* that is, and in line with what we observed in the introduction) God is not one more thing in the universe (*ST* 1a. 12, 12).

Whatever its caveats, the tradition of natural theology was to come under the same criticism in the twentieth century as the liberal Protestant tradition because of its risk of confusing 'what is constituted *by* human beings [as reliable knowledge of God] with what is constituted *for* human beings' (Schwöbel 2000: 32). This criticism was delivered above all by our second broad tradition of thought about revelation in the modern period, to which we now turn.

'Positivist'

Dismayed by the reductionist view in which, broadly speaking, the knowledge and experience of the believer become more a *source* of revelation than a *response* to it, a major strand of twentieth-century theology has sought to recover God's sovereign independence of our human faculties. It articulated forcefully the weaknesses in the reductionist position, especially its loss of genuine transcendence. Against the Schleiermacherian school it insisted that '[t]he "beyond" of God is not the "beyond" of the mind' (Schwöbel 2000: 26), and against the Ritschlian school it denied that '"history" is a more comprehensive and well-founded reality than "revelation"' (Webster 2000: 10–11). On the basis of these convictions, many theologians of the twentieth century (Karl Barth foremost amongst them) asserted with renewed vigour that theology's task of speaking about God depends upon God himself speaking. This is a legacy which continues to be very influential today.

Barth's position is summed up by Trevor Hart as follows:

> God does not belong to the world of objects with which human apprehension and speech ordinarily have to do and to which they are fitted to pertain. God's reality transcends this realm in such a way that human knowing could never aspire to lay hold of it and render it into an 'object'. God is beyond human classification, understanding and description. (Hart 2000: 42; see Barth 1975: 295–489 and 1956: 1–537).

But for God not to be an object in human terms does not entail that he has no reality. God is, for Barth, the true subject of creation and its history—thus too the true subject of the event of revelation. The viability of theology as a science is grounded in its responsiveness to this, the only really real reality: the existence and character of God. This led Barth to an extraordinary feat of theological renewal, central to which was his relentless emphasis on a wholly non-worldly objectivity that confounds all our conventional categories of the objective: the *objective reality of God the subject.*

But if God's disclosure of himself, to which theology is to respond in obedience, is not objective in any ordinary sense, and if God always remains subject, then it seems that the content of revelation will resist access by human knowledge. Barth is fully aware of this difficulty, and in rejecting the strategies of the liberal Protestant tradition as also of natural theology, he is determined to find another way to do justice to God's knowability. God *is* known, after all—so it must be a possibility, even if not an ordinary human one. More specifically, Barth recognizes, God is known *in Jesus Christ.* So 'the heart of [Barth's] enterprise is to place Jesus Christ, God become man, where Schleiermacher placed religious experience' (Gunton 2001: 222).

Jesus Christ is, for Barth, the self-presentation of God. This self-presentation then becomes theology's object, as witnessed to in scripture and attested by the Spirit in a God-given correlation. And what is presented by the *incarnate one* to the eyes of faith in the event of revelation is nothing less than the *triune one*—God the Trinity. The very *structure* of revelation, and not only the *content* of revelation, discloses this triunity. For God to 'self-objectify' is for him to act as both source, substance, and sensorium of revelation. In Barth's words, he is revealer, revelation, and revealedness. There is absolute unity between the event and the content of revelation, for both are God himself (God's being and God's act are one). God is thus safeguarded as the ground of his own knowability, rather than any creaturely capacity. For any 'visibility or graspability to human capacities, whether intellectual, sensory or affective', if it were somehow the human being's possession or achievement, would be 'by definition . . . a violation of the integrity (unconditionedness) of transcendence' (Janz 2004: 117).

There is a risk of seeming to do an injustice to Barth by characterizing his position as positivist (though this characterization owes itself to one of his more sympathetic interpreters, Dietrich Bonhoeffer). What is intended by the label is the designation of a tradition stemming from Barth (Barth is not its only representative, though he is easily its most refined) that seeks to establish the priority, independence, and autonomy of God's initiative in revealing himself, thus giving revelation (as we have seen) its own, *sui generis,* positive objectivity. Even though knowledge of God is beyond access by historical investigation, God nonetheless actualizes himself in such a way as to be accessible through a unique sort of participatory knowledge for which God himself posits the conditions. Human beings participate in God's truth 'not independently but only insofar as our ways of doing so are adopted by God in grace. . . . This fulfillment is intensely real (as we might say) because it is based in the existence of God' (Hardy 2005: 32).

Where this position is vulnerable to critique (although it is usually a juster criticism of a certain sort of Barthianism than it is of Barth himself) is in the fact that it is the *theology* that can sometimes seem to be doing the positing. A Barthian style of theology is accused of arbitrarily *positing God* as the real referent of theological discourse, 'in a way that entirely overrides questions of rational authority and responsibility, and declares itself utterly free of its scrutiny, while fundamentally appealing to rational authority in other ways' (Janz 2004: 213). Revelation is set up as something having full authority over the insights of reason and sensibility, and as not in any way subject to them. It is completely exempt from the need to justify itself at their bar. This theological approach can be read as saying both that God is 'a possible referent of rational discourse or thinking' and that he is also 'entirely immune from the intrinsic obligations of the very rational discourse into which revelation posits itself': 'God "gives" himself in the kind of "aboutness" or intentional reference required for intelligible discourse without thereby becoming susceptible to the fundamental requirements of rational integrity' (Janz 2004: 120). It seems like trying to have one's cake and eat it too. A further serious effect of this model of revelation, if crudely handled, is that it renders lonely and passive the finite consciousness which receives revelation. It is divine agency alone which 'lifts the veil', or else miraculously delivers non-worldly truth into the human mind.

There is a risk in this variety of positivism that theological language will become essentially heteronomous, determined, as Rowan Williams puts it, 'from an elusive "elsewhere"': it is detached from any of the ordinary events on which we depend for 'the "authorizing" of our usual speech' (Williams 2000: 131). Williams's argument, by contrast, is that because Christian revelation constitutes a new and social reality, a new way of being, a new 'world', then it must be capable of being rooted or embedded in that world. In attempting to conform themselves to God's authoritative communication (his revelation), Christian structures of thought do not therefore need to deny their social rootedness. In the case of revelation, social rootedness and conformity to God's authoritative communication are compatible. Indeed, Christian structures of thought owe themselves (precisely *in* their social rootedness) to God's communication of a new world, a new way of being, which is more than instantaneous and more than individual-centred, and which allows for the growth and development of persons in community. So there is the development, as part of the new world of redeemed life in Christ, of a world of discourse in which Christians in their language about God 'develop meaningful constructs out of historical process and decision' in interaction with 'ordinary events' (Williams 2000: 132). And this ought not to be seen as an obstacle to a properly God-centred doctrine of revelation.

As noted earlier, Barth's theology is sufficiently aware of the dangers of a crude heteronomy to excuse it from some of these criticisms, which (like those of the reductionist view we have already laid out) are in any case criticisms of a somewhat typologized position here rendered 'ideal' for the sake of simplicity. The following things need to be said in favour of Barth's position. First, he does not think that revelation resolves all human questions and dilemmas by some sort of intellectual short circuit. Second, he does not have a crude view that revelation is just data. Third, he does not suppose that revelation is just an epistemic matter.

On the first point, Barth has his own highly developed sense of the unknowability of God. Jesus is not God's decisive revelation because he makes 'a dimly apprehended God' clearer to us than he was before (Williams 2000: 138). God is veiled in flesh and not to be discerned there without the light of faith. Moreover, there remains an unknowability of God even when he is revealed to faith, which is in part a mark of God's absolute freedom to decide when and how to communicate himself to us. A key point here is Barth's insistence that the unknowability of God is itself something revealed, not postulated by the mind as it comes up against the limits of its own ignorance.

Second, the fact that revelation is not just data is central to Barth's insistence on God's action in revelation. Revelation is not just a deposit—something left behind after a prior act of revealing. For Barth, as we have seen, revelation is the act of revealing, and what is revealed is indistinguishable from this acting. Both the act and the content are God himself. This retains a proper regard for God's continuous divine authorship in making himself known—always in free, personal encounter; never by proxy or at a distance.

Third, *contra* an oft-levelled criticism, Barth's doctrine of revelation is not just about cognition. The epistemic is not a substitute for the soteriological in his thought. There is something more than the merely epistemic going on in Barth's connection of soteriology and the doctrine of revelation. Salvation is not reduced to 'the dispelling of ignorance through the bestowal of "knowledge"' (Hart 2000: 54). On the contrary, Barth shows the intrinsic link between revelation and the event of reconciliation, for 'God reveals himself in reconciling acts': '[T]o be the recipient of "revelation"... is actually to be drawn into fellowship with (reconciled to) the Father through the self-objectifying form of the crucified and risen Son and in the power of the Holy Spirit who now indwells one's life in a redemptive manner' (Hart 2000: 54–5). There is certainly a new knowledge involved in this, for the restoration of human beings by their participation in fellowship with God must include the dimension of knowledge. But the restoration of the image of God in human beings is not reducible to that dimension. For Barth therefore, 'revelation and reconciliation/atonement are two aspects of the same reality: they are both ways of referring to what happens and what must happen' in order for human beings to be drawn into 'self-involving and transforming communion with God as personal Other' (Hart 2000: 42).

As noted already, there is an important distinction to be made between Barth's own positivism and that of a certain kind of Barthianism which closes the gap between the eschatological and the historical in a way that Barth himself never did. Barth talks of revelation (in the context of reconciliation) as being the arrival of an eschatological reality in which the human being is liberated in the whole of his or her being to correspond properly to God's own freedom and love. Barth is at the same time aware of an ongoing historical reality in which sinful human beings are constantly assimilating God to their own systems. Faced with these two realities, Barth proves reticent about exactly how the eschatological reality of new life in Christ really beds itself in the historical (or realizes itself in history). He holds the gap between the eschatological and the historical open. To his credit, this can be read as a concern not to obliterate the historical and as a refusal to claim an overconfident understanding of the mechanism by which the eschatological and the historical are related. There is a tendency in some Barthian positions, however, to talk less hesitantly about the relation, in terms which (for example) make the arrival of the eschatological a repeated, punctiliar interception of the historical (rather than a whole new creation that somehow overtakes it in its midst). Barth would not agree with such moves.

Nonetheless, though creditable in one respect, Barth's reticence about the exact relation of the eschatological and the historical has its own vulnerabilities. Principal amongst these is perhaps that he stops short of showing how revelation can be something with which human beings are in a collectively creative relationship through time, inasmuch as he isolates the revelatory event from any historical conditioning (it occurs in, but not as part of history). He sidesteps that aspect of revelation which Rowan Williams calls 'learning about learning'. To talk about the peculiar sort of learning that occurs in revelation, without thinking about how that learning is achieved and reachieved in time through its renewed and critically reflexive and deepening reappropriation by God's grace in ever-new circumstances and through its instantiation in concrete and transmissible practices in the church—this is to want learning without 'learning about learning'. It is to celebrate the 'achievedness' or consummation of revelatory truth in a model where 'truth [is] something ultimately separable in our minds from the dialectical process of its historical reflection and appropriation' (Williams 2000: 132). The objection that, to get involved in dialectical processes of historical reflection is to wrest revelation back from being always and only God's gift, may represent a failure to see the role of the Holy Spirit in its fullness, unfolding the truth of revelation over time and in the life of the community of the redeemed. Might it not be possible to see 'learning about learning'—just as much as 'learning'—as being God's work? This would be to insist as vigorously as Barth does that a good doctrine of revelation must be fully trinitarian, but to make that trinitarianism work in a significantly different way. Following Williams, it would be to say (against revelation's being either a 'generative point' in the past or an extrinsicist insertion into the present) that revelation is also the process of its interpretation—even in confusion, disagreement, and debate. It would be to make the passage of time internal to the event of revelation and to justify this with a doctrine of the Spirit. Our seeing of God is an ongoing process. It is made possible by Christ but is not exhausted in a single moment, not 'contained', 'placed', or 'left behind'. Instead, the seeing continues, as with the aid of the Spirit Christian believers find Christ in new places and in the exploration of new, concrete possibilities of ethical existence. There is an integration of revelation with history, with active and continuous scriptural interpretation, and with lived life, by means of which our ideas of God will be continually challenged and enlarged. In this account, there is an affirmation that 'the same radical renewing energy as is encountered in the event of Jesus' is also encountered in that 'generative power' which enables 'continuing participation in the foundational event—the forming of Christ in the corporate and individual life of believers' (Williams 2000: 141). Interpretation being central to this continuing participation and formation, we might say with Williams that the 'hermeneutical spiral' can itself be authentically revelatory (as also, presumably, redemptive), and that 'the revelatory aspect of the "hermeneutical spiral" is, in Trinitarian perspective, what we mean by the illuminating or transforming operation of the Spirit. "He will take what is mine and give it to you"' (Williams 2000: 143). This is as determined an attempt as Barth's to see the structure of revelation as corresponding in fully trinitarian fashion to God's own being, while retaining in a way that seeks to correct Barth a strong sense of its dimension of process.[4] Additionally, it offsets from a different angle the tendency to treat revelation in too 'noun-like' a way (the 'deposit' model of revelation once again, habituating us to think of revelation as some commodity—scripture, or apostolic truth, or a body of ecclesial doctrine—after which there is only (non-revelatory) interpretation and exposition). As we have seen, Barth resisted the temptation to make revelation more noun than verb on the basis of his emphasis on divine act; this corrective model opens a fuller dimension of the ongoing activity, simultaneously divine and human, which is intrinsic to revelation.

The legacy of Barth's doctrine of revelation, like Schleiermacher's, may be traced in the works of many subsequent Protestant and Catholic theologians. The Protestant line of succession includes Eberhard Jüngel, George Hunsinger, T. F. Torrance, John Webster, Colin Gunton, Bruce McCormack, Trevor Hart, and many others. Barth's theology also had a very particular fruitfulness in the so-called

[4] Another fascinating framework for a thoroughgoingly trinitarian doctrine of revelation, which we cannot treat fully here, is Oliver Davies's model of revelation as our being permitted to *hear* and *join in with* the inner-trinitarian 'conversation' of the persons of the Trinity. The conversation 'between God and God' which we overhear at Jesus' baptism, in Gethsemane, on the cross, and elsewhere, becomes 'the content of God's speaking *in* Jesus' (Davies 2004: 85), and our joining in with this conversation enables our human speaking to be penetrated by and formed within 'the creative rhythms of revelatory divine speech' (Davies 2004: 75).

Yale School (Hans Frei, George Lindbeck, Stanley Hauerwas, and their pupils), which is notable for its development of Barth's thought to show how revealed Christian truth is practice-based and ecclesially mediated—thus going a long way towards meeting concerns like those of Rowan Williams. Wolfhart Pannenberg is perhaps deserving of special mention amongst those downstream from Barth for the particular centrality he gives to the doctrine of revelation. He makes the bold attempt to think through the doctrine in thoroughgoing engagement with history. He follows Barth in insisting that revelation is the revelation of God's very self, not of truths about God at one remove. But he departs from Barth in his affirmation of the usefulness to theology of the tools of historical science. God does not reveal himself directly (for example, by his Word), according to Pannenberg. Rather, God reveals himself in his historical acts (indirectly), and these are verifiable by reason—for '[t]he revelation . . . of the biblical God in his activity is no secret or mysterious happening' (Pannenberg 1969: 135). Above all, it is the event of the resurrection in time and space that stands as the historical evidence of the divinity of Christ and of God's salvific intentions. The resurrection is the proleptic presence of God's ultimate future in time, and it is therefore of eternal and universal significance. Humans could not by themselves attain to knowledge of God and his future without such an event having occurred. Given that it *has* occurred, the event can be perceived as God's communication with 'natural eyes' (Pannenberg 1969: 135).

In a Catholic framework, the 1965 Dogmatic Constitution on Divine Revelation, *Dei Verbum*, is a landmark statement on the doctrine, and although it would be presumptuous to claim a direct Barthian influence on it, it nonetheless shares some key features of the positivist as opposed to the reductionist tendency. It links revelation to participation in reconciled relationship with God. God reveals himself 'so as to invite and receive [human beings] into relationship with himself' and so that 'through Christ, God's Word made flesh, and in his holy Spirit, human beings [might] draw near to the Father and become sharers in the divine nature' (*Dei Verbum* §2, in Tanner 1990: ii. 972). It emphasizes revelation as springing from God's free choice to show forth and communicate himself, which occurs above all in the 'total reality' of Jesus Christ's 'presence and self-manifestation—by his words and works, his symbolic acts and miracles, but above all by his death and his glorious resurrection from the dead, crowned by his sending of the Spirit of truth' (*Dei Verbum* §4). It is distinctly un-Protestant in the high status it gives to sacred tradition as the necessary interpretative counterpart to holy scripture—suggesting that they ought to be treated with equal reverence as flowing from 'the same divine wellspring' (*Dei Verbum* §9)—but the close identification of revelation with scripture is nonetheless one of its central concerns, which Barth would surely have endorsed: 'The holy scriptures contain the word of God and, since they are inspired, really *are* the word of God; therefore the study of the "sacred page" ought to be the very soul of theology' (*Dei Verbum* §24). The role which *Dei Verbum* gives to sacred tradition may, however, offset some of the risk that it construes revelation as a simply static body of material which does not need illumination and ongoing interpretation though time.

The effects of Barth's positivist approach to revelation in a Catholic framework can more directly be traced to the individual theologian Hans Urs von Balthasar, who owes much to Barth's insistence on the priority of God's self-positing initiative. Balthasar's approach to the question of God's self-disclosure begins with the object of faith—God in Christ—and then thinks outwards from it. This makes his theology contemplative as opposed to critical, concrete rather than abstract. Like Barth (and in opposition to the reductionist position), he will not treat revelation as simply a set of modifications of the believer's own self-understanding. Revelation is an encounter with other-worldly glory, in the context of entry into an all-involving relationship with God. Balthasar shares Barth's concern with scripture, whose underlying unity is given to it by its witness to the Christological *deus dixit* ('God has spoken'). Against Rahner and others, Balthasar sees the revealed Word as the 'peak' inserted into the world from above, such that 'the "peak," which is God's revelation in Christ and its proclamation, is not the outcome of the "base," the world and human nature, but is the peak *of* the base' (Balthasar 1989: 243). Balthasar saw in Rahner's description of a natural spiritual dynamism in human beings, and in his identification of it with the life of faith, a fatal blurring of the distinction between human apprehension of the divine and the divine self-revelation itself. To speak thus was, in Balthasar's terms, to confuse the natural searching of men and women for the truth with that ultimate vision of God which both fulfils and transcends those intimations of the divine. It was above all to lose sight of the way in which true Christian belief flourishes as a response to the encounter with the revelation gestalt of Christ. This is redolent of Barth. That said, Balthasar perhaps retains in his category of the theodramatic, and in his conviction that the church and the saints participate in the overall event of revelation, a stronger sense than Barth has of the historical unfolding of revelation in a way that has traceable continuities and institutional forms that participate in the fullness of Christ's revealed glory in an abiding way.

Balthasar is as significant as Barth for the way in which he resists, in his doctrine of revelation, a limiting concentration only on its epistemological dimensions. There is a strong tendency, at least in the modern period, to look at the doctrine of revelation only in terms of truth, and to disregard what the medievals would have recognized as its fellow transcendentals: goodness and beauty. We have seen how Barth sought to avoid that narrowness by his setting of revelation in its full and proper relationship with the fact of reconciliation. He thus safeguards the essential role played in revelation by right relationship (goodness). Balthasar has this safeguard too, but goes one step further in his attempt to recover the *attractive* role played in this by the vision of God's glory. By analogy with the aesthetic, God's perfect 'form' in Christ draws us into goodness (right relationship) as our perceptions are educated to see and appreciate him—and this is the full context of revelation. The instincts of the modern forensic intellect to make revelation an object of neutral enquiry are rebuffed in both cases.

At this point we may take stock by looking back to Caravaggio and the issues raised right at the beginning of this essay with the help of his *Calling of St Matthew.*

Summary

The reductionist and positivist alternatives in their extreme forms leave us in an unsatisfactory position. The reductionist tendency veers towards the idea that God's self-disclosure is perceptible in principle to all people (general revelation at the expense of special revelation). The positivist tendency veers towards the idea that it is not perceptible at all except by an act of God that must in some way overcome or bypass our normal rational and sensible faculties and our regular experience of the world (special revelation at the expense of general revelation). A reductionist looking at Caravaggio's painting might wonder why more of the people sitting round the table haven't noticed the light, or the pointing finger of Jesus, and deduced the divine presence from it. Surely these indicators ought to be enough? On this particular point, the positivist might reply to the reductionist that after all there is nothing in the shaft of light or the human figure *per se* to lead anyone to the firm conclusion that something miraculous is taking place, that Levi is receiving new sight. This same positivist, meanwhile, might be asking larger questions about what is gained by trying to paint such a scene at all. Revelation cannot be depicted. Divine reality cannot be reduced to the humanly imaginable. The painting as a painting can only show us a group of men, a dingy wall, a pointing finger, a shaft of light. To which the rejoinder might be: was the presence of an empirically real man (Jesus Christ) in a particular setting at a particular point in time merely incidental to the moment of revelation Levi underwent? Were whatever words were said and whatever gestures were made just some sort of irrelevant 'front' for 'some deeper supra-sensible reality in which the mystery of Christ [was] "really" hidden as something "subterranean" within immanence' (Janz 2004: 220)? Even if the material indicators are not in themselves enough, are they not at least in some way intrinsic to the event of revelation, rather than a distraction from its supposedly true nature as pure other-worldly divine act? What status, if any, should one accord the empirical when giving an account of revelation?

III. Revelation and Christology

It is in the person of the incarnate one above all that the issue of God's 'appearance' becomes acute for Christian theology, and this is a reminder of the centrality of Christology for any Christian doctrine of revelation. To be fair, both reductionist and positivist approaches in the modern period have acknowledged this in their own way (Schleiermacher and Barth are both extremely Christocentric theologians), even though with very differing results.

The facts of Jesus' life as brute facts are not revelation-bearing (*contra* a certain sort of reductionist). '[I]n apprehending the man Jesus, we do not as such and without further ado lay hold of God.... [T]he vehicle of revelation, even when it is hypostatically united with God, is not itself God' (Hart 2000: 52). But nor will the advent of revelation dispense with these facts, or obliterate their importance (*contra* a certain sort of 'positivist'). We might say that the facts are made transparent to something in excess of themselves. The Christological form of this claim would be that the veil of Jesus' humanity can to the eyes of faith become a transparent veil. But what is true specifically of the role played by the humanity of Christ in the happening of revelation is true for revelation *tout court*:

> [B]oth the recipient and the medium of revelation are lifted up beyond the limits of their own natural capacities and drawn into an epistemic triangulation, the third term in which is God himself. A person, an event, a text which in itself is not God and veils God nonetheless becomes transparent to faith and refers faith beyond itself appropriately to God.... The mystery is never fathomed but rather indwelt in the relation of faith. (Hart 2000: 47)

The Christian belief that in the hypostatic union the humanity of Christ is assumed eternally by the divinity, and never set aside, is the basis for an important defence of the empirical, for '[i]f the revelation of the transcendent God is truly to be the revelation of God to God's creation in any meaningful sense of the term, then it has to be the revelation of the transcendent God-with-us' (Janz 2004: 214). The veil of material things is not somehow in the way. If there is a way through the impasse of too narrowly reductionist and positivist views of revelation, it lies here, with an insistence that empirical history is the locus of the revelation of transcendence, and that without it transcendence is merely a speculative projection.

A good doctrine of revelation will prevent attention to the empirical from becoming only a concern with brute facts such that we cannot discern *God* with us, and such that there is no genuine transcendence to revelation. It will also forbid a concern with transcendence from being abstract such that we do not see God *with us*, and such that there is no real reference in revelation. What is needed is a mode of reference that is not circumscription by our own systems and categories—not comprehension, though respectful of the integrity of the operations of our reason and its capacity to remain 'in reference to' that over which it cannot exercise full jurisdiction. This mode of reference will allow itself to find its empirical object opening out to something more than reason can possess, while still having some recognizable relation to that object (even in its 'moreness'). Human perception and human reason will thus find themselves simultaneously dispossessed and affirmed. They will be propelled into a self-involving, self-questioning, and transformative process which will be an education in new desire and new goodness as well as new truth.

The opening up of a 'third term' in the confrontation between the recipient(s) and the medium of revelation is something that all good theologies of revelation in the modern period have had to attempt in different ways. Dietrich Bonhoeffer has left us with what is arguably one of the most suggestive and fruitful,[5] with his affirmation of the penultimate (the rational, empirical, social domain) in its intimate closeness-in-distinction to the ultimate. The ultimate opens up within the penultimate in the form of a question, as we confront and examine the phenomena of our earthly existence. It is not our own question—it is given to us. And although it is given to us phenomenally (in the penultimate), its answer is not. The question is 'Who is Jesus Christ for us today?' (Bonhoeffer 1966: 30; 1971: 279). This question draws us along the way of the cross into dispossessive relationship with one who is the non-circumscribable ultimate of existence. We find him incognito, 'hidden in empirical history *as* empirical reality, "in the likeness of sinful flesh" (Romans 8:3)' (Janz 2004: 220). He is the definitive revelation of God by allowing himself to be pushed out of the world onto the cross, in this way showing us the God who is not an agent in competitive relation to other agents in the world—not just one who makes particular differences—but one who makes all the difference, in but not in addition to all the differences that there already are.

The shadowy figure of Christ in Caravaggio's painting can be read as the one who provokes this 'who' question. His tangible presence is the condition for this question being asked, but not the resolution of the question. The question will only be answered by allowing some greater possibility to open up within the creaturely material (within the predicates) in which he is humanly present. This greater possibility, if it is worthy of the description 'revelatory', will be a converting possibility, one by which we are changed and embark on the eternal process of being opened from the midst of the penultimate to the fullness of the ultimate: to God's truth, beauty, and goodness.

[5] Paul Janz argues this well in *God, the Mind's Desire* (2004) to whom I am indebted in these closing remarks.

References

Aquinas, St Thomas (1975). *Summa Theologiae.* London: Blackfriars.

Balthasar, Hans Urs von (1989). *The Word Made Flesh: Explorations in Theology I.* San Francisco: Ignatius.

Barth, Karl (1975). *Church Dogmatics* I/1. Edinburgh: T. & T. Clark.

—— (1956). *Church Dogmatics* I/2. Edinburgh: T. & T. Clark.

Bonhoeffer, Dietrich (1966). *Christology.* London: Collins.

—— (1971). *Letters and Papers from Prison: The Enlarged Edition.* London: SCM.

Davies, Oliver (2004). *The Creativity of God: World, Eucharist, Reason.* Cambridge: Cambridge University Press.

Gunton, Colin E. (2001). 'Can we know anything about God anyway?: Introductory Essay'. In Colin E. Gunton, Stephen R. Holmes, and Murray A. Rae (eds.), *The Practice of Theology: A Reader,* London: SCM.

Hardy, Daniel W. (2005). 'Karl Barth'. In David F. Ford and Rachel Muers (eds.), *The Modern Theologians: An Introduction to Christian Theology since 1918,* 3rd edn., Oxford: Blackwell.

Hart, Trevor (2000). 'Revelation'. In John Webster (ed.), *The Cambridge Companion to Karl Barth,* Cambridge: Cambridge University Press.

Janz, Paul D. (2004). *God, the Mind's Desire: Reference, Reason and Christian Thinking.* Cambridge: Cambridge University Press.

Kelsey, David H. (2005). 'Paul Tillich'. In David F. Ford and Rachel Muers (eds.), *The Modern Theologians: An Introduction to Christian Theology since 1918,* 3rd edn., Oxford: Blackwell.

Kilby, Karen (2005). 'Karl Rahner'. In David F. Ford and Rachel Muers (eds.), *The Modern Theologians: An Introduction to Christian Theology since 1918,* 3rd edn., Oxford: Blackwell.

Lash, Nicholas (1988). *Easter in Ordinary: Reflections on Human Experience and the Knowledge of God.* London: SCM.

Pannenberg, Wolfhart (ed.) (1969). *Revelation as History.* London: Sheed and Ward.

Rahner, Karl (1978). *Foundations of Christian Faith: An Introduction to the Idea of Christianity.* London: Darton, Longman & Todd.

Schleiermacher, Friedrich (1988). *On Religion: Speeches to its Cultured Despisers, 1821.* Cambridge: Cambridge University Press.

—— (1999). *The Christian Faith.* Edinburgh: T. & T. Clark.

Schwöbel, Christoph (2000). 'Theology'. In John Webster (ed.), *The Cambridge Companion to Karl Barth,* Cambridge: Cambridge University Press.

Swinburne, Richard (1992). *Revelation: From Metaphor to Analogy.* Oxford: Clarendon.

Tanner, Norman P., SJ (ed.) (1990). *Decrees of the Ecumenical Councils.* 2 vols. Georgetown: Sheed and Ward.

Ticciati, Susannah (2007). 'The Castration of Signs: Conversing with Augustine on Creation, Language and Truth'. *Modern Theology* 23/2: 161–79.

Tillich, Paul (1953). *Systematic Theology,* i. London: Nisbet.

Webster, John (2000). 'Introducing Barth'. In id. (ed.), *The Cambridge Companion to Karl Barth,* Cambridge: Cambridge University Press.

Williams, Rowan (2000). *On Christian Theology.* Oxford: Blackwell.

Suggested Reading

Baillie, John (1956). *The Idea of Revelation in Recent Thought.* New York: Columbia University Press.

Dei Verbum. 'The Dogmatic Constitution on Divine Revelation'. In Tanner (1990: ii. 971–81).

Dulles, Avery (1983). *Models of Revelation.* Dublin: Gill & Macmillan.

Gunton, Colin E. (1995). *A Brief Theology of Revelation.* Edinburgh: T. & T. Clark.

Hart (2000).

Helm, Paul (1982). *The Divine Revelation: The Basic Issues.* London: Marshall, Morgan & Scott.

Janz (2004).

Lash (1988).

Schwöbel, Christoph (1992). *God, Action and Revelation.* Kampen: Kok Pharos.

Swinburne (1992).

Thiemann, Ronald (1985). *Revelation and Theology: The Gospel as Narrated Promise.* Notre Dame: University of Notre Dame Press.

Williams (2000).

CHAPTER 19

SCRIPTURE

STEPHEN E. FOWL

This essay will cover two interrelated sets of issues. The first set of issues concerns how Christians ought to think theologically about scripture. The second set of issues concerns the ways in which such theological thinking about scripture shapes the ways in which Christians might interpret scripture theologically. Of course, it is not always clear how to separate theological thinking about scripture from theological interpretation of scripture, since much theological thinking about scripture is closely connected to Christian views of God, the world, and God's relations with the world that are themselves drawn in various ways from scripture. Indeed, as Origen's *On First Principles* (Origen 1973) and Augustine's *On Christian Teaching* (Augustine 1997) indicate, these issues were traditionally treated together. It is not my aim to separate what belongs together conceptually and theologically. Rather, I am simply treating these as two distinct topics for the sake of organizational clarity.

I. Thinking Theologically about Scripture

Initially, then, I want to begin by thinking about scripture in theological terms. Most modern attempts to address the place and status of scripture begin by asking what sort of book scripture is (e.g., Work 2002: 1–14). On the one hand, modern historical studies have made it all too clear that scripture is a human work. The original texts which comprise the Bible were written by a variety of human authors (known and unknown) in diverse historical, linguistic, and cultural settings. Both the human authors of these texts and those who preserved, edited, and ordered these texts participated in and were subject to a host of social, material, and institutional forces which undoubtedly affected the composition of the Bible, even if scholars are not altogether sure how and to what extent this happened.

At the same time, Christians are committed to the notion that scripture is the word of God. In, through, or in spite of its clearly human, historical characteristics, Christians confess that scripture repeats, conveys, or reflects the words of the living God. At the very least, this makes scripture the standard against which Christian faith and practice need to measure up.

If one begins by focusing on scripture's status as both the word of God and the work of human hands, it seems quite natural to extend a Christological analogy to scripture in order to account for its status as both divine and human writing. That is, in ways that are analogous to the confession that Christ has two natures, scripture is taken to be both human and divine. Although there are some pre-modern theologians who deploy a Christological analogy to account for various ways in which scripture might function, the use of a Christological analogy to account for scripture's status seems to be quite modern (Ayres and Fowl 1999). Moreover, although this analogy is fairly common across theological and denominational differences, it is less clear that theologians use this Christological analogy in the same way.

For example, Karl Barth applies a Christological analogy as a way of taking scripture's 'writtenness' seriously: 'there is no point in ignoring the writtenness of Holy Writ for the sake of its holiness, its humanity for the sake of its divinity' (Barth 1956: 463; see also Work 2002: 68–74). Taking scripture's writtenness seriously in Barth's eyes seems to allow for some types of historical exegetical methods (Barth 1956: 469).[1] Because Barth fundamentally orders his views about scripture in the light of his doctrine of God, treating scripture's writtenness seriously means primarily treating scripture as the hermeneutical lens through which one views all other things (Barth 1956: 468). As a result, Barth's use of the Christological analogy does not demand any specific interpretative practices.

Vatican II's Dogmatic Constitution on Divine Revelation (*Dei Verbum*) also relies on a Christological analogy in its reflection on scripture. In this case, the analogy works to show that human language can be a suitable vehicle for conveying God's word. 'God's words, expressed through human language, have taken on the likeness of human speech, just as the Word of the eternal Father, when he assumed

[1] Barth clearly is appropriately wary of the exhaustive claims of historical criticism. He seems to avoid theologically corrosive historical critical claims by stressing scripture's role as human witness to a divine 'subject matter'. Barth takes this subject matter as self-evident. Subsequent Marxist or feminist biblical critics, however, simply extend the suspicion that the historical critics of Barth's day applied to the text of scripture to the Bible's 'subject matter'. See Fowl (1998: chs. 3–4).

the flesh of human weakness, took on the likeness of human beings' (*Dei Verbum* §13, in Tanner 1990: ii. 977).

Over the past forty years, however, it has become much more common for this Christological analogy to be applied to scripture in the way advocated by Ernst Käsemann. For Käsemann (1967), this application of a Christological metaphysic to scripture results in or justifies a further set of arguments and practices. First, scripture's human, historical status necessitates the wide variety of practices commonly known as historical criticism. Failure to see this is to lapse into a sort of docetism. Because the Bible is a human book, it should be subject to the same interpretative practices and standards as any other ancient text. In this light, the interpretative practices and theories of biblical scholars should be accessible to all regardless of one's disposition to the claims of Judaism or Christianity. Should an interpreter be a Jew or a Christian, those convictions need to be abstracted as much as possible from one's interpretative work as a biblical scholar. Biblical interpretation becomes an end in itself whose goal is either the unearthing or the construction of textual meaning(s).[2]

Upon deciding to treat the Bible as a human, historical text to be read like any other, the remaining issue for theologians, and Christians more generally, is how to treat the Bible as the word of God. Once interpreting the Bible as a human book becomes its own end, the question is how to move from the results of that work either to theological claims, or to the moral and ascetical formation of Christians, or to any other edifying practice which Christians have traditionally based upon scripture.

Attempts to distil the timeless truths of scripture from the historical particularities of the biblical texts and those texts' production represent simply one form of the attempt to figure out how to treat the Bible as the word of God after already treating it as the work of human hands. The so-called 'biblical theology movement' represents another form of the same attempt (Brett 1991: ch. 4).

Such attempts rarely stand the tests of time. It is usually just a matter of a few years before any given proposal about a unique or timeless scriptural theme is shown to have some sort of cultural or temporal antecedent. When scholars adopted the Christological analogy as a justification for reading the Bible as any other book, it became evident that critical scholarly activity would seek to fit the texts of the Bible into their historical and cultural milieu without remainder. The fact that contemporary theologians find so little in contemporary biblical studies to be theologically interesting further reinforces this view. This is not to relieve theologians of responsibility for attending to scripture and even to the work of professional exegetes. Rather, the failures of theological approaches to scripture

[2] Adam (1996) has noted the comprehensive failures of Käsemann's position. The Pontifical Biblical Commission's report, *Interpretation of the Bible in the Church*, is the Catholic version of this way of taking the Christological analogy. For a critical analysis of that document, see Ayres and Fowl (1999).

that primarily operate on this Christological analogy suggest that one should try an alternative starting point.

In his recent work, *Holy Scripture: A Dogmatic Sketch*, John Webster points out that doctrines about scripture must begin with and depend upon doctrines about the triune God (Webster 2003: ch. 1). The Christian God is the Trinity, whose inner life is reflected in the gracious and peaceful self-giving and self-communication of Father, Son, and Spirit. In creation God freely wills not simply the existence of humans created in the image of God, but God also desires fellowship with humans, offering them a share in the divine life. This is both the intention with which God created and the end for which God created. Given this, God's self-presentation or self-communication is an essential element in establishing the fellowship God freely desires to have with humans. Thus, God's self-revelation to humans is both the source and content of a Christian doctrine of revelation. Revelation is directly dependent upon God's triune being and it is inseparable from God's freely willed desire for loving communion with humans (Webster 2003: 13–15). In this light, the written text of scripture is subsidiary to and dependent upon a notion of revelation that is itself directly dependent on God's triune being (*Dei Verbum* §2). This recalibrates the relationships between God, scripture, and Christians in several interesting ways. For Christians, the ends of reading, interpreting, and embodying scripture are determined decisively by the ends of God's self-revelation, drawing humans into ever deeper communion with the triune God.

In this way, scriptural interpretation is not an end in itself for Christians. One might even say that the mediation of revelation through written scripture is not God's best desire for believers but a contingent response to human sinfulness. Recall that God speaks with Adam and Eve with an unbroken immediacy. This is also reflected in the description of God's interactions with Moses as speaking with a friend face to face (Exod. 33: 11). Further, Jeremiah 31: 31–4 indicates that the written covenant will ultimately be replaced by a covenant written on the heart so that teaching, remembering, and interpreting scripture will be a thing of the past. In addition, when confronted with Moses' permission of divorce in Deuteronomy 24: 1–4, Jesus makes it quite clear that there is a gap between God's best intentions for humans and the scriptural words of Moses which are offered as a concession to human sinfulness (Matt. 19: 1–9). These texts indicate that scripture is the result of God's condescension to human sinfulness. At the same time, scripture is absolutely important since it reveals the mystery of God's reconciling of all things in Christ. Thus, although the interpretation and embodiment of scripture is not an end in itself, as Christians engage scripture 'for teaching, for reproof, for correction, and for training in righteousness', they can confidently advance toward their proper ends in God, 'proficient [and] equipped for every good work' (2 Tim. 3: 16–17).

Another avenue which opens up when Christians think of scripture in the light of their convictions about the triune God is in relation to the history and processes of the formation of scripture. An emphasis on scripture's dual nature will obviously recognize that the text of scripture as we know it today is tied to a variety of historical, political, and social processes. Scholars may disagree about the nature of these processes, but it is hard to deny that a variety of forces known and not known shaped and were shaped by the text of scripture.

This recognition becomes difficult to square with a doctrine of revelation if that doctrine is divorced from its subsidiary role in relation to the doctrine of God. As Webster argues, just such a divorce occurred in the history of modern theology. Rather than a doctrinal assertion related to God's triune identity, theologians came to think of revelation as an epistemological category requiring philosophical rather than theological justification. 'Understood in this dogmatically minimalistic way, language about revelation became a way of talking, not about the life-giving and loving presence of the God and Father of our Lord Jesus Christ in the Spirit's power among the worshipping and witnessing assembly, but instead of an arcane process of causality whereby persons acquire knowledge through opaque, non-natural operations' (Webster 2003: 12). In this light, attempts to defend the divine nature of scripture tend to focus their attention on establishing either the incorruptibility or the benign nature of the processes by which the texts of scripture come to us. The most extreme manifestation of this concern is found in those theories or doctrines of scripture that require some form of divine dictation where the human authors of scripture simply record the words the Spirit speaks to them. Even though scholars probably know much less about the processes which shaped the final form of scripture than we are willing to admit, it is indubitable that every stage of this process was fully historical and fully human. Indeed, if this epistemologically founded doctrine of revelation persists, it really becomes impossible for the Christological analogy of scripture's dual nature to hold. It would seem that at this particular point the divine and human natures of scripture simply cannot coexist. 'Both naturalism and supernaturalism are trapped... in a competitive understanding of the transcendent and the historical' (Webster 2003: 21).

Alternatively, if revelation is seen as the triune God's self-communication, an activity that flows from the very nature of the Trinity, an activity that is graciously directed toward drawing humanity into ever deeper communion with God, then one can be more relaxed about the human processes that led to the formation of Christian scripture. This is because the triune God is not simply the content of revelation, but the one who directs and sustains the revelation of God's very self with the aim of drawing humanity into ever deeper communion. The conviction that God's revelation is ultimately directed towards bringing about our salvation also entails a view of God's providential ordering of history so that God's ends ultimately will be achieved. In this way, Christians can fully recognize the human processes (whatever they may have been) that led to the formation of scripture. At the same time, their convictions about God's providence should lead Christians to understand that, however scripture came to look the way it does, scripture reveals all that believers need to sustain a life of growing communion with God.

In this respect, Christians would do well to take on the disposition displayed by Paul in Philippians 1: 12–18. In this passage the imprisoned Paul begins by noting that, contrary to what one might expect, the gospel has advanced even in the midst of his imprisonment (1: 12). Indeed, Paul's use of the passive voice here makes it clear that God, and not Paul, is the agent advancing the gospel. Paul then goes on to note that many believers in Rome (most likely) have become bold in proclaiming the gospel. Paul further observes that among these newly emboldened preachers, some preach from good motives and others preach from selfish motives (1: 15). After commenting on each of these groups (1: 16–17), Paul surprisingly goes on to announce that, no matter what the motives of these preachers, Christ is being proclaimed, and Paul rejoices in this (1: 18).

The motives of the preachers, while important, seem secondary to the act of proclamation. It may appear that Paul pragmatically prefers to see the gospel preached than to wait until everybody's motives are pure. I do not think Paul sees the choice in quite this way. Ultimately, Paul is convinced that God is directing both his personal circumstances and the more general spread of the gospel. Thus, he need not be overly concerned about the motives of any particular set of preachers. Paul is able to see in the midst of his own circumstances that, despite appearances and contrary to expectations, God is advancing the gospel. Rather than expressing a preference for preaching from selfish motives over no preaching at all, this phrase is an expression of faith in God's providential oversight of the gospel's progress.

From a theological perspective it is important to note that a very particular doctrine of providence underwrites Paul's account here. Paul is confident that God will bring the good work started in his own and the Philippians' lives to its proper completion (1: 6). Paul's view of God's providence leads him to fit himself and his various circumstances into a larger ongoing story of God's unfolding economy of salvation. Within this larger context, and only within this context, Paul's circumstances can be seen as advancing the gospel. This view of providence enables Paul to rejoice even in the face of a gospel proclaimed from selfish motives. This is because the advance of the gospel is subject to the larger ends of God's economy of salvation. If this disposition is extended to scripture, Christians can both recognize the vicissitudes in the historical formation of scripture and still treat scripture as God's providentially ordered self-revelation.

Obviously, one cannot sustain any notion of God's providence apart from a fairly robust notion of the Spirit's role in the various aspects of scripture's formation. One can see this initially by looking in John's Gospel at the role Jesus anticipates for the Spirit in the lives of those who will come to produce scripture. The Spirit is the one who calls to mind all that Jesus taught (John 14: 26). Jesus also promises that the Spirit will lead his followers into all truth, truth that they simply could not bear on that side of the crucifixion and resurrection (John 16: 2–15). In addition, the Spirit will guide and direct the disciples concerning what is to come so that they can continue to abide in Christ (John 15: 1–11). In remembering the past words of Christ, leading and confirming the disciples in all truth, and speaking about the things yet to come, the Spirit's role in the lives of believers and thus in the production of scripture is comprehensive. The Spirit's work as the operation of God's providential ordering of things sanctifies the means and processes which lead to the production of scripture, turning them to God's holy purposes without diminishing their human, historical character. Thus, in calling scripture 'holy' Christians are not making a comprehensive claim about the purity of the motives of the writers and editors of scripture. These may well have been decidedly unholy. Nevertheless, Christians are committed to the belief that the triune God has revealed a passionate desire to have fellowship with them, even in the light of their manifest sin. Scripture is chief among God's providentially ordered gifts directed to bringing about reconciliation and fellowship with God despite human sin. Thus, scripture is holy because of its divinely willed role in making believers holy.

II. Interpreting Scripture Theologically

This recognition leads to a second main topic. If Christians see scripture as intimately connected to their beliefs about the triune God and his deepest desire for fellowship with us, then what implications are there for the ways in which Christians ought to interpret scripture?

Just as it is important to think of doctrines about scripture as connected to and dependent upon trinitarian doctrine, it is equally important for Christians to understand that scriptural interpretation is inseparable from and dependent upon God's desires for humanity. In this light, scriptural interpretation is one of a set of practices Christians engage in in order to enhance their growth into ever deeper communion with God. Scriptural interpretation is not an end in itself for Christians. Rather it is one of the ways (if not the chief) in which they can deepen their fellowship with God.

Although he uses a different set of images, Augustine nicely displays the instrumental status of scripture and scriptural interpretation in Book 1 of *On Christian Teaching* (1997), where he likens scripture to a vehicle graciously provided by God to bring us to our true home. With regard to this image, Augustine is concerned that Christians could find the vehicle of scripture so appealing and the ride so smooth that they forget the importance of reaching their destination. This is part of his larger concern that Christians need to order their relationships with their surroundings in such a way that they love the right things in the right way so that ultimately their love is properly directed to God.

Keeping both Augustine's specific and general concerns in mind here will be important in thinking about how Christians should interpret scripture. Initially, however, just as with doctrines about scripture, it may prove instructive to contrast this position with one that deploys a Christological analogy in order to think about how Christians ought to interpret scripture.

In the modern period both Protestant and Catholic biblical scholars have relied on Christological analogies to claim that proper attention to scripture's human nature requires that Christians practice historical criticism and, in particular, seek to uncover the intention of the human authors of scripture (Käsemann 1967; Pontifical Biblical Commission 1994). The Christological aspect of this argument is in fact quite limited. What one finds is more of a philosophical-hermeneutical argument which gets its initial momentum from a small Christological nudge. There are a great variety of conceptual, historical, and theological problems with this position which have received a good deal of attention elsewhere (Adam 1996; Ayres and Fowl 1999). For my purposes, I simply want to indicate a theological tension that results from deploying Christological analogies in this way. If attending to the human nature of scripture requires interpretation to focus on the intentions of the human authors of scripture, then what is one to make of attempts to interpret the servant songs of Isaiah Christologically or to read John 1 or Philippians 2: 6–11 in the light of the Trinity? It seems most unlikely that the original authors of these texts could have intended their writing to refer to Christ or the Trinity. Theologically, Christians have a significant stake in asserting that Isaiah does point to Christ (even if not exclusively to Christ) and that the assertions of John 1 and Philippians 2: 6–11 can only be properly ordered within the grammatical boundaries set by trinitarian doctrine. This sets up the same difficulty of relating the two 'natures' of scriptural interpretation noted above with regard to doctrines of scripture. Once one uses assumptions about scripture's human nature to argue for the primacy or necessity of historical-critical interpretative practices, the relationship between the divine and human becomes either viciously parasitic or competitive. Such a situation further encourages interpreters to think of scriptural interpretation as an end in itself.

Alternatively, shifting the focus from Christological analogies to a set of judgements dependent upon a doctrine of God will provide more resources for theological interpretation of scripture. If one begins from the theology of scripture already laid out above, one must start with the triune God's desire to enter into friendship with the world that God freely created. In the light of human sin, the Son of God takes flesh in order to bring about our healing and reconciliation with God. Through the Spirit's guidance and vivifying power, believers are led into a life of transformation whereby they become more deeply conformed to Christ.

These transformations enable them to deepen their communion with God and each other as they await the consummation of the ages. As they await this consummation, Christians are called to participate in the body of Christ, the church. As the locus of Christian worship of and witness to God, the church provides a context within which believers are formed through the Spirit's working to be the people God calls them to be and that the world needs them to be.

This brief overview of God's drama of salvation is most comprehensively and concretely revealed to the world in scripture. Scripture becomes the primary vehicle through which believers learn of this drama. Thus, scripture plays a significant role in this drama of salvation and definitively reveals the contours of that drama.

Assertions about scripture's definitive revelation of God's economy of salvation, however, do not mean that scripture is a self-interpreting text. All texts require and call forth interpretation. In day-to-day encounters we interpret in relatively unreflective ways without much difficulty or dispute. Texts written in other languages from the distant past are more complex. Adding the stipulation that scriptural texts require believers, because of their place in the drama of salvation, to shape their belief and practice in particular ways is a further level of complexity. Scripture calls forth interpretation. Until that time anticipated by Jeremiah 31 when there will be no more need for interpretation because all will know the Lord, Christians are called to interpret scripture. It is crucial, however, to recognize that, because of scripture's relationship to the ends of the Christian life, Christian interpretation of scripture is not primarily governed by hermeneutical concerns with philosophical conceptions of textual meaning.[3] Rather, Christians interpret scripture as part of their ongoing struggle to enter into ever deeper communion with God. That is, Christians interpret scripture primarily in the light of the triune God's own desires for communion with them.

Interpreting scripture in the light of God's ultimate intentions for communion with them provides Christians with an overall set of aims and purposes they should bring to their various engagements with scripture. This does not thereby necessitate any particular hermeneutical strategy; it does not require a general theory of textual meaning. Rather, this overarching aim opens up and regulates the various ways in which Christians will interpret, debate, and seek to embody scripture.

The remainder of this essay will consider several ways in which God's ultimate purposes for humanity situate Christian interpretation of scripture first and foremost within the body of Christ, the church. As a way of specifying the properly ecclesial context of Christian interpretation, it will show how Christian interpretation of scripture as an ecclesially based practice is integrally tied to other practices,

[3] For two philosophically sophisticated but ultimately mistaken attempts to do this, see Vanhoozer (1998) and Wolterstorff (1995). For the most part, these types of approaches are primarily concerned with ruling out interpretative anarchy or interpretative emotivism. For a specific response to this fear see Adam (2006).

thus indicating that, at its best, Christian interpretation of scripture is theologically regulated and ecclesially located. The essay concludes by trying to articulate what this means given the fractured state of the church.

Once one allows the triune God's desire to draw believers into ever deeper communion to function as the primary hermeneutical concern for Christian approaches to scripture, Christians must also recognize that they cannot deepen their communion with God and others through brief or sporadic encounters with scripture. The Christian life is an ongoing, lifelong process of formation and transformation. In this process Christians will engage scripture in a variety of ways, but with the overall aim of deepening their communion with God. Moreover, as God calls Christians to participate actively in the church as a means of deepening their communion with God, it is reasonable to assume that Christian interpretation of scripture will not be the work primarily of isolated individuals. Rather, if Christians are successfully to engage scripture in all of the various ways they seek to do, this will generally happen in the context of their participation in Christian communities. Further, contemporary Christians should recognize that they are participants in a tradition that is geographically and historically extended and culturally diverse. In countless and often subtle ways, Christians' engagements with scripture are (and should be) shaped by the successes, failures, debates, discussions, and prayers of previous generations of Christians.

Of course, the church does not exist solely to interpret scripture. The church is the proper home of numerous Christian practices. Thus Christian interpretation of scripture is intimately connected to a host of other ecclesial practices all of which need to be in good working order. Failure or distortion in one of these practices is likely to invite failure or distortion in the others. One could not hope to enumerate all of these ecclesial practices that touch upon scriptural interpretation. I will simply cover a few that seem particularly significant.

Truth-seeking and truth-telling in Christ must be towards the top of any list of ecclesial practices crucial to interpreting and embodying scripture in the body of Christ. On the one hand, this seems obvious. Debates, discussions, and arguments about scripture or anything else cannot be life-giving apart from issues of truthfulness. If truth-telling is to be a practice essential to Christians' arguments about scripture, we will need to think of it in Christological terms.

Here is a brief account of what that might mean. In a passage filled with military images, the apostle Paul commands the Corinthians (and all believers) to bring every thought captive in obedience to Christ (2 Cor. 10: 5). It is not that Christ aims to obliterate all thoughts. Rather, they are to be subjected to Christ's penetrating, healing gaze. Bringing all thoughts captive to Christ is a way of establishing or restoring their right relationship to the one who is the Truth. For example, think of the risen Christ's engagement with Peter around a charcoal fire in Galilee. Peter's deceit and betrayal is purged and he is restored in the course of being questioned by the resurrected one who is feeding him at the same time he interrogates him.

The truth about Peter is never glossed. Nevertheless, the resurrected Christ uses this truth to transform Peter (John 21).

I mention truth-telling initially for two related reasons. The first is that truth is the first casualty of sin. This, of course, makes it much more difficult to recognize sin, and our own sin in particular. The second reason is that truth-telling is the primary component of the practices of forgiveness and reconciliation. I want to turn to these two practices as essential for Christians' engagements with scripture.

To engage in the communal discussion, argument, and debate crucial to faithful embodiment of scripture, Christians must be capable of recognizing and naming sin, particularly their own sinfulness. This ability to recognize and name sin is not a one-time achievement but an ongoing process of transformation and repentance. Recall that the first of *The Ninety-Five Theses* is, 'When our Lord and Master Jesus Christ said, "Repent," he willed the entire life of believers to be one of repentance' (Luther 1957–86: xxxi. 25). Without a community well practiced at asking for and offering forgiveness, and without a community committed to the penitential work of reconciliation, Christians have little reason to recognize their sin, much less to repent of it. If believers think that sin is both the first *and last* word on their lives, then self-deception will always appear the easiest and best option.

When Christians' convictions about sin and their practices of forgiveness and reconciliation become distorted or inoperative, then Christians will also find that they cannot discuss, interpret, and embody scripture in ways that will build up rather than tear apart the body of Christ.

A community whose common life is marked by the truthfulness of Christ and regularly engaged in practices of forgiveness and reconciliation will be able to engage in the discussion, argument, and debate crucial to interpret and embody scripture faithfully in ways that deepen their communion with God. One further practice crucial to engaging scripture is patience. As a way of teasing out some issues around patience I want to turn again to Philippians. I will focus on what seems to be an inconsequential line in this letter. In 3: 15 Paul wraps up a long plea to the Philippians to adopt a pattern of thinking, feeling, and acting that is focused around the patterns displayed to them by the crucified and resurrected Christ. This pattern of thinking, feeling, and acting will lead the Philippians to do certain things and avoid other things. Developing such patterns of thinking, feeling, and acting will enhance the Philippians' prospects of attaining their true end in Christ. Paul then turns to himself. He does not claim that he has attained this end yet. Rather, he presses on to the finish line so that he might win the prize of the heavenly call of God in Christ Jesus. Instead of stopping there and moving on to something else, Paul adds that, to those inclined to adopt a different pattern of thinking, feeling, and acting, God will reveal the proper mindset to adopt (cf. 3: 15). After this impassioned plea, Paul seems willing to allow that others may think differently. This is not because Paul is a good liberal and thinks that in matters of faith people should be allowed their own opinions. Instead, as I noted above, Paul can display a certain detachment from his own argument because he is convinced that God is directing and enabling the advancement of the gospel. Paul does not have to coerce the Philippians into adopting his pattern of thinking, feeling, and acting because he is confident that God will bring both him and the Philippians to their proper end in Christ. This sort of patience must underwrite all theologically regulated, ecclesially located interpretation of scripture.

If Christian interpretation of scripture is ecclesially located and dependent for its success on its proper connection to a variety of ecclesial practices, then what is one to say about scriptural interpretation in the light of the fractured state of Christ's body? What sort of location does a divided church provide for Christian interpretation of scripture? Indeed, might one further argue that it is precisely Christians' interpretation of scripture that has served as the catalyst for church division?

III. Theological Interpretation in and of the Divided Church

First, as Christians and Christian communities seek to interpret and embody scripture faithfully in the contexts in which they find themselves they should expect to engage in discussion, argument, and debate with each other. This is simply a feature of Christian life between the cross and resurrection on the one hand, and the return of Christ on the other. For the most part, these discussions and debates do not divide and have not divided the church. Long before the Reformation, Christians engaged in rather sharp and substantial disagreements about scriptural interpretation without tearing the body of Christ apart. I would like to suggest that when such divisiveness occurs in debates over scripture it is not so much an issue of scriptural interpretation as the result of a separation of scriptural interpretation from a variety of other practices such as those mentioned above. These are the practices needed to keep the body of Christ whole in the midst of the inevitable debate, discussion, and argument that is part of the Christian community's ongoing engagement with scripture. More fundamentally, these practices are held together and properly maintained by love, by the love Christ has for believers and which Christ commands believers to have for each other. Thus, all church division is fundamentally a failure of love. All division proceeds from believers assuming that they are better off apart from each other than together (Radner 1998). Doctrinal or scriptural differences cannot divide the church unless there is this prior failure of love.

Although disagreements over scripture did not directly cause church divisions, the church in the West is quite clearly divided. It is therefore important to understand how those divisions might affect theologically regulated and ecclesially located scriptural interpretation.[4] In the course of doing this I will explore a variety of scriptural passages. Hence, addressing a theological issue I also hope to display a form of theological interpretation of scripture.

First, contemporary Christians should recognize that church division is a very different issue today than it was for Catholics, Lutherans, Calvinists, and others in the sixteenth century. At that time the issues were focused on where the true church was located and how to know this. Once the true church was found, all other options simply were not church. The problems of a divided church as we know it today are really the result of ecumenism. The more that Catholics and non-Catholics, for example, recognize each other as true Christians, the greater the problem of their division, the sharper the pain of this fracture. In this light, I would like to turn to some scriptural texts which might help us think better about this situation.

I will take my initial bearings from Ephraim Radner's difficult and challenging book, *The End of the Church* (1998). Radner encourages believers to read their current situation through the scriptural image of divided Israel. Without rehearsing Radner's views in great detail, I want to take up his invitation to begin to read our situation of church division through lenses provided by biblical Israel and her divisions.

Israel's division into northern and southern kingdoms was one of the results of Israel's persistent resistance to the Spirit of God (cf. Ps. 106; Jer. 3). Division is simply one manifestation of this resistance along with such things as grumbling against God and Moses in the wilderness, lapses into idolatry when Israel occupies the land, and the request for a human king. Interestingly, each of these manifestations of resistance tends also to become a form of God's judgement on Israel.

Take the example of Israel's request for a human king in 1 Samuel 8. Although Samuel takes this as a personal affront, God makes it clear that it is simply part of a pattern of Israel's rejection of God's dominion which has carried on from the moment God led the Israelites out of Egypt. This rejection of God results in the granting of a king. The granting of this request becomes the form of God's judgement on Israel as kings become both oppressively acquisitive and idolatrous (cf. 1 Sam. 8: 10–18; 12: 16–25).

We see here that one of the forms of God's judgement is giving us what we want. If we treat division in this light it becomes clear that division is both a sign that we are willing to, and even desire to, live separate from our brothers and sisters in Christ, and also God's judgement upon that desire. This separation in the form of church division is God's judgement on our failure to love as Christ commands.

[4] For a discussion of how church division might affect the gospel's overall claims to truthfulness see Marshall (1993).

One of the by-products of the Israelites' resistance to God's Spirit was that their senses became dulled so that they were increasingly unable to perceive the workings of God's Spirit. As the prophets indicate time and again, this sort of stupefaction and blindness is a precursor to judgement. Judgement, however, leads to restoration. Importantly, it is restoration of a unified Israel as noted in passages such as Jeremiah 3 and Ezekiel 39. This restored, unified Israel is so attractive and compelling that the nations are drawn to God because of what they see God doing for Israel. This blessing of the nations fulfils God's purposes in calling Abraham out from among his own people (cf. Isa. 2: 1–4).

If one reads the divided church in the light of biblical Israel and her division, then one faces several conclusions. First, division is one particularly dramatic way of resisting the Spirit of God. Such resistance further dulls our spiritual senses. Believers thus become further crippled in hearing and interpreting God's word. The response called for throughout the prophets is repentance. Whether believers' senses are so dulled that they cannot discern the proper form of repentance, or whether God's judgement is so close at hand that they cannot avoid it, one cannot say. Instead, believers are called to repent and to hope in God's unfailing plan of restoration and redemption in Christ.

The second set of scriptural texts one might look at are those New Testament passages which deal with unbelieving Israel. Romans 9–11 comes immediately to mind. Instead of devoting time and energy to figuring out which part of the divided church is the natural vine, which parts are only grafted in, and which are simply cut off, believers should remember that the God who grafts in also can lop off. There is no place for presumption or complacency here. Instead, Christians in their divisions should try through ever greater works of love to provoke their divided brothers and sisters to return to the vine. As Cardinal Ratzinger, now Benedict XVI, argued, 'Perhaps institutional separation has some share in the significance of salvation history which St Paul attributes to the division between Israel and the Gentiles—namely that they should "make each other envious", vying with each other in coming closer to the Lord (Rom 11: 11)' (Ratzinger 1988: 87).

In each of these passages believers can see some of the consequences of church division. Division is seen as a form of resistance to the Spirit of God. It dulls believers' abilities to hear and respond to both the Spirit and the word, which, in turn, generates further unrighteousness. Division provokes God's judgement and is not part of God's vision for the restoration of his people. While both presumption and complacency are real temptations, neither is an appropriate response to division. Rather, we are called to sustained forms of repentance, 'vying with each other in coming closer to God' with the aim of drawing the other to God. Finally, I want to look at the consequences of church division for the world. In this case the key text is in Ephesians.

At the beginning of the epistle one learns that God's plan for the fullness of time is that all things should be gathered together under Christ's lordship. Just as God's restoration of Israel brings a reunion of divided Israel and the inclusion of Gentiles, so in Christ, God will bring all things together in their proper relationship to Christ. It is important to note that this includes those principalities and powers which are not yet under Christ's dominion (1: 10).

For Paul's purposes, the paramount activity of Christ's gathering of all things is the unification of Jews and Gentiles in one body through the cross and resurrection. Ephesians 2 is focused on just this activity by which those near and those far off are brought together into one. This is both the 'mystery... made known to me by revelation' (Eph. 3: 3) and the good news which Paul has been commissioned to proclaim. As he reflects on this Paul notes that God has given him the charge 'to make everyone see what is the plan of the mystery hidden for ages in God who created all things; so that through the church the wisdom of God in its rich variety might now be made known to the rulers and authorities in the heavenly places' (Eph. 3: 9–10). The church, by its very existence as a single body of Jews and Gentiles united in Christ makes God's wisdom known to the rulers and authorities. As it appears here in Ephesians, the church's witness to the rulers and authorities is integrally connected to and may even depend upon its unity.

Seen in its most extreme light, this passage suggests that the church's witness to the rulers and authorities is falsified or undermined by division. At the very least, one must say that the church's witness is hindered and frustrated by division.

Here, then, are a variety of scriptural passages which help us to understand and speak theologically about church division. Each passage requires a different style of reading. Israel and its resistance to the Spirit are interpreted as a figure of the church to call the divided church to repentance. The reading of Romans expands on this to provide some admonitions by way of analogy about how to live in a divided church. Finally, Ephesians implicitly warns of some of the consequences of division for the world at large, especially for the rulers and authorities. No single hermeneutic or theory of textual meaning can validate all of these. Rather they are held together because they work in service of a common theological purpose. Describing that purpose will help to clarify and summarize the type of theologically regulated and ecclesially located interpretation discussed in this essay.

Although the above comments are only a preliminary sketch, it should be clear that I am not trying to plumb what scripture 'says' about church division. That would be to take the presence of the divided church as a sort of self-evident datum that Christians can best comprehend on some other grounds and then to try to correlate that datum with some set of scriptural texts. Rather, these and other scriptural texts, theologically understood, can help Christians begin to develop a scripturally shaped language and set of categories for comprehending church division and its consequences in theological terms. Such comprehension is but a more technical way of speaking about the truthfulness that comes from bringing every thought captive to Christ. Moreover, the assumption that scripture provides believers with the conceptual, descriptive, practical, and ascetical resources for bringing every thought captive to Christ is, perhaps, the most fitting way to reassert the central claim of the first section of this essay. That is, scripture is chief among the trinue God's providentially ordered gifts for drawing believers into ever deeper communion.

References

Adam, A. K. M. (1996). 'Docetism, Käsemann, and Christology: Why Historical Criticism Can't Protect Christological Orthodoxy'. *Scottish Journal of Theology* 494: 391–410.

—— (2006). *Faithful Interpretation: Reading the Bible in a Postmodern World.* Minneapolis: Fortress.

Augustine (1997). *On Christian Teaching.* Oxford: Oxford University Press.

Ayres, L., and Fowl, S. (1999). '(Mis)Reading the Face of God in *Interpretation of the Bible in the Church*'. *Theological Studies* 603: 513–28.

Barth, Karl (1956). *Church Dogmatics* I/2. Edinburgh: T. & T. Clark.

Brett, Mark (1991). *Biblical Criticism in Crisis?* Cambridge: Cambridge University Press.

Fowl, Stephen (1998). *Engaging Scripture.* Oxford: Blackwell.

Käsemann, E. (1967). 'Vom Theologischen Recht historisch-kritisch Exegese'. *Zeitschrift für Theologie und Kirche* 64/3: 259–81.

Luther, M. (1957–86). *Luther's Works.* 55 vols. St Louis: Concordia.

Marshall, Bruce (1993). 'The Disunity of the Church and the Credibility of the Gospel'. *Theology Today* 50/1: 78–89.

Origen (1973). *On First Principles.* Gloucester: Peter Smith.

Pontifical Biblical Commission (1994). 'Interpretation of the Bible in the Church'. *Origins* 23: 497–524.

Radner, Ephraim (1998). *The End of the Church: A Pneumatology of Christian Division in the West.* Grand Rapids: Eerdmans.

Ratzinger, J. (1988). 'Anglican-Catholic Dialogue: Its Problems and Hopes'. In id., *Church, Ecumenism and Politics.* New York: Sheed and Ward.

Tanner, Norman P., SJ (ed.) (1990). *Decrees of the Ecumenical Councils.* 2 vols. Georgetown: Sheed and Ward.

Vanhoozer, K. (1998). *Is there a Meaning in this Text?* Grand Rapids: Zondervan.

Webster, John (2003). *Holy Scripture: A Dogmatic Sketch.* Cambridge: Cambridge University Press.

Wolterstorff, N. (1995). *Divine Discourse.* Cambridge: Cambridge University Press.

Work, Telford (2002). *Living and Active: Scripture in the Economy of Salvation.* Grand Rapids: Eerdmans.

Suggested Reading

Dei Verbum. 'The Dogmatic Constitution on Divine Revelation'. In Tanner (1990: ii. 971–81).

Fowl (1998).

VANHOOZER (1998).
VANHOOZER, K. (ed.) (2005). *Dictionary for Theological Interpretation of the Bible*. Grand Rapids: Baker.
WATSON, F. (1994). *Text, Church and World: Biblical Interpretation in Theological Perspective*. Edinburgh: T. & T. Clark.
—— (1997). *Text and Truth: Redefining Biblical Theology*. Edinburgh: T. & T. Clark.
WEBSTER (2003).
WORK (2002).

CHAPTER 20

TRADITION

A. N. WILLIAMS

Discussion of tradition in a Christian context has often focused on the 'problem' of tradition. Tradition has often been perceived to raise vexatious theological questions more immediately and inherently than many other topics in theology. In reality, the 'problem' of tradition is not one, but a set of interrelated issues: how to define tradition; whether it is to be viewed as normative, and if so, how it is related to scripture; how tradition is related to the church as sustained and vivified by the Holy Spirit; whether, if tradition is living, there is not the possibility of corrupt accretions to it, and if so, how these would be distinguished from legitimate developments. Finally, there is a problem of the one and the many: although theologians often speak of tradition in the singular, substantial differences exist between theologies considered authoritative by various Christian churches, and even (though this is less often acknowledged) within individual ecclesial traditions. The problem then arises of how to adjudicate conflicts between traditions, or strands of a tradition: if tradition is normative to some degree, *which* tradition is normative? Christian reflection on all these questions has proved ecclesially divisive, although the sharp polarities asserted in the sixteenth century are less frequently maintained as black-and-white positions; today, the spectrum appears more as variations of grey.

The first problem arising in connection with tradition is that of how to define it: definitions have varied so widely that no consensus can be discerned even on this preliminary point. Yves Congar, for example, simply asserted that what tradition designates is too large and complex to admit of any capsule definition (Congar 1966: 234). Commentators do not agree as to whether tradition is written or oral, or whether it is a process of handing on doctrine, the doctrine that is handed on, or both. Some conceptions of tradition are so broad that they are not in any sense doctrinal or even clearly normative: tradition can, for example, be identified with the church's life or faith, its collective understanding and consciousness, or even with the abiding presence of the Holy Spirit in the church. Other views identify tradition with the Bible, or its interpretation, while yet others insist that it encompasses liturgy, canon law, or the church's life of prayer. Some regard mutability as virtually constitutive of it; on these accounts, it is precisely the fact that tradition is able to reflect intellectual and societal change which makes it a necessary companion to scripture.

While there is undoubtedly an element of truth in all these conceptions of tradition, those which identify it outright with the Bible, the church, or the Christian life effectively obliterate the category altogether; if we are to speak of tradition at all, it makes sense for the term to designate something that these other terms do not. There is broad consensus that tradition represents communal interpretation of the Bible which is above all, though not exclusively, doctrinal in content. The vast majority of commentators moreover specify that tradition's relation to the Bible is derivative, and in that sense, tradition is secondary in authoritative status, though it can still be regarded as normative: tradition is the *norma normans* (the rule that stipulates) while scripture is the *norma normans non normata* (the rule that stipulates but is not stipulated by any other rule than itself). For our purposes, then, we may define tradition as the church's sacred teaching, which undergoes at least linguistic reformulation over time, and which interprets the Bible in light of the church's worship, experience of the living God, and practice of the Christian life. Although tradition encompasses both dogma and theologoumena, it seems more appropriately applied to the latter when the theology in question is that of a thinker with some claim to authoritative status within a particular community.

If there is wide agreement over the necessary relation of tradition to scripture, identifying the precise nature of this relation has nevertheless proved one of the thorniest of the problems surrounding the issue. The question of when this problem first arose is itself difficult. Appeal to tradition itself implies—although via an argument that is necessarily circular—that one would look to older theology for guidance regarding the relation of scripture and tradition. As far back as Irenaeus, Christian theologians were insisting on scripture's need, not merely for interpretation, but for interpretation that was in some sense ecclesially sanctioned. Tradition in this sense did not function as an independent warrant in its own right, and the early church never formally accorded normative status to individual theologians or ruled on the status of ecclesial authorities outside their own jurisdiction, though the determination of heresy did function as a negative criterion of what lay outside normative tradition. In this period, then, there could be no question of any opposition of scripture and tradition.

Where one locates the beginning of such opposition is debatable. Commentators differ over whether a breach first develops in the Middle Ages. George Tavard pinpoints the moment of divorce in the question of Henry of Ghent: given a difference between scripture and the teaching of the church, which ought we to believe (Tavard 1959: 23)? Other medieval theologians avoided the difficulty of potential conflict by identifying the two in a way that few theologians of any stripe would unreservedly endorse today. Hugh of St Victor, for instance, claimed that, like the Old Testament, the New was divided into three parts: the Gospels, the apostles, and the church fathers. On this account, there could be no opposition between scripture and the patristic tradition, because the canon of scripture included what would now be considered tradition. In the early days of the Reformation, using a different argument, but ultimately to similar effect, Thomas More claimed that the words of God are both written and unwritten and that both must be believed with equal faith, an endorsement which, at least in its exaltation of what is unwritten, exceeds what modern Roman Catholic theologians have been inclined to claim on tradition's behalf (Tavard 1959: 16, 132).

Conventional wisdom holds that it was with the Reformation that Christian theologians first insisted on the scripture as the sole doctrinal authority (although some, like Tavard, trace such insistence to earlier eras, maintaining that theologians of the High Middle Ages were faithful to what he terms the 'patristic conception of scripture alone') (Tavard 1959: 20). In theory, the Reformers' cry of *sola scriptura!* denied any authority to tradition whatsoever, as long as it were taken to be, at least in part or in some sense, extra-biblical. The *sola scriptura* principle relies in significant part on the assumption that scripture is self-interpreting, not needing a body of attendant doctrinal commentary in order to stipulate answers to disputed questions. Calvin viewed scripture as such, and is on this point followed by some modern-day evangelicals.

In practice, the Reformers did not abandon patristic codifications of Christology or the doctrine of the Trinity, even though these are not found explicitly in the Bible, and most churches of the Reformation accorded normative status to the major creeds. According to George Lindbeck, the Reformers reconciled the authority they accorded to the creeds and confessions with their proclamation of scripture alone as authoritative for theology simply by ignoring the fact that the creeds and confessions *were* developments (Lindbeck 1967: 65). Lindbeck was not alone in pointing to advances in historical understanding as invalidating the *sola scriptura* principle or in calling for a deeper investigation of history in order rightly to understand development of doctrine. Jaroslav Pelikan summarized the finding of a World Council of Churches commission on tradition in three theses: that theological history makes the Reformation's rejection of tradition obsolete, that theological historiography makes the Reformation's depreciation of tradition untenable, and that theological historicism makes the Reformation's affirmation of tradition impossible (World Council of Churches 1961: 36).

In addition to those criticizing the *sola scriptura* principle on historical grounds, some theologians from Reformation traditions have also maintained that this principle is unworkable even in theory. Edward Farley and Peter Hodgson point out that the Reformers themselves created an authoritative interpretative key to scripture in the form of the Lutheran and Reformed confessions, 'an ersatz teaching authority in Protestant dress', and maintain that despite the Reformers' appeal to the *sola scriptura* principle, the differences between the Reformers' and Roman Catholic versions of authority were more apparent than real (Farley and Hodgson 1985: 72).

One indication of the unworkability of the Reformers' attempts to deny tradition authoritative status lies in the fact that *sola scriptura* was not the sole Reformation *sola*: the assertion that *sola gratia*, for example, was the heart of the gospel—or as has been more recently affirmed, the metalinguistic principle governing all Christian theology—represents an attempt to locate a core or foundation of the gospel and, as such, arguably reflects an implicit affirmation of the status of tradition: the Bible itself does not proclaim any such doctrinal 'canon within the canon', and those churches that have identified such a criterion have taken an extra-scriptural principle of the unique status of one doctrine as the norm of the interpretation of scripture—which is exactly one of the functions of tradition. That such a principle is extra-scriptural is attested by the fact that Christians have never agreed on what the core of the gospel is—if indeed there is one such principle—and the putative core is therefore rather less than self-evident.

Today it is hard to find even theoretical proponents of the *sola scriptura* principle. Writers from Reformation churches have increasingly acknowledged that scripture requires interpretation, and if one takes tradition to be simply the body of interpretation of scripture acknowledged as authoritative by the church, it becomes impossible to oppose scripture and tradition as sharply as they have sometimes been in the past. It is, however, possible to acknowledge scripture's need for interpretation and grant some degree of normative status to some of its interpreters, while still maintaining that scripture is the supreme authority, a position which is increasingly characteristic of evangelicals such as Geoffrey Bromiley.

If disengaging scripture from tradition seems all but impossible, the opposite impulse, to identify the two, seems no more feasible. If scripture is taken to be a part of tradition (so Bulgakov 1988: 12), and if the understanding of scripture *must* be based on tradition, then tradition is functioning as a control on the biblical message and any possibility of tradition's being shown to be corrigible becomes remote. Certainly, there could be little question of any Barthian notion of scripture's confronting the believer and the church with a message she resists hearing, although ecclesial history has all too often demonstrated the church's capacity to turn a deaf ear to even quite straightforward scriptural dicta.

If the estimation of tradition in the eyes of the Reformers' successors can no longer be straightforwardly summarized in a slogan, the Roman Catholic view of the matter is no more clear-cut. The Council of Trent has been widely regarded as holding that there are two independent sources of revelation, scripture and tradition; such was Cardinal Bellarmine's view of it. Whether Trent itself actually decreed as much has, however, been disputed by some Roman Catholic scholars. Vatican II, while rejecting the notion of two sources of revelation, affirmed both that scripture and tradition flow from the same divine wellspring, and that the church does not draw her certainty of revealed truth from scripture alone; hence tradition must be accepted and honoured with the same devotion and reverence accorded to scripture.

However, even scripture and tradition jointly are not authoritative in the Roman Catholic view. *Dei Verbum*, Vatican II's constitution on revelation, proclaims that scripture and tradition together make up the sacred deposit of the Word of God, but the task of giving an authentic interpretation to that Word is entrusted solely to the living teaching office of the church; this magisterium is, however, the servant, rather than the superior, of the scriptural Word (*Dei Verbum* §10, in Tanner 1990: ii. 975). In this respect, Vatican II extended well beyond Trent, which did not even mention a magisterium. Nevertheless, Vatican II declined to answer the crucial question of whether the whole of revelation is contained in scripture, a question previously left open by both Trent and Vatican I.

One especially problematic way in which the problem of tradition's relation to scripture arises is in connection with the formation of the scriptural canon. The word 'canon' can itself be taken in two quite different ways, as Bruce Metzger notes (Metzger 1987: 283). The books within the canonical collection can be regarded as possessing an intrinsic worth prior to their having been collected together, in which case their authority is grounded in their nature or source. Looked at another way, the collection itself is taken as giving the books an authority they did not possess before they were designated as belonging to the collection. In the first instance, the canon is *norma normans*, and in the second, *norma normata*.

Whatever view is taken, both the lateness of any attestation of the New Testament canon and the abiding differences over the parameters of the Old pose serious questions to the notion of scripture as solely authoritative. Those who appeal to the norm of the Hebrew Bible (as opposed to the Septuagint) to determine the canon of the Old Testament have simply pushed the problem of canonicity back onto an earlier community. Those who cite a doctrinal criterion—the extra books included in the Septuagint being deemed non-authoritative because they have been used to ground doctrines such as purgatory—effectively elevate tradition to a status above scripture, inasmuch as a predetermined scope of doctrine now functions to decree what is scriptural.

The scope of the New Testament canon has not generally been subject to such sharp disagreement—with the notable exception of the great advocate of the *sola scriptura* principle, Martin Luther, who questioned the inclusion of James and Revelation, and relegated both to the back of his translation of the Bible, again on doctrinal grounds. However if the parameters of the New Testament canon are clear, the late date of its earliest attestation and the murkiness of the process of its formation remain awkward questions for those who would insist on the priority of scripture, let alone its self-sufficiency. The first list of New Testament books that matches the one we know today is found in a festal letter of Athanasius in 367. He seems to regard this list as already agreed, yet there would have been little reason for him to enumerate it if the matter were entirely settled in his day. Unfortunately, he does not tell us where the list came from or on what basis it was determined. Knowing as little as we do about the origin of the New Testament canon, there is as little ground to assert the church as the servant of the canon as to assert the church as its master.

Part of what is at stake in the debate over the relative authority of scripture and tradition is the issue of the extent to which the very parameters of the New Testament were determined by the church and whether scripture is not therefore necessarily subordinate to tradition in at least one important sense. Advocates of tradition point—rather gleefully—to the church as the author of that canon, or at least as the codifier of its parameters, and accordingly insist that the church and its tradition cannot be subordinated to scripture. Upholders of scripture as the final authority in matters doctrinal acknowledge the church's role as articulator of the canon, but deny that the church formed the canon, properly speaking.

An examplar of the second position is Bromiley, who maintains that the definition of the canon meant no more than the recognition of an authoritative status that some works enjoyed by objective and inherent right. He denies the church had the authority to make its own canon; rather, its role was merely to recognize, endorse, and proclaim a canon that was already there. According to Bromiley, the criterion on the basis of which the church made these endorsements was apostolicity: gradually it determined which texts were written by the apostles of Jesus Christ and which were not (Bromiley 1983: 205). Whether such a view can withstand historical scrutiny is debatable. Modern scholars question whether all the writings of the New Testament are of apostolic origin: virtually no contemporary scholar accepts that Hebrews, to take one example, was written by either Paul or one of the Twelve. If one accepts that some of the letters traditionally ascribed to Paul are in fact deutero-Pauline, or not in any sense Pauline, then the parameters of the canon are not determined by which documents were written by apostles and which were not. Whatever the origins of these letters, it is still of course true that they were *considered* apostolic by the early church and on that basis deemed canonical. Nevertheless, if they were not in fact written by an apostle, it would appear that the canon is based on a false premiss, a possibility at least as problematic as what the appeal to apostolicity seeks to avoid.

One might avoid these difficulties by insisting upon the divine inspiration, not simply of the content of the books of the Bible, but also of the canon that enumerates them. On this account, over the process of time, the Holy Spirit guided the mind of the church, so that the canon was formed, not by the church as the arbiter of scripture, but as the recipient of the divine gift of self-disclosure, a gift that includes the wisdom to know what is authentic divine revelation. This account need not deny that there may have been obviously human, indeed less than edifying, factors in the formation of the canon, because it can point to the possibility of God's working through human frailty and sin—which scripture in any case claims over and over again. The difficulty is that on this account the process of forming the canon is formally and materially exactly the same as the formation of dogma.

Both the process and the principles by means of which the canon of the New Testament was formed remain rather murky, but the three principles Metzger identifies as determinative—conformity to the rule of faith, apostolicity, and *consensus ecclesiae*—were all determinations of the church (Metzger 1987: 251–3); scripture itself does not yield any such criteria. It is equally true, however, that the very existence of the church was attributable to that proclamation of the life and teaching of Christ that became crystallized in the writings of the New Testament, and that the tenets expressed in the rule of faith are drawn from the apostles' testimony, whose written form is the New Testament. The church and the Bible are probably best regarded as mutually constitutive, therefore, and it is unlikely, even if our historical information were better, that data concerning the formation of the biblical canon could 'solve' the scripture–tradition debate.

If the boundaries of what counts as scripture are decreed by the church, though, is not such an ecclesial determination already evidence that scripture has never and can never stand alone? Does it not in fact imply that the church stands above scripture, and that scripture, dependent for its very composition on the church, cannot be *norma non normata*? Here the advocates of the normative status of tradition face an awkward problem, inasmuch as some commentators point out that the fathers themselves regarded scripture as the criterion of tradition and knew no concept of the priority of tradition. Interpretations of the fathers on this point have varied widely, however: others maintain that for some of the earliest Christian theologians, such as Irenaeus and Tertullian, scripture is simply apostolic tradition in written form. Moreover, even the most ardent modern supporters of tradition tend to resist suggestions of scripture's insufficiency, despite the insistence on scripture's need for authoritative, communally endorsed interpretation appearing to imply as much. Commentators tend to resolve the dilemma by pointing to the propensity of individuals to come up with divergent interpretations and, in light of this consideration, maintain both the sufficiency of scripture and its need for ecclesially sanctioned interpretation.

Farley and Hodgson point out that a tradition of authoritative interpretation of scripture is something Christianity inherited from Judaism, so that the *regula fidei*, and subsequently dogma, functioned in the Christian context in an analogous way to that in which the Mishnah and Talmud functioned in a Jewish one (Farley and Hodgson 1985: 70). As Christianity inherited a canon from Judaism, so it inherited methods of interpretation of scripture, along with the very notion of methods and interpretations pronounced authoritative by the community. The issues of canonicity and the self-sufficiency of scripture are thus necessarily related.

Hence, although Congar insists that tradition is no more than the interpretation of scripture, he also maintains that the relation of scripture and tradition is one of mutual conditioning (Congar 1966: 37, 45). On such accounts, scripture is held to be materially sufficient but unable by itself adequately to present its own meaning; on this ground, scripture, tradition, and the church are deemed either inseparable or mutually inclusive, and the priority of scripture is expressed simply through one formulation or another of the *norma normans non normata* formula. Nevertheless, to the extent that scripture is deemed to be not understandable without the hermeneutic key of the tradition's exegesis, a commentator's protestations of its sufficiency may seem merely contradictory. It seems no more coherent to claim that the church never added its own doctrinal definitions to scripture, since the developed theology of the church can only be shown to be grounded in scripture rather than directly extracted from it. Those like Bulgakov who claim the absence of any opposition between scripture and tradition because both belong to the life of the church (Bulgakov 1988: 11) simply refuse to acknowledge the problems posed by the development of doctrine or by the possible difference of meaning between an idea couched, for example, in poetry or narrative, and one expressed in expository prose.

It may be helpful to distinguish between an apodictic norm and what one might call a monitory one: with the possible exceptions of conciliar decrees, few items of tradition have been accorded the status of norms in any absolute or finally binding sense: it is possible to view tradition as normative in the sense that it counsels theological directions and even conclusions without regarding it as furnishing propositions that are binding for all time. (The other possible exception would be papal pronouncements satisfying the conditions of infallibility, but these fall more under the heading of magisterium than tradition proper.)

The historically conditioned nature of tradition implies some element of development, but the notion that this development itself presents a theological problem is relatively recent. John Henry Newman expends a great deal of energy in his *Essay on the Development of Christian Doctrine* furnishing tests for the legitimacy of particular developments, a task which in itself acknowledges a potential problem, yet despite this meticulousness he is arguably rather cavalier in his confidence that the Christianity of the second and fourth centuries, let alone the twelfth, sixteenth, and all the intervening centuries, is 'in its substance' the very religion taught by Christ and his apostles, particularly given that there is scarcely unanimity in any one of these eras (Newman 1989: 5). Likewise, much of Newman's argument proceeds from axioms whose tenability is debatable: for example, the notion that the more claim an idea has to be living, the longer and more eventful its course will be, or that the whole Bible is written on the principle of development. In other respects, Newman uncannily portends the theological developments of the next century, as when he notes that a necessary corollary of Christianity's being a universal religion is the fact that in the course of its dealings with the world around it, it will develop. Here is a faint anticipation of the contextual and liberation theologies that arose in the second half of the twentieth century.

Newman's sanguine attitude to the development of doctrine has some modern counterparts, and for some, like G. L. Prestige, the notion that the tradition is actually expanding, and not merely spelling out what was always implicit in it, is scarcely troubling (Prestige 1948: 2). Such advocates of tradition tend to portray the mounting body of dogma as uniformly authoritative and, indeed, internally coherent. Others point to the very evidence of development as grounds for theological scepticism; of these, Maurice Wiles may serve as an example. Wiles notes two quite distinct approaches to development: those claiming that it represents the process of making explicit what had always been implicit and those claiming it is the process of discovering truths of which the church had not been fully conscious (Wiles 1967: 2–3). These do not seem quite as mutually exclusive as Wiles would have it: what is merely implicit may well be something of which one is not aware. Likewise, in contending that if the *depositum fidei* is propositional in form, later formulations reached through a process of deductive logic from the original propositions must contain an element of novelty, Wiles ignores the fact that in a process of deductive logic, the conclusion is supposedly contained in the premisses from which one starts (thus, at least, Aristotle). Nevertheless, Wiles provides a sobering counter to the contextual argument advanced by Newman, noting that although a truth can never lose its truth, it can lose its relevance, so that if its truth or falsity can only be determined in terms of a world view that is dead, it cannot be directly relevant to later societies (Wiles 1967: 9). Appeal to contextualization can therefore serve as a warrant both for dogmatic accretion and for dogmatic redundancy.

Vatican II sought a more moderate, middle way than Newman's: it speaks of a 'growth in understanding' and an advance towards 'the fullness of God's truth' (*Dei Verbum* §8). In either case, however, the need to affirm the truths of the gospel means that limits must be placed on the possibility of development. As Bernard Lonergan noted, the development of Christian doctrine is not subject to the revolutions that characterize the history of science (Lash 1973: 168), and conceivably one might go further still, holding that doctrine *cannot* be subject to such revolutions, inasmuch as it attempts to articulate eternal truths. Karl Rahner maintained that progress in doctrinal development is becoming progressively slower (Rahner 1966: 43), and if he is correct, then this is presumably due not only to the codification of more official dogma within the Roman Catholic Church, but also because many of the key doctrines of the faith have already reached a form considered irreformable. The implication of this gradual slowing would appear to be that the tradition would eventually come to a complete standstill, and so become as static as tradition's defenders insist it ought not to be, although presumably proponents of the retardation theory could still point to the *lex orandi* and *lex agendi* (the laws of prayer and of right action) as areas where tradition could continue to be lively and developing.

If tradition adapts itself to the need of different epochs, the possibility lies always at hand for some of its adaptations to represent corruptions rather than legitimate developments of any variety. This concern Newman was at pains to counter, providing his famous seven tests for distinguishing true developments from corruptions; he defines the latter as false or unfruitful developments, contrasting them with faithful developments, which retain both the doctrine and the principle from which they started. Newman's concern to show false developments are distinguishable from legitimate ones may be in part attributable to the circumstances of his time and the apologetic character of his work. Rahner, writing roughly a century later and in a more ecumenical climate, exhibits less concern to prove that developments can be preserved from corruption. For him the potential for error in theology is a by-product of its historicity. That truth should have a history, he points out, is far from self-evident, even astonishing, yet this history is inevitable given that revelation is addressed to us and that theology is, as it were, the dialogue with scripture that is always unfolding in the life of the church (Rahner 1972: 65). At an even deeper level, theology must always fall short of the God it seeks to describe and praise, simply because of the radical ontological discontinuity between humanity and God. Rahner's position is not so much the consequence of insouciance at the prospect of false development as his acknowledgement of the inherently human dimension of all talk about God. Rahner's freedom to admit the 'humanity' of Christian doctrine is perhaps related to the lack of any apologetic dimension to his consideration of the issues. Unlike Newman, who was not only advocating the position of his own church, but defending it against attackers, Rahner was concerned principally to articulate a position that would be consonant with the self-understanding of modern Roman Catholics. Nevertheless, justifying doctrinal development at the bar of internal consistency does not necessarily mean holding it to a lower standard; as MacIntyre warns, it is possible for a tradition to fall into a state of epistemological crisis, recognizable as such by its own criteria of rational justification (MacIntyre 1988: 364).

Newman's concerns have not simply faded from the debate over tradition. Some see the problem of false development as so acute that the only way to avoid it is through reversion to the *sola scriptura* principle. R. P. C. Hanson offers a modern variant of this approach, claiming that after the middle of the fourth century any appeal to the uniformity or consistency of Christian tradition is increasingly liable to be rendered invalid by 'forgery or invention or self-delusion' (Hanson 1962: 186). Tradition's inferiority to scripture rests in its vulnerability to corruption: scripture, once it has been deemed canonical, is incorruptible. On this account, however, scripture's imperviousness to corruption lies precisely in the fact that, its parameters being closed, it is in some sense static. In addition to the problems of the relation of the church and the canon, the difficulty with this approach lies in the open nature of the community which scripture addresses. As Rahner points out, revelation is always addressed *to* someone, and tradition represents the handing on of these revealed truths, spoken to the church (Rahner 1974: 24). As the addressed community changes, so the scriptural message in some degree changes as it is heard anew by each successive generation. The fixity of the scriptural canon—in itself problematic in one sense—is countered by the fluidity of scripture's reception, even though the historicity implicit in this fluidity is the condition of the possibility of false development. One answer to this dilemma is to face the problems of the articulation of doctrine frankly and enjoin, as Walter Kasper does, the self-awareness and self-examination always commended to the school for sinners that is the church: because the church is always a church of sinners, dogma may be true and yet be formulated in a manner which is too prescriptive, historically culpable, or ambiguous (Kasper 1967: 77).

The problem of corrupt development only arises because there is development at all. Without such development, tradition would be dead, and on Hanson's account, scripture comes perilously close to attaining the status of artefact, preserved pristine, to be sure, but not able to be related to new problems and questions as they arise. No more could scripture furnish what Congar calls the 'ever growing treasury of spiritual reflection' (Congar 1966: 7)—an important dimension of tradition, albeit often overlooked—than it could lend a basis to Christian ethical, social, or political life. False development might therefore be viewed as a risk that must be taken if Christians are to live their lives in faithful response to the Bible. On this account, the possibility of false development arises because of the comprehensive nature of tradition: tradition is comprised not only of the *lex credendi* (that which is to be believed), but also the *lex orandi* and the *lex agendi.* The insistence that the rule of faith needs more than solely doctrinal explication is old: Prosper of Aquitaine appealed to the rule of prayer as indispensable to understanding the rule of faith (Pelikan 1984: 17).

Equally, however, doctrine must avoid that form of corruption which is mere traditionalism. As Pelikan wrote: 'Tradition is the living faith of the dead, traditionalism the dead faith of the living', noting 'it is traditionalism that gives tradition such a bad name' (Pelikan 1984: 65). Such a theology of repetition is not merely misguided; it is, as John Meyendorff bluntly notes, dead (Meyendorff 1978: 7). The difficulty, then, is to find a way to confess the faith in the present, while avoiding the Scylla and Charybdis of either repeating dead formulae or reducing that confession to a 'mere declaration of existential attitudes' (Lash 1973: 57). Yet if Daniel Jenkins is correct that traditionalism comes into play when tradition becomes absolute (World Council of Churches 1961: 27–8), then there would appear to be no way that tradition could both be living and normative.

The tendency to contrast 'living tradition' with 'dead traditionalism', to connect development to liveliness and to deplore that which is static, is nevertheless based on a set of assumptions that are questionable. To begin with, these determinations proceed from a dubious analogy with living organisms. It is not clear why that which is growing is intrinsically better than the static, nor why that which is static or unchanging is necessarily inadequate, uninteresting, or bad, any more than it is clear that an idea that does not change is dead or irrelevant simply because it is unchanging. It is far from clear that key doctrines of the faith, those of the person of Christ or of the Trinity, for instance, have changed significantly over time and yet few would claim they are irrelevant to the Christian life.

As the problems of canonicity are perhaps avoidable by appeal to the Spirit's custody of the church, the traps of traditionalism and false developments may also be avoided through appeal to the Spirit's abiding presence in it. In Rahner's view, the danger of false developments cannot be excluded by human means, but only through the promise of the Spirit (Rahner 1966: 43). The Spirit's role can be taken as yet more positive and more fundamental: not only to guard against false developments, but as the only means by which the message of the Bible may be understood at all. As David Kelsey puts it, tradition names a process that embraces both the church's use of scripture and the presence of God, which are together essential to the church's identity, so that tradition and the concept of the church are dialectically related (Kelsey 1975: 95). This kind of conception of tradition is therefore inseparable from an ecclesiology: a positive, indeed normative, conception of tradition follows from an ecclesiology that assumes the church as the authoritative context for the interpretation of the Bible, and the Spirit as the giver of life and truth to the church.

The presence of the Spirit in the church guarantees also that her risen and ascended Lord will be present to her, and those who stress this point sometimes reach conclusions that have far-reaching ramifications for the question of the relation of scripture and tradition. Hans von Campenhausen, for example, goes so far as to claim that, for Christians, the Bible is not normative in the sense that it is for Jews, because in the church, Christ himself accompanies and takes possession over the book, and as a result, Christianity is no longer a religion of the book in the strict sense (Campenhausen 1972: 1).

A final cluster of questions concerning tradition springs from its diversity: if tradition is normative at all, then whose tradition and which theology may lay claim to this authority? If Christians have been unable to agree on which scriptural canon to use, there is even less agreement over which theology of the past possesses authoritative status, although there has been little overt debate of the issue: the canon of tradition has tended to be tacit. The fathers of the early church have the widest and strongest claim to authoritative status, yet their very antiquity means they wrote before the problem of tradition had presented itself as acutely as it would to later generations. The claim of medieval and Byzantine theology to normativity is limited to particular churches, and in the West there is in the Middle Ages already evidence of the signs of fissure that would erupt into the polemic of the sixteenth and seventeenth centuries. The most widely accepted items of tradition are the ecumenical councils of the early church. The first four of these (Nicaea I, Constantinople I, Ephesus, and Chalcedon) possess, in many Christian churches, either an explicitly acknowledged normative weight, or a *de facto* equivalent status: even the Reformers who claimed to reject tradition as a theological norm operated with a Christology that is scarcely imaginable without the developments of the first five centuries and their conciliar decrees. Eastern Orthodox churches accord normative status to the next three ecumenical councils as well, and the Roman Catholic Church, to the councils up through Vatican II. Although many churches of the Reformation would hesitate to accord normative weight to the decisions of the fifth through seventh ecumenical councils on such matters as iconodulia, the decree of the sixth council (Constantinople III) on monothelitism stipulated a theology of two wills in Christ which is again, *de facto*, the theology of all western churches, as well as of the Eastern Orthodox.

If there is only minimal consensus with respect to which councils are explicitly accepted as authoritative, there is still less agreement over which theologians speak normatively. The fathers of the early church enjoy the most widespread regard: even those churches professing to spurn tradition regard them with a respect bordering on recognition of normative status. The patristic period, then, enjoys a respect and authority accorded no other, and it is no accident that it was that era in which the doctrines of the Trinity and Christology were forged in their classical form.

Even within the patristic period, though, there is disagreement over which fathers are regarded as authoritative. Augustine is the most highly regarded theologian by the West, but the East pointedly refers to him as 'the blessed Augustine' and will no more consider his theology authoritative than his sainthood a given. Even in the West, there is an often unacknowledged division in regard to Augustine, stemming from a 'canon within a canon' in his works: those of Catholic proclivities tend to cite his earlier works, while the Reformation-minded cite the later, especially over issues of grace and freedom. The eastern fathers, conversely, function largely as normative for the Orthodox, but tend not to be treated as such in some of the churches of the Reformation. While the East has never acknowledged divergences among its doctors with the candour common in the West, it is nonetheless not uncritical of them. Many later figures in the patristic period, though still read and appreciated by professional theologians, have not in fact functioned as normative in any Christian tradition.

The question of what tradition is to be considered normative has sometimes been answered by appeal to the so-called 'Vincentian canon': *quod ubique, quod semper, quod ab omnibus creditur est* ('that which has been believed everywhere, always, and by everyone') (*Commonitorium* 2. 6, in Schaff 1980: xi. 132). The difficulty is that even in Vincent's time, it would have been hard to locate a doctrine that enjoyed such uncontroverted reception. One could point to the Christological and trinitarian dogmas which had settled into place by the end of the patristic period, but to claim that Christ's full divinity was believed by all is not quite accurate, given the predominance of Arian or semi-Arian views for large portions of the period. If one claims that these were not the views of the church, but of heretical sects, one is merely using a doctrinal criterion to determine membership of the church, and one that can only function criteriologically by appeal to an obviously circular argument. The problem is not solved simply by noting, as Pelikan does, that Vincent did not mean the *quod ubique* in any statistical sense (Pelikan 1971: 6): there has to be some sort of dividing line between what is viewed as universal and local, what has been believed always and what has been believed only sometimes, what has been believed by everyone and what has been believed only by some, and some form of quantification necessarily enters into this determination.

The difficulty of ascertaining which theologians function normatively within a given ecclesial tradition is exacerbated by the West's open acknowledgement of disagreements among its fathers and doctors. This candid admission of fissure stretches back to Abelard's *Sic et non*, often regarded as the first work of scholastic theology. *Sic et non* compiled apparently contradictory statements from past authorities, itself an exercise that cast doubt on their collective normative status. As Abelard acknowledged in his preface, the fundamental problem with which he wrestled is that the past doctors of the church present an array of views that seem not only diverse from one another, but even adverse to one another. In the face of this diversity, the Vincentian canon can scarcely function, although some of these divergences are more apparent than real, as one of the successors to Abelard's work, Aquinas's larger *Summa*, often shows to be the case.

It is undeniable that the theologians of the past do not speak with one voice, and any appeal to tradition as norm must confront this fact. Some churches have mechanisms for declaring a theologian to be authoritative (such status was accorded by the Roman Catholic Church to Aquinas in the nineteenth century). Other churches have *de facto* authorities (as Calvin is for various Reformed churches). Whether such status is explicit or implicit, however, it would be difficult to cite any theologian whose work functions in unambiguously normative fashion in any church. Despite Aquinas's status, for example, his view of the Immaculate Conception did not determine the shape of later Roman Catholic theology, and Calvin's influence in many modern Reformed churches has arguably diminished to the point that they can scarcely be considered Calvinistic in any sense.

Tradition, once the preserve of the more Catholic-minded churches and the root of some of the Reformation's major divisions, has attained to quiet acceptance as a theological norm. Whether or not it is conceded openly, the fact that very few modern theologians have found a way to articulate and defend the *sola scriptura* principle convincingly has *de facto* underwritten some form of normative status for tradition. The issue being faced by all Christian churches of the historically conditioned nature of the biblical writings and the challenge to their authority posed by this acknowledgement applies equally to authoritative interpretations of scripture (and indeed to other possible theological warrants, such as reason and experience), and a finally determinative theological norm, a last court of appeal for *quaestiones disputatae*, seems further out of reach than ever before. If the status of tradition was once a bone of contention between churches, its determinations are now disputed intra-ecclesially, dividing them from within. The current status of tradition is therefore in all churches markedly different from what it was in the past: its acceptance across the range of Christian traditions is broader than ever before, yet radical challenges to its conclusions are being issued from within even those churches in which its position was once secure. To a degree, this state of affairs is a function of the radical challenge to authority posed by societal change and intellectual movements such as postmodernism in the West, which has led to a general decline in the acceptance of any form of authority. However the general problem is more acute in the case of tradition, inasmuch as tradition imputes normative value to the past, a past that can be dismissed on the grounds of sheer irrelevance. Perhaps the best hope for avoiding the twin traps of naive biblicism and dead traditionalism lies in stressing the dialogical nature of tradition: it is the ever-unfolding dialogue of scripture with the community it addresses, the dialogue of the past with the present, the dialogue of the diverse voices of the communion of saints. To understand tradition in this way is to see it as the voice *of* the Christian community, and not merely as a 'disembodied' authority speaking legalistically to it and in the process exerting a moribund influence.

References

Bromiley, Geoffrey W. (1983). 'The Church Fathers and Holy Scripture'. In D. A. Carson and John D. Woodbridge (eds.), *Scripture and Truth*, Leicester: InterVarsity, 199–220.

Bulgakov, Sergius (1988). *The Orthodox Church*. Crestwood: St Vladimir's.

Campenhausen, Hans von (1972). *The Formation of the Christian Bible*. London: Black.

Congar, Yves M.-J. (1966). *Tradition and Traditions: An Historical and a Theological Essay*. London: Burns and Oates.

Farley, Edward, and Hodgson, Peter C. (1985). 'Scripture and Tradition'. In Peter C. Hodgson and Robert H. King (eds.), *Christian Theology: An Introduction to its Traditions and Tasks*, Philadelphia: Fortress, 61–87.

Hanson, R. P. C. (1962). *Tradition in the Early Church*. London: SCM.

Kasper, Walter (1967). 'The Relationship between Gospel and Dogma: An Historical Approach'. *Concilium* 1: 73–9.

Kelsey, David H. (1975). *The Uses of Scripture in Recent Theology*. Philadelphia: Fortress.

Lash, Nicholas (1973). *Change in Focus: A Study in Doctrinal Change and Continuity*. London: Sheed and Ward.

Lindbeck, George A. (1967). 'The Problem of Doctrinal Development and Contemporary Protestant Theology'. *Concilium* 1: 64–72.

MacIntyre, Alasdair (1988). *Whose Justice? Which Rationality?* Notre Dame: University of Notre Dame Press.

Metzger, Bruce M. (1987). *The Canon of the New Testament: Its Origin, Development and Significance.* Oxford: Clarendon.

Meyendorff, John (1978). *Living Tradition: Orthodox Witness in the Contemporary World.* Crestwood: St Vladimir's.

Newman, John Henry (1989 [1878]). *An Essay on the Development of Christian Doctrine.* Notre Dame: University of Notre Dame Press.

Pelikan, Jaroslav (1971). *Historical Theology: Continuity and Change in Christian Doctrine.* London: Hutchinson.

—— (1984). *The Vindication of Tradition.* New Haven: Yale University Press.

Prestige, G. L. (1948). *Fathers and Heretics: Six Studies in Dogmatic Faith.* London: SPCK.

Rahner, Karl (1966). *Theological Investigations*, i. London: Darton, Longman and Todd.

—— (1972). *Theological Investigations*, ix. London: Darton, Longman and Todd.

—— (1974). *Theological Investigations*, iv. London: Darton, Longman and Todd.

Schaff, Philip (ed.) (1980). *A Select Library of the Nicene and Post-Nicene Fathers of the Christian Church.* 2nd ser. Edinburgh: T. & T. Clark.

Tanner, Norman P., SJ (ed.) (1990). *Decrees of the Ecumenical Councils.* 2 vols. Georgetown: Sheed and Ward.

Tavard, George H. (1959). *Holy Writ or Holy Church: The Crisis of the Protestant Reformation.* London: Burns and Oates.

Wiles, Maurice (1967). *The Making of Christian Doctrine: A Study in the Principles of Early Doctrinal Development.* Cambridge: Cambridge University Press.

World Council of Churches, Faith and Order Commission (1961). *The Old and the New in the Church.* London: SCM.

Suggested Reading

Bromiley (1983).

Congar (1966).

Farley and Hodgson (1985).

Lash (1973).

Lindbeck (1967).

Meyendorff (1978).

Newman (1989 [1878]).

Pelikan (1971).

Rahner (1966).

—— (1972).

—— (1974).

Tavard (1959).

Wiles (1967).

World Council of Churches (1961).

CHAPTER 21

WORSHIP

BRYAN D. SPINKS

WRITING in the 1960s, the Eastern Orthodox theologian Alexander Schmemann stated, 'the problem of the relationship between worship and theology is on the theological agenda of our time' (Schmemann 1963: 165). Some forty years on and at the beginning of the new century, Schmemann's words still hold good. The importance of worship for theological discourse was pinpointed by J.-J. von Allmen when he wrote that worship is 'the sphere *par excellence* where the life of the church comes into being, that the fact of the church first emerges. It is there that it gives proof of itself, there where it is focused, and where we are led when we truly seek it, and it is from that point that it goes out into the world to exercise its mission' (Allmen 1965: 44). A similar point was made from the very different perspective of the Constitution on the Sacred Liturgy of Vatican II: 'the liturgy is . . . the high point towards which the activity of the church is directed, and, simultaneously, the source from which all its power flows out' (*Sacrosanctum Concilium* §10, in Tanner 1990: ii. 823). Whatever else the church engages in—be it detailed biblical exegesis, dogmatic formulation, ethical discussion, exploring methods of spirituality—it is made visible in its greatest numbers when it assembles for worship. Worship summons the church and makes it visible. And it is in worship that theology is articulated as doxology. A popular adage of the twentieth century was *lex orandi, lex credendi*, with the implication that it is worship which determines the common faith by which the church lives. The adage is in fact a modern précis of the words of Prosper of Aquitaine, *ut legem credendi lex statuat supplicandi* (*Capitula de gratia* 8, in Migne 1844–65: 5. 555). With 1 Timothy 2: 1–2 in mind, Prosper appealed to the prayers of the church to rebut semi-Pelagianism. In twentieth-century liturgical discussion

Prosper's words prompted renewed discussion of the place of worship in relation to systematic theology.

Aidan Kavanagh in his celebrated book *On Liturgical Theology*, in which he distilled some of his methods together with some of his frustrations of teaching liturgics at the Yale Divinity School, argued that worship is the locus of *theologia prima*, where, somewhat like the encounter of Moses with Yahweh at the burning bush, the 'ordinary' Christian and academic theologian alike are confronted by the experience of God which is always the substance for reflection on God (Kavanagh 1984). Week by week faith is built up by this continuing encounter. And this is the source and substance of most Christians' theology. All other forms of theological activity are *theologia secunda*. That is, they derive from reflection on the primary experience. Cult precedes creed, and gives rise to it. Or, to use the title of the book by Leonel Mitchell, 'praying shapes believing' (Mitchell 1985). However, the relationship between worship and doctrinal formulation is somewhat more complex than Kavanagh suggests. In his *Method in Theology*, Bernard Lonergan describes the interrelated steps which lead from human experience to human understanding. Experience ultimately leads to dialectic and judgement (Lonergan 1972). However, Lonergan notes that the resulting judgement is not final, because it is taken to experience which as a result now appears in a new way. When Lonergan's observations are applied to worship, they suggest that belief can and does shape worship; or, to invert the popular adage, *lex credendi, lex orandi*. Geoffrey Wainwright, in his book *Doxology*, argues that although worship is a crucial source for systematic theology, worship nevertheless needs the rigour of theological study to discipline its rhetoric. Wainwright, a British Methodist, points to the need of St Basil the Great to correct the doxologies then in use to exclude an Arian or at least subordinationist Christology and to promote a Constantinopolitan doctrine of the Trinity. Wainwright also suggests that it was unbridled *lex orandi* and popular devotion to Mary which led to the declaration of the immaculate conception (1854) and bodily assumption (1950), both doctrines which, for a Methodist, are unable to withstand the scrutiny of *theologia secunda* (Wainwright 1980: 238). For Wainwright, the closer a liturgical item comes to the universality of the Vincentian canon, *quod ubique, quod semper, quod ab omnibus creditur est*, the greater will be its importance as a doctrinal locus (Wainwright 1980: 243). While conceding that Wainwright had a valid point, some reviewers have noted that it was unclear which and whose *theologia secunda* should be regarded as normative. Wainwright sometimes appealed to Nicaean and Chalcedonian orthodoxy, sometimes to the Faith and Order Commission of the World Council of Churches, and sometimes to the hymns of the Wesleys. Certainly not everyone would accept the hymns of the Wesleys as any more an authoritative doctrinal standard than the apocryphal books on which much Marian teaching was based. Furthermore, it could be argued that, but for the use of the title *theotokos* in devotion and worship in some parts of fourth- and fifth-century Egyptian and Syrian churches, there would not be a Chalcedonian orthodoxy for Wainwright to appeal to.

More recent studies such as those of David Fagerberg and Kevin Irwin have attempted to bridge the chasm between the approaches of Kavanagh and Wainwright. Fagerberg seeks to develop a methodology to distinguish 'liturgcal theology' (Kavanagh) from both a theology *of* worship (Allmen; cf. Brunner 1968) and a theology *from* worship (Wainwright) (Fagerberg 1992). The weakness of Fagerberg's advocacy of 'liturgical theology' is that it fails to engage with the words actually spoken in worship and promotes a generic 'worship'. This weakness (at least, so it seems to those trained in liturgical study) is shared by many systematic theologians who have attempted to spell out the theological implications of doxology. Daniel Hardy and David Ford (1985) make a valiant attempt in *Praising and Knowing God.* Central to this book is the conviction that praise is the decisive mode of relating to God, and therefore the decisive way of knowing God. The authors argue their case from Old Testament psalmody and the *Divine Comedy* of Dante as well as from the Irish poet Patrick Kavanagh. The rise of the Pentecostal movement features in their discussion, with the observation that the mark of this movement is 'its worship and all that flows from it' (Hardy and Ford 1985: 67). However, there is no actual evidence of engagement with and analysis of Pentecostal worship, or the actual worship of any other tradition, but only a general invoking of generic 'praise'. The more recent work by Bernd Wannenwetsch (2004), which argues that worship is the locus for Christian citizenship and Christian ethics, acknowledges the insight of Aidan Kavanagh that *theologia prima*, liturgical theology, is communitarian, a joint enterprise springing from the regular performance of liturgical acts. However, despite the engagement with the Lutheran tradition and citation from eighteenth-century Enlightenment liturgical texts, 'worship' remains, as with Hardy and Ford, a generic term without solid illustration from actual worship. Kevin Irwin (1994) has attempted to overcome this weakness by engaging with the texts. The recent essays, *A More Profound Alleluia*, are a more successful attempt to show how doctrines such as the Trinity, sin and grace, revelation and Christology, eschatology and ethics find expression in worship, and how liturgy and doctrine illuminate each other (Van Dyk 2005). Nevertheless, a precise, agreed understanding of the relationship between *lex orandi* and *lex credendi* remains a matter of debate, and although many systematic theologians indicate the importance of worship in theology, and many liturgical scholars attempt to evaluate the theologies of worship, all too frequently a great gulf still remains.

Coupled with the question over what might constitute liturgical theology is that of the method or methods of assessing worship. Much liturgical study has been perceived to be only a study of historical forms—a branch of archaeology. Certainly, on analogy with biblical study there is concern to establish critical editions of manuscript texts. Unlike the biblical books which constitute a fixed canon, there are myriads of manuscript liturgical texts, including some which are known to exist but which are not accessible to western scholars. In many ways liturgical 'lower criticism', establishing critical texts, is still in its infancy compared with biblical studies. An example of this approach is Robert Taft, whose ongoing work on the history of the Liturgy of St John Chrysostom involves comparing as many manuscripts as possible, Greek, Old Slavonic, and others, together with ancient commentaries and other relevant sources in order to reveal a developmental history (Taft 1975; 1991; 2000). This development through manuscripts and commentaries helps to reveal changes in both the liturgy and theology over the centuries. Methods akin to biblical 'higher critcism' and redaction criticism are also used. For example, comparison of the many versions of the eucharistic prayer of Basil yields that the Egyptian and early Armenian fragments preserve the earliest recensions. The Byzantine version has undergone considerable expansion and rewriting—possibly by Basil himself—reflecting the theological changes of the 380s (Capelle 1960). The same applies to the East Syrian eucharistic prayer of Nestorius, which draws on the eucharistic prayers of Basil and Chrysostom, but has theological additions reflecting the Christological concerns of a school of Theodore of Mopsuestia (Spinks 1996). Important also is the sociocultural context of worship. For example, although some feminists have castigated the old service of churching or thanksgiving after childbirth for denigrating women as unclean, the work of David Cressy (1997) shows that in Tudor and Stuart England it was an important and popular social occasion for women.

These methods tend to presuppose some written text. However, worship is something which is to be done or performed. A written or printed text is always only a score awaiting performance; and in many traditions the worship score is entirely oral and linguistically variable. More recently, therefore, terminology and grids from anthropological ritual studies have been pressed into service in attempts to give further clarity to the deep ritual structures of worship. Performance theory—be it from theatre or from linguistic theory such as that set forth by J. L. Austin—has furthered understanding of both movement and ceremonial as well as the function of language in worship. Jean Ladrière (1973) argues that liturgical language cannot be analysed in terms of information theory because it does not consist in the reporting of events, the description of objects, or the handling of data. Rather, the language of worship is characterized by a certain form of action. It puts something into practice or operation. The language of worship does not merely give expression to attitudes; it itself creates them. Lessons for worship have also been drawn from Ricoeur and Gadamer. Bridget Nichols (1996), for example, uses Ricoeur to analyse different Anglican rites, and argues that liturgy enshrines the promises of the kingdom and invites participants to appropriate for themselves the promises of the discourse. Siobhán Garrigan (2004) has used Habermas's theory of communicative action to suggest two things. First, a method by which theology can access the ritual symbols by which faith is formed;

and secondly, a metaphor of intersubjectivity with which theology can propose an interpretative, rather than an instrumental, understanding of sacrament. Combining these two in fieldwork studies of both marginal and mainstream Christian eucharists leads Garrigan to suggest a radical intersubjectivity as a key contemporary way of speaking of God.

From the question of methodologies there has emerged at the beginning of the twenty-first century some controversy over the place and authority of historic forms of worship. The liturgical movement, which was in origin Roman Catholic, but which both spread to and had counterparts in other western churches, was originally a movement for renewal of worship as the place of formation for the church as the body of Christ. As it progressed, it became a movement which called for liturgical reform based on historical development. The Constitution on the Sacred Liturgy of Vatican II resulted in complete revision of Roman Catholic forms of worship, which until then, apart from minor changes, had been in place since the revisions set forth by the Council of Trent. Throughout the 1960s, 1970s, and 1980s, most western churches revised their liturgical forms, at least once, and sometimes two or three times. Those decades saw an unprecedented level of new liturgical compilation. However, one strange phenomenon was the almost unchallenged assumption that pre-seventh-century liturgical forms were authoritative for twentieth-century churches; they were given almost unconscious privileged status as sources and inspiration for worship revision. Alan Hayes has described it as a 'meta-narrative of a liturgical golden age before Nicaea, followed by medieval deformity, capped by Protestant error, and happily concluded by the recovery of true tradition by the Liturgical Movement' which controlled much subsequent liturgical research and was repeatedly cited by liturgists and denominational leaders as a rationale for liturgical revision (Hayes 2000: 31). A major document has been the so-called *Apostolic Tradition* (*c.* 215), attributed to Hippolytus, (anti-) bishop of Rome. In 1551 a headless statue was uncovered in Rome, containing a plinth with a list of works, some of which were known to be by someone called Hippolytus. It was assumed that there was only one Hippolytus and that all the works on the plinth were by this person. One work listed, but unknown, was entitled *Apostolic Tradition.* A large number of church orders, associated mainly with Egypt, but also with Syria, and one existing in Latin, were known to share a large body of material in common. At the beginning of the twentieth century, E. Schwarz and R. H. Connolly, apparently working independently, isolated the common material in these church orders, a sort of liturgical 'Q', and identified it as a missing work by Hippolytus. Popularized in editions by B. S. Easton in the USA, Gregory Dix in the UK, and Dom Bernard Botte in the world of Catholic liturgical scholarship, liturgical scholars and revisers took it for granted that the document outlined representative forms of worship found throughout the western church, and even perhaps the East, *c.* 215. It seemed self-evident that what was used in 215 should be reused in the twentieth century. Thus the eucharistic prayer of

Hippolytus—even though the document cites it as one suitable for a bishop to use on the occasion of his ordination—was adopted by many denominational worship books either wholesale or in adapted form. The ordination prayer for bishops was adopted by the Roman Catholic Church and the Episcopal Church of the USA. The *Apostolic Tradition*'s instructions regarding the catechuminate and baptism were used in conjunction with the mystagogical catecheses and lectures of Cyril of Jerusalem, Theodore of Mopsuestia, John Chrysostom, and Ambrose to structure new rites of Christian initiation.

The question posed more recently is twofold. First, why should this era have been singled out as something of a 'golden age'? Secondly, and more devastatingly, what happens when subsequent scholarship indicates that an ancient and authentic source is not so ancient and not so authentic after all?

Recent scholarship has called into question the authenticity and normativity of the so-called *Apostolic Tradition*. The statue is now regarded as having been of a woman, and thus not Hippolytus; there are a number of shadowy figures with the name Hippolytus in third-century Rome; and the group which seems to have owned the statue and library seems to have been a conservative dissident group. The actual liturgical material is seen to consist of at least three redactions. Although one recent work has attempted to date the latest redaction in 235, the extensive commentary by Paul Bradshaw, Maxwell Johnson, and Edward Phillips (2002) suggests that the composite document dates from the fourth century and is not representative of any church of the time. When this document, which formed the cornerstone of the 'golden age', is removed from the picture, the result is that we know very little of how the church worshipped prior to the fourth century. This debacle arising from drastic revisionist historical study raises a fundamental question of whether scholarly opinion regarding historical texts should be given so much weight in the revision of forms of worship. Antiquity and tradition were promoted over questions of doctrine and pastoral suitability. The contemporary church may wish to draw on many areas of historic liturgy, but to privilege one particular document, or one particular era, for no other reason than its supposed antiquity, seems a highly questionable methodology and theology. In terms of postmodernist parlance, the metanarrative that the church of the first four centuries was a golden age, and everything thereafter was 'downhill', appears to be modernist prejudice at its worst. The whole role that historical studies and reconstructions can play in revision of worship, unquestioned in the 1960s and 1970s, is now under debate.

Related to this is the question of the role of culture in worship. In recent debate it has taken at least three forms. First, in terms of global Christianity, is the question of how far western forms of worship and, with them, alien forms of western culture have been unnecessarily imposed on other cultures. Second, in terms of popular western culture, is the desirability or otherwise of adopting modern entertainment methods and marketing techniques in worship. Third, from the more esoteric and intellectual western academe, the question has been raised concerning the implications of postmodernism for worship, in particular, in assessing worship forms authored in the late twentieth century.

The question of culture and its relation to western and non-western liturgy has been the occasion of a number of conferences and books, many of which generate more heat than light. Frequently, discussions remain at a theoretical level, discussing culture and worship in broad terms.

Since the gospel and the worship which it calls forth are not acultural, but are always embodied in particular cultures, it is evident that certain cultural characteristics will be reflected in worship—in its language and performance. Thus for example the East Syrian eucharistic prayer of Addai and Mari, being a Syriac composition which perhaps pre-dates Nicaea, has certain expressions which mark it as early Syrian rather than late Byzantine. Or again, Edmund Bishop, in a celebrated essay entitled 'The Genius of the Roman Rite', drew attention to the simplicity and sobriety of the Roman prayers in contrast to the more exuberant form of the Gallican and Mozarabic rites, illustrating 'a style, a run of thought, and a mode of expression so clearly different as to declare the two things to be the product of the mind, spirit, and genius of two different peoples' (Bishop 1917: 14). However, these examples come from a time of oral, or at least fluid, forms. With the advent of the printing press, together with both Catholic and Protestant versions of uniformity, the natural tendency for inculturation of liturgy was severely curtailed.

It is generally recognized that missionaries—be they Syrians in India in the fifth century, English in Africa, or American Presbyterians in Korea in the nineteenth century—import not only the gospel, but the gospel in the cultural dress of their world. It might be argued that Syrian Christianity, which retains Semitic characteristics, may also have retained something akin to the culture of first-century Palestine. Catholic missionaries brought with them the Tridentine forms of worship with a fairly rigid text and style of celebration. English missionaries brought with them either a Tudor/Stuart form of worship, or, in the case of Methodists, nineteenth-century revisions of Wesley, together with their hymnals and European style of music. In the late twentieth century, conscious efforts have been made to inculturate the forms of worship. Thus for example in India the Catholic National Biblical, Catechetical and Liturgical Centre at Bangalore pioneered a mass for India which included prayers using Sanskrit religious concepts, readings from Hindu scriptures, and ceremonial associated with Hindu devotional customs. In Africa a mass was prepared for Zaire, again attempting to reflect concepts and gestures more in keeping with the country's culture than the corridors of the Vatican. This quest raises questions of at what point a particular culture, especially when it is closely tied with a religion, so invades worship as to make it syncretistic or obscure the gospel and Christian faith. Here theolgians have appealed to the classic work of H. Richard Niebuhr, *Christ and Culture.* Of the five categories Niebuhr proposed, three seem to be important ingredients for assessing theologically balanced worship:

Christ of culture. The incarnation confirms the creation as God's deliberate act and as intrinsically good. Worship will affirm those things in human culture which are in harmony with the gospel: law and order, peace and justice, 'neutral' religious customs such as gesture or symbolism (e.g., the Advent wreath).

Christ against culture. God in Christ judges the world and convicts it of sin. The incarnation and the divine affirmation of the world cannot be separated from the atonement, the resurrection, and the eschaton. There are aways human activities which are called in question by the gospel and worship.

Christ the transformer of culture. God's forgiveness and the call to repentance implies a transformation of culture in which Christian theology, and Christian worship, should play a part. The Ditchingham Faith and Order report (World Council of Churches 1995: 16) offers the following:

> Liturgical inculturation operates according to basic principles emerging from the nature of Christian worship, which is
>
> i. trinitarian in nature and orientation;
> ii. biblically grounded; hence the Bible is one indispensable source of worship's language, signs, and prayers;
> iii. at once the action of Christ the priest and of the church his people; hence it is a doxological action in the power of the Holy Spirit;
> iv. always the anamnesis of the mystery of Jesus Christ, a mystery which centers on his death, resurrection, the sending of the Holy Spirit, and his coming again;
> v. the gathering of the priestly people who respond in faith to God's gratuitous call; through the assembly the one, holy, catholic, and apostolic church is made present and signified;
> vi. a privileged occasion at which God is present in the proclaimed Word, in the sacraments, and in the other forms of Christian prayer, as well as in the assembly gathered in worship; and
> vii. at once remembrance, communion, and expectation; hence its celebration expresses hope of the future glory and dedication to the work of building the earthly city in the image of the heavenly.

Western scholars have found it easy to theorize and encourage churches in non-western cultures to embark upon a de-westernization of their worship. As commendable as this is, it overlooks the impact of modern western global culture on all other cultures, which are constantly absorbing and adapting the global culture into their own. Furthermore it is easy for western scholars to be oblivious to just how far their own worship is influenced by, and even at times compromised by, the modern global culture.

Whereas many mainstream churches were busy drawing on historic forms and authoring new prayers for traditional structures and presentation styles of worship, other churches, mainly evangelical in nature, have turned to other sources for inspiration, and have produced 'seeker' services. Perhaps the most famous of these is Willow Creek Church near Chicago USA. The models seem to be the shopping mall, Disney, and customer-sensitive companies, with the conviction that both non-churched and traditionally churched people need to be made comfortable and entertained. In one sense this is simply a continuation of the approach of the nineteenth-century evangelist Charles Finney, who abandoned what was then the traditional Presbyterian form of service and proclaimed that the worship leader should use whatever it takes. The worship of seeker services reflects a culture which is used to contemporary (MTV) music and the television and video screen, with the ability to switch channels if something is deemed uninteresting. It is the culture of the fun and fantasy of a Disney world, as well as of the mall, and the international corporation. Kimon Sargeant observes:

> Seeker churches want to surprise, to move, and eventually to captivate the hearts of their attenders. And they claim that by mirroring the forms of contemporary culture and by deemphasizing the outdated traditions of church services they have found a new way to cultivate more genuine, less ritualistic worship. (Sargeant 2000: 56)

Opponents point out that ultimately the challenge of the gospel is watered down and even excised. There are parts of the gospel message which are disturbing and uncomfortable; indeed, the demand for repentance leaves no one unmoved. Furthermore, worship should be a Godward act, not entertainment for an audience. It may be that this style of worship has so compromised with the prevailing culture that it is not true worship at all, but simply an exaggerated form of a cultural incantation.

Sargeant has suggested that seeker churches and seeker worship are forms of postmodernism. That may be correct, but it would be postmodern culture at the popular, marketplace level. A more intellectual discussion has come from the self-styled Radical Orthodoxy group, and also from some Roman Catholic scholars.

In an extremely provocative book, Catherine Pickstock of Cambridge University challenged Derrida's interpretation of Socrates' *Phaedrus*, arguing that liturgy (here with a fluid meaning) is the highest representation of language. She then turned to attack modernity, the invention of which is placed at the door of Duns Scotus, and which is then propagated by Pierre Ramus. In a final section Pickstock criticizes modern forms of worship, advocating instead a reading of the pre-modern Catholic mass (Pickstock 1998). As intriguing as this is, her advocacy is flawed because the medieval mass she expounds is that of a scholarly critical text, not a real medieval mass, and is as artificial as Disneyland castles. There is no generic mass which floats about in some metaphysical world. There are only performed masses with specific manuscripts and ceremonials of particular places and times. To present an ahistorical mass is singularly unhelpful. From the Roman Catholic side one may cite David Torevell's *Losing the Sacred: Ritual, Modernity and Liturgical Reform* (2000), which purports to be a postmodern liturgical critique of the

Vatican II liturgies. He appeals to Durkheim, Weber, Turner, Tambiah, and Rappaport for the importance of ritual in religious formation and of understanding 'person' as body and soul, or body and mind, and as being part of a wider social body. Zygmunt Bauman and Michel Foucault are invoked as postmodern liberators of a flawed modernity. The resulting reforms of Vatican II are seen as a surrender of divine transcendence in favour of anthropocentricity. Torevell too hankers after the pre-modern as seen through the eyes of John Bossy and Eamon Duffy. What is methodologically odd here is that Torevell appeals to a vast number of late modernist writers and their theories in order to indict modernism; he has a thoroughly modernist view of the Reformation and Enlightenment. Such studies are flawed by their own inconsistency. A slightly more nuanced approach has been set forth by the present writer in the Pitt Lecture at Yale in 2001 (Spinks 2002: 8–13). Here it is argued that the church needs to return to the *analogia fidei* of which the liturgy is an expression and upon which it rests. There is no room for metanarratives other than the one overriding metanarrative of the canon of scripture, or narrative of redemption. Or, to use Richard Lints's words, 'The church's story is the story of God's redeeming presence as narrated in and through the scriptures and which therefore interprets all of reality' (Lints 2000: 99). The church must not attempt to find golden ages of worship, but rather must use all knowledge of worship in order to author and evolve worship which retains the transcendent, speaks of the Other, and engages the present age. In this respect the medieval period—not the artificial medieval period of Pickstock, nor the idealized medieval culture of Torevell—may prove suggestive as providing examples of a self-confident liturgy which developed in the belief that the Christian interpretation of reality was real and capable of a viable, universal interpretation. Medieval liturgies were able to adapt to regional and cultural diversity without loss of a common core or loss of orthodoxy. They show how worship, preaching, and social application can all be integrated. They might therefore serve as an inspiration (and no more than that) for (post)modern forms of worship.

Another phenomenon particularly in English-speaking churches has been the critique of worship by feminist theologians. This has ranged from calls for rituals which express women's concerns, to calls for inclusive language in regard to both humans and God. The latter has tended to be dominated by demands to avoid male pronouns for the deity, and the quest for alternative trinitarian names for Father, Son, and Holy Spirit. It is strongly disputed as to whether Father, Son, and Holy Spirit should be regarded as names, or mere metaphors which can be changed according to fashion and gender egalitarianism. The issue is far from settled, and is often perceived as a struggle between conservatives and liberals. Outside the English-speaking world, it appears to be a white, middle-class, self-indulgent power struggle, which is chauvinistically oblivious to the fact that in many languages grammar carries no gender, and so simply irrelevant to the rest of the world. It has led to some infelicitous English prose, with frequent repetition of the word God to avoid the masculine pronoun; the introduction of natural gender in place of grammatical gender by calling God 'she'; and, given that there is no such thing as a reflexive noun, the invention of the totally ungrammatical word 'Godself'. Ecclesiastical communities are also often unaware that generic use of such words as 'man' and 'mankind' is alive and well in scientific and much political discourse. The question arises as to just how different ecclesiastical language, and in this case, worship language, can become before it loses touch with the secular world with which it has to do.

The interplay between theology, ecclesiology, and worship has been underscored by the Lima report of the Faith and Order Commission of the World Council of Churches, *Baptism, Eucharist, and Ministry* (World Council of Churches 1982). Here an ecumenical theology was unveiled along with a eucharistic liturgy authored to reflect what the document said about the eucharist. The implications have been explored more deeply in the Ditchingham report and the Faverches statement. In these documents there is less concern to find or author a common text as to find a common *ordo* of preaching, eating and drinking with thanksiving, the bath, and sending out into the world. The problem with the concept of a common *ordo* is akin to the problem of talking about the sacraments of baptism and eucharist. Kenan Osborne (1999) appeals to the Scotist word *haecceitas*, 'thisness', to argue that there is no generic baptism or eucharist, but only actual baptisms and eucharists. There is no generic liturgical *ordo*, but only actual celebrations of worship. As interesting as the idea of a common *ordo* might be, ultimately most churches are judged on the forms of their worship, i.e., the text (whether printed and fixed, suggested as a guide, or entirely oral), because it is here that a more obvious theology is articulated. This is illustrated by the recent work on worship in the Baptist tradition by Christopher Ellis (2004), who argues that it is a cluster of values and spirituality which unlocks the heart of worship in that particular tradition.

In terms of baptism, many modern western rites are the result of a number of issues. One has been the debate over infant baptism versus believer's baptism, and here the Lima document warned against the practice in many churches of indiscriminate baptism—particularly by state or established churches. This has given rise to articulating parental promises and undertakings as part of the baptismal rite. Allied with this has been a tendency to emphasize baptism as initiation *into* the church rather than *from* original sin. In the Roman Catholic rites, the prayer for blessing the font emphasizes the paschal concept of Romans 6, and this has been copied by a number of churches. More recent revisions in some churches (Church of Scotland, Church of England) have restored the new birth imagery alongside the paschal imagery. One particular debate has been over whether the term 'covenant', preferred in the sixteenth-century Reformed tradition to defend infant baptism, should be the overriding hermeneutic for understanding baptism. The Episcopal Church of the USA uses the term 'baptismal covenant' for the recital of the creed and other promises and undertakings given prior to the act of baptism, echoing the concern found in other Anglican, Lutheran, and the Roman Catholic churches about parental undertakings on behalf of their children. The resulting liturgical sequence suggests that baptism becomes dependent upon a covenant agreement or contract made by parents or the candidate, with baptism following as the reward. The older sequence in the Roman Catholic, Lutheran, and Anglican rites was a liturgical sequence of creed (the faith of the church), baptism (grace), and admonition to godparents (the response to grace).

In the Church of Scotland, Church of England, and New Zealand Prayer Book one sees a return to this liturgical sequence which avoids semi-Pelagianism, and reflects the prevenient grace of God which calls forth a response. Related to this has been the move to eliminate confirmation as a rite of admittance to communion, and instead to see initiation complete in baptism, therefore allowing infant and children's communion. Part of the problem has been that ever since the episcopal rite of hand-laying became detached from the Roman initiation rite (which was quite different in eastern and other western churches), confirmation has been a rite in search of a theology. The Reformation churches redefined it as a graduation ceremony after successful catechesis, suggesting or implying some standard of intellect as necessary for receiving communion. But moves towards infant and children's communion have left confirmation even more beleaguered.

One of the results of the twentieth-century liturgical movement has been more frequent celebrations of the eucharist. In many churches weekly communion as the main service has become the norm, and in many others at least a monthly celebration as the main service occurs. In the mainline churches there has also been a remarkable agreement on the structure of the rite, together with a recovery of eucharistic prayers modelled on those of the classical rites. Yet theological differences obviously continue. One significant difference between East and West has always been the importance of the *epiklesis* (calling on the Holy Spirit) over against the stress upon the recital of the words of institution. Behind this lie concepts regarding what constitutes the consecration or setting apart of the elements as well as their sacramental nature. This was heightened at the Reformation when Lutherans and the Reformed, with different understanding of sacramental presence, both removed the words of institution and recited them separately and apart from any prayer. The new eucharistic prayers which were set forth in a post-Vatican II missal include an *epiklesis*, though still with manual acts which highlight the words of institution. Liturgical scholars have tended to suggest that whatever is meant by consecration, it is, following Jewish practice, by the whole prayer and not specific words. Systematicians have tended to emphasize sacraments as occasions of personal encounter with the divine, or of a disclosure of God. Together, these point to less concern with particular words. In 2002 the Vatican acknowledged the validity of the Church of the East's eucharistic prayer, Addai and Mari, which has no institution narrative, and therefore in theory there can no longer be a Catholic objection to the Lutheran and Reformed practice (e.g., Church of Scotland) of having eucharistic prayers separate from the words of institution. However, the western Protestant churches still seem at times to be haunted by the theory of transubstantiation, and this is reflected in the *epiklesis.* Whereas some churches ask that the Holy Spirit be sent upon the bread and wine that they may be the body and blood of Christ, others are reticent about asking for the Spirit to come upon inanimate objects and are anxious that any 'real presence' not be too real! Coupled with this is a difference in how, if at all, the eucharist is related to the concept of memorial and sacrifice. *Baptism, Eucharist, and Ministry* (*BEM*) (World Council of Churches 1982) stated:

> The biblical idea of memorial as applied to the eucharist refers to this present efficacy of God's work when it is celebrated by God's people in a liturgy. Christ himself with all that he has accomplished for us and for all creation (in his incarnation, servanthood, ministry, teaching, suffering, sacrifice, resurrection, ascension and sending of the Spirit) is present in this anamnesis, granting us communion with himself. The eucharist is also the foretaste of his parousia and of the final kingdom. (*BEM* Eucharist 5)

The Eastern and Catholic churches tend to understand anamnesis as implying 'offering' the eucharistic sacrifice, whereas many Protestant churches with a modern, western, subjective interpretation of the word 'remembrance' still prefer to make the memorial of an absent Lord. *BEM* noted that 'The eucharist is the sacrament of the unique sacrifice of Christ, who ever lives to make intercession for us'. Here at least the Church of Scotland's 'pleading the eternal sacrifice' and the recent Church of England's 'we plead with confidence his one sacrifice' both express *BEM*'s understanding of eucharistic memorial and sacrifice.

Studies on the development of marriage rites reveal a considerable distinction between eastern and western forms. The eastern rites centre on celebrating a marriage in the presence of Christ, blessing it, and crowning the bride and groom as temporary royal lovers. There are an exotic blessing of rings and generous use of the language of the Song of Songs. Vows are confined to the betrothal rite. In contrast, the West developed rites which were suspicious of sexuality and far more concerned to establish a valid contract than celebrate marriage. This was taken to its logical conclusions in the Reformation rites, where the vows become the centre of the rite. Most modern western rites, having bequeathed this understanding of marriage to the culture, seem unable or unwilling to break with it. There are signs of enrichment in some recent marriage rites. The centrality of the vows are mitigated by separating the consent from the exchange of vows by the liturgy of the word. The blessing of rings is being restored, and the blessings enriched. Rich nuptial blessings are being provided, and formulae and intercessions introduced which express the role of the wider family and community. Attempts to borrow from the eastern rites—anointing (Coptic and Maronite traditions), crowning with garlands, drinking from a common blessed cup—seem so far not to have become popular options.

In funerals there has been a marked distinction between, on the one hand, the eastern and Catholic rites, which provide for a twofold rite of passage for the deceased and the mourners; and Protestant rites on the other, which have seen the funeral as a rite of passage mainly for the mourners. In more recent revisions some Protestant traditions have recovered a baptismal ecclesiology and eschatology and have introduced prayers concerned with the departed person as being still a member of the church, albeit the church triumphant.

A great deal of liturgical revision took place in the latter part of the twentieth century, much of it reflecting the state of scholarship and the cultural needs of the time. In an age which regards itself as postmodern, and very different from the 1960s and 1970s, it is likely that the western churches may well be in for another round of new liturgical forms. Once again, current historical scholarship, culture, ecumenism, and theological fashion will all filter into the crafting of those new forms. Clearly, worship is still on the theological agenda.

References

Allmen, J.-J. von (1965). *Worship: Its Theology and Practice.* London: Lutterworth.

Bishop, Edmund (1917). *Liturgica Historica.* Oxford: Oxford University Press.

Bradshaw, Paul F., Johnson, Maxwell E., and Phillips, L. Edward (2002). *The Apostolic Tradition.* Minneapolis: Fortress.

Brunner, Peter (1968). *Worship in the Name of Jesus.* St Louis: Concordia.

Capelle, B. (1960). 'Les Liturgies "basiliennes" et saint Basile'. In J. Doresse and E. Lanne (eds.), *Un témoin archaïque de la liturgie copte de S. Basile*, Louvain: Université de Louvain.

Cressy, David (1997). *Birth, Marriage and Death: Ritual, Religion, and the Life-Cycle in Tudor and Stuart England.* Oxford: Oxford University Press.

Ellis, Christopher J. (2004). *A Theology and Spirituality of Worship in Free Church Tradition.* London: SCM.

Fagerberg, David W. (1992). *What is Liturgical Theology? A Study in Methodology.* Collegeville: Liturgical.

Garrigan, Siobhán (2004). *Beyond Ritual: Sacramental Theology after Habermas.* Aldershot: Ashgate.

Hardy, Daniel, and Ford, David (1985). *Praising and Knowing God.* Philadelphia: Westminster.

Hayes, Alan L. (2000). 'Tradition in the Anglican Liturgical Movement 1945–1989'. *Anglican and Episcopal History* 69: 22–43.

Irwin, Kevin W. (1994). *Context and Text: Method in Liturgical Theology.* Collegeville: Liturgical.

Kavanagh, Aidan (1984). *On Liturgical Theology.* New York: Pueblo.

Ladrière, Jean (1973). 'The Performativity of Liturgical language'. *Concilium* 2: 50–62.

Lints, Richard (2000). 'The Vinyl Narratives: The Metanarrative of Postmodernity and the Recovery of a Churchly Theology'. In Michael Horton (ed.), *A Confessing Theology for Postmodern Times*, Wheaton: Crossway.

Lonergan, Bernard (1972). *Method in Theology.* New York: Herder and Herder.

Migne, J.-P. (1844–65). *Patrologia Latina.* Paris.

Mitchell, Leonel (1985). *Praying Shapes Believing.* Minneapolis: Winston.

Nichols, Bridget (1996). *Liturgical Hermeneutics: Interpreting Liturgical Rites in Performance.* Berlin: Peter Lang.

Osborne, Kenan B. (1999). *Christian Sacraments in a Postmodern World.* New York: Paulist.

Pickstock, Catherine (1998). *After Writing: On the Liturgical Consummation of Philosophy.* Oxford: Blackwell.

Sargeant, Kimon Howland (2000). *Seeker Churches: Promoting Traditional Religion in a Nontraditional Way.* New Brunswick: Rutgers University Press.

Schmemann, Alexander (1963). 'Theology and Liturgical Tradition'. In Massey H. Shepherd (ed.), *Worship in Scripture and Tradition*, New York: Oxford University Press.

Spinks, Bryan D. (1996). 'The Anaphora of Nestorius: Antiochene Lex Credendi through Constantinopolitan Lex Orandi?' *Orientalia Christiana Periodica* 62: 273–94.

—— (2002). 'Berkeley, Liturgical Scholars and the Liturgical Movement'. *Berkeley at Yale* 20: 8–13.

Taft, Robert (1975). *The Great Entrance: A History of the Transfer of Gifts and Other Preanaphoral Rites of the Liturgy of St John Chrysostom.* Orientalia Christiana analecta 200. Rome: Pontifical Oriental Institute.

—— (1991). *A History of the Liturgy of St John Chrysostom*, iv. *The Diptychs.* Orientalia Christiana analecta 238. Rome: Pontifical Oriental Institute.

—— (2000). *A History of the Liturgy of St John Chrysostom*, v. *The Pre-Communion Rites.* Orientalia Christiana analecta 261. Rome: Pontifical Oriental Institute.

Tanner, Norman P., SJ (ed.) (1990). *Decrees of the Ecumenical Councils.* 2 vols. Georgetown: Sheed and Ward.

Torevell, David (2000). *Losing the Sacred: Ritual, Modernity and Liturgical Reform.* Edinburgh: T. & T. Clark.

Van Dyk, Leanne (ed.) (2005). *A More Profound Alleluia: Theology and Worship in Harmony.* Grand Rapids: Eerdmans.

Wainwright, G. (1980). *Doxology: The Praise of God in Worship, Doctrine and Life: A Systematic Theology.* London: Epworth.

Wannenwetsch, Bernd (2004). *Political Worship: Ethics for Christian Citizens.* Oxford: Oxford University Press.

World Council of Churches (1982). *Baptism, Eucharist, and Ministry.* Geneva: World Council of Churches.

—— (1995). 'Towards Koinonia in Worship: A Consultation on the Role of Worship within the Search for Unity, held at All Hallows Community, Ditchingham, England, 20–27 August, 1994'. *Studia Liturgica* 25/1: 1–31.

Suggested Reading

Bradshaw, Paul F. (2002). *The Search for the Origins of Christian Worship.* New York: Oxford University Press.

Calivas, Alkiviadis (2003). *Essays in Theology and Liturgy*, iii. Brookline: Holy Cross Orthodox Press.

Costen, Melva (2004). *In Spirit and in Truth*. Louisville: Westminster/John Knox.

Fenwick, John, and Spinks, Bryan (1995). *Worship in Transition: The Liturgical Movement in the Twentieth Century*. Edinburgh: T. & T. Clark.

Ward, Pete (2005). *Selling Worship: How What We Sing has Changed the Church*. Milton Keynes: Paternoster.

White, James F. (2000). *Introduction to Christian Worship*. Nashvile: Abingdon.

CHAPTER 22

REASON

ANDREW MOORE

I. Faith and Foundationalism

In 'The Epistle to the Reader' of his *Essay Concerning Human Understanding*, the philosopher John Locke briefly alludes to the circumstances of the work's conception. He and a handful of friends had met at Exeter House in London early in 1671. They were 'discoursing on a subject very remote' from the concerns of the *Essay* and 'found themselves quickly at a stand, by the difficulties that arose on every side'. One of those present records that they had talked 'about the principles of morality and revealed religion' (Cranston 1957: 141). Locke continues: 'After we had a while puzzled ourselves, without coming any nearer a resolution of those doubts which perplexed us, it came into my thoughts, that we took a wrong course; and that before we set our selves upon an enquiry of that nature, it was necessary to examine our own abilities, and see, what objects our understandings were, or were not fitted to deal with' (Locke 1975: 7). Some eighteen years later, Locke's *Essay* was published.

This episode matters for our understanding of reason as a source of systematic theology because it is important to appreciate that ideas have origins and that this is particularly the case with our topic. Locke's *Essay* was composed at a time when England was riven by questions about how the Bible was to be interpreted; was its best interpreter the private reader, the priest, or the church? Locke was brought up in a Puritan home but became a Latitudinarian. He had lived through the execution of Charles I and longed for a church free of divisions and for a tolerant society. He was a close associate of the early experimental scientist Robert Boyle. Those matters concerning 'the principles of morality and revealed religion' were discussed in this context. Locke could have chosen to consult the Bible for guidance, but this seemed to risk begging the question in favour of one particular doctrine of scripture. So instead he directed himself to human cognitive abilities, to the topic of how we come to believe what we believe and how we should decide what to believe. In doing so he put epistemology at the centre of rational enquiry in a new, even revolutionary way.

Locke's answer to the hermeneutical question is in the climactic Book IV of the *Essay*. There is one unerring mark of the lover of truth: 'The not entertaining any proposition with greater assurance than the proofs it is built upon will warrant' (Locke 1975: IV. xix. 1). God has endowed us with reason, but with regard to a claim to revelation, Locke's maxim implied that 'it still belongs to reason, to judge of the truth of its being a revelation, and of the signification of the words, wherein it is delivered. Indeed, if any thing shall be thought revelation, which is contrary to the plain principles of reason... there reason must be hearkened to' (Locke 1975: IV. xviii. 8). Locke was no enemy of Christianity, but he believed that faith should only assent to that which is consistent with the deliverances of reason and evidence.

Locke's empiricism has had a decisive influence on the role of reason in systematic theology. For along with his rationalist predecessor René Descartes, he bequeathed to the western world the account of epistemology known as foundationalism. According to this, for any belief to be held rationally, for it to be elevated to the epistemically superior status of knowledge, it must be justified by being shown to be founded upon that which is either evident to the senses (Lockean foundationalism), immune from error insofar as it is self-evident or incorrigible (Cartesian foundationalism), or validly inferred from beliefs which display these features. If one is to be rational in what one believes, one must show that one's beliefs have been formed according to foundationalist principles. Faith, by contrast, is seen as untrustworthy and is therefore not a source of knowledge. It is apparent that Christian doctrine—even with respect to such a basic matter as God's existence, let alone concerning the Trinity or Chalcedonian Christology whose source is unquestionably in divine revelation—is going to be hard put to show that it is rational on foundationalist principles. The story of the way in which reason has functioned as a source of contemporary systematic theology is that of how theologians have responded to the challenge of foundationalism.

The second reason why the episode at Exeter House matters is because it launched upon the world a very different view of the relationship between reason and revelation from that which had obtained before the dawn of modernity. The claims of reason had not been foreign to Anselm and Thomas Aquinas. Each used reason with exemplary rigour and precision, but they did so in a way that was dedicated to understanding and communicating the substance of Christianity to which the assent of faith had already been given, or which, as in the case of Anselm's *Cur Deus Homo*, set the terms for debate. Anselm writes 'from the point of view of one trying to raise his mind to contemplate God and seeking to understand what he believes'; he does not 'seek to understand so that I may believe, but I believe so that I may understand' (Anselm 1979: preface). Aquinas has been, and in some circles continues to be, read as a precursor of and/or an antidote to modern epistemology. However, the later decades of the twentieth century have seen a trend to regard him not as an apologist or philosopher but as a theologian of the Christian life whose work found its animating centre in Christology and its source in scripture. In contrast to Descartes and Locke, Anselm and Aquinas found both the sources and the norms of Christian theology in scripture and the church's teaching. Reason was seen as a human faculty used in the orderly exposition of what was given in scripture and tradition; it was not an independent source or norm of Christian belief. Reason and revelation were not distinct and potentially competing sources of knowledge in the way that foundationalism has taught us to think of them. Only since modernity have theologians seen it as necessary to provide epistemological justification (in the form of methodological prolegomena) for the claims of revelation before embarking on the task of constructive theology.

So the place of reason in relationship to Christian faith has not been static and fixed throughout the history of the church. Once we recognize that ideas have origins in specific historical settings, and in particular that our concept of reason and the use of our rational faculties in theology are shaped by the settings in which they have arisen, then perhaps we can be free from unhelpful or distorting influences from the past. One of the burdens of this essay is to raise the question whether, with respect to reason, theologians need be bound by an intellectual settlement concerning its use that has tended to eclipse other, uniquely ecclesial sources of theology, and thereby distorted its content (cf. Jenson 1997–9). On the other hand, if we think that the influence of modernity's view of reason has been baleful, does this mean that we can or should retreat behind it to (a possibly nostalgic vision of) the past? Can we, should we, seek to retrieve a pre-modern understanding of the relationship between faith and reason? Even if we can chart a genealogy of the secularization of reason, identify false turnings on the road that led from the past to the present (as John Milbank has argued with respect to Scotus), and reorder the relationship between epistemology and ontology on a properly Christian metaphysical footing, is this sufficient to restore to vitality the church's obligation to speak faithfully about God's acts (cf. Milbank 2003: 61–105; 2000)? Many of the decisive turns in the articulation of the substantive issues in systematic theology treated elsewhere in this volume have their origin in how Christians have construed the relationship between reason and (the various sources of) revelation.

II. Inferential Reason and the Self-Alienation of Religion

The rise of foundational rationality is only one instance of a larger historical trend, what Michael Buckley has referred to as the 'self-alienation of religion' (1987: 341). The key thinkers here are the Flemish Jesuit Leonard Lessius and the French friar Marin Mersenne. Buckley traces the rise of modern atheism and the alienation of Christianity from its own properly theological subject matter to the attempts of Lessius and Marsenne in the early seventeenth century to rebut nascent atheism.

> Whatever the metaphysical judgements of such attempts, the theologian will look in vain for a critical position accorded to Christology or religious experience. Both Lessius and Mersenne treated the atheistic question as if it were a philosophic issue, not a religious one. Both acted as if the rising movement were not a rejection of Jesus Christ as the supreme presence of god [*sic*] in human history, whose spirit continued that presence and made it abidingly evocative, but a philosophic stance toward life.... Whatever the causes, neither theologian indicated that the understanding of god's [*sic*] self-revelation in the person of Jesus and in the depths of human religious experience had anything to contribute to this most critical issue for the Church. (Buckley 1987: 65–6)

Instead of appealing to Christology to rebut the atheism he saw as the outcome of heresy, Lessius goes to the arguments of natural theology proposed by the pagan philosopher Cicero. Thus, '[a]s theology generated apologetic philosophy and philosophy generated Universal Mathematics and Universal Mechanics, and as these in turn co-opted theology to become the foundation of [generically] theistic [as opposed to specifically Christian] assertions, theology itself became a *disciplina otiosa* in the justification or establishment of its own subject matter' (Buckley 1987: 358). Theological reasoning became subordinate to the demands of atheism and apologetics.

The universal mathematics and mechanics of Descartes and Newton gave rise to modern science. The epistemic obligations imposed by foundationalism are usually held to apply indifferently to all fields of human enquiry, hence, since science is characterized by the foundationalist virtues of empirical observation, logical inference from observation, and mathematically precise modelling, scientific practice is widely held to be the supreme paradigm of rational cognition. This has had a significant impact on theological method and to a lesser degree on substantive proposals in the field of Christian doctrine,[1] but the way in which it has caused theology to become alienated from its own sources and norms in scripture and church teaching is best

[1] On theological method see Torrance (1969), van Huyssteen (1989), and Murphy (1990). For doctrinal proposals see Peacocke (1993) and Polkinghorne (1994). Scientific conceptions of reason and evidence have also had a major impact on historical knowledge and therefore on the place of the Bible as a source of Christian doctrine. This is best seen in the relationship between the quest for the historical Jesus and Christology; see Pannenberg (1968: 21–37).

shown by looking—as we shall do shortly—at the use of inferential reason in contemporary philosophy of religion's contributions to theological reflection.

Strictly speaking, in the modern period there have been few who have regarded reason as a *source* of theology. The view that it could flourished in the heyday of natural religion, and one of its enduring legacies, due in no small measure to the shift in the relationship of theology to its proper subject matter described by Buckley, is the view that, Hume's and Kant's arguments to the contrary notwithstanding, belief in God can be justified by rational argument, and not only that it can, but that, in accordance with foundationalist precepts, it must be (cf. Plantinga 2000). This is the apologetic use of reason. It includes not only the traditional tasks of natural theology in demonstrating God's existence without appeal to supernatural revelation but also the application of it in developing accounts of traditional doctrinal *loci*.

The arguments of natural theology continue to be deployed by philosophers and theologians who believe that it is important for Christians to provide epistemological foundations for faith. For the theologians of the seventeenth century, 'the warrant for the personal god was the impersonal world: the strongest evidence for the personal god was the design within nature.... The Christian God was to be justified without Christ' (Buckley 1987: 343, 350). Then as now, apologetic reason, when alienated from the substance of belief, finds the grounds for believing in God external to Christian doctrine and practice. The most notable example of this is in relation to the doctrine of creation. In confessing its faith 'in God the Father Almighty, maker of heaven and earth', the church locates the doctrine of creation *within* the structure of the creed: it is ingredient within that faith. By contrast, under the pressure of the search for rational justification for Christianity, Christian natural theologians have sought to argue from the world to its having been brought into being by a creator. Belief that the world has been created by God migrates from being of the substance of faith to being a condition of faith. But in doing so, what had been part of the church's confession becomes prolegomenal and external to that confession; inferential reason becomes an independent source of belief.

One of the most significant and influential contemporary exponents of apologetic reason is the philosopher of religion Richard Swinburne, who regards Christianity as a species of that genus of metaphysical theory known as 'theism'. Swinburne has developed sophisticated inductive arguments for the probable existence of God and in more recent works has explored the meaning and coherence of central Christian doctrines (cf. Wiles 1974). A common feature of his treatment of topics in the field of systematic theology has been to argue for a general philosophical position—in metaphysics in the case of the doctrine of the Trinity—and then to argue *a priori* for the doctrine under consideration. (The structure of his book *The Christian God* (1994) is notable: the first part is 'Metaphysics'; the second is 'Theology'.) Of the doctrine of the Trinity, he writes that there are 'arguments of pure reason in favour of the necessary truth of the doctrine of the Trinity' which back up arguments from scripture and church tradition for the truth of the doctrine (Swinburne 1994: 1). This approach shares the same basic problem as Lessius': the success of the doctrinal case depends on the success of the philosophical argument. The truth of the former depends epistemically on the truth of the latter. Overall, Swinburne's argument conveys the impression that had the church taught that God is four persons in one substance, then an *a priori* argument would have been found for that teaching.

The problems in Swinburne's account arise from the fact that, although he argues for the consistency of his position with that which the church has held, he fails to penetrate into the reasons why the church has come to believe what it does. Neither the dynamics of salvation history (especially of the Christ-event), their distinctive intellectual and conceptual demands and challenges, nor the witness of scripture have any determinative role in shaping his doctrine of the Trinity. It is not these but an apologetic response to the demands of foundational rationality upon a too static view of Christian doctrine that drive his argument. There is therefore a strong sense of abstraction surrounding his doctrinal exposition.

Wittgensteinian philosophy of religion has argued against the apologetic use of reason in favour of an account of religious belief and its content that pays closer attention to the forms of life within which religious discourse is used, and theologians with an interest in analytic philosophy have found Wittgenstein's own work liberating and congenial. However, the work of his philosophical epigones also tends in practice to abstract from the doctrinal content of religious beliefs and their sources. Like Swinburne, it argues about a generic 'theism'. D. Z. Phillips's work continues to be notable in this respect, even though in his later work he showed more interest in the specificities of Christianity.[2]

The problem of abstraction arises because reason has become detached from the matrix of events, beliefs, and practices from which doctrines arose; the task of reason is not to penetrate into and to articulate the inner logic of that matrix but to demonstrate at the bar of neutral, universal reason the rationality of the doctrines in their authoritative forms. In this process, the problematics that gave rise to the doctrines are changed: defending the doctrine of the Trinity can, for example, be seen more as a matter of the correct handling of a particular instance of a more general difficulty, for example, in mereology, than as one of saying what the church has to say in order to speak of the God who raised Jesus from the dead and poured out the Holy Spirit. By abstracting from the economy of salvation, apologetic reason risks creating the impression that the doctrine has an independent standing as a problem to be solved or that the logic of trinitarian discourse is at risk unless and until Christians can show that it is not subject to philosophical objections. But this is to mistake the role of a doctrine for that of an explanatory theory which

[2] See, e.g., his understanding of God's covenant in his most theologically engaged work (2004: 147–62, 230–2). Wittgenstein's influence on contemporary theology is widespread; notable examples of it are found in Holmer (1978) and Lindbeck (1984).

should only be accepted on condition that it can be shown to be coherent, not only with the scriptural witness, but with neutral reason. Philosophical defences of Christian doctrine can have apologetic value in the witness of the church, but they need correctly to represent not just what Christians believe, but why they believe it and how they have come to believe it (cf. Marion 2002: 53–70).

There is a further problem with abstracting Christian doctrines from their natural habitat in the church's reflection on and witness to God's saving acts. The concept of God itself is thereby changed and distorted as it becomes part of the metaphysical or explanatory theory within which it occurs. The concept becomes 'useful' for solving metaphysical problems—witness, for example, the purpose that God serves in Descartes's search for certainty in his *Meditations* (Descartes 1984: 24–36, 44–9; cf. Jüngel 1983: 108–26). Some theologians see the God of this philosophical theism in stark contrast with the God of Abraham, Isaac, and Jacob, even describing it as heretical and idolatrous (Kasper 1984: 294–5). Others, for example Eberhard Jüngel, regard the distinction as 'irresponsible', for even if, as Jüngel thinks, Descartes's work lies at the heart of modern atheism's criticism of the metaphysical concept of God, nevertheless, 'we should incorporate modern criticism of the metaphysical concept of God into the questioning process of faith as it understands itself, so that, through the modern crisis of the metaphysical idea of God, God will be *thinkable in a new way*, on the basis of the certainty of faith' (Jüngel 1983: 110). The core question in these debates is whether, when philosophical reason argues for the *existence* of God in abstraction from salvation history, it arrives at a concept of God denuded of those features of his *essence* in virtue of which the God of the Bible is God. For example, in much philosophy of religion, God's existence is established on the basis of his supposed causal relationship to the world; his essence is thus that of primal cause. But as Wolfhart Pannenberg has argued, 'the idea of a first cause is so general that it does not carry with it the specific view of God as personal power, let alone the characteristic features of the biblical God' (Pannenberg 1991–8: i. 349). By contrast, in classical Christianity, God's essence and existence are given together in his self-revealing in Christ and through the Spirit, and therefore when God's existence is given to human cognition his essentially personal and loving being are given also.

III. The Legacy of Kant

The view that belief in God can be justified by inferential reason is held in defiance of Kant, whose influence on contemporary theology cannot be overestimated. The great philosopher of the Enlightenment held that in the past humans had laboured under a 'self-incurred... tutelage' whose cause lay 'not in lack of reason but lack of resolution and courage to use it without direction from another' (Kant 1985: 3). By contrast, enlightened humans are those set free for autonomy by the critical use of reason on those putatively authoritative sources of knowledge that once had held them in heteronomy—notably tradition, the Bible, and ecclesiastical authority. Kant's use of critical reason is displayed at its greatest power in his masterpiece, the *Critique of Pure Reason*, and his arguments there are generally taken to have sounded the death knell for the traditional arguments for God's existence (Kant 1998: A584/B612–A642/B670). Kant believed that in his metaphysics he had shown that the only knowledge it is possible for human beings to have is of what is given through the senses; knowledge of that which is not thus given—the traditional subject matter of metaphysics and theology—is not available to us. It is therefore impossible for human beings to have any knowledge of God. This did not mean that he denied the existence of God or that he sought to abolish religion, only that 'religion is a purely rational affair' (Kant 1996: 287). For Kant, God was a postulate of *practical* reason: God was the necessary but unknowable foundation of morality, and religion its practical realization.

Kant's extensive writings on religion are characterized by a systematic demythologization of Christian doctrine that reinterprets its metaphysical claims in favour of their practical relevance. 'The only thing that matters in religion is *deeds*, and this final aim and, accordingly, a meaning appropriate to it, must be attributed to every biblical dogma. Dogma is not what we ought to believe (for faith admits of no imperative), but what we find it possible and useful to admit for practical (moral) purposes, although we cannot demonstrate it and so can only believe it' (Kant 1996: 267). Whilst the Bible retains a central place as a source in his view of Christianity, it is subject to the normative control of critical reason. Thus scripture cannot 'be accredited as the word of God'. 'For if God should really speak to a human being, the latter could still never *know* that it was God speaking. It is quite impossible for a human being to apprehend the infinite by his senses, distinguish it from sensible beings, and *be acquainted with* it as such' (Kant 1996: 283). The outworking of Kant's metaphysics is clearly shown in his view of the doctrine of the Trinity:

> The doctrine of the Trinity, taken literally, has *no practical relevance at all*, even if we think we understand it, and it is even more clearly irrelevant if we realize that it transcends all our concepts.—Whether we are to worship three or ten persons in the Deity makes no difference.... On the other hand, if we read a moral meaning into this article of faith... it would no longer contain an inconsequential belief but an intelligible one that refers to our moral vocation. (Kant 1996: 264)

Kant's critique of traditional metaphysics has found widespread acceptance, and his influence on subsequent theology has been lasting and profound. For if it is denied that supra-sensible being can be known on the basis of or amongst sensible beings, the problem arises as to how God can be known. It has been the task of the doctrine of revelation to meet this challenge. This explains why the centrality of revelation to theological epistemology—indeed, the concept of theological epistemology itself—is a surprisingly recent arrival on the theological scene (Pannenberg 1991–8: i. 214–29). That revelation has this role, that it is called upon to do so much work, and that it is generally seen as being in conflict with reason, is owing to the impact of foundationalism and Kant. Two of the most striking and divergent examples of Kant's continuing influence on systematic theology are represented by the works of Gordon Kaufman and by those of Karl Barth and Hans Urs von Balthasar.

Gordon Kaufman

Gordon Kaufman represents in clear form a dominant tendency in post-Enlightenment theology: he believes that the theologian's task has to be undertaken in dialogue with and accommodated to the demands of secular culture. Theologians of this kind believe that in mediating between theology and secularity they will be able to show that faith and critical enquiry need not be at loggerheads, that the claims of transcendence can still appeal to autonomous rationality (cf. Michalson 1999). For Kaufman, theology must therefore learn from, address, and if need be, radically reconceive itself in face of the challenges posed by global injustice, ecological crisis, and religious pluralism. The reasons for this lie, first, in an awareness—derived from Hegel—that human reality is 'radically and profoundly historical' (Kaufman 1993: 103) and that consequently our ideas and systems of thought are historically shaped and mutable. Theology should therefore be continually revising itself in the light of the problems with which the world is faced; it cannot be a static tradition or final deposit of orthodoxy. The second is Kantian in character: the human mind unavoidably structures its knowledge of reality. Kant came to hold that 'objects must conform to our cognition' (Kant 1998: B xvi). In other words, our minds shape not only *how* we know what we know, but *what* we know. Briefly and crudely put: the mind actively constructs reality. For Kant this does not mean that we cannot know reality. Rather, we can only know it as it appears to us through our senses and the concepts or categories by which the mind shapes our sensory experience. We can only know things as they appear to us (their 'phenomenal' reality) but not as they are in themselves (their 'noumenal' reality). Now if Kant is correct about this, Christians need to be very careful to distinguish between God as God is in himself and the ways in which our minds construct concepts of God, for if we do not we are at risk of mistaking an idol for God.

It is just this concern that lies behind Kaufman's *In Face of Mystery: A Constructive Theology* (1993), and in this book he proposes two ways by which we can distinguish God from idols. The first is to understand 'God' as

> an X which is positively... related to life and its problems: the True God, in contrast to idols, is the one who brings genuine salvation or liberation to men and women. This is the

> deepest existential reason for human interest in, search for, and devotion to God; and it provides an important criterion for distinguishing God from idols. On the basis of this criterion we can assert that any kind of human devotion or activity, any institution or social order, which is oppressive or destructive of human beings must be regarded as idolatrous; it is not grounded upon faith in or obedience to what is intended by the word 'God'.... [Thus] theologians should attempt to construct conceptions of God, humanity, and the world appropriate for the orientation of contemporary life. (Kaufman 1993: 79–80, 31)

The second is that we should avoid reifying our concept of God. On Kaufman's view, we must not suppose that our concept of God refers to a reality independent of us. God is 'an "ultimate point of reference"' constructed by us, and we should 'think of this X... as transcending everything in our world of experience and knowledge' (Kaufman 1993: 327, 328). It is perhaps unsurprising given his Kantianism that Kaufman concludes his argument by stressing that 'the trinity [is] a *practical* notion having to do with the way in which life is to be lived (not a speculative concept pretending to set forth the inner structure of the divine being—something about which we can have no knowledge)' (Kaufman 1993: 457).

This response to the Kantian problematic faces two difficulties. Let us grant to Kaufman that our senses and the categories by which we come to such knowledge of reality as we can have are themselves shaped by our historical experience. It follows that they will have been shaped by devotions and activities, institutions and social orders that have proved 'destructive or oppressive of human beings'. If this is the case, then the basis on which we construct our revisionary concept of God will be tainted by just those categories which, on his view, lead to idolatry. It is therefore hard to see how, without recourse to an unacceptable essentialism, his argument can produce a conception of God that is not itself distorted by, in traditional terms, human sinfulness and who is therefore genuinely worthy of human devotion. Nor will refusing reification solve the problem, for by Kaufman's strategy all we shall have avoided reifying is an idolatrous conception of God. The second difficulty is this: do we in fact know enough about human life to be able to state what or who it is that 'brings genuine salvation or liberation to men and women'? The history of the twentieth century discourages confidence that we do. Kaufman's view of human ability to master our own nature and our environment is too optimistic and overly reliant on (Enlightenment) conceptions of human progress. If, *contra* Kaufman, we cannot confidently state who or what brings salvation, again, by Kaufman's argument, we cannot distinguish the true God from an idol. And if we believe we can confidently state this, have we done anything more than written large ourselves and our autonomous rationality?

Karl Barth and Hans Urs von Balthasar

Such views of Enlightenment rationality as Kaufman's have been described as 'titanism' by both Karl Barth and Hans Urs von Balthasar, who represent the second way theologians have resolved the Kantian dilemma. Not only have they subjected enlightened reason to powerful critiques, but they have turned their backs on it by denying that its epistemological and metaphysical demands have any valid claim on Christian theology. They have therefore embarked on the theological (and as a consequence, especially in the case of Balthasar, the metaphysical) enterprise on the basis of God's action for us in Christ and the Holy Spirit, which, in light of our sinfulness and the fallenness of our rational faculties, we are unable to argue for or to grasp by unaided reason in any case (cf. Webster 2003: 10–30; Westphal 1990). Though they have different assessments of the role and value of natural theology, both insist that theology can only be done on the basis of the entirely free and gracious prior work of the triune God. Thus, as Balthasar puts it,

> Theology... is possible, but it will primarily be, not a human achievement, but an achievement of the divine Father, who is able truly to exposit himself and make himself understood in his incarnate Word, albeit only to those whom he equips for understanding this exposition by the gift of the Holy Spirit. And in all of this, something curious happens: the God who truly and unreservedly ex-posits himself does not therefore cease to be a mystery. (Balthasar 2000: 22)

Or to quote Barth, '*God* reveals himself. He reveals himself *through himself*. He reveals *himself*' (Barth 1975: 296). God is both the subject and the object of revelation who makes human beings capable of being in relationship with himself. Hence:

> Dogmatics as an enquiry presupposes that the true content of Christian talk about God can be known by man. It makes this assumption as in and with the Church it believes in Jesus Christ as the revealing and reconciling address of God to man.... Hence it does not have to begin by finding or inventing the standard by which it measures. It sees and recognizes that this is given with the Church. It is given in its own peculiar way, as Jesus Christ is given, as God in his revelation gives himself to faith. But it is given. It is complete in itself. It stands by its claim without discussion. It has the certainty which a true standard or criterion must have to be the means of serious measurement. (Barth 1975: 12)

God's self-revelation is a unique event and so cannot properly be judged or measured by human standards, such as those of critical reason. Since theology takes its noetic rise from the God-man, Jesus Christ, it cannot be treated as a species of a larger, more encompassing metaphysical genus. Revelation governs human thought about its object.

Yet though they deny that the Kantian problematic sets a fundamental and insuperable obstacle for Christian faith, neither Barth nor Balthasar refuse rational argument or indulge in wilful irrationalism. For Balthasar, even though theology has to do with that which is not knowable by other means than revelation, the philosophical understanding of the world offered by phenomenology is indispensable to the theological task of displaying God's glory in it and love for it and thereby declaring its redemption. 'A Christian has to conduct philosophical enquiry on account of his faith. Believing in the absolute love of God for the world, he is obliged to understand Being in its ontological difference as pointing to love, and to live in accordance with this indication' (Balthasar 1991: 646). For Barth, 'Theology means rational wrestling with the [triune] mystery'. 'All dogmatic formulations are rational and every dogmatic procedure is rational to the degree that in it use is made of general concepts, i.e., of the human *ratio*. It can be called rationalistic, however, only when we can show that the use is not controlled by the question of dogma, i.e., by subordination to Scripture, but by something else, most probably by the principles of some philosophy' (Barth 1975: 368, 296). Theology is free to use philosophy, but it surrenders its freedom when it conforms to a measure or standard of rationality external to it. It has no need to be underwritten or confirmed by 'neutral' or 'critical' reason. Both theology and the conceptual resources it uses are measured by the standard of truth given to it in God's self-revealing. '[T]he truth that God has made known to us about himself through revelation... becomes the ultimate norm of all truth in the world' (Balthasar 2000: 30). There can be no higher norm—which is why theological work is carried out, not just in gratitude and astonishment at God's love, but also in fear and trembling.

Theology is rational because it follows the intrinsic rationality of its object—and hence, in Barth's view, theology is properly termed a 'science' (Barth 1975: 4–11). Barth's most sustained treatment of these themes is in his commentary on chapters 2–4 of Anselm's *Proslogion* (Barth 1960). There he explains that 'The element of reason in the knowledge of the object of faith consists in recognition of the rationality that is peculiar to the object of faith itself. Ontic rationality precedes noetic' (Barth 1960: 50). One of the more fateful consequences of foundationalist conceptions of reason and Kantian metaphysics has been that they have inverted the traditional ordering of the relationship between knowing and being. Here, however, Barth, like Balthasar, seeks to restore it: the *ordo essendi* precedes the *ordo cognoscendi*. (And it may well be that the only way of construing theology on realist lines, rather than on idealist or constructivist lines such as are exemplified by Kaufman, is to return to this kind of traditional ordering.) Theology 'follows after' the rationality of God's being and it knows God and is rational to the extent that it does so (Barth 1960: 53).

Wolfhart Pannenberg

The obvious and frequently raised objection to this second way of dealing with the Kantian dilemma is that it is subjectivist and that it involves circular reasoning. Wolfhart Pannenberg believes that, since Christian theology claims that God is the creator of the whole of reality and since these claims have since the Enlightenment been contested, theology is under an internal and an external obligation to test and confirm both its truth and the deity of God. These are genuinely open questions, not only in the logical sense that their truth cannot be assumed but also in a theological one: 'Only God's final revelation at the end of history will bring with it final knowledge of the content and truth of the act of God in Jesus of Nazareth' (Pannenberg 1991–8: i. 16).[3] So although faith has its own certainty, the universal and eschatological character of theology's truth claim rules out the subjectivism and irrationality of a 'retreat to commitment' (Pannenberg 1991–8: i. 47). 'Theologians . . . cannot begin . . . with a firm presupposition of the truth of Christian revelation. If they did, they would make this truth a matter of mere subjective conviction, which would be little more than an objective untruth and perhaps even an in many ways attractive fable' (Pannenberg 1991–8: ii. xiii). Pannenberg is severely critical of Barth on just these grounds as well as those of begging the question (Pannenberg 1991–8: i. 45; cf. Barth 1957: 37, 43 and 1975: 42, 130–1), that is, of assuming that which is required to be proved—here, the universal claim of the gospel—and hence discrediting that for which one claims truth.

Pannenberg seeks to avoid this logical fallacy by sophisticated appeal to a natural knowledge of God that is available to all human beings and which can therefore establish the rationality of theology. Although Kant destroyed 'the arguments of speculative reason . . . for a supreme being' (Pannenberg 1991–8: i. 90), Pannenberg follows Kant in finding in the cosmological argument a basis for conceiving the unity of empirical reality. Thus, although cosmological arguments 'cannot decisively change the situation regarding the debatability of God's existence . . . they are not without significance as descriptions of the reality of humanity and the world which make talk about God intelligible and can thus establish criteria for it' (Pannenberg 1991–8: i. 95). Pannenberg wishes not only to establish a common ground in human reasoning for the intelligibility of talk about God, but also to recover a patristic view of the function of natural theology. 'God can be known only through God himself' (Pannenberg 1991–8: i. 94), but cosmological arguments for God's existence help ensure that speech about God is adequate to God's divine nature, untainted by the projection of human interests which besets modern versions of natural theology (Pannenberg 1991–8: i. 76–82).

Pannenberg's account of how systematic theology should be undertaken is also orientated towards showing its universal rationality. Precisely because the statements of theology claim to be true, they can only be made true by the God about whom they claim to speak: 'They stand or fall with his reality' (Pannenberg 1991–8: i. 59). However, because God will only be fully revealed at the eschaton, the truth of our knowledge of God will only be confirmed as true, if it is true, at the eschaton. Moreover, our knowledge of reality is finite and incomplete. So until the eschaton, our knowledge of God and its theological statement are provisional. Although theological statements are grounded in the confident assertions of faith, at the level of reflection they have a hypothetical character. The task of systematic theology is thus to offer

[3] While Pannenberg has been deeply influenced by Hegel, this influence is less strong now than at an earlier period. See Pannenberg (1969: 125–58; 1991–8: i. 249–57).

> a model of the world, humanity, and history as they are grounded in God, a model which, if it is tenable, will 'prove' the reality of God and the truth of Christian doctrine, showing them to be consistently conceivable, and also confirming them, by the form of presentation. In this way dogmatics expounds the truth claim of Christian teaching. (Pannenberg 1991–8: i. 60)

Now although Pannenberg succeeds in overcoming the problems of subjectivity and circular reasoning by appeal to natural theology and by refusing to assume the truth of systematic theology, he does so at a cost that puts his project in question. First, from the internal perspective of faith: on the one hand, 'Christians should have such confidence in the truth of their faith that they can let its divine truth shine forth from the content without any need for preceding guarantees' (Pannenberg 1991–8: i. 52). Therefore, 'by the convicting ministry of the Spirit of God' (Pannenberg 1991–8: i. 56), Christians can make a provisional decision concerning the truth of Christian doctrine. Faith is thus entitled to operate in an assertoric mode. Yet on the other hand, as we have seen, systematic theology itself is conducted in a hypothetical mode. The difficulty here is that whilst due weight seems to be given to the work of the Holy Spirit in producing faith, this does not carry over into Pannenberg's account of systematic theology. This apparent lack of close integration between faith and reflection seems to carry the risk that, whilst theological reflection can make out a case for its rationality, the assertions of faith still carry a whiff of subjective commitment. If Barth's theology can appear to be insufficiently alert to its own provisionality, in his desire to correct this Pannenberg—who is deeply influenced by Barth—errs by going too far in the opposite direction.

Nor is it easy to see how this concession will persuade unbelievers. Theology is logically coherent because it 'follow[s] in thought the divinely grounded unity of all that is true' (Pannenberg 1991–8: i. 53). But it is precisely this commitment to the precedence of the order of being over the order of knowing at which secular thought, sceptical of metaphysics, will baulk. For modernity, 'rational argumentation [is] a court which decides for (or against) the truth of faith' (Pannenberg 1991–8: i. 52), yet Pannenberg denies this by his claim that the truth of theology will be decided by God at the eschaton. So although Pannenberg offers the unbeliever the criterion of rational coherence with one hand, with the other he bids her to ground this in God's action and hence to defer to a theological criterion of truth: that theological hypotheses will be eschatologically confirmed. It therefore appears that in fact Pannenberg himself faces the charge of begging the question in favour of God.

Karl Rahner

But perhaps the charge can be sidestepped by an argument to the effect that all human beings are always already orientated towards God, whether they acknowledge this or not. This is what Karl Rahner set out to show in his 'metaphysical anthropology'. (Pannenberg proposes a similar argument—based on Romans 1: 19–20, Descartes's

Third Meditation, and our experience of the finitude of the world—in favour of our having a 'nonthematic', implicit knowledge of God (Pannenberg 1991–8: i. 107–18).) Rahner's major philosophical work *Hearer of the Word* (1994) opens with the problem of finding a non-circular basis for theology, and he proposes that it is found in a metaphysics of being that analyses the human situation. This engagement with metaphysics is motivated by a desire to communicate Christianity to modern culture: theological work 'should be . . . conditioned by the problematic of *today's* philosophy' (Rahner 1968: lii)—hence his massively sophisticated and technically accomplished correlation between Aquinas and Kant (Rahner 1968). Unless philosophy acknowledges its fulfilment in theology, Rahner thinks it will become existentially 'irrelevant'. Conversely, if theology ignores enquiry into its metaphysical basis (as he suggests Barth's does), 'it can logically be no more than God's No to humanity', for it will not be able to affirm human beings as having a positive capacity to receive revelation as anything other than judgement (Rahner 1994: 18, 20; cf. 153–4).

Rahner's approach to metaphysics is a very good example of the Cartesian 'turn to the subject'—a pervasive and much-contested motif in modern theology (Jüngel 1983: 108–26)—for in his view, since metaphysics is a human activity, 'it is necessarily an inquiry into human nature itself' (Rahner 1994: 3). Nevertheless, though philosophy of religion seeks 'to establish, on the basis of human nature, . . . an epistemological foundation for theology', it does not prescind from the autonomy of revelation by founding a contemporary 'natural religion' or by seeing it, with Schleiermacher, as 'but the objective counterpart of our human religious disposition' (Rahner 1994: 11, 92). Rather, since theology consists in free listening to God's free Word, theology must find 'validation' through establishing the conditions under which it is possible for us to hear this Word of revelation.

It is at this point that Rahner's metaphysics becomes controversial. Instead of offering, with traditional natural theology, a positive argument for God's existence and for his revealing himself, or, like Barth and Balthasar, refusing the demand for external validation and beginning with God's givenness in Christ, Rahner argues indirectly (or, in technical language, 'transcendentally') from anthropology and epistemology to the possibility of God's revealing himself and our being able to receive that revelation. Theology, 'as a listening to the personal revelation of the supremely free and transcendent God to humanity, cannot be set up in function of humanity', and therefore 'it always rests on the fact of such a Logos of God' (Rahner 1994: 145). However, theology's metaphysical validation is found in human beings' asking themselves the question of 'the being of beings' (Rahner 1994: 25) and their being unable not to go on asking it.

> Every answer is just the beginning of a new question. Man experiences himself as infinite possibility because in practice and in theory he necessarily places every sought-after result in question. He always situates it in a broader horizon which looms before him in its vastness. He is the spirit who experiences himself as spirit in that he does not experience himself as *pure* spirit. Man is not the unquestioning and unquestioned infinity of reality.

> He is the question which rises up before him, empty, but really and inescapably, and which can never be settled and never adequately answered by him. (Rahner 1978: 32)

So humans have a capacity for self-transcendence that is established in the question of being, but Rahner rejects the Heideggerian option of grounding the question of being in nothingness. Instead, metaphysical enquiry anticipates a final, absolute being as the ground of being.

> To be human is to be spirit, i.e., to live life while reaching ceaselessly for the absolute, in openness toward God. And this openness . . . is the condition of the possibility of what we are and have to be and always also are in our most humdrum life. Only that makes us human: that we are always on the way to God, whether or not we know it expressly, whether or not we will it. We are forever the infinite openness of the finite for God. (Rahner 1994: 53)

In this openness of humans for God Rahner finds both the condition of possibility for God's self-revelation and for humans receiving it and practising theology. But here lie two problems. First, with regard to anthropology it can be asked whether Rahner gives sufficient attention to the fact that human beings are sinners who refuse God's revelation, who crucified the Lord of glory. If we are 'always on the way to God . . . whether we will it or not', whence sin? This theme is inadequately treated in Rahner's philosophy of religion. Second, although he stresses God's freedom in revelation, in his philosophy of religion Rahner defines the conditions of its possibility in terms of his anthropology. This raises the question as to whether it is properly grounded in the unique, concrete events of Christ's incarnation, ministry, death, and resurrection or whether it is being understood, and therefore being qualified by, Rahner's metaphysical anthropology (cf. Marshall 1987). Is it 'the Logos of God' that gives the final and determinative shape to Rahner's metaphysics and theology, or is it anthropology? Does his treatment of the demand that theology validate itself leave Rahner open to Barth's charge that 'God's Word is no longer grace, and grace itself is no longer grace, if we ascribe to man a predisposition towards this Word, a possibility of knowledge regarding it that is intrinsically and independently native to him' (Barth 1975: 194)?

IV. Conclusion

With these questions we come to the basic question that has shaped the use of reason in systematic theology since the seventeenth century. Do humans have any power of their own by which they can come to some, albeit shadowy and incomplete, knowledge of God? As we have seen, our answer to this question has profound consequences for the doctrine of God, for Christology, for pneumatology, for anthropology, for soteriology, and for the mission of the church. Can theology and anthropology be brought into correlation in a way that does not so stress the sovereignty of God that humanity is diminished, or, on the other hand, so stress human capacity that God's free grace is diminished? Are Barth and Balthasar right in finding the solution to this dilemma in Christology? Here we seem to face two choices: either obligation to the demands of foundationalism and Kantian metaphysics, or obedience to what God has done in Jesus Christ and in the outpouring of the Holy Spirit; either a circular reasoning in which God is not assumed and perhaps never reached because fallen, finite, and sinful intelligence has no capacity to know God, or a circular reasoning that begins, continues, and ends with the sheerly given *logos* incarnate in Jesus Christ as he is attested in scripture and the teaching of the church (cf. Alston 1993).

References

Alston, William (1993). 'On Knowing That We Know: The Application to Religious Knowledge'. In C. Stephen Evans and Merold Westphal (eds.), *Christian Perspectives on Religious Knowledge*, Grand Rapids: Eerdmans, 15–39.

Anselm (1979). *Proslogion*. Notre Dame: Notre Dame University Press.

Balthasar, Hans Urs von (1991). *The Glory of the Lord: A Theological Aesthetics*, v. *The Realm of Metaphysics in the Modern Age*. Edinburgh: T. & T. Clark.

—— (2000). *Theo-Logic: Theological Logical Theory*, i. *Truth of the World*. San Francisco: Ignatius.

Barth, Karl (1957). *Church Dogmatics* II/1. Edinburgh: T. & T. Clark.

—— (1960). *Anselm: Fides Quaerens Intellectum: Anselm's Proof of the Existence of God in the Context of his Theological Scheme*. London: SCM.

—— (1975). *Church Dogmatics* I/1. Edinburgh: T. & T. Clark.

Buckley, Michael (1987). *At the Origins of Modern Atheism*. New Haven: Yale University Press.

Cranston, Maurice (1957). *John Locke: A Biography*. London: Longmans.

Descartes, René (1984). *The Philosophical Writings of Descartes*, ii. Cambridge: Cambridge University Press.

Holmer, Paul (1978). *The Grammar of Faith*. San Francisco: Harper and Row.

Jenson, Robert W. (1997–9). *Systematic Theology*. 2 vols. New York: Oxford University Press.

Jüngel, Eberhard (1983). *God as the Mystery of the World: On the Foundation of the Theology of the Crucified One in the Dispute between Theism and Atheism*. Edinburgh: T. & T. Clark.

Kant, Immanuel (1985). 'What is Enlightenment?' In Lewis White Beck (ed.), *Kant: On History*, New York: Macmillan, 3–10.

—— (1996). 'The Conflict of the Faculties'. In id., *Religion and Rational Theology*, Cambridge: Cambridge University Press, 239–327.

—— (1998). *Critique of Pure Reason*. Cambridge: Cambridge University Press.

Kasper, Walter (1984). *The God of Jesus Christ*. London: SCM.

Kaufman, Gordon (1993). *In Face of Mystery: A Constructive Theology*. Cambridge: Harvard University Press.

LINDBECK, GEORGE (1984). *The Nature of Doctrine: Religion and Theology in a Postliberal Age.* Philadelphia: Westminster.

LOCKE, JOHN (1975). *An Essay Concerning Human Understanding.* Oxford: Clarendon.

MARION, JEAN-LUC (2002). *Prolegomena to Charity.* New York: Fordham University Press.

MARSHALL, BRUCE (1987). *Christology in Conflict: The Identity of a Saviour in Rahner and Barth.* Oxford: Blackwell.

MICHALSON, GORDON E., JR. (1999). *Kant and the Problem of God.* Oxford: Blackwell.

MILBANK, JOHN (2000). 'The Programme of Radical Orthodoxy'. In Laurence Paul Hemming (ed.), *Radical Orthodoxy? A Catholic Enquiry,* Aldershot: Ashgate, 33–45.

—— (2003). *Being Reconciled: Ontology and Pardon.* London: Routledge.

MURPHY, NANCEY (1990). *Theology in the Age of Scientific Reasoning.* Ithaca and London: Cornell University Press.

PANNENBERG, WOLFHART (1968). *Jesus—God and Man.* London: SCM.

—— (1969). 'Dogmatic Theses on the Concept of Revelation'. In id. (ed.), *Revelation as History,* London: Sheed and Ward, 123–58.

—— (1991–8). *Systematic Theology.* 3 vols. Grand Rapids: Eerdmans.

PEACOCKE, ARTHUR (1993). *Theology for a Scientific Age: Being and Becoming—Natural, Divine and Human.* London: SCM.

PHILLIPS, D. Z. (2004). *The Problem of Evil and the Problem of God.* London: SCM.

PLANTINGA, ALVIN (2000). *Warranted Christian Belief.* Oxford: Oxford University Press.

POLKINGHORNE, JOHN (1994). *Science and Christian Belief: Reflections of a Bottom-Up Thinker.* London: SPCK.

RAHNER, KARL (1968). *Spirit in the World.* London: Sheed and Ward.

—— (1978). *Foundations of Christian Faith: An Introduction to the Idea of Christianity.* London: Darton Longman & Todd.

—— (1994). *Hearer of the Word: Laying the Foundation for a Philosophy of Religion.* New York: Continuum.

SWINBURNE, RICHARD (1994). *The Christian God.* Oxford: Oxford University Press.

TORRANCE, THOMAS F. (1969). *Theological Science.* Oxford: Oxford University Press.

VAN HUYSSTEEN, WENTZEL (1989). *Theology and the Justification of Faith: Constructing Theories in Systematic Theology.* Grand Rapids: Eerdmans.

WEBSTER, JOHN (2003). *Holiness.* London: SCM.

WESTPHAL, MEROLD (1990). 'Taking St Paul Seriously: Sin as an Epistemological Category'. In Thomas P. Flint (ed.), *Christian Philosophy,* Notre Dame: University of Notre Dame Press, 200–26.

WILES, MAURICE (1974). *The Remaking of Christian Doctrine.* London: SCM.

SUGGESTED READING

BALTHASAR (1991).

—— (2000).

—— (2004). *Theo-Logic: Theological Logical Theory,* ii. *Truth of God.* San Francisco: Ignatius.

Balthasar (2005). *Theo-Logic: Theological Logical Theory*, iii. *The Spirit of Truth*. San Francisco: Ignatius.

Barth (1957).

—— (1960).

—— (1975).

Buckley (1987).

Dalferth, Ingolf (1988). *Theology and Philosophy*. Oxford: Blackwell.

Frei, Hans (1992). *Types of Christian Theology*. New Haven: Yale University Press.

Kant, Immanuel (1996). *Religion and Rational Theology*. Cambridge: Cambridge University Press.

Kaufman (1993).

MacKinnon, Donald (1987). *Themes in Theology: Essays in Philosophy, Politics and Theology*. Edinburgh: T. & T. Clark.

Marshall, Bruce (2000). *Trinity and Truth*. Cambridge: Cambridge University Press.

Milbank (2003).

Murphy (1990).

Pannenberg (1991–8: vol. i).

Rahner (1978).

—— (1994).

Swinburne (1994).

Wiles (1974).

CHAPTER 23

EXPERIENCE

ELLEN T. CHARRY

Of all the sources of authority for Christian theology, experience is the most awkward and ambiguous. To close in on this contested and fluid topic we begin with a discussion of the questions surrounding it. By responding to them we will define experience for Christian theology as Christian theological experience (CTE), ruling out claims to experience that fall beyond this parameter. Having done that, the third section of our attempt will identify the variety within CTE using four classic examples: St Teresa of Avila, Robert Barclay, Jonathan Edwards, and Karl Rahner. Following that we will offer some suggestions for future developments.

I. Questions Surrounding Experience in Theology

We begin with questions surrounding experience as a source for theology with a prefatory note. It is not accidental that experience often falls last in the list of sources and norms for Christian theology. Since theology is conversation about God and the things of God, sources or bases for undertaking that conversation are generally understood to be places to which we turn to gain insight into and knowledge of the truth about God and things with which God has to do. That is, in a broad sense, sources of theology are places of revelation understood as knowledge of God. With this understanding of sources in mind, the reasons why experience sometimes fits awkwardly with scripture, tradition, reason, and the rest become more evident.

First, formal recognition of experience as a source of knowledge of God is relatively new for theology as well as philosophy. For this reason, we will consider examples of CTE in the sixteenth, seventeenth, eighteenth, and twentieth centuries. Although we will consider a salient example of CTE from the sixteenth century, it only becomes a formal category in the seventeenth century in England with the beginnings of modern science and philosophy.

Francis Bacon advocated experimental science as a way of gaining empirical knowledge about the world. His ideas were explored and expanded by the Royal Society, officially founded in 1660 to study his work and advance experimental science. At that point, science and philosophy began to part ways as separate means to knowledge and perhaps as different visions of knowledge. On the way to separation, 'experimental philosophy' depended on matters of 'fact', either events of daily life that were common knowledge and publicly observable, or laboratory procedures that were contrived but verifiable in front of witnesses (Dear 1990: 46–7). To know something 'experimentally' was to claim authenticity for it by appeal either to common experience or to publicly verifiable scientific observation that apparently amounted to the same thing. Experience and experiment (a particular form of experience) radically reshaped both philosophy and science at that time, particularly through the psychological empiricism proposed in John Locke's *Essay Concerning Human Understanding* of 1689 (Locke 1964).

A second reason for putting experience last is that it is slippery. As the unity of what would later be separated into personal experience and scientific experiment suggests (to us), it is too broad a category to be specific. In current uses of the term, locutions like 'in my experience' can become so detached from the knowledge of God that virtually any human experience can be proposed as experience of God. The term becomes either theologically empty or simply a personal objection to an interlocutor, a cipher (Schner 2003: 110–13). The problem here is that if all human experience qualifies as divine revelation, there is no revelation, let alone divine illumination, as Augustine called it, or special calling, as did Calvin. Here the problem is not the subjectivity of the interpretation of experience so much as mistaking human for divine experience. Group or individual reports of political, economic, and social experience as experience of God—rather than as man-made conditions—make knowledge of God difficult to discriminate from general experience. It raises the question of what counts as an experience of divine illumination and revelation.

The slipperiness of experience in theology is illustrated by the rise of North American theologies of identity in the late twentieth century that claim group experiences of suffering as the primary norm for theological reflection, subordinating tradition, scripture, and reason to it. Although only black and feminist theology will be discussed here, since their creation many more racial, ethnic, and other communities have followed their lead.

Black theology was created by James Cone in the late 1960s. His *Black Theology and Black Power* (1969) picked up the orientation of the black power movement that split off from the integrationist civil rights movement for school desegregation, which was sparked by Brown v. Board of Education (1954) and carried forward by Martin Luther King, Jr. In 1970 Cone published *A Black Theology of Liberation*, in which his training in the theology of Karl Barth was radicalized by a Marxist interest. Under criticism that he was still under the influence of 'white theology', Cone later sought to ground his theology in black cultural sources and 'the black experience', understood as the experience of slavery and its after-effects in the US. Thus, black theology lifts up a generalized picture of the distinctive experience of the descendants of African slaves in the US as the central datum for theology—or for black theology if it understands itself to be sectarian, which is not always clear.

Feminist theology followed in the late 1970s. It entered the scene as a North American expression of 'second wave' feminism that traces itself to Simone de Beauvoir. When de Beauvoir's *The Second Sex* was translated into English in the early 1950s, writers like Valerie Saiving (1960) and Betty Friedan (1963) picked up her work and expressed a feminine outlook on sin and on life in the workplace respectively. By the late 1960s the term 'feminist' had replaced feminine, suggesting an ideological outlook on women's issues. In the late 1970s and early 1980s, politically aroused Christian and Jewish women began to challenge their traditions in a trenchant manner that often focused on scriptural and church teaching on the subordination of women and on a notion of sin that seemed to stigmatize them by associating women with lust and licentiousness. Comparable to 'black experience', 'women's experience' was defined in terms of patriarchy, the idea that almost all societies are hierarchical social systems structured by men that do not admit 'the full humanity of women'.

The cry for freedom expressed by these early writers was transformed both politically, by the black power movement that radicalized and broke with the civil rights movement, and intellectually, by deconstruction, especially in its French forms. Michel Foucault, for example, integrated Marx, Freud, and Nietzsche, who sharpened our understanding that knowledge is power, or, more specifically, that power generates knowledge. Knowledge then is not discovered or uncovered, but shaped to the interests of those with the power to do so. Black and feminist theology thus came to see classical theology as the patriarchal, hegemonic expression of a white, European, male elite that constructs reality to suit its own needs, including the suppression of non-Europeans and women. Accordingly, the discourse of liberation shifted from the call for freedom of opportunity to participate in culturally powerful institutions to the quest for power to transform them.

With this turn, there is no longer truth that comes from God but only competing visions of power. This paved the way for theological construals of women's experience, black experience, Hispanic experience, Jewish experience, and so on as sources of theological authority—authority once thought to reside in scripture, the creeds, philosophy, and so on.

A question arises, however, when group experiences of trauma and suffering are claimed as CTE. What exactly is being claimed? Is the point that knowing God or experiencing God now resides exclusively in the trauma or in vicarious suffering by historically disadvantaged groups? Or, is it, as the US Roman Catholic bishops put it, that God has a preferential option for the poor and loves them more than the wealthy because of their economic status? If so, this is a radically new vision of theological authority or, perhaps, of election. The implications for theology are far-reaching. Personal or group experience becomes the will of God over against scripture, tradition, reason, worship, and so on (Charry 1991).

The slipperiness of special group reports of experience of God is visible in phrases like 'women's experience', or 'the black experience', or to expand the case a bit, 'the experience of war', or 'the experience of motherhood'. These conceptual construals may capture certain experiences of many individuals, but they are unavoidably reductionist generalizations. They inevitably essentialize and simplify a set of experiences and then claim to represent a group of persons whose actual experiences are far broader than any snapshot can capture. Such phrases have the effect of flattening and squeezing those who qualify to speak to the issue at hand—women, blacks, veterans, mothers—into predefined types that may be helpful for some purposes but inevitably foreshorten and misrepresent the experiences of some of those on whose behalf they seek to speak. In order to count as a woman one must have a certain experience of or at least outlook on patriarchy; to be 'black enough' one must have a certain outlook on race; to be a true mother one must have a certain sense of self-sacrifice; to count as a true war veteran one must experience some degree of post-traumatic stress disorder; and so on.

One result of this movement of the past forty years is that the notion of CTE has been transformed from personal intimacy with God, or personal experience of the comfort of divine grace, into a political tool for advancing the agenda of special-interest groups who rewrite the Christian map along sociological, cultural, and bioethnic lines.

A third reason for experience's last place in the list is that it is contended within theology, and this for two reasons, each of which offers a different reading of the topic. First is the question of what kind of experience is appropriate as a source for theology. While modern liberal Roman Catholic theologians like Karl Rahner and Bernard Lonergan make strong appeals to the necessity of understanding the knowing subject in order to understand divine revelation (Rahner 1979; Lonergan 1958), Reformed theologian Karl Barth robustly objects to any theological appeal to general human experience or to a universal aspect of human nature that enables us to understand or know God (Barth 1975). For Barth, there is no *homo religiosus*; knowledge of God comes exclusively from divine initiative (basically, the incarnation). While coming to know Jesus Christ through Barth's threefold account of revelation is a proper experience for those confronted by the Word of God and thus for a theology that reflects on such experience, no other type of experience is. For Roman Catholics, on the other hand, all are *homines religiosi* by dint of the divine grace of our creatureliness.

One source of such contention is disagreement over whether experience in theology is of common or special revelation. Yet, even if this were to be settled, another question arises. Many of those who claim experience as having theological authority are not referring to experiences available to everyone, either through common or special Christian scriptural revelation, but to immediate, individual, private, or semi-private experiences of divine illumination, visions, epiphanies, or flashes of clarity, insight, or understanding that are claimed to be personally transforming, often as moments of conversion from nominal Christianity to evangelical faith. This is a problem shared by Catholic mystics and Protestant evangelicals who challenge ecclesiastical authority and established custom and ways of thinking. This is the same problem for religious authority as that posed by the Montanist movement as early as the second century. Medieval mystics were often scrutinized because of their claims to immediate experiences of God in the form of visions, revelations, or openings which threatened to undermine established ecclesiastical authority. In the early fourteenth century, Marguerite Porete was burned at the stake as a heretic and Meister Eckhart posthumously condemned.

In the modern period, the derogatory term for individual or group experience claimed as an immediate basis for knowing God is 'enthusiasm' (Knox 1950). John Locke criticized the 'enthusiast' claimants to independent inspiration or revelation in his *Essay* (4. 19, in Locke 1964: 428–33). R. A. Knox charted enthusiasm in Protestantism from the Quakers to the German Lutheran Pietists, the Moravians, the Camisards in France, the Shakers in America, and back to the Methodists in England. Within Catholicism he cites the Jansenists and the Quietists and Molinists. His outline is classic.

Distinguishing private or sub-group revelation from daydreams, wish-fulfilment, (self-)delusion, a simple mistake, political aspiration, or mental illness has proven difficult, especially for observers who are asked to take such reports seriously as theological data. The question here is what authenticates or qualifies the specific experience of any particular individual or group to have their reported experience count as a source of the knowledge of God. Debate is frequently intense because individual and group claims (often seen as sectarian by others) may be perceived as undermining or subordinating other more central claims to theological authority, like scripture or church teaching, while the reporters of idiosyncratic experience of divine illumination often want to reform or purify religious establishments that they deem to have lapsed into formalism or corruption or succumbed to bureaucratic efficiency, and therefore to be lacking in religious verve.

In response, as black and feminist theologies were gaining strength, another but softer marginalized voice was beginning to speak. The Society of Christian Philosophy was organized in 1978 and began their journal *Faith and Philosophy* in 1984. Over the past twenty years, a reawakened Christian philosophy has attended to justifying the validity of religious belief in general and more recently to the justification of claims to individual experience of God, especially claims of mystical experience (Alston 1991; Jantzen 1987; Mason 1987; Salamon 2004; Swinburne 1979). Among these works, the most significant for a discussion of CTE is that of William Alston. He supplies philosophical argumentation to support the epistemological validity of Christian mystical experience. In *Perceiving God* he argues that it is 'rational to engage in any socially established doxastic practice that we do not have sufficient reasons for regarding as unreliable' (Alston 1991: 6). A 'doxastic' practice is a way of forming beliefs and epistemically evaluating them that relies upon sense perception, introspection, memory, rational intuition, various kinds of reasoning, and mystical experience. He argues that no cogent argument can be brought against mystical experiences that claim to be of God, and that these experiences therefore cannot be declared irrational or unreliable on the basis of evidence.

Altson is responding directly to the general Christian anxiety over mysticism that besets those who claim admittance to the company of theologians on the basis of their direct experience of God rather than publicly approved sources like scripture, creeds, and reason. The first major skirmish between spiritual theologians and scholastic theologians was between St Bernard of Clairvaux and Abelard in the twelfth century (Evans 1980: 79–90). Abelard won the debate and his view of theology came to preclude spiritual theology as theology at all. Dogmatic theology, commonly understood as exclusively the province of minds trained in the scholastic intellectual tradition has, until quite recently, excluded most women theologians as well as men from the lower classes. Such exclusion of the untrained would relegate thinkers like Teresa of Avila, Catherine of Siena, and Julian of Norwich to the category of spiritual writers or mystics, as if mystics are not also theologians. (In fact, the Vatican in 1970 named Teresa and Catherine doctors of the church on account of their theological writings.) Exclusion of spiritual writings as theological on the grounds that these voices did not come from professional theologians has two consequences for our understanding of CTE. First, it denies precisely the point of theological experience as a source of the knowledge of God: that it is the spontaneous working of the Holy Spirit and not simply the application of the trained mind to data supplied by scripture, creeds, canons, and so on. Second, it has the effect of distancing systematic theology, or any theology that relies on experience, from the vast majority of Christian believers.

II. Parameters of Christian Theological Experience

To wend our way through this contended and unstable topic, we will confine the discussion to CTE that we define as knowledge of the God Christians worship, received as a gift of grace or divine illumination, frequently attributed to the Holy Spirit. This does not at all suggest that CTE is not subject to all the conditions and philosophical questions relating to other types of experience, although it is distinguished from them in that it is attributed to God. For example, St Augustine, in his account of his decision to embrace Christianity in a Milan garden, interprets the child's voice that he heard saying 'take and read' 'as a divine command' (Augustine 1991: 153). St Catherine of Siena experiences a union with God which she expects on the basis of John 14: 21–3 through 'continuous humble prayer'. 'For by such prayer the soul is united with God, following in the footsteps of Christ crucified, and through desire and affection and the union of love he makes of her another himself' (Catherine of Siena 1980: 25). Note that it is not the prayer that effects the union, but God who effects the union through the one who prays. For his part, Calvin views CTE as the result of preaching and treats it under his doctrine of 'special calling'. It is an interpretation of Matthew 22: 14. Special calling 'he deigns for the most part to give to the believers alone, while by the inward illumination of his Spirit he causes the preached Word to dwell in their hearts' (*Institutes*, 3. 24. 8, in Calvin 1960: 974). In all cases—and this is significant for our definition here—the recipient is prepared for the specific experience by prior familiarity with and practice of the Christian tradition. The recipient applies mental and emotional resources to interpret it.

Although CTE is an inward illumination or special calling, it is not discontinuous with other experience. The frequent deployment of 'mysticism' to dismiss such reports of spiritual vivification is surely an abuse of the term and cannot explain such reported experiences that are central to the evangelical tradition, for example. CTE is at once psychological, intellectual, and religious, and to that extent, continuous with other types of experience that modern psychology, epistemology, and comparative religion appropriately examine from their perspectives.

Nor does limiting the discussion to CTE suggest that spiritual experiences reported by non-Christians cannot be interpreted Christianly. It only serves to identify Christian experience theologically, just as theologians identify Christian revelation, Christian scripture, Christian tradition, and Christian worship—that is, as sources of knowledge of the God Christians confess. Reason will be discussed at the end of this section.

To examine this definition further, let us consider the work of the young Friedrich Schleiermacher, the five famous speeches *On Religion*—often considered to be an appeal to religious experience. Schleiermacher described what he called a pure or natural religion that is prior to, separable from, and more general than what we are calling CTE (Schleiermacher 1996). He clearly intended this: the speeches are not on Christianity but on religion. (The fourth speech, on religious associations and their leadership, while it takes its point of departure from Christian forms, is still meant to be understood generically.) In the second and most important speech, religion is not knowledge but a pious affection: 'It wishes to intuit the universe, wishes devoutly to overhear the universe's own manifestations and actions, longs to be grasped and filled by the universe's immediate influences in childlike passivity' (Schleiermacher 1996: 22). He elaborates a formal and pre-thematic vision of the infinite or the eternal beneath, behind, or throughout the finite world, reminiscent of the ancient Stoic, Christian, and Plotinian notions of the logos. He calls upon his readers to cultivate an attitude of contemplative piety toward this transcendent vision, an insight or ability to set aside 'the extraneous parts', to 'read between the lines', to 'crack open this shell' of the positive or actual religion that the highly educated distrust and disrespect (Schleiermacher 1996: 21–2). He urges them to press on to the deeper, 'pure' intent of actual religion that is always altered and corrupted in its practice and articulation. Only in the last of the five speeches does he urge his readers to forbear with the positive religions with which they are familiar, including Christianity.

Schleiermacher does not claim that the pious affection that he confusingly defines as religion and that he urges as an orientation to the world is an experience or epiphany of God; it is rather a spiritual attitude that he pleads ought to structure one's manner of apprehending things. Now, that spiritual attitude can produce moments of apprehending the unity of 'infinite and living nature' and excitement at being a part of it (Schleiermacher 1996: 24). The memory of such intense moments of feeling is the basis of piety and the moral life; they are emotional experiences. Such pure religion 'proceeds from an influence of the intuited on the one who intuits, from an original and independent action of the former, which is then grasped, apprehended, and conceived by the latter according to one's nature' (Schleiermacher 1996: 24–5).

From the point of view of CTE, there are several problems with Schleiermacher's proposal. What Schleiermacher fails to note is that his ability to make this last claim is the result of his familiarity with that very positive religion that he will not admit into the discussion. This hidden assumption is at work all along the line. The ability to attribute feeling to God is only possible because of the ideas and principles of a positive religious tradition (for example, Judaism, Christianity, or Islam) that he has previously dismissed as belonging to the realm of science, that is, the science of philosophical rationalism to which his Romanticism objects. Feeling must be articulated in some terms, and for Schleiermacher, whether he admits it or not, those terms are precisely the Christian ones that he says he is setting aside in order to appeal to Christianity's cultured despisers. But it cannot be done. Feelings and attitudes that structure the moral life, or the intellectual life for that matter, are articulated and shaped by ideas and principles that are culturally accessible, even if these be stated in inventive ways.

Schleiermacher follows the same pattern in his great dogmatic presentation of Christianity, *The Christian Faith* (1986). Here religious feeling is further specified as a particular feeling, that of utter dependence. It is now a religious self-consciousness, and it is from that foundation that Christian doctrines derive their articulation, meaning, and authority for individuals (Schleiermacher 1986: 76–8). Now, we have argued that Schleiermacher has stated the case backward. It is not feeling that provides doctrines with meaning, but quite the reverse. Doctrines (including vague and imprecise notions carried from childhood or gleaned from casual conversation or the media) shape feelings into attitudes that provide guidance for life and appreciation of the world, even if unselfconsciously so. Indeed, it can also be argued that the feeling of utter dependence which Schleiermacher thought universal is an expression of the salient Christian virtue of humility with a particularly Protestant emphasis on the utter helplessness of man to save himself. The insistence on feeling as religious self-consciousness was far more deeply formed by his Moravian upbringing than Schleiermacher seems to be aware of. He generalizes from it to all persons as prior to doctrinal expression.

In short, Schleiermacher sustains the basic mistake of *On Religion* in his dogmatics. When he says that 'man is born with the religious capacity' (Schleiermacher 1986: 124), he is not really saying that we have an innate ability to know God without revelation, as Barth may have read him. He is only saying that we have feelings that lead us to cultivate attitudes and values that guide us through life. What he fails to see is that these are shaped by 'positive' religious traditions as well as any number of other possibilities: ideologies, folklore, consumer culture, and so on. This criticism was raised against Schleiermacher's *Glaubenslehre* early on by one Dr. Bretschneider. In his first letter to Dr. Lücke, Schleiermacher rejects it 'because that conception is not a knowledge of the mode of determination of my being, nor does it develop first out of that knowledge' (Schleiermacher 1981: 38).

What do we conclude from the previous discussion for our understanding of experience for Christian theology? We have argued that Schleiermacher failed to offer a persuasive account that the attitude he asks his readers to adopt prior to Christian content is an experience or that it is religion. Rather it is an attitude of awe toward the world and a subsequent sense of dependence. His liberal Protestant desire to offer a universal religious framework, of which Christianity is but one—although the best—example, failed. All religions do not simply promote awe and connectedness to it. Each set of religious claims seeks to be taken on its own terms, even though there are considerable overlaps and concerns that many share.

Inadvertently, Schleiermacher supports the position we have adopted here. Experience for Christian theology can only be CTE, that is, experiences of the God Christians talk about, shaped by interactions with revelation, scripture, tradition, worship, and Christian thought itself.

Further, because he advocates an attitude rather than confirming a universal experience, Schleiermacher has not successfully argued that the attitude he commends can contend as an epiphany of God or source of revelation. It is not by the grace of God that one experiences the truth of God but a posture that one ought to adopt in order to see religiously. In short, in *On Religion*, Schleiermacher may appear to be talking about religious experience, but he is more interested in advocating a stance toward or way of interpreting the world. What Schleiermacher is advocating is not intentionally CTE, or knowledge, or either experience or knowledge of God; implicitly, however, it is these things, because he has inadmissibly sneaked in Christian presuppositions despite the stated parameters of his inquiry.

This inquiry, by contrast, focuses on a certain type of psychological, intellectual, and religious experience: that of God and things with which God has to do according to Christian claims to know him. So, we begin by defining experience for Christian theology as divine illumination or special calling of individuals or groups by the triune God known through Christian revelation, including scripture, tradition (canons, creeds, and theology), and worship. This is the fourth and perhaps most important reason that experience is listed last among the sources; it relies on those that have come before. Indeed, it is a subset of special revelation.

This definition of experience for systematic theology specifies CTE beyond any vague, prearticulate sensation or perception of a *mysterium tremendum*, an aesthetic dimension of reality, or a broadly transcendent dimension of existence with moral overtones that one may come in contact with in discrete moments of life: at the edge of the ocean, in a sudden violent thunderstorm, a sunrise or sunset, a mass crowd experience, or moments of death or birth. Such experiences may give one pause by evoking a sense of awe in the observer: an awareness of one's smallness and helplessness in the face of powerful currents of life, or forces of nature that even experts cannot control. Or, on a more religious note, they may arouse awareness that there is a great scheme of things into which we have no choice but to fit or perish in despair. Such evocative moments may stimulate a personal search for a religious or spiritual framework that can accommodate such experiences in a way that provides meaning and moral direction for life. We may call these spiritual, but they must be interpreted within the confines of the Christian theological tradition for them to be considered CTEs.

While such immediate experiences may arouse what can be called spiritual feelings of awe or anxiety, they are as yet without the historically conditioned context of the Christian religion by means of which they are structured and interpreted. These do not yet qualify as CTE because they are too vague and imprecise to be considered experiences either of God as Christians know him or the things with which God has to do, although if they suggest a creator, for example, the individual is already within the sphere of western theism. CTE is never unstructured, but takes shape and finds meaning as it is articulated through the sources and norms of Christian theology (Tilley 1994). So, it is no denigration of or sign of distrust in experience to put it at the end of the list. Rather, this is most appropriate, for, as Schner notes, there is no religious experience that is not 'constructed' by the persons undergoing it (Schner 2003: 114). For example, by the time I realize that I am having a headache, I realize that the sensation I so name may have been going on for some time, but until I become aware of it, I was not experiencing a headache. Unless I have had a headache before, or have read or heard about these sensations from others, the sensations within my body have no meaningful context within which to be named, interpreted, and understood. So it is with CTE: it functions within the parameters established by the other sources. Experiences that stray beyond these parameters may be theological, Christian, spiritual, liberating, or any number of other things, but the meaningfulness of CTE is circumscribed and constrained by Christian theology's other sources of self-understanding. Before we close this section, however, there are two objections to this suggestion that must be answered.

One objection to the suggestion of limiting experience for theology to CTE is that the claim that reason is a source of theological authority is not confined to a special Christian vision of reason and so neither should experience. Since there is no particularly Christian handle on reason, claiming a particularly Christian handle on experience is an inappropriate stricture. Any experience should be admissible as a source of theological authority, just as any careful use of reason is.

This objection raises a larger question as to what counts as data for any field of inquiry: alchemy, astrology, astronomy, biology, phrenology, psychology, and so on. Each type of inquiry has interests, and data to be considered in advancing the field must fit within those interests. Some data will simply fall outside its parameters and be irrelevant. Theology too has a field of interest: the God of Israel revealed again as Jesus Christ. And so it is just as appropriate for theology to limit what counts as data for its inquiry to matters pertaining to this God as it is for astronomy or astrology to limit admissible data to matters pertaining to the stars. Indeed, fields of inquiry differentiate themselves from one another by what they examine and the perspective from which they examine it.

Another objection to CTE is that such confinement may exclude criticism from the activity of theology. This poses a serious problem. The history of Christian self-criticism teaches us that theology must always be a self-critical undertaking even when it is an apologetic undertaking. Experience that counts against Christian claims should not be excluded *a limine*, lest theology become isolated from salutary counsels that come from outside its guarded corridors. As the examples below will show, those attesting to CTE are often doing so in the service of loving Christian self-examination.

Here we finally come to the positive task of experience for theology within the various sources and norms. Heretofore, we have examined objections to experience *per se*, queries about what counts as authentic Christian experience, and concerns that experience may manipulate theology to particular political ends. Now we come to see the constructive contribution of experience to the Christian theological conversation.

Acknowledging individual or even group experience of the God of Israel revealed again as Jesus Christ has usually functioned as a corrective to school theology that prides itself on not attending to the testimony of individual or particular group experience and insight but reason, scripture, and tradition alone. Guided by these three since the twelfth and thirteenth centuries, school theology has claimed a universal authority that has yet been regularly challenged by the voices of mystics, contemplatives, and pastors who are their proper other-voice. A careful definition of experience will offer an internal corrective to other sources of theological authority, keeping it apprised of and sensitive to loving dissent from those committed to the tradition and to the wellbeing of the church catholic. This was the case with the Franciscan controversy over poverty in the thirteenth and fourteenth centuries, in which the rigorous spiritualists censured the wealth of the medieval church and stood as a beacon of light in the midst of confusion about the identity of the church even if only recognized as such in retrospect. The strongest criticism of a field of inquiry comes from within rather that from without. In this regard, CTE will better serve the needs of Christian theology than will experience that is not explicitly Christian. That experience-in-general is excluded as a source for Christian theology does not compromise the important critical and corrective role that experience plays in Christian theology.

III. Varieties of Christian Theological Experience

Having set parameters on experience for theology as CTE we now will examine its breadth by looking at the writings of several significant figures: St Teresa of Avila (1515–82), Robert Barclay (1648–90), Jonathan Edwards (1703–58), and Karl Rahner (1904–84). Chronologically, they represent Christian mysticism, the Radical Reformation, Protestant evangelicalism, and contemporary Roman Catholic theology. Only in retrospect does the theology of St Teresa qualify as advancing CTE as a source of theological authority. For, as noted previously, experience became a topic of interest first in seventeenth-century England. To the best of this writer's knowledge, the first formally to elevate direct divine illumination as the central source of direction of the church and the Christian life was George Fox, the founder of the Society of Friends, or 'Quakers' (initially a term of derision). Robert Barclay was to Fox as Philip Melanchthon was to Martin Luther. Jonathan Edwards appropriated individual experience as a central feature of evangelicalism that did not separate cognition from affect. Finally, as modernity turned to the knowing subject, examination of that subject was incorporated into theology. Karl Rahner will be our representative here. Looking at the notion of CTE these figures will illustrate some of the reasons for the anxiety and confusion surrounding experience as a source or norm for theology.

Probing the Inner Life: St Teresa of Avila (1515–82)

Teresa of Jesus sought nothing less than spiritual perfection. She was a tortured soul who considered herself evil and sinful, yet she was committed as a religious to love God with all that she was. She is well known for her role in reforming and founding convents and monasteries in Spain during the Catholic Reformation. Here, however, we are interested in her analysis of her own religious experience, generally regarded by history as mystical. It is recorded in her autobiography and evident in her most important work, *The Interior Castle*, both written under obedience for the sake of guiding the inner life of other nuns and interested persons (Teresa of Avila 1979; 1960).

In a religious culture that recited its prayers in community, Teresa became committed to 'mental' or silent prayer and, like Hannah before her, raised eyebrows with her internalized prayer life. She analysed her emotional life and her setting theologically in the context of her prayer life. She was embarrassingly blessed with special favours from God—intuitions, visions, and locutions—some of which she referred to as raptures. Some of these comforted her, but others tormented her, and she sought spiritual guidance from experts. She was perhaps too trusting of respected authorities, listening to their advice and interpretations of her inner life perhaps too readily. This often left her fearful and worried as to whether the favours she received were from God or the devil. She knew that people around her thought she was mentally ill—to the extent that they had such a category—or in their categories, that her soul was caught in a conflict between God and the devil. She tried to quit the life of prayer and to obey her advisers and confessors. She abandoned friendships that were spiritually bad for her, and sought solitude and the companionship of books or, alternatively, accepted the advice of others never to be alone and to stop reading books. She wanted only to please God and not arouse the jealousy of those not favoured with the raptures she enjoyed. In her autobiography, Teresa gives us an intimate picture of these epiphanies, visions, and locutions. She tells us how to recognize them, how to resist them (as she is ordered), how to interpret them, and how to distinguish a vision or locution from God from one from the devil.

From St Teresa's experience it is easy to see why individual CTE is so volatile. It offends the existing order not only of the ecclesiastical power structure and the theological guilds, but of convention. Because such experience is both private and personal it appears to be of little use to a systematic theology that seeks to be public and communal. Yet, Teresa and those who ordered her to write realized that her experience of exceptional intimacy with God, although idiosyncratic, was inspired and would therefore be instructive to others who were similarly favoured.

Illumination for Reforming the Church: Robert Barclay (1648–90)

Since our interest here is in systematic theology, it is appropriate to turn to Robert Barclay, a Scot, rather than to the fiery Englishman George Fox, to appreciate the formal entrance of CTE into theology. The reason is that Barclay wrote a classic *Apology* for Quakerism, an orderly presentation of doctrine that follows the order of the *Westminster Shorter Catechism* (Barclay and Freiday 1967).

Barclay's *Apology* elaborates fifteen theological theses that set forth the theological doctrine of the Friends. These resonate with Puritan concerns, but go further in their resistance to outward religion. Four of them set forth the Friends' doctrine of CTE. The *Apology* is clear that Friends organize around the third article of the creed. CTE is often Spirit-oriented, since the Holy Spirit is the most accessible, unprogrammed, and continuingly dynamic way that God reveals himself, unites believers with Christ, and guides and comforts them.

The first two theses of the *Apology* are on the true knowledge of God and inward, unmediated revelation. They are explicit that the agency of the Holy Spirit, who makes Christ live in the hearts of contemporary believers, is the central authority for Friends. Barclay put this thesis on inward and unmediated revelation before that on the authority of scripture, suggesting that individual inward experience of and direct knowledge of God have their own authority. Friends were heavily criticized and persecuted for this 'subversion' of accepted standards of theological authority.

Following Fox, Barclay read specific New Testament passages in light of the modern interest in the power of direct experience, concluding that authentic faith requires a personal inward experience of Christ whose agent is the Holy Spirit. Barclay was theologically literate and traced the divine illumination theme through Augustine, Clement of Alexandria, Tertullian, Athanasius, Cyril of Alexandria, and Bernard (in that order). The Holy Spirit verifies souls in true, that is, inward, knowledge of God. Against this, all outward forms and formal expressions of piety, worship, and obedience pale; sacraments, preaching, singing, clergy, and liturgy crumble. Scripture is retained, but takes a backseat to immediate spiritual knowledge: 'these inward illuminations possess their own clarity and serve as their own evidence' (Barclay and Freiday 1967: 5). The early Friends were persecuted, jailed, publicly punished, and even executed for their theological views and the style of worship that followed from them.

Conversion: Jonathan Edwards (1703–58)[1]

The American Puritan preacher, theologian, and philosopher Jonathan Edwards worked out a view of CTE as spiritual perception, offering an interpretation of the affections that avoids both enthusiasm on one hand and strong rationalism on the other.

At the heart of eighteenth-century revivalism was the centrality of personal conversion stirred by passionate preaching. Revivals are a crowd phenomenon. This form of religious experience is personal and public rather than personal and private as in the case of St Teresa. One of Edwards's greatest philosophical contributions lay in his working out an epistemology of spiritual perception, a specific form of Christian religious experience, to give intellectual respectability to the revival. He insisted that feeling and mental judgements are integrated, but he distinguished passions which overpower the mind from religious affections in which the mind is not overpowered but fully engaged (Edwards 1959: 98). Conversion or regeneration involves normal emotional and cognitive processes, but the indwelling of the Holy Spirit provides 'a new foundation . . . for a new kind of exercises [*sic*] of the same faculty of understanding' (Edwards 1959: 206).

In his review of scholarship on Edwards's 'new sense', 'spiritual sense', or 'sense of the heart', Michael J. McClymond argues that it has three aspects. It is a perception of the excellence of the divine (also called 'holiness', 'beauty', or 'amiability'); it proceeds by illumination of the grace of the Holy Spirit (along Augustinian lines); and it is essentially a feeling of delight and joy in God and in the beauty of the things of God (McClymond 1997: 208). To apply this affective epistemology to the evangelistic setting, a whole audience may hear a fine sermon, and all understand rationally what is being said. Yet, only some—the regenerate—will grasp the story of the life, death, and glorification of Christ in terms of the divine beauty or excellency itself and be thrilled by it. This illumination is morally transforming because the Holy Spirit provides the regenerate with a new disposition and guides their human actions as properly godly and holy.

Edwards, then, upheld Calvinist doctrines of grace and election and yet also recognized the role which emotion plays in thought, thus grounding Protestant evangelicalism in its Puritan heritage while employing the empirical psychology of his day. Here we have not only a far more public account of Christian

[1] With thanks to Professor Sang Lee for help and suggestions in distilling the work of Edwards.

religious experience than we have seen hitherto, but a philosophically sophisticated presentation as well.

Openness to God: Karl Rahner, SJ (1904–84)[2]

Although working in a completely different context and tradition, Karl Rahner sustained Edwards's insight that experience is both cognitive and affective (Rahner 1979). He began his theology with the encouraging view that one great gift of divine grace is that God has created us to be united with his own life. All persons are open to and in search of their own fulfilment, a fulfilment which lies in and is enabled by God, which comes through his self-communication to us, and which is unconditionally and irreversibly assured as historical possibility in the paschal mystery of the incarnate Word. God's gift of himself is received through embodied experience of it. For this reason, analysing human experience as embodied transcendent experience is central to Rahner's understanding of theological knowledge.

Experience and knowledge are closely linked. Rahner sees experience in general as imaginative, cognitive, and affective together, and he distinguishes knowledge or experience that we cannot yet name and by means of which we live unselfconsciously (unthematic knowledge) from that which we think we realize and understand so that we live and choose responsibly (thematic knowledge).

Rahner's conviction of the transcendent nature of the human spirit is that we all face the divine mystery as a gift of God's love. That experience is central not only to Rahner's view of human psychology but also to his understanding of the task of theology. His orientation to experience challenged the Roman Catholic hierarchy of his day. 'He urged the hierarchical magisterium not to reduce faith to a mere blind affirmation of official teachings coupled with the minimum requirements of church attendance' (Kelly 1992). The pastoral challenge for the professional theologian is to help both the churched and the unchurched, all of whom are addressed by God at the level of everyday experience, to come to interpret that experience in theologically conceptualized or thematized Christian terms: the trinitarian vision of God and the hypostatic union of the incarnate Christ.

Rahner's interest is in construing human nature as seeking to know and find the fullest possible reality that presses beyond itself toward God. This is a result of divine grace. God is always choosing us and wishes to choose us for himself forever. Every human word can be oriented Godward because God has already communicated himself to us in the incarnation of the Word. This and the paschal mystery convey to us God's longing for us. Because he has created us to know him and acted graciously so that we can know him, unselfconscious living may rise to the conscious level at which life is lived toward God.

[2] With thanks to Professor Leo O'Donovan for help and suggestions in distilling the work of Rahner.

IV. Conclusion

The previous discussion suggests that the current status of the discussion of CTE is complex and ambiguous. It is complex because it spans many interpretations and historical periods. It is ambiguous because it has been variously co-opted for reform of the church, control of popular outburst, and political programmes. The four examples of CTE illustrate why ambivalence swirls about it. Although all of our writers understood religious experience as a means to reform or transform both individuals and the church structures they were part of—St Teresa to reform and found convents, Barclay to enliven the Church of England, Edwards as part of the great movement of eighteenth-century evangelicalsm, and Rahner as a critic of the Roman Catholic hierarchy—no clear pattern emerges, although they share a common conviction. The hope of CTE is to internalize and personalize the doctrines, practices, decrees, and ordinances of the church.

Rahner's dogmatic use of religious experience is controlled by the doctrines of creation and divine grace and so is regularized for systematic theology; for the other writers, CTE is irregular. It presses at the edges or limits of doctrinal and ecclesiastical authority because it is spontaneous, emotional, unpredictable, perhaps even disconcerting, and, in its more evangelical forms, associated with the most dynamic and spontaneous person of the Trinity, the Holy Spirit. Further, while an evangelical like John Wesley gained a deep sense of peace and comfort from his conversion experience, immediate insights believed to be from God can also induce grave self-doubt and often call people to unconventional attitudes and actions. These in turn can bring both social censure as well as censure from threatened religious authorities—as St Teresa, the Quakers, and the revivalists well knew. All, however, understand their religious experiences to call for responsible obedience, even though it lead them into narrow pathways. In sum, our examples suggest that CTE is the most destabilizing of the sources of authority because it cannot be easily controlled. Perhaps it is important precisely for this reason.

Precisely because it is destabilizing, CTE is important and needs to be protected from cursory dismissal as 'natural theology' or merely 'personal' experience. CTE is one of Christianity's most enduring mechanisms of self-correction and needs to be protected even as its particular expressions need to be carefully weighed and adjudicated. As Rabban Gamaliel said of the earliest followers of Jesus, 'If this plan or this undertaking is of human origin, it will fail; but if it is of God, you will not be able to overthrow them—in that case you may even be found fighting against God!' (Acts 5: 38–9).

The growing criticism of the modern epistemology that ruled out CTE as irrational and therefore invalid suggests that CTE will increasingly be taken seriously. If this is the case, it suggests that Christian theology will be continuously pressed to discern and adjudicate claims of genuine CTE from mere self-interest masquerading as the will or calling of God. In this case, the reawakening of Christian philosophy should prove to be a great blessing, for it can provide tools for this daunting and delicate task.

It is clear that CTE has moved beyond individual confirmation of the grace of God narrated in the Christological mystery. The Foucauldian discourse of power, if employed in conjunction with the older Christian rhetoric of guilt and shame, could reorder the hierarchy of Christian piety by morally privileging political powerlessness, racial minorities, and the poor. To submit to this dynamic would be understandable, morally attractive as it is, but unfortunate, for by retaining the same hierarchical structure but changing the cast of characters it would impoverish the richness of CTE, reframing it as little more than power politics among competing individuals and groups. This would undo the very heart of the Pauline message of the cross as stated in 1 Corinthians 1: 18–31, where nobility of birth as well as political powerlessness and social weakness are equally irrelevant to righteousness, sanctification, and redemption.

References

Alston, W. P. (1991). *Perceiving God: The Epistemology of Religious Experience.* Ithaca: Cornell University Press.

Augustine (1991). *Confessions.* Oxford: Oxford University Press.

Barclay, R., and Freiday, D. (1967). *Barclay's Apology in Modern English.* Alburtis: Hemlock.

Barth, K. (1975). *Church Dogmatics* I/1. Edinburgh: T. & T. Clark.

Calvin, J. (1960). *Institutes of the Christian Religion.* Philadelphia: Westminster.

Catherine of Siena (1980). *The Dialogue.* New York: Paulist.

Charry, E. T. (1991). 'Literature as Scripture: Privileged Reading in Current Religious Reflection'. *Soundings* 74: 65–99.

Dear, P. (1990). 'Miracles, Experiments, and the Ordinary Course of Nature'. *ISIS: Journal of the History of Science in Society* 81: 663–83.

Edwards, J. (1959). *The Religious Affections.* New Haven: Yale University Press.

Evans, G. R. (1980). *Old Arts and New Theology: The Beginnings of Theology as an Academic Discipline.* Oxford: Clarendon.

Friedan, Betty (1963). *The Feminist Mystique.* London: Penguin.

Jantzen, G. M. (1987). 'Epistemology, Religious Experience, and Religious Belief'. *Modern Theology* 3/4: 277–91.

Kelly, G. B. (1992). 'Introduction'. In id. (ed.), *Karl Rahner: Theologian of the Graced Search for Meaning*, Minneapolis: Fortress.

Knox, R. A. (1950). *Enthusiasm: A Chapter in the History of Religion, with Special Reference to the XVII and XVIII Centuries.* New York: Oxford University Press.

LOCKE, J. (1964). *An Essay Concerning Human Understanding.* New York: New American Library.

LONERGAN, B. J. F. (1958). *Insight: A Study of Human Understanding.* London: Longmans.

MCCLYMOND, MICHAEL J. (1997). 'Spiritual Perception in Jonathan Edwards'. *Journal of Religion* 77/2: 195–216.

MASON, D. R. (1987). 'Selfhood, Transcendence, and the Experience of God'. *Modern Theology* 3/4: 293–314.

RAHNER, K. (1979). *Experience of the Spirit: Source of Theology.* New York: Crossroad.

SAIVING, VALERIE (1960). 'The Human Situation: A Feminist View'. *Journal of Religion* 40: 100–12.

SALAMON, J. (2004). 'On Cognitive Validity of Religious Experience'. *Forum Philosophicum* 9: 7–24.

SCHLEIERMACHER, F. D. E. (1981). *On the Glaubenslehre: Two Letters to Dr. Lücke.* Chico: Scholars.

—— (1986). *The Christian Faith.* Edinburgh: T. & T. Clark.

—— (1996). *On Religion: Speeches to Its Cultured Despisers.* Cambridge: Cambridge University Press.

SCHNER, G. P. (2003). 'The Appeal to Experience'. In id., *Essays Catholic and Critical.* Aldershot: Ashgate, 109–24.

SWINBURNE, R. (1979). *The Existence of God.* Oxford: Clarendon.

TERESA OF AVILA (1960). *The Life of Teresa of Jesus.* Garden City: Image.

—— (1979). *The Interior Castle.* New York: Paulist.

TILLEY, T. W. (1994). 'The Institutional Element in Religious Experience'. *Modern Theology* 10: 185–212.

SUGGESTED READING

ALSTON (1991).

GELLMAN, J. I. (1997). *Experience of God and the Rationality of Theistic Belief.* Ithaca: Cornell University Press.

—— (2001). *Mystical Experience of God: A Philosophical Inquiry.* Aldershot: Ashgate.

GODIN, A. (1985). *The Psychological Dynamics of Religious Experience: (it doesn't fall down from heaven).* Birmingham: Religious Education Press.

JAMES, W. (2003). *The Varieties of Religious Experience: A Study in Human Nature.* New York: Penguin.

LANE, D. A. (1981). *The Experience of God: An Invitation to do Theology.* New York: Paulist.

LONG, E. T. (1980). *Experience, Reason, and God.* Washington, DC: Catholic University of America Press.

SCHLITT, D. M. (2000). *Theology and the Experience of God.* New York: Peter Lang.

TILLEY (1994).

PART III

CONVERSATIONS

CHAPTER 24

BIBLICAL STUDIES

C. KAVIN ROWE
RICHARD B. HAYS

WERE the early Christians to hear of 'systematic theology', they would probably be astonished to find that it is something different from 'biblical studies', to discover that in contemporary theological education one usually encounters systematic theology and biblical studies as two separately conceived disciplines, each with its own rules of inquiry and corresponding community of discourse. In the postmodern period, we may experience the opposite surprise upon finding a biblical studies article in a handbook of systematic theology. Are these not two different disciplines?

This article will analyse the relationship between biblical studies and systematic theology by surveying the history of their original unity and subsequent separation. It is impossible to trace every detail of this complex development, but a strategic selection of crucial figures and critical moments will provide the background for reflection about the relation between the two disciplines today.

I. UNITY: THE NEW TESTAMENT THROUGH THE POST-REFORMATION PERIOD

In the earliest period of Christianity, theology was essentially reflection upon the significance of the life, death, and resurrection of Jesus Christ in connection with scripture. In one of the oldest fragments of Christian tradition, Paul states explicitly that he passed on what he had received, namely that 'Christ died for our sins *in accordance with the scriptures*, and that he was buried, and that he was raised on the third day *in accordance with the scriptures*' (1 Cor. 15: 3–4). This basic conviction—that of the inseparability of Jesus Christ from Israel's scripture—is not peculiar to Paul, or to the tradition that he preserves, but is indigenous to the New Testament as a whole. In the Gospel of Matthew, for example, one encounters again and again the formula citation, 'this took place to fulfil what had been spoken' (Matt. 1: 22, etc.). Likewise, the Gospel of Luke, long considered by modern scholars to be the most 'Gentile' of the four canonical Gospels, begins its narrative with a seamless transition from the tone and atmosphere of the Old Testament to 'the events that have been fulfilled' (Luke 1: 1) and ends the story with two successive scenes in which Jesus himself instructs his followers in how to interpret the scriptures Christologically (Luke 24: 13–35, 36–48). Even in the Letter to the Hebrews, where the 'law' is regarded as only 'a shadow of the good things to come' (Heb. 10: 1), the imagery used for Christological construction is itself derived from the Old Testament and Jewish tradition; the Christology of Hebrews is unintelligible—indeed, inconceivable—apart from the deep theological well of the Old Testament.

This basic unity between theological reflection and the interpretation of scripture continued through the patristic period, though with the substantial difference that the writings of the New Testament itself were now placed alongside Israel's scripture to form a two-testament hermeneutical matrix. Even so, the integration of theological reflection and scriptural interpretation remained. Irenaeus' *regula fidei*, for example, is not simply identical with scripture. Yet, neither is it a deposit of doctrine logically independent of scripture; instead, the rule of faith is the very content of scripture itself as understood in the apostolic tradition. Only so can it function as the criterion of correct interpretation (Irenaeus, *Against Heresies* 1. 9. 4, in Roberts and Donaldson 1990: i. 330).

> [T]he quest which Irenaeus accomplishes is basically the discovery of a principle of interpretation in the apostolic Rule of faith. At the same time... it is in another sense scripture itself that supplies the categories in which the principle of interpretation is expressed. Text and interpretation are like twin brothers; one can scarcely tell the one from the other. (Greer 1986: 157)

Similarly, in his *Adversus Marcionem*, Tertullian does not attempt to refute Marcion first on a philosophical or theological level and then draw out the implications of his argument regarding the accurate interpretation of scripture. Rather, his overall polemic is inextricably bound to both the Old and the New Testament. To separate Tertullian's use of scripture from his 'systematic' theological argument is to dismantle the argument altogether.

One might object that, in light of his *De principiis*, we ought to consider Origen an early exception. On this construal of the evidence, *De principiis* would be read as a systematic or philosophical theology, while Origen's commentaries and homilies would be taken as his biblical, exegetical work. Yet such a view is inaccurate, for Origen's treatment of 'first principles' is not a general systematic construction but rather a hermeneutical defence of the proper (i.e., Christian) understanding of scripture. Moreover, the treatments of the theological topics of Books I–III are unthinkable without the manner of exegesis described in Book IV. *De principiis* thus attempts to justify established, if controversial, exegetical practice and in this way both arises out of and is written for the interpretation of scripture (Young 2003: esp. 335–8).

So, too, as his preface to the work makes clear, Augustine's *De doctrina christiana* is not a systematic treatment of Christian doctrine articulated independently of scripture: 'There are certain rules for the interpretation of Scripture which I think might with great advantage be taught to earnest students of the word.... These rules I propose to teach' (*De doctrina christiana*, preface 1, in Schaff 1980: ii. 519). Indeed, for Augustine, Christian doctrine is itself derived from scripture taken as a whole—the 'sense' of its 'wording'—even as the 'doctrinal tradition provides the principal criterion' for correct exegesis and understanding (Young 2005: 130–1).

To highlight the unity of exegesis and theology is not to say that reflective theology was *only* exegetical commentary. That would be an exaggeration. Yet Greer's point that 'for the church fathers the true meaning of scripture was a theological one' can hardly be overstressed (Greer 1986: 177). As Robert Wilken notes, in the patristic period

> biblical exegesis was not a specialized discipline carried on independently of theology; it *was* theology. The church thought about the mysteries of the faith by expounding the text of the Bible. In the church fathers one will seldom find arguments that stand on logical or philosophical grounds alone. Behind most theological discussions was a biblical text or texts, and it was on the basis of these texts that the church's first teachers gave expression to the central truths of faith and morals. (Wilken 2000: x)

As Henri de Lubac has demonstrated, this interdependence of theology and exegesis continued throughout the medieval period. This is not to imply that the theological ratiocinations of Anselm, Abelard, and Aquinas are, to those who read with modern eyes, recognizably biblical. Nonetheless, the Bible and ecclesial theology were still assumed to exist in a complementary relationship, if not one of synonymity.

We may take Aquinas's *Summa Theologiae* as an example. Aquinas's metaphysical articulations of *sacra doctrina* are intimately intertwined with his reading of scripture. If we focus, for example, upon questions of 'being' in relation to God's identity, it would be a gross misunderstanding of Aquinas to view his theology as simply a kind of Christianized Aristotelian metaphysics. As Matthew Levering has argued, the name YHWH 'does not on Aquinas' interpretation trap Israel's God within the limitations of Aristotle's (idolatrous) prime mover. Rather, the name belongs to the history of Israel's and the church's striving *against* idolatrous conceptions of the divine being' (Levering 2004: 65). Aquinas does not, in other words, contemplate God 'generically, but specifically as revealed through Moses to Israel' (Levering 2004: 53).[1] The God about whom Aquinas speaks metaphysically is at every point—to the properly trained eye—the God of the Bible.

Despite the considerable ecclesial upheaval engendered by the Reformation, the essential unity between biblical interpretation and theological reflection remained unbroken. It is true, of course, that cries of *sola scriptura* and *ad fontes* were employed in an effort to reform and simplify the church's practices. Yet, this corrective effort took place essentially within the parameters given by the early church's theological canon. Reformation exegesis was not interested, for example, in overturning the Christological claims made at Nicaea. Nor, despite certain criticisms of 'allegory', were the authorities of the patristic period spurned. Augustine is cited frequently not only in Aquinas's *Summa* but also by Calvin; indeed, in Calvin's *Institutes of the Christian Religion*, Augustine is cited more often than any source except scripture itself.

For Calvin, moreover, systematic theology was itself derived from scripture. Thus conceived, it was not a separate field in which deliberation could take place apart from scripture. Rather, the *telos* of systematic theology was in fact hermeneutical; it existed for the sake of biblical interpretation:

> [I]t has been my purpose in this labor [writing the *Institutes*] to prepare and instruct candidates in sacred theology for the reading of the divine Word.... For I believe I have so embraced the sum of religion in all its parts, and have arranged it in such an order, that if anyone rightly grasps it, it will not be difficult for him to determine what he ought especially to seek in scripture and to what end he ought to relate its contents. (*John Calvin to the Reader*, in Calvin 1960: 4)

The unity envisioned by Calvin between doctrine and exegesis—the 'sum of religion' and the 'divine Word'—was not a simple hermeneutical circle of biblical proof-texts employed in the service of already-known doctrine. Nor was theology arranged in 'order' merely to underwrite a particular mode of Reformed exegesis. Instead, the unity described here was in practice deeply dialogical: there was a mutually interactive relationship between the biblical text and the systematizing or ordering of theology. On the one hand, Calvin's theology was in effect *biblical* theology, and, on the other, his exegesis operated under the guidance of systematic theology. This dialogical unity allowed Calvin to attend concurrently to the shape and particularities of the biblical texts themselves and to the larger attempt to relate his exegetical findings ('contents') to the 'sum of religion'.

There was, however, a crucial point at which the exegesis of the Reformation did prefigure modern developments: the notion of *Sachkritik* in relation to the biblical canon. *Sachkritik* is a type of criticism that exposes theological inconsistencies

[1] Levering's thesis is articulated in conscious opposition to Rahner's well-known criticism of Aquinas's discussion of the divine essence as unbiblical (Rahner 1998).

within a text and criticizes an author's contingent formulations in light of the allegedly more fundamental truth (or subject matter) to which the text points. Clear indications of such an approach are found in Luther, though *Sachkritik* is hardly the sum of his hermeneutics.

To be sure, the earlier history of exegesis amply demonstrates interpreters' uneasiness with a wide range of biblical problems. Yet, before Luther, the tradition's characteristic strategy for dealing with intracanonical tensions was harmonization (e.g., the Gospel harmonies of Tatian, the *Diatessaron*, and Augustine, *De consensu evangelistarum*). No hermeneutical move had been made from within the Christian tradition that entailed a plain theological rejection of parts of scripture that were long considered canonical. In his preface to the Epistle of James, however, Luther made just such a move.[2]

Luther criticizes James on the grounds that (1) 'it is flatly against St Paul and all the rest of scripture in ascribing justification to works', and (2) 'in all this long teaching it does not once does mention the Passion, the resurrection, or the Spirit of Christ. He names Christ several times; however he teaches nothing about him' (Luther 1957–86: xxxv. 395–7). It is well known that for Luther the central doctrine of the Christian faith is justification by faith (not works) and that the centre of scripture is Christ: 'all the genuine sacred books... preach and inculcate Christ' (Luther 1957–86: xxxv. 396). Thus, in Luther's reading, James 'mangles the scripture, and there by ture, and thereby opposes Paul and all scripture'. In this light Luther concludes: 'Therefore, I will not have him in my Bible to be numbered among the true chief books.... How should this single man alone avail against Paul and all the rest of scripture?' (Luther 1957–86: xxxv. 397 nn. 54–5).

Thus, even though Luther does not regard biblical interpretation and theology as different disciplines, his doctrine of justification and his conviction that 'all the genuine sacred books... preach and inculcate Christ' are separated from explicit exegetical engagement and are worked out on a reflective level with considerable sophistication. At least in the preface to James, Luther approaches the exegetical task with a pre-understanding that is construed systematically. In light of this pre-understanding, he then moves to criticize a portion of scripture as theologically deficient.

Still, the theological position that leads Luther to criticize James is conceivable only on the basis of a prior unity between biblical exegesis and constructive theology. Luther's hermeneutical process moves from his exegesis of Paul to his view of justification, which he then develops systematically into a doctrinal criterion for right reading of the Bible. Subsequently, he returns to (canonical) scripture with this systematic structure in place. Even if Luther's particular interpretation of

[2] Luther's rather negative view of Jude, Hebrews, and especially Revelation is also well known (see the prefaces in Luther 1957–86: xxxv). But '[w]hat is not so well known is that in the table of contents of his September Bible of 1522 he openly separated them from the other twenty-three and according to him true New Testament writings, thus characterizing them at once as deutero-canonical' (Barth 1998: 476).

Paul would not find wide support among New Testament scholars today (at least outside Germany: cf. Harink 2004: 13–65), Luther himself evidently endeavours to speak theologically with the voice of the biblical Paul. Thus, if we may say that Luther operates under the guidance of a systematically developed *Sachkritik*, we must also say that this is for him emphatically biblical.

In his willingness to criticize canonical texts in light of doctrinal criteria, Luther differed from other Reformation leaders (e.g., Calvin). But, in that his criteria were biblically funded, he also differed widely from many scholars in the so-called 'post-Reformation' period for whom—to oversimplify the matter—theology overran exegesis: the Bible functioned largely as a set of proof-texts (the *dicta classica* or *collegia biblica*) or a springboard for established doctrine.[3] This insertion of biblical texts into doctrinal schemata and discussions did not amount to a strict disciplinary separation between biblical studies and systematic theology. Viewed retrospectively, however, it allowed systematics to swallow up exegesis: no longer did the biblical narratives decisively impart their shape to dogmatic constructions (Frei 1974; cf. Blowers 1997). Thus, in the midst of the burgeoning philosophies of the Enlightenment, when the early historical critics (e.g., Reimarus) returned to the Bible, it is no great surprise that what they found there bore scant resemblance to the systematic theology of the post-Reformation period.

II. Separation: The Eighteenth to the Early Twentieth Century

The beginnings of a fundamental separation between biblical exegesis and theology are notoriously difficult to determine with any precision. What is clear in general is that in light of certain philosophical-theological developments in Britain (especially deism) and the subsequent bloom of the Enlightenment in Germany, two interrelated possibilities arose: a historical, biblical exegesis set in conscious opposition to established ecclesial theology and of a 'systematic' theology whose content was distinguished from that of the Bible. The unity between the Bible as a whole and the theological content prescribed by the *regula fidei* was dissolved. This is not to say that historical exegesis was devoid of ecclesial elements, or that constructive theology had entirely rid itself of biblical content. In practice, many of the emerging historical critics saw their biblical work as theologically significant and, conversely, theologians even in the speculative

[3] e.g., H. Diest's *Theologica biblica* of 1643, the earliest extant 'biblical theology', organizes variously collected biblical texts under twenty-three different dogmatic topics.

Hegelian tradition continued to grapple with at least parts of the Bible. Yet, biblical exegesis and systematic-theological reflection increasingly became two different disciplines.

Johann Philipp Gabler's famous inaugural address (1787) is often treated as the starting point for modern, descriptive biblical study. This perception doubtlessly oversimplifies the matter but is not without foundation. Gabler's address does evidence a particularly clear collocation of convictions and presuppositions that led to the erection of a wall between biblical studies and systematic and dogmatic theology. If the materials for this dividing wall were shaped earlier during the seventeenth and eighteenth centuries, it was here at the end of the eighteenth century that the wall itself began to be built.

In his address Gabler argued for the necessity of three crucial distinctions. First, he distinguished between 'religion' and 'theology'. Religion is 'every-day, transparently clear knowledge', whereas theology is 'subtle, learned knowledge, surrounded by a retinue of many disciplines' (Gabler 1980: 136). The Bible was the former rather than the latter, though scripture could furnish dogmatics with the material to be explained. Second, Gabler distinguished between historically conditioned statements and timeless, universal truths, and he affirmed that the Bible contained both. Finally, Gabler distinguished between 'true' and 'pure' biblical theology. The task of 'true' biblical theology was carefully 'to collect and classify' the 'sacred ideas' of the biblical authors (Gabler 1980: 139–40). In other words, it was conceived as a *historically descriptive* discipline—although the 'history' in question was strictly a history of ideas. On the basis of this classification, 'pure' biblical theology would then differentiate the historically conditioned ('true') material from the ('pure') timeless, 'universal ideas'. As a result of this final differentiation, which 'peel[ed] off everything local and temporal, everything individual and particular' (Bultmann 1951–5: ii. 243), dogmatics was provided with a secure foundation upon which to build: '[A]fter we have separated those things which in the sacred books refer most immediately to their own times from those pure notions which divine providence wished to be characteristic of all times and places, let us then construct the foundation of our philosophy [i.e., systematic theology] upon religion' (Gabler 1980: 138).

Although later scholars were not necessarily seeking to work out Gabler's programme, his crisp delineations exemplify a certain way of conceptualizing the larger theological task that framed the ensuing history of discussion through the early twentieth century. Gabler's distinctions (1) split cleanly the discipline of historical exegesis of the Bible from dogmatic and systematic theology; (2) assigned a proper order to the relationship of the two disciplines that consisted of stages: first historical exegesis, then systematic reflection on the basis of the results; and (3) designated the contents of the Bible as 'religion' in explicit contrast to reflective theology.

Taking these matters together, it becomes apparent that Gabler's model of the theological enterprise mandates a wall between historical exegesis and systematic reflection, since systematic theology in itself is *in principle* incapable of inquiring into the biblical text. It is the wrong tool for the task—like trying to eat soup with a fork—for the Bible is not theology but religion. Systematic theology is thus removed from the Bible and placed in a separate sphere of inquiry. Systematic theology, if it seeks to be 'biblical', will have to wait for the completed results of historical exegesis.

The corollary, furthermore, to the notion that *historical* exegesis is the science proper to biblical interpretation is that the biblical texts are situated first of all not in the immediate life of the church but in the past. A sense of the vast chronological distance between the genesis of the texts and present theological reflection thus became a constitutive feature of biblical interpretation. In that the Bible could no longer speak directly from its time to ours—it needed mediation through historical research—the space was opened for the (now perennial) question of 'development' to arise: how did we get from there to here? It was but a short step from this question to the inference that truly historical interpretation—that which attends to phenomena in their proper chronological sequence—not only entails the bracketing out of later ecclesial doctrine and systematic theology but also potentially undermines it.

By the middle of the nineteenth century, the separation between biblical studies and systematic theology had become firmly institutionalized in the disciplinary structure of European universities. This is not to say that theologians entirely shied away from interpreting the Bible (Schleiermacher, for example, wrote on source-critical questions in his essay on Luke) or that biblical scholars were unaware of the theological implications of their research (Strauss was acutely aware of the impact of his 1835 *Life of Jesus*). Nonetheless, both systematicians and exegetes, many of whom differed widely in the particulars of their theological perspective, agreed that accurate historical examination of the biblical texts divided these texts, in their original meaning, from later Christian systematics. In *The Christian Faith*, for example, Schleiermacher assumes historical distance between the Gospel of John and later systematic theology. By focusing on the Gospel prologue, he elucidates the noetic difference between the Gospel's author and those who fashioned the doctrine of the Trinity:

> If the Trinity had been in the Apostle's mind, his exposition would very easily have lent itself to a similar introduction of the Holy Spirit, whose name occurs so often in ... John; nor would John have lacked opportunity ... to speak here of the Spirit as that which was 'in the beginning with God and was God'. Assuming, however, that John here declares that the dual nature of Christ existed in God in distinct form from all eternity, it would still not follow by any means that this was meant in the sense of the doctrine of the Trinity, and that that doctrine is therefore the true and the only natural completion of the Johannine statements.... John was not on the way to the doctrine of the Trinity as we have it. (Schleiermacher 1928: 740; cf. 2003: ii. 517)

Even where there was a push to see the roots of doctrinal development in the New Testament itself, such as in the work of Ferdinand Christian Baur, the distance between the biblical texts and later systematic theology was assumed, and thoroughgoing historical study was considered the method appropriate to biblical interpretation. In practice, of course, Baur's Hegelian philosophy functioned as the unifying factor for the various pieces of the historical puzzle, but in principle Baur knew no method other than radical historical criticism by which to interpret the New Testament texts. Speaking of biblical theology, Baur wrote that 'one calls this branch of theological science "theology" in order to distinguish it with this general and non-specific name from "dogmatics," i.e., *systematic* theology. As distinct from dogmatics and other similar modes of inquiry, biblical theology should be a purely historical discipline' (Baur 1973: 1, emphasis added).

By the end of the nineteenth and beginning of the twentieth century, the disciplinary divisions were taken for granted to the point that the New Testament scholar William Wrede could declare to a group of German pastors that historical study of the New Testament should be 'totally indifferent to all dogma and systematic theology' (Wrede 1973: 69). Reading the Bible in light of later dogmatic or systematic theology perverted the truth of historical conditioning and development and therefore was a hindrance to historical study of the biblical documents. On this latter point, if not on others, Albert Schweitzer agreed with Wrede:

> Chalcedon... cut off the last possibility of a return to the historical Jesus.... This dogma had first to be shattered before men could once more go out in quest of the historical Jesus.... That the historical Jesus is something different from the Jesus Christ of the doctrine of the Two Natures seems to us now self-evident. (Schweitzer 1998: 3)

Later ecclesial theology, he wrote in a memorable phrase, binds the historical Jesus 'like Lazarus of old... [in] the grave-clothes of the dogma of the Dual Nature' (Schweitzer 1998: 3). Thus was Gabler's programmatic distinction carried forward, as doctrinal theology was taken to be the wrong instrument for investigation of the Bible.

The conviction that later theological categories were inappropriate for biblical exegesis found sophisticated systematic expression in the work of Ernst Troeltsch, the recognized 'dogmatician' of the history-of-religions school. In an essay designed to introduce American theology to 'a dogmatics working with the presuppositions and in the spirit of this school', Troeltsch argued forcefully for the historical determination of theology: 'Jesus' life and teaching must be interpreted not by reference to later Christology and metaphysics but exclusively in the light of prophetism and late eschatological Judaism' (Troeltsch 1991: 93). Troeltsch's point was that all knowledge is fundamentally historical in character; theological knowledge (dogmatic theology), therefore, was dependent upon historical reality. For Troeltsch, the 'history' in question was of course that which could be reconstructed by the historical-biblical scholars. In this sense, in principle if not in practice, the historical determination of dogmatic theology conformed to Gabler's two-stage process in which the task of the dogmatician followed and was dependent upon that of the historian. The obvious effect was to remove dogmatic concerns further from the mind of the historians. As Wrede put it, '[h]ow the systematic theologian gets on with the results [of historical criticism] and deals with them—that is his own affair' (Wrede 1973: 69).

Around the turn of the century, there was, of course, considerable debate about these matters within wider academic theology, and one can sense, looking back through Karl Barth, an almost prophetic tone in the dissenting voices of Martin Kähler (1896) and Adolf Schlatter (1909). Yet, the conviction that historical exegesis and systematic theology were independent and separate disciplines—each with its own primary sources of knowledge and rules of inquiry—dominated across the larger theological spectrum.

III. Unity and Separation: The Twentieth Century through the Present

Despite the virtual consensus in the late nineteenth and early twentieth century, the relation of biblical studies to systematic theology underwent profound change later in the twentieth century. The complexity involved in this change can best be seen by concentrating on the way in which Karl Barth and Rudolf Bultmann attempted to reintegrate theology with exegesis, the subsequent reaction to Barth and Bultmann, and finally, in this light, the more recent and competing tendencies within the field of biblical studies.

Karl Barth's break with the liberal Protestantism of his day changed decisively the course of both biblical studies and theology for the twentieth century. This shift, however, was arguably not a new direction as such. Indeed, on Barth's own terms, it was more of a return to a well-worn ecclesial path, walked first by the biblical writers themselves and subsequently by certain doctors of the church. Barth's was a return, to switch the metaphor, to an 'ancestral line which runs back through Kierkegaard to Luther and Calvin, and so to Paul and Jeremiah' (Barth 1957: 195).

The crucial difference between the historians in the exegetical disciplines and himself, so Barth maintained, was that the former attempted mainly to think *about* Paul whereas Barth's attempt was to think *with* Paul. 'The reigning biblical science saw [Paul] as an object of interest in his own right; Barth saw him as *witness*' (McCormack 1991: 327). Historical-critical interpretation as practised in the early twentieth century concentrated upon matters anthropological—human religious experience as reflected by the biblical texts. This concentration, in Barth's view, neglected the true subject matter (*die Sache*) of scripture, that to which Paul and Jeremiah witnessed and with which Calvin and Luther had attempted to grapple actively in their exegesis. Barth insisted that, in its character as witness to God, the Bible itself called for explicitly *theological* exegesis. In this way, Barth reversed Gabler and maintained that dogmatic theology was in principle required for the interpretation of scripture. To eliminate the theology of the church from biblical exegesis was to ignore the subject matter of scripture and, hence, not to *interpret* scripture at all.

Yet, dogmatic or systematic theology was not itself an independent discipline in which a preconceived system was forced upon the biblical texts with a heavy hand. Despite charges to the contrary, Barth himself claimed never to have called for the abandonment of historical exegesis.

> The demand that the Bible should be read and understood and expounded historically is, therefore, obviously justified and can never be taken too seriously. The Bible itself posits this demand: even where it appeals expressly to divine commissionings and promptings, in its actual composition it is everywhere a human word, and this human word is obviously intended to be taken seriously and read and understood as such. To do anything else would be to miss the reality of the Bible and therefore the Bible itself as the witness of revelation. (Barth 1998: 464)

His protests were 'not directed against historical research as such but against the *historicism* of the historians who sought to reduce... explanation of the biblical texts to historical explanation and that alone' (McCormack 2002: viii–ix). In point of fact, as Bruce McCormack has argued, Barth can be understood to view historical exegesis as both a starting point for and a 'relative control' over the interpretative proposals of theological exegesis (McCormack 1991: 333–4).

Moreover, the 'science' of dogmatics was itself to be biblical, both in the sense that it was dependent upon the pointing of the biblical witness for its view of the subject matter and in the sense captured by the old ecclesial notion of the relation between the *norma normans* (scripture) and the *norma normata* (dogmatic and systematic theology): systematic or dogmatic theology was subject to the formative and corrective witness of scripture. As opposed to 'modern biblicism'—a proof-texting application of 'what one thinks one has already heard from [the Bible] simply by repeating its words'—truly theological exegesis displays a 'posture', or 'a way of human thinking shaped by the Bible... in which those cultivated by its "rule of thought" learn to think its thoughts and hear its message again and again' (Burnett 2004: 58). Thus did Barth return to an earlier ecclesial mode of interpretation (e.g., Calvin's) in which there was a unity of biblical exegesis and theological reflection that derived ultimately from the unity of the subject matter itself: even within the distinction between *normans* and *normata*, the Bible and dogmatic theology were part of one dialectical theological conversation.

Rudolf Bultmann, probably Barth's only rival in influence, also interpreted scripture in light of its perceived subject matter and also believed that authentic interpretation was impossible apart from direct theological engagement with the witness of the Bible. In this way, Bultmann, too, returned to an earlier mode of interpretation in which biblical exegesis was believed to have 'something to say to the present' (Bultmann 1951–5: ii. 251).

In particular, Bultmann's reading of scripture in light of its subject matter resembled Luther's, in the sense that both interpreters moved to criticize portions of scripture as theologically deficient in light of their understanding of scripture's subject matter (*Sachkritik*). As Barth warned, 'Those who throw stones at Bultmann should be careful lest they accidentally hit Luther, who is also hovering somewhere in the background' (Barth 1962: 123). For Bultmann, as for Luther, there was a deeply unified interpretation in which exegesis and theological reflection were brought into a synthetic relationship. On the basis of his exegesis of certain parts of the Bible (notably Paul and John)—and with considerable help from the early Heidegger—Bultmann developed a theological criterion (authentic believing self-understanding) with which he then returned to perform the exegetical task. If in reality Heidegger's existentialism provided the essential link between Bultmann's exegesis and his theology, in theory at least, Bultmann's highly sophisticated theology was exegetically shaped, even as his exegesis received its direction from his theological reflection.

(In this respect there is a strong, though rarely recognized, family resemblance between Bultmann's theology and the theologies of many feminist and liberationist theologians today who likewise discover within the Bible an anthropologically oriented theological criterion—whether a principle such as justice or freedom, or the divinely given dignity of marginalized groups—and then employ this criterion in critically interrogating the biblical texts. The work of Elisabeth Schüssler Fiorenza (1983) is a particularly clear example of this method: a theologically grounded critical hermeneutics that thoroughly engages the historical exegetical task.)

Yet, the conceptualization of the interface between exegesis and theology in Bultmann's interpretative vision was substantively different from Karl Barth's. Where Barth challenged the primacy of historical critical investigation, Bultmann could write that 'the one presupposition that cannot be dismissed is *the historical method* of interrogating the text. Indeed, exegesis as the interpretation of historical texts is a part of the science of history' (Bultmann 1960*a*: 291). And though he could agree with Barth against Troeltsch that Christian faith is not a phenomenon of the history of religion, Bultmann could also characterize his *Theology of the New Testament* as one which stood within the history-of-religions tradition of investigation (Bultmann 1951–5: ii. 250).

Furthermore, where Bultmann differed from the history-of-religions school, he also differed from Barth in a way that drew significant criticism from the latter (Barth 1962). Bultmann accused the history-of-religions approach of tearing apart 'the act of thinking' and 'the act of living', by which he meant that Bousset, Wrede, and others failed to understand the theological thoughts in the New Testament as expressions of 'believing self-understanding', i.e., the explication of 'man's understanding of himself' from the perspective given by faith (Bultmann 1951–5: ii. 249–51). For Barth, however, to read the biblical texts as witnesses to human self-understanding—even if the change in one's self-understanding could be attributed to God—was to return to an anthropologically centred exegesis and, hence, to forfeit criticism of the history-of-religions paradigm at the place where it was most needed.

It is important to stress, however, that Barth and Bultmann were united in a common endeavour to read the Bible theologically in the face of a legacy which, in large part, maintained the inappropriateness of such an endeavour. Despite the far-reaching differences between these two giants, in both Barth and Bultmann biblical studies and systematic theology were once again brought into dialogue. Though it is an oversimplification, it may not be too much to suggest that most, if not all, subsequent attempts to deal with the relationship between biblical studies and systematic theology swim with, or against, the wakes generated by Barth and Bultmann.

Despite its real differences from the theological scene in Germany, for example, the emphasis on the theological content of the Bible in the so-called 'biblical theology movement' in America is practically inconceivable apart from Barth and Bultmann (Childs 1970: 18–22). Further, when in 1962 Krister Stendahl famously advocated the necessity of a clear distinction in exegesis between 'what it meant' and 'what it means', Barth and Bultmann were the primary targets of his attack:[4]

> [It] appears that the tension between 'what it meant' and 'what it means' is of a competitive nature, and that when the biblical theologian becomes primarily concerned with the present meaning, he implicitly (Barth) or explicitly (Bultmann) loses his enthusiasm or his ultimate respect for the descriptive task. (Stendahl 1962: 421)

In its overall shape, Stendahl's own position was hardly a new one, even in North America (Cadbury 1949). Indeed, the sharp divide between 'meant' and 'means' was in essence a return through Wrede to Gabler, though Stendahl recognized in a way the others did not the difficulty in moving from the past to the present. He thus called for an intermediate stage in which attention would be given to the hermeneutical principles involved in rendering the past relevant for the present: 'With the original in hand, and after due clarification of the hermeneutic principles involved, we may proceed toward tentative answers to the question of the meaning here and now' (Stendahl 1962: 422). Nonetheless, in conceptualizing the exegetical and systematic tasks as different modes of inquiry, sequentially ordered so that interpretation runs in one direction only—from the 'original' to the 'here and now'—Stendahl's programme was Gabler's programme *redivivus*.

The influence of Stendahl's proposals was such that almost twenty-five years later, in a critique of the meant/means division, Ben Ollenburger could write that 'the distinctions for which Stendahl pleaded have come to be seen as virtually axiomatic, and self-evidently so, particularly for distinguishing biblical from systematic theology' (Ollenburger 1986: 61). There was of course the occasional appreciation of Barth from

[4] Oscar Cullmann was the third figure treated by Stendahl, but Cullmann came in for much less criticism than Barth and Bultmann. Indeed, Stendahl considered Cullmann's work to be largely accurate on the descriptive level.

a biblical scholar (Minear 1974), and, methodologically speaking, the historical-critical aspect of Bultmannian exegesis had legions of followers among New Testament scholars (in contrast to the theological or existential dimension of Bultmann's work). But Ollenburger's statement was not unfair: well into the 1980s biblical studies and systematic theology were thought of as two different disciplines. The former worked on a strictly 'descriptive' level and dealt with the historical problems and literary diversity encountered in the exegesis of a text in its original context ('meant'). The latter worked on a 'normative' level with the abstract conceptual and philosophical issues that arise in the attempt to reflect theologically upon the content of the Christian faith in its connection to contemporary life ('means').

In more recent years, Stendahl's programmatic suggestions have lost the virtually universal, if subconscious, acceptance within biblical studies they once enjoyed. The learned publications of Old Testament scholar Brevard Childs, for example, have displayed sophistication in both biblical exegesis and systematic theology and relentlessly called into question the necessity of their separation, as have those of his former Old Testament colleague Christopher Seitz (1998). In New Testament studies, Richard Hays's book on New Testament ethics (1996) exhibits wide-ranging theological analysis and construction, while Francis Watson has in two successive works (1994; 1997) mounted extensive arguments for 'biblical interpretation in theological perspective'. Stephen Fowl's book, *Engaging Scripture: A Model for Theological Interpretation* (1998), found its way to a panel review session at the Society of Biblical Literature's 1999 Annual Meeting. Perhaps most impressive in its scale is the ongoing, multi-volume work of N. T. Wright on 'Christian Origins and the Question of God' (1992; 1996; 2003). As the overall title of the series suggests, Wright is pursuing historical exegesis of the New Testament with explicitly theological ends in view. The Roman Catholic New Testament scholars Luke Timothy Johnson and William S. Kurz, SJ have called for biblical scholarship to 'imagine the world that scripture imagines' in ongoing conversation with the Catholic Church's rich tradition of theological interpretation (Johnson 2002: 119). Moreover, an ecumenical and interdisciplinary consultation of scholars, under the name The Scripture Project, has likewise offered a programmatic summons to the practice of biblical interpretation as a seamlessly integrated theological activity that speaks directly to the needs of the church (Davis and Hays 2003). The appetite for such work is evidently considerable: two new commentary series have of late been launched with the express purpose of bringing biblical exegesis and theological reflection into close relation.[5] Finally, from the side of systematic theology, it is significant that one of the most important contemporary systematic theologies claims that its success should be measured by its achievement or failure 'as a hermeneutical principle for scripture taken as a whole' (Jenson 1997–9: i. 33).

[5] See the Two Horizons Commentary series (a prospectus of which can be found in the collection of essays in Green and Turner 2000) and the Brazos Theological Commentary on the Bible.

A particularly noteworthy development within this resurgence of theological integration has been a newly intensified interest, among both systematic theologians and biblical scholars, in *narrative* as the distinctive medium for the articulation of the Christian message. As Robert Jenson explains:

> The message of Jesus' resurrection, the gospel, is a message about an event and so itself has the form of a narrative. Therefore, when the church sets out to read scripture as a whole, the kind of unity by which she construes this whole is narrative unity. The church reads her scripture as a single plotted succession of events, stretching from creation to consummation, plotted around exodus and resurrection. (Jenson 2003: 29)

This approach to biblical interpretation, obviously consonant with ancient patristic tradition, received new impetus through the work of Karl Barth and the theologians influenced by him. Especially significant for more recent theology have been the contributions of Hans Frei (1974; 1975) and George Lindbeck (1984). These theologians have advocated an understanding of theology as what Lindbeck calls an 'intratextual' enterprise, through which the community of faith retells and interprets its foundational story.

So long as 'theology' was conceived in terms of systematically ordered propositions, whether by Protestant scholasticism or by scholars pursuing the Enlightenment's ideal of pure, generalizable universal truth, the biblical narratives appeared as limited and limiting texts, inconvenient in their crude particularity. Even Paul's letters, perhaps the most apparently theological writings in the Bible, were in fact, as read by historical criticism, contingent pastoral advice for ancient readers, not systematically constructed theological treatises. Theology had to be somehow *distilled* from the raw material of these texts, and the relation between descriptive biblical study and systematic-theological discourse was a fairly distant one.

If, however, the task of theology is understood in the post-liberal mode as the reflective renarration of the community's identity-defining story within a particular historical moment, then not only Paul but also the canonical evangelists were practising 'theology' in a way that is exemplary for theologians in the church at any time, including ours. Consequently, the gap between the biblical scholar's close descriptive reading of the text and the theologian's constructive reflection about the text becomes indistinct; both are engaged in imaginative construal of one and the same story.

In other circles, however, the basic disciplinary divide promoted by Gabler, Wrede, and Stendahl continues strongly in force, as some erudite biblical scholars insist—in the face of postmodernism's erosion of 'objectivity' in the doing of history—on the independence and priority of descriptive, historical exegesis in opposition to 'dogmatic abstractions' (e.g., Meeks 2005). 'Gabler', as Räisänen put it, 'was basically right' (Räisänen 1990: 137). Exegesis and dogmatics 'are to be kept apart'. There is room, of course, within today's Gablerian approach, for broadly theological concerns—e.g., the use to which historical exegesis of the Bible is put—but systematic theology itself is, at best, seen to be of little help for exegesis.

At the present moment, then, with respect to the question of the relation between biblical studies and systematic theology, there are competing tendencies within the field of biblical studies that arise naturally out of the history of this field's unity with and separation from systematic theology. On one side, there is a conscious push toward theologically interdisciplinary work, in which biblical exegesis is related positively to systematic or dogmatic theology and in which systematic theology is considered an indispensable tool for the exegetical task. This tendency corresponds to the hermeneutically integrated interpretation of earlier ecclesial exegesis and, in more recent history, to the Barthian endeavour as well as to certain aspects of the Bultmannian theological programme. The rapprochement between biblical exegesis and theology has been aided particularly by systematic theology's renewed interest in the narrative character of Christian convictions. On the other side, however, there is a rueful memory of the long history of dogmatic proof-texting in the modern period, a recognition of the reality of the historical situatedness and diversity of the biblical texts, and a resultant desire to steer exegesis clear of the threatening systematic rocks. This tendency corresponds to the rise of a particular form of academic historiography in the Enlightenment, to the efforts of Gabler, Wrede, and Stendahl to achieve methodological distinction and clarity, as well as to the history-of-religions tradition in Bultmannian exegesis.

IV. Concluding Reflections

In light of the tension in the present situation, we offer some concluding reflections on the basis of the foregoing history. First, it would greatly aid discussion to dispense with the idea that exegesis can be done without dogmatic interests. On this point at least, biblical scholars should—with help from postmodern criticism if necessary—be ready to grant Barth his point: every exegete has dogmatic interests and presuppositions. Or, as Adolf Schlatter put it: 'The connection between historical science and dogmatics... cannot be set aside until historical work is complete.... The relationship between the two functions is there right from the beginning of historical work.... It does not simply come in at the end, but permeates the whole course of historical work' (Schlatter 1973: 126). The task, then, is to acknowledge and probe the theological (or anti-theological) interests involved in exegetical work and, hence, to ask whether some interests are more fruitful for biblical interpretation than others.

Second, to speak of various texts together as the 'Bible' or 'New Testament' is in fact to make a dogmatic judgement. As Heinrich Schlier once wrote with respect to New Testament theology, 'from a purely "historical" stand-point... there is no justification for restricting it to the collection of books in the New Testament. Such a restriction is *already* a piece of theology' (Schlier 1968: 5). Inherent in the name 'biblical studies', in other words, is the theological decision that the particular documents that constitute the Bible are in some way related to one another, as distinct from their relation to other pieces of literature, and are therefore to be treated together. '[O]utside the church, no such entity as the Christian Bible has any reason to exist' (Jenson 2003: 27). This does not so much settle as raise the question of how the documents relate to one another, but to read at least sixty-six texts together is to make a dogmatic theological judgement.

Third, such a judgement is not merely ideational abstraction; rather, it locates us socially in a community of interpretation. Indeed, as Wrede saw clearly, to interpret the 'Bible' is to situate oneself within a specific set of ecclesial decisions: 'Anyone who accepts... the idea of the canon places himself under the authority of the bishops and theologians of [the second to fourth] centuries' (Wrede 1973: 71). To admit that there is an interpretative arena called the Bible places the interpreter (whether self-consciously or not) within a community of interpretation that evaluates positively the theological decision to read these disparate documents together. Conversely, to reject the necessity of the 'Bible' or, as did Wrede, the appropriateness of the name 'New Testament', is to situate oneself within a different community of interpretation on the basis of a different but equally 'dogmatic' judgement. Thus the question of social location, or community of interpretation, is raised by the name we give to what we interpret, and the name we give to what we interpret is inseparably bound with theological decisions of one kind or another. Let us at least be consistent: if we say we study the 'New Testament' but desire to do so free of doctrinal or dogmatic decisions, we are involved in a contradiction at a basic level, since in fact dogmatic decisions constitute in a crucial way the very object we claim to study. And if we reject the notion of the 'Bible', let us say on what dogmatic grounds we do so and in which community of interpretation we are thereby located.

Fourth, however much the previous points press for a recognition of the implicit unity between biblical studies and systematic theology, they do not preclude an emphasis within biblical studies on the distinctiveness and particularity of the diverse texts. In fact, it may not be too much to suggest that the careful delineation of the manifold and richly varied emphases of the individual witnesses within scripture is one of the unique contributions of modern biblical studies to the overall reception of the gospel. In this light, the insistence of Gabler and Stendahl upon descriptive exegesis is indispensable, even if their view of a separation from dogmatics is untenable. Descriptive exegesis always involves theological decisions with respect to the object described, but the content of particular descriptions is not for that reason predetermined or rendered irrelevant for theological reflection. Indeed, even Karl Barth was quick to say that there was no 'path to the whole gospel except the one through the comprehension of the particular, for no one has yet displayed all sides simultaneously' (Barth 1947: xvi).

We thus come, finally, to the question with which the essay began: the relation of biblical studies to systematic theology. The history of the relationship outlined in this essay suggests that where the subject matter of biblical exegesis and of dogmatic theology is not taken to be the same, there exists no real ground for mutual interaction between the two disciplines. Indeed, such interdisciplinary interaction may even be logically precluded, and the point of a biblical studies essay for this handbook would then be to say 'Hands off!' to the systematicians. At best, systematic theology could attempt to appropriate the 'results' of biblical exegesis. Such an essay would consist of a simple summary of the most significant advances in biblical studies, which the systematicians could then put to use—a contemporary remnant of the older proof-texting approach.

However, where the subject matter of biblical exegesis and of dogmatic theology is thought to be the same, the two disciplines are of necessity inseparable. In this respect, to refuse interdisciplinary work between biblical interpretation and constructive theology is to deny the coherence of the subject matter itself. Today, however, the complexity of the interpretative task may warrant a continued, though always provisional and cooperative, division of labour between biblical scholars and systematicians. The exegete concentrates upon the refraction of the subject matter through particular witnesses, thereby penetrating more deeply into the particular shape of the subject matter and helping to avoid banal theological generalities (Childs 2004: xi). And the theologian concentrates more upon the whole of the subject matter as it is expressed through the understanding of scripture in the dogmatic tradition, thereby helping to avoid the tendency toward fragmentation in exegesis (the old problem of losing the forest for the individual trees).

Yet, in continuity with the ancient church, there is no final division between biblical interpretation and theological reflection, for they are united in the common task of attending to the subject matter of scripture. Their actual relationship is thus dialectical, in the sense that within their respective foci there exists a constant movement between the particulars of the biblical text and the whole of systematic reflection in an effort to do justice both to the exegetical thickness of doctrine and the theological coherence of biblical exegesis.

References

Barth, K. (1947). 'Vorwort zur zweiten Auflage'. In id., *Der Römerbrief*, Zurich: Evangelischer Verlag, pp. vi–xviii.

—— (1957). 'The Word of God and the Task of the Ministry'. In id., *The Word of God and the Word of Man*, New York: Harper & Row, 183–217.

—— (1962). 'Rudolf Bultmann: An Attempt to Understand Him'. In H.-W. Bartsch (ed.), *Kerygma and Myth: A Theological Debate*, ii. London: SPCK, 83–132.

—— (1998). *Church Dogmatics* I/2. Edinburgh: T. & T. Clark.

Baur, F. C. (1973 [1864]). *Vorlesungen über neutestamentliche Theologie.* Darmstadt: Wissenschaftliche Buchgesellschaft.

Blowers, P. M. (1997). 'The Regula Fidei and the Narrative Character of Early Christian Faith'. *Pro Ecclesia* 6/2: 199–228.

Bultmann, R. (1951–5). *Theology of the New Testament.* 2 vols. New York: Scribner.

—— (1960*a*). 'Is Exegesis without Presuppositions Possible?' In id., *Existence and Faith: Shorter Writings of Rudolf Bultmann*, New York: Meridian, 289–96.

—— (1960*b*). 'Autobiographical Reflections'. In id., *Existence and Faith: Shorter Writings of Rudolf Bultmann*, New York: Meridian, 283–8.

Burnett, R. E. (2004). *Karl Barth's Theological Exegesis: The Hermeneutical Principles of the* Römerbrief *Period.* Grand Rapids: Eerdmans.

Cadbury, H. J. (1949). 'The Peril of Archaizing Ourselves'. *Interpretation* 3: 331–7.

Calvin, J. (1960). *Institutes of the Christian Religion.* Philadelphia: Westminster.

Childs, B. S. (1970). *Biblical Theology in Crisis.* Philadelphia: Westminster.

—— (2004). *The Struggle to Understand Isaiah as Christian Scripture.* Grand Rapids: Eerdmans.

Davis, E. F. and Hays, R. B. (eds.) (2003). *The Art of Reading Scripture.* Grand Rapids: Eerdmans.

De Lubac, H. (2000). *Medieval Exegesis.* Grand Rapids: Eerdmans.

Fowl, S. E. (ed.) (1997). *The Theological Interpretation of Scripture: Classic and Contemporary Readings.* Malden: Blackwell.

—— (1998). *Engaging Scripture: A Model for Theological Interpretation.* Malden: Blackwell.

Frei, H. W. (1974). *The Eclipse of Biblical Narrative: A Study in Eighteenth and Nineteenth Century Hermeneutics.* New Haven: Yale University Press.

—— (1975). *The Identity of Jesus Christ: The Hermeneutical Bases of Dogmatic Theology.* Philadelphia: Fortress.

Froehlich, K. (1991). 'Church History and the Bible'. In M. Burrows and P. Rorem (eds.), *Biblical Hermeneutics in Historical Perspective: Studies in Honor of Karlfried Froehlich on His Sixtieth Birthday*, Grand Rapids: Eerdmans, 1–15.

Gabler, J. P. (1980 [1787]). *De iusto discrimine theologiae biblicae et dogmaticae regundisque recte utriusque finibus.* In J. Sandys-Wunsch and L. Eldredge (eds. and trans.), 'J. P. Gabler and the Distinction between Biblical and Dogmatic Theology: Translation, Commentary, and Discussion of his Originality', *Scottish Journal of Theology* 33/2: 133–58.

Green, J. B. and Turner, M. (eds.) (2000). *Between Two Horizons: Spanning New Testament Studies and Systematic Theology.* Grand Rapids: Eerdmans.

Greer, R. A. (1986). 'The Christian Bible and Its Interpretation'. In J. Kugel and R. Greer (eds.), *Early Biblical Interpretation*, Philadelphia: Westminster, 107–208.

Harink, D. (2004). *Paul among the Postliberals.* Grand Rapids: Eerdmans.

Hays, R. B. (1996). *The Moral Vision of the New Testament. Community, Cross, New Creation: A Contemporary Introduction to New Testament Ethics.* San Francisco: Harper.

Jenson, R. W. (1997–9). *Systematic Theology.* 2 vols. New York: Oxford University Press.

—— (2003). 'Scripture's Authority in the Church'. In E. Davis and R. Hays (eds.), *The Art of Reading Scripture*, Grand Rapids: Eerdmans, 27–37.

Johnson, L. T. (2002). 'Imagining the World that Scripture Imagines'. In L. T. Johnson and W. Kurz (eds.), *The Future of Catholic Biblical Scholarship: A Constructive Conversation*, Grand Rapids: Eerdmans, 119–42.

Kähler, M. (1988 [1896]). *The So-Called Historical Jesus and the Historic Biblical Christ.* Philadelphia: Fortress.

Levering, M. W. (2004). *Scripture and Metaphysics: Aquinas and the Renewal of Trinitarian Theology.* Oxford: Blackwell.

Lindbeck, G. A. (1984). *The Nature of Doctrine: Religion and Theology in a Postliberal Age.* Philadelphia: Westminster.

Luther, M. (1957–86). *Luther's Works.* 55 vols. St Louis: Concordia.

McCormack, B. (1991). 'Historical Criticism and Dogmatic Interest in Karl Barth's Theological Exegesis of the New Testament'. In M. Burrows and P. Rorem (eds.), *Biblical Hermeneutics in Historical Perspective: Studies in Honor of Karlfried Froehlich on his Sixtieth Birthday,* Grand Rapids: Eerdmans, 322–38.

—— (2002). 'The Significance of Karl Barth's Theological Exegesis of Philippians'. In K. Barth, *Epistle to the Philippians: 40th* Anniversary Edition with Introductory Essays by Bruce L. McCormack and Francis B. Watson. Louisville: Westminster/John Knox v–xxv.

Meeks, W. A. (2005). 'Why Study the New Testament?' *New Testament Studies* 51/2: 155–70.

Minear, P. S. (1974). 'Barth's Commentary on the Romans, 1922–1972, or Karl Barth vs. the Exegetes'. In M. Rumscheidt (ed.), *Footnotes to a Theology: The Karl Barth Colloquium of 1972,* Waterloo: Corporation for the Publication of Academic Studies in Religion in Canada, 8–29.

Ollenburger, B. C. (1986). 'What Krister Stendahl "Meant": A Normative Critique of "Descriptive Biblical Theology"'. *Horizons in Biblical Theology* 81: 61–98.

Rahner, K. (1998). *The Trinity.* New York: Crossroad.

Räisänen, H. (1990). *Beyond New Testament Theology: A Story and a Programme.* London: SCM.

Roberts, A., and Donaldson, J. (eds.) (1990). *Ante-Nicene Fathers: The Writings of the Fathers down to A.D. 325.* Edinburgh: T. & T. Clark.

Schaff, P. (ed.) (1980). *A Select Library of the Nicene and Post-Nicene Fathers of the Christian Church.* 1st ser. Edinburgh: T. & T. Clark.

Schlatter, A. (1973 [1909]). 'The Theology of the New Testament and Dogmatics'. In R. Morgan (ed.), *The Nature of New Testament Theology,* Naperville: Allenson, 117–66.

Schleiermacher, F. D. E. (1928). *The Christian Faith.* Edinburgh: T. & T. Clark.

—— (2003). *Der christliche Glaube: nach den Grundsätzen der evangelischen Kirche im Zusammenhange dargestellt, Zweite Auflage.* In R. Schäfer (ed.), *Kritische Gesamtausgabe,* I. 13, 1 and I. 13, 2, Berlin: Walter de Gruyter.

Schlier, H. (1968). 'The Meaning and Function of a Theology of the New Testament'. In *The Relevance of the New Testament,* New York: Herder and Herder, 1–25.

Schüssler Fiorenza, E. (1983). *In Memory of Her: A Feminist Theological Reconstruction of Christian Origins.* New York: Crossroad.

Schweitzer, A. (1998 [1906]). *The Quest of the Historical Jesus: A Critical Study of its Progress from Reimarus to Wrede.* Baltimore: The Johns Hopkins University Press.

Seitz, C. R. (1998). *Word without End: The Old Testament as Abiding Theological Witness.* Grand Rapids: Eerdmans.

Stendahl, K. (1962). 'Biblical Theology, Contemporary'. In *Interpreter's Dictionary of the Bible* 1: 418–32; rep. (1984), as 'Biblical Theology: A Program', in *Meanings: The Bible as Document and as Guide,* Philadelphia: Fortress, 11–44.

Troeltsch, E. (1991 [1913]). 'The Dogmatics of the History-of-Religions School'. In J. Adams and W. Bense (eds.), *Religion and History,* Minneapolis: Fortress, 87–108.

Watson, F. (1994). *Text, Church and World: Biblical Interpretation in Theological Perspective.* Edinburgh: T. & T. Clark.

—— (1997). *Text and Truth: Redefining Biblical Theology.* Edinburgh: T. & T. Clark.

Wilken, R. L. (2000). 'Foreword'. In H. de Lubac, *Medieval Exegesis,* Grand Rapids: Eerdmans.

Wrede, W. (1973 [1897]). 'The Task and Methods of "New Testament Theology"'. In R. Morgan (ed.), *The Nature of New Testament Theology,* Naperville: Allenson, 68–116.

Wright, N. T. (1992). *The New Testament and the People of God.* Minneapolis: Fortress.

—— (1996). *Jesus and the Victory of God.* Minneapolis: Fortress.

—— (2003). *The Resurrection of the Son of God.* Minneapolis: Fortress.

Young, F. M. (2003). 'Alexandrian and Antiochene Exegesis'. In A. Hauser and D. Watson (eds.), *A History of Biblical Interpretation,* i. *The Ancient Period,* Grand Rapids: Eerdmans, 334–54.

—— (2005). 'The "Mind" of Scripture: Theological Readings of the Bible in the Fathers'. *International Journal of Systematic Theology* 7/2: 126–41.

Suggested Reading

Barth, K. (1968). 'Prefaces'. In id., *The Epistle to the Romans.* London: Oxford University Press.

Bultmann, R. (1951–5: vol. ii, 'Epilogue'). New York: Scribner.

Childs, B. S. (1993). *Biblical Theology of the Old and New Testaments: Theological Reflection on the Christian Bible.* Minneapolis: Fortress.

Davis and Hays (2003).

Fowl (1997).

Gabler (1980).

Lash, N. (1986). *Theology on the Way to Emmaus.* London: SCM.

Meeks (2005).

Räisänen (1990).

Schlatter (1973).

Stendahl (1962).

Watson (1997).

Wrede (1973 [1897]).

Yeago, D. S. (1997). 'The New Testament and the Nicene Dogma: A Contribution to the Recovery of Theological Exegesis'. In Fowl (1997), 87–100.

—— (2001). 'The Bible: The Spirit, the Church, and the Scriptures: Biblical Inspiration and Interpretation Revisited'. In J. Buckley and D. Yeago (eds.), *Knowing the Triune God: The Work of the Spirit in the Practices of the Church,* Grand Rapids: Eerdmans, 49–93.

Young, F. (1997). *Biblical Exegesis and the Formation of Christian Culture.* Cambridge: Cambridge University Press.

CHAPTER 25

MORAL THEOLOGY

DUANE STEPHEN LONG

THE term 'moral theology' (*theologia moralis*) originated at the end of the sixteenth century as part of a Thomistic renaissance in Catholic theology. Aquinas himself did not use the term, nor did any of his predecessors; but it became a distinct discipline within Christian theology after the Council of Trent (Mahoney 1987: vii). Moral theology is one of two systematic-theological disciplines within Catholic theology, the other being speculative or dogmatic theology (Grisez 1983: 3–6). This division shows the influence of Aristotle's understanding of the virtues, which were divided between the intellectual (speculative theology) and the moral (moral theology). Practical wisdom was the only virtue in both categories. Because practical wisdom is a primary concern of moral theology, and because it is both an intellectual and a moral virtue, moral theology cannot be decisively separated from dogmatic theology and its attendant intellectual virtues. Moral theology differs from dogmatic theology in that it focuses on the practical living out of Christian doctrine. Germain Grisez states, 'Moral theology helps us better to understand and so better to do the work of redeeming which our Lord Jesus has assigned to us' (Grisez 1983: 6). Or, as Romanus Cessario puts it in his *Introduction to Moral Theology*, 'moral teaching is located within a larger picture of saving doctrine' (Cessario 2001: xiii).

Protestant theology also bears the mark of this twofold division, although it usually divides into systematic theology and Christian ethics. Ethics is primarily a discipline of the later modern era that seeks to provide unity across confessional traditions. The difference between moral theology and Christian ethics will be explored below; however, these terms are not significant in themselves. Some works bearing the title

'Christian ethics' fit better within moral theology, and some works bearing the title 'moral theology' fit better within Christian ethics. The main difference between them is that moral theology recognizes Christian dogma as essential to the moral life, while Christian ethics sees dogma as less important for its task.

Moral theology assumes an explicit doctrinal context. Its basic structure draws on Aquinas's work, since he established a tradition of setting the moral life within the context of Christian doctrine, thus both confirming and perpetuating the patristic tradition that presented morality according to specific Christian teachings. His discussion of Christian morality in the second part of his *Summa Theologiae* both depends upon the first part, where he sets forth the doctrines of the Trinity and creation, and requires the third part on Christology, church, and sacraments for its completion. Unfortunately, the second part circulated on its own, giving the false impression that Christian morality could be taught independent of doctrine. This was ironic, for Aquinas thought the moral life had become too separated from doctrine, which is why he placed the Christian life—the virtues, gifts, beatitudes, commandments, laws, sins, and vices—within an overarching systematic theology focused on happiness understood as the human creature seeing the vision of God and thus being restored into God's image. To understand the tradition of moral theology, we will need to examine this basic theological structure. But first it is useful to contrast moral theology with the more modern theological discipline of Christian ethics.

I. Moral Theology or Christian Ethics?

Moral theology and Christian ethics represent different approaches to the Christian moral life. Although the term 'moral theology' was first used in the early modern era, it refers to an ancient theological tradition, especially the practices of penance and confession. Christian ethics began to be taught in the modern era after the scientific revolution of the seventeenth century; it assumes a more decisive break with the Christian past in order to make ethics relevant to the changing intellectual environment of modernity. It often assumes that Christian ethics is to be applied to public issues through the social sciences.

This produces a distinction in audience: moral theology addresses primarily the church, while Christian ethics addresses primarily more modern social formations such as the nation state, corporation, global market, or the university. It tends to focus on policies which those in charge of such institutions could implement irrespective of any particular faith or lack thereof. Thus, Christian ethics tends to focus on 'ethics' as a more universal category than doctrine. The term 'Christian' is used to let those within the Christian community know they are included within and can fit their particular claims into the more universal ethics. A prime example of this would be the tradition of ethics associated with the University of Chicago and exemplified by James Gustafson, who wrote, 'The theologian addressing many issues—nuclear war, social justice, ecology, and so forth—must do so as an outcome of a theology that develops God's relations to all aspects of life in the world, and develops those relations in terms which are not exclusively Christian in a sectarian form. Jesus is not God' (Werpehowski 2002: 121). This tradition assumes that doctrine divides whereas ethics unites. Thus Christian ethics becomes a public discourse that includes people of faith, but it also seeks to temper their confessional, doctrinal claims in order to make common cause with those who seek to be ethical but who do not accept Christian doctrines. It assumes that the good is a more universal category than a confessional doctrine such as that God is triune. Every individual can be good; every individual cannot confess that God is triune. The moral life should not be presented in terms of something that will be controversial among the earth's inhabitants when we can develop it in less controversial terms.

Moral theologians, however, deny that ethics is a more universal category than Christian doctrine. This divides them from Christian ethicists. For instance, Stanley Hauerwas and Samuel Wells, moral theologians associated with the Duke Divinity School, state that 'attempts to distinguish ethics from theology in modernity have distorted the character of Christian convictions and practices' (Hauerwas and Wells 2004: 35). Like Aquinas, they seek to read ethics in terms of doctrine. In an essay entitled, 'How the Church Managed Before There Was Ethics', they explicitly draw on the work of Aquinas, who situated the Christian life within the narrative structure of creation, fall, and redemption (Hauerwas and Wells 2004: 46). Hauerwas and Wells might agree that doctrine divides and ethics unites, but they want no part of the 'unity' which the modern discipline of ethics produces, for it requires us to abstract from Christian teaching some putatively universal ethical kernel.

Several reasons exist as to why moral theologians do not assume that the good is a more universal and inclusive category than the categories of dogma. Many philosophers and theologians now claim that no neutral and universal space is available to any human creature's unaided intellect. Thus a certain suspicion emerges concerning those who claim to be doing ethics solely from a neutral, public space and who indict others for doing it from a particular, confessional space. Related to this is a claim such as Alasdair MacIntyre's that every ethics presupposes a sociology (MacIntyre 1984: 22). Ethics assumes some kind of social formation. If it is true that every ethics presupposes a sociology, then some form of doctrine will undergird every ethic; for the 'teaching' of some institution will be necessary for that ethics' intelligibility. The very claim that 'ethics unites but doctrine divides' is itself a dogma that serves certain political interests. To adopt that dogma is to adopt those interests. The question then is not whether doctrine makes ethics possible, but which doctrine. All ethics assumes specific doctrines. Moral theology and Christian ethics differ on which doctrines are most significant.

Moral theology begins with a vision of God. Christian ethics tends to begin with the commanding God. The distinction here should not be overdrawn. Moral theologians do not deny that God commands; that is a central part of the revelation given to Moses and fulfilled in Jesus. But moral theology emphasizes first who this God is who commands and thus subordinates the giving of the commands to the vision of God. Take for instance John Wesley's moral theology, which can be found in his 'Discourses on the Sermon on the Mount'. Before he begins to discuss the obligations that the beatitudes bring, he finds it imperative that one know who it is that pronounces certain ways of life blessed.

> Let us observe who it is that is here speaking, that we may 'take heed how we hear'. It is the Lord of heaven and earth, the Creator of all, who, as such, has a right to dispose of all his creatures; the Lord our Governor, whose kingdom is from everlasting, and ruleth over all: the great Lawgiver, who can well enforce all his laws.... It is the eternal Wisdom of the Father who knoweth whereof we are made, and understands our inmost frame.... It speaks the Creator of all—a God, a God appears! Yea, *ho ōn*, the being of beings, Jehovah, the self-existent, the supreme, the God who is over all, blessed for ever! (Wesley 1984: 470–6)

The vision of God comes first; only then can the significance of ethical obligations arise. This is less the case with Christian ethics, where the command itself becomes just as or even more important than the vision of the one who issues it. Thus obedience to something like the 'golden rule', or Kant's translation of it into his categorical imperative, becomes more basic than the vision of the triune God who issues the command.

This leads to another important distinction. Moral theology tends to draw on an ethics of virtue while Christian ethics emphasizes an ethics of obligation, which is one reason Christian doctrine plays a more significant role in moral theology than in Christian ethics. An ethics of virtue finds the good in both the intellect and the will. The intellect, in grasping truth, offers a vision of what is true to the will, while the will, in pursuing the good, moves the intellect as well. The moral life is about both the will willing the good and the intellect pursuing truth. In fact, the two cannot finally be divided; they come together in practical wisdom.

Christian ethics tends to focus primarily on the will. What is good is a good will; one is not accountable for being foolish or ignorant or for failing to pursue truth as long as one wills the good. An ethics of obligation logically follows, whose decisive question is, Have you kept the law? An ethics of virtue, on the other hand, while not denying the importance of keeping the law, sets the law within a framework of the vision of God and the virtues, gifts, and beatitudes that allow us to see God. It begins with the question, Have you seen God? It assumes that the law can only truly be kept if God is seen. Because of the importance of vision, moral theology tends to emphasize the sacraments and scripture. Because of the importance of commands, Christian ethics tends to focus on scripture alone. This might lead one to think that moral theology is primarily Catholic and that Christian ethics is Protestant. While there is some truth to such an assumption, the Catholic tradition has generated its share of ethics of obligation, and Protestants such as John Wesley and Jonathan Edwards clearly described the Christian moral life on the basis of the vision of God (Long 2005). Even a theologian as committed to the God who commands as Karl Barth nevertheless fits more easily within moral theology, for he never wrote an ethics independent of Christian confessional claims. For Barth, like the tradition of moral theology, dogmatics is ethics. Thus he stated, 'We can speak about man only by speaking about God' (Webster 1998: 104).

II. The Theological Basis for Moral Theology

If moral theology begins with a vision of God, then it fits best within a systematic theology where ethics is neither an appendix to doctrine nor a discipline that makes sense apart from doctrine. Within the tradition of moral theology, ethics is neither the 'application' of doctrine, nor is it a public and more universal presentation of otherwise parochial and confessional claims. Ethics requires an explicit presentation of doctrine.

The moral life has its origin in our creation in the image of God and its end in our restoration and return into that image. Jesus Christ is the image of God from whom, through whom, and toward whom creation exists. To be restored into God's image is to be restored into the image of God that Jesus is. For this reason, who God is must first be recognized before the moral life can be delineated. Moral theology finds completion in this particular vision of God, which is known by faith, but this is not where it begins. It begins with the assumption that all creatures, because they are creatures, have a natural desire for God. This desire produces an intellectual quest to know God, but the most that can be naturally known is *that* God is, not *who* God is. To know who God is, the theological virtue of faith is necessary. Faith teaches us that God is triune and that we have glimpsed this in the incarnation. The triune God is complete goodness and therefore in need of nothing. The triune God is the perfect fullness of being. Our creation adds nothing to God's being. Why then creation? Why is there created being rather than nothing? Solely because of God's love. God loves his own goodness such that he seeks to share it. This occurs in creation through the second person of the Trinity, who is the image of God. All creation exists within the 'space' of the second hypostasis. Thus this image of God is the origin as well as the end of creation. The gift of the Holy Spirit invites us to participate in the life of God by drawing us into the life of the Son. This occurs through the gifts and the virtues of divine goodness which the Spirit shares with us.

Moral theology assumes the doctrines of creation and salvation, which are grounded both in the procession of that love which is the 'gift' of the Holy Spirit and in the procession of the image, which is the Son. Although creation is purely gratuitous and non-necessary, it is not arbitrary. It has a purpose which is both disclosed by and accomplished in the incarnation of the Son, 'the Image' of God. 'Image' is a 'personal name' for the second person, just as 'gift' is for the third person (*ST* 1a. 35, 1, in Aquinas 1948). The two processions form the basis for Aquinas's reflections on the moral life in the second part of his *Summa*. To see these two processions would be to see God. This is the human creature's true end, for only this makes such creatures truly happy. Moral theology, like much of ancient moral teaching, finds that human action always tends toward some good and that the pursuit and achievement of that good will produce in us happiness. Happiness here is not to be confused with pleasure and the absence of pain, as with the utilitarians. Rather, happiness is associated with holiness and the vision of God.

We cannot see the invisible God through natural means alone. Such a vision requires the theological virtues, gifts, and beatitudes. They perfect the natural passions and virtues. Because they come from the Holy Spirit, they allow us to participate in God's life. Because they perfect our natural created dispositions, they allow this participation to occur without blurring the boundary between God and creatures. The theological virtues, gifts, and beatitudes restore us into the image of God, Christ, whose life is the foundation for this restoration. Through his incarnation and its mediation through the church in word and sacrament, we participate in his righteousness. Once we know how we are to be ordered toward God, we can then know the reason for both the law's positive commands as well as its prohibitions of those sins and vices that would destroy us.

Although moral theology is not primarily an ethics of obligation, it has an important place for law. The virtues, gifts, and beatitudes help us understand the purpose of the law. Aquinas states, 'The precepts of the Law are about acts of virtue' (*ST* 1a2ae. 62, 1). Law directs human action toward virtuous ends. Baptist theologian James McClendon explained this well in his *Ethics* when he noted that the Ten Commandments assume virtuous practices without which they become unintelligible. If we did not have the virtue of fidelity, founded upon the practice of lifelong monogamous marriage, then the seventh commandment not to commit adultery makes little sense (McClendon 1986: 182). Law is not an end in itself; it orders us toward our proper end. This does not mean that the law can be treated arbitrarily.

Moral theology acknowledges that certain things, such as directly intending to kill the innocent, are never to be done. Such actions are 'intrinsically evil' because they cannot be ordered to humanity's true end in God. Therefore by definition they cannot make us happy. John Paul II explained 'intrinsically evil' actions in his 1993 encyclical on moral theology, *Veritatis Splendor*:

> Reason attests that there are objects of the human act which are by their nature 'incapable of being ordered' to God, because they radically contradict the good of the person made in his image. These are the acts which, in the Church's moral tradition, have been termed 'intrinsically evil' (*intrinsece malum*): they are such *always and per se*, in other words, on account of their very object, and quite apart from the ulterior intentions of the one acting and the circumstances.... The Second Vatican Council itself, in discussing the respect due to the human person, gives a number of examples of such acts: 'Whatever is hostile to life itself, such as any kind of homicide, genocide, abortion, euthanasia and voluntary suicide; whatever violates the integrity of the human person, such as mutilation, physical and mental torture and attempts to coerce the spirit; whatever is offensive to human dignity, such as subhuman living conditions, arbitrary imprisonment; deportation, slavery, prostitution and trafficking in women and children, degrading conditions of work which treat labourers as mere instruments of profit and not as free responsible persons....' (*Veritatis Splendor* §80, in Wilkins 1994: 150)

This is not an ethics of obligation that makes the commands more important than the vision of the God who issues them; nor is it a deontological ethic like Kant's categorical imperative. These acts can only be understood as 'intrinsically evil' when they are placed within a doctrine of God and our creation in God's image. If there were no journey into that image, we could not identify such intrinsic evils.

As the virtues and gifts can become principles of movement of the soul's natural passions, so can the vices. Whereas the grace found in the virtues and gifts presupposes and perfects nature, the evil found in the vices trades on the same goodness of nature but disorders it. The seven deadly or capital vices disorder our nature by treating something finite as an infinite end. Pride, covetousness, envy, lust, gluttony, anger, and sloth all trade on something good, but order it toward an improper end. Each of these takes a passion that should be a means and makes it an end in itself.

The above is a brief sketch of the basic theological structure of moral theology. Mostcontemporary moral theologians either engage directly with this theological structure or assume it as they develop variations upon it. Of course, not every moral theologian agrees with this basic structure or even interprets it in the same way, since ambiguities exist within it. One such important ambiguity is the role of nature. Moral theology assumes that grace perfects nature, but what does this mean? Is nature sufficient in itself while grace merely adds to it? A Reformed theologian like Karl Barth had significant reservations about the system precisely because of such an assumption.

III. Karl Barth: Dogmatics is Ethics

Like Aquinas, Barth recognized that dogmatics is ethics, which is to say, the Christian life cannot be abstracted from the church's teaching. Ethics cannot exist independent of dogma. Although he was not following Aquinas explicitly, Barth comes closer to a recovery of moral theology than any other twentieth-century Protestant theologian. Without his work, we would not have seen a renaissance in both Catholic and Protestant moral theology. Barth situated ethics within a theological structure similar to that of Aquinas, beginning with the doctrine of God as triune, moving to creation, and concluding with reconciliation and Christology.

Like Aquinas, the theological virtues are central for Barth. When he discusses the work of Christ and the doctrine of reconciliation, he correlates Christ's priestly work with the virtue of faith confronting the deadly vice of pride (Barth 1956). He then correlates Christ's kingly work with the virtue of love confronting the deadly vice of sloth (Barth 1958). Finally, he correlates Christ's prophetic work with the virtue of hope confronting the deadly vice of falsehood (Barth 1961; 1962). Although Barth puts the pieces together differently than does Aquinas, many of the basic elements of Barth's moral theology connect with the tradition derived from Aquinas. But Barth also poses an important question to this tradition: Does its account of nature take on too much that remains pagan? When he tells us that the Roman Catholic 'analogy of being' is 'the invention of Antichrist', he challenges the notion that nature could be sufficient unto itself (Barth 1975: xiii). This is always the temptation when incorporating Aristotle's moral philosophy into theology as the tradition of moral theology does. The temptation is to think that 'nature' itself gives us access to God in such a way that we finally 'lay hands' on God and reduce him to what we think is 'natural' rather than allowing the incarnation to confront our pride and even lead us to reconsider what constitutes 'nature'. Barth's work thus raises an important question about the function of the concept of 'nature' within moral theology. We will look first at the moral-theological renaissance inspired by Barth and then at the concept of nature.

IV. Moral Theology's Modern Renaissance

Moral theology underwent a renaissance in both Catholic and Protestant circles in the twentieth century. Dissatisfaction with the discipline of Christian ethics contributed to this renaissance. Criticisms of ethics as a neutral, universal discipline as well as a retrieval of the church's ancient wisdom on moral matters encouraged renewed interest. The ecumenical movement also contributed to it as churches began to recognize the truth and beauty in traditions besides their own.

Paul Ramsey was one of the Protestant contributors to this renaissance. He became increasingly dissatisfied with the utilitarian character of much that passed for modern Christian ethics (perhaps including his own early work). In 1965, one year before the publication of his own *Situation Ethics*, Joseph Fletcher wrote to Ramsey and acknowledged that this work 'had a great deal to do' with what had been 'planted' in his mind by Ramsey's *Basic Christian Ethics* (Long 1993: 105). But Ramsey was no situational ethicist; he thought it contributed to the 'wasteland of utility' into which much of twentieth-century Christian ethics had fallen. In opposition to this drift in Christian ethics, Ramsey began to look back into the Christian tradition to see if it did not have more to offer for thinking through questions of war and peace, abortion, cloning, and medical care at the edges of life. He did this by recovering natural law and reading it through 'love'. For this reason Ramsey set out to do Christian ethics through a new paradigm called 'love transforming the natural law'. It assumed certain 'natural' institutions such as the market and political government. But Christ's victory transformed them so that the natural laws by which they operated could not alone provide resources for ethical reflection. The love of Christ must transform them. Yet Ramsey was not always attentive as to how his love-transforming natural law might fit within a more comprehensive theological programme. When pressed to explain its theological basis, he cited Barth's claim that the covenant is the internal basis of creation and creation is the external basis of the covenant. For Ramsey, the doctrine of creation identifies certain natural structures within which medicine, politics, and economics must be pursued. These structures include the possibility of exceptionless moral principles. However, Christ has transformed these structures so that they must now be read as falling under the vindication of his life, which Ramsey called 'agape'.

Much of modern Protestant ethics prior to Ramsey was a not-so-veiled effort to replace the truth of doctrine with the good of morality because ethicists no longer found Christian doctrine defensible. Walter Rauschenbusch's *A Theology for the Social Gospel* explicitly argued that ethics should replace eschatology (Rauschenbusch 1978). While Reinhold Niebuhr reacted against what he saw as Rauschenbusch's neglect of sin and easy identification of Christianity and moral progress, he nevertheless produced a 'moral theology' in which moral good was no more rendered intelligible by the truth of Christian doctrine than it was in Rauschenbusch's account. For instance, Niebuhr rejected as 'logical nonsense' any understanding of the incarnation that would 'affirm both [Christ's] divinity and humanity in the sense that they ascribe both finite and historically conditioned and eternal and unconditioned qualities to his nature' (Niebuhr 1943: 61). Ramsey's contribution to moral theology was to follow Karl Barth and make room for the truth of Christian doctrine as that which would once again render intelligible the moral good.

No moral theologian has developed Ramsey's insights better than Oliver O'Donovan. What Ramsey left implicit, O'Donovan makes explicit. Ramsey's appeal to 'agape' left too much ambiguity regarding the theological truth of the moral life. O'Donovan, on the other hand, has consistently emphasized Christ's resurrection and ascension as the true context within which Christians produce moral and political theory. 'A belief in Christian ethics', O'Donovan states, 'is a belief that certain ethical and moral judgments belong to the gospel itself; a belief, in other words, that the church can be committed to ethics without moderating the tone of its voice as a bearer of glad tidings' (O'Donovan 1994: 12). This is a marked difference from the tradition of Christian ethics that appealed to ethics because doctrine was indefensible.

A number of other Protestant ethicists are well known for refusing to separate theology and ethics, including John Howard Yoder, James William McClendon, Jr., and Stanley Hauerwas. I consider each of them moral theologians because they do not set the moral life over against Christian doctrine. Yoder and McClendon were both Anabaptist/Baptist theologians who did not always claim to be bound by conciliar creeds, even though their work never conflicted with the truth of the councils. Yoder presented a restitutionist theological ethics that sought to retrieve a biblical presentation of Jesus without the necessary mediation of tradition. What is striking is how similar Jesus is in Yoder's work to that of conciliar, creedal Christianity. Like Barth, Yoder presented Jesus as prophet, priest, and king. For Yoder, however, Christ must first be understood as king, while his 'royal priesthood' is to be understood eschatologically (Yoder 2002: 240–81). If we lose eschatology, we lose the way of life Christ blessed and vindicated, a way we are called to imitate. Yoder argued that there can be no ethics without eschatology.

McClendon offers another form of moral theology. His three-volume work does not begin with Christian doctrine, but with ethics, moving from there to doctrine and concluding with witness. Yet he assumes that the Christian life and doctrine are interdependent. In the second volume, he states, 'Without Christian life, the doctrine is dead, without Christian doctrine the life is formless' (McClendon 1994: i). His ethics begins with ecclesiology, emphasizing 'the story-formed or narrative shape of the shared life of the Christian church' (McClendon 1986: 45). It begins with descriptions of what it means to be the church.

McClendon distances his work both from the decisionism found in the Protestant ethicist J. Philip Wogaman (1989), who constructs a method for making ethical decisions, and from the Catholic ethicist Timothy E. O'Connell (1978), who offers a form of decisionism known as 'the fundamental option'. This is a revisionist natural law ethic that argues the task of the moral life is to take a fundamental option for God and life and that this is possible without any explicit acknowledgement of Christian doctrine. It is a tacit decision one makes in the core of one's being. While both Wogaman and O'Connell offer an ethics that 'exceeds' Christian doctrine, McClendon does not find such a position to be theologically responsible. Instead, he appeals to a 'biblical morality' that is 'viewed as a multistranded rope' (McClendon 1986: 64). This rope has three strands: the organic, the communal, and the anastatic, which are 'three ways of talking about morality'. Christians are '(1) part of the natural order, organic beings; but also (2) part of a social world that is constituted first by the corporate nature of Christian existence, the church, and thereby by our share in human society, God's social creation as well; and (3) part of an eschatological realm, the Kingdom of God, the "new world" established by

God's resurrection of Jesus of Nazareth from the dead' (McClendon 1986: 66). McClendon's moral theology proceeds on the basis of these three strands.

Stanley Hauerwas also has re-energized the tradition of moral theology within Protestantism. He finds any distinction between theology and ethics to be mistaken; ethics becomes primarily for Hauerwas ecclesiological description. He is well known for his axiom, 'the church does not have a social ethic, it is a social ethic' (Hauerwas 1983: 99). Hauerwas's work has also made some Catholic moral theologians rethink their own tradition. For instance, Immanuel Katongole develops Hauerwas's insight to show how 'uninspiring' certain aspects of Catholic moral theology have become. According to Katongole, many moral theologians begin by assuming they know what ethics is and then ask how God can relate to it. The result, he suggests, has become all too predictable: the God of relevance in contemporary moral theology finally becomes nothing other than a projection of what we think we need in order to secure an otherwise autonomous moral order (Katongole 2000: 16). Katongole finds an alternative to this kind of moral theology by developing Hauerwas's claim that 'to begin by asking what is the relation between theology and ethics is to have already made a mistake' (Katongole 2000: ix). In opposition to an ethics that seeks to bridge two distinct things called 'religion' and 'ethics', both Katongole and Hauerwas begin with Christology and ecclesiology and ask what difference this makes for how we see and live in a world viewed as God's good creation. Hauerwas recognizes that the historical body of the risen Christ is no longer with us in the way it was with the disciples; nevertheless, it is mediated to us through word and sacrament in the church. Because Jesus Christ is the one in whom, through whom, and toward whom all things are created, Hauerwas cannot allow for a category of creation or nature to be larger than Christological and even ecclesiological claims. Thus when he offers Christological and ecclesial descriptions as the basis for the moral good, only someone who either does not understand basic Christian doctrine, or who tacitly rejects it, could possibly ask for something more universal than Jesus and his church as the basis for the moral life. Much of the confusion and debate over contemporary moral theology has less to do with a universal or sectarian ethics, and more to do with the explicit and implicit Christian doctrines that do or do not render those ethics intelligible.

Jean Porter is a Roman Catholic moral theologian who seeks to mediate between, on the one hand, the 'proportionalism' which is found in Joseph Fuchs, Bernard Häring, Richard McCormick, and Charles Curran, and, on the other, a 'radical reinterpretation of the traditional doctrine of the natural law' as is found in the work of Germain Grisez and John Finnis (Porter 1990: 17). The proportionalists draw upon an important essay by Peter Knauer entitled 'The Hermeneutic Function of the Principle of Double Effect' (Knauer 1979). The principle of double effect states that an action can have a directly intended effect and an unintended effect. The unintended effect, even though it is foreseen, does not count as the object of the moral act; only the intended effect counts. Proportionalists use the principle of double effect to argue that proportionate reason sometimes permits or requires 'pre-moral evils' in order to achieve some other moral good (Knauer 1979). John Paul II took this position to task in *Veritatis Splendor* (1993), producing a flurry of debate in both Protestant and Roman Catholic moral theology concerning whether or not his critique rightly presented proportionalism. The second position, that of Grisez and Finnis, interprets Aquinas in Kantian terms. It develops an account of practical reason which states that every action must formally be ordered toward some good. It then seeks to stipulate the categorical character of those goods. Like Kant's categorical imperative, these goods are intrinsic to a properly good action.

Porter attempts to develop a 'general theory of goodness' which can guide Christian moral action and which has neither the problems of proportionalism nor the categorical claims of Grisez and Finnis. However, like both of these positions, and unlike Hauerwas, McClendon, and Yoder, Porter seeks to develop this theory of goodness based on nature and not simply as a description of ecclesiology. She suggests that we must find a category of truth and goodness that goes beyond the church (Porter 1990: 31). At this point the difference between Porter and Hauerwas becomes clear. Hauerwas is committed to traditional teaching regarding the threefold form of Christ's body. First is his historical, risen body, which is ascended. Second is the eucharist (including the word), through which his body is mediated to the world. Third is the church, which receives its being as the body of Christ from word and sacrament. All of creation has its presupposition in Christ's body. Thus Hauerwas could never admit something called 'nature' that is outside of, larger than, or beyond Christ. Porter, on the other hand, would seem to be committed to claiming that there are transcendentals that are somehow greater than the procession of the second person of the Trinity. Once moral theologians begin to see systematic theology as essential to their task, such differences and their underlying doctrinal assumptions will hopefully begin to emerge.

Martin Rhonheimer and Servais Pinckaers represent a Catholic moral theology that fits neither with proportionalism, nor with Grisez and Finnis, nor with the transcendental Thomist tradition. Rhonheimer understands the natural law to be 'a discourse on practical reason'. It is 'not simply receptive', but also 'a power that is constitutive of the human good' (Rhonheimer 2000: ix). Natural law, then, is not the discovery of an objective order over and against us, as much as it is 'constituted' by our use of our natural reason as it participates in the eternal law (Rhonheimer 2000: 5). Rhonheimer suggests that a virtue ethic is necessary to understand how this works. We do not live in a world of non-moral goods that are then made moral through our own agency. Instead, the exercise of our practical reason forms our moral character, and when it is done well it constitutes a natural law that is consistent with eternal law. Like much of the Catholic natural law tradition in moral theology, how this fits within Christian doctrine does not seem to be clear. In fact, this question does not even seem to arise for Rhonheimer, who writes primarily as a Catholic philosopher.

Servais Pinckaers brings together ethics, theology, and spirituality in such a way that one cannot be had without the others. He works against any notion of an autonomous ethics, or an ethics of obligation, and argues that the rise of both stems in part from the Catholic manualist tradition which gave an 'exaggerated emphasis to the study of justice, resulting in an overly juridical presentation of morality' (Pinckaers 1995: 35). He recovers much more than virtue for moral theology in his emphasis on the work and gifts of the Holy Spirit in relation to the beatitudes pronounced by Jesus in the Sermon on the Mount. He shows how Augustine and Aquinas correlated the seven gifts of the Spirit with the first seven beatitudes; the eighth beatitude ('blessed are those who are persecuted') was the fruit of a life embodying the beatitudes and gifts (Pinckaers 1995: 157). These were then correlated with the seven petitions of the Lord's Prayer. Pinckaers seeks to 'reestablish the relation between Scripture and moral theory so that the latter may become once more truly Christian' (Pinckaers 1995: 109).

While the recovery of moral theology moves much of the discipline of Christian ethics back in a more confessionally Christian direction, not all ethicists are pleased with this. Some find it insufficiently 'emancipatory' because it is insufficiently universal. Others find that the quest for universal criteria denies the inevitable social and contextual character of our knowledge. The debates between these two positions have played themselves out in feminist Christian ethics as well. Thus Susan Frank Parsons presents three kinds of feminist Christian ethics that do not reject Christian doctrine, but give it a significantly different place. The first is liberal feminism. It offers paradigms for ethical reflections that 'drive us on to a universal perspective applicable to all regardless of circumstance'. It offers women a 'framework' to use 'for emancipation throughout the world' (Parsons 1996: 64). The second is a 'social-constructivist' feminist paradigm that recovers something akin to Aristotle's practical moral reasoning. It eschews looking for universal criteria for ethics; instead 'what one should do may be derived from a social understanding of who one is' (Parsons 1996: 76). But the aim of this position is less the preservation of a social order and more its reconstruction. The third is a 'naturalist paradigm' that finds a natural basis for moral behavior intrinsic to being human, which is not so much transcendental as it is 'a process of deepening awareness of what is already the case, so that its many facets and possibilities are opened to the increasing sensitivity of the moral consciousness' (Parsons 1996: 131–3). Parsons offers criticisms of all of these positions and then seeks to 'pick up some threads' in all of them in order to set forth a feminist Christian ethics in terms of a 'redemptive community' (Parsons 1996: 200–21).

V. Happiness and a Natural or Supernatural End

While Christian ethicists raise the question whether there is an ethics independent of Christian doctrine, moral theologians dispute whether, for reasons of faith, a natural basis for ethics can be found upon which all persons could agree independent of their confessional stances. The difference in these two questions is subtle, but significant. The first questions the relevance of Christian doctrine. The second questions whether there can exist, within Christian doctrine, a doctrine of pure nature, common grace, or human dignity that all reasonable people should be able to intuit independent of their formation into the life of the church. Answers to these questions will largely determine the context in which such thinkers address significant moral issues of economics, war, the family, marriage, and gender. The Christian ethicist, for example, who seeks an ethics independent from Christian doctrine will find the church either problematic or at best neutral in addressing these issues. The moral theologian who finds within Christian doctrine some basis for a common moral life with those outside the church may find the church significant, but not always necessary. Christian doctrine, on this view, concedes to those outside the church an independence and even autonomy from specific church teachings. The moral theologian, finally, who finds Christian doctrine essential for the narration of the good life will find the church indispensable for addressing these issues.

On the face of it, the first two of these examples seem most satisfying when it comes to everyday life. One does not expect a secular anaesthesiologist, an Islamic police officer, a Jewish judge, or a Protestant or Catholic bus driver to act differently from other persons in discharging the moral duties of their various vocations. We hold each of them to moral expectations and are shocked when we find those expectations violated. Seldom do Christians say, 'That is what you get with people who do not confess the Nicene Creed.' If the third example suggests that we should in fact say something like this, it is difficult to square with everyday life. A common ability to function morally in neighbourhoods, schools, cities, workplaces, and various and sundry forms of transportation is part of our everyday life. Who could deny this?

However, at times this ability to function in common is strained. Does the prohibition against contraception make sense outside the Roman Catholic Church? Should all right-thinking persons intuit by nature that contraception is intrinsically evil? Is there a natural inclination to help the innocent that makes war a moral endeavour? Can opposition to war make sense outside the Christian confessions Anabaptists make? Should marriage be monogamous and exclusively between a man and a woman? If Christ is not confessed as faithful to the church, fidelity as a virtue of marriage could seem unnatural. Abortion, suicide, economic policy, taking money on usury, capital punishment, family structure, participation in warfare, policing, business practices such as pornography or buying and selling luxury cars, racial and ethnic identity: on these and many other matters, finding a common morality is difficult if not impossible, and many people cannot make sense of their everyday lives without reference to the teachings of some church or other community.

The ability to function in common morally is both present in our everyday activities and also strained by confessionally grounded moral practices. The question is how to relate these two everyday realities. One way is to ask which is the surface reality, and which lies beneath. Should we make sense of the ability to function in common morally in terms of deeper confessional practices, as moral theology suggests? In other words, even a 'common' morality emerges out of confessional practices. Or should we regard confessional practices as unnecessary surface disturbances to an underlying common morality and seek to find in this morality the 'deeper' meaning of such practices, as ethics suggests? The debate over which is the depth and which the surface reality divides moral theologians and ethicists. Moral theologians often find in Christian ethics a rationalism indebted to the Enlightenment that assumes a disengaged subject capable of willing the good without that subject being constituted communally. Christian ethicists find moral theologians to be fideists who withdraw from larger public and political issues. Both deny such charges. But even when moral theologians agree that only doctrine can render ethics intelligible, they often disagree over the precise nature of this doctrine and hence disagree as well over which virtues are appropriate for moral and political matters.

This difference among moral theologians goes back to sixteenth-century interpreters of Aquinas and centres on the question whether humans have a single or a double end. In other words, does moral theology teach that there is both a natural and a supernatural end, either of which can make us happy; or does it teach that only the supernatural end accomplishes this? These moral theologians agreed that our primary end is supernatural: the vision of God. They disagreed, however, over our natural end. Some thought that a distinct natural end provides the basis for a universal common morality potentially known to all people by reason alone. Others feared that this relativized the role of the church, the sacraments, and the theological virtues, actually allowing for that secular space within which a Christian ethics could be developed.

The point of contention is found in passages from Aquinas such as this: 'Man was happy in paradise, but not with that perfect happiness to which he was destined, which consists in the vision of the Divine Essence. He was, however, endowed with "a life of happiness in a certain measure," as Augustine says, so far as he was gifted with natural integrity and perfection' (*ST* 1a. 94, 1 ad 1). Because the moral life tends toward happiness, this suggests that human creatures have a kind of natural happiness separate from the supernatural gift of faith, which would have been the situation of Adam in paradise. This natural end would explain the common basis for the moral life that brings a certain degree of happiness in everyday life. But notice that Aquinas also speaks of the 'perfect happiness' to which the human creature is 'destined'. This is the vision of God. Does this suggest that human creatures have two ends, one natural and one supernatural? If so, are they distinct, are they related, or are they finally the same end where the latter must perfect the former for it to achieve its end?

One answer is provided by those theologians who assert a *duplex ordo cognitionis* (a twofold order of knowing). Thus Romanus Cessario states, 'the very doctrine of the incarnation implies a twofold order of being, truth and knowledge: that of created nature (assumed by the Word) and that of the uncreated God and his grace.... the order of nature is distinct from and has no claim upon the supernatural' (Griffiths and Hütter 2005: 332, 336). Others find this twofold order problematic—the basis for much that went wrong in theology. Colin Gunton, following Karl Barth, censured Aquinas as 'the father of all those who hold that theology requires some basis in independent rational thought' (Gunton 1997: 16–17). This implies that we can think not only about God but also about the good outside of the gift given in revelation.

The Catholic theologian Henri de Lubac challenged the twofold order of knowing because he thought that it produced a rationalist morality that separates the supernatural—including the church, sacraments, theological virtues, gifts, and beatitudes—from everyday life. Joseph Komonchak explains this when he writes that the twofold order against which de Lubac wrote 'so insisted on the radical distinction between nature and grace that it lost the sense of their intimate relationship, of the finality of nature for grace. It thus provided others the opportunity to separate the supernatural off into a distant realm, into an exile where Christians might care for it, while they proceeded to construct the world on "natural," that is secular, grounds' (Komonchak 1990: 584). If de Lubac is correct, then the rise of Christian ethics was less a reaction against moral theology and more a development within it based on the strong distinction taught in the twofold order of knowing. But what would it mean to reject this *duplex ordo* in favour of a single end?

Gustavo Gutiérrez and John Milbank both find the *duplex ordo* problematic and develop a theology in terms of a single supernatural end; they differ, however, over the significance of this end. Gutiérrez argues that the sixteenth-century moral theologian Cajetan was a 'less-than-faithful' interpreter of Aquinas in reading him in terms of this *duplex ordo* (Gutiérrez 1988: 43). Gutiérrez rejects this reading and insists there is 'one call to salvation' which overcomes any sharp distinction between the natural and the supernatural. This theological move animates most of his work. He writes, 'The affirmation of the single vocation to salvation, beyond all distinctions, gives religious value in a completely new way to human action in history, Christian and non-Christian alike. The building of a just society has worth in terms of the Kingdom, or in more current phraseology, to participate in the process of liberation is already, in a certain sense, a salvific work' (Gutiérrez 1988: 47). Here even secular processes that work for justice are given theological significance whether they intend it or not.

John Milbank's development of a single vocation to salvation moves in a very different direction. He thinks that two possibilities emerge once a double finality no longer serves as the human creature's end. On the one hand, one could 'naturalize the supernatural', which is what he finds theologians such as Karl Rahner and Gustavo Gutiérrez doing. Or one could 'supernaturalize the natural', as did de Lubac and Balthasar and as he himself attempts to do (Milbank 1990: 207). This increases the role played by the church and by the theological virtues, gifts, and beatitudes. Milbank writes, 'there can be no true justice without charity, and no true social order without transformation by the supernatural society which is the Church' (Milbank 1990: 223). But this does not mean that Milbank denies the possibility of natural inclinations which are shared beyond the precincts of confessional doctrine. For instance, we possess natural intuitions 'to protect the innocent' which are 'rooted in our animality, embodiment and finitude' and which mandate a moral use of violence and make pacifism immoral (Milbank 2002: 39). This differs from Hauerwas, who also rejects the *duplex ordo* but finds a deeper 'clash' between the 'political (and essential) claims of Christianity' and the 'Greek understanding of virtue' (Hauerwas and Pinches 1997: 63). For Hauerwas, peace is an essential and natural Christian virtue.

David Schindler follows the intricacies of de Lubac's thought and avoids either a strong distinction between nature and grace or collapsing nature into grace. He refers to de Lubac's position as 'organic-paradoxical': '"Organic" signifies that nature is (in the one and only order of history) created with a single final end, which is supernatural, that relation to this end (to the God of Jesus Christ) therefore orients nature from the beginning of nature's existence.' 'Paradox', on the other hand, signifies the 'radical distinction between nature and grace' (Schindler 1996: 52). While there is a single supernatural end, namely, Jesus Christ, this end does not turn all nature into grace; for then being itself would already be salvation.

This contemporary debate among moral theologians bears on the role which the church, the sacraments, scripture, and the theological virtues, gifts, and beatitudes should play in the moral life. Are they the deep structure which renders everyday life intelligible? If so, then we should at least expect family resemblances between Christian doctrine and a life well lived inside and outside the faith. Or is there a natural morality, either given in and through the faith or outside of it, upon which moral theology or Christian ethics can proceed?

Moral theology raises questions such as how we should think and act when it comes to all those aspects of an everyday life that is both driven by passions and ordered by virtues. How should we do this given the teachings entrusted to us as

Christians? These are questions that require a theological analysis of economics, sexuality, politics, family, etc. that draws upon virtues, gifts, beatitudes, commandments, and foundational Christian doctrines. Moral theology is not an exact science; it is more a matter of practical wisdom, which is wisdom that can be other. While there are certainly errors in moral theology, answers are not to be had apart from interpretation. Moral theology is the interpretation of human life within the context of God's economy in which he redeems the world in Jesus Christ.

References

Aquinas, St Thomas (1948). *Summa Theologica.* Notre Dame: Ave Maria.

Aristotle (1985). *Nicomachean Ethics.* Indianapolis: The Library of Liberal Arts.

Barth, Karl (1956). *Church Dogmatics* IV/1. Edinburgh: T. & T. Clark.

—— (1958). *Church Dogmatics* IV/2. Edinburgh: T. & T. Clark.

—— (1961). *Church Dogmatics* IV/3.1. Edinburgh: T. & T. Clark.

—— (1962). *Church Dogmatics* IV/3.2. Edinburgh: T. & T. Clark.

—— (1975). *Church Dogmatics* I/1. Edinburgh: T. & T. Clark.

Cessario, Romanus (2001). *Introduction to Moral Theology.* Washington, DC: Catholic University of America Press.

Griffiths, Paul J., and Hütter, Reinhard (2005). *Reason and The Reasons of Faith.* New York: Continuum.

Grisez, Germain (1983). *Christian Moral Principles,* i. *The Way of the Lord Jesus.* Chicago: Franciscan Herald.

Gunton, Colin (ed.) (1997). *The Cambridge Companion to Christian Doctrine.* Cambridge: Cambridge University Press.

Gutiérrez, Gustavo (1988). *A Theology of Liberation.* Maryknoll: Orbis.

Hauerwas, Stanley (1983). *The Peaceable Kingdom: A Primer in Christian Ethics.* Notre Dame: University of Notre Dame Press.

Hauerwas, Stanley, and Pinches, Charles (1997). *Christians among The Virtues.* Notre Dame: University of Notre Dame Press.

—— and Wells, Samuel (2004). *The Blackwell Companion to Christian Ethics.* Oxford: Blackwell.

Himes, Kenneth R., and Himes, Michael J. (1993). *Fullness of Faith: The Public Significance of Theology.* New York: Paulist.

John Paul II (1993). *Veritatis Splendor—The Splendor of Truth.* Boston: Pauline.

Katongole, Immanuel (2000). *Beyond Universal Reason: The Relation between Religion and Ethics in the Work of Stanley Hauerwas.* Notre Dame: University of Notre Dame Press.

Kirk, Kenneth (1931). *The Vision of God: The Christian Doctrine of the Summum Bonum.* London: Longmans, Green and Co.

Knauer, Peter (1979). 'The Hermeneutic Function of the Principle of Double Effect'. In Charles E. Curran and Richard A. McCormick (eds.), *Readings in Moral Theology*, no. 1, New York: Paulist.

Komonchak, Joseph A. (1990). 'Theology and Culture at Mid-Century: The Example of Henri de Lubac'. *Theological Studies* 51: 579–602.

Long, D. Stephen (1993). *Tragedy, Tradition and Transformism: The Ethics of Paul Ramsey.* Boulder: Westview.

—— (2005). *John Wesley's Moral Theology.* Nashville: Kingswood.

McClendon, James (1986). *Ethics: Systematic Theology.* Nashville: Abingdon.

—— (1994). *Doctrine: Systematic Theology.* Nashville: Abingdon.

—— (2000). *Witness: Systematic Theology.* Nashville: Abingdon.

MacInytre, Alasdair (1984). *After Virtue: A Study in Moral Theory.* Notre Dame: University of Notre Dame Press.

Mahoney, John (1987). *The Making of Moral Theology.* Oxford: Clarendon.

Milbank, John (1990). *Theology and Social Theory: Beyond Secular Reason.* Oxford: Basil Blackwell.

—— (2002). *Being Reconciled: Ontology and Pardon.* London: Routledge.

Niebuhr, Reinhold (1943). *The Nature and Destiny of Man*, ii. *Human Destiny.* New York: Charles Scribner's Sons.

O'Connell, Timothy E. (1978). *Principles for a Catholic Morality.* New York: Seabury.

O'Donovan, Oliver (1994). *Resurrection and Moral Order: An Outline for Evangelical Ethics.* Grand Rapids: Eerdmans.

Parsons, Susan Frank (1996). *Feminism and Christian Ethics.* Cambridge: Cambridge University Press.

Pinckaers, Servais (1995). *The Sources of Christian Ethics.* Washington, DC: Catholic University of America Press.

Porter, Jean (1990). *The Recovery of Virtue: The Relevance of Aquinas for Christian Ethics.* Louisville: Westminster/John Knox.

Rauschenbusch, Walter (1978 [1917]). *A Theology for the Social Gospel.* Nashville: Abingdon.

Rhonheimer, Martin (2000). *Natural Law and Practical Reason: A Thomist View of Moral Autonomy.* New York: Fordham University Press.

Schindler, David (1996). *Heart of the World, Center of the Church.* Grand Rapids: Eerdmans.

Warner, Michael (1995). *Changing Witness: Catholic Bishops and Public Policy, 1917–1994.* Grand Rapids: Eerdmans.

Webster, John (1998). *Barth's Moral Theology: Human Action in Barth's Thought.* Grand Rapids: Eerdmans.

Werpehowski, William (2002). *American Protestant Ethics and the Legacy of H. Richard Niebuhr.* Washington, DC: Georgetown University Press.

Wesley, John (1984). 'Upon the Lord's Sermon on the Mount, Discourse the First'. In id., *The Works of John Wesley*, i, Nashville: Abingdon.

Wilkins, John (1994). *Considering Veritatis Splendor.* Cleveland: Pilgrim.

Wogaman, J. Philip (1989). *Christian Moral Judgement.* Louisville: Westminster/John Knox.

Yoder, John (2002). *Preface to Theology: Christology and Theological Method.* Grand Rapids: Brazos.

Suggested Reading

Cessario (2001).

Gallagher, Joseph (1990). *Time Past, Time Future: An Historical Study of Catholic Moral Theology.* New York: Paulist.

Grisez (1983).

Häring, Bernard (1963). *The Law of Christ: Moral Theology for Priests and Laity,* i. *General Moral Theology.* Cork: Mercier.

Hauerwas and Wells (2002).

Kirk (1931).

Mahoney (1987).

May, William E. (2003). *An Introduction to Moral Theology.* Huntington: Our Sunday Visitor.

Melina, Livio (2001). *Sharing in Christ's Virtues: For a Renewal of Moral Theology in Light of Veritatis Splendor.* Washington, DC: Catholic University of America Press.

O'Donovan (1994).

Parsons (1996).

CHAPTER 26

HISTORY

REBECCA LYMAN

'Words are superfluous, when the works are more manifest and plain than words', declared Eusebius of Caesarea at the opening of his ambitious apologetic survey of ancient culture, *Praeparatio Evangelica* (1. 3, in Eusebius 1982). This provocative claim rested on confidence in the concrete events and texts which historians display, and thus the superiority of historical proof to mere myth or opinion. As inheritors of the Jewish biblical world view, Christians over the centuries have preserved and interpreted human history as evidence of the relationship between God and God's people. The living presence of the past as an authoritative guide for the present and future has also been a characteristic part of Christian practice from earliest apocalyptic expectations to the cult of the saints to the Reformed insistence on biblical norms in worship to liberation theology. History as an interpretation of the past has therefore been both a conceptual tool for telling the story of God and God's people, and also a spiritual practice woven into the very language and structures of devotion and institution. In these ways history has played a double role of ensuring the veracity and continuity of salvation history and, equally important, shaping theological reflection on creation, incarnation, and resurrection in light of human events and devotional patterns.

If history is then another 'book' of revelation, its exegesis can be as contested as that of scripture. Eusebius' confidence in works over words rested in part on his editorial abilities to select the events and texts he wished to include in his account. History like memory is a reconstruction of past events with attendant problems of selectivity, coherence, and verification. Over the centuries, historical methodologies in the West have shifted often in close proximity to Christian religious concerns and practices. For example, the Enlightenment affirmation of secular progress was indebted to Christian conviction that history has a *telos*. In eastern Christianity, the affirmation of the eternal and the unchanging presence of the divine in reality created another view of the past which contrasts to the western focus on change and development. Many contemporary Asian and African churches are making theological sense of ancestors or inherited practices in ways which both preserve their past and also challenge western Christian doctrine. Theologically, history is best understood within the practices of particular communities and cultures and as an intellectual discipline. In each case we see that history is a story told about the past for the sake of present meaning and the identity of a community, but it is also a cultural practice of memory, inquiry, and authority.

At present in western intellectual culture, questions of historical method have gained in complexity, often as an echo of shifts in hermeneutics and literary method, but also in response to increasing global communication, cultural exchange, and social reform. The questions of current historiography with regard to definitions of narrative, textual interpretation, and culture, though highly creative and provocative, are hardly settled among historians. Since these questions are both the extension and critique of modern historical criticism which has had a profound impact on theology in the West, they are particularly critical contemporary theological questions and methodologies. This essay will provide a brief chronological introduction to western and Christian historiography, and then examine contemporary historiographical problems and theological responses.

I. Issues and Ideas in Western and Christian Historiography

Biblical Judaism structured its identity through a story which began with the creation and proceeded in the events of fall, bondage, deliverance, and restoration. This narrative focused on the divine and human relationship revealed and shaped within historical existence. Based on the covenant between God and God's people, such a view was never static, as expressed in the daily duty to keep the law which embraced all of life or the regular retelling of the story of Abraham and the exodus as a source of present identity and future hope. In the face of political crisis or destruction, the prophets renewed and shifted spiritual expectations. After the destruction of the temple during the wars with Rome, the diaspora of the Jewish people reinforced this religious and material sense of contingency and dynamism in Jewish life. Rabbinic thought itself may be seen as 'diasporic' in its provisional and continuing dialogue like the experience of history itself (Boyarin 1994: 259).

Although Jewish concepts of history are often contrasted to those of Greece and Rome, both traditions had aspects of cyclical and linear time; they were distinguished by a chronology which began with creation, by the distinction between mythical and historical time in Graeco-Roman tradition and the religious nature of remembering the past in Judaism, and by the acceptance of prophetic interpretations of the past (Momigliano 1977: 195). In Graeco-Roman thought the actions of humans in struggle with fate shaped narratives of the past. Antiquity was treasured and preserved as a time of origins, yet time also had a tragic dimension in revealing human mistakes and final mortality. Historiographically, Herodotus and Thucydides placed 'inquiry' at the centre of historical work as a repudiation of myth and a concern for sources and historical time. The Hellenistic period saw the rise of the writing of universal history which reflected the unity and exchange of diverse cultures through the expansion of the empires of Alexander the Great and, later, the Romans. This imperial perspective stimulated the growth of universalistic philosophies as well. Roman historians focused on recent events of history, writing explicitly in the service of the empire and for the moral formation of its citizens (Momigliano 1992).

As Jews who embraced a radically eschatological *telos* in which history and covenant were consummated by the divine presence and agency of Jesus, the earliest Christian authors included both apologists for the continuity of salvation history, such as Luke, or preachers of the collapse of the past and expectation of the future, such as Paul. In ancient Christian literature we find the prophetic teaching of Jesus concerning the reign of God translated in varied ways through the events of crucifixion and resurrection into communities of eschatological expectation. Christian practices such as prayer for the coming kingdom or celibacy were expressions of the expected end of history. Persecution periodically heightened the sense of the apocalyptic as reflected in the acts of the martyrs. In the second century theological arguments concerning the nature of continuity in salvation history and the spiritual interpretation of material life created divisions with so-called 'gnostics' and 'Montanists'. Eschatological energy also poured into the intellectual work of the Apologists, in which providence was seen as completed in the incarnation and resurrection of Jesus so that all of intellectual and cultural history was at a climax, thus echoing the universal histories of the Hellenistic period. Ancient Christians therefore affirmed, sometimes in conflict, both the continuity of salvation history and the radical newness of eschatological expectation.

The eventual differences between the concept and practice of history in eastern and western Christianity may be illustrated by contrasting Eusebius of Caesarea and Augustine of Hippo. Writing at a critical time of transition from persecution to imperial conversion, Eusebius seemingly witnessed the fruition of apologetic universal history in the legalization of Christianity within Roman society. Christian belief to him was therefore the culmination and correction of the many streams of Mediterranean culture which preceded it. The transformation of Hellenism into Christianity focused on the centrality and finality of the incarnation, which revealed the true structures of reality and the purpose of history. Practically speaking, material existence and the past were therefore converted into a sort of cultural 'realized eschatology'. The chronicles of sacred history which had emphasized both distinction and synchronisms with Graeco-Roman history were slowly translated into existing sacred places and calendars. This created a new religious topography in the Mediterranean which was a spatial projection of sacred history; a different history made a new physical reality and topography (Markus 1990: 142). Eastern liturgical practices therefore represented time and history as a permeable barrier to the divine, accessible through spiritual practices and material objects such as pilgrimage and icons.

Augustine, a century after Eusebius, seemed to be witnessing the disaster of the fall of Rome under Christian rule. In contrast to the apologetic fulfilment of Eusebius, Augustine in *The City of God* outlined a story of historical pilgrimage in which the ways of God remained largely hidden and unidentified with concrete human institutions. Time was not a transparency to be erased by practices, but rather a testing process for moral development in which struggles were expected until the final restoration of perfection and completion in the reign of God. The often chaotic and profound political transformations of the West would certainly support this view of history. Gregory of Tours wrote a history of the Franks to show their place in the divine plan as a newly converted people; divine retribution and the active power of miracles were reassuring markers of divine presence and continuity in a chaotic world (Van Dam 1993).

The appearance of a historical horizon in the early modern period had profound consequences for the study of history as well as for Christian life and thought. Lorenzo Valla's famous proof of the forgery of the Donation of Constantine showed the falsity of an official church document as well as the power of scholarship to test the intellectual and, in this case, economic validity of tradition. Textual criticism with its aims of restoration and authenticity became part of the engine of religious reform in the Reformation. The *Magdeburg Centuries* and *Ecclesiastical Annals* ushered in duelling church histories which revealed not only sectarian spirit, but also early critical scholarship which emphasized the difference of the past. History could be used either to show illegitimate corruption of primitive practice which justified or demanded new current practices or else to show how changes were continuous under the guidance of the Holy Spirit. Popular history such as Foxe's *Acts and Monuments of These Latter and Perilous Days* described the spiritual continuity between ancient martyrs and present Protestant sufferers (Breisach 1983: 166–9). Critical historical practice then could erase or invalidate certain parts of the past and seemingly establish or restore others to a different ecclesiastical future. As a modern sensibility this sense of disdain or defence of tradition could and did result in both amnesia and nostalgia as part of the reaction to the distance of the past (Lowenthal 1985).

Not surprisingly, Christian historiography fractured with the West, reflecting the diversity of stories of denominations and rising nationalism. The history of the church became in fact many histories of many churches. While theories of divine providence had of course reflected the ideas of specific theologians, now such theories echoed particular theological schools such as those associated with Luther or Calvin (Hodgson 1989: 19–20). This diversity of church histories was echoed and supported by the rise of national histories. In Germany, ecclesiastical history was separated from secular history. Inevitably, the razor of historical criticism together with the religious wars and polemics between Christians issued in a critique of salvation history itself. Christian providence was translated into a secular progress whose own development needed the destruction of religion as irrational and an impediment to freedom and enlightenment (Breisach 1983: 194). Equally important, the philosophical developments of the Enlightenment promoted 'reasonable religion', while at the same time increasingly widening the gulf between reason and revelation. As famously expressed by Gotthold Lessing, 'The accidental truths of history can never become the proof of the necessary truths of reason' (Welch 1972–85: i. 50). Theologically, Schleiermacher demythologized supernatural versions of salvation history to describe a God of absolute causality and to trace descriptions of human consciousness within the piety of the church.

In the nineteenth century the professional study of history was increasingly wedded to empirical methods of science, most notably in Germany. With cautious optimism, historians such as von Ranke believed that an objective history could be written on the basis of a disciplined positivism. This allowed a *Geschichte*, a grand narrative of the development of one idea, often of a significant institution which shaped the rest of society. In thinkers such as Hegel and Marx this evolving narrative was synonymous with western progress and institutions; non-western peoples therefore had no history (Iggers 1997: 142–3). Within the study of history these trends increased claims of a scientific discipline based on disinterested evaluation of evidence and therefore an objective method. This definition strengthened the intellectual authority of historical criticism as a form of rational inquiry distinct from bias or ideology, and formed the basis for professional identity and practice well into the twentieth century (Novick 1988).

In Christian circles revelation and doctrine began to meet the force of biblical and historical criticism. Could Christianity be both a historical and an eternal religion? Early in the nineteenth century Ferdinand Christian Baur promoted the development of doctrine as a historical process, and used textual criticism to evaluate the motives and perspective of theological texts. He set out to establish a historical basis for belief. History was the self-mediation of the divine life which allows a penetration into the course of reality. Therefore theology had a history, and universal history was the proper place of theological inquiry (Welch 1972–85: i. 159–60). Following the work of Albrecht Ritschl, Adolf von Harnack also had more confidence in the use of history rather than metaphysics to discover and establish the continuing essence of Christianity. Grounded in his reconstruction of a messianic Jesus, he could then separate later cultural additions to outline an authentic development of dogma. The historian was to 'intervene in the course of history' in order to purify and renew (Welch 1972–85: ii. 177). The breadth and depth of his scholarship in uncovering the complexity of the past led to not 'a predictability of progress, but an opportunity and necessity for decision' (Welch 1972–85: ii. 181). At the beginning of the twentieth century, Ernst Troeltsch explored the problem of historical consciousness in several important sociological and historical works. Historical method became the foundation of his theological studies, and for him there was no longer any supernatural certainty based on the contingency and variation of history. Neither dogma nor evolutionary history nor a permanent essence could suffice, but rather the creative act of the interpreter within historical context and thus giving different answers at different times. Faith ultimately decided validity (Welch 1972–85: ii. 300–1). The division between faith and history initiated by Lessing seemed complete.

In contrast to the liberal Protestant confidence in historical criticism, others in the nineteenth century sought to preserve authority and tradition in ecclesiastical continuity. John Henry Newman's famous *Essay on the Development of Doctrine* argued against what he perceived as the rationalism and relativism of the liberals. Rather than search for an unchanging essence, Newman argued for notes which would chart authentic developments as organic growth of a recognizable organism. The idea of Christianity did not develop, but articulations of doctrine did (Tilley 2004: 86). The condemnations of modernism by the Roman Catholic Church and the rise of biblical fundamentalism in the United States were repudiations of the authority of historical or biblical criticism with regard to tradition or scripture.

The twentieth century saw varied theological responses to the challenge of historical criticism, especially in light of the violence and conflict of the world wars. 'Neo-orthodox' thinkers such as Karl Barth, Richard Niebuhr, and Reinhold Niebuhr affirmed the transcendence of God and the centrality of revelation, sharing a pessimism and reserve about human experience or capability and especially about secular ideas of progress. For Barth the history of theology was a theological task in which the theologian engaged past authors as living Christians in asking critical and systematic questions. Those who could achieve disengagement were 'theological Philistines'; history therefore was never 'past', 'completed', or distant in the church, for all were part of the spiritual community: 'They are in search of the answer to a question that concerns us, too' (Barth 1972: 18–27). The reception or rejection of past ideas both exposed the quality of the character of the theologian as a fellow Christian as well as tested the structure of his own theology. Historical criticism was therefore essential to Barth's systematic-theological task, but only as a step to encountering divine revelation. For Reinhold Niebuhr the events of history reflected only the irony of human effort and the persistence of evil; God's action and plan were not easily discernable and separate from any institution. Henri de Lubac, Jean Danielou, Yves Congar, and Hans Urs von Balthasar also emphasized a creative recovery of the past which avoided both detachment and repristination. Called *ressourcement* theology, this movement examined the connection of spirituality and theology, especially in liturgy, exegesis, and symbol rather than the philosophical systems of neo-scholasticism. Their goal was ecclesiastical revitalization through historical scholarship at the service of faith (Congar 1950).

For many theologians in the twentieth century, confessional history became the essential resource to preserve Christian identity in a secular world and to reject the dominance of a scientific reductionism with regard to religious topics. If history is a story which conveys identity, then church history is properly the story of the church and is evaluated and narrated primarily according to its principles with some attention to critical method (Williams 2005). Theologians drew on historical study in order to explicate and examine the development and significance of Christian belief. Thomas Torrance argued that one could find the framework and logic of Christian belief by studying the classic figures of Christian history; salvation history could offer glimpses of God's nature (Torrance 1984). Wolfhart Pannenberg also looked to history as the source of indirect revelation of God; the theologian must seek the true significance of Jesus as Christ in history, but this examination is illuminated by looking back from later events (Pannenberg 1991–8: vol. i). Jürgen Moltmann reconnected the modern ideal of progress to Christian eschatology in order to formulate a radical theology of hope as part of salvation history (Moltmann 1993). Indeed, the retrieval of past practices and traditions for Christians who had rejected or lost them could be a necessary corrective to the narrowness of modern denominational practice (Williams 1999; Webber 1999). Eastern Orthodox theologians also emphasized the recovery of their spiritual legacy, rescuing the fathers from the historical field of 'late antiquity' (Behr 2001: x).

Others would see the role of critical historical method as essential to theological understanding for purposes of both veracity and continuity in broader dialogue with contemporary culture. Even if the practice of history cannot finally adjudicate doctrinal claims, the reconstruction of the meaning of the past may alter present understandings of theological principles. Maurice Wiles described 'doctrinal criticism' as parallel to 'biblical criticism' as a means of examining theological history critically as a genuinely open rather than an orthodox narrative; changed understandings of the origins or formations of doctrines may affect the reasonableness or form of belief in such doctrines in the present (Wiles 1967). David Tracy offered a correlational approach to understanding the continuity of doctrine in the midst of historical change and multiple interpretations; the continuing power of a 'classic' practice, text, or person sustains the identity of the tradition (Tracy 1981: 231). George Lindbeck described a set of rules which underlay developing theologies and practices (Lindbeck 1984: 94). Brian Gerrish claimed that all theology was in fact historical theology, since especially Protestant theology is inextricably woven into the web of particular and changing historical conditions: 'Precisely because the model is experiential, it is also inescapably revisionary: faith, unlike dogmas, is a matter of adaptation and change' (Gerrish 1992: 302). Clearly, historical contexts shape belief, but the degree of influence seems to lie in the varied models of theological method. The arguments of Gadamer and Habermas concerning hermeneutics reflect a similar tension that absolute scepticism regarding tradition is as implausible as uncritical obeisance (Hamilton 1996: 98).

In western twentieth-century church history the reliance on a common historical method together with the rise of the ecumenical movement created new comprehensive histories such as Jaroslav Pelikan's *The Christian Tradition* (1971–89), which intentionally surpassed contesting confessional accounts, and drew on the fruit of historical labour. The discipline of detachment and contextual understanding also allowed branches of Christendom to understand some of their differences as distinct developments within communities rather than necessarily opposing doctrines. Additionally, the application of Christian insight and faith could also bring new help to the 'historiographical crisis' of the nineteenth century not by denying their own values and perspectives, but by combining the practices of critical history with the Christian search for understanding, faith, and hope (McIntire and Wells 1984).

However, developments within historiography in the latter half of the twentieth century have shifted the ground upon which western theology and history have commonly worked since the nineteenth century. Many of the modern assumptions concerning epistemology and language have been subjected to critical revision. The growth of social history has challenged the claims of 'objective' history as well as the Enlightenment assumption of progress. The development of 'cultural history', with its adaptation of literary theory, has equally threatened the usual tools of inquiry by questioning the criteria and veracity of facts and narrative. The discipline of history remains fragmented by methodological conflicts, presenting new opportunities and challenges for theology.

II. Whose Story? Social History

In the twentieth century, historians continued the work of Karl Marx and Max Weber in using new concepts in sociology to broaden their work from a history of literary sources or elites to a more inclusive and comprehensive understanding of the past. The growth of the sophistication of these tools and methodologies together with contemporary political reform movements gave rise to histories focused on class, race, or gender as well as everyday experience. The retrieval of long-ignored histories and perspectives challenged and reshaped more conventional historical narratives, especially the claim of objectivity in analysis, and has led to increasingly complex theoretical questions. Political commitments were often woven into the evolving methodologies which prompted critical examination of older 'objective' histories.

The recent development of post-colonial theory, which combines insights from literary and cultural theory, is a further step in broadening our understanding of the complexities of culture and especially power in the writing of history.

An influential series of works in modern social history came from the *Annales* school in France. Historians such as Marc Bloch, Fernand Braudel, and Emmanuel Le Roy Ladurie set out to do justice to the chronological plurality and cultural streams within one civilization or place. In this way they rejected the linear and progressive history of earlier historical sociology represented by Karl Marx and Max Weber in order to explore the regional and the individual. Geography, economics, and psychology as well as language and culture gave these historians important access to material culture and everyday life. Unlike many social historians in the United States or Germany, their reliance on art, folklore, and customs encouraged a more subtle and broad construction of the operation of culture (Iggers 1997: 56–7).

For many historians in the 1970s, 'popular history' became more appealing than the usual focus on notable individuals or institutions. The work of Keith Thomas, *Religion and the Decline of Magic: Studies in Popular Beliefs in Sixteenth and Seventeenth Century Europe* (1971) is an important example. In Italy historians such as Carlo Ginzburg looked to restore a human face and individual experience to history by writing *microstoria* such as *The Cheese and the Worms: The Cosmos of a Sixteenth-Century Miller* (1980) and therefore avoid what they considered to be the failed macrohistory of Marxism or the impersonal forces of the *Annales* school. However, they retained a conviction of the inequality in society, the importance of economics, and the need for rigorous method and empirical analysis (Iggers 1997: 108).

The use of these methods of social analysis as well as contemporary political changes also encouraged histories of women as a form of recovery of repressed voices and experiences. In several decades this field moved from a more conventional recovery of lost history to highly sophisticated problems of retrieval and textual analysis as well as new definitions of gender itself. Especially when historians are working with mainly literary sources, tools which focus on the 'representation' of women to produce ideological effects can be more useful in retrieval than conventional historical analysis (Clark 2004: 173–81). The combination of social analysis with cultural and linguistic methods has created new understanding of both the social functions and constructions of gender as well as restoring the history of women as historical agents.

The integration of such studies into the inherited narrative has happened slowly and inevitably has a political edge in both secular and Christian histories. Not only may centres of interest shift, but older historical narratives and theologies may be discredited. Justo González described the recovery of the breadth of the past and the global present as means of restoring an understanding of Christianity as universal, diverse, and marginalized rather than at the centre of social power (González 2002). Liberation theology and history tell a different story of God and community than many conventional western narratives or traditions. The

African-American rejection of a white gospel of divinely sanctioned slavery led to an emphasis on spiritual and political liberation; the recovery of this involves the repudiation of other moments of Christian history and theodicy (Hopkins and Cummings 1991; Bascio 1994). In a similar way the telling of Asian history focuses on different cultural forms and emphasizes the meaning of suffering in history (Phan 2003: 109). African church history and theology may desire to incorporate the spiritual practices of ancestors as a parallel to the western cult of the saints (Hood 1990). Feminist historiography and theology has challenged institutional and theological norms which some have seen as essential to Christian identity (Chopp and Davaney 1997; Wiesner-Hanks 2002). The development of both categories of gender and women's history creates new narratives of western theology (Shaw 2004) or theological conflict (Burrus 2000). The current writing of the popular history of Christianity therefore reveals a diversity of methodologies in order to locate and explain previously unexplored territory (Burrus 2005).

Most recently, post-colonial theory has combined literary theory and social science methodology to examine structures of power and culture particularly in the contemporary global context. Edward Said's *Orientalism* (1978) was an early attempt to examine the pervasive and subtle operation of political and economic power as well as the discursive influence of the western division of the world into Occident and Orient: 'It is rather a *distribution* of geopolitical awareness into aesthetic, scholarly, economic, sociological, historical, and philological texts;... it not only creates but also maintains; it *is*, rather than expresses, a certain *will* or *intention* to understand, in some cases to control, manipulate, even to incorporate, what is a manifestly different... world' (Said 1978: 12). Indebted to Foucault and Derrida, these authors intended to investigate the shape of history and culture as locations for political, economic, and ideological European colonization. Particular histories and cultural contexts as well as theoretical forms are therefore critical to these authors and to some degree resistant to the construction of trans-historical categories of the 'colonial' or the 'patriarchal'. In the rejection of forms of modern definition such as essentialism or progress, categories such as ambivalence, border, hybridity, and mimicry are investigated in order to show the complexity of social and cultural relationships. According to Homi Bhabha, the simultaneous resistance and complicity in the relation of power reveal important and creative negotiations; hybridity rather than diversity offers a way of recovering and understanding contemporary culture (Bhabha 1994: 34–8). The focus on the non-elite called (following Gramsci) the 'subaltern' has provoked more theoretical reflection on how models of dominant discourse, both theoretical and political, can constrain a recovery of marginal voices (Spivak 1999: 272–3).

These conceptual models bring breadth and depth to the study of Christian theology and history by restoring and including omitted or new insights into Christian reflection and experience. Although these recent accounts challenge the often narrow basis of confessional histories, they are in themselves a form of particularized storytelling. The focus on the dynamic of power and difference may also allow a more subtle understanding of the interweaving of Christianity and culture in social ideas and practices (Grau 2004; Kwok 2005; Lyman 2003).

III. What Story? The Problem of Narrative and the Cultural Turn

Growing from linguistic and philosophical study, another feature of contemporary historiography, especially in the United States, has been the 'cultural turn', in which post-structural and postmodern theory has been applied to the writing of history. If the production of history is literary, i.e., a narrative involving texts and imagination, then critical theories of language are essential to the practice of history. Through engagement with structuralism, semiotics, and post-structuralism, some historians began to treat texts as closed systems with no necessary reference to an outside reality; they contained an abundance of meaning, but this was not necessarily linked to the author's intention. In postmodern philosophy the modern ideals of rationality and progress, with their underlying assumption of continuities, were rejected as inadequate or as masking a dominant and repressive ideology. The combination and development of these methodological trends produced the 'cultural turn', which some believed signalled 'the end of history'.

Structural linguistics, semiotics, and post-structuralism rested in part on the ideas of Ferdinand de Saussure from the turn of the twentieth century and were developed over the course of the century, especially by Jacques Derrida. Language in these models is key to understanding the social construction of reality, since all understanding or description is mediated by language. Documents therefore cannot transparently reflect the world outside themselves; they can only reflect a system of discourse. If words are arbitrary 'signs' capable of multiple meanings, semiotics focused on the performative nature of language in the production of meaning. The relations of the signs to one another constituted codes of meaning apart from the intention of the author. As pointed out by Gabrielle Speigel, 'by denying the importance of a historically situated authorial consciousness, a dehistorization of the literary text [occurred] that was tantamount to the denial of history' (Speigel 1997: 6). By decoding and 'deconstructing' the codes, one was able to discover a surplus of meaning, especially in the silences of the text. History then becomes 'not a presence, but an effect of presence created by textuality' (Speigel 1997: 8).

For historians, two works were particularly important in translating these theories into historical practice. In 1973, Hayden White's *Metahistory: The Historical Imagination in Nineteenth-Century Europe* argued that historical narratives were fictions constructed via individual rules of language without any reference to an 'objective reality'. They were poetic acts in which the structures of language shaped modes of explanation. Verification of outside data therefore lay outside the possibilities of historical practice. Clifford Geertz's *The Interpretation of Cultures: Selected Essays* (1973) described the study of culture from an anthropological view as 'semiotic': the interpretation of rituals, artefacts, and belief systems were all 'texts' to be examined for semiotic structure. The linguistic model had therefore been extended to social material. Anthropological models soon were increasingly used by social historians to understand the structures of pre-modern societies (Iggers 1997: 118–23).

Michel Foucault's *Discipline and Punish* (1977) and *Madness and Civilization* (1973) were also essential in the turn of many historians to cultural analysis. Some of the reason for this included a dissatisfaction with the universal categories of the social-science models, the post-structuralist insistence that such categories were dependent on a specific culture, and the insistence on a range of explanatory paradigms as well as attention to issues of power (Bonnell and Hunt 1999: 8–10). Looking back in part to Friedrich Nietzsche's *The Use and Abuse of History*, theorists were conscious of the social power implicit in 'neutral' languages of analysis and description, and therefore of the need for the hermeneutic of suspicion. For Foucault this called for a new history of ideas which acknowledged the limits of language. His investigation of power in discourse and society could be done by 'archaeology', that is, by digging below the surface of a discourse and not looking for the causes or contexts, but rather for the rules of the discourse itself. These rules were not fixed, but were called 'episteme', the discursive practices underlying relations or systems. The purpose was to challenge the modern narrative of progress and clarity by exposing the structures of power: 'I know how irritating it is to treat discourses in terms not of the gentle, silent intimate consciousness that is expressed in them, but of an obscure set of anonymous rules..., how unpleasant it is to reveal the limitations and necessities of a practice where one is used to seeing, in all its pure transparency, the expression of genius and freedom' (Foucault 1972: 210). The purpose was to undo traditional modernist history which affirmed privilege, progress, power, and history as 'living and continuous,... a place of rest, certainty, reconciliation, a place of tranquilized sleep' (Foucault 1972: 14). By focusing on discontinuities or oppositions, such as reason and madness or crime and prisons, Foucault explored how social categories become 'natural' and therefore objects of study as objective realities.

Drawing on such theorists, some historians have therefore argued that no master narrative can properly exist, since any attempt to create one out of the contingent events of human experience is only an arbitrary choice of a particular ideology. Conflict of interest is therefore a better rule in interpretation of past events, and the dismemberment of narrative is in fact a necessary means of historical reconstruction. One can recover significant changes or events which may have been obscured by a narrative by emphasizing discontinuities.

The 'new historicism' represents an attempt to practise these textual conceptions concerning representation and reality with attention to historical problems. Stephen

Greenblatt described 'cultural poetics' in which social or political practices are analysed by the same procedures as texts: political, institutional, and social practices are read as 'cultural scripts' (Speigel 1997: 16). In such a view, historical events are 'artefacts' to be 'salvaged' rather than pieces in a puzzle. The breaks are more important than continuity (Hamilton 1996: 205–6). Defined more by practices and eclecticism than one particular theory, 'new historicism' is revisionist and deconstructive, opening up possibilities in the study of particular cultures and attentive to 'resistance as much as replication, friction as well as assimilation, subversion as well as orthodoxy. . . . Accordingly, we mine what are called sometimes counterhistories that make apparent the slippages, cracks, fault lines, and surprising absences in the monumental structures that dominated a more traditional historicism' (Gallagher and Greenblatt 2000: 16–17). What may seem to be a loss and undue confinement to a text in understanding the past can also be seen as an invitation to an 'infinite universe' (Martin and Cox Miller 2005: 18).

Critics of these positions note that these revisions of modernity seem in fact to be an extension of certain aspects of the older historical criticism, such as the hermeneutic of suspicion, but without attendant self-criticism. As Wayne Meeks commented in defence of a 'corrigible' history, the self-critical gaze on all methodologies must be professionally constant. 'It may be not that we have doubted too much, but that we have doubted too little' (Meeks 2002: 259). More tartly, Ernst Breisach observed that we have given up progress as artificial only to arrive at a petrified present in which we observe ceaseless and rather pointless change and exchange of revealed diversities (Breisach 2003: 195). Clearly, much of the force of the development of these epistemologies has been dissatisfaction with modern certainties and therefore criticism as much as construction. Spiegel notes that 'alterity' can be a watchword of the new understanding of the loss and grief of the positivist old historicism, and the sense of the otherness of the past now studied (Spiegel 1997: 80). Many historians would argue that the present practice of history as interdisciplinary and collegial has its own set of checks and balances to discourage overconfidence; the eclectic practice of history has always been an uneven collection of theories and methods with the myth of objectivity long modified. Theory at its best can suggest new questions or answers for historians to ask of their periods (Burke 1992: 165). Spiegel offers a middle way of theory and construction of a historical reality as a practice, even if the old certainties of objectivity are past. By focusing on the historical and social context of the creation of the text, one can insist on history itself as an active constituent of the elements of the text (Spiegel 1997: 26–7). D. Brakke has suggested that one of the virtues of cultural studies is the less abstract and more detailed analysis of specific stories and symbols; this may rejuvenate a study of Christianity 'as a diachronic culture in which these elements both persisted and are contested' (Brakke 2002: 490). Most historians believe past reality exists outside a text or interpretation, however changeable or incomplete it remains in retrieval. 'This assertion has not denied the value of those ways of thinking about the world. . . . But neither would or could history concede its place to them' (Breisach 2003: 207). If rumours of the death of history have been greatly exaggerated, the need for dialogue and exchange across theoretical lines remains critical for the health and unity of the field.

The initial theological responses to the use of postmodernity for Christian history inevitably reveal differences in theological traditions and methodologies. In the current study of ancient Christianity David Brakke outlined 'post-liberal nostalgia', 'post-orthodox subversion', and 'early Christian discourse studies' (Brakke 2002: 482). Robert Wilken has defended the importance of 'engaged scholarship' in the history of Christianity (Wilken 1995). In the 'radical orthodoxy' movement, the criticism of the dominance of secular positivism and progress may create space for the particularity of the Christian story itself as authoritative (Milbank, Pickstock, and Ward 1999). On the other hand, postmodernity encourages a breadth of Christian perspective and commitment which challenges either a nostalgia for the pre-modern or a narrow reframing of unity or orthodoxy (Ruether and Grau 2006). Alain Le Boulluec used Foucault to illuminate the literary construction of heresiology in the first three centuries (Le Boulluec 1985). By defining religion as a necessary and coherent part of culture, cultural criticism allows historians to examine past practices often ignored or spurned with fresh insight as well as inviting theology into public discourse as a legitimate discourse (Brown, Davaney, and Tanner 2001: 14). Kathryn Tanner has used the dynamism of cultural studies to put forward an understanding of a continuity of Christian practices focused on God, not tradition: 'God's own control of Christian history is not identifiable with some historical aspect of what Christians say or do that is nevertheless exempt from history's vicissitudes. . . . Christian history itself would replace God's own directives to human beings' (Tanner 1997: 136). Sheila Davaney has argued for a combination of pragmatic philosophy and imaginative historicism as a means of both grounding and expanding contemporary Christian thought (Davaney 2000). More recently, Terence Tilley has argued for attention to the actual practices of history and theology as a means of focusing on judgements which necessarily shape our interpretation of inherited faith and doctrine (Tilley 2004).

IV. The Practice of History

Among professional historians the struggles between theory and practice are necessary in the performance of a task which necessarily remains elusive and always mediated by present interests. The current range of methodologies allows possibilities of new insights into historical questions beyond the nineteenth-century polarities of scientific proof or narrative myth-making by proposing new relations between material and literary sources. Historians may divide among those practising rhetorical or theoretical performance as a means of mediating a past and those interested in more broadly assembled narratives, but such diversity of perspective and method can potentially enrich our interpretation and understanding of the past.

As both eschatological and traditional, historical Christianity has engaged in nostalgia, antiquarianism, amnesia, and ceaseless revision. To borrow a post-colonial term, such a hybrid can be seen positively as leading to openness and renewal as well as continuity. Equally important, since contemporary Christianity has a diversity of expressions in its global manifestations, not surprisingly various methods or insights will have to be used for narratives of identity. Post-colonial and cultural studies of history offer varied ways to think about such diversity in light of theological narratives and faith commitments. The sophistication of social history also allows the integration of insights and social practices of ordinary people into theology which have been often neglected or ignored in past narratives (Taves 1999). History as a conceptual problem and a practice shares with theology the provisional nature of its task, and therefore can be put into an important dialogue. Histories, like experiences, bring in the particular human condition which is a legitimate and necessary part of theological reflection as part of the material and personal relationship to God. The successful story in the end is founded on both persuasion and illumination, and historical practices have for centuries attempted to include both. Humility and dialogue can be shared professional virtues for historians and theologians.

References

Ashcroft, B., Griffiths, G., and Tiffin, H. (2000). *Post-Colonial Studies: The Key Concepts.* London: Routledge.

Barth, K. (1972). *Protestant Theology in the Nineteenth Century: Its Background and History.* London: SCM.

Bascio, P. (1994). *The Failure of White Theology: A Black Theological Perspective.* New York: Peter Lang.

Behr, J. (2001). *The Way to Nicaea.* Crestwood: St Vladimir's.

Bhabha, H. (1994). *The Location of Culture.* London: Routledge.

Bonnell, V., and Hunt, L. (eds.) (1999). *Beyond the Cultural Turn: New Directions in the Study of Society and Culture.* Berkeley and Los Angeles: University of California Press.

Boyarin, D. (1994). *A Radical Jew: Paul and the Politics of Identity.* Berkeley and Los Angeles: University of California Press.

Brakke, D. (2002). 'The Early Church in North America: Late Antiquity, Theory, and the History of Christianity'. *Church History* 71/3: 473–91.

Breisach, E. (1983). *Historiography: Ancient, Medieval and Modern.* Chicago: University of Chicago Press.

—— (2003). *On the Future of History: The Postmodern Challenge and its Aftermath.* Chicago: University of Chicago Press.

Brown, D., Davaney, S., and Tanner, K. (2001). *Converging on Culture: Theologians in Dialogue with Cultural Analysis and Criticism.* Oxford: Oxford University Press.

Burke, P. (1992). *History and Social Theory.* Ithaca: Cornell University Press.

Burrus, V. (2000). *'Begotten Not Made': Conceiving Manhood in Late Antiquity.* Stanford: Stanford University Press.

Burrus, V. (ed.) (2005). *Ancient Christianity: A People's History of Christianity,* ii. *Late Ancient Christianity.* Minneapolis: Augsburg Fortress.

Cairns, E. E. (1979). *God and Man in Time: A Christian Approach to Historiography.* Grand Rapids: Baker.

Chopp, R., and Davaney, S. G. (1997). *Horizons in Feminist Theology: Identity, Tradition, and Norms.* Minneapolis: Fortress.

Clark, E. (2004). *History, Theory, Text: Historians and the Linguistic Turn.* Cambridge: Harvard University Press.

Coakley, S., and Pailin, D. (eds.) (1993). *The Making and Remaking of Christian Doctrine.* Oxford: Clarendon.

Congar, Y (1950). *Vraie et fausse refórme dans l'Église.* Paris: Éditions du Cerf.

Davaney, S. G. (2000). *Pragmatic Historicism: A Theology for the Twenty-First Century.* Albany: State University of New York Press.

Eusebius (1982). *Preparation for the Gospel.* Grand Rapids: Baker.

Foucault, M. (1972). *The Archaeology of Knowledge and the Discourse on Language.* New York: Pantheon.

—— (1973). *Madness and Civilization. A History of Insanity in the Age of Reason.* New York: Vintage.

—— (1977). *Discipline and Punish: The Birth of the Prison.* New York: Pantheon.

Gallagher, C., and Greenblatt, S. (2000). *Practicing New Historicism.* Chicago: University of Chicago Press.

Geertz, C. (1973). *The Interpretation of Cultures: Selected Essays.* New York: Basic.

Gerrish, B. (1992). 'Postscript to "Theology and the Historical Consciousness"'. In M. P. Engel and W. E. Wyman (eds.), *Revisioning the Past: Prospects in Historical Theology,* Minneapolis: Fortress, 297–302.

Ginzburg, C. (1980). *The Cheese and the Worms: The Cosmos of a Sixteenth Century Miller.* Baltimore: Johns Hopkins University Press.

González, J. (2002). *The Changing Shape of Church History.* St Louis: Chalice.

Grace, Marion (2004). *Of Divine Economy: Refinancing Redemption.* Edinburgh: T. & T. Clark.

Hall, R. G. (1981). *Revealed History: Techniques for Ancient Jewish and Christian Historiography.* Sheffield: Sheffield Academic.

Hamilton, P. (1996). *Historicism.* London: Routledge Press.

Hinchliff, P. (1992). *God and History: Aspects of British Theology 1875–1914.* Oxford: Clarendon.

Hodgson, P. (1989). *God in History. Shapes of Freedom.* Nashville: Abingdon.

Hood, R. (1990). *Must God Remain Greek? Afro Cultures and God Talk.* Minneapolis: Fortress.

Hopkins, D., and Cummings, G. (1991). *Cut Loose Your Stammering Tongue: Black Theology in the Slave Narratives.* Maryknoll: Orbis.

Iggers G. G. (1997). *Historiography in the Twentieth Century: From Scientific Objectivity to the Postmodern Challenge.* Hanover, NH and London: University Press of New England.

Kinzig, W., Leppin, V., and Wartenberg, G. (eds.) (2004). *Historiographie und Theologie: Kirchen- und Theologiegeschichte im Spannungsfeld von geschichtswissenschaftlicher Methode und theologischem Anspruch.* Leipzip: Evangelische Verlagsanstalt.

Kwok, Pui-Ian (2005). *Postcolonial Imagination and Feminist Theology.* Louisville: Westminster John Knox.

Le Boulluec, A. (1985). *La Notion d'hérésie dans la littérature grecque* IIe–IIIe *siècles.* Paris: Études augustiniennes.

Lindbeck, G (1984). *The Nature of Doctrine: Religion and Theology in a Postliberal Age.* Philadelphia: Westminster.

Lowenthal, D. (1985). *The Past is a Foreign Country.* Cambridge: Cambridge University Press.

Lyman, R. (2003). 'The Politics of Passing: Justin Martyr's Conversion as a Problem of "Hellenization"'. In K. Mills and T. Grafton (eds.), *Conversion in Late Antiquity and the Early Middle Ages: Seeing and Believing*, Rochester: University of Rochester Press, 36–60.

McIntire, C. T. (ed.) (1977). *God, History and Historians: An Anthology of Modern Christian Views of History.* New York: Oxford University Press.

McIntire, C. T. and Wells, R. A. (1984). *History and Historical Understanding.* Grand Rapids: Eerdmans.

Markus, R. (1990). *The End of Ancient Christianity.* Cambridge: Cambridge University Press.

Martin, D. B., and Cox Miller, P. (eds.) (2005). *The Cultural Turn in Late Antique Studies: Gender, Asceticism and Historiography.* Durham, NC: Duke University Press.

Meeks, W. (2002). *In Search of the Early Christians: Selected Essays.* New Haven: Yale University Press.

Milbank, J., Pickstock, C., and Ward, G. (1999). *Radical Orthodoxy: A New Theology.* London: Routledge.

Moltmann, J. (1993). *Theology of Hope: On the Ground and Implications of a Christian Eschatology.* Minneapolis: Fortress.

Momigliano, A. (1977). *Essays in Ancient and Modern Historiography.* Oxford: Basil Blackwell.

—— (1992). *The Classical Foundation of Modern Historiography.* Berkeley and Los Angeles: University of California Press.

Novick, P. (1988). *That Noble Dream: The 'Objectivity Question' and the American Historical Profession.* Cambridge: Cambridge University Press.

Pannenberg, W. (1991–8). *Systematic Theology.* 3 vols. Grand Rapids: Eerdmans.

Patterson, L. (1967). *God and History in Early Christian Thought.* New York: Seabury.

Pelikan, J. (1971–89). *The Christian Tradition.* 5 vols. Chicago: University of Chicago Press.

Phan, P. C. (2003). *In Our Own Tongues: Perspectives from Asia on Mission and Inculturation.* Maryknoll: Orbis.

Ruether, R. Radford, and Grau, M. (2006). *Interpreting the Postmodern: Responses to 'Radical Orthodoxy'.* London: T. & T. Clark.

Said, E. (1978). *Orientalism.* New York: Vintage.

Shaw, J. (2004). 'Women, Gender and Ecclesiastical History'. *Journal of Ecclesiastical History* 55/1: 102–17.

Spiegel, G. (1997). *The Past as Text: The Theory and Practice of Medieval Historiography.* Baltimore: Johns Hopkins Press.

Spivak, G. (1999). *A Critique of Postcolonial Reason: Toward a History of the Vanishing Present.* Cambridge: Harvard University Press.

Tanner, K. (1997). *Theories of Culture: A New Agenda for Theology.* Minneapolis: Fortress.

Taves, A. (1999). *Fits, Trances and Visions: Experiencing Religion and Explaining Experience from Wesley to James.* Princeton: Princeton University Press.

Thomas, K. (1971). *Religion and the Decline of Magic: Studies in Popular Beliefs in Sixteenth and Seventeenth Century Europe.* New York: Scribner.

Tilley, T. (2004). *History, Theology and Faith: Dissolving the Modern Problematic.* Maryknoll: Orbis.

Torrance, T. (1984). *Transformation and Convergence in Forms of Knowledge.* Grand Rapids: Eerdmans.

Tracy, D. (1981). *The Analogical Imagination: Christian Theology and the Culture of Pluralism.* New York: Crossroad.

Trompf, G. W. (2000). *Early Christian Historiography: Narratives of Retributive Justice.* London: Continuum.

Van Dam, R (1993). *Saints and their Miracles in Late Antique Gaul.* Princeton: Princeton University Press.

Webber, R. (1999). *Ancient-future Faith: Rethinking Evangelicalism for a Postmodern World.* Grand Rapids: Baker.

Welch, C. (1972–85). *Protestant Thought in the Nineteenth Century.* 2 vols. New Haven: Yale University Press.

White, H. (1973). *Metahistory: The Historical Imagination in Nineteenth-Century Europe.* Baltimore: Johns Hopkins University Press.

Wiesner-Hanks, M. (2002). 'Women, Gender, and Church History'. *Church History* 71/3: 600–20.

Wiles, M. (1967). *The Making of Christian Doctrine.* Cambridge: Cambridge University Press.

Wilken, R. (1995). *Remembering the Christian Past.* Grand Rapids: Eerdmans.

Williams, D. (1999). *Retrieving the Tradition and Renewing Evangelicalism: A Primer for Suspicious Protestants.* Grand Rapids: Eerdmans.

Williams, R. (2005). *Why Study the Past? The Quest for the Historical Church.* Grand Rapids: Eerdmans.

Suggested Reading

Ashcroft, Griffiths, and Tiffin (2000).

Bonnell and Hunt (1997).

Breisach (1983).

—— (2003).

Burke, P. (ed.) (1992). *New Perspectives on Historical Writing.* University Park: Pennsylvania State University Press.

Clark (2004).

Davaney (2000).

Hodgson (1989).

Iggers (1997).

McIntire (1977).

Tilley (2004).

CHAPTER 27

HERMENEUTICS

OLIVER DAVIES

Hermeneutics concerns the act of interpretation. It is closely related to, though not to be identified with, the science of semiotics, which is the study of meaning. Semiotics reflects upon how meaning comes about; it deals with signs and the ways in which they signify. Hermeneutics, on the other hand, already presupposes that the act of meaning will be plural, requiring choices to be made. Hermeneutics is inherently problematic in its conception therefore, and tends towards the question not only of how meaning is constituted but also, and more importantly, how we should seek to find the right meaning in any particular case.

Judged from the perspective of systematic theology, interpretation appears to be a deeply Christian exercise. After all, on many accounts faith begins with the question that Jesus poses to Peter (Matt. 16: 15): 'Who do you say that I am?' The implication here is that there was more than one way of understanding the identity of Jesus. When Peter answers, 'You are the Messiah', and Jesus tells him that it is not flesh and blood but the Father in heaven who has revealed this to him, then the issue of *how* the right answer is to be arrived at is already made thematically present. According to Christian tradition, in the post-resurrection period it was the Holy Spirit who took on this function of guiding the judgements of those who encounter Jesus so that they will understand or interpret him in the right way.

In the account that follows, we will discover that hermeneutical questions have arisen, and do arise, in all kinds of different Christian contexts. The Bible itself has moments of interpretation built within it. The New Testament writers were inevitably engaged at critical points in devising new ways of interpreting the Jewish scriptural tradition they had inherited, and some Pauline texts, for instance, thematize their own hermeneutical practices. The story to be told about hermeneutics will move between exegesis and doctrine, exegesis and theology, and extra-biblical philosophies of interpretation. There was something indeterminate about the Greek god Hermes, who gave his name to the discipline of hermeneutics. Hermes was known as the god of those who wander or travel. He was the divine shepherd: the god of paths. But he became known also as the god whose skills were felt in the rhetor's art, and in practices of financial transaction. His cunning also won him a reputation as god of deceit. We shall find that the practice and theory of interpretation is no less polymorphic than this winged god of the Greeks.

Despite the hermeneutical nature of so many of the early Christian doctrinal debates, which sought foundation in their varied readings of scripture, hermeneutics as a formal discipline only began at the end of the eighteenth century, with the work of F. D. E. Schleiermacher. Prior to this point the principles of deciding between interpretations (as we have defined hermeneutics) were manifested implicitly, within Christian practices of interpretation. The theoretical justification of these practices was generally attributed to the action of the Holy Spirit. In 1810 the University of Berlin was founded, an event in which Schleiermacher took a prominent part. Within this new environment of a professional academic community working within different disciplines but united around the principles of *Wissenschaft*, or the dispassionate, public, and evidenced pursuit of knowledge, such an implicit and internal hermeneutics was bound to raise more questions than it answered. It was Schleiermacher who thematized and made reflexive the act of interpretation, and in doing so, perhaps inevitably, set the question of deciding between the possible meanings of scripture within a broader context of hermeneutics as such. In other words, Schleiermacher believed that the hermeneutical question could only be addressed from within an overarching account of the rules which govern the proper understanding of all texts, especially those which were composed in societies very different from our own. A distinction can usefully be drawn therefore between Christian hermeneutics before and after Schleiermacher.

In the first section of the discussion which follows, we shall focus upon the premodern hermeneutical tradition, when issues to do with the interpretation of texts were implicitly present and functioned either as biblical hermeneutics in engagement with scriptural texts or as an extended form of biblical hermeneutics in engagement with the world. We shall then pass on to a discussion of the modern hermeneutical tradition, when specifically theological kinds of hermeneutics were embedded within a more general account of interpretation and needed to negotiate their proper validity in dialogue with secular accounts of meaning. We shall conclude with a discussion of the state of hermeneutics today, when Christian claims to validity in interpretation are shaped by community, narrative, tradition, and concern for the 'real'.

I. The Pre-Modern Tradition

The pre-modern tradition of Christian hermeneutics began in the requirement felt by the early church fathers to read the Jewish scriptures they had received, which came to be called the Old Testament, in the light of the church's faith in Jesus Christ. This led to the rise of different kinds of typological readings whereby Jewish prophetic or messianic texts, together in some cases with other biblical genres, were read as making anticipatory reference to the messianic advent and significance of Jesus Christ. In the anti-Marcionite writings of theologians such as Irenaeus and Tertullian, we also find the evolution of a more sophisticated type of Christian hermeneutic grounded in the fuller unity of doctrine and scripture. Concealed within such early reading practices were further practical hermeneutical judgements about how to interpret those passages of scripture which resisted easy inclusion within an overarching Christian history of salvation. Such 'difficult' texts were to be read in the light of other, more accessible and tractable passages. The use of allegory also served as an interpretative tool for refiguring Old Testament texts in the light of New Testament affirmations.

Allegory is in itself the most distinctive characteristic of pre-modern hermeneutics. It represented a multilayered, generally non-competitive sequence of readings and attained a considerable notoriety in the modern period on account of its alleged arbitrariness. In practice, the allegorical method led to a rampant diversity of possible readings on the one hand and to a painful constraint through the authority of precedent on the other (as theologians laboriously repeated each other's readings). But within the contexts of its own times, allegory was a way of understanding that was based upon a combination of ancient cognitive and ontological principles which constituted its basic coherence. The hermeneutical importance of allegory comes into view in the insistence of this tradition that there exists a graspable continuity between the ways in which we can discern the possible meanings of scripture on the one hand, and the structure both of the human mind and of the perceptible world on the other.

The character of pre-modern hermeneutics, hovering between Bible and world, becomes evident as we glance at two of the greatest hermeneutical theologians of the ancient world: Origen and Augustine. Origen believed that he could discern a process of reading and understanding that was internal to scripture itself, above all in the Pauline texts. In 1 Corinthians 10: 1–11 Paul himself reads passages from Exodus and Numbers concerning the wanderings of Israel in the desert as 'examples', or *tupoi* ('types'), for us today. In Galatians 4: 21–31 Paul understands Hagar and Sarah, Abraham's concubine and wife, to represent the old and new covenants respectively. Hagar 'corresponds to the present Jerusalem' while Sarah is 'the Jerusalem above'. On this occasion, their symbolic meaning is described as an 'allegory' (*allegoroumena*).

At the root of Origen's hermeneutic is his belief that the gospel itself exists on two levels. Drawing upon Revelation 14: 6, Origen holds that it is simultaneously a 'temporal' and an 'eternal gospel'. Although in themselves one, the existence of these two faces of the gospel reflects our own inability to comprehend the divine self-communication in its purity. We are forced to rest upon the earthly or fleshly gospel, with its material signs, as a point of access to the eternal or heavenly gospel, which is the truth as it exists before God and in the presence of the saints (*On First Principles* 4. 25, in Origen 1973). The human mind, which rises from Old Testament signs to the mediated meanings of the temporal gospel and finally to the truth of the eternal gospel, is itself substantially changed in the process. Having received a participation in the divine Logos through the creation, the mind, in its 'logos-like' characteristics, becomes conformed to the divine, creative Wisdom. As Origen likes to point out, Christians can only read scripture in the right way by virtue of their possession of what is called at 1 Corinthians 2: 16 the 'mind of Christ' (*Commentary on John* 10. 27, in Origen 1989; *Commentary on Matthew* 14. 11, in Roberts and Donaldson 1990: ix. 501).

The Origenist view of scripture was one which placed the interpretative act, as a modality of both human and divine knowing, at the centre of Christian identity. But it was grounded in the relation between the self and the objects of its knowing in general, and not just in the reading of scripture. Indeed, the act of interpretation, for Origen, was itself a participation in the cosmological and Christological heart of the world. An important theme here is Origen's development of the concept of the *epinoiai* ('titles'). In Book One of his *Commentary on John*, he argues that *Sophia* or Wisdom is prior to all the other names or 'titles' of Christ. In an exegesis of John 1: 1, 'In the beginning (*arche*) was the Word (*logos*)', Origen laid down the principle that *arche* here signifies 'Wisdom' and that, as the site or place of the *logos*, it is clearly prior to and distinct from it (*Commentary on John* 1. 22). Wisdom designates the nature of Christ as the one who understands the manifold and generative 'speculations' of the Godhead which are identified with primal creation. *Logos*, on the other hand, designates Christ in so far as he *makes known* to us the 'secret things of His Father' (*On First Principles* 1. 2, §§2–3; *Commentary on John* 1. 22, 42). This distinction between generation and revelation is further strengthened by Origen's attribution of 'power' specifically to Wisdom. He repeatedly points to 1 Corinthians 1: 18–31, where Christ is linked with the divine power and wisdom, and to the Wisdom of Solomon, which speaks of Wisdom as the breath of the power of God (*On First Principles* 1. 2, §§4–12; *Commentary on John* 1. 23). Origen's identification of Wisdom with the *energeia* of God draws out the extent to which Christ as Wisdom is not only the final term of our knowledge, as the highest mystery, but also the generative ground of the creation. Wisdom is thus also the dynamic principle of our own return to that ground through exegesis of the created order in the light of scripture's revelation of its ultimate origin and end.

We find the same link between scriptural exegesis and our understanding of the world in Augustine's theology, albeit in a more pessimistic register. The Johannine description of Jesus as 'the true light' (John 1: 9) is a central text for Augustine's reflections on knowledge, signs, and the world. We find that Augustine first developed textual strategies of allegorization for countering the literalistic claims of the Manichees. This exegetical practice was later coloured by Platonic hierarchalism, though, paradoxically, Augustine's exegesis tends to place greater emphasis upon the literal sense of scripture than we find in Origen, with a clear commitment to history and to the created world as the ultimate semiosis of the divine creativity.

In both *De magistro* and *De trinitate*, Augustine views human knowledge under the aspect of subjectivity, and does so in ways that show our dependence upon the internal presence of the power of Christ for the correct functioning of our understanding. But in *De doctrina christiana* and, more importantly, in his commentaries on Genesis, the focus of his attention lies on the exterior aspect of the act of understanding, on the nature of the world itself. One of the functions of Augustine's emphasis upon the literal sense of scripture is that it allowed him to read the biblical signs as literal signs which point to events in history, thus transposing the primary act of interpretation away from the biblical text to the world itself, in its historical manifestations. Such textual signs, or *signa translata* as Augustine called them, can be received by the reader in an entirely literal mode while at the same time they point to events in the real world which called for a radical and Spirit-filled act of interpretation. The thrust of this hermeneutic was to show that Christ himself was the true meaning of history, and that the demonstration of this was the true meaning of scripture.

In an exegesis of Vulgate Psalm 103, which occurs in both the *Enarrationes* and the *Confessions*, Augustine understood the phrase 'like a skin it is stretched out' (v. 2) to refer to the claim of Isaiah 34: 4 that 'the heavens shall be folded together like a book', and thus to be an allusion to the scriptures, which are 'your words which are not mutually discordant, and which you have placed over us by the ministry of mortal men' (*Confessions* 13. 15. 16, in Augustine 1991: 282). Scripture stands over the creation, and creation itself is a scriptural semiotic, as appears from the many passages in which Augustine speaks of the way in which created things point to their creator. In *De civitate dei*, for instance, he speaks of the 'eloquence' of events which point to divine action in the world (*City of God* 11. 18, in Augustine 1998: 472).

Our own subjective state is an essential precondition for our capacity to understand the true meaning of the world as the creation of God which is transcendentally open to him. As Augustine elaborates in *De doctrina christiana*, we can either 'enjoy' (*frui*) the world in God and thus grasp it in its ground in him, or 'use' it (*uti*) according to our own limited and self-centred purposes. The world, like signs in general, constitutes for Augustine an opportunity to be transformed by the grace of God, which is given with the sign. We can respond positively to the ways in which God speaks with us through signs, in what Augustine calls *admonitiones*, events in life which seem to us to communicate God's providence. This serves to remind us that it is through signs and creatures, whose meaning is ultimately realized through scripture, that God summons us to the highest and most spiritual love.

Origen and Augustine are not representative of pre-modern hermeneutics as a whole, which is a highly diverse phenomenon. But emphases within their work show the pre-modern concern of Christian hermeneutics with the question of how we are to understand scripture when we read it within a world that is itself theophanic in ways which scripture teaches and illustrates (according to the pre-modern mind). Within such a context, the issue of the relation between the hermeneutic of scripture and the hermeneutic of the world comes to the fore. Indeed, the act of reading scripture has a cosmological resonance, and the world itself is read from within the scriptural text. The multilayered character of both world and text is, through allegory, realized also in the human mind. Thus to be a Christian is in some fundamental sense to be one who interprets, and to be part of a community whose acts of interpretation are necessarily open to, and dependent upon, the sanctifying illumination of the trinitarian God, who is author of text and world alike.

The consummate representative of a pre-modern Christian hermeneutic is not in fact a theologian but a writer. In the *Divine Comedy* of Dante Alighieri (1993), we find the richest and most complex representation of the Christian universe. The human act of interpretation is once again at the centre of this view of the cosmos. Dante had already highlighted the theme of interpretation in his early work, *De vulgari eloquentia*. Here he gave a definition of language which showed that he understood language to be material and thus itself to be part of the sensible universe (I. 3, in Dante 1996). Therefore, when he came to represent that universe as a continuity between the material and spiritual dimensions of the cosmos, language itself—the language in which he himself composed the *Divine Comedy*—came to participate in the world-reality he was depicting.

The *Divine Comedy* is a multi-sided work which has been read in very many different ways. But at the centre of its meaning is a continuity between the physical world that surrounds us and the heavenly world of God, angels, and saints. That this is not merely the 'physicalization' of what should be left incorporeal is shown by the fact that Dante, at the end of his upward journey, receives a glimpse of the Trinity itself. What is proposed here then is that the world is rooted in God and, by its very nature as the creation, can communicate God in a cosmic, theophanic display. This model of the universe, which is so alien to modern thinking, is in fact the classical model of the pre-modern world. It is not Dante's invention but reflects that fusion of Genesis, Ptolemaic astronomy, and Aristotelian physics which gave the patristic and medieval world its distinctive, Christian cosmology. Nor is it Dante's own idea that the world in its materiality should be thought of as sign, ordered to the creator. But what is particular to Dante is the understanding that, since language is material, and since the human body is intimately bound up both with language and the material world of which it is a part, the linguistic act of interpretation stands at the heart of what it is to be human: to be a speaking creature in a signifying world of God's making.

The *Divine Comedy* is a massive work but Dante's hermeneutics can be lightly sketched. When Dante, as the figure in his own work, loses his way in mid-life 'in a dark forest' (*Inferno* 1. 1–2) early in the morning of Good Friday, he enters the underworld. He discovers that it is a dark and fragmented place of shattered rocks and hideous landscapes (or perhaps 'habitats' would be a better word), where severely contorted human figures are imprisoned. Their contortions and misformations are not arbitrary but closely correspond to the nature of their sins, so that those guilty of concupiscence for instance in the second circle of Upper Hell are buffeted in the gales like 'starlings' and 'cranes' (*Inferno* 5), while the simoniacs in Lower Hell are inverted (*Inferno* 19) and the fortune-tellers have twisted necks (*Inferno* 20). They thus symbolize the divine justice. This establishes a continuity between the human body, the world or environment, and the moral state of the subject. But language also comes into play here, for it too is broken. Dante speaks of 'sighings, complaints and howlings' in Upper Hell (*Inferno* 3. 22), and among the thieves of Lower Hell there is a dislocation of voice and speech such that Dante hears 'a voice, which did not seem designed for forming words' (*Inferno* 24. 65–6). The lack of language reflects the isolation of the sinners. In purgatory the light begins to return. The human body is now also manifest as an instrument of penance, as the sinners labour uphill towards the ever-increasing light. The landscape is severe and exhausting, but it also contains brief episodes that seem to promise heavenly beauty. The penitents engage each other in conversation, and music is present in the singing of penitential psalms. What we find here is the return of a kind of community between human beings which is grounded in a cosmic *consonantia* (to use Robert Grosseteste's word) or harmony that is itself the cosmic expression of a sovereign divine order of creation, fall, and redemption. By the time Dante reaches the heavenly spheres, we can speak of a topography of light. As Dante ascends through these spheres, the human bodies become increasingly light and diaphanous: in fact, they become increasingly angelic. Language itself is manifest primarily in what the medievals understood to be an angelic mode. (Since angels do not need to use language in order to communicate, the angelic modes of speaking are purposeful praise of God and teaching of the divine truth.) Music, song, praise, and instruction permeate the light-filled air of the higher realms. When finally Dante comes to the highest sphere, the *Divine Comedy* presents the sense of a complete harmonization of divine light, divine love, and divine life. Human communication (with its concomitant task of interpretation) becomes rarified until it takes on the characteristics of angelic community and finally finds itself in praise and awe before the Blessed Trinity, which is the ineffably radiant and living enactment of the perfect love 'which moves the sun and other stars' (*Paradiso* 33. 145).

Dante's understanding of language as material, and thus as part of the world rather than something which is set over against it, allowed him to present his own work as an instrument of what we may call 'right interpretation' under God.

In other words, his own creation took on something of the role played by scripture in Origen and Augustine. Indeed, he makes very abundant use of scriptural allusion throughout the *Divine Comedy*. He writes himself as author into his own account of how the world works, as someone who paramountly receives teaching and *learns*. And Dante makes the point about the artist that his art is not the child of God (which is nature) but 'the grandchild of God' (*Inferno* 11. 99–105).

II. The Modern Tradition

The nature of Christian theological hermeneutics is such that it is impossible to offer an overview without taking account of the literary strand to that tradition. There are also many literary figures of the modern period who put their art at the service of Christian faith (John Milton and John Donne, to name only two), but two outstanding theologians in particular chose to integrate artistic creativity into their own highly original contributions to theology. J. G. Hamann and Søren Kierkegaard both show the influence of early Romanticism, with its intensified understanding of the transcendental possibilities of art, language, and the poetic. But both need also to be seen against the background of the many fundamental changes in science, culture, and politics which came to characterize the emergence of the modern world from the sixteenth century.

In the history of hermeneutics, we can see two moments which seem both to contribute to those world-historical changes and to reflect them. The first is Luther's affirmation of the perspicuity of scripture, which led to a privileging of the plain or literal sense of scripture (while of course preserving the Spirit's role in both the origin of scripture and its true understanding). The second was the evolving disjunction between history as depicted in the Bible and the sense of history that was developing among the European peoples during the eighteenth century (to which Hans Frei drew our attention in his critical study *The Eclipse of Biblical Narrative* (1974)). The former moment opened the door to Pietism in exegesis but also to later explorations of the literal meaning of scriptural texts from an un-Spirited perspective (e.g., Strauss and Semler), while the latter led to narrativist readings which take the Bible to have no necessary connection with history or the empirical world (e.g., Bultmann and the postmoderns).

Luther's proclamation of the principle of *sola scriptura* led to a deep-rooted change in the understanding of the relation between scripture and the church and that between scripture and theology. Protestant dogmatics would later give clearer expression to the hermeneutical principles which Luther articulated or practised in diverse forms throughout his voluminous writings. Scripture now had 'normative authority', which meant that it was the sole source of theology. It also had 'causative' authority in that it became itself, as mediator of divine truth, the primary vehicle of the divine power to judge and to save. The authority of scripture, which was self-authenticating and independent of any criteria other than those implicit in it as the Word of God, was evidenced by its divine origins. The biblical authors were commanded or impelled to write, and, for the early Lutherans, what they wrote was inspired by the Holy Spirit both in terms of the *forma* (or meaning) of the words and their *materia* (or particular character). This theory of the 'verbal inspiration' of the Bible in its entirety came to be frowned upon in later Lutheran tradition, but it was a seminal part of the early post-Reformation period which both took the authority of scripture away from the ecclesial mediations of their Catholic interlocutors while also defending its inerrancy against the Socinians. The Lutheran tradition also came to stress the role of the Holy Spirit at work within the mind and heart of the faithful reader. To some extent this can be seen as a response to the Catholic emphasis upon the role of the Spirit in the church, as an intrinsic part of scriptural authority. The early Lutherans likewise denied that the canon, to which they strongly held, though in a new form, resulted from any act on the part of the church. It was rather given by God and was independent of any human judgement.

It was also against the Catholic understanding of the role of the church in the reception of scripture that the Lutherans stressed the *sufficiency* of scripture. This meant that nothing other than scripture was necessary for salvation; it was an elaboration of *sola scriptura.* Sufficiency led further to scripture's *clarity,* which perhaps meant little more than that the mediation of the church was not required for the individual believer to understand the Bible's meaning. The words in themselves were perspicuous enough, and the light of Christ sufficiently active. It did not mean that the Bible was without difficulties, which required application of the principle that scripture interprets scripture. But it did signal a Lutheran emphasis upon the plain sense of scripture which under all circumstances was to be given priority over allegorized or mystical readings of the text. Any text could have only one plain-sense meaning (although of course there could be figurative meanings where this was intended by the author). As far as possible therefore Lutheran theologians sought to preserve the text of scripture from criticism or relativization by establishing its ultimate authority and truthfulness. As the Word of God, scripture mediated Christ directly to the believer, through the Spirit, and was thus the guarantee of our salvation in this world.

The Reformation turn to the plain-sense meaning and to history led on the one hand to a Spirit-guided hermeneutic which replaced the role of the church as authoritative mediator of scripture's many meanings, and it established exegetical practices which strongly reflected the new spirit of individual commitment and piety. On the other hand, it also led to more rationalist and individualistic forms of exegesis. These could raise sharply critical questions about the content of scripture and its traditional interpretations, as shown by the work of the deist Reimarus, which was first published by G. E. Lessing in 1774–8. But it could also be harnessed to new kinds of large-scale theological projects of the kind set out by Schleiermacher. Indeed, the contribution of Schleiermacher, who founded hermeneutics as a formal discipline in the modern sense, turned on the contemporary notion of *Wissenschaft*. As a commitment to a new 'science of knowing' (to borrow Fichte's phrase), *Wissenschaft* seemed to promise a hermeneutical turn with far-reaching consequences for Christians. *Wissenschaft* would dictate that biblical texts be approached from within a hermeneutical horizon which was effectively indistinguishable from that which needed to be applied generically for the responsible reading of all manner of ancient texts. The text as such was seen to be the product of a particular mind or minds which required precise localization within the intermeshing fields of reliable knowledge concerning the contexts in which the text was produced. Responsible reading of the biblical text entailed the recreation of a historical environment within which the original meaning of the text was formed. Originality constituted authenticity. This evidently contrasted starkly with the Spirit-led allegorizing hermeneutic of the classical period of Christianity on the one hand and with the Spirit-centred plain-sense hermeneutic of Pietism on the other. It was Schleiermacher too who drew the natural consequences of this reorientation. Effectively, Schleiermacher applied the concept of *Wissenschaft* in its other contemporary sense, as 'system' or 'systematic knowledge', in order to defend Christian belief against excessive vulnerability to the kinds of radically secular outcomes which were likely to follow from the application of a secular hermeneutic to the scriptural word. Powerful, 'scientific', philosophical systems were in the air, stemming from the work of Immanuel Kant and its idealist and Romantic aftermath. Part of Schleiermacher's achievement therefore was the realization that, with the emergence of the historical-critical method in biblical exegesis, to which he himself in no small degree contributed, a commensurate turn to 'system' would be required if Christian faith was to retain its authenticity and accountability without recourse to a positivist reading of scripture as unadulterated 'history'.

The insights which Schleiermacher had brought to bear came into play again when, in 1835, David Friedrich Strauss published his highly influential *Life of Jesus*. This drew extensively upon historical-critical sources and came to the conclusion that very little can be known about the actual historical life of Jesus of Nazareth. But, Strauss argued, the biblical text remained an intensely historical document nevertheless, since it could be viewed as an expression of the historical consciousness of early believers. What this text was essentially *about*, then, was not the historical detail of a particular life, but rather the historical nature of human consciousness itself, incorporating elements of both the infinite and the finite into a self-realization of new profundity.

The tension between philosophical ideas and the historical character of scripture, the historical reliability of which was increasingly being put into question, came into view again in the work of F. C. Baur. Baur was a Hegelian, but against both Hegel and Schleiermacher he argued for a unity of the 'ideal Jesus' with the historical one. What mattered to Hegel was the idea of the unity of the infinite and the finite manifested historically in the finite spirit of those who believed that Jesus Christ embodied this union (it does not have to be a genuine embodiment). Baur disagreed and stressed the importance of the historical Jesus as the one in whom this realization was first accomplished and therefore first entered history. As a result of these new strategies, principally Lutheran theologians working in nineteenth-century Germany moved further away from the exegetical project, constructing ever more 'systematic' accounts of faith which accorded with the felt need to express the Christian faith in terms of *Wissenschaft* as a 'scientific system'. At the same time, they accepted that *Wissenschaft* as *historical* method would increasingly remove the text of scripture from the interests of theology, leaving it finally as a resource for a 'theological' or 'subjectivist' homiletics and the fostering of Christian belief among the faithful.

In the first half of the twentieth century two important new voices were heard. Rudolf Bultmann was a New Testament specialist who also became the chief advocate of a new kind of theology based upon the influential existentialist philosophy of Martin Heidegger (Bultmann 1961). Heidegger had presented a powerful new model of the self as being fundamentally temporal, hermeneutical, and language-centred. Bultmann's achievement was to link with the New Testament texts this new anthropology (which he certainly believed to have a relevance and applicability far beyond the immediate contexts in which Heidegger was writing). Bultmann did so through the principle of *kerygma*. Scripture itself thus became an instrument of supernatural disclosure of a kind which made sense within a Heideggerian account of the self. The radical openness towards death which characterized human authenticity for Heidegger, for instance, became for Bultmann the eschatological *telos* of scriptural hermeneutics. This was a text which mediated radical human authenticity, and thus fulfilled its kerygmatic promise. It is important to note that, for Bultmann, scripture did not find its principal anchorage in historical events which were independent of it, but rather, and somewhat like Baur—who shared Bultmann's scholarly interest in text and theology alike—in the kind of historical consciousness which came to expression in it. The *Christus praesens* of Bultmann's biblical theology is primarily a modality of disclosive existence which is manifest in the text of scripture itself.

The second voice was that of Karl Barth. Barth's use of scripture is an extensive topic, but, like Bultmann's, it includes a turn to the kerygmatic (Barth 1956: 457–740). The kerygmatic in Barth's case is not supported by, or articulated as, an extra-biblical system. Barth rejects the very possibility of such an alignment. But it remains kerygmatic nevertheless in that Barth does not seek to justify his particular readings of scripture in terms of any consensual readings of the day or in terms of any current debates. Barth's reading of scripture has to be seen as being at one with his theology: if his theology is in itself and reflexively proclamation, centring in his theology of the Word, then the Bible is its principle resource and the medium of its transmission. Barth's theology therefore *is* his exegesis, a deeply systematic, generative, and expansive inhabiting of scripture in the service of a theologically reflexive return to proclamation.

Bultmann and Barth point the way to further significant changes in the relation between text, interpretation, and theology in the modern world. But we cannot get a grip on the kind of changes which have taken place in recent decades, and which continue to be formative in our culture, without also taking account of the work of non-theologians such as Hans Georg Gadamer and Paul Ricoeur.

In an important essay published in 1966 on 'The Universality of the Hermeneutical Problem', Gadamer argued against Schleiermacher's view that hermeneutics is about clarifying communication, proposing instead that 'being' is coterminous with 'world' and both are reducible to language, which 'is the fundamental mode of operation of our being-in-the-world and the all-embracing form of the constitution of the world' (Gadamer 1976: 3). This marked a key point in the evolution of hermeneutics, since it sought to establish that hermeneutics is not about texts, or not only about texts, but is also about the way we experience the world.

Gadamer took up and developed the notion of the centrality of interpretation in his classic work *Truth and Method.* He argued that world is itself given by, or is a function of, language: 'In every view of the world the existence of the world-in-itself is implied' (Gadamer 1979: 406). Here too we find the celebrated formula: 'Being that can be understood is language' (Gadamer 1979: 432). Gadamer's contribution was the idea that interpretation is engaged in every act of understanding. If the classical position was that the human mind perceives and understands its objects within a horizon which traverses a spectrum from inerrant objectivity to arbitrary subjectivity, then Gadamer established the principle that our understanding is always from a point in a historical process: it is therefore never free of subjectivity. We understand things from the ground of our own situatedness. Gadamer spoke of understanding in terms of 'a fusion of horizons' whereby our own situatedness could become reconciled with the situatedness of another, the author of a text, for instance. It is important to note that, for Gadamer, our subjectivity or inescapable 'point of view' was not a weakness in understanding to be avoided at all costs, but was rather the sole means by which we can arrive at an understanding of some other 'point of view'. In historical terms (which Gadamer himself set out), the universalization of interpretation had its roots in Kant's account of aesthetics. Kant allowed that it is only from within a tradition of interpretation, which presupposes some degree of subjectivity, that we can come to an understanding or appreciation of a work of art. Kant contrasted this with other kinds of cognition. Gadamer's achievement was to rethink Kant's account of aesthetic judgement, the third *Critique*, in terms of a general theory of understanding, grounded in a much keener sense of the extent to which language shapes both the world and our knowledge of the world—one of the characteristic insights of the modern period.

The second contemporary philosopher who has profoundly influenced hermeneutics, and particularly theological hermeneutics, is Paul Ricoeur. Ricoeur's hermeneutics grew from his early engagement with the phenomenology of Edmund Husserl, in whom he identified the contrasting instincts of an idealist and a realist. The conclusion Ricoeur drew was that the way forward for philosophy lay between these two. In other words, in our experience we are confronted with the real, though not directly. If we are to study the real in depth, we need therefore to identify the place in our experience where there is most *resistance* (hence Ricoeur's early interest in the will), and we need to be alert to what he later calls 'the arduous detours' of analytical interpretation (Ricoeur 1992: 19).

Ricoeur differs from Gadamer to the extent that he engages as a hermeneutical philosopher with scripture itself (perhaps on account of his Protestant background). Ricoeur is careful to define his own work as 'philosophical' and not 'theological'; nevertheless, the kinds of insights he brings to texts and to scriptural texts continue to have a pervasive influence upon many areas of theological concern. One of his chief contributions is the idea of 'second naïveté', which he coined as a riposte to the 'masters of suspicion' (Nietzsche, Marx, and Freud). The tendency of these thinkers was to deconstruct the text against the background of extra-textual drives or forces. The text thus lost something of its autonomy and imaginative potentiality by being reduced or held to account by powerful ideologies of origination, which invite us to understand the text as being itself under the control of or subject to more fundamental powers of culture, society, or the unconscious mind. Ricoeur's 'second naïveté' (in contrast with a 'first naïveté' of uncritical reading) acknowledged the existence of deconstructive critique but turned our gaze back again to the text in its integrity and inviolability. The second outstanding contribution Ricoeur made to the understanding of texts is linked with the first and finds its fullest expression in the article 'Towards a Hermeneutic of the Idea of Revelation' (1981). Here he argues that the revealing moment is not something outside the text, nor is it the historical referent of the text, but is rather what he calls the 'world of the text'. That is the whole sphere of reference and interconnection which unfolds for the one who reads the text. This denotes not the world as given, in a first order reference, but the world as possibility, in a second order reference (Ricoeur 1981: 43). Ricoeur sets forth an argument for the 'poetic' text as revelation, which 'alone restores to us that participation-in or belonging-to an order of things which precedes our capacity to oppose ourselves to things taken as objects opposed to a subject' (Ricoeur 1981: 101). Poeticity contests the teleological systems which bind language to the world and restores the sentient self to a new and originary engagement with world as an opening of *possibilities*. The distinctively religious character of the opening engendered by biblical texts resides, for Ricoeur, in the circulation of all the different biblical discourses around the name of God: 'narration that recounts the divine acts, prophecy that speaks in the divine name, prescription that designates God as the source of the imperative, wisdom that seeks God as the meaning of meaning, and the hymn that invokes God in the second person' (Ricoeur 1995: 227). God remains unknown, however, as the 'vanishing point' of the circulating voices that testify to him, and as term of all the extravagant and hyperbolic 'limit-expressions' that are testimony to him (Ricoeur 1995: 228–30).

There is no doubt that Ricoeur's hermeneutical philosophy constitutes a powerful aid to theological hermeneutics (as well of course to philosophy more generally). But there are some areas of difficulty. It is the case for instance that Ricoeur understands 'poeticity' to be a property of all texts, or at least of all texts which have the capacity to cause a world of 'second reference' to emerge for the reader. This will include texts other than those of scripture. Ricoeur does in fact comment on the problems this raises in an intriguing article in which he draws attention to the extent to which sacred texts reverse the ordinary order of interpretation. In other words, most texts represent the deposit of fixed signs from an oral environment of speech and present interaction. As a hermeneutical philosopher, Ricoeur understood himself to be engaged with written utterance, which could not be illumined by the authorial voice. In the case of sacred texts (Ricoeur is thinking of liturgy) the movement is the other way, however. Here the written text is taken back into some kind of orality and spoken relation. Ricoeur the philosopher designates this domain as the province of the theologian (Ricoeur 1995: 68–72).

III. Hermeneutics Today

And so we come to the question of Christian faith, systematic theology, and hermeneutics today. From some perspectives very little will seem to have changed. The problematic of the relation between scripture, assessed by the historical-critical method, and theology remains. There are signs of a significant recontextualization of the problem, however. There are biblical scholars who affirm the role of the church community as the prime community of interpretation (e.g., Francis Watson 1994). This serves to reduce the possible tensions between 'scientific' exegesis and the living, worshipping community who actually receive the scriptural texts (and who will indeed often include in their number the practitioners of the historical-critical method). In harmony with this we have also seen the emergence of more theological modes of reading scripture (e.g., Brueggeman 1997; Moberly 2000). There is often an explicit or implicit debt to Paul Ricoeur. It may be that we will continue to see a softening of the divide between systematic theology and biblical science.

One reason why this might be so is that the rise of narrativity as a primary mode of knowing in our society is providing an incentive for theologians to revisit scriptural sources. The questioning of the traditional conceptuality of reasoning which is pervasive in our society, and which obtains also in the domain of formal logic with its 'vagueness' and 'fuzzy set logic', have made it more difficult for theologians to rely purely upon the kind of systematic knowledge which was characteristic of, for instance, nineteenth-century Lutheran theologians or indeed of the highly influential Protestant and Catholic theologians of the mid-twentieth century. Their work was perhaps conceived at a time when epistemology rather than deconstructive language and culture-centred forms of thinking were in the ascendancy.

The greater understanding of the role of tradition in the formation of knowledge proposed by Gadamer (and the social scientists) and 'theologized' by Hans Frei (1974) and George Lindbeck (1984) makes it more difficult for biblical scholars to detach themselves from the contexts in which the books they study are used and read, namely, the churches or what we might call scriptural communities. Paradoxically, it is pressures such as these which have led scholars such as John Webster (2003) to argue for a return to the kind of 'dogmatic ontology' of scripture which was developed during the Reformation on the one hand, and advocates of the neo-Rabbinic hermeneutics of Peter Ochs (1998) and 'scriptural reasoning' to argue for a radical reshaping of Christian hermeneutics through Jewish-Christian-Muslim encounters on the other.

The third element in all this is the question of interpretation and the real. In the pre-modern texts we looked at, the assumption could always be made that, however semiotic and therefore interpretative the Christian understanding of the world became, it would always retain a dimension of resistance and of universality which required the philosophical terminology of the 'real'. Reality in this sense belonged to the meaning of the creation. If that has been called into doubt by the modern primacy of language, with its inherent multiplicity and divergence, then it nevertheless remains the case that Christianity is a religion which needs to make certain kinds of historical claims. Are we comfortable with theologies which efface not just the ontological urgency of doctrine about the life, death, and resurrection of Christ, but which also might serve to lessen the imperative to meet the (real) needs of the suffering other? Perhaps also there are pressures from globalization which lead to the need to re-establish the values of practices and norms which may give communities of contrasting beliefs grounds on which to meet? The language of the real goes far beyond the narrow concerns of verificationalism and rationalism. It can also serve to ease what is one of the most difficult Christian problems of all: if interpretation is at the heart of Christian existence, shaping it from within, then how are we to justify practising one interpretation rather than another? If all is interpretation, is all interpretation wrong?

The Christian community today has one task before it which earlier times either did not have or did not experience with the same keenness. We live in a society which understands interpretation to be both a necessity and a right. There is no greater misconception about who we are today than that we are anti-foundationalist. We are not. But our foundationalism is not any one interpretation or set of interpretations: it is rather interpretation itself. The structures of the democratic state assume and safeguard the primacy of the interpretative act. If interpretation has always been at the heart of Christianity ('Who do you say that I am?'), then we now live in a culture for which interpretation is also foundational, though interpretation which is not in general constrained by tradition and community, as it is in the Christian case.

It is axiomatic therefore that the challenge before the churches is to articulate the grounds on which any one interpretation is to be preferred to another. It is to explore the boundaries of legitimate diversity both within the Christian communities themselves, and between them, and it is to explore the fluid boundaries and new interpretative relations between Christianity and the multiplying worlds in which it sits. This is perhaps an invitation to link doctrine more closely with the practices of holiness and the self-communicating wisdom and Christ-shaped virtues of discipleship which can most claim to be a universal language of meaning among humankind.

References

Augustine (1991). *Confessions*. Oxford: Oxford University Press.

—— (1998). *The City of God against the Pagans*. Cambridge: Cambridge University Press.

Barth, K. (1956). *Church Dogmatics* I/2. Edinburgh: T. & T. Clark.

Brueggemann, Walter (1997). *Theology of the Old Testament*. Minneapolis: Augsburg Fortress.

Bultmann, Rudolf (1961). 'How does God speak to us through the Bible'. In id., *Existence and Faith*, London: Hodder and Stouton, 196–201.

Dante Alighieri (1993). *The Divine Comedy*. Oxford: Oxford University Press.

—— (1996). *De Vulgari Eloquentia*. Cambridge: Cambridge University Press.

Frei, Hans (1974). *The Eclipse of Biblical Narrative*. New Haven: Yale University Press.

Gadamer, Hans-Georg (1976). 'The Universality of the Hermeneutical Problem'. In id., *Philosophical Hermeneutics*, Berkeley and Los Angeles: University of California Press, 3–17.

—— (1979). *Truth and Method*. London: Sheed and Ward.

Lindbeck, George (1984). *The Nature of Doctrine: Religion and Theology in a Postliberal Age*. Philadelphia: Westminster; London, SPCK.

Moberly, R. W. L. (2000). *The Bible, Theology and Faith: A Study of Abraham and Jesus*. Cambridge: Cambridge University Press.

Ochs, Peter (1998). *Peirce, Pragmatism and the Logic of Scripture*. Cambridge: Cambridge University Press.

Origen (1973). *On First Principles*. Gloucester: Peter Smith.

ORIGEN (1989). *Commentary on the Gospel of John.* Washington, DC: Catholic University of America Press.

RICOEUR, PAUL (1981). 'Towards a Hermeneutic of the Idea of Revelation'. In id., *Essays on Biblical Interpretation*, London: SPCK, 73–118.

—— (1992). *Oneself as Another.* Chicago: University Press of Chicago.

—— (1995). *Figuring the Sacred: Religion, Narrative and the Imagination.* Minneapolis: Fortress.

ROBERTS, A., and DONALDSON, J. (eds.) (1990). *Ante-Nicene Fathers: The Writings of the Fathers down to A.D. 325.* Edinburgh: T. & T. Clark.

WATSON, FRANCIS (1994). *Text, Church and World.* Edinburgh: T. & T. Clark.

WEBSTER, JOHN (2003). *Holy Scripture: A Dogmatic Sketch.* Cambridge: Cambridge University Press.

SUGGESTED READING

DAVIES, OLIVER (2004). *The Creativity of God: World, Eucharist, Reason.* Cambridge: Cambridge University Press.

FREI (1974).

GADAMER, HANS-GEORG (1979). *Truth and Method.* London: Sheed and Ward.

JEANROND, WERNER (1991). *Theological Hermeneutics.* New York: Crossroad.

LINDBECK (1984).

OCHS (1998).

PREUS, ROBERT DAVID (1970–2). *The Theology of Post-Reformation Lutheranism.* St Louis and London: Concordia.

WEBSTER (2003).

CHAPTER 28

PHILOSOPHY

GORDON GRAHAM

I. Historical Background

The history of the relationship between theology and philosophy in the western tradition is one of convergence, divergence, reconvergence, and finally a more prolonged separation. The origins of philosophy are to be found in the Presocratic thinkers of ancient Greece, but the surviving fragments of their writings do not distinguish questions that we would now classify as philosophical from those now regarded as theological or scientific. It is with Socrates as represented by Plato, his most famous pupil, that we find philosophy distinguishing itself as a special kind of inquiry, a development accelerated first by Plato himself and then by Aristotle. This is why the writings of Plato and Aristotle are today regarded as primarily philosophical, though in both there remain elements of theological reflection as well as scientific speculation.

With the rise of Christianity the philosophy of ancient Greece was brought into intellectual contact with the very different ideas of Jewish sacred history for the first time. The process of integration began with Justin Martyr. Trained in philosophy, Justin continued as a teacher of philosophy after his conversion to Christianity. His *Dialogue with Trypho the Jew* and two *Apologies* established it as a major part of the purpose of the earliest Christian thinkers to articulate Christian theology in a way that would make it accord with the intellectual standards set by Greek philosophical thought. While this is perhaps less true of one of the greatest of them, Origen, who was for the most part a biblical scholar of prodigious learning, another major figure, Clement of Alexandria, was a philosopher by training and his *Miscellanies* quotes from the Greek philosophers. Clement held philosophy to be an avenue to faith, though inferior to revealed truth, for which it should accordingly be abandoned. Nevertheless, it is St Augustine who is usually identified as the first Christian philosopher, mainly for two reasons. Augustine expressly attempts to demonstrate the superiority of Christian thought when compared with Platonism, and in the course of doing so he reflects at length upon such perennial philosophical issues as free will, the nature of knowledge, and the existence of evil.

After Augustine, theology and philosophy were effectively indistinguishable as part of the same inquiry, partly because metaphysical analysis was inescapable in forging a theology that included such doctrines as the incarnation and the Trinity. In the formulation and discussion of both, philosophical distinctions like that between 'substance' and 'property' took on great theological importance. The zenith of this integration was the work of Thomas Aquinas, whose *Summa Theologiae* presented an extended series of arguments in which appeal is made to the authority of scripture, the church fathers, and Aristotle ('the Philosopher') whose works had recently been rediscovered. Aquinas was both capitalizing upon and giving important stimulus to a tradition of scholastic inquiry that brought techniques of logical analysis and strictly conceptual inquiries to new heights of sophistication, and though Aquinas's intention and influence were both principally theological, many of the questions the *Summa* addresses would now be regarded as falling within the province of philosophy rather than theology.

The French philosopher René Descartes is usually identified as the thinker with whom began the new 'modern' philosophy that eventually emerged from medieval scholasticism. Descartes's philosophy lent special importance to the issue of the foundations of knowledge, and though by no means hostile to theology, he importantly made philosophical reasoning more foundational to human thought than theological doctrine. That is to say, in his *Meditations* (1641) philosophical argument is offered as a basis for religious belief in preference to any appeal to the authority of scripture.

Of the other major contributors to the development of modern philosophy, only Thomas Hobbes, who expressly set himself to abandon Aristotelian scholasticism, can be described as a religious sceptic. John Locke, the founding father of philosophical empiricism, was himself a devout adherent of the Christian religion and thought that clear evidences could be offered for its truth. Gottfried Wilhelm Leibniz, the great rationalist philosopher, was also a believing Christian. Nevertheless, all these philosophers treated philosophy as an autonomous intellectual inquiry that was neither subservient to nor restricted by revealed theology.

In the eighteenth century the divergence of philosophy and theology may be said to have quickened its pace. An important figure in this respect was the Scottish philosopher David Hume. Hume's major philosophical work *A Treatise of Human Nature* had little impact at first, and with an eye to finding a larger readership he rewrote and republished it in two later *Inquiries*. In the first of these he included a new section on the subject of miracles, and its effect was to establish his reputation as the author of a philosophy positively hostile to theology and religion. His most extended discussion and criticism of the rational basis of religion, the *Dialogues Concerning Natural Religion* (1779), confirmed this reputation, though it did not in fact appear until after his death.

In the same century the towering figure of Immanuel Kant, writing partly in response to Humean scepticism, was much less evidently hostile to religion. His only work devoted exclusively to theological topics was significantly entitled *Religion within the Boundaries of Mere Reason* (1793), and this reflects the sharp distinction he draws between what reason can show to be true, and the sphere of 'rational faith' which necessarily acknowledges that we must remain largely in theological ignorance. Kant does offer versions of some traditional Christian doctrines, including, somewhat surprisingly, the doctrine of original sin. But they undergo a radical reconception. Thus the incarnate Christ becomes a 'prototype' of 'humanity in its full moral perfection', an ideal which it is 'our universal duty to elevate ourselves to' (II. 1. A, in Kant 1998). This sort of transformation of doctrines is characteristic, and for Kant demonstrable truths properly called theological are few, very general, and not notably Christian. His *Groundwork to the Metaphysics of Morals* (1785) attempts to found morality not on God, but on the principles of pure practical reason. Most importantly, Kant's three great *Critiques*, which comprise his mature and enduring thoughts on the fundamental questions of existence, make no appeal to theology or scripture. Indeed, in the second of these, the *Critique of Practical Reason* (1788), while Kant does invoke the ideas of God and immortality, he does so as the solution to a more basic problem about morality and human action, rather than as fundamental concepts in their own right.

The nineteenth century saw a measure of reconvergence between philosophical and theological thinking, but of a special kind. The encyclopaedic philosophy of G. W. F. Hegel was hugely influential across Europe in the second half of the century, and Hegel identified religion and philosophy (along with art) as manifestations of 'Spirit', that is to say, the principal modes of the progressive development of mind to self-consciousness. Within the Hegelian framework, then, theology and philosophy can be thought of as allied or complementary forms of inquiry and understanding, and Hegel was passionate in his defence of a rational and philosophically sophisticated version of Christian belief that stood in opposition both to the dogmatic evangelical Protestants of his day and to the hugely influential theology of Friedrich Schleiermacher, which rooted religion in feeling rather than reason. Moreover, in formulating an explanation of the relation between logic, nature, and mind, Hegel makes these the precise philosophical correlates of Father, Son, and Holy Spirit. Nevertheless, even his more sympathetic contemporaries wondered if Hegel's philosophy was not ultimately atheistic. Since it is philosophy that reveals the rational inner core of religion, there appears to be a sense in which Hegelian idealism renders theology redundant: 'God the Father' is a picture or metaphor to be replaced by the concept of the logical structure of the world.

While it was common to find idealist philosophers of the late nineteenth century seeking solutions to philosophical problems in theological (or at any rate spiritual) conceptions of mind and matter, the rapid decline of Hegelian idealism early in the twentieth century ushered in a period in which the divergence of philosophy from theology seems to have been complete and confirmed. Two schools came to dominate philosophy, both of which were antithetical to religion. The dominant voice in Anglo-American philosophy was a powerful combination of empiricism and logical positivism, and its analysis of language rendered theological language meaningless. Meanwhile, in Europe, existentialism came to dominate, and though its origins can be traced to the Protestant thinker Søren Kierkegaard, in the hands of its major representatives, Jean-Paul Sartre and Martin Heidegger, it rapidly assumed the task of providing a satisfactory explanation of the significance of human existence in a godless world (though some theologians have identified valuable intellectual resources in Heidegger).

It was not philosophical developments alone, however, that caused the radical and seemingly permanent divergence of theology and philosophy. A long-standing tradition in Protestant theology was also an important contributor. By placing heavy emphasis on both the free grace of God's revelation and the corruption of human reason, it made all forms of natural theology suspect. Since it was largely in the context of natural theology that the two disciplines had met hitherto, a long-standing point of contact was abandoned. In particular the highly influential theology of Karl Barth welcomed a separation from natural theology, and since it was in the sphere of natural rather than revealed theology that philosophy had a part to play, this was a separation that both logical empiricism and existentialism were only too willing to concede.

Despite this eventual separation, any adequate survey of the issues with which both theology and philosophy continue to deal will reveal that there must remain substantial common ground in at least three important areas: metaphysics, moral philosophy, and epistemology. This may explain the re-emergence of a measure of intellectual conversation between the two in the late twentieth century.

II. Metaphysics

Perhaps the most fundamental question human beings can ask is this: Why is there something rather than nothing? This is an ontological question, a question about existence itself. Once we have set off along this path, other related questions quickly present themselves. It seems evident that there are quite different *kinds* of thing in existence—material things like sticks and stones, mental entities such as desires and ideas, social entities like clubs and societies, and abstract objects such as an isosceles triangle or the number three. There are also different *levels* of existence—particular objects such as the chair I am sitting on and classes of objects such as the 'furniture' to which my chair belongs. Furthermore some of these classes of object appear to be 'given' in nature. While motor cars and mobile phones are human creations, lions and lemons are *natural* kinds.

How are all these aspects of existence to be related? Do some 'things' (stones, say) really exist while others do not (numbers, perhaps)? Are some kinds of thing more basic or fundamental forms of being than others, the material than the mental, say, so that the existence of a mind is ultimately reducible to the existence of a brain? Is a class of things simply the totality of all the individual things in that class, as a mathematical set is the totality of its members? Are manufactured objects simply rearrangements of natural objects? Is a club any more than the individuals who belong to it? These are metaphysical questions, and they may be said to concern both the ground and the nature of being or existence itself.

Closely related to the question of being, however, and for the Greeks inseparable from it, is the question of becoming, or the problem of change. How can one thing become another thing, an acorn become an oak tree for example? Surely at any given moment it is either one or the other, and there is no moment at which it is both. But if this is the case, then while it is not so difficult to see how an acorn might be *replaced* by an oak tree, it is hard to see how it could *become* one. Furthermore, while anything could replace anything else, it is not the case that anything can become anything else. An acorn could disappear and be replaced by a cow, but it is calves, not acorns, that become cows. So in addition to a principle or ground of being, there must be some principle of change.

Any such principle of change will have to deploy the distinction between what is essential to a thing and what is not. The cow does not simply replace the calf because, unlike the cow and the acorn, both calf and cow share an essential nature. Their appearances change, of course, and we must say, therefore, that some aspect of their existence is essential to them, while others are merely contingent. One way of conceiving this difference is to identify a fundamental substance to which accidental properties adhere. This is a distinction familiar to Greek metaphysics, but (as the language of the Nicene Creed reveals) it takes on great theological relevance when we try to formulate the doctrine most distinctive of Christianity—the Trinity.

It is evidently also of singular relevance to the doctrine of the real presence in the eucharist. How is it possible for bread and wine to change into the body and blood of Christ while retaining the appearance of bread and wine? We generally believe that change can take place in our perception of things as well as in things themselves and that the two are distinct. As an object recedes into the distance, it appears to contract in size, but (or so we believe) this is not the same as its actually contracting in size. This implies that reality and appearance are different. But how then are they related? Does the way things appear to us correspond with how they really are, or are we systematically subject to illusory appearances? Or is it the other way about, perhaps? Is the fundamental role to be given to appearance, so that what we call 'reality' is nothing more than a fabrication or construction by the human mind out of sense perceptions?

These are all questions which troubled the ancient Greek philosophers, and which they tried to resolve. Some of their solutions seem strange to us; faced with the difficulty of explaining change, Zeno of Elea (*c.* 470 BC) appears to opt for an outright denial that it ever happens. But the relevant point here is that in their grappling with these metaphysical questions ancient philosophers fashioned concepts that subsequently were of special relevance to the theological debates in which Christians soon found themselves embroiled. More than that, the two most influential Greek philosophers formulated answers to them that are quasi-theological.

Both Plato and Aristotle find the ultimate cause of reality in a divine spirit of somewhat indeterminate sort. In combination with Judaeo-Christian theology, this solution to Greek metaphysical questions assumes greater precision and explanatory power. The claim that the world is the work of an intelligent, omnipotent creator by whose will it was brought into existence both explains why something exists rather than nothing and how change is both possible and ordered. Things exist because the divine will says that they should, and the world is governed by laws which are also an expression of the ordering will of its creator.

The identification of the divine will as a single principle of both being and becoming is thus one potential answer to the philosopher's questions. But the relation between philosophical question and theological answer is a dialectical one. That is to say, to test the adequacy of such answers, we have to subject the theology invoked to further questions of a philosophical sort. How does the existence of God explain the existence of other things? Surely it just shifts the original question along a little, with the result that we have to ask why there is God, rather than no God. One reply invokes the idea that God has necessary and not merely contingent existence. He does not merely happen to exist; he has to exist. The distinction between 'necessary' and 'contingent' is a philosophical distinction, so that if it is to be sustained it has to be made philosophically coherent. If it is to be employed to good effect in the present context, however, we have to be able to say that existence is one of God's properties. To say this, however, is to turn from philosophy to theology again, because theology can most adequately be characterized just as the attempt to discern the properties of God.

III. Moral Philosophy

These metaphysical questions about being and change constituted only half the philosophical agenda of the ancient Greeks. Of equal or, to some philosophers, greater concern was the question of goodness. In Plato's earlier dialogues it is moral philosophy rather than metaphysics that figures most prominently. In many of them Socrates is the chief protagonist and is ranged against the Sophists, a philosophical school characterized by the doctrine that there is a fundamental difference between *physis* and *nomos*, or as we might say today, between fact and value. The Sophists held that whereas the physical world is real, all claims about good and bad are either subjective (an expression of personal taste and desire) or conventional (a reflection of political power and social conformity). Plato contended strenuously against this view, and through the mouth of Socrates formulated detailed arguments to show that good and evil are in fact fundamental to reality itself.

But how can good and evil be real entities, or even properties of things? We can count and measure physical objects and access their properties through the five senses; we cannot do this for their moral or other evaluative qualities. Besides, if good and bad were indeed properties of things like yellow or square, how could they be connected to action and choice? The fact that something is yellow does not imply that there is anything we ought to do about it. But is it not precisely the implications for action that make it important to tell good from bad?

In the eighteenth century these two points were built upon to sceptical effect by David Hume. In a famous passage in his *Treatise of Human Nature* he questions the legitimacy of inferring 'ought' from 'is', thereby beginning a debate on the 'is/ought' question that has continued ever since. Hume was a sentimentalist. That is to say, he held that evaluative properties like good and bad, beautiful and ugly, are not really properties at all. Common speech is to this extent misleading. Although evaluative statements have the form of an assertion about an object—'He is a good person', 'That was a bad thing to do'—they are in fact expressions of approval or disapproval on the part of the person uttering them. It is this that explains the connection with action; we choose the things we approve of, and shun the things we disapprove of.

Hume's position (in more sophisticated versions) is now widely shared, though there are still philosophers who dispute it. One of the chief problems it confronts is its seeming inability to ground what we might call the seriousness of morality. It seems acceptable that, in *some* matters of taste and preference, there is only normal and abnormal and not right and wrong. The person who prefers eating chalk to cheese is highly unusual, but that's all there is to it. In moral matters, however, the normal/abnormal distinction seems insufficient. Hume himself provides a striking example. There is nothing contrary to reason, he tells us, in someone who would rather that the whole world were destroyed than that he hurt his little finger. Such monstrous egoism is highly unusual (happily) but cannot be shown to be objectively wrong because morality is matter of feeling, not reason. Yet if it is true that there is no rational check on our beliefs and feelings about right and wrong, the result is a state of radical amorality in which anything goes. Worse, it implies that actions cease to be wrong when people in general cease to disapprove of them. The wrongness of slavery or the sexual use of children disappears wherever and whenever human beings cease to disapprove of them, and courageous self-sacrifice loses its value when it is no longer well regarded by others.

It was this implication of Hume's view that his contemporaries found most objectionable, and among the ways in which they sought to counter it was an appeal to God as the foundation of right and wrong. But how could this help? Several centuries before Christ, in a short dialogue entitled *Euthyphro*, Plato set out the difficulty confronting any such appeal. If we try to root good and bad in divine approval and disapproval, we make them contingent on the things that God happens to approve or disapprove of. Yet it seems evident that there is something *intrinsically* wrong about slavery and sex with infants, and something good *in itself* about running great personal risks to save others, whether God approves or not.

Any straightforward appeal to God, then, will not provide a suitable answer to Humean sentimentalism. A much more sophisticated reply is to be found in Kant's moral philosophy. Kant founds his argument on the very premisses that are stumbling blocks for Hume. Human action is not the outcome of feelings and desires, but the exercise of a rational will. If this were not so, human beings would not be free agents but creatures causally moved by the instincts they happen to have, like cows in search of water. The essence of action is to be found precisely in our freedom to choose whatever rationality shows we ought to do, in preference to what we simply find ourselves inclined to do. That we are truly free in this sense is not something that can be proven. The best we can do is offer a 'transcendental argument', an argument which shows that for us as acting beings choice is inescapable, and choice presupposes freedom.

Action then, is an exercise of freedom and reason, but rational action is not co-extensive with moral action. I ought to study for my forthcoming examination, say, rather than yield to the inclination to abandon my books for the cinema. But this is not the 'ought' of moral obligation. What is it, then, that marks out moral oughts? Kant's answer (in brief) is that they are overriding. That is to say, moral requirements trump all other calls on our will: honesty has to be preferred over profitability, truthfulness over personal advantage, and so on. This special status arises because moral obligations are the product of *pure* practical reason, i.e., reason directed at action without special appeal to feeling or desire. The person who acts out of pure practical reason is in effect formulating rules of behaviour that have universal application to all rational agents.

Kant's account of overriding moral obligation rooted in pure practical reason is impressive and has been highly influential, partly because it captures and articulates some very deep intuitions that we have about morality. Among these is the old idea, *fiat justitia, ruat coelum* ('let justice be done though the heavens fall'). But what if there is a real prospect of the heavens falling? If we want to object to Hume's egoist, who would prefer the destruction of the whole world to a little bit of personal pain, why is it not equally irrational to be so obsessed with moral obligation that we would prefer the destruction of the whole world to a single violation of principles of justice? It is at this point that Kant turns to 'rational faith'. It is rational for us to treat moral obligations as overriding only if we presuppose that the right and the good, justice and wellbeing, virtue and happiness, will not ultimately conflict. But clearly this is not something that human beings can themselves ensure. So morality must in the end be underwritten by two other presuppositions: the existence of an omnipotent, benevolent God, and the existence of an afterlife in which virtue *is* rewarded with happiness. It is thus by means of transcendental deductions that Kant's famous triad—God, freedom, and immortality—comes to comprise the most fundamental concepts of philosophy.

Kant's basic moral principle or 'categorical imperative' is commonly referred to as 'respect for persons': people ought always to be treated as ends in themselves and never simply as means to somebody else's purpose. In the course of defending this principle, Kant derives some moral applications relating to suicide, promising, being charitable, and making the most of personal aptitudes. Impressive though Kant's philosophical achievement is, few people have been convinced by these derivations, and fewer still by the transcendental moral argument for the existence of God. But even if we were convinced by these, his moral philosophy would have made an important break with theology, because neither the principle of respect for persons, nor its applications, nor the appeal to God as the guarantor that virtue and happiness will ultimately coincide, requires any specific knowledge of God and his will. In other words, what we need to know in order to live a good life does not depend directly on any demonstrable theological truths. This is why Kant thinks of it as rational *faith*, a conclusion in keeping with his own Pietist upbringing, but one which renders theological inquiry practically redundant.

Moral philosophy subsequently followed this path. The most prominent alternative to Kantianism—utilitarianism—is still a morality within the limits of reason and makes no appeal to divine revelation. Even when moral philosophers have uncovered deep difficulties in both of these alternatives, they have rarely sought solutions in revealed or systematic theology. No doubt there are a number of explanations for this indifference, but one of them is the conviction that theology cannot help because knowledge claims about God and his will are inescapably insecure. Theological propositions may well express sincerely held *beliefs*, but they cannot meet the criteria of knowledge proper.

IV. Epistemology

The question of what counts as knowledge proper is also a very long-standing philosophical concern. Although the technical term 'epistemology' (the rationale of knowledge) dates from the nineteenth century, the theory of knowledge goes back to the ancient world. In fact, Plato expounds and discusses what is undoubtedly the most familiar and intuitively plausible theory of knowledge, namely that knowledge is justified true belief, often shortened to 'JTB'. Two of the elements in this threefold criterion seem relatively unproblematic; to know something is to believe something to be true. Take any simple case—knowing that the redwood is native to North America, for example. If it were not true that the redwood is native to North America, then while we might *claim* to know it, we would not *in fact* know it. Ergo, truth is a necessary part of knowledge. Secondly, it makes no sense to claim to know it, while asserting one's own disbelief in this proposition about the redwood. Ergo, knowledge implies belief.

But I might believe that the redwood is native to North America for no reason at all, and even express my doubts about it, even though it is as a matter of fact true. From this it follows that justification is a crucial part of the JTB theory, and is indeed the element which has attracted most philosophical attention. What is to count as justification? It is evident that a true belief must rest upon something or be derived from something more secure than itself, if the result is to be knowledge. That is to say, knowledge, it seems, must have some foundation, and the only question is what that foundation should be. Two candidates have dominated modern philosophy. The first is pure reason; belief is converted into knowledge if it is derived by the rules of reason from incontrovertible first premisses. Descartes, who championed this sort of rationalism, provides the most famous example of such a foundational proposition: *Cogito ergo sum* ('I think, therefore I am'). The alternative to rationalism is empiricism, whose most enthusiastic adherent was David Hume. The human mind, Hume held, is composed entirely of 'impressions' and 'ideas'. Impressions come to us through the senses and are primary. Ideas are merely copies of impressions. Accordingly, knowledge proper must be rooted in and derived from sense impressions.

These two possibilities are not entirely exclusive. John Locke, for example, who is usually thought of as the founding father of empiricism because, like Hume after him, he thought that the contents of the mind must be derived from experience, nevertheless gave a crucial role to reason in the acquisition of knowledge. And unlike Hume, Locke's empiricism was not developed in opposition to theology, but worked out within a theological framework. Even so, both rationalism and empiricism seek a foundation to knowledge that leaves no role for revelation. Whereas for Aquinas one mark of truth was what the Bible says, for modern philosophy, beginning with Descartes and Locke, the Bible must itself be tested against reason and/or experience.

This important shift was the first step in a more lasting separation between philosophy and theology. The second was the increasing dominance of empiricism over rationalism, a dominance both begun and confirmed by the spectacular success of natural science as a form of knowledge. The achievements of Francis Bacon and Isaac Newton led philosophers like Hume to advance a philosophy in which experimentalism and empirical observation are the only adequate methods for all subjects of study. But once this position is adopted, it is not hard to see how God and the supernatural fail to qualify as objects of knowledge, since they admit of neither observation nor experiment.

The emptiness of theological propositions is not an immediate implication of empiricism. It is possible to claim that theological truths are to be derived in some way from empirical observations. This is in fact the presupposition of natural theology in general, and of the teleological argument for God's existence in particular. It is precisely this argument (also known as the argument from design) that Hume subjects to devastating critical analysis in the *Dialogues Concerning Natural Religion.* Powerful though this analysis is, the argument nonetheless continued to attract intellectual support. It received one of its most famous expositions twenty-five years after Hume's death in the work of English clergyman William Paley, *Natural Theology* (1802). What seemed eventually, and finally, to destroy any remaining credibility in theological accounts of the natural world was the arrival of a compelling non-theological alternative, namely, the theory of biological evolution as expounded in Charles Darwin's *The Origin of Species.* The profound challenge presented to Judaeo-Christian theology by Darwinian biology arises from two features. By replacing intentional design with natural evolution, it seems to explain everything that hitherto theology was called upon to explain. But more importantly (since rival explanations can be equally good), Darwinian biology has empiricism's epistemological stamp of approval.

In the late nineteenth century, empiricism was somewhat briefly displaced from its pre-eminent position in English-speaking philosophy by idealism. Both in Britain and America, idealist philosophers, for the most part taking their inspiration from Hegel, rejected empiricism as a doctrine that rested upon the false and distorting practice of treating the relative distinction between perceiver and perceived as though it were absolute. Sense perceptions, they held, were intelligible only in relation to the mind of the perceiver, so that to attribute ultimate justificatory authority to empirical 'data', was to make human knowledge rest upon a mere abstraction. Of course, lending such authority to the reflective mind itself, as Descartes does, was equally one-sided and hence mistaken. The answer was to pursue a true absolute, within which all these relative distinctions can be satisfactorily encompassed. Many (though not all) identified this absolute with the God of theism.

It is surprising to discover just how widely and strongly this version of absolute idealism was held. But only for a time. At the hands of Bertrand Russell and G. E. Moore, British empiricism re-established itself, to be powerfully reinforced by the logical positivism of the Vienna Circle, many of whose members, fleeing Nazism, took residence in the United States. The application of logical positivism to religious belief was yet more destructive. Theological propositions were not merely indemonstrable by the standards of natural science, they were meaningless, and of interest only to that 'linguistic' philosophy which interests itself in the different ways in which language is used.

This 'victory' however, was not confined to theology. Metaphysics was also to be declared meaningless. Since metaphysics lies at the heart of philosophy, this has the important result that philosophy and theology are once again in the same position, and both have a powerful motive to find ways of rebutting the contention that empirical science encompasses the whole of what may be thought and known. An obvious move is to explore once more the presuppositions of positivism and empiricism. Once this move is made, albeit on behalf of philosophy in the first instance, it can be shown to reopen the possibility of theology.

V. Contemporary Philosophical Theology

It is worth emphasizing that while there is a widely shared perception in the modern world that science and religion are in conflict, this conflict does not arise directly. (What possible conflict could there be between the Psalms of David and a chemistry textbook?) It depends crucially on an underlying epistemology, one that gives natural science a privileged position. Such a position becomes less privileged, however, once this epistemology is questioned. One aspect worth questioning, an aspect empiricism shares with rationalism, is the supposition that epistemological justification is essentially foundational. That is to say, both rationalism and empiricism suppose that any belief accorded the status of knowledge must have a foundation. They dispute what this foundation should be, of course, the self-evident truths of pure reason, or the observations of sense perception. But what if we question the idea of a foundation?

Foundationalism holds that real knowledge has to be based on something properly basic. But why does the 'properly basic' have to be just specific kinds of proposition or perception? This is the question that gives rise to what is now known as 'Reformed epistemology', an avenue of inquiry begun by Alvin Plantinga. Plantinga observes that our knowledge of minds other than our own is not based upon and cannot be derived from empirical observation. We engage directly with other human beings, and to insist that our knowledge of other minds has to be based upon empirical observation is not to make us more secure in that knowledge, but to put us at the mercy of solipsism, forever enclosed within the confines of our own minds. Knowledge of other minds, then, is as 'properly basic' as knowledge of the world of atoms and molecules. But once we are freed from the tyranny of empiricism, we can openly explore the possibility that our knowledge of God is also properly basic, and hence that Christian belief is 'warranted'.

We might even go further and abandon foundationalism altogether. This is the conclusion some interpreters have drawn from the philosophy of Ludwig Wittgenstein. Wittgenstein's own philosophical position on religion is somewhat elusive, but in several places he resists the idea that our everyday beliefs are in order only if their truth can be demonstrated on the basis of some incontrovertible and conclusive chain of reasoning. But if such a demand is unsatisfiable with respect to beliefs about the everyday, why should it be a demand which religious beliefs and theological propositions should be required to be satisfy?

In any event, even where reasoning from empirical evidence is in order, it is rarely if ever a matter of proof or conclusive demonstration. This is true of science no less than religion, as evidenced by the fact that a scientific theory can hold sway for a very long time, only to be displaced by some alternative. Such was the case with Newtonian physics, whose universal acceptance over more than two centuries eventually gave way to Einstein's theory of relativity. It is also important to observe that the relation between the two is not a simple one of contradiction. Under the pressure of continuing investigation, Newtonian physics encountered more and more phenomena that it had difficulty in explaining, and relativity came to be preferred because it explained them better. In other words, the deciding factor between the two was not simple empirical observation which declared one to be false and the other true, but inference to the best explanation.

Once this move is made, however, it seems that natural theology can re-enter the discussion. This is because claims about God need not be regarded as empirically vacuous 'observation statements' that lack any confirming observations. They can now be understood in the way that traditional cosmological and teleological arguments understood them, as putative explanations of the existence of the universe, of the order we find in it, and of the existence of mental as well as material phenomena. At the same time there are important differences between the traditional arguments and this new way of interpreting theological propositions. Inferences to the best explanation are not deductions. The best explanation of some phenomenon or other may not in the end be true, so that choosing the best out of a number of competing explanations is a judgement of probability. Applied to natural theology, this means that the quest for proof or disproof of God's existence must be abandoned. The issue is whether the postulation of the existence of a God of a certain kind is the best explanation we can come up with for the evidence presented to human experience. Any conclusion we reach on these grounds will be a judgement about the greater or lesser probability of God's existence. The same point can be made about disproving God's existence. Following Plantinga's 'free will defence', contemporary philosophical argument has largely rejected attempts to deduce the non-existence of God from the facts of evil, but gives considerable credence to inductive versions of the argument that find the existence of such a being highly improbable.

The philosopher principally associated with this revitalization of natural theology is Richard Swinburne, whose highly influential book *The Existence of God* (1979) was the first of several major works devoted to the traditional topics of God's existence and attributes. Swinburne's strategy has this special feature. Whereas Reformed epistemology and anti-foundationalism construct their defences of theology and religious belief by challenging the presuppositions of logical positivism, Swinburne makes substantial use of one of the methods of scientific reasoning specially devised and endorsed by positivists, namely, Bayesian confirmation theory. In the minds of positivistic critics of religion, Swinburne's strategy has special attractions. At the same time, it obviously brings with it the problems that Bayesianism is known to have—chiefly the rather arbitrary assignment of the 'prior' probabilities that the theory requires. It also faces a difficulty that traditional natural theology has always encountered—that it seems to misconstrue religious belief. People live by religious belief and die for the sake of theological claims. By comparison, natural science, however intellectually impressive, is of theoretical interest only. Consequently, it seems less objectionable (if anything) to construe the beliefs of saints, mystics, and martyrs as profoundly mistaken, than to interpret them as the explanations of empirical phenomena judged most probable, given the evidence.

VI. Contemporary Theology and Philosophy

Whatever the objections to the work of Plantinga, Swinburne, and others, there can be little doubt that they have brought renewed strength and vigour to the philosophical discussion of religion and theology. It would not be true to say, however, that the separation of theology and philosophy which began with modern philosophy has been reversed to any great extent. Alongside this separation, certainly, and to some extent indifferent to it (a notable exception being Karl Rahner), Roman Catholic theologians within the Thomist tradition, especially Etienne Gilson, continued to think in a highly philosophical manner and to engage with those philosophers for whom Aquinas is also a major influence. However, while within the analytic tradition that looks to Descartes, Locke, and Hume the great era of logical positivism has receded and metaphysics has once more become a respectable area of inquiry, metaphysicians in general have not turned back to theology. The philosophical investigation of theological topics has become a branch of philosophy in its own right, and even includes the investigation of strictly doctrinal subjects such as the incarnation, the Trinity, original sin, and predestination (Quinn and Taliaferro 1997). But the closeness of this engagement with doctrinal subjects, while being accorded intellectual respect, has further displaced philosophical theology from the heart of philosophy. Whereas formerly it encompassed and influenced the core areas of metaphysics, moral philosophy, and epistemology, contemporary philosophy of religion is to be ranked alongside other respected but more peripheral branches, such as aesthetics and political philosophy. Both these areas look back to a venerable history they can claim as their own, and both can name figures past and present as major contributors to the western philosophical tradition. Nevertheless, neither would take precedence over metaphysics, moral philosophy, or epistemology in the story of that tradition, and this is reflected in the 'optional' status of both in the typical curriculum.

Though in a different way, the relation between theology and philosophy within the contemporary hermeneutic or continental tradition is not much closer. This is for a number of reasons. Those theologians who have most evidently turned to the existentialist philosophy of Heidegger (despite its deeply humanistic character)—John Macquarrie and Eberhard Jüngel, for example—cannot be said to have been major influences in either philosophy or theology. More influential figures like Wolfhart Pannenberg and Edward Schillebeeckx are highly eclectic in their use of philosophical sources. The most influential of all—Barth and Rahner especially—can be said to be philosophically informed, and even philosophical in style, but by placing the self-revelation and experience of God at the centre of their thought, they have given systematics the role formerly occupied by metaphysics. In addition, some of the major new movements in modern theology—liberation theology, feminist theology, postmodern theology, and theology of mission—draw more on lived experience than rational reflection and are thus largely indifferent to strictly philosophical questions. The legacy of Schleiermacher, we might say, has been far more powerful than the legacy of Hegel.

References

Aristotle (1941). *Basic Works.* New York: Random House.

Barnes, Jonathan (1990). *The Pre-Socratic Philosophers.* London: Routledge.

Evans, G. R. (ed.) (2004). *The First Christian Theologians.* Oxford: Blackwell.

Gilson, Etienne (1941). *God and Philosophy.* New Haven: Yale University Press.

Hegel, G. W. F. (1992). *Lectures on the Philosophy of Religion.* Berkeley and Los Angeles: University of California Press.

Hume, David (1990). *Writings on Religion.* Peru: Open Court.
Kant, Immanuel (1997). *Critique of Practical Reason.* Cambridge: Cambridge University Press.
—— (1998). *Religion within the Boundaries of Mere Reason.* Cambridge: Cambridge University Press.
Plantinga, Alvin (2000). *Warranted Christian Belief.* New York: Oxford University Press.
Plato (1975). *Collected Dialogues of Plato.* Princeton: Princeton University Press.
Pringle-Pattison, A. S. (1917). *The Idea of God in the Light of Recent Philosophy.* Oxford: Clarendon.
Quinn, Philip L., and Taliaferro, Charles (eds.) (1997). *A Companion to Philosophy of Religion.* Oxford: Blackwell.
Swinburne, Richard (1979). *The Existence of God.* Oxford: Clarendon.

Suggested Reading

Allen, Diogenes (1985). *Philosophy for Understanding Theology.* Atlanta: John Knox.
Davies, Brian (2000). *Philosophy of Religion: A Guide and Anthology.* Oxford: Oxford University Press.
Evans, C. Stephen (1985). *Philosophy of Religion.* Downers Grove: InterVarsity.
Flew, A. (1955). 'Theology and Falsification'. In A. Flew and A. MacIntyre (eds.), *New Essays in Philosophical Theology,* London: SCM, 96–130.
Hick, John (1989). *Philosophy of Religion.* Englewood Cliffs: Prentice-Hall.
Inwagen, P., and Zimmerman, D. (eds.) (1998). *Metaphysics: The Big Questions.* Oxford: Blackwell.
Peterson, M. L. (ed.) (2003). *Contemporary Debates in the Philosophy of Religion.* Oxford: Blackwell.
Taylor, Richard (1991). *Metaphysics.* 4th edn. Englewood Cliffs: Prentice-Hall.

CHAPTER 29

CULTURAL THEORY

KATHRYN TANNER

The study of culture suggests a great deal about the nature of the theological enterprise and about how to address a number of the basic issues that arise when deciding upon an appropriate way to do theology (Tanner 1997).

I. Culture as the 'Meaning Dimension' of Social Action

If theology is a cultural activity, it is bound up with social practices and therefore more than a rarefied, merely intellectual activity. Culture, as the contemporary discipline of anthropology understands it, is not primarily located in the intellectual or spiritual achievements of a community—its great works of art, philosophy, or literature. Instead, culture refers to the whole social practice of meaningful action, and more specifically to the 'meaning dimension' of such action—the beliefs, values, and orienting symbols that suffuse a whole way of life. This meaning dimension of social action cannot be localized in some separate sphere specifically devoted to intellectual or spiritual concerns. It accompanies all social action as a constitutive aspect of it; it is what makes action socially meaningful and not merely a biological reflex (say, a twitch) or a purely personal idiosyncrasy (say, an aversion to peas).

Thinking of theology in cultural terms does not, therefore, suggest the placement of theology primarily in a high-culture realm, as, say, a religious form of literature or philosophy. Christian theology has to do, instead, with the meaning dimension of Christian practices, the theological aspect of all socially significant Christian action. Christian theology in this primary sense would, accordingly, be found embedded in such matters as the way altar and pews are arranged. Their placement usually has a meaning, a theological aspect, in that it embodies a sense of the difference between clergy and laity, or the difference between God and human beings. All Christian activities would have a meaning or theological dimension in this sense—going to church, protesting poverty, praying, and helping one's neighbour. They are socially significant Christian actions in virtue of the way they are constituted by a sense of what Christians believe and of how they should lead their lives. They are all, then, theologically informed actions in a very fundamental way.

As a matter of day-to-day practice, the beliefs, values, and orienting symbols of Christian life can, of course, also be directly expressed. They do not remain a merely implicit dimension of social action. Christian social practice essentially involves making theological affirmations about God and Jesus and about human life in their light. One does that, for example, when one prays, confesses one's beliefs, exhorts oneself and others to properly Christian forms of action, preaches, or laments the injustices of life before God. In the ordinary course of Christian life, occasions also arise for engaging in theological investigation about those beliefs, values, and symbols. One does that when one's beliefs are directly challenged, or when it simply becomes clear that others do not agree. One is prompted to engage in theological investigation when situations seem difficult to reconcile with one's beliefs, or when trying to interpret novel circumstances in light of one's Christian commitments. Occasions for theological reflection arise, too, when the theological dimension of social practices in different areas of Christian life seem to conflict, or when one considers whether changes to Christian practice are justified.

When it becomes a specialized intellectual activity, with some people devoting a great deal of their lives to it as a matter of professional commitment, theology still raises the same sort of questions occasioned by the same sort of problems in Christian practice, but often in a more general and abstract way. It investigates these questions, moreover, in a sustained fashion according to criteria less attuned to the urgencies of everyday life—criteria, for example, which put a premium on clarity, systematic coherence, and consistency of expression. This sort of sustained inquiry often requires a level of intellectual training and institutional support unavailable to most people. For all the differences, however, such specialized theological investigation is appropriately placed on a continuum with theological activity elsewhere, as something that arises in an organic way out of Christian practice; theology at work in the everyday lives of Christians, shaping and forming the character of their social action, remains the root and ground of theology as a more specialized activity.

II. Culture and Basic Issues in Theological Method

Besides these implications for a general understanding of the theological enterprise, the study of culture is important for theological work because certain notions of culture have already infiltrated discussion of basic issues in theological method as a kind of taken-for-granted common sense. 'Culture' is one of the most widely used terms in the English language, incorporating within its range of associations such notions as context, community, convention, and norm. To talk about any human activity, with a recognition of its self-fashioning capacities and its historically and socially conditioned character, is inevitably to talk of culture. It is not surprising then that the notion has come to figure centrally in theological work. Theologians across a wide range of contemporary methodological perspectives all frame their methodological preoccupations in ways informed by notions of culture. This includes those who approach theology with a concern to retain the distinctiveness of the Christian message and prevent its submersion within the ideas of the day (for example, post-liberals); those who look for a method that will ensure the meaningfulness of the Christian message in a new situation (for example, followers of Paul Tillich's method of correlation); those who worry that Christianity has become irrelevant in a world going its own way (for example, Protestant liberals); and those who make it their priority to learn from and collaborate with contemporary movements for greater equality and inclusion (for example, liberation theologians). The contemporary trends and situations to which theology must attend are cultural matters—cultural trends and situations susceptible of cultural analysis. The non-Christian 'world', which Christianity is either to set itself against or show its relevance to, can now be identified as 'culture'. In the influential terminology of H. Richard Niebuhr (1951), Christians who are 'of' the world have a 'Christ of culture', while those opposed to it affirm a 'Christ against culture'. What Christianity stands for, moreover, becomes itself a cultural matter. Is there, behind all the diversity of Christian self-expression, some unified identity to be put forward as a specifically Christian way of looking at things—a specifically Christian culture to be brought into conversation with the culture that is the world? If such a Christian culture exists, how might one understand differences within it—internal disagreement on the fundamental question of what Christianity stands for? Are such differences, for example, always the product of cultural differences across the times and places of Christianity's spread? Concerns about both the distinctiveness and relevance of Christianity become cultural matters, matters of the putative intersection and difference of cultural forms—Christian forms on the one side, the cultural forms of the wider world or other religious traditions on the other. How might a Christian cultural form be set off from others in ways that ensure its distinctiveness, or how might it be brought into connection with other cultural forms so as to either prove its plausibility or demonstrate its broader cultural importance?

The ways these questions have been asked and answered in modern theology, however, show the influence of a now outmoded understanding of culture. The rest of this chapter will detail the change from a modern to a postmodern view of culture and its significance for basic issues of theological method.

III. The Modern View of Culture and its Postmodern Critique

The usual understanding of culture, the commonsensical view that has infiltrated Christian understandings of theological method, presumes that cultures are self-contained and clearly bounded units, internally consistent and unified wholes of beliefs and values, which are simply transmitted to every member of their respective society or social group as principles that maintain the social order and ensure the regular functioning of the organized behaviours characteristic of the group (Benedict 1934; Boas 1982; Malinowski 1954). Let us briefly examine each of these aspects of the common view of culture before subjecting them to postmodern critique.

The differences that make cultures many are assumed to follow differences in social groups. If cultures differ from one another, this is because they are the cultures of different societies. The boundaries of a particular culture line up in this way with the boundaries of a particular society. Where a network of social interaction breaks off, so does its culture. Cultures therefore tend to be discussed as isolatable units in geographical space.

There is a nationalist rhetoric underlying such a view. Centralized states in modern Europe typically used the idea that those within their territories form a nation or people with a distinctive culture—their own language, customs, and religion—to solidify allegiance to the state. In order to serve the purpose of solidifying allegiance to the state (a great worry when states were initially consolidating their power and citizens' allegiance could not be taken for granted), the culture of the people had to be coterminous with the territorial boundaries of the state, marked off from that of others by the same geographical borders that delimit the territorial jurisdiction of the state.

Because cultures are group-specific, they are associated with social consensus. If it is the culture of a group, a culture is evidently what every member of the group shares. What all the members of a particular group agree upon—their shared norms and values—constitutes their culture. Differences in culture, disagreements about fundamental beliefs and values, fall between social groups and not within them. The various elements of a culture are bound up with one another to form an integrated whole, and this means that the boundaries that make for a culture's distinctiveness are not simply a function of the spatial limits of a culture's social group. A culture's own internal organization—the way everything is bound up with everything else—establishes a culture's boundaries as an integral sum total. The character of a culture can therefore be summed up as a whole, in terms, for example, of the general quality that all elements or components of a culture typically exemplify.

The elements of a culture must hang together as a whole if culture is to integrate or hold a society together, and, indeed, this is viewed as culture's prime function—to be a kind of social cement. Social order requires what a shared culture provides: a group consensus on beliefs, attitudes, appropriate dispositions, and so on. Social order, coordinated action among the many members of a society, requires a willingness on the part of each to do as others expect, and this ultimately requires that everyone share the same body of beliefs, values, and attitudes. Culture could not work as a principle of social order if the elements of a culture were not all of a piece. If a culture is to integrate or hold a society together, it must itself be integrated and hang together. Social coherence implies cultural coherence.

Typified as wholes, different cultures tend to become qualitatively distinct incommensurables; between cultures there is only a discontinuity of kind. Similarities in the elements that make them up tend to be overshadowed by their differences in fundamental character as wholes. And therefore to understand one element of a culture, it is sufficient to pay isolated attention to the other elements within the same culture. There is no need to look further afield: a culture's meaning is generally self-contained. This sort of holistic interpretative stance tends indeed to view influences from other cultures as a source of cultural disruption; outside influences that add to or subtract from a culture potentially disrupt the coordinated integration of its elements that make a culture a whole. Those influences need to be either repulsed or neutralized in ways that allow a culture's overall character to remain unchanged.

The postmodern direction of recent work in cultural studies and theory contests all these assumptions, and subjects them to a rather severe reinterpretation, according to the usual postmodern stresses on interactive process and negotiation, indeterminacy, fragmentation and internal conflict, porosity of boundaries, and hybridity of character (Clifford 1988; De Certeau 1984; Rosaldo 1989). These now become the baseline assumptions guiding postmodern understanding of culture—assumptions which run directly contrary to those of the modern view of culture explained above.

Underlying most of these postmodern assumptions is an attack on the dehistoricized character of the modern, common-sense view of culture. Culture, on the common view, appears as a given, right from the start, something already formed and finished. The character of a finished product is wrongly ascribed to culture because the ongoing historical processes through which culture emerges are not taken with sufficient seriousness. The messy real-life character of these historical processes undermines all that the common view of culture tends to presume. For example, rather than being an internally consistent whole, a culture in use is likely to display a disaggregated quality. No one is likely to know all of it, and the whole of it is never mobilized on any one occasion. Only bits of a culture appear at any one time, according to the dictates of the situation and the various interests of the actors in it. The elements of a culture are integrated not in some tight logical relationship but in a loose fashion befitting the complex and changing character of actual social relations over the course of time.

Moreover, connections that have been established between elements of culture are always in principle susceptible of being taken apart. Social processes have given rise to these connections and can also undo them. This is particularly true of the stability and sense of unity presumed by the common view of culture as a kind of social cement. Any belief or value, no matter how central to a cultural outlook, is subject in principle to renegotiation and contest since all cultural elements are the temporary precipitates of social interactions that are ongoing. Indeed, the greater the investment in a belief or value and the more central it is to a particular culture, the more likely that disagreements will surface around it. Political fights, engaged on a cultural terrain, will tend to centre on it, leading to some degree of diversity in the interpretation of what all parties affirm. The historical processes in and through which cultural forms emerge are often conflict-laden because there are political stakes in how the beliefs and values of a culture are interpreted and interrelated. For example, by defining the situations at issue and the nature of the actors in them, beliefs about the character of the world and the people in it encourage only certain forms of social relations. What one thinks establishes in great part what one can think of doing. Fights about social policy therefore often involve a contest over the interpretation and associations of well-respected beliefs and values such as (in the USA) freedom, faith, and family.

Even apart from overt political conflict, the wider the social group covered by a culture the more likely that cultural agreement will be shallow. What people agree about remains vague and unelaborated, more a matter of form than substance, more a matter of vocabulary and manner of expression than articulated belief or clearly defined sentiment. This very lack of definition is what enables cultural forms to be shared, to be the focus of interactions among a whole group of differently situated people. If, however, participants in the same culture do not hold common beliefs and sentiments at any real depth of meaning, and if what they share is as much a common reference point for conflict as for agreement, the idea of culture as a principle of social order becomes tenuous. What everyone agrees about does not have a sufficiently well-defined meaning to constitute a clear directive for social behaviours. The social effects of a cultural form cannot be simply read off from it; in between the cultural form and its influence on action come differently situated historical agents who make different things of it. Cultural forms may be intended as norms directing behaviour, but that does not mean they succeed in orchestrating it.

Advocates of the old view of culture tend simply to assume, without a great deal of empirical testing, that where a stable social order exists it is shored up by a common culture, by shared beliefs and values. They therefore overlook a whole host of other forms of social control that are not similarly mediated by beliefs or values: coercion and the threat of force, the lack of alternatives, the lure of monetary and social benefits for compliance, isolation from others in similar straits, sheer physical exhaustion among an exploited and disgruntled work force, and so on.

Cultures always have internal sources of risk and therefore cultures need not be protected from external influences in the way the old view presumes. Change, conflict, and contradiction do not simply beset a culture from the outside but are usually generated internally. Indeterminate cultural forms are susceptible of diverse interpretations; loosely connected elements can be pulled apart and rearranged to subvert existing social arrangements. Because they emerge piecemeal in rather unpredictable fashion, cultures are liable to contain items at odds with one another, to be pushed and pulled against one another by opposed political factions—in the USA, for example, the value placed on equal opportunity runs up against the value placed on laissez-faire libertarianism. Because change, conflict, and contradiction are now admitted within a culture, it makes little sense to insist on sharp boundaries between cultures to protect them from mutual corruption. Cultures are not tightly bounded entities, essentially unaffected by relations with one another and in that way sustaining their respective characters. They instead come to be themselves in and through processes of exchange with one another.

The kind of closed-system analysis favoured by the common-sense notion of culture has to give way before a more relational, cross-cultural understanding of cultural meaning. What something means, its significance for a particular culture, cannot be understood without attention to how that cultural form relates to what is going on elsewhere, in other cultures. Cultures are not adequately understood simply on their own terms but need to be set within the broader field of competition and alliance with other cultures.

Because cultures are not sharply bounded from others in fear of contagion or indifferent isolation, the postmodern view does not share the tendency of the common-sense view to identify different cultures with social units localized in geographical space. The more or less objective boundaries of a social group—where social interactions break off—need no longer establish the boundaries of a culture. A culture need not correspond to a particular society. Some social networks are formed among people of radically different cultures: educated governing elites and peasant farmers may share very little culturally and yet form interdependent links in the same social order. Cultures can also cross the territorial boundaries of social groups—nothing could be clearer in the internet age. Finally, social networks that sustain a particular culture are unlikely in this day and age to be localized in space; transnational social networks cross widely dispersed spaces in ways that prevent any simple territorial delimitation of a culture.

In any case, cultural forms are no longer viewed as the natural possessions of particular groups of people. Cultural forms instead are associated with a particular group only through an effort of interpretation and alignment with their activities. The same cultural forms are therefore available to other groups. And this means that cultures are different from one another not so much because of a divide in cultural forms—because they believe and do, for example, totally different things—but because of a different use of much the same cultural items that recur across cultural boundaries.

To sum up, the old presumptions about culture are not necessarily undermined entirely by postmodern trends in cultural studies and theory. But what the old view is always looking for must be resituated now according to a very different baseline of change, conflict, and instability. Cultural uniformity and agreement, for example, might very well exist in some times and places. Cultural consensus might indeed shore up the social order, in which case political factions would be fighting to impose their cultural view as a consensus view. But such cultural uniformity and agreement must always be seen as the merely provisional achievements of historical processes whose character continues to put them in jeopardy.

What might this postmodern perspective on culture—particularly some of the last criticisms of the idea of tightly bounded, self-contained cultures corresponding to particular social groups—suggest about the formation of a Christian culture, about how a Christian culture is to be demarcated and understood? What might it suggest about what Christians share and about the character of their disagreements?

IV. Christian Culture and Social Groups

The common-sense understanding of culture leads to an understanding of the character of Christian culture in terms of the social group with which Christianity is aligned. A culture corresponds to a distinct people or community. The boundaries of that community establish a culture's difference from others. Christian culture would then be the culture of a particular Christian society with clearly demarcated social boundaries. The difference between what is Christian and what is not would follow a division between Christian and non-Christian social groups. Christianity would have its cultural distinctiveness ensured through the existence of a social world distinct from others.

Postmodern objections to making the culture of Christianity a function of a social group differ to some extent depending on how one understands the society of which Christianity is the culture. Theologians who worry about losing the distinctiveness of Christian culture tend to identity that society with the church as an independent society, a society forming an alternative to others such as the nation state. The church is comparable to other societies in the range of its functions, but remains qualitatively different in its principles: the Christian community is one of peace, joy, and cooperation; all others are characterized fundamentally by conflict and violence. Followers of the Radical Orthodoxy movement tend to talk of Christian culture in terms of a church understood along these lines (Milbank 1990). On the other hand, theologians who worry about maintaining the cultural importance of Christianity for the nation, or for the West generally, tend to think of the society with which Christian culture is aligned in much broader terms: the church may be at issue here, but only as it overlaps with, say, a nation state that officially sanctions it. Christian culture and the fortunes of that broader society tend to rise and fall together; if western Christian culture is to have a future, it is tied up with the future of the West. A preoccupation like this is at the heart of the work of one of the foremost cultural analysts of Christianity, the theologian Ernst Troeltsch, in his magisterial and enormously influential *Social Teaching of the Christian Churches* (1976 [1912]).

The objection to the first view (the church as a separate society) is that it overemphasizes the self-contained social functions of the church as an organization. The church is not an independent, separate society, the sort of full-service social organization that one might talk about as having its own culture, but an organization whose members continue to participate in many of the social functions of the wider society. Christian culture does shape the behaviours of its members, but not primarily for the purpose of guiding their interactions among themselves in the way the culture of a self-contained social network would. What is often at issue for Christian culture as an action-guiding mechanism is how Christians are to act in their ordinary lives which take place in the main outside of the church. And unlike a self-contained social group, the character of activities in the wider society always infiltrates the church; activities in the church have to manage, for example, the differences in rank and status that its members bring to them in virtue of their participation in other social fields.

The problem with the second view, defining Christian culture in broader social terms, in terms of, say, a state or European Union which sanctions and promotes Christianity, is that Christian culture is too closely tied to a particular social group. Christian culture, like any culture, can always be untied from the particular social group with which it has been associated; this association is not a natural, inseparable relationship but a historically contingent 'articulation' (to use postmodern jargon). No social group has a monopoly on the Christian culture with which it is associated; these forms of Christian culture can be loosened from its hold and migrate to other groups, or in any case be brought into a more antagonistic or critical relationship with a previously established social allegiance. It does not make sense to define a particular Christian culture simply with reference to social allegiance if it always has this potential to slip its social moorings.

A shared problem for both views is that a strategy for delimiting Christian culture according to social group assumes that social groups are much more clearly bounded than they often are. Social groups are pictured as if they were discrete objects in space lying next to one another. While there may be social groups that lead a completely self-contained existence, social groups are generally not demarcated from one another by a sharp break in social relations such that members of a group only have to do with one another. In the main, there are no sharp breaks like that; there is just one huge pool of social interaction, and divisions among discrete social groups are made on some other basis, as a matter of group identification or allegiance. In other words, members of one group might interact with members of another group as much as or more than with their own. These interactions, however, need not jeopardize group identity, because that identity is a matter of allegiance to certain standards or value orientations, a matter of self-definition. Turning one's attention to discrete social groups or communities, then, is not the way to answer questions about the character of Christian culture. One needs to have already determined what makes someone or something (some belief or action) Christian in order for Christians and non-Christians to be seen as forming discrete social groups to begin with.

To put the point another way, this manner of answering the question of Christian culture in social terms seems to think of the relations between social groups in terms of relations between physical objects in space. But while two different objects cannot be made up of the same parts in the same space, two social groups can. People waiting to buy movie tickets make up only one queue but they might constitute any number of different social groups—the movie group from the old-folks home, the film noir society, and so on. Against those who think of Christian culture (the church) as the culture of a separate society, it must be emphasized that Christian identity need not exclude overlapping activities and memberships. Against those who identify Christian culture by reference to a state or wider territorial governance, it must be emphasized that Christian identity should not be simply conflated with any one social membership it overlaps with.

V. Christian Culture at the Boundaries

Let us turn now to the question of how Christian culture might be established, not by a social boundary, but by a cultural boundary between what is Christian and what is not. We can say a little less here since we have already hinted at much of what there is to say about this from a postmodern point of view differences in religious culture need not be maintained by sharp boundaries holding apart self-contained religious cultures. On a postmodern understanding, cultural elements may cross the boundaries between cultures without jeopardizing the distinctiveness of those different cultures. What establishes and sustains the distinctive character of cultures in this case is the way in which common elements are used, how they are handled and transformed.

Most cultures, religious ones included, share a great deal with other secular and religious cultural forms; differences in culture are maintained in more subtle ways. Imported cultural forms, for instance, need not threaten a culture's identity; a difference can be maintained by interpreting these forms differently. Water rites, for example, figured in both Christianity and the Graeco-Roman religions of the first few centuries: they just meant different things.

Differences in religious culture are therefore often established by differences of use and not by the distribution of entirely discrete cultural forms on one side or the other of a cultural boundary. A difference between cultures does not require there to be two entirely different sets of cultural materials with nothing in common. Cultural difference is more a matter of how than of what; it is not so much what cultural materials are used as how they are used to establish identity. Moreover, identity-establishing differences in the use of the same materials do not simply sit side by side in supreme indifference to one another. Rather, a difference between cultures is established in a kind of tussle over what is to be done with shared materials. The distinctiveness of a culture emerges out of tension-filled relations with what other cultures do with much the same cultural stuff.

Christian culture can still be formed by a cultural boundary between what Christians believe and value that is different from what other religions or secular groups believe and value, but this is not the sharp boundary of independent cultural contents. The boundary is instead one of use, allowing Christian culture to be essentially impure and mixed, possessing the identity of a hybrid that always shares cultural forms with its wider host culture and with other religions. The distinctiveness of a Christian culture is not so much formed *by* a cultural boundary as *at* it. Christian distinctiveness is something that emerges in the very cultural processes occurring at the boundary, processes that construct a Christian identity through the distinctive use of cultural materials shared with others.

No matter how sharp the cultural boundary between what is Christian and what is not, no matter how oppositional, what is on the other side of that boundary is not thereby rendered irrelevant to Christian identity. Christian culture remains essentially relational; it is not intelligible apart from the way Christian culture situates itself vis-à-vis others. Christian identity therefore tends to shift—it is continually in process—depending upon the other cultures in relation to which it comes to be defined, in relation to which it actively sets itself apart.

This relational account of Christian culture sits uneasily with a post-liberal theological method which suggests that the only relevant criteria of meaningfulness and plausibility are internal to a Christian outlook and which cautions against efforts to convey the meaning and plausibility of Christianity in other terms as a threat to Christian distinctiveness (Lindbeck 1984). Here Christian and non-Christian cultures seem to amount to discontinuous wholes without any common ground between them. Christian culture is a spontaneous self-creation, establishing its own web of meaning, to be understood in its own terms, without the need for reference to anything outside itself. Christian culture seems properly maintained by avoiding the influences and alterations that might accrue from intimate involvement with other ways of doing, feeling, and understanding. Following a common-sense understanding of culture, a post-liberal theological method suggests that Christian culture is a tightly bounded entity, essentially unaffected by relations with others and thereby sustaining its distinctive character.

Surprisingly similar assumptions about culture extend to liberal theological method of a correlationist sort (Tracy 1975). Liberal theologians, in contrast to post-liberals, think that connections with wider cultural spheres must be developed for purposes of assessing a Christian outlook, but that these connections do not help establish its Christian character. While opposing post-liberals with the demand that the meaningfulness and plausibility of Christian claims be proved with reference to general criteria that are not specifically Christian, liberal theologians share with post-liberals the view that Christian cultural forms generate a cultural world of themselves. The self-generation of a distinctly Christian cultural world—for example, through classic texts with the capacity to disclose their own world—is indeed necessary to prevent the loss of Christian distinctiveness in the process of correlation. Christianity must already make its own claims to meaning and truth—seemingly indigenous and self-originating claims in virtue of its classic texts—before being brought before the bar of standards of intelligibility and plausibility in the wider culture, if its distinctively Christian character is not to be threatened thereby. For a method of correlation to work, therefore, it seems it must involve a meeting of independently generated wholes—one constituted by way of a hermeneutical analysis of specifically Christian texts, the other by way of a phenomenological description and transcendental analysis of general human processes. The need for their meeting is disputed by post-liberals, but the general idea of such independently specifiable wholes is fully compatible with post-liberal ideas about Christian culture.

If Christian culture is an essentially relational affair, then both post-liberal and liberal theologians bring relations with the wider culture into the picture too late. Relations with the wider culture are not, as post-liberals claim, at best a secondary or, at worst, a purely optional matter of apologetics. Nor are relations with the wider culture merely part of a subsequent task of application, in which one works out the implications of an already established Christian perspective by re-envisioning other world views in its terms. And, contrary to what liberal theologians maintain, the boundary between Christian and non-Christian outlooks is not crossed for the first time with arguments to determine whether, in light of wider cultural norms, what Christians believe makes sense, seems plausible, or proves illuminating. The boundary has already been crossed in and through the very processes by which Christians come to believe anything at all. A Christian culture is formed through the reworking of borrowed materials; it is the culture of others made odd. At one end of the spectrum the new twist given to prior cultural forms might involve affirmation on new grounds—for example, new movements for the equality of women are the Christian thing to do in light of Christ's mission of love to all. At the other end of the spectrum, the twist might involve something closer to reversal; thus, in the very odd Christian use of an honour-code ethics, humility rather than worldly glory might be cause for honour before God.

Because it is always present from the start, Christian engagement with other cultures rarely involves a face-off between distinct wholes in the way both liberal and post-liberal theologians tend to imagine that engagement. Transforming the use of shared items from a non-Christian to a Christian one is a piecemeal process; the items of another culture are not taken up all at once but one by one or block by block. Indeed, if they are to be used differently, the elements of another culture cannot be taken up as they form a whole; a form of selective attention is necessary in which they are wrested out of their usual contexts so as to be put to new use. Cultural forms that are already in use must be disarticulated, so to speak, taken apart in order to be put together again in new ways, to form a new pool of associations or a new organization of elements with weightings different from what they had elsewhere. Thus, Christians formed a new moral code in which many pagan virtues were wrested from their usual philosophical context and set in a religious one, thereby weaning them of their associations with virtuoso achievement and turning them into an ideal to which all may aspire by God's grace.

Because this is a piecemeal process, and because cultures are not all of a piece in any case on a postmodern view of them, the Christian transformation of culture—say, of the wider culture in which Christianity is set—is not a blanket affair in which each item of that wider culture is treated in the same way. Contrary to the usual theological worries, therefore, Christian relations with the wider culture are unlikely to take the simple form of either accommodation or resistance. The relationship is bound to be more complex, to involve not a characterization of the whole of the other culture, but a variety of cross-cuts through it, some features of that culture being affirmed, perhaps, but oddly weighted for unusual reasons, and others repudiated as incompatible with a Christian way of life, with a whole host of more subtle cultural transformations between these extremes.

Finally, a postmodern understanding of culture suggests that shared beliefs and values are not what hold a Christian culture together as a coherent whole. Christian culture can no more be easily typified as a whole than the cultures with which it is in constant communication. Because a Christian culture is constructed piecemeal in the messy course of social relations, its various elements are not likely to show a great deal of consistency among themselves; they have to be made consistent through, for example, some effort of selection and emphasis. Those cultural elements that are not selected for inclusion or are under-emphasized in a given construction of Christian culture remain resources for radically different views of what Christianity is all about.

Moreover, because of the reach of Christian culture—its common ambition being to include the whole of humanity within its compass—the cultural materials that are the unifying focus for such a diverse array of differently situated people are bound to be rather vague. Christians are unlikely to agree at any deep level about what they mean. Just to the extent they remain ambiguous, subject to a variety of interpretations, are they able to unify a highly diverse membership. When these meanings take a more developed form, the result is quite often disagreement about them. The rather vague beliefs that all Christians share—for example, that Jesus saves—need to be elaborated if they are to influence the shape of human life, but Christians are unlikely to agree on how to do that. How the different materials of Christian culture are interpreted and put together is crucial for determining what a Christian way of life involves in any more concrete sense. But Christians tend never to agree on this because the materials themselves are too vague, too many, and too loosely organized of themselves for this ever to be very clear.

What brings Christians together then, across the wide array of times and places covered by Christian cultural forms, is their common concern to figure this all out. Christian culture amounts to a joint project of making something out of the rather underdeveloped and quite disparate cultural materials that all their lives revolve around. The unity of Christian culture is sustained by a continuity of fellowship, by a willingness, displayed across differences of time and place, to admonish, learn from, and be corrected by all persons similarly concerned about the true character of Christian living.

Theologians have the task, then, of formulating an account of what Christianity is all about while recognizing the great difficulty of the task and the essentially contestable nature of the conclusions they draw. The character of Christian culture itself propels internal diversity and disagreement over how to characterize what it is all about. Diversity in the fundamental understanding of Christianity is not, then, the overlay of external cultural influences on a Christian culture that is fundamentally uniform and homogeneous in its own right, as post-liberal theologians tend to presume. Disagreements over the meaning of Christianity, in other words, are not simply the product of the way a consistently formed Christian culture spreads to new times and places and comes to be refracted by them. Nor with liberal theologians can one presume that any one shape of Christian culture is peculiarly suited to today. When Christian culture meets a particular historical context, no single understanding of Christianity naturally arises from their confluence; instead, an argument usually breaks out over the meaning of Christian culture for that time. If the sort of culture that Christianity is prompts diversity in its own self-understanding, diversity is as likely to erupt within the same time and place as across different ones.

VI. Conclusion

We have been looking at how an approach to theology is impacted by postmodern challenges to the idea that cultures are group-specific, established by sharp cultural boundaries, and marked by homogeneity of practices; and we have come to the following conclusions. First, the distinctiveness of Christian culture should not be thought of as the product of a self-contained or self-sufficient social group. The character of Christian social relations is sustained, it is true, by some fairly isolated social activities, ones, that is, that involve in the main only Christians—for instance, church services. But Christians always bring with them on such occasions their other social roles and commitments. By infiltrating Christians' activities with other Christians, by being brought inside, those other roles and commitments are reworked in the course of such activities. Christians, moreover, remain engaged in sites of social interaction with non-Christians. Their Christian commitments remain relevant to these arenas, too, and therefore operate to transform the character of social relations in them. In such fashion, Christian opposition to the wider society is maintained, not by isolation, but by the indefinitely extended effort to alter, where necessary, whatever one comes across through sustained engagement with it, in or out of church.

Second, while there are boundaries between Christian and non-Christian ways of life, those boundaries are fluid and permeable. Claims and values that are outside are brought inside (or, much the same thing, what is inside is brought outside) in processes of transformation at the boundary. Christian culture is therefore no longer a matter of unmixed purity, but a hybrid affair established through unusual uses of materials found elsewhere. Nor can Christian culture be understood from isolated attention to Christianity *per se*; understanding it now requires the careful situating of Christian beliefs and values within the wider fields of cultural life with which it interacts.

Third, what Christians have in common, what unites them, is not some baseline of shared beliefs and values forming some coherent whole. Agreement on the substance of Christian culture is not what they start from but what they are moving towards in a shared project of attempting to figure out what the beliefs and values, which mean so much to all of them, are all about. Such a project of cultural construction—the project of determining what Christianity is all about—is the principal theological task, both as a specialized intellectual activity and as an ingredient in the everyday effort to lead a Christian life. It is to be undertaken with due consideration of the essentially hybrid character of every Christian form and of the complexity of social relationships appropriate to Christianity as a world-transforming force.

References

Benedict, R. (1934). *Patterns of Culture.* New York: Houghton Mifflin.

Boas, F. (1982). *Race, Language and Culture.* Chicago: University of Chicago Press.

Clifford, J. (1988). *The Predicament of Culture.* Cambridge, Mass.: Harvard University Press.

De Certeau, M. (1984). *The Practice of Everyday Life.* Berkeley and Los Angeles: University of California Press.

Lindbeck, G. (1984). *The Nature of Doctrine.* Philadelphia: Westminster.

Malinowski, B. (1954). *Myth, Science and Religion and Other Essays.* New York: Doubleday Anchor.

Milbank, J. (1990). *Theology and Social Theory: Beyond Secular Reason.* Oxford: Basil Blackwell.

Niebuhr, H. R. (1951). *Christ and Culture.* New York: Harper and Row.

Rosaldo, R. (1989). *Culture and Truth.* Boston: Beacon.

Tanner, K. (1997). *Theories of Culture: A New Agenda for Theology.* Minneapolis: Fortress.

Tracy, D. (1975). *Blessed Rage for Order.* New York: Seabury.

Troeltsch, E. (1976 [1912]). *The Social Teaching of the Christian Churches.* Chicago: University of Chicago Press.

Suggested Reading

Benedict (1934).

Clifford (1988).

De Certeau (1984).

Kroeber, A. L., and Kluckholm, K. (1952). *Culture: A Critical Review of Concepts and Definitions.* Cambridge: Harvard University Press.

Lindbeck (1984).

Marcus, G., and Fischer, M. (1986). *Anthropology as Cultural Critique.* Chicago: University of Chicago Press.

Milbank (1990).

Niebuhr (1951).

Rosaldo (1989).

Tanner (1997).

Tracy (1975).

CHAPTER 30

NATURAL SCIENCE

NANCEY MURPHY

I. Historical Overview

A common misconception, particularly in the United States, is that science and theology have been at war. In fact, modern natural science first developed within a theological context. Early scientists and philosophers produced assorted systems of 'physico-theology'. Johannes Kepler took geometry to be the language of God's thought. Isaac Newton's mechanics was as much an argument to the divine first cause and it was science. The Galileo affair is better understood as a clash of personalities and approaches to scriptural interpretation than a clash between science and religion.

While science itself has generally been no direct threat to theology, two intellectual changes associated with science have had a major impact. One was a change in the meaning of the word 'probable'. Medieval thinkers distinguished between *scientia* and *opinio*. *Scientia* was a concept of knowledge modelled on geometry; *opinio* was a lesser but still respectable category of knowledge, not certain but probable. But for them 'probable' meant subject to approbation by the authorities. Theological knowledge fared well in this system, being that which is approved by the highest authority of all, God.

However, the multiplication of authorities that occurred with the Reformation made resort to authority an increasingly inapplicable criterion for settling disputes. The transition to our modern sense of probable knowledge depended on recognition that the *probity* of an authority could be judged on the basis of *frequency* of past reliability. Furthermore, if nature itself has testimony to give, then the testimony of a witness may be compared with the testimony of nature. Thus there are two kinds of facts pertaining to a witness's testimony to the occurrence of an event: external facts having to do with the witness's personal characteristics, and internal facts having to do with the character of the event itself, that is, with the frequency of events of that sort. Given the problem of multiple authorities, the task became one of deciding which authorities could be believed, and the new sense of probability—of resorting to internal evidence—came to predominate.

Jeffrey Stout traces the fate of theism after this epistemological shift (Stout 1981). In an early stage of development it became necessary to provide evidence for the truth of scripture. If such evidence could be found, then the content of scripture could be asserted as true. In a later stage it was asked why the new canons of probable reasoning should not be applied to the contents of scripture as well. Claude Welch writes that by the beginning of the nineteenth century the question was not merely *how* theology is possible, but whether theology is possible *at all* (Welch 1972: 59).

The second indirect effect was a change in the understanding of causation. In the Middle Ages, *scientia* was knowledge of a subject matter in terms of its properties. Medieval writers imposed order on reality by fitting a phenomenon into a pattern of similar items. The scientific revolution embodied a new form of explanation, fitting events into causal accounts, and causation came to be understood in terms of laws of nature, especially those that could be expressed mathematically. While this change was motivated theologically—it was an answer to the question of how God governs the universe—the concept of nature as entirely determined by strict causal laws soon made God's ongoing involvement seem both unnecessary and problematic.

Immanuel Kant's system was largely a response to recognition of the threat which Newtonian determinism posed to human freedom and morality and thus to religion. One aspect of his strategy led to the birth of modern liberal theology. He made the sharpest possible distinction between the spheres of knowledge (science and metaphysics) and ethics. These involve different forms of reason and different objects (the world of experience versus the world of things in themselves). Religion belongs to the sphere of ethics, and there is no valid way to argue from science or metaphysics to theological conclusions. Friedrich Schleiermacher, founder of the liberal theological tradition, kept Kant's notion of independent spheres but located religion in a third sphere, the aesthetic. The consequence was an understanding of theology that bore no intellectual relation whatsoever to science. For example, the doctrine of creation says nothing about how the universe came into existence, but speaks rather of human religious awareness of the dependence of everything on God. This also freed theologians from the demands of the new probable reasoning and created a gulf between the liberal tradition and theologians still holding to a more traditional understanding of theological *knowledge*. This accounts for the fact that it is only conservative

Christians who have seen science as a threat, even though many conservative theologians have made impressive moves to reconcile theology with scientific developments.

The indifference of liberal theologians to science has recently begun to give way to a new round of engagement. Scholars with dual training in science and theology, such as Ian Barbour and Arthur Peacocke, have contributed to a growing movement to relate theology to developments in science, and have also argued for significant epistemological similarities between the two sorts of disciplines. At present there is scarcely a topic in Part I of this volume that does not provide an interesting point of contact with the natural sciences.

II. Creation, Cosmology, and Eschatology

Julian Hartt speaks of a theological consensus from Origen to Calvin regarding creation and providence (Hartt 1982: 115). Points of agreement included the conviction that the universe was created by God out of nothing, that God alone can create, that God created freely for the sake of love, that creation involves temporal origin, and that the universe is essentially good. This consensus provided components of the western world view until the Enlightenment. A variety of developments, philosophical and scientific, have led to rejection of these assumptions in secular culture and have so eroded the place of the doctrine of creation in theology that it no longer has a vivid and compelling life in the churches.

The historical factors leading to the loss of consensus on the meaning of creation are many. Michael Buckley argues that the way was prepared by pre-Enlightenment theologies in which foundations for Christian faith were sought in natural philosophy sundered from theology (Buckley 2004). Such foundations could at best support *thin* doctrines of God and creation. The most significant response was the liberal strategy, described above, to immunize theology from science. Schleiermacher's relocation of religion within the aesthetic sphere, the world of human feeling, was symptomatic of a Copernican revolution in theology, the 'turn to the subject'. In a rich variety of ways mainline theologies up to the present, both Protestant and Catholic, have followed this anthropocentric tendency. This has had two negative effects. First, as already noted, it has resulted in the marginalization of the doctrine of creation. Second, it has left contemporary Christians without adequate guidance for relating to nature.

Much popular writing by scientists and philosophers today might be described as reflections on the theological significance of current debates in scientific cosmology. The importance of these discussions in contemporary culture suggests that theologians can no longer reduce the doctrine of creation to reflection on humankind's relation to God, but must return to the questions of origins, temporality, and finitude that were once thought of as central to the doctrine. While science does not always support traditional Christian convictions, it certainly shows that most of the issues comprising the earlier consensus are back on the table.

The most obvious theological issue that has been reopened is the question of whether God created the universe in time or from eternity. Confronting Aristotle's argument for the eternity of the universe, Thomas Aquinas argued that, while scripture teaches that the universe was created in time, the notion of an eternal universe is not incompatible with the doctrine, which is essentially about the contingency of the universe and its dependence for existence on the will of God (*ST* 1a. 46, 1–2, in Aquinas 1975; cf. Copleston 1950: 366). Thus, God could have created from all eternity. Bonaventure, by contrast, argued that the eternity of the universe is inconceivable, in that it is impossible to add to an infinite number or to pass through an infinite series. Thus, if time were eternal the world would never have arrived at the present day; yet it is clear that it has (Copleston 1950: 263).

Copernicus overturned the Ptolemaic conceptions of the organization and motion of the universe but not the conception of the universe as eternal and static. However, the development of the science of thermodynamics in the mid-nineteenth century presented problems for the assumption of an *eternal* universe—problems that Bonaventure would have appreciated. If physical systems can undergo irreversible change at a finite rate, then they will have completed those changes an infinite time ago and we could not be observing any such changes today.

In the 1920s astronomers had to give up the idea that the universe is *static*. Its observable expansion forms the basis for the big-bang theory of the origin of the universe. This sudden explosive origin was immediately interpreted by some—believers and atheists alike—as confirmation of the traditional account of creation as temporal origination. Cooler heads refused the temptation to claim that science had shown the truth of the doctrine; Ernan McMullin's account of science and theology as 'consonant' has been judged by many to be most reasonable. He says, 'if the universe began in time through the act of a Creator, from our vantage point it would look something like the Big Bang that cosmologists are now talking about' (McMullin 1981: 39).

More recent (highly speculative) developments in theories of origins threaten this tidy consonance. Cosmologists have attempted to go beyond what was once thought to be the absolute explanatory limit of science and explain the origin of the big bang itself. One is Andrei Linde, who theorizes that our universe started out as a small bubble in space–time; the bubble's swift inflation produced the big bang (Linde 1983). While the notion of a 'fantastic' rate of expansion at the beginning is widely accepted, Linde's assumption that our universe is but one small bubble in an infinite assemblage of universes is controversial. For our purposes it is interesting to see how the very possibility raises again the centuries-old questions of whether the universe is eternal and whether an infinite universe is even conceivable—in this case, whether an infinite series of universes is conceivable.

If something like Linde's cosmology were to become accepted it would occasion major rethinking of Christian assumptions. For example, it is not only fools (as Augustine said) who are tempted to ask why an eternal God would create only one comparatively short-lived universe. The 'principle of plenitude', used by Augustine to account for the variety of forms of being in the universe, could easily be extended to allow for the expectation that a God who creates as many forms of being as possible would also create as many universes as possible.

Another development is the 'quantum cosmology' developed primarily by Stephen Hawking. This theory, whether or not it is ever confirmed scientifically, reopens several traditional theological debates. Hawking's work depends on recognition that very early in the history of the universe it would have been compressed enough in size for quantum effects to be significant. Because quantum events occur without causes in the classical sense, this raises the question of whether the origin of the universe can be explained without cause, that is, as the result of quantum fluctuations. In addition, at this scale, the fluctuations would affect space–time itself. Hawking argues that before 10^{-47} seconds into the universe's existence, space and time would not have been distinguishable. Paul Davies says, 'one might say that time emerges gradually from space', so there is 'no actual "first moment" of time, no absolute beginning at a singular origin' (Davies 1992: 67). Nevertheless, this does not mean that the universe is infinitely old; time is limited in the past but has no boundary.

A number of authors have commented on possible theological implications of Hawking's work, including Hawking himself (Hawking 1988: 141): 'So long as the universe had a beginning we could suppose it had a creator. But if the universe is completely self-contained, having no boundary or edge, it would have neither beginning nor end: it would simply be.' Hawking is mistaken in believing that the absence of a temporal starting point eliminates any necessity for a creator since traditional accounts such as Aquinas's focus on contingency: the doctrine of creation is *essentially* an answer to the question of why there is a universe at all, and only *accidentally* about its temporal origin.

The most subtle response to quantum cosmology is Robert Russell's (Russell 1993). He points out that Hawking's theory requires theologians to make conceptual distinctions that have been passed over in earlier discussions. First, the concept of a temporally finite creation is distinguishable from the claim that there was a first event, designated as occurring at time zero ($t = 0$). Second, it forces theologians to grapple with the very concepts of time that they presuppose. Thus, theologians can no longer make a simple distinction, as Aquinas and Bonaventure did, between creation 'in time' and 'from eternity'.

Hawking's cosmology also raises questions about the traditional emphasis on God's creating *ex nihilo*, out of nothing. This notion is based on Old Testament texts that reflect rejection of Babylonian creation myths, according to which the world is made of the severed body of a goddess, and it was developed in the second century in response to a variety of Greek cosmologies. The doctrine serves a variety of purposes in Christian theology. It maintains God's transcendence against views that the universe is somehow a part of or an emanation from God. It maintains God's sovereignty against the view that God's creative activity was constrained by the limitations of pre-existing matter. It thus provides grounds for the goodness of the created world against views based on the essential evil of matter itself. Finally, it emphasizes the contingency of the universe—there could have been nothing but God.

Hawking's proposal does not provide a genuine analogy to the universe's origination out of nothing, since the coming into being of the universe, on his theory, presupposes the existence of a quantum vacuum as well as the laws of quantum physics. It does provoke some thought about what 'nothing' means, and more importantly it provokes thought about the nature and status of the laws of nature themselves. It also confirms Augustine's insight that space and time must be part of the created order.

Current work in scientific cosmology deals not only with the beginning of the universe but with predictions about its future. For years it was an open question whether there was enough mass in the universe so that the force of gravity would eventually overtake the force of the original explosion, resulting in the universe ceasing its expansion and then collapsing, or whether the mass was such that it would expand and cool forever. Current estimates favour the latter.

The attempt to reconcile scientific pictures of the end of the universe with hope for human survival has led to the development of what Freeman Dyson calls 'physical eschatology' (Dyson 1988). Dyson's theory postulates an open universe that continues to expand and cool forever. It depends on the premiss that a living creature can be characterized as a type of organization that is capable of information processing. Given this definition of life, he argues that life can continue, throughout the universe, without the conditions needed for terrestrial biochemistry.

Russell points out that theories such as Dyson's can remind theologians that eschatology pertains to the whole of the cosmos, not just humans. These theories should prompt us in the church 'to rethink the cosmological implications of just what is at stake if we claim... that the groaning of *all* nature will be taken up in and healed by the transfiguration of the universe which has already begun with the Resurrection of Christ' (Russell 1994: 571).

Nonetheless, attempts such as Dyson's to tack 'eternal life' onto the timeline of the universe's history miss the point of Christian eschatology; they overlook the radical discontinuity between this life and resurrection life, between the present aeon and the one to come. Wolfhart Pannenberg argues that what we see in Jesus' resurrection is a foretaste not only of the transformation that awaits us all, but of transformation of the entire cosmos (Pannenberg 1968).

Eschatology is a point where science and theology must part company. Our knowledge of future physical processes is based on projections using current laws of nature. But we also know that the 'laws of nature' in the eschaton cannot be the same as we have now, both because of the scriptural witness to the *transformation* involved in Jesus' resurrection and because of the fact that the travail of this life is tied so directly to the physics of this world.

Although the New Testament knows nothing of the modern conception of laws of nature, there are passages that can be taken to say that the laws of nature of the present aeon are imperfect and will be perfected in the eschaton—fully subjected to the lordship of Christ. It is now widely accepted that the Pauline concept of the 'principalities and powers' (*exousiai* and *dunameis*) refers not to the angels and demons of the medieval world view, but rather to (largely) social and political powers. (There is nonetheless an echo of the alien gods of Old Testament understanding.)

These powers were seen by New Testament authors as subordinate to God—they are God's creatures (Col. 1: 15–17), yet they are fallen and rebellious (Eph. 2: 1–3; Gal. 4: 1–11). Jesus' mission is understood as conflict with and conquest of these powers. In the Epistles, Jesus' victory over the powers is typically represented in summary and proclamatory form as in Colossians 2: 15: 'He disarmed the principalities and powers and made a public example of them, triumphing over them in him' (RSV). In the Gospels, the conflicts are presented in narrative form and the opponents are no longer called 'principalities and powers'; they are the Herods and Caiphases and Pilates. Wherever Christ's victory is proclaimed, the corrupted reign of the powers is challenged; yet the powers remain in being, for social life is impossible without them. There are hints in the New Testament that the final destiny of all the powers will be not their abolition but their full restoration, 'a plan for the fullness of time, to gather up all things in [Christ], things in heaven and things on earth' (Eph. 1: 10).

The relevance of this material is that, while most of the 'power' terms can easily be read as referring to institutional or social realities—thrones, dominions, rulers, powers, the law—there are some oddities, in particular the *stoicheia.* This term occurs seven times in the New Testament. Translations include the four physical elements, the first principles of philosophy, basic religious rituals, the precepts of Jewish law, and the stars conceived as demonic powers. The most common translation in contemporary versions is 'elemental spirits'. Walter Wink notes that the English term 'element' is a formal category that can refer to the most basic constituents or principles of anything; if *stoicheia* is used similarly, this explains the variety of referents and means that context is crucial for an interpretation (Wink 1984: 67). Wink argues that *stoicheia* in Colossians 2: 8 ('See to it that no one takes you captive through philosophy and empty deceit, according to human tradition, according to the elemental spirits of the universe, and not according to Christ') refers to the philosophical search for the first elements or founding principles of the physical universe (Wink 1984: 74). In current terminology, we could speak of subatomic particles as first elements and the laws of nature as founding principles.

My suggestion, then, is that we can read our concept of the laws of nature *back* into the New Testament texts and so find support for the following theses: The laws of nature of this aeon are God's creatures. Yet, in contrast to early modern understandings of them as perfect expressions of God's will, they are fallen—not in the sense that they once were perfect and then changed, but in the sense that, while they are meant to be our servants, they are instead our masters; they do not enable humankind to live a genuinely free, loving life. Thus, the completion of Christ's work must include a radical transformation of the laws of nature such that they do permit the life that God intends.

III. Fine-Tuning, the Existence of God, and Evil

A more recent area of research that has occasioned theological speculation is referred to as the anthropic principle. A number of factors in the early universe had to be adjusted in a remarkably precise way to produce the universe we have. These factors include the mass of the universe, the strengths of the four basic forces (electromagnetism, gravitation, and the strong and weak nuclear forces) and others. Calculations show that if any of these numbers had deviated even slightly from its actual value the universe would have evolved in a radically different manner, making life as we know it—and probably life of any sort—impossible. An example of the 'fine-tuning' required: if the ratio of the strength of electromagnetism to gravity had varied by as much as one part in 10^{40} there would be no stars like our Sun (Barrow and Tipler 1986).

Many claim that this apparent fine-tuning of the universe calls for explanation. To some, it appears to provide grounds for a new argument for design. Others believe that it can be explained in scientific terms, for example, by suggesting that there are vastly many universes, either contemporaneous with our own or in succession, each of which instantiates a different set of fundamental constants. One or more of these universes would be expected to support life, and it is only in such a universe that observers would be present to raise the question of fine-tuning.

Whether or not the fine-tuning is taken as evidence for the existence of God, it has important consequences for understanding human and animal suffering. It is common to distinguish among moral, natural, and metaphysical evil, and the theological task has been to reconcile these with the assumption of the ultimate (or original) goodness of the created order. Moral evil, that is, human sin, has always been the easiest to account for. I shall focus here both on natural evil, that is, the (apparent) disorder in nature and the suffering that it causes for humans and animals, and on the closely related topic of limitation or metaphysical evil.

Augustine, over the course of his lifetime, produced an elaborate set of answers to these three interrelated problems, in all cases drawing heavily on the doctrine of creation *ex nihilo*. Unfortunately, his answer to the problem of natural evil was also dependent on an account of the human fall as a historical event and especially on the notion of the fall of the angels; both premisses are highly questionable on both biblical and scientific grounds.

A first step in providing a credible treatment of natural evil is to recognize that all purely natural evil is a simple consequence of the regular working of the laws of nature. Children fall and injure themselves because of the law of gravity; mountain-climbers freeze and people starve to death because of the laws of thermodynamics; deadly bacteria and viruses evolve by means of the same biological laws that have produced ourselves. Of course, much suffering is a result of both natural and moral evil. For example, famines are often produced by a combination of factors such as drought and war.

G. W. Leibniz was much maligned for his claim that this is the best of all possible worlds. He argued that the more we understand the interconnectedness among events the less we can imagine a world that preserves the goods of this one and eliminates the evils (*Discourse on Metaphysics* §1, in Leibniz 1998). This observation can be all the better supported in light of current science, especially by noting the *connections* that can be drawn among the laws of the various sciences, from physics to sociology. More pertinent to Leibniz's argument is the issue of fine-tuning. These calculations have led to reflections on the abstract possibility of a vast number of different sets of physical laws. These reflections, in turn, allow us to make sense of Leibniz's notion of God selecting the best of all possible worlds. Here God selects, from among a number of possible worlds, one of the incredibly small number in which the development of life would be possible.

'Metaphysical evil', in the tradition, refers to the basic fact of finitude and limitation. Metaphysical evil has regularly been seen as a condition or occasion for both natural and moral evil. Light can be shed on this ancient idea by focusing on one particular law of nature, the second law of thermodynamics, the law of entropy. Russell notes that '[e]vil is likened to a disorder, a disfunction in an organism, an obstruction to growth or an imperfection in being. Entropy refers to such disorder, measuring the dissipation of a system, the fracturing of a whole.... [T]he pain and cost of natural disasters... are rooted in the press of entropy, the relentless disintegration of form, environment, organism' (Russell 1984: 457). The constant need to replenish the human body with food and other forms of energy is the cause of much moral evil. While we may dream of a world without this constant loss and degradation of energy, Russell argues on the basis of the work of Ilya Prigogine that the second law plays a necessary catalytic role in the development of higher forms of order, particularly the development of life.

These scientific considerations give theologians additional resources for an understanding of natural evil: natural and metaphysical evil are both necessary but unwanted *by-products* of conditions necessary to fulfil God's purposes, including particularly the existence of beings who could freely return his love. One obvious condition for such beings is an orderly, regular universe. Now we can see, in addition, that human life could *only* exist in a universe that operates according to laws practically indistinguishable from those we observe.

IV. Reductionism, Providence, and Divine Action

In the years following Newton's formulation of the laws of mechanics, modern philosophers and scientists came to think of the universe as a gigantic machine. The most striking proponent of this view was Pierre Simon de Laplace, who envisioned every atom in the universe as a component in an unfailingly precise cosmic clockwork mechanism. He was not unaware of the theological implications. There is a famous story in which Napoleon is said to have asked Laplace about the role of God in his system. Laplace's reply: 'I have no need of that hypothesis.'

Laplace's response is an extreme example of a problem that has plagued theologians throughout the modern period: that confluence of scientific and philosophical factors which make an account of divine action difficult. The first of these, already mentioned, was the development of the concept of laws of nature. The second was the development of a modern form of *atomism*. This is in the first instance a scientific theory regarding the nature of matter, but the success of the scientific theory has led to a general view of reality (a metaphysical theory) to the effect that in any system, the functioning of the parts accounts for the characteristics of the whole. This metaphysical thesis is a form of *reductionism*. When atomism and reductionism are combined with the assumption that deterministic laws apply in the domain of physics, the consequence is a determinist view of the universe. That is, the laws of physics determine the behaviour of the atoms, and the atoms determine the behaviour of all larger wholes.

Determinism presents two problems. One has to do with free will. If the body is nothing but an arrangement of atoms whose behaviour is governed by the laws of physics, then how can free decisions arise? Second, if science gives a complete and adequate account of the causes of all events, where, if at all, is there room for God to act?

The simplest solution to reconcile divine action with the clockwork universe was deism, a popular option in the eighteenth century. Deists concluded that while God was the creator of the universe and author of the laws of nature, God was not involved in ongoing natural processes or in human affairs. They maintained a notion of God as the source of moral principles, but rejected the rest of positive religion.

Modern theologians who would stay within the Christian fold have found only two strategies for reconciling their accounts of divine action with the Newtonian-Laplacian world view. 'Interventionism' has generally been the doctrine of choice for conservative theologians. These theologians hold that in addition to God's creative activity, which includes ordaining the laws of nature, God occasionally violates those laws in order to bring about extraordinary events. So it is a mistake to think that the laws, once 'created', are immutable; they merely reflect God's ordinary way of working. Note that an assumption held by some contemporary Christians, that an event is an act of God only if it cannot be explained by natural laws, is a degenerate view of divine action by these standards. God works in the regular processes just as much as in miraculous interventions.

The liberals' 'immanentist' view was a reaction against both deism and the conservative theologians' view that God performs special, miraculous acts. The liberal view emphasizes the universal presence of God in the world, and God's continual, creative, and purposive activity in and through all the processes of nature and history. This view made it possible to understand progress, both evolutionary progress in the natural world and human progress, as manifestations of God's purposes.

A primary motive for emphasizing God's action *within* natural processes was the acceptance of the scientific view of the world as a closed system of natural causes, along with the judgement that a view of divine activity as intervention reflected an inferior grasp of God's intelligence and power. It suggested that God was unable to achieve all of the divine purposes though an original ordering, and that God was inconsistent in willing laws and also willing their violation. The higher view of divine action was one in which God did not need to intervene. The interpretation of divine activity in terms of miracles tended to disappear in the liberal tradition.

We find variations on these themes from Schleiermacher up through the present. Schleiermacher claimed that divine providence and the operation of causal laws entirely coincide; the word 'miracle' is just the religious word for 'event'. A more recent example is Maurice Wiles's claim that, once God is no longer needed to explain the irregularities in Newton's model of planetary motion, the problematic concept of a 'God of the gaps' is also removed. This does not mean that it is impossible to speak at all of God in relation to the natural world. Rather, 'it has made possible the reaffirmation of a more profound concept of God as the transcendent ground of there being a world at all' (Wiles 1983: 183). To speak of God acting *in history* is in fact to speak of the varying human response that is elicited by the unvarying divine presence in historical events. Some events more than others elicit the response of faith, especially the events surrounding Jesus Christ. Thus the distinction between general and special acts of God does not pertain to a difference in God, but to a difference in human perception.

Thus, the atomist, reductionist, determinist view of the universe left theologians with the unhappy alternatives of abandoning either special providence or the integrity of the scientific world order. The choice one makes here has consequences for the whole of theology. For instance, an immanentist view contributes to the anthropocentrizing of doctrine noted above and requires a theological method that avoids taking scripture as a product of divine intervention.

Fortunately a variety of developments in physics since the end of the nineteenth century have called into question the determinist world view, with its dire consequences for accounts of divine action. Quantum physics has introduced indeterminacy into the world view of physics. Quantum theory allows only for probabilistic predictions regarding classes of events, not for prediction of individual events. Most interpreters do not believe that this is merely a limit of human knowledge; rather it signifies genuine indeterminacy in nature. Thus, most physicists reject the determinism of the Newtonian world view, at least at this level.

'Quantum non-locality' refers to the peculiar fact that electrons and other subatomic entities that have once interacted continue to behave in coordinated ways, even when they are too far apart for any known causal interaction in the time available. This phenomenon radically calls into question the Newtonian picture of the universe as composed of discrete particles in motion, interacting by means of familiar physical forces.

If Newtonian determinism had strong implications for theories of divine action, these developments in quantum physics must have theological implications as well. What these implications are is still an open question (Russell et al. 2001).

A more recent development, which cuts across physics and the other natural sciences, is chaos theory. This is the study of systems whose behaviour is highly sensitive to changes in initial conditions. What this means can be illustrated with an example from classical dynamics: the movements of a billiard ball are governed in a straightforward way by Newton's laws. However, very slight differences in the angle of impact of the cue stick have greatly magnified effects after several collisions. Initial differences that make for large differences in later behaviour are too small to measure, so the system is intrinsically unpredictable. Chaotic systems are found throughout nature—in thermodynamic systems far from equilibrium, in weather patterns, and even in animal populations.

Chaos theory is relevant to discussions of divine action not because chaotic systems are causally undetermined and thus open to divine action without violation of laws of nature. Rather, the recognition of the ubiquity of chaotic systems shows the intrinsic limitations of human knowledge, and leads to the negative but important conclusion that one is usually not in a position to know that God is *not* acting in natural processes (Russell et al. 1995).

Another development throughout science with important implications for the issue of determinism and divine action is the recognition of 'top-down causation'. This calls into question the *reductionism* of the modern world view. Causal reductionism is the thesis that all causation in the hierarchy of the sciences is 'bottom-up'. However, it is now apparent that the behaviour of entities at various levels of the hierarchy of complexity cannot always be understood entirely in terms of the behaviour of their parts: it also requires attention to their interaction with non-reducible features of their environments. Thus, the state or behaviour of a higher-level system exercises top-down influences on its components.

Arthur Peacocke has used this development in scientific thought to propose new directions for understanding divine action. In his 'panentheist' view, the universe is 'in' God, and God's influence on the cosmos can then be understood by analogy to top-down causation throughout the hierarchy of natural levels (Peacocke 1993). While this proposal does not answer questions about how God affects specific events within the cosmos, it does dissolve the long-standing problem of causal determinism.

V. Evolution, Design, and the Fall

Physics and astronomy were the main scientific foci for theologians in the seventeenth and eighteenth centuries; geology and biology have been in the nineteenth and twentieth. For centuries, the biblical narrative from creation to Christ and to the projected last judgement provided the skeletal outline for accounts of natural as well as human history. For instance, the story of Noah and the flood served as a useful explanation for marine fossils found high above sea level. However, by the seventeenth century, the short span of history calculated from the Bible was being challenged from a number of directions. Although sporadic attempts to reconcile geologic history with Genesis continue up to the present, a large number of geologists, already in the eighteenth century, recognized that the flood hypothesis could not explain the growing body of knowledge regarding rock stratification and the placement of fossils. A much longer history of the Earth, prior to human history, had to be presumed.

While some contemporary opposition to evolutionary theory involves 'young earth' chronology, negative reactions in the nineteenth century to Charles Darwin's *The Origin of Species* (1859) were more often objections to the claim that humans were kin with the 'lower animals' and to the fact that natural selection provided an alternative to divine design for explaining the fit of organisms to their environments, thus undermining an important apologetic argument. Nonetheless, many theologians and other believers readily accepted the theory and have judged the changes it required in theology to be salutary rather than mere accommodation.

Evolution is a surprisingly hot issue at the beginning of the twenty-first century. Polls regularly show that a majority of North American Christians are sceptical of the macroevolutionary paradigm, and there are increasingly popular attempts to have 'intelligent design' added to school curricula. One explanation for resistance to evolutionary theory is the fact that the issue has come to be framed in terms of creation *versus* chance as an account of the origin of the human species. That the issues can be formulated in these terms is due to a defective theory of divine action that *contrasts* God's creative acts with natural processes, rather than allowing that God works through natural processes, including those that involve random events. The controversy is exacerbated by scientists and philosophers who use evolutionary theory in the popular press to argue for atheism.

Another source of resistance to evolutionary theory is the implication that there could not have been a single first couple to have committed the first sin. Biblical critics called the historicity of the first chapters of Genesis into question centuries ago, interpreting the fall as a picture of the condition of everyman and everywoman. Yet many Christians fail to distinguish our fallen condition from the Augustinian complex of (historic) first sin and inherited corruption and guilt. Thus, no first sin, no fall, no need for salvation.

VI. Neuroscience and the Human Creature

While biblical scholars and historians have long questioned whether anthropological dualism is biblical, these discussions have evidently not reached the Christian in the pew. Most Christians (according to my casual surveys) believe that dualism (humans consist of body and soul) or trichotomism (body, soul, and spirit) is essential Christian teaching. Thus, an important point of intersection between theology and science is the change that the cognitive neurosciences are making in human self-understanding. In short, all of the functions once attributed to the soul (perception, reason, emotion, moral awareness, even religious experience) are yielding to brain studies.

The rejection of dualism in favour of physicalism presents interesting opportunities for rethinking a number of theological issues. While dualism was not part of the earliest Christian teaching, most systematic theology has been written in contexts where dualism was presupposed. All that physicalism strictly requires is a change in one's view of life after death. As the notion of an immortal soul became accepted in Christianity it was combined with the very different concept of resurrection. The standard account became one in which the body dies, the soul departs, and at the general resurrection the soul receives a new body. For a physicalist there is no soul existing in the 'intermediate state' between death and resurrection.

There are, however, subtler theological implications of physicalism. Nicholas Lash notes that a doctrine of God is always correlative to anthropology (Lash 1986). When the human person is identified with a solitary mind, God tends to be conceived as a *disembodied* mind, as in the case of so-called classical theism. Consider, by contrast, the correlation between certain aspects of the Hebraic anthropology and doctrine of God. Aubrey Johnson emphasizes an aspect of the Hebraic conception of personhood that contrasts sharply with modern individualism (Johnson 1961). For moderns, individuals are thought to be 'self-contained' in two senses: The first is that they are what they are apart from their relationships. The second is the idea that the real self—the soul or mind or ego—is somehow contained within the body. In contrast, the Hebraic personality was thought to be extended in subtle ways throughout the community by means of speech and other forms of communication. 'In Israelite thought the individual, as a [*nephesh*] or centre of power capable of indefinite extension, is never a mere isolated unit' (Johnson 1961: 7). Johnson uses this conception of personhood to elucidate various modes of God's presence. *Ruach*, Spirit, is an extension of Yahweh's personality. Hence God is *genuinely* present in God's messengers (the angels), in God's word, and in God's prophets when they are moved by God's Spirit. '[T]he prophet, in functioning, was held to be more than Yahweh's "representative"; for the time being he was an active "Extension" of Yahweh's Personality and, as such, *was* Yahweh "in Person"' (Johnson 1961: 33). This understanding of God's presence is crucial for understanding the later development of trinitarian theology and Christology.

Questions that often arise in connection with a physicalist account of humans suggest that the questioner is assuming that the divinity of Christ is somehow connected with his soul. Deny the existence of human souls in general and this is tantamount to denying Christ's divinity. However, the assumption lurking behind this question conflicts with the Chalcedonian conclusion that Jesus is both fully divine and fully human. A Christology consistent with physicalism requires attention to the doctrine of the Trinity as well.

There has always been tension in trinitarian thought between those who emphasize the unity of God and those who emphasize the three-ness. In the eyes of one, the others appear to verge on tri-theism; in the eyes of the other, on unitarianism. An alternative approach to now-popular social trinitarianism emphasizes that the word 'person' in formulations of the doctrine of the Trinity has shifted its meaning. Whereas it now refers to an individual rational agent, the Latin *persona* from which it was derived referred to masks worn by actors and, by extension, to the roles they played. Consequently, Robert Jenson argues that in order to understand the origin of the understanding of God as triune, Christians need to 'attend to the plot of the biblical narrative turning on these two events [the exodus and resurrection], and to the *dramatis personae* who appear in them and carry that plot' (Jenson 2000: 716). Here we see how we are led to speak of God as Father, Son, and Spirit. '[T]hroughout scripture we encounter *personae* of God's story with his people who are neither simply the same as the story's Lord nor yet other than he. They are precisely *dramatis dei personae*, the personal carriers of a drama that is God's own reality' (Jenson 2000: 716).

With this understanding, we can say that there is one God, Israel's LORD. God at work in the world and in the human community is Spirit; the Hebrew word *ruach* suggests not a substance but an event. God at work (as Spirit) in Jesus is Messiah, incarnate Word, Son of God. This 'Spirit Christology' sees the Holy Spirit as the divine aspect of the person of Christ. While Spirit Christology can, perhaps, be reconciled with a three-person account of the Trinity, it accords more easily with a oneness trinitarianism.

An equally important doctrine to rethink in light of physicalism is the doctrine of salvation. What might theology be like today, and how might Christian history have gone differently, if physicalism had predominated rather than dualism? Much of the Christian spiritual tradition would be different. There would be no notion of care of the soul as the point of Christian disciplines—no concept of depriving the body so the soul might flourish. As feminist thinkers have said, dualist anthropology too easily leads to disparagement of the body and all that goes with being embodied. Without the Neoplatonic notion of the goal of life as preparing the soul for its proper abode in heaven, would Christians have devoted more attention to working for God's reign on earth? Would Jesus' teachings be regarded as a blueprint for that society? Would the creeds *not* have skipped from birth to death, leaving out his teaching and faithful life? Would Christians see a broader, richer role for Jesus Messiah than facilitator of forgiveness of sins? If Christians had been focusing more, throughout all of these centuries, on following Jesus' teachings about sharing, and loving our enemies at least enough so as not to kill them, how different might world politics be today? What *would* Christians have been doing these past two thousand years if there were no such things as souls to save?

REFERENCES

AQUINAS, ST THOMAS (1975). *Summa Theologiae*. London: Blackfriars.

BARROW, JOHN D., and TIPLER, FRANK J. (1986). *The Anthropic Cosmological Principle*. Oxford: Clarendon.

Buckley, Michael J. (2004). *Denying and Disclosing God: The Ambiguous Progress of Modern Atheism.* New Haven: Yale University.

Copleston, Frederic, SJ (1950). *A History of Philosophy,* ii. *Medieval Philosophy: From Augustine to Duns Scotus.* Mahwah: Paulist.

Darwin, Charles (1859). *On the Origin of Species by Means of Natural Selection, or the Preservation of Favoured Races in the Struggle for Life.* London: John Murray.

Davies, Paul (1992). *The Mind of God: The Scientific Basis for a Rational World.* New York: Simon and Schuster.

Dyson, Freeman J. (1988). *Infinite in All Directions.* New York: Harper and Row.

Hartt, Julian (1982). 'Creation and Providence'. In P. C. Hodgson and R. H. King (eds.), *Christian Theology: An Introduction to its Traditions and Tasks,* Philadelphia: Fortress.

Hawking, Stephen W. (1988). *A Brief History of Time.* London: Bantam.

Jenson, Robert W. (2000). 'Trinity'. In Adrian Hastings et al. (eds.), *The Oxford Companion to Christian Thought: Intellectual, Spiritual, and Moral Horizons of Christianity,* Oxford: Oxford University Press.

Johnson, Aubrey R. (1961). *The One and the Many in the Israelite Conception of God.* 2nd edn. Cardiff: University of Wales Press.

Lash, Nicholas (1986). *Easter in Ordinary: Reflections on Human Experience and the Knowledge of God.* Charlottesville: University of Virginia Press.

Leibniz, Gottfried Wilhelm (1998). *Philosophical Texts.* Oxford: Oxford University Press.

Linde, Andrei D. (1983). 'The New Inflationary Universe Scenario'. In G. W. Gibbons et al. (eds.), *The Very Early Universe,* Cambridge: Cambridge University Press.

McMullin, Ernan (1981). 'How Should Cosmology Relate to Theology?'. In A. R. Peacocke (ed.), *The Sciences and Theology in the Twentieth Century,* Notre Dame: University of Notre Dame Press.

Pannenberg, Wolfhart (1968). *Jesus—God and Man.* Philadelphia: Westminster.

Peacocke, Arthur R. (1993). *Theology for a Scientific Age: Being and Becoming—Natural, Divine, and Human.* Minneapolis: Fortress.

Russell, Robert J. (1984). 'Entropy and Evil'. *Zygon* 19/4: 449–68.

—— (1993). 'Finite Creation without a Beginning: The Doctrine of Creation in Relation to Big Bang and Quantum Cosmologies'. In Russell et al. (eds.), *Quantum Cosmology and the Laws of Nature: Scientific Perspectives on Divine Action,* Vatican City: The Vatican Observatory Foundation.

—— (1994). 'Cosmology from Alpha to Omega'. *Zygon* 29/4: 557–77.

Russell, Robert J., Murphy, Nancey, and Peacocke, Arthur R. (eds.) (1995). *Chaos and Complexity: Scientific Perspectives on Divine Action.* Vatican City: The Vatican Observatory Foundation.

—— et al. (eds.) (2001). *Quantum Mechanics: Scientific Perspectives on Divine Action.* Vatican City: The Vatican Observatory Foundation.

Stout, Jeffrey (1981). *The Flight from Authority: Religion, Morality and the Quest for Autonomy.* Notre Dame: University of Notre Dame Press.

Welch, Claude (1972). *Protestant Thought in the Nineteenth Century,* i. New Haven: Yale University Press.

Wiles, Maurice (1983). 'Religious Authority and Divine Action'. In O. C. Thomas (ed.), *God's Activity in the World: The Contemporary Problem,* Chico: Scholars.

Wink, Walter (1984). *Naming the Powers: The Language of Power in the New Testament.* Philadelphia: Fortress.

Suggested Reading

Barbour, Ian G. (1966). *Issues in Science and Religion.* New York: Harper and Row.

Buckley (2004).

Davies (1992).

Lindberg, David, and Numbers, Ronald L. (eds.) (1986). *God and Nature: Historical Essays on the Encounter between Christianity and Science.* Berkeley and Los Angeles: University of California Press.

Murphy, Nancey (2005). *Bodies and Souls, or Spirited Bodies?* Cambridge: Cambridge University Press.

Murphy, Nancey, and Ellis, G. F. R. (1996). *On the Moral Nature of the Universe: Theology, Cosmology, and Ethics.* Minneapolis: Fortress.

Peacocke (1993).

Peters, Ted, Russell, Robert J., and Welker, Michael (eds.) (2002). *Resurrection: Theological and Scientific Assessments.* Grand Rapids: Eerdmans.

Rolston, Holmes (1987). *Science and Religion: A Critical Survey.* New York: Random House.

Russell (1993).

Russell, R. J., Stoeger, William R., and Coyne, George V. (eds.) (1988). *Physics, Philosophy and Theology: A Common Quest for Understanding.* Vatican City: The Vatican Observatory Foundation.

—— et al. (1995).

—— et al. (1999). *Neuroscience and the Person: Scientific Perspectives on Divine Action.* Vatican City: The Vatican Observatory Foundation.

—— et al. (2001).

CHAPTER 31

THE ARTS

WILLIAM A. DYRNESS

In the last two centuries Christian theologians have revived a conversation on the role of art and aesthetics in theology that had been eclipsed during the Reformation. Many medieval thinkers saw the arts as theological practices that were intimately related to worship. Music, architecture, altarpieces, and, later, smaller devotional images, were understood to communicate the presence of God. The world as God's creation, the incarnation of Christ in human form, and the reading and interpretation of scripture all stimulated the practices of art and literature.

All this changed at the Reformation. The Reformers did not object to art objects in themselves but to the use to which these objects had been put, and, especially, the religious implications of such uses. Luther was not opposed to the use of art even in the church, but insisted that images had no religious power: the believer trusted God alone for salvation. Once faith was properly fixed on God, images could be used for teaching and enjoyment, though Luther did not spend much time reflecting positively on the role of imagery in the Christian life or worship. Calvin reflected more constructively on how worship should be arranged, though he insisted that imagery could not convey spiritual reality. Only the word of God, preached and heard, was capable of constituting God's people into the body of Christ. Art was a gift of God, but since it only appealed to the emotions, it was of no use in teaching and edifying believers. At the same time Calvin believed that the events of creation and redemption constituted a drama of the highest order, in which humans were invited to participate as players. Creation itself was a theatre of the glory of God. These emphases suggested new ways of reflecting on art and its relation to theology. During the last two hundred years in particular, theologians have explored these new possibilities even as they have revisited medieval conversations.

This chapter will explore these modern discussions. Exactly how the arts are thought to relate to God varies widely, as we will see, but all the writers we explore agree that aesthetic reality incorporates a critical component of our created life and can not only contribute to spiritual health, but may, in some sense, reflect or embody God's presence. Art and aesthetics will be used here in the broad sense, including both object and experience.

It may be helpful to place views relating art and theology on a spectrum. Beginning on the left, one might describe theologians who have privileged symbols or aesthetic impulses as either deriving from or dependent on God, or some transcendent ground; those in the centre want to hold together the symbol and the transcendent ground (or the natural and the subjective); and those on the right believe that art objects can only model or reflect theological truth. One might say that, on the left, theological meaning is *intensive*, suggesting contemplation; while, on the right, meaning is *extensive*, stimulating faithful practice. One focuses on God's immanence, the other on divine transcendence. The groups that follow provide a general overview of the range of views along this spectrum—they are meant to be suggestive rather than definitive. While we will suggest strengths and weaknesses of these views, the aim is to understand them as viable theological options and assess their significance for systematic theology.

I. Theology and Aesthetics after Kant

The theologians considered in this first section reflect the influence of the German Enlightenment philosopher Immanuel Kant. Kant's major contribution in this field was to argue that knowledge is constructed from the perceptions given in our experience and the shaping power of our imagination. From this he drew two conclusions that influenced how theologians thought about art. First, since God does not appear in our experience, we cannot have true knowledge of him: our experience of God had to be mediated. Second, our experience of art and beauty is a matter of taste which is an expression of feeling. Our judgement about beauty is subjective rather than objective, even if we mean it to have universal validity.

The theologian who first followed up these Kantian insights in thinking about aesthetics and theology was Friedrich Schleiermacher. Raised in a strong Moravian environment, Schleiermacher had come to understand faith in a deeply emotional way. When he came to Berlin in 1796, he was dismayed to encounter artists and writers who had no interest in religion. In 1799 he published his famous speeches *On Religion*, in which he sought to show that these artists' understanding of beauty was a kind of implicit faith in God. In the third speech, he appeals to their aesthetic experience. Encountering a great work of art, 'the sense of the universe opens up, in a moment as if through an immediate inner illumination, and surprises a person with its splendor' (Schleiermacher 1996: 68). Perhaps, he tells these cultured despisers, since religion and art stand together as kindred beings, the artistic treatment of the outer world can reflect the divine.

As Schleiermacher later developed these ideas it became clear that aesthetics was much more than an apologetic strategy for him. Indeed, the fundamental impulse to knowledge, he was to argue in his *Dialectic* (1814), was aesthetic in nature. Though, following Kant, he believed that God could not be simply an object of knowledge, some such transcendent reality must be assumed as the basis of all thinking and willing. And since this is so, the basic shaping of knowledge was an 'artwork [*Kunstwerk*]', and the picture one forms is 'art [*Kunst*]' (Schleiermacher 1839: 12). Even before knowledge there is this prior aesthetic impulse, reflected in what Schleiermacher called an 'image [*Bild*]', even before it passes over into language and becomes 'signs [*Zeichen*]' (Schleiermacher 1839: 41). The basic impulse to knowing and willing for Schleiermacher was aesthetic in character in that it was based on a sense of dependence on unconditioned reality that issues in feelings and perceptions.

Knowledge not only begins with an aesthetic sense, it also finds its highest expression in aesthetic objects. He understood human consciousness to be a kind of organ by which the absolute comes to expression. Individuals in their creativity can become mediators of God's reality in the same way that the unified system of nature is a kind of 'symbol' of God. These ideas come to early expression in his *Christmas Eve Dialogue* (1805), in which the celebrants recognize they are bound together in the joy they share over the Redeemer's birth. Such experiences suggested to Schleiermacher that human life could become, both individually and communally, a kind of ethical work of art, displaying the Christian life in its purest form.

Even if Schleiermacher avoided pantheism directly, the being of God and the world are so closely correlated that the freedom of God, or of the creature for that matter, seems curtailed.[1] Commentators have wondered whether history, for Schleiermacher, is simply an internal development of this relationship between creature and creator and whether anything genuinely new can intervene. But Schleiermacher advanced the discussion by arguing that creativity is fundamental to human knowing and willing. Though he referred to this sense as 'feeling', he did not mean simply emotions, but the pre-theoretical sense of being dependent on God. On this basis he could go on to develop a deep understanding of the creative process as fundamental both to the human person and, even more, to the believer.

If Schleiermacher could be said to have an heir in his view of art's relation to God, it would surely be Paul Tillich, perhaps the most prominent theologian of art

[1] Though earlier he was influenced by Schelling's identity philosophy, Schleiermacher later broke with this implicit pantheism, arguing that God could not be the absolute source of thought without being transcendent over the world (Schleiermacher 1839: 186; Redeker 1973: 105–6).

in the twentieth century. If Schleiermacher proceeded from our relation to God to an understanding of art and creativity, Tillich went the other direction, from reflection on the meaning of art to seeing its relation to God. In part this reflected their different biographies: Schleiermacher went from a background of deep faith to a later exposure to art and artists, whereas Tillich's experience with modern art during the first World War was seminal in the development of his theological ideas. As he says of this period: 'The visual arts became my hobby in the trenches of the First World War.... they became for me a realm of human creativity from which I derived categories both for my philosophical and my theological thought' (1987*a*: 126). He proceeded initially to develop these categories by an analysis of culture (Tillich 1987*b*: 22). Religion he defined as the 'experience of the unconditioned... of absolute reality' (Tillich 1987*b*: 24).[2] Since art, when it is worthy, expresses human meaning, it is an indicator of the spiritual situation of a given culture, and therefore it is essentially religious.

But how does art participate in what Tillich called the ground of being? Here his famous notion of 'symbol' is key. Unlike 'signs' which point to reality, symbols participate in the power of what they represent. As he put it: 'They open up dimensions of reality which cannot be grasped any other way' (Tillich 1987*a*: 133). Art as symbolic of this religious ground can help us understand that we are grasped by the power of being in a way that parallels the function of symbolic statements like 'Christ is the Saviour'.

Tillich's study of art gave him the vocabulary to express these ideas. He believed the notion of 'style' was key to understanding these artistic symbols. For an encounter with style is 'an encounter of man with his world, in which the whole man in all dimensions of his being is involved' (Tillich 1987*a*: 129). Here he saw in the progression from naturalism to idealism and finally to expressionism a growing freedom from the encountered reality. The last of these styles is the highest, in that the artist does not simply represent the natural world but shows something that cannot be expressed in any other way. This progression began, he believed, with Cezanne, whose still lifes 'embody a cosmic power which is religiously far superior to sentimental Jesus portraits' (Tillich 1987*a*: 133). Of all styles, Tillich preferred expressionism, because he saw in it a 'strong religious passion... striving... after expression' (Tillich 1987*b*: 30).

Tillich believed that the production of specifically religious symbols is important, providing a counterweight to seeing culture as simply secular. These symbols resonate with the religious meaning that is found in the art of a culture. In both cases, however, it is the religious meaning that is important, not the religious or symbolic forms (Tillich 1987*b*: 35–6).

[2] He later came to define this experience famously as 'ultimate concern about the ground and meaning of being', which in his *Systematic Theology* he admits is 'rather near' to Schleiermacher's 'feeling of absolute dependence' (Tillich 1951: 42).

This final statement indicates both the strength and weakness of Tillich's programme. On the one hand no one has done more to underline the 'religious' dimension of culture, arguing that cultural forms express deep concerns which are often implicitly religious. In some sense then it is wrong to speak of 'secular culture' as though cultural forms could exist apart from the value commitments of the people who make up that culture. But at the same time Tillich's tendency to privilege the meaning over the form—reflecting his Protestant concern over idolatry—issues in a symbolism without cognitive traction and a vagueness that finally undermines definitive meaning.

II. Neo-Romantic Aesthetics

For both Schleiermacher and Tillich, aesthetic language is essentially theological: the aesthetic impulse or the symbol are both grounded in God's being. The figures to be addressed in the present section believe that art has theological significance in that it draws one toward God. We refer to these as neo-Romantic or neo-medieval in that they continue the Romantic quest to participate in the transcendent, and they frequently revisit much of the medieval discussion of God and beauty. Rather than privileging the experience of the symbol or aesthetic impulse, as Schleiermacher and Tillich did, these privilege the divine subject to which the symbol or story draws us, and who is the personal source of its power. The art object and practice of art are not thought of as theological in any direct sense. What is important is the divine joy and beauty these might evoke.

C. S. Lewis, though not a theologian or a philosopher of art, was one of the most widely read and influential writers on these topics in the last century. He also resisted association with Romanticism, a movement which he believed represented a '*Sehnsucht* awakened by the past, the distant and the imagined, but not believed, supernatural' (Lewis 1967: 16). Lewis's own experiences of longing were more fleeting and elusive, perhaps because, unlike the Romantic poets, he had a greater sense of God's transcendence. Owen Barfield has said that Lewis 'in his theological utterances always emphasized the chasm between the creator and creatures, rather than anything in the nature of participation' (Barfield 1989: 111). But in the end Lewis could say of his experiences of desire, 'I still cannot help thinking... that the experiences themselves contained, from the very first, a wholly good element. Without them my conversion would [to Christianity] have been more difficult' (Lewis 1967: 23).

But what are these experiences to which he refers? And in what sense are they aesthetic? Or religious? Lewis frequently recalled the first experience he remembers, when he was about 6, a sensation of an 'enormous bliss of Eden... of desire' (Lewis

1955: 19). He also described other glimpses that carried unspeakable desire: the green hills of his childhood, an island, music that ravishes the soul, stories of faeries. But desire for what? With his conversion, Lewis came to believe that this desire was ultimately for the vision of God. But as he said in the essay 'Transposition', in experiences of this kind this higher desire has been 'transposed' onto lower ones. Art, like sex, can convey a joy that cannot be explained merely in aesthetic or erotic terms—although it surely has an aesthetic or erotic side. At present, our desire for the beatific vision cannot simply displace our desire for beauty, sex, even food. But what if every transposition is the reverse side of a higher fulfilment? What if this provides a background for understanding the theological virtue of hope? Of this vision of God, he concluded tellingly, our present embodied life may be the diminution, the symbol (Lewis 1965: 86–90).

The human experience of longing or hunger served as the starting point for Lewis's understanding of art and religion. He was convinced that if the experiences of this world give rise to longings which nothing in this world can satisfy, satisfaction must lie outside the world. Such longings are 'news from a country we have not yet visited' (Lewis 1965: 98). So the images and stories he shapes are meant as bearers of such news. What is important is that these images, replete with their aesthetic attractions, participate in the higher programme of God's drawing people to himself, just as our lower feelings find their fulfilment in their ('sacramental') participation in higher ones (Lewis 1965: 83).

Lewis by no means disparaged the role of the image or the power of the aesthetic, nor did he belittle the emotions connected with sex and food. Scott Carnell argues that, unlike T. S. Eliot, Lewis seemed to exult in the pleasures of the senses (Carnell 1974: 129–30). Lewis treasured the images that he shaped; he believed myth to be one of the only ways that the fallen imagination could be healed. Indeed he argues that the aesthetic quality of stories, as a shaper of the imagination, is their most important feature.

Lewis did not give much attention to his work as 'art'; he frequently said he was a writer who happened to be a Christian. He did not intend to make any contribution to 'Christian aesthetics'—something he doubted even existed. But he felt that his myth-making was getting at something that was really there. But this something, this longed-for paradise, existed on the other side of the door. Meanwhile we live in the world of diminution and symbol. This 'knobbly' world is not necessarily an illusion, as Plato said; it is a figure of paradise, but it is still irreparably other. Art can speak of this region, even, like sex, stimulate our desire for it, but in the end it cannot participate in it.

Orthodox theologian David Bentley Hart believes, like Lewis, that art, beauty, and image speak of something that is really there. While he is also no Romantic, he believes with Lewis that desire is constitutive of our being: 'Desire is the energy of our movement and so of our being' (Hart 2003: 190). And at a deep level, desire corresponds to the call of God. But unlike Lewis he insists that beauty speaks directly of God because it expresses the participation of all things in God. Hart has relatively little to say about the practices and objects of art; but he shapes an aesthetic framework with significant implications for art-making as well as for the broader practices of Christian living.

Hart's argument centres on the question of beauty and its place in the Christian tradition. Beauty is important, he believes, because it 'adheres to every moment of the Christian story' and is one with its truth (Hart 2003: 4). In fact, he believes the Christian faith is ethical because it is first aesthetic, which for him means that it opens one up to love and knowledge. It invites a desire that is moral because it is *not* disinterested (Hart 2003: 15); it is poetic before it is rational (Hart 2003: 132–3). Hart's discussion—so at odds with the Kantian tradition of disinterested beauty—connects beauty with both morality and knowledge. For him, beauty is always interested because it is analogical, that is, intimately related to God as its source and end. As a result, it is objective, since it is given in creation and thus has phenomenological priority. It is the true form of distance, filling and embracing intervals with that plenitude of love and peace which has its source in God. And for this reason beauty evokes desire, eros and agape together, that 'delights in the distance of otherness' (Hart 2003: 20).

This participatory view of beauty leads Hart to develop a unique view of symbolism, one that has great significance for art and faith. He proposes a symbolism that arrests the surface force of the aesthetic in order to disclose the depths in which it participates—one that is more important for what it does than what it is (Hart 2003: 24–35). By contrast, he notes, Tillich's symbolism does nothing to clarify the concrete but reduces it to abstractions—which Hart suggests is no less idolatrous than the belief that God's gracious acts in history are really acts (Hart 2003: 27). 'Christian faith abounds in particularities... which cannot be dissolved into universal truths of human experience.... The "symbol," extracted from the complexities of its many contexts, is... the paralysis of beauty' (Hart 2003: 27–8).

Hart seeks an alternative rhetoric, and a fuller vision, than that which has resulted from the abyss which he believes Kant opened. 'The Christian story', he writes in words that Lewis would approve, 'is the true story of being, and so speaks of that end toward which all human thought and every natural act are originally oriented' (Hart 2003: 31). Hart proceeds to sketch out a systematic theology that is grounded in God's works, which are 'perfectly expressive signs of his delight' (Hart 2003: 131). Christ is the form that persuades, made visible in the resurrection, and brightened by the Spirit (Hart 2003: 147, 335, 203). The Trinity is a perichoresis of love, infinite and—contrary to much recent discussion of God—apathetic, precisely so that God can be 'the fullness of love dwelling within our very being' (Hart 2003: 166).

Over against typical Protestant theology and unlike Lewis, it is the gaze, not insight, that controls Hart's theology. He wants to reverse Kant's revolution. He wants to turn away from the subject toward the 'sun of the good' (Hart 2003: 137). He wants a gaze that positively embraces the splendour of God's gifts. 'And what one sees and hears, if desire seeks it, is the creature's participation in God, the fountainhead of being' (Hart 2003: 144). But desire seeks often the wrong object; the gaze can be controlling. A weakness of Hart's bracing vision is that the creature seems drawn toward the light as a fact and not simply as an invitation. Sin is merely the suppression of the gift, something which dulls the senses (Hart 2003: 268). What then is the reason for the evil so visible on every hand? And what is its aesthetic potential?

III. Neo-Thomist Theology of Beauty

While discussions of Thomas Aquinas appear throughout Hart's work, it is a third set of thinkers who have done more to bring medieval discussions to life. We refer to these as neo-Thomist theologians of art and beauty because they represent the tradition of thought that goes back to that period. Rather than focusing on the beauty and joy that humans desire as Hart and Lewis did, these thinkers, taking their cue from the incarnation and sacraments, focus on the object of beauty itself as carrier and extension of God's presence. In the object itself, in the form, the visible and invisible are fused in a way that can mediate the presence of God—the object itself can be theophanic in a sense neither Lewis or Hart nor subsequent theologians in their tradition would allow. The most obvious exception would appear to be role of the icon for Hart, though, interestingly, he does not engage in any extended discussion of this in his study.

In the Middle Ages the arts existed only as 'craft' (*ars*) or as the liberal arts taught at the university. Nevertheless, discussions of beauty and what we call aesthetics were prominent and have been revisited in the last century. Thomas Aquinas held that goodness and beauty are related. He wrote: 'goodness expresses perfection, which is something desirable, and hence it expresses something final' (*ST* 1a. 5, 1 ad 1, in Aquinas 1975). Beauty and goodness are fundamentally identical, he went on to say, in that they are based upon the same form of the good, but they differ logically. He writes:

> Goodness properly relates to appetite (goodness being what all things desire), . . . on the other hand, beauty relates to a cognitive power, for those things are said to be beautiful which please when seen [*id quod visum placet*]. Hence beauty consists in due proportion, for the senses delight in things duly proportioned, as in what is like them—because the sense too is a sort of reason, as is every cognitive power. (*ST* 1a. 5, 4 ad 1)

In this famous definition Thomas connects the good (and thus morality) with desire and appetite, but designates beauty as a cognitive power. Seeing colours, shapes, and forms is recognized as a kind of knowing, involving a cognitive process in its own right. As Umberto Eco explains: 'Aesthetic knowledge has the same kind of complexity as intellectual knowledge, because it has the same object, namely, the substantial reality of something' (Eco 1986: 73).

The most substantial modern exponent of these medieval ideas is the French philosopher Jacques Maritain. In an early essay *Art and Scholasticism* (1920), Maritain noted that in the Middle Ages, 'The sphere of making is the sphere of Art, in the most universal sense of this word' (Maritain 1962: 8). The end of making is inherent in the work; everything done is done for the sake of the work. So though art belongs to the intellectual order, it is 'a habitus of the practical intellect' (Maritain 1962: 12). Following certain fixed rules, what Maritain calls a 'lived participation in logic' (Maritain 1962: 49), the artisan of that day created more beautiful things, while 'he adored himself less' (Maritain 1962: 22). This beauty was an object of intelligence but it was also a reflection of divine beauty. Though made *from* the creation, it drew its soul from *beyond* the created order.

Later, Maritain drew out many of the implications of this early work. Art, he noted, is 'the creative or producing, work-making activity of the human mind' (Maritain 1954: 3). When there is a genuine interaction between humanity and nature, beauty is involved (Maritain 1954: 4–5). The critical notion of the self in western art, he claims, emerged in relation to theological formulations of the person of Christ. The self first was seen as object in the revelation of Christ's divine self (especially in the great councils that defined that self), then humanity came to understand the self as subject, and finally it came to see the creative subjectivity of the person as poet or artist (Maritain 1954: 20). So even in the modern promotion of the self, the artist cannot escape the influence of Christ. Modern art then brings with it a new potential by which the inner meaning of things is grasped through the interaction with the artist's self: both are manifest in the work (Maritain 1954: 25).

This theological grounding of the artist's work, both in creation and in the selfhood of Christ, makes possible a striking view of the process of art-making. Working out a lived logic (*habitus*), the artist ferrets out the inner workings of nature, which is 'in its own way the labor of divine creation' (Maritain 1954: 50). This knowledge-with things Maritain termed 'con-naturality'. That is, the soul of the artist seeks itself by 'communicating with things', effecting knowledge through 'affective union' (Maritain 1954: 83).

Beauty emerges out of this 'connatural' knowledge of the self and things. It 'spills over or spreads everywhere, and is everywhere diversified' (Maritain 1954: 124). Notice that beauty emerges from the work—from below, as it were, not from above. Even if it reflects the radiance of the transcendent, it is a spontaneous product of the affective union of self and nature which comes to expression in the work. This unique union suggested the promise of modern art, but also its peril. Modern art's temptation, Maritain believed, was to favour the anti-rational rather than the super-rational, to seek beauty at the expense of the beauty of the human form, or to choose the self over the thing seen—distortions amply illustrated in the history of modern art.

This focus on the form as carrier of deep meaning is picked up also by the best known of the later twentieth-century Catholic writers on aesthetics, Han Urs von Balthasar, especially in his seven-volume work, *The Glory of the Lord: A Theological Aesthetics* (1961–9). While Hart acknowledges his dependence on Balthasar—he calls his own work a '*marginalium* on some page' of Balthasar (Hart 2003: 29)—he does not give the beauty of form the centrality that it has for Balthasar, nor does Hart share with Balthasar the latter's admiration for Karl Barth. In fact Balthasar takes the starting point for his discussion of beauty from Barth's treatment of glory in *Church Dogmatics* II/1 (Barth 1957). In these pages one sees the central themes of Balthasar's work. God's being is eternal in glory, Barth claims. It is God's dignity 'to make himself conspicuous and everywhere apparent as the One he is' (Barth 1957: 641). God's glory 'expresses itself in the force of his appearance and activity, in the impression that he makes on others. *Kabod* is light, both as source and radiance' (Barth 1957: 642). Barth goes on to stress that this radiance 'reaches all other beings and permeates them' (Barth 1957: 646), though he characteristically adds that we must wait for this revelation. 'The creature has no voice of its own' (Barth 1957: 648). Still, beauty is the unique form and 'explanation' that this glory takes and which awakens joy. If this is missing, Barth asks, 'What becomes of the evangelical element of the evangel?' (Barth 1957: 655). In words that particularly anticipate Balthasar, Barth stresses that the persuasive, convincing form of God is to be seen in Jesus Christ. 'What is reflected in this determination of the relationship between the divine and human nature in Jesus Christ is the form, the beautiful form of the divine being' (Barth 1957: 664), and the Son in his relation to the Father is the 'eternal archetype and prototype of God's glory in his externalization' (Barth 1957: 667).

Barth's Protestant reticence in the end places him closer to figures we will explore later. For him the form of beauty is not self-evident, it is only given to us via the cross and resurrection (Barth 1957: 665–6). Barth knew, moreover, that the danger of aestheticism was real; the study of beauty is, after all, a 'parenthesis' to the study of theology (Barth 1957: 653, 666; cf. Viladesau 1999: 26–9). Meanwhile, as we await the final revelation of beauty we are surrounded by the earthly form of beauty, the church (Barth 1957: 676).

Balthasar finds inspiration in Barth's theology, but corrects the fundamental weakness of Barth's tradition: its denial of the analogy of being. Balthasar thus begins his reflection by recovering a Thomist doctrine of being. That is, the form appears beautiful only because the delight it arouses is 'founded upon the fact that, in it, the truth and goodness of the depths of reality itself are manifested and bestowed' (Balthasar 1982–9: i. 118). Moreover, the beauty of this form is visible in the epiphany of God in salvation history, and supremely in the incarnation of the form of God in Christ (Balthasar 1982–9: i. 124). This theological aesthetics Balthasar develops in two senses. One is a theory of vision, which is a 'theory about the perception of the form of God's self-revelation'; the other is a theory of rapture which is a theory about the incarnation of God's glory and 'the consequent elevation of man to participate in that glory' (Balthasar 1982–9: i. 125). The former is fundamental theology; the latter is dogmatic theology. This venturing forth of God and the human return to God constitute the very core of Balthasar's theology. It is a fully human act of encounter through the senses, because 'in Christianity God appears to man right in the midst of worldly reality' (Balthasar 1982–9: i. 365); and it is an objective revelation in Christ precisely in its quality as form, 'the perfection of the form of the world' (Balthasar 1982–9: 1.432).

Balthasar's consistent focus on biblical material—here too he follows Barth—disciplines his reliance on the Greek philosophical tradition, though both contribute to his theology. From these materials he fashions an aesthetic theory (the power of beauty speaks of the divine beauty in which it is grounded) and a theological aesthetics (the highest art is the revelation of God in history especially as seen in the form of Christ). Unlike Maritain, who focuses on the act of creative intuition, Balthasar believes the beauty of God is discovered in the act of reception and adoration, which for Balthasar is not only the centre of theology but 'also the heart of the individual's existential situation' (Viladesau 1999: 33). However striking, Balthasar's formulation bears all the marks of its twentieth-century European origin and of the heavy hand of philosophy from Plato to Heidegger. For those at home in such a context, Balthasar has much to offer, but for those accustomed to reading scripture in other contexts, the attraction may be diminished.

One who makes use of this Catholic imagination in a wholly different setting is the Hispanic American theologian Roberto Goizueta. Using the terminology of liberation theology, Goizueta argues that the true end of the person is an intersubjective 'praxis' (Goizueta 1995: 81–5). The key category for understanding such experience, which Goizueta proposes in contrast to liberation theology, is not transformation but aesthetics—the former a by-product, the latter of the essence of human action. Here Goizueta makes use of the Mexican philosopher José Vasconcelos, who argued (over against the positivism of Comte) that true understanding involves the 'empathic fusion' between subject and object in order to enjoy and celebrate (Goizueta 1995: 91–2). We are to work out the oneness that we share with God (and which God shares with the world) by exploring those forms of life which are fused with action and motivated by love, which is the law of aesthetics (Goizueta 1995: 92). Like art-making, rather than dealing with the general and abstract, such practices deal with particularities.

Goizueta goes on in subsequent chapters to ground this praxis in the religious popular culture which expresses Latino religiosity. Processions and images connect these people with the aesthetic dimension of life, as an end and not simply an instrument to other ends. The goal is that all human action take on the character of a liturgical celebration in which both affective and domestic life—and the marginalized and 'useless' persons who inhabit these worlds—are affirmed. 'In daily life we learn to value human relationships as ends, and therefore as liberating and empowering' (Goizueta 1995: 113). Though the aesthetic is prior, liberation follows.

Here is a rich and subtle application of important themes of the Catholic tradition: the theological and aesthetic nature of human relations and the priority of love in a new setting that reflects the changing and diverse nature of the contemporary world. But some may wonder whether the impulse to celebrate the quotidian and popular expressions of faith, though rightly seen as intrinsically aesthetic, do not risk diluting the salvific presence of God and the special narrative shape of this presence.

IV. Protestant Theologies of Art

The Protestant attempts to reflect theologically on the arts, to which we now turn, uniformly reflect the desire to preserve the particularity of God's special work of salvation. Their worry is not about the connection between aesthetics and theology—they too want to root aesthetics in the good creation and gracious acts of God. But their convictions about sin and fallenness lead them to believe that one cannot simply read off God's radiance from the world as it is. Indeed, they worry with Barth that one may well be led astray by the splendours one sees there. We will explore first those who continue the Reformed tradition of Calvin, and, second, those who seek to understand art and aesthetics in terms of some of the newer insights into the trinitarian character of God. These all share the Reformers' suspicion of medieval notions of participation and analogy and therefore see art as fundamentally metaphoric and illuminating of, rather than transparent to, the divine presence. The heirs of Calvin's theology continue that theologian's emphasis on the priority of the preached word and its unique ability to convey the transformative power of God's actions. Preaching for these is theophanic in a way art could never be. Calvin, however, had a robust sense of the power of images used in preaching and of the dramatic course of God's redemptive working in creation and history—which he often called a theatre for God's glory (Dyrness 2004). These emphases have continued to influence discussions of art and theology in this tradition.

The language of beauty was at the centre of the massive theological work of Jonathan Edwards because it expressed for him the inner nature of God. Edwards believed that the loving nature of God from eternity desired to communicate the 'excellencies' of this nature. Creation itself is an expression of this fullness and beauty, and therefore the elements of creation are types of the higher, spiritual excellencies of God (Lee 1988: 52, cf. 81). The excellencies, or beauty, which reflect God's inner being are of two kinds: primary and secondary. Secondary beauty is the larger and more general category and consists in various kinds of beauty which are seen in creation or even in the works of architects or in just rulers of nations. These objects 'consent' or agree with each other in the sense that they reflect the harmony and proportion appropriate to them. As Edwards says, 'When one thing sweetly harmonizes with another, as the notes in music, the notes are so conformed and have such proportion one to another that they seem to have respect one to another, as if they loved one another' (Edwards 1980: 380).

The higher or primary beauty is based on actual consent or love between spiritual beings. Edwards writes, 'The highest excellency... must be the consent of spirits one to another. But the consent of spirits... in their mutual love one to another, and the sweet harmony between various parts of the universe is only an image of mutual love' (Edwards 1980: 337–8). This mutual love is of course ultimately to be found in love of the members of the triune Godhead, but it is communicated to the creature whose continued existence depends on God. The basic structure of being then is relational, and thus reflects in its being this primary beauty (Mitchell 2003: 7). Humans all naturally delight in secondary beauty, but those whose eyes are opened by the Spirit can see in this the deeper beauty of God.

In his writings on the revival, Edwards stressed that there can be no pure spiritual experience, because such experiences, in our earthly condition, are always mixed with impure and carnal elements (Edwards 1980; 1972: 459). Even genuinely Christian experience has layers of impurity that must be discarded. The ability to see beauty, then, may be diminished both by a lack of spiritual vision and by the limitations of the body. Edwards concluded that the imagination, in its bodily context, tends to tarnish the spiritual affections and exaggerate fanciful elements so that the spiritual part is lost. Thus the vocation of the artist is inherently flawed, dependent as it is on the constitution of the body. While there is a deep and lively sense of the beauty that is resident in God and that is communicated to the creature, in the end Edwards leaves us with an experience of beauty that is entirely spiritual. Spiritual rebirth may result in a new and lively sense for the beauties of creation, but in the end only an echo of beauty remains, and for these at least, the project of shaping that created order into reliable images of this beauty is not encouraged (Edwards 1980: 461–7).

The Dutch theologian and politician Abraham Kuyper was perhaps the first person in this tradition not only to think about God and aesthetics, but directly to address the project of making art as a serious human calling. In his 1898 *Lectures on Calvinism*, Kuyper recognized that art is 'a most serious power in our present existence'. How can such a power be independent from 'the deepest root which all human life has in God' (Kuyper 1931: 151)?

But what would an art properly rooted in God look like? Taking his cue from Calvin, Kuyper notes that any art that 'does not watch the forms and motions of nature nor listen to its sound' is in danger of deteriorating into fantasy (Kuyper 1931: 154). But an art that does this sensitively will 'discover in those natural forms the order of the beautiful... reminding us in its productions of the beautiful that was lost, and of anticipating its perfect coming luster' (Kuyper 1931: 154–5).

Kuyper believed that the Reformers, in making a clean break from medieval religious art, actually advanced the development of art. In releasing art from its religious guardianship, they freed it to explore the common lot of humanity, reflecting the 'emancipation of our ordinary earthly life' (Kuyper 1931: 166). Rather than focusing attention on the crucified Christ, 'some now began to understand that there was a mystical suffering also in the general woe of man' (Kuyper 1931: 166). Further, in discovering the joys and sorrows of the people and their lives, art could reflect a religion that has 'graduated from the symbolical into the clearly-conscious life' (Kuyper 1931: 146). So Protestants should not lament the emptiness of their churches, bereft as they are of images and symbols, for in maturity a person does not return to 'the playthings of... infancy' (Kuyper 1931: 149).

Many in the Reformed tradition have found both inspiration and warning in the work of Kuyper. The warning follows from his insistence that all of life flows from the principle of faith. This led to Kuyper's notion of the 'antithesis' between those whose faith rests in God and those whose faith rests elsewhere. While Kuyper, as Calvin before him, was clear that all of life lies open before God and shares the common blessing of God (what Kuyper called 'common grace'), he insisted more strongly than Calvin on the antithesis that faith creates. This led subsequent thinkers to stress the difference between world views, and to look, for example, at the development of modern art and culture as illustrating this antithesis.

The person who applied Kuyper's critique most consistently to modern art was Hans R. Rookmaaker. What is involved in modern developments in the arts, he argued, 'is a whole way of thinking that leaves out of account... vital aspects of our humanity' (Rookmaaker 1970: 9–10). He traced this decline to the loss of ideals in the nineteenth century, which led to expressionism and Dada in the twentieth century. Rookmaaker believed that the German expressionists, as Tillich had argued, were searching for a universal unity that transcended the particular and overcame the barrenness of positivism (Rookmaaker 1970: 110–12). But in the course of this quest, artists like Picasso lost the human and the personal. Rookmaaker concluded that 'modern art in its more consistent forms, puts a question mark against all values and principles. Its anarchist aims of achieving complete human freedom turn all laws and norms into frustrating and deadening prison walls' (Rookmaaker 1970: 161).

For Christians who had never thought about modern art, Rookmaaker offered a vocabulary for thinking critically about it. While he failed to provide tools for constructively engaging with the period, as Maritain for example had done, he did continue Calvin's emphasis on seeing art as a part of the larger work of obeying and glorifying God. He closed his book by noting: 'Christian art is nothing special. It is sound, healthy, good art. It is art that is in line with the God-given structures of art, one which has a loving and free view on reality, one which is good and true' (Rookmaaker 1970: 228).

Other contemporary Reformed thinkers have developed this humble aesthetics of everyday life. Calvin Seerveld avoided giving any transcendental reference to art, such as Maritain had done (Seerveld 1980: 122; 1968). Art, like all other Christian callings, has the modest task of opening up creation, of moving all things, from politics to sex, under the leading of the Holy Spirit, toward what Seerveld called a 'saved normality' (Seerveld 1980: 90). But what is the special contribution of the aesthetic realm? Its central moment is what Seerveld calls 'allusiveness', a disciplined making that stimulates the senses and emotions with its free play of suggestions (Seerveld 1980: 126–35). Similarly, philosopher Nicholas Wolterstorff suggests that art finds its greatest meaning when it is located within the larger world of purposive human action. Modern developments isolated art in museums and diminished aesthetics by removing it from its natural context in real life (Wolterstorff 1980: 36). Artists, in their special vocation of promoting human livelihood and delight, have the same calling as everyone else to serve their neighbour and to praise God (Wolterstorff 1980: 77). This leads him to propose an aesthetic category he calls 'fittingness'. Good art, he believes, projects a world that suits the context and feelings that produced the artistic vision and that finally reflects something of the goodness and health that God intends the world to show.

These themes have encouraged many to think about and participate in the arts in helpful ways. Taking their cues from God's good creation and God's final purposes of shalom in that creation, these thinkers have suggested that carrying on a deep and careful conversation with one's materials (as Wolterstorff puts it) may lead one to discover something about oneself and the world that is worthy, perhaps even transformative. But a basic question remains. However worthy art may be, can it reflect God? Or what can it teach us about God?

This is a question other Protestants have recently asked. They have made use of the wealth of recent trinitarian reflection to enrich the conversation about art and to correct what they see as a weakness in reflection on the arts. One of the important voices in this conversation is Colin Gunton, who sought to use aesthetics to understand the dual nature of Christ and the Trinity more generally. He notes that our experience is overly dominated by visual patterns of perception, which encourage us to see objects in isolation from one another (Gunton 1997: 114; cf. Begbie 1991: 225). Music, he suggests, helps us see the way in which two accounts of an event can be juxtaposed without one precluding the other. Gunton claims that this has implications for the way the world exists (Gunton 1997: 116). Understanding these interpenetrating presences helps us to overcome an epistemology inherited from Plato and to see the world in a way more consistent with modern physics—objects can in fact exist simultaneously in different modes and places (Gunton 1997: 116–17). This illustrates Gunton's more general view that art is intrinsically metaphoric. Elsewhere Gunton argues that creation is made real in great art. Art enables the world to take meaningful form; the world and its structures speak 'words' in the arts. The gospel as the greatest story of art helps us see that truth and beauty take shape not by escaping from the world but by action within it (Gunton 1985: 8, 14, 17).

Jeremy Begbie followed up these ideas in his 1991 book *Voicing Creation's Praise*. When he asks what bearing theology has on the arts he finds reflection on the Trinity crucial: 'The metaphor of Christ as the agent, sustainer, and goal of creation has in fact considerable potential to illuminate both the acts and the eternal being of God as triune, and, by extension the nature of the created world' (Begbie 1991: 170). Taking our cue from the trinitarian mutuality reflected in God's creative work, we find that we are involved in a common history with the world—its redemption and ours are vitally connected. Moreover, in the human voice the inarticulate nature speaks (Begbie 1991: 177). Human creativity, then, is about sharing through the Spirit in the 'creative purpose of the Father as he draws all things to himself through his Son' (Begbie 1991: 179).

This emphasis on the trinitarian mutuality and exchange has proven to be a fruitful model for thinking about the arts. In a later book edited by Begbie, Trevor Hart asks how the application of human imagination can enhance the good of creation, while avoiding the Promethean pretensions of modern artists (Hart 2000; cf. Sherry 1992). Here the model that is most helpful, Hart believes, is the incarnation, especially as seen, for example, in Galatians 4: 4–7. Here the free response of the incarnate Jesus, who by the power of the Spirit calls out in intimacy to the Father, 'Abba', models the way in which the artist can offer the gifts of creation back to God by the Spirit. As Christ takes our flesh, with all its flaws, transfigures it through Spirit-inspired artistry, and offers it back to us to the glory of the Father, so the artist can take the goods of creation and transform them into images that glorify God.

For these thinkers, objects of art function metaphorically, proposing a dynamic juxtaposition into which we are drawn as in a game. We come out of this process changed. Begbie, like Gunton, proposes that music best expresses 'the temporal morphology of creation as we encounter it' (Begbie 1991: 245). This insight is greatly expanded and elaborated in Begbie's later work *Theology, Music and Time* (2000). Here he reiterates his goal, not of understanding art via theology, but of revitalizing theology through the arts. Art, in the form of music, advances theology by 'enacting theological wisdom' (Begbie 2000: 5). Music as a socially embedded and bodily practice, by its temporal and material character, makes important claims about the world (Begbie 2000: 55). For example, music shows the created order to be interpenetrating, temporally limited but meaningful, and displaying promise and fulfilment. Begbie claims that music not only gives insight into the world but also reorders human sympathies; in worship and witness it is involved in the very salvific processes of God (Begbie 2000: 127). In music the 'process of salvation can be conceived... as an ongoing healing of our time through participation in the temporality established in Jesus Christ' (Begbie 2000: 150–1). The experience of music gives one a deeper insight into, for example, the initial appearance of a theme and its eucharistic repetition, but also shows its 'potential to be taken up into the process of shaping a mature Christian identity' (Begbie 2000: 169, 152).

Begbie gives us helpful tools to explore the temporal and interpenetrating dynamics of God's creation which reflect God's triune reality (Begbie 2000: 271). He claims these patterns allow us to be shaped by and in this temporality, thus allowing music, and art more generally, to play a role by the Spirit in God's process of redemption.

By means of this brief and limited survey, we have discovered some who want to see art function as symbolic objects transparent to the presence of God or the unconditioned. Others see art objects as 'sacramental' by virtue of their participation in God. Still others want to affirm both the goodness of creation and the transcendence of God and thus limit art to a sign or metaphor of meaning. For the latter, art can generate theological knowledge and insight, but it may not represent and actually convey the presence of God, as Schleiermacher would have claimed. Where God is discovered phenomenologically, aesthetic value is measured experientially; where God is transcendent, mirrored in the good creation or the words of scripture, art can only be an instrument of response and obedience. But in either case aesthetic language has established itself as a legitimate means of expressing both the mystery of God and the depth of Christian experience.

References

Aquinas, St Thomas (1975). *Summa Theologiae.* London: Blackfriars.

Balthasar, Hans Urs von (1982–9 [1961–9]). *The Glory of the Lord: A Theological Aesthetics.* New York: Crossroad.

Barfield, Owen (1989). *Owen Barfield on C. S. Lewis.* Middletown: Wesleyan University Press.

Barth, Karl (1957). *Church Dogmatics* II/1. Edinburgh: T. & T. Clark.

Begbie, Jeremy S. (1991). *Voicing Creation's Praise: Towards a Theology of the Arts.* Edinburgh: T. & T. Clark.

—— (2000). *Theology, Music and Time.* Cambridge: Cambridge University Press.

Carnell, Scott (1974). *Bright Shadow of Reality: C. S. Lewis and the Feeling Intellect.* Grand Rapids: Eerdmans.

Dyrness, William (2004). *Reformed Theology and Visual Culture: The Protestant Imagination from Calvin to Edwards.* Cambridge: Cambridge University Press.

Eco, Umberto (1986). *Art and Beauty in the Middle Ages.* New Haven: Yale University Press.

Edwards, Jonathan (1972). *The Works of Jonathan Edwards,* iv. *The Great Awakening.* New Haven: Yale University Press.

—— (1980). 'The Mind'. In *The Works of Jonathan Edwards,* vi. *Scientific and Philosophical Writings,* New Haven: Yale University Press.

Goizueta, Roberto S. (1995). *Caminemos con Jesus: Toward a Hispanic/Latino Theology of Accompaniment.* Maryknoll: Orbis.

Gunton, Colin E. (1985). 'Creation and Re-Creation: An Exploration of some Themes in Aesthetics and Theology'. *Modern Theology* 2/1: 1–19.

—— (1997). *Yesterday and Today: A Study of Continuities in Christology.* London: SPCK.

Hart, David Bentley (2003). *The Beauty of the Infinite: The Aesthetics of Christian Truth.* Grand Rapids: Eerdmans.

Hart, Trevor (2000). 'Hearing, Seeing and Touching the Truth'. In Jeremy Begbie (ed.), *Beholding the Glory: Incarnation through the Arts*, Grand Rapids: Baker, 2–25.

Kuyper, Abraham (1931 [1898]). *Lectures on Calvinism: The Stone Foundation Lectures.* Grand Rapids: Eerdmans.

Lee, Sang Hyun (1988). *The Philosophical Theology of Jonathan Edwards.* Princeton: Princeton University Press.

Lewis, C. S. (1955). *Surprised by Joy.* London: Fontana.

—— (1965). 'Transposition'. In id., *Screwtape Proposes a Toast, and Other Pieces*, London: Fontana.

—— (1967). 'Christianity and Culture'. In id., *Christian Reflections*, Grand Rapids: Eerdmans.

Maritain, Jacques (1954). *Creative Intuition in Art and Poetry.* New York: Meridian.

—— (1962 [1920]). *Art and Scholasticism: and The Frontiers of Poetry.* New York: Scribners.

Mitchell, Louis J. (2003). *Jonathan Edwards on the Experience of Beauty.* Studies in Reformed Theology and History 9. Princeton: Princeton Theological Seminary.

Redeker, Martin (1973). *Schleiermacher: Life and Thought.* Philadelphia: Fortress.

Rookmaaker, Hans R. (1970). *Modern Art and the Death of a Culture.* Downers Grove: InterVarsity.

—— (2002–3). *Collected Works of H. R. Rookmaaker.* Carlisle: Piquant.

Schleiermacher, F. (1839 [1814]). *Dialektik.* Berlin: G. Reimer.

—— (1996 [1799]). *On Religion: Speeches to its Cultured Despisers.* Cambridge: Cambridge University Press.

Seerveld, Calvin (1968). *A Christian Critique of Art and Literature.* Toronto: Association for Reformed Studies.

—— (1980). *Rainbows for the Fallen World.* Toronto: Tuppence.

Sherry, Patrick (1992). *Spirit and Beauty: An Introduction to Theological Aesthetics.* Oxford: Oxford University Press.

Tillich, Paul (1951). *Systematic Theology*, i. Chicago: University of Chicago.

—— (1987*a*). *On Art and Architecture.* New York: Crossroad.

—— (1987*b*). 'On the Idea of a Theology of Culture'. In Victor Nuovo, *Visionary Science: A Translation of Tillich's 'On the Idea of a Theology of Culture' with an Interpretive Essay*, Detroit: Wayne State University Press.

Viladesau, Richard (1999). *Theological Aesthetics: God in Imagination, Beauty, and Art.* New York: Oxford University Press.

Wolterstorff, Nicholas (1980). *Art in Action: Toward a Christian Aesthetic.* Grand Rapids: Eerdmans.

Suggested Reading

Begbie, Jeremy (ed.) (2000). *Beholding the Glory: The Incarnation through the Arts.* Grand Rapids: Baker.

Brown, Bruce Birch (1989). *Religious Aesthetics: A Theological Study of Making and Meaning.* Princeton: Princeton University Press.

De Borchgrave, Helen (1999). *A Journey toward Christian Art.* Philadelphia: Fortress.

Drury, John (1999). *Painting the Word: Christian Pictures and their Meanings.* New Haven: Yale University Press.

Dyrness, William (2001). *Visual Faith: Theology, Art and Worship in Dialogue.* Grand Rapids: Baker.

Jensen, Robin (2004). *The Substance of Things Seen: Art, Faith and the Christian Community.* Grand Rapids: Eerdmans.

Miles, Margaret (1985). *Image as Insight: Visual Understanding in Western Christianity and Secular Culture.* Boston: Beacon Press.

Morgan, David (2005). *The Sacred Gaze: Religious Visual Culture in Theory and Practice.* Berkeley and Los Angeles: University of California Press.

Scarry, Elaine (1999). *On Beauty and Being Just.* Princeton: Princeton University Press.

Steiner, George (1989). *Real Presences: Is there anything in what we say?* London: Faber and Faber.

Zenenski, Elizabeth, and Gilbert, Lela (2004). *Windows to Heaven: Introducing Icons to Protestants And Catholics.* Grand Rapids: Brazos.

PART IV

PROSPECTS

CHAPTER 32

THEOLOGIES OF RETRIEVAL

JOHN WEBSTER

ANY work in constructive systematic theology, whether it be a comprehensive account of Christian doctrine as a whole or a more restricted treatment of a single topic within the corpus of Christian teaching, requires the articulation of judgements. These may be announced and defended in a formal criteriology, though they often simply emerge in the course of theological exposition. Such judgements include, most obviously, judgements about the material content of Christian doctrine, as part of a larger construal of the nature of Christian faith and its objects. Pervading these substantive judgements, however, are other, apparently more formal, judgements in which theologians articulate decisions about the character, setting, and goals of the intellectual inquiry in which they are engaged. Among these are: judgements about the sources and norms of Christian doctrine, usually involving some sort of hierarchical arrangement to establish a final court of appeal; judgements about the procedures ('methods') to be followed in theological construction, often in relation to what are taken to be prestigious modes of intellectual activity in other fields of inquiry considered to carry weight in theology, such as philosophy or hermeneutics; judgements about the social location(s) and audience(s) of doctrinal work; judgements about the ends of systematic theological inquiry, such as the critical investigation of Christian truth claims or the edification of the church; lastly, judgements about systematic theology's historical situation, both its more immediate circumstances and its relation to the longer trajectory of the Christian tradition.

This chapter examines the prospects held out by a cluster of theologies which reach a broadly similar set of judgements about the nature of systematic theology. These theologies are too diverse (chronologically, confessionally, and in terms of theological style) to constitute a movement, still less a school. Terms often used to label them—post-liberal, post-critical, restorationist, palaeo-orthodox, intra-textual, even postmodern—tend to fasten on one or other feature of some of their practitioners and thus lack the necessary generality (the term used here, 'theologies of retrieval', is simply a convenience in the absence of a better designation). If for the purposes of exposition these theologies can be brought together under a single head, it is because they exhibit a set of common concerns and share some ways of addressing the theological task. These theologies are differently occasioned: some are generated by dissatisfaction with the commanding role played by critical philosophy or by historical and hermeneutical theory in mainstream modern theology; some derive more directly from captivation by the object of doctrinal reflection as unsurpassably true, good, and beautiful. All, however, tend to agree that mainstream theological response to seventeenth- and eighteenth-century critiques of the Christian religion and Christian religious reflection needlessly distanced theology both from its given object and from the legacies of its past.

'Retrieval', then, is a *mode* of theology, an attitude of mind and a way of approaching theological tasks which is present with greater or lesser prominence in a range of different thinkers, not all of them self-consciously 'conservative' or 'orthodox'. Although here we concentrate upon strong versions of this approach, it can be found in less stringent forms and in combination with other styles of theological work. A rough set of resemblances between different examples of this kind of theology would include the following: these theologies are 'objectivist' or 'realist' insofar as they consider Christian faith and theology to be a response to a self-bestowing divine reality which precedes and overcomes the limited reach of rational intention; their material accounts of this divine reality are heavily indebted to the trinitarian, incarnational, and soteriological teaching of the classical Christianity of the ecumenical councils; they consider that the governing norms of theological inquiry are established by the object by which theology is brought into being (the source of theology is thus its norm); accordingly, they do not accord final weight to external criteria or to the methods and procedures which enjoy prestige outside theology; their accounts of the location, audience, and ends of Christian doctrine are generally governed by the relation of theology to the community of faith as its primary sphere; and in their judgements about the historical setting of systematic theology they tend to deploy a theological (rather than socio-cultural) understanding of tradition which outbids the view that modernity has imposed a new and inescapable set of conditions on theological work. For such theologies, immersion in the texts and habits of thought of earlier (especially pre-modern) theology opens up a wide view of the object of Christian theological reflection, setting before its contemporary practitioners descriptions of the faith unharassed by current anxieties, and enabling a certain liberty in relation to the present. With this in mind, we begin by considering the study of history as a diagnostic to identify what are taken to be misdirections in modern theology, and then the deployment of history as a resource to overcome them.

I. Theological Genealogies of Modernity

From at least the second half of the seventeenth century, Christian (and especially Protestant) theology found itself increasingly in competition and conflict with critical philosophy, as the latter put forward a claim to be able to present a better account of the Christian faith and of its purported objects than could be offered by positive Christian dogmatics and exegesis. As the intellectual prestige of Christian theology waned and the explanatory reach of critical philosophy waxed correspondingly, the latter was often perceived to be uniquely competent to furnish a comprehensive metaphysical and epistemological framework within whose limits alone theology was entitled to operate. Alongside this, and partly as a result of these developments, Christian theology found itself faced by two claims which had a profound impact on its historical awareness. The first was the contention that intellectual inquiry in the 'modern' (i.e., critical) era is qualitatively different from intellectual inquiry in the past, from which it constitutes a profound and liberating break. The second claim concerned the superiority of critical history, that is, of the reconstruction of the Christian past, especially of the past of Christian thought, in terms of natural conditions and agencies to the exclusion or at least the suspension of the divine. On this basis, Christianity's canonical writings and its post-canonical traditions could be investigated and assessed without appeal to such contaminating notions as inspiration, illumination, providence, or church, and instead judged from the standpoint of the rational sufficiency of the present. The effect of both these claims was to disrupt modern theology's sense of continuity with its past, a past habitable only with difficulty and ill-equipped to instruct theology about its contemporary responsibilities.

Theologies of retrieval resist this view of the situation of theology by proposing different genealogies of modernity and by treating pre-modern Christian theology as resource rather than problem. These genealogies exhibit some variety, partly as a result of confessional divergence. Nevertheless, they converge in a broadly accepted conviction that Christian teaching about God and God's relation to the world must be deployed if the cultural-historical situation of Christian theology is to become comprehensible. Christian theology, that is, is not required or authorized to adopt non-theological descriptions of its situation, nor may theology operate as if context were transparent, requiring no special Christian theological teachings for its illumination. Rather, it is incumbent upon theology to give a theological account of its present and of the developments from which it issues.

There are two corollaries of this approach to the matter. First, it means that the history of modern theology is not recounted as simply one of the defencelessness of Christian self-description against the onslaught of critical reason, but as the failure to marshal specifically theological resources to meet its detractors. Having allowed itself to be drawn away from its own ground, theology found itself forced to engage its antagonists on terms which almost inevitably led to its collapse. From this point of view, the insecurity of theology in modern intellectual culture has much to do with theology's alienation from its own subject matter. Its material substance came to play only a slender role, as fundamental aspects of Christian teaching about God (notably trinitarian and incarnational doctrine) were considered to be less fundamental and so replaceable by something more generic and apparently more defensible before critical reason's tribunal. This forgetfulness of theology's own *Sache*, along with gradual dislocation from the ecclesial settings and practices which support and lend plausibility to Christian teaching, is a basic aspect of the way in which theologies of retrieval often explicate the current theological situation.

A second corollary is that such a reading of the modern situation requires the availability of robust versions of Christian teaching. A theological interpretation of the position of modern theology can only be accomplished on the basis of accounts of Christian doctrine which are sufficiently cogent and have sufficient imaginative appeal to be able to generate an alternative, less concessive narrative. To speak of the history of modern theology as, for example, forgetfulness, alienation, or compromise, rather than as theology's defeat at the hands of its adversaries, demands access to a store of texts and ideas which are considered to be able to outpace those who would declare them redundant or ineffectual in the establishment of Christian claims. Genealogy presupposes description.

Both of these features are present in a first example of theological genealogy, Jüngel's highly suggestive, if at times rather sketchy, study *God as the Mystery of the World* (1983). The book is best read as a set of analytical soundings in the modern history of the relation between theology and philosophy, seeking to show how the rise of atheistic philosophy is parasitic upon decay in Christian thought about God. Its chief theological sources are those which maximize the contrariety of theological and non-theological conceptions of deity: Luther's theology of the cross and Barth's doctrine of the incarnation, in both of which the figure of Jesus is basic to the doctrine of God proper. Jüngel's portrayal of the history of modernity is chiefly indebted to Heidegger's attempts to unearth the corruptions of ontotheology. At the book's heart is a proposal that the modern situation of theology is best elucidated by tracing the declension of the Christian confession of God's self-identification in the death of Jesus.

Accordingly, Jüngel traces the *theological* failures of metaphysics since Descartes. The Cartesian grounding of certainty about God in the self-certainty of the cognitive subject means that, even as the most necessary being, God is contingent upon the *cogito* of whose continuity he acts as guarantor. Or again, Fichte's identification of 'existence' with existence under the conditions of time and space means the inevitable breakdown of the identity of God's essence and existence in the 'metaphysical' accounts of God with which Christian theology had associated itself. Taken as a whole, Jüngel's genealogy is an attempted demonstration that 'the modern grounding of thought in the Cartesian *cogito* is the initiation of the destruction of the metaphysically based certainty of God' (Jüngel 1983: 109). Underlying the historical argument is a conviction that the *proprium* of the Christian apprehension of God—the identity of God with the crucified—no longer serves to determine theology's engagement with metaphysics, with the result that a Christianly unspecific theism acquires increasing theological prestige. Alongside this investigation of thought about God, Jüngel also traces the erosion of the possibility of authentic speech about God. The same pattern of argument recurs: an internally corrupt tradition lacks access to the resources needed to maintain integrity under interrogation. In the matter of language about God, the historical trajectory is longer, reaching back to Aquinas, whose Neoplatonic emphasis upon divine ineffability makes divine revelation in human speech acutely problematic.

Jüngel's response to the modern predicament of Christian theology is to appeal for renewed attention to the inner substance of Christian faith, above all to 'the word of the cross' and 'the humanity of God' (shorthand terms for God's identification with worldly existence and language in the history of Jesus). Thus the modern fate of thought about God can only be overcome by consideration of God's 'unity with transience' at the cross; or again, human speech about God is contingent upon the revelatory speech-events in which God makes himself a presence in the linguistic structures of the world.

What is most noteworthy in Jüngel's diagnosis is its focus on the mismatch between the authentic content of Christian faith and the conceptual version of itself by which it sought to retain its authority in face of modern critiques. 'Atheism' is as much a child of theology's theistic self-alienation as of philosophical unbelief. Jüngel's presentation of this authentic content is undoubtedly dogmatically compressed, appealing to only a narrow selection of doctrinal material; and his historical narrative can lack complexity and nuance. The book's appeal is, indeed, as much kerygmatic as historical. What gives strength to his account is his insistence that the crisis of Christian thought and speech about God 'is to be worked through in terms of the particular character, the *proprium* of the Christian faith' (Jüngel 1983: 229). What is required is not a more effective apologetic strategy but a better dogmatics.

For a second example, we turn to a set of theological mappings of modern theology, all of which owe a good deal, whether directly or indirectly, to the work of the Jesuit Henri de Lubac. Like that of Jüngel, these accounts censure the atrophy of properly Christian teaching about God and God's relation to the world, and regard the disarray of modern theology as one of the deleterious effects of that atrophy. But there are some pivotal differences, all of which indicate a more 'catholic' orientation. These accounts are deeply appreciative of the theological-spiritual traditions of patristic and earlier medieval Christianity; they tend to take a longer view, often tracing the fall of Christian theology to Scotus or Ockham; they commonly identify the theology of the Protestant Reformation as an expression of the deformation of Christian authenticity, not a source of correction; above all, they counter modernity not by reasserting grace over aggrandized nature but by reintegrating nature and grace after their disastrous separation.

In *Surnaturel* (1946), de Lubac sought to excavate what he regarded as a primary Christian insight, namely that 'natural' being is ordered to participation in God. What made the excavation necessary was the calamitous notion of 'pure nature' which had lodged itself in nineteenth century neoscholasticism but which could be traced back through Cajetan to strands of late medieval and early modern scholastic thought. The resultant separation of nature from grace made the patristic and earlier medieval tradition virtually inaccessible. 'Pure nature', knowledge of which is attainable by philosophical inquiry independent of theology, is mirrored by a conception of supernatural realities which are the domain of an equally 'separated' theology. Identifying this isolation of an extrinsicist positive dogmatics from a philosophy whose concern is with natural being considered purely *in se* is for de Lubac fundamental to placing the modern project. Protecting the supernatural by isolating it from the natural, on his account of the matter, serves to encourage the flowering of naturalism and deism and restricts theology to an increasingly tight sphere of operations in which revelatory events have little to do with the dynamic of immanent creaturely being.

De Lubac thus explicates modernity by placing it at the end of a long defection of Christian theology from its native vision of the end of created being in participation in God. On this basis, he, along with others like Yves Congar (1966), was able to claim that the neoscholastic theologies of the nineteenth and early twentieth centuries, far from conserving ancient tradition, were in fact thoroughly modern, trapped by the antithesis between the extrinsicism of grace and the immanence of pure nature. De Lubac's influence has been strongly present in writings clustered around the designation 'Radical Orthodoxy' (Milbank, Pickstock, and Ward 1999), particularly in the work of Pickstock (1998) and Milbank (1990; 1997; 2003; 2005) where the attempt to unmask the historical and systematic dimensions of the separation of theology and philosophy and the invention of the secular are especially prominent.

Both these genealogies serve (very different) constructive proposals. Running parallel to them are a number of more detailed historical studies which resist the progressive idiom of liberal histories of modernity, in which the paradigmatic episode is the Enlightenment's release of reason from the tutelage of ecclesiastical faith. In these investigations (Buckley 1987; 2004; Dupré 1993; 2004) a good deal of attention is devoted to the long-range effects of some mutations in western theological and philosophical culture in the early modern period: the breakdown of the synthesis of God, nature, and self; the effective withdrawal of God into a supernatural sphere, acting only as a remote causal force; the exaltation of subjectivity to the status of the epistemologically and metaphysically basic. Underpinning them all is a claim that '[t]he origin of atheism in the intellectual culture of the West lies... with the self-alienation of religion itself' (Buckley 1987: 363). Such accounts can be reinforced by T. F. Torrance's many attempts to expose the effects of dualism in theological and scientific thought (Torrance 1969) or by Hans Frei's history of the decline of the role of the realistic narratives of the Bible in shaping the cultural imagination (Frei 1974).

At their most mature, these various genealogies are not simple gestures of opposition but exercises in historical understanding and responsibility for which theology is not the unsullied victim of cultural decay but the co-creator of circumstances in which it cannot flourish. They consider modernity, however understood, to be a contingent, not an absolute, phenomenon, and suggest that whatever misdirections have occurred can be corrected by skilful deployment of the intellectual and spiritual capital of Christianity. In this, they differ radically from other theological interpretations of modernity which believe that the survival of Christian theology depends upon abandonment of the ruined intellectual house it has so far occupied, and the search for an entirely new habitation. 'The house of authority has collapsed' (Farley 1982: 166). For Farley, genealogical work discloses the sheer impossibility of modern theology continuing to operate by the criteria of the classical Christian tradition, which have been exposed as 'the occasion and framework for human pathology, sin and grief' (Farley 1982: 168). If theologies of retrieval disagree with this judgement, it is in part because they offer a different explanation of how and why it has come about that theology finds itself in such straitened circumstances, and because they retain greater confidence in its capacity to be reformed without abandonment of its texts and traditions.

II. History as *Ressourcement*

Historical work enables theologies of retrieval to place, interpret, and in some measure transcend the constraints of modern theology by unearthing the neglect and disorder by which they are imposed. This, of course, places considerable reliance upon the plausibility of authentic Christian teaching and upon its availability apart from degraded versions. And this, in turn, necessitates a further historical task, namely the reclamation of tracts of the Christian past as a resource for present constructive work.

Ressourcement is a mode of theology particularly associated with some leading Roman Catholic theologians of the middle third of the twentieth century. But many of its underlying assumptions—that the history of Christian thought and practice is a field of the Spirit's operation; that the communion of the saints across time is of greater consequence than the synchronic relation of theology to contemporary culture; that attentiveness to the Christian past is a spiritual responsibility and joy—are widely shared. For Roman Catholics like de Lubac, Congar, or Chenu, the spiritual and exegetical writings of the fathers and earlier medievals afforded liberation from the theology of the modern schools with its heavily conceptual idiom and its detachment of dogma from the church's life in the paschal mystery. More recently, significant strands of Protestant theology have looked for alternatives to the critical history of doctrine which dominated writing on *Dogmengeschichte* from the early decades of the nineteenth century. This critical historical enterprise, exemplified by a tradition from Strauss (1840–1) and Baur (1878–9) through to Harnack (1894–9), Bauer (1971), and Werner (1957), tended to maximize the inauthenticity of an array of orthodox doctrines by explicating them in terms of the influence of speculative Hellenism and so demonstrating their distance from the teaching of Christianity's founder. This model of doctrinal criticism survived in British patristic scholarship in the work of Lampe (1977) and Wiles (1976), who often concluded that classical incarnational and trinitarian doctrine is both accidental and largely unusable.

Theologies of retrieval 'decentre' (the word is Rowan Williams's (Williams 2005: 110)) this sort of critical judgement by trying to stand with the Christian past which, precisely because it is foreign to contemporary conventions, can function as an instrument for the enlargement of vision. Classical sources outweigh modern norms. Theologies of retrieval are not alone in making this move, of course. Sophisticated work in systematic theology always involves rereading the tradition: if the achievement of a theologian like Balthasar (whose work is assuredly a 'theology of retrieval') is unthinkable without his immersion in Origen or Gregory of Nyssa, the same has to be said of such a characteristically modern thinker as Rahner, whose indebtedness to Aquinas is immense. The Christian tradition is cumulative, and its theology does not start *de novo* but with 'classics' (Tracy 1981: 99–154). What distinguishes theologies of retrieval is that its practitioners do not regard these classics as only one element, however authoritative, in a process of correlation or negotiation between the Christian past and modernity. Classics come first; they exceed the possibilities of the present and have the capacity to expose and pass beyond its limitations.

Chief among the commanding sources of displacement and revitalization is the Bible, which in theologies of retrieval commonly plays a self-evidently authoritative role in determining the theological agenda and in the construction of doctrinal claims. The mutual isolation of biblical and doctrinal work is a telling example of what happens when theological sub-disciplines align their self-definition to those of neighbouring non-theological disciplines (biblical studies to literary history and the history of religions, doctrine to philosophy). Lacking a common theological rationale for their different undertakings, they drift apart. The renewed convergence between biblical scholarship and systematic theology indicates a reconception of the unity of theology on the basis of agreement about its vocation and tasks (Braaten and Jenson 1995; Fowl 1997). The much-canvassed term 'theological interpretation of scripture' embraces a range of attitudes and projects—a desire to go further than critical-historical investigation of text and context, an interest in readers and reading communities, an orientation of biblical and dogmatic theology to revelation. They converge to the extent that they treat the Bible as scripture, that is, as more than a set of clues to the history of antique religious culture, and so as a text which may legitimately direct theological reason because in some manner it affords access to God's self-communication. This, for theologies of retrieval, is sufficient to overturn Kant's relegation of the biblical theologian to the status of mere guardian of the domestic culture of ecclesiastical faith, leaving universality to the philosophical theologian (Kant 1996: 247–93). Far from being merely the raw material of theological problems, scripture can effect their resolution.

Alongside this, theologies of retrieval have invested deeply in expectant rereading of tracts of the post-biblical Christian tradition. The renewal of patristics as a field of theological, rather than purely historical, inquiry, is a good instance. *Ressourcement* theologians proper derived much of their impetus from an awed rediscovery of the inseparability of theology, exegesis, and spirituality in the texts of the fathers which they made available in *Sources chrétiennes* and explicated in their writings. Slightly later, in the quite different theological world of Reformed dogmatics, T. F. Torrance immersed himself in the texts of Athanasius and the Cappadocians, whom he regarded as quasi-normative exponents of the conceptual structure of Christianity (Torrance 1988; 1995). To study them alongside Calvin and Barth, whom he considered their heirs, is not only to be shown 'the inner theological connections which gave coherent structure to the classical theology of the ancient Catholic church' (Torrance 1988: 2) but also to see how Nicene theology thought its way out of dualisms similar to those which afflict modern culture. Though not all would share Torrance's confidence in finding unified habits of mind amongst the early theologians, his sense that the fathers demand theological and not simply archaeological attention is widely shared even by those who have developed much more complex historical accounts (Ayres 2004), particularly of the centrality of exegesis among patristic writers (Young 1997; O'Keefe and Reno 2005).

One of the most fruitful suggestions of *ressourcement* theologians and of others like Peter Brunner (Brunner 1968) was that the separation of (conceptual) dogma from the practices of liturgical sharing in the mystery of Christ is symptomatic of the modern hypertrophy of critical reason. This suggestion—and a parallel conception of an earlier shared tradition of worship and teaching which precedes the sixteenth-century dismantling of western Christendom—has generated some very substantial accounts of Christian doctrine: from a liturgical perspective, the work of the Methodist systematician Geoffrey Wainwright (1980), and from an ecumenical outlook, the still somewhat neglected dogmatics of Edmund Schlink (1983).

Later texts from the Christian tradition can effect the same renewal. The reinvigoration of Roman Catholic theology which began before the Second World War and bore fruit at the Second Vatican Council is inconceivable without the discovery of a different Aquinas from that of the manualist tradition—more biblical, more soteriological and ecclesial, a great deal less philosophical: in effect, a theologian of the divine mysteries rather than an official apologist for dogma or an analytical philosopher *avant la lettre* (Healy 2003; Kerr 2002). Similar moves can be found amongst Protestant theologians. The most intense period of development in Barth's thought coincided with his astonished discovery of the confessional and dogmatic traditions of early Calvinism (Barth 2002; 2004). Or again, fresh study of Luther has enabled some Lutheran theologians to break free of the soteriological extrinsicism of nineteenth-century theologies of justification and propose an account of Christian doctrine centred on creaturely participation in God (Mannermaa 2005).

In short, though theologies of retrieval are widely divergent, they entertain a common attitude to the biblical and theological traditions which precede and enclose contemporary theology: more trustful, more confident in their contemporary serviceability, unpersuaded of the superiority of the present age. There are consequences here for the genres of theology. If 'systematic' theology means the organization of Christian doctrine into a consistent structure on the basis of a founding principle, theologies of retrieval will rarely count as systematic, for the term suggests a higher degree of conceptual determinacy and arrangement than most think desirable (an exception might be Robert Jenson's tightly systematic work (1997–9)). Instead, they have often preferred looser, less conceptually elaborated, and more commentarial genres. Much *ressourcement* theology took the form of historical studies (de Lubac's *Catholicism* (1950) or Congar's *Tradition and Traditions* (1966) are representative). A more recent project, van Beeck's *God Encountered* (1989–), draws on an extraordinary range of 'the Great Tradition'; again, Oden's substantial systematics is, in essence, a work of Christian midrash, using the topics of dogmatics to make available materials from the biblical, theological, and confessional traditions with relatively little concern for a further level of analysis (Oden 1987–92). Such works express the conviction that Christian doctrine is not (as it has often become) the study of problems but rather the descriptive elucidation of faith's objects, introducing its readers to those realities by commending persuasive versions of them. A further consequence is that these theologies eschew saying anything new—not in the sense that they content themselves with formulaic repetition, still less in endorsing everything the tradition has ever said—but in the sense that they operate on the presupposition that resolutions to the questions which they address may well be found already somewhere in the inheritance of the Christian past.

III. Re-Envisaging Systematic Theology

In light of these overlapping conceptions of the theological task, how is the task and content of systematic theology to be reconceived?

Most work in this mode has a well-developed sense of the integrity and distinctiveness of Christian theology. This is why theologies of retrieval decline to adopt one of the most well-tried strategies by which systematicians have engaged modern culture, namely theological construction through correlation (Tillich 1951–63; Buri 1956–78; Macquarrie 1977; Siegwalt 1986–) or mutually hospitable conversation (Ford 1999) between received tradition and the possibilities offered by the contemporary situation. One important factor here is resistance to what is perceived to be a pervasive preference for the generic in modern understandings of religion. This preference is sometimes traced to the rise in the seventeenth century of theories of natural religion and natural theology which envisaged a common substrate (usually some kind of ethical theism) beneath positive religious traditions and their competing claims to be bearers of revelation. Into this common religious essence, apprehensible by natural reason and the natural moral sense, the texts, practices, and doctrines of particular religious traditions can be resolved as contingent, though possibly useful, expressions. In more contemporary guise, this preference for the generic can take the form of appeal to 'common human experience' or to a general theory (hermeneutical, symbolic, anthropological) which can ground theological construction.

Theologies of retrieval, by contrast, do not consider Christianity as a version of anything: it is irreducible. For some, this irreducibility may be a silent assumption; in such cases systematic theology proceeds descriptively (Berkouwer's dogmatic work is an example (1954–76)). Others, especially those seeking to counter the dominance of correlation in North American theology, have been more self-consciously 'unapologetic', resisting the pressure of the generic by elaborating theories of knowledge or religion which emphasize the fundamental status of the positive or external (texts, practices, forms of common life). Notable exponents (Lindbeck 1984; Christian 1987) draw attention to the roots of doctrine in the cultural-linguistic world of Christian practice. Their dismantling of the authority of natural religion is, curiously, often achieved not primarily by appeal to inner-theological materials but by use of philosophical, anthropological, or literary theory (Wittgenstein, Geertz, Auerbach). This indicates something of a division within theologies of retrieval, between those of a more descriptive orientation and those more confident in the possibilities of non-theological theory. Despite this, theologies of retrieval are generally agreed that Christian doctrine is a positive science. Some more readily account for this positivity by appeal to the splendour of divine revelation in generating faith and quickening reason; others connect it more directly to the historical and social determinacy of the Christian religion as a set of practices: the work of Christian doctrine cannot take place in the absence of competence in the habits of the ecclesial community and without the exercise of certain virtues (Hütter 2000; Marshall 2000). The differences here reflect differing understandings of the ways in which revelation is mediated, and so about the measure of directness with which theology's object presents itself. But the differences are embraced by a common emphasis that, because theology works from a *positum*, its tasks cannot be formulated in terms of general *Wissenschaftstheorie* (*contra*, e.g., Pannenberg 1976).

In terms of the substantive content of Christian doctrine, theologies of retrieval again exhibit extensive variety. But although (say) Barth, Congar, and Jenson have conflicting conceptions of Christian teaching, they share broad similarities. Systematic theologies of retrieval are usually concerned to ensure that the proportions of an overall account of Christian teaching are not governed by the constraints of circumstance but by the object of Christian doctrine, that is, God and the economy of God's grace. Consequently, certain doctrines which acquired high profile in dominant strands of modern theology are accorded less significance or relocated so that they no longer enjoy the same prominence. The most telling instance is theological anthropology, which occupied a central position in much post-Enlightenment systematic theology, expressing the axiomatic status of the knowing, experiencing, or interpreting self as that *from* which theology moves. In theologies of retrieval, the hypertrophy of anthropology is countered by refusing to allow anthropology to ground doctrines such as creation or Christology. This does not mean the elimination of anthropology, but it does require that the topic be kept within its limits and in subordination to conceptions of the nature and ends of human creatures derived from elsewhere in the corpus of Christian teaching (Barth 1960).

If some doctrinal topics require contraction, others demand expansion: two exemplary *loci* are the doctrine of the Trinity and the doctrine of creation.

Trinitarian doctrine has long suffered from the cramping effects of, on the one hand, the assumption that theistic construals of God are more basic than trinitarian teaching, and, on the other hand, critical histories of orthodoxy which appeared to relegate it to the status of an accidental development. Particularly in English-language theology, the last thirty-five years have witnessed the doctrine's renewal. It is not that the doctrine ever disappeared from view (it is basic to Roman Catholic school dogmatics and massively present in, for example, Protestant dogmaticians like Dorner and Bavinck); and its rehabilitation has occurred across a range of theologies, including some with little investment in classical orthodoxy and others not typically considered as theologies of retrieval, such as that of Rahner (1970). Nevertheless, theologies of retrieval have often urged the foundational status of the doctrine of the Trinity, which must be allowed to govern the entire corpus of systematic theology (Gunton 1991; Torrance 1996). Three features of these accounts are worth noting. First, they make much of pre-modern theology, particularly the Cappadocians, widely considered to have developed the most penetrating accounts of divine personhood in the Christian tradition. (Because this Cappadocian theology is often mediated by émigré Orthodox theology, it is frequently associated with severe criticism of Augustine and his heirs such as Aquinas or Barth as 'monist' and so liable to infection from theism.) Second, trinitarian doctrine is the *discrimen* of Christian doctrine, preventing the adoption of a notion of deity generated by philosophy or the study of religion. Third, therefore, other doctrines are shaped by trinitarian teaching, of which they are corollaries or extensions.

A related expansion takes place in the doctrine of the church, especially in theologies of retrieval of a more 'catholic' orientation. In a standard correlationist systematics such as Macquarrie's, ecclesiology appears late in the exposition, under the heading of 'applied theology', and does not shape the preceding philosophical theology (Macquarrie 1977: 386–419). Some theologies of retrieval resist this disconnection of the foundational from the ecclesial on the grounds that the condition of possibility of Christian doctrine is the mystery of salvation which is equiprimordially the mystery of the church (Congar 1966; Jenson 1997–9). Because the church is intrinsic to salvation as communion with God, ecclesiology is not concerned merely with external structures and acts but with the human historical forms of participation in God. Not all would accept radical versions of this such as that of Milbank (1997: 145–68), fearing a blurring of the dogmatically necessary demarcation between creator and creature; but even Barth wrote a *church* dogmatics.

Other doctrines are relocated and reconceived. A good instance is the doctrine of creation: a number of recent accounts of the topic attempt to detach it from what is taken to be a distorting modern frame and let it emerge in its own Christian integrity (Tanner 1988; Gunton 1998). Once again, there is a sense of discrepancy between the biblical and classical materials and the expectations placed on the doctrine by modern cosmology and philosophy. The doctrine's viability rests upon its success in specifying the identity of the creator and the nature and ends of the creator's acts; once this is undertaken, then the creator's action can be seen neither as a tyrannous power competing with creaturely agency, nor as an opaque causal force, but as that which sustains and perfects the creature's integrity.

IV. Conclusion

The major achievements of theology in the mode of retrieval have been to commend a more celebratory style of theological portrayal and to rehabilitate classical sources of Christian teaching and draw attention to their potential in furthering the theological task. For systematic theology, this suggests that exegetes and historians often prove more congenial and valuable neighbours than critical philosophers, especially when the history of Christian thought is studied through the lens of tradition and church. To look at the past in this way brings some substantial benefits; most of all, it can encourage resistance to immanentist explanations of Christian doctrine which, after the manner of Troeltsch, subsume historical and dogmatic theology under social processes (Rendtorff 1972). Adopting this stance is not without its perils. A providential understanding of the history of orthodoxy can overwhelm its material, most of all by eliding the processes of negotiation which are part of the doctrinal life of the Christian tradition (Tanner 1997; Williams 2005). Especially when deployed in reaction to an apparently unyielding ideology of criticism, 'the' tradition might easily be viewed as a fully realized whole rather than as an unfinished assemblage of products, however providentially ordered. At their best, theologies of retrieval have eschewed excessive stability and determinacy; but a reminder of the danger is important, because in any 'positive' theology much hangs on what *kind* of givenness is being recommended. A revelatory or ecclesial given which is entirely unaffected by the conditions of its reception, wholly free from the poetics of church and culture, is scarcely imaginable. On the other hand, theologies of retrieval have argued with some success that to expect critical reason to deliver theology from the sclerosis of tradition is not to solve but to inflame the problem of ideology. What is required are, once again, skills of theological judgement schooled by the Christian past, alert to present opportunity, and enacted with deference and hope.

A further temptation for theologians of retrieval is to subscribe to a myth of the fall of theology from Christian genuineness at some point in its past (fourteenth-century nominalism, the sixteenth-century Reformation, seventeenth-century Cartesianism, or wherever 'modernity' is considered to have first presented itself). The oversimplifications which attend epochal interpretations of history are well known. But there is a deeper point here. However necessary 'anti-modern' protest may be on certain occasions, however much it may empower the re-engagement of neglected constructive tasks, it should not betray theology into the illusion that all that is required for successful dogmatics in the present is the identification and repudiation of an error in the past. Such a stance can indicate the same illusion of superiority as that sometimes claimed by critical reason. Moreover, it can fail to grasp that the problem is not *modern* theology but simply *theology.* All talk of God is hazardous. Modern constraints bring particular challenges which can be partially defeated by attending to a broader and wiser history, but there is no pure Christian past whose retrieval can ensure theological fidelity.

This does not in any way call the project of retrieval into question or minimize its impact. The recovery of the present ecclesial vocation of systematic theology, as well as the renewal of its public functions, surely require persuasion of the weightiness of its past. But however basic a task, retrieval cannot constitute the entirety of theological work. 'In... obedience to the church's past it is always possible to be a very *free* theologian. But it must be borne in mind that, as a member of the church, as belonging to the *congregatio fidelium*, one must not *speak* without having *heard*' (Barth 1962: 181).

References

Ayres, Lewis (2004). *Nicaea and its Legacy: An Approach to Fourth-Century Trinitarian Theology.* Oxford: Oxford University Press.

Barth, Karl (1960). *Church Dogmatics* III/2. Edinburgh: T. & T. Clark.

—— (1962). *Credo.* New York: Scribner's.

—— (2002). *The Theology of the Reformed Confessions.* Louisville: WJKP.

—— (2004). *Die Theologie Zwinglis.* Zurich: TVZ.

Bauer, Walter (1971). *Orthodoxy and Heresy in Earliest Christianity.* Philadelphia: Fortress.

Baur, Ferdinand Christian (1878–9). *Church History of the First Three Centuries.* 2 vols. Edinburgh: Williams and Norgate.

Berkouwer, G. C. (1954–76). *Studies in Dogmatics.* 18 vols. Grand Rapids: Eerdmans.

Braaten, Carl, and Jenson, Robert (eds.) (1995). *Reclaiming the Bible for the Church.* Grand Rapids: Eerdmans.

Brunner, Peter (1968). *Worship in the Name of Jesus.* St Louis: Concordia.

Buckley, Michael (1987). *At the Origins of Modern Atheism.* New Haven: Yale University Press.

—— (2004). *Denying and Disclosing God: The Ambiguous Progress of Modern Atheism.* New Haven: Yale University Press.

Buri, Fritz (1956–78). *Dogmatik als Selbstverständnis des christlichen Glaubens.* 3 vols. Bern: Haupt.

Christian, William (1987). *Doctrines of Religious Communities.* New Haven: Yale University Press.

Congar, Yves (1966). *Tradition and Traditions: An Historical and a Theological Essay.* London: Burns and Oates.

De Lubac, Henri (1946). *Surnaturel: Études historiques.* Paris: Aubier.

—— (1950). *Catholicism: A Study of Dogma in Relation to the Corporate Destiny of Mankind.* London: Burns and Oates.

Dupré, Louis (1993). *Passage to Modernity: An Essay in the Hermeneutics of Nature and Culture.* New Haven: Yale University Press.

Dupré, Louis (2004). *The Enlightenment and the Intellectual Foundations of Modern Culture*. New Haven: Yale University Press.

Farley, Edward (1982). *Ecclesial Reflection: An Anatomy of Theological Method*. Philadelphia: Fortress.

Ford, David (1999). *Self and Salvation: Being Transformed*. Cambridge: Cambridge University Press.

Fowl, Stephen (1997). *The Theological Interpretation of Scripture*. Oxford: Blackwell.

Frei, Hans (1974). *The Eclipse of Biblical Narrative: A Study in Eighteenth and Nineteenth Century Hermeneutics*. New Haven: Yale University Press.

Gunton, Colin (1991). *The Promise of Trinitarian Theology*. Edinburgh: T. & T. Clark.

—— (1998). *The Triune Creator: A Historical and Systematic Study*. Edinburgh: Edinburgh University Press.

Harnack, Adolf von (1894–9). *History of Dogma*. 5 vols. Edinburgh: Williams and Norgate.

Healy, Nicholas M. (2003). *Thomas Aquinas: Theologian of the Christian Life*. Aldershot: Ashgate.

Hütter, Reinhar (2000). *Suffering Divine Things: Theology and Church Practice*. Grand Rapids: Eerdmans.

Jenson, Robert W. (1997–9). *Systematic Theology*. 2 vols. Oxford: Oxford University Press.

Jüngel, Eberhard (1983). *God as the Mystery of the World*. Edinburgh: T. & T. Clark.

Kant, Immanuel (1996). *The Conflict of the Faculties*. In A. W. Wood and G. Di Giovanni (eds.), *Religion and Rational Theology*, Cambridge: Cambridge University Press, 233–327.

Kerr, Fergus (2002). *After Aquinas: Versions of Thomism*. Oxford: Blackwell.

Lampe, G. W. H. (1977). *God as Spirit*. Oxford: Clarendon.

Lindbeck, George (1984). *The Nature of Doctrine: Religion and Theology in a Postliberal Age*. Philadelphia: Westminster.

Macquarrie, John (1977). *Principles of Christian Theology*. London: SCM.

Mannermaa, Tuomo (2005). *Christ Present in Faith: Luther's View of Justification*. Minneapolis: Fortress.

Marshall, Bruce (2000). *Trinity and Truth*. Cambridge: Cambridge University Press.

Milbank, John (1990). *Theology and Social Theory: Beyond Secular Reason*. Oxford: Blackwell.

—— (1997). *The Word Made Strange: Theology, Language, Culture*. Oxford: Blackwell.

—— (2003). *Being Reconciled: Ontology and Pardon*. London: Routledge.

—— (2005). *The Suspended Middle: Henri de Lubac and the Debate Concerning the Supernatural*. Grand Rapids: Eerdmans.

Milbank, John, Pickstock, Catherine, and Ward, Graham (eds.) (1999). *Radical Orthodoxy*. London: Routledge.

Oden, Thomas (1987–92). *Systematic Theology*. 3 vols. San Francisco: Harper and Row.

O'Keefe, John, and Reno, R. R. (2005). *Sanctified Vision: An Introduction to Early Christian Interpretation of the Bible*. Baltimore: Johns Hopkins University Press.

Pannenberg, Wolfhart (1976). *Theology and the Philosophy of Science*. London: Darton, Longman and Todd.

Pickstock, Catherine (1998). *After Writing: The Liturgical Consummation of Philosophy*. Oxford: Blackwell.

Rahner, Karl (1970). *The Trinity*. New York: Herder and Herder.

Rendtorff, Trutz (1972). *Theorie des Christentums: Historisch-theologische Studien zu seiner neuzeitlichen Verfassung*. Gütersloh: Mohn.

Schlink, Edmund (1983). *Ökumenische Dogmatik: Grundzüge.* Göttingen: Vandenhoeck und Ruprecht.

Siegwalt, Gérard (1986–). *Dogmatique pour la catholicité évangélique.* 8 vols. Paris: Cerf.

Strauss, David Friedrich (1840–1). *Die christliche Glaubenslehre in ihrer geschichtlichen Entwicklung.* 2 vols. Tübingen: Osiander.

Tanner, Kathryn (1988). *God and Creation in Christian Theology: Tyranny or Empowerment?* Oxford: Blackwell.

—— (1997). *Theories of Culture: A New Agenda for Theology.* Minneapolis: Fortress.

Tillich, Paul (1951–63). *Systematic Theology.* 3 vols. Chicago: University of Chicago Press.

Torrance, T. F. (1969). *Theological Science.* Oxford: Oxford University Press.

—— (1988). *The Trinitarian Faith: An Evangelical Theology of the Ancient Catholic Church.* Edinburgh: T. & T. Clark.

—— (1995). *Divine Meaning: Studies in Patristic Hermeneutics.* Edinburgh: T. & T. Clark.

—— (1996). *The Christian Doctrine of God: One Being Three Persons.* Edinburgh: T. & T. Clark.

Tracy, David (1981). *The Analogical Imagination: Christian Theology and the Culture of Pluralism.* New York: Crossroads.

Van Beeck, Frans Josef (1989–). *God Encountered: A Contemporary Systematic Theology.* 5 vols. San Francisco: Harper and Row.

Wainwright, Geoffrey (1980). *Doxology: The Praise of God in Worship, Doctrine and Life.* London: Epworth.

Werner, Martin (1957). *The Formation of Christian Dogma.* London: Black.

Wiles, Maurice (1976). *Working Papers in Doctrine.* London: SCM.

Williams, Rowan (2005). *Why Study the Past? The Quest for the Historical Church.* London: Darton, Longman and Todd.

Young, Frances (1997). *Biblical Exegesis and the Formation of Christian Culture.* Cambridge: Cambridge University Press.

CHAPTER 33

REVISIONISM

IAN S. MARKHAM

THE task of theology is difficult. And any responsible theology needs to recognize this. For all the talk about the 'simple' gospel, evangelical scholars are acutely aware of the challenge of how to read the text of the Bible in a consistent way. Roman Catholic scholars do not simply appeal to an authoritative magisterium but recognize the challenge of reconciling the received tradition with contemporary insights (Markham 2004). Every form of theology recognizes that there are intrinsic methodological problems. Revisionism as a form of theology is distinctive in two ways. First, it acknowledges that methodological problems need to be faced at the outset. Before one can start the work of theology one must construct a methodological prolegomenon. Second, revisionism recognizes the importance and significance of modernity for theology. Our texts were constructed in a pre-modern age. And the dramatic changes since the western Enlightenment need to be faced. The result of this is that the theologian lives much more on the edge of the ecclesial community. There is a stronger sense of the constructive challenge that the 'world' poses for the church. Revisionism wants to push the hard questions: What sort of Christology makes sense of our contemporary experience of the biblical text in our context? Is the traditional account of providence intelligible and plausible in our scientific world? Revisionist theologians look at many other approaches to theology and suspect that these questions are not being faced. Revisionists are suspicious of what Edward Farley calls 'authority theology' (Farley 1996: xv). Farley explains that for authority theology 'that which initially establishes the truth or reality of a belief is simply its presence in the text of an authority, for instance, a biblical, conciliar, or papal text' (Farley 1996: xv). He goes on to admit that 'to depart from authority theology leaves the work of the theologian and the articulation of a theology of God with severe problems' (Farley 1996: xv). But this is required of us. And the net result, explains Farley, is that 'the theologian does not work directly *from* the texts but attempts to discover what is at work to prompt the ancient authors to bespeak God as they do' (Farley 1996: xv). Farley speaks for all revisionist theologians at this point. There is a recognition that the theological task is a struggle. One must struggle with the past, engage with the present, and create anew an account of God and God's relations with the world that makes sense of our historical moment. Every word of our theology is born of struggle.

The key text for understanding revisionism is David Tracy's *Blessed Rage for Order* (1996). This chapter will start by looking at this book in some detail and drawing from it an outline of the key features of revisionism. Since this book was originally written in 1973, we shall then look at the various ways in which Tracy wants to amend his project. Using his second edition, published in 1996, we identify four ways in which the project needs to be developed. I shall suggest that the key area, underpinning three of the four ways, is in his attitude to reason and modernity. Moving out from Tracy's book, we then examine the roots of revisionism, especially the impact that Paul Tillich and A. N. Whitehead have had on the movement. After this look back, we then look at fellow-travellers, with particular attention being given to Robert Neville, Edward Farley, Peter Hodgson, Schubert Ogden, and Gordon Kaufman. In conclusion, the chapter examines the future of revisionism. We shall see that, although it is clear that the impact of revisionism is largely confined to North America and Europe, some revisionist theologians are hoping that, appropriately modified, the revisionist project can have a wider appeal. Particular attention is paid to the work of the English theologian Keith Ward. In addition, I shall show that the underlying impulse of revisionism is important for all forms of theology.

I. David Tracy's *Blessed Rage for Order*

In this book, Tracy compares his revisionist model with four alternatives. These alternatives are: orthodox theology, which concentrates exclusively on the internal logic of the Christian drama; liberal theology, which concentrates on the conversation between the tradition and secularism; the neo-orthodox theology of Karl Barth and others, which Tracy interprets as a continuation of the liberal tradition; and finally, radical theology as advocated, for example, by the 'death of God' theologians, and which wants the traditional God to die so that human life can be liberated.

For Tracy, the revisionist model is one grounded, albeit in a critical way, in the work of Paul Tillich. Tracy describes the approach thus:

> With the relative strengths and limitations of liberalism, orthodoxy, neo-orthodoxy, and radical theologies in mind, the revisionist theologian is committed to continuing the critical task of the classical liberals and modernists in a genuinely post-liberal situation. By that commitment, the revisionist will also try to rectify earlier theological limitations both in the light of the new resources made available by further historical, philosophical, and social scientific research and reflection and in the light of the legitimate concerns and accomplishments of the later neo-orthodox and radical theological alternatives. In short, the revisionist theologian is committed to what seems clearly to be the central task of contemporary Christian theology: the dramatic confrontation, the mutual illumination and corrections, the possible base reconciliation between the principal values, cognitive claims, and existential faiths of both a reinterpreted post-modern consciousness and a reinterpreted Christianity. (Tracy 1996: 32)

So for Tracy it is an approach which takes our current situation seriously. Much as we might prefer to be living in a different time with different questions, we have to recognize where in fact we are. We need a theology, argues Tracy, that challenges both secularism and supernaturalism. Revisionist theologians, explains Tracy, 'believe that neither secularism nor supernaturalism can adequately reflect or appropriately ensure our commitment to the final worthwhileness of the struggle for truth and honesty in our inquiry, and for justice and even agapic love in our individual and social practice' (Tracy 1996: 9). For Tracy, the commendable values of secularity (e.g., the equality of all persons and the evil of patriarchy) need to be sustained by a proper understanding of the Christian drama. For Tracy, the supernaturalism of the Christian tradition needs to engage and be modified by the insights offered by the modern world.

The revisionist model is described in five theses. The first is this: 'The two principal sources for theology are christian texts and common human experience and language' (Tracy 1996: 43). For Tracy, the world of the Christian tradition needs to encounter, make sense of, and be modified by our shared human experience. The second thesis is: 'The theological task will involve a critical correlation of the results of the investigations of the two sources of theology' (Tracy 1996: 45). Here Tracy acknowledges his debt to Paul Tillich. However, he modifies Tillich's own method of correlation. In Tillich, it is the questions of our situation that need to correlate with the tradition; for Tracy, it is the entire situation that needs to be correlated with the tradition. The idea here is that the Christian texts must be correlated with the complexity of the human situation. The third thesis is: 'The principal method of investigation of the source "common human experience and language" can be described as a phenomenology of the "religious dimension" present in everyday and scientific experience and language' (Tracy 1996: 47). When one is making sense of the complexity of human life, the ultimate and most important discourse is the religious one. The fourth thesis is: 'The principal method of investigation of the source "the christian tradition" can be described as an historical and hermeneutical investigation of classical christian texts' (Tracy 1996: 49). So the revisionist theologian does apply the historical-critical method to the Bible. And the final thesis is: 'To determine the truth-status of the results of one's investigations into the meaning of both common human experience and christian texts the theologian should employ an explicitly transcendental or metaphysical mode of reflection' (Tracy 1996: 52). This he admits is the most contentious thesis. However, he wants to affirm that the ultimate mode of description required to make sense of our complex human experience is a religious one. He cites with approval both process philosophers, who affirm that our basic trust in scientific processes is linked with a basic faith, and Paul Tillich, who sees faith as a universal phenomenon because all people have some sort of ultimate concern (Tracy 1996: 53).

II. Development in Tracy

In the second edition, published in 1996, Tracy identifies four areas in which the revisionist model needs development. First, he argues for the imperative of absorbing the feminist paradigm more effectively. As Tracy himself notes, the theologian of his original text was almost always a 'he'. But more substantively, he argues that 'the whole self-corrective and self-critical character of the revisionary position of the book...turned out to be entirely open to that critical feminist revolution' (Tracy 1996: xiv). One difficulty with such assertions is that Tracy is assuming that feminism is itself a monolithic entity. While it is true that certain forms of feminism would find the revisionist model attractive (e.g., Ruether 1983), other feminists might feel that liberation and oppression are insufficiently central. Sharon Welch argues that we must engage with actual contexts of resistance and solidarity to enable a genuine theological critique to emerge (Welch 1985). Although Tracy can accommodate this idea, it is not central in the way that Welch seeks.

The second area of development concerns the hermeneutical task. The task of understanding the world theologically has become much harder for Tracy. Hermeneutics became a theme of much of his subsequent work, especially *Plurality and Ambiguity: Hermeneutics, Religion, and Hope* (1990). This is very significant. His growing sensitivity to hermeneutics changed his attitude to reason. Tracy explains:

> Indeed, a hermeneutical understanding of reason, history, and theology has defined, for me, how to understand reality and thought most adequately. Inevitably, as all my subsequent work on hermeneutics argues, modern 'rationality' cannot be, therefore, as straightforwardly

clear and controlled as 'rationality' frequently functions in *Blessed Rage for Order*. I still firmly believe in the self-correcting power of reason (as Bernard Lonergan nicely names it). However, I am not as sure as I once was that modern reason can produce so unproblematically the kind of uncomplicated metaphysical and transcendental arguments needed for fundamental theology. (Tracy 1996: xiv)

Tracy's increasingly sophisticated understanding of reason is a much-needed development to his original model. 'Modern reason' (as Tracy calls it) has been undermined by several different scholars and movements. Alasdair MacIntyre, in *Whose Justice? Which Rationality?* (1988), argued that reasoning is 'tradition-constituted' and 'tradition-located'. Both theoretical and practical reasoning is done differently in different traditions. Meanwhile some feminist theologians have argued that modern reason can be deeply oppressive. Grace Jantzen, for example, argues in her *Becoming Divine* (1998) that the traditional model of western reasoning is deeply problematic. This recognition of the complex nature of reason is linked with the third and fourth ways in which Tracy feels the project needs developing.

The third way is that modernity, as a category, is more complex than Tracy assumed:

[T]he ambiguity of the modern project seems far greater to me now than this 1973 book foresaw. Ambiguity, of course, is not simply a negative term. Ambiguity involves both truth *and* falsehood, goodness *and* evil, and even, in the religious dimension, the holy *and* the demonic. The modern project surely has involved all of these realities. On the one hand, modernity, as Jürgen Habermas and Schubert Ogden have persuasively argued, remains the great unfinished project of emancipation and demystification in Western and, increasingly, global culture.... On the other hand, as many analyses under the rubric of 'post-modernity' have justly argued, we now need even more studies of the profound ambiguities of the modern project than those articulated in *Blessed Rage for Order*. (Tracy 1996: xv)

So along with a much more nuanced view of reason, Tracy is now insisting that we need a more nuanced view of modernity. In one sense, revisionism always implied a nuanced attitude to modernity. While liberal theology celebrates the secular, the revisionist model wants to suggest that such celebration is incomplete unless it also recognizes the significance of the religious. However, Tracy does want to recognize the achievements of modernity (especially in terms of emancipation and demystification). 'A thinker today can only go through modernity, never around it, to post-modernity' (Tracy 1996: xv).

It is the recognition of the significance of postmodernity which constitutes Tracy's fourth way in which revisionism must be modified. It is interesting to see how Tracy states it:

Post-modern thought also makes it easier than a great deal of modern thought once did to appropriate positively many aspects of pre-modern thought: such as the pre-modern links between theory and 'spiritual exercises'...; such as greater attention to a range of forms beside concept and argument for theological content—metaphor, symbol, narrative, ritual, and many more; such as the need to heal the modern separation of feeling and thought...; such as Bernard Lonergan's fine interpretation of 'faith' as best understood as 'knowledge born of love'.

All of these pre-modern realities—and more—can be appropriated by post-modern thinkers as crucial fragments from our plural and ambiguous pre-modern past. (Tracy 1996: xv)

For Tracy, then, the attraction of the postmodern is that it becomes possible again to use pre-modern concepts and categories. Many who are sympathetic to post-modernism are arguing that modernity's emphasis on science, rationality (especially the significance of logical argument), technology, and control need to be displaced with pre-modern outlooks and dispositions.

So where does that leave the revisionist model? Tracy starts the second edition with the following claim:

The fundamental arguments of this book remain, I believe, as necessary now as then: the need to focus in theology on an ever increasing pluralism; the need to develop a genuinely public theology—available, in principle, to all intelligent, reasonable, responsible persons; the usefulness of some form of a correlation method as a heuristic guide for theology; the signal importance of fundamental theology to the entire theological enterprise; the importance, therefore, of reason and its critical, self-correcting function for all theology. These are the principal positions of this book. They were crucial then and they are crucial now for any serious critical theology. (Tracy 1996: xiii)

Revisionism is an approach to theology that takes the challenge of modernity (and postmodernity) seriously. Theology needs to be a discourse that is intelligible to those outside the Christian tradition. It needs to engage constructively with the reality of pluralism (i.e., the existence of many different traditions and world views in our society). For a revisionist theology, there is an explicit recognition that an uncomplicated authoritative revelation is not available. Instead, theology is a struggle—one that starts where we are—which seeks to understand anew how the symbols of the Christian drama speak to the age we live in.

III. The Roots of Revisionism

For many theologians, there is a complex web of influences that shape their thought. It is not easy to identify a straightforward trajectory from one particular person to another. There is a clear debt that revisionism owes to the nineteenth-century giant Friedrich Schleiermacher (1999). However, rather than concentrating on its nineteenth-century roots, I propose to focus on two twentieth-century theologians who are key for understanding contemporary revisionism.

The first is Paul Tillich. As we have already noted, Tillich's explicit contribution to revisionism (as advocated by David Tracy) is the concept of correlation. But there is a wider set of dispositions that Tillich provides. The challenge and complexity of theology is brilliantly captured by Tillich, when he writes:

No one can call himself a theologian, even if he is called to be a teacher of theology. Every theologian is committed *and* alienated; he is always in faith *and* in doubt; he is inside *and* outside the theological circle. Sometimes the one side prevails, sometimes the other; and he is never certain which side really prevails. Therefore, one criterion alone can be applied: a person can be a theologian as long as he acknowledges the content of the theological circle as his ultimate concern. (Tillich 1953: 13)

This theologian lives with doubt and alienation. And this is partly because the theologian should treat the subject matter with uttermost seriousness. When Tillich talks of faith as 'ultimate concern', he means that it matters ultimately. And this is the condition for Tillich's participation in theological conversation. Add to this Tillich's insistence that we should approach our subject matter with an appropriate humility—very aware of the limitations of our God-talk, we find a rather attractive picture of the theologian who struggles with humility to articulate the truths of the Christian tradition to the modern world.

Along with this set of dispositions, there are methodological insights and concepts, which are derived from Tillich's theology. On method, Tillich's emphasis that theology needs to be shaped by (and to shape) contemporary culture has been widely recognized. As regards concepts, many revisionist theologians share Tillich's stress on the challenge of God-talk. For Tillich, there is only one sentence about God which is non-symbolic: 'God is being itself.' All other assertions are symbolic:

There can be no doubt that any concrete assertion about God must be symbolic, for a concrete assertion is one which uses a segment of finite experience in order to say something about him. It transcends the content of this segment, although it also includes it. The segment of finite reality which becomes the vehicle of a concrete assertion about God is affirmed and negated at the same time. It becomes a symbol, for a symbolic expression is one whose proper meaning is negated by that to which it points. And yet it is also affirmed by it, and this affirmation gives the symbolic expression an adequate basis for pointing beyond itself. (Tillich 1953: 265–6)

Now it is not the case that David Tracy or Robert Neville or any other contemporary revisionist theologian would concur entirely with Tillich's account of the symbolic nature of religious language. However, it is the case that they share with Tillich the recognition of the indirect and difficult nature of God-talk. Unlike the English philosopher Richard Swinburne, one cannot take a human quality (for example, love) and simply stretch it out and apply it to God (Swinburne 1977). Tillich has loomed like a vast shadow over every revisionist project since.

Where Tillich provides the mood, the other major figure inspiring much revisionist theology is A. N. Whitehead. Process theology, especially the form it took at Claremont Graduate School with such people as John Cobb, David Ray Griffin, and Margaret Suchocki, was inspired by A. N. Whitehead. Whitehead's key achievement was to offer a sophisticated vocabulary that weaved together modern science and metaphysics. The net result was to contrast an imminent God, firmly located in time and embedded at the heart of the universe, with the classical account of God as timeless, incorporeal, and simple. The direct impact on the Claremont theologians is apparent, but Whitehead's reach is much further. David Tracy also celebrates and endorses the insights of the process theologians. He shares a rejection of the 'monarchical God' (as the God of classical theism is often described) and talks of God as the soul of the world and as dipolar or panentheistic (Tracy 1996: 185). And even in those who would never be labelled as process theologians, one finds an echo of these arguments. Keith Ward, for example, argues for a 'dynamic infinity', which involves 'a move which requires the admission of potency and temporality in God, but which can be reconciled with a properly interpreted doctrine of eternity and necessity' (Ward 1982: 3).

Tillich, then, provided primarily the approach, the disposition, and, for some, the method, while Whitehead provided the direction. A key issue for many revisionist theologians is to provide an account of God which links God more effectively with the world. This is true not simply of David Tracy, but also of many of his fellow-travellers.

IV. Other Revisionist Theologians

All labels have problems. Although all theologians emerge out of a tradition of inquiry, the thought of each one takes a particular shape which often transcends the tradition out of which he or she writes. Therefore, in considering the work of Robert Neville, Edward Farley, Peter Hodgson, Schubert Ogden, and Gordon Kaufman, we should recognize that, to an extent, the label revisionist is an imposition on their work. From the outside, it is clear that there are broad similarities and sympathies across their work; from the inside, however, there are significant differences.

Robert Neville of Boston University sees the task of theology as primarily one of making connections in all sorts of different ways—between popular and academic theology, between ancient and modern, and between different faith traditions. In *The Truth of Broken Symbols* (1996), Neville explores the fundamental location and understanding of God-talk. Starting with the ways that religious symbols helped our forebears cope with their problems, Neville argues that these ancient symbols, appropriately reconstructed or revised, can also help us cope with our problems. This is the work of theological semiotics. For Neville, as for most revisionist theologians, truth is mediated via these religious symbols. Although there are some revisionist theologians who place considerable emphasis on the human role in constructing our God-talk (e.g., Gordon Kaufman), none go as far as non-realist theologians such as Don Cupitt (1987).

While these symbols are the discourse of lived, experienced religion, the theologian needs to develop a discourse that enables cross-comparison between traditions. This for Neville is the work of philosophical cosmology and metaphysics. Neville explains:

> Only when theological ideas are addressed with metaphysical generality can any fair way be found to compare different religious traditions or find common ground with science, the arts, and practical disciplines such as law. Metaphysical ideas are so abstract as to be vague with respect to how they can be instantiated in various less abstract conceptualities. They should be able to register just how each of those less abstract ways of thought are specifications of the metaphysical abstractions, thus making it possible to tell how they relate to one another, for instance as identical, complementary, or contradictory. A good metaphysical system allows all plausible less abstract conceptualities to be registered without bias, and facilitates connecting them. (Neville 2005: 147)

For Neville, then, the primary role of the theologian is to *translate* various religious discourses from one type to another. One translates the underlying significance of religious symbol into a discourse that is intelligible to our time and place; and one translates all religious symbols into a metaphysical discourse that enables cross-cultural and interdisciplinary comparison. The theologian, for Neville, is seen very much in-between—in-between the discourses of religion and of the worlds of science, arts, and society.

The impact for systematic theology is best seen in his *A Theology Primer* (1991). Written as a textbook for systematic theology courses, it is an outstanding example of how the revisionist approach makes a difference. On the one hand, it is a traditional systematic theology with chapters on revelation, God, the human condition, salvation, justification, sanctification, Christology, and the Holy Spirit. It is, as Neville points out, 'The general outline of topics . . . typical of Christian systematic theology from Thomas Aquinas in the thirteenth century down to Paul Tillich in the twentieth' (Neville 1991: xiii). On the other hand, the way he frames a problem and the range of sources he is willing to consider in attempting to engage the problem is very different from more traditional presentations of systematic theology. So when Neville introduces the problem of God, he does so in the following way: 'The problem of God is thus to develop conceptions of the divine that provide interpretations for the various symbolic representations in religious life and at the same time cope with the conception of the universe as having closure' (Neville 1991: 28). The phrase 'symbolic representations in religious life' captures the sense of God that we have received. The phrase 'conception of the universe as having closure' captures for Neville the challenge of modernity, the very definition of which includes closure (i.e., the ease with which we see the universe as a closed set, describable in a certain way that excludes certain entities). In posing the problem of God in this way, Neville places the past in conversation with modernity (the present). When it comes to the range of sources he is willing to use to solve the problem of God, he does not confine himself to the Christian community or story, but is happy to consider insights and arguments from other faith traditions.

> The element of form or order has been expressed in the history of religions, as well as in the Judeo-Christian tradition, in the guise of the Sky God who imposes order on chaos.... Of course, in the Christian tradition God is the creator of the stuff or chaos ordered as well as of the order. Therefore, there is a divinity in the power and careers of the components of any given order. This is associated with the religious impulses of Mother Nature, the Earth Mother. (Neville 1991: 46)

As Neville admits, he wants to incorporate insights of 'feminist theology, liberation theologies, and the history of the dialogue between Christianity and other world religions, including many of the major positions of the other religions themselves' (Neville 1991: xxiv). And in his discussion of God he is drawing on both feminist sources (the male aspect needs the female aspect) and the discourse of other religions.

Staying with the impact of revisionism on the doctrine of God, we turn to the work of our second contemporary revisionist theologian Edward Farley from Vanderbilt Divinity School. All revisionist theologians are in critical conversation with the tradition, and Farley is no exception. In *Divine Empathy: A Theology of God* (1996), he describes the 'classical catholic theology of God'. There are, he suggests, four ambiguities embedded in this account. The first is its foundationalism: this is best illustrated by its use of Anselm's ontological argument, which is sometimes treated as a traditional argument intended to persuade the non-believer, even though Anselm made this argument in a prayer. The second is its confusion over whether God is a being or being itself. Popular piety, which tends to think of God as an object out there, gets mixed up with more formal theology, which is hostile to the idea of God as an object. The third is 'a tension between a set of attributes derived from God as the necessary and perfect self-existent and the discourse that attributes activity, responsiveness, and personality to God' (Farley 1996: 36). This is the ground on which the battle between more classical accounts of God and process accounts is fought. The final ambiguity concerns theodicy. For the catholic account of God, the theodicy problem is an inevitable and unresolvable *a priori*, built into the definition of God and the relation of that God with the world.

It is in conversation with these ambiguities that Farley starts to construct his alternative. The revisionism is explicit. In a move sympathetic to Anselm's ontological argument (read firmly located in its prayer setting), Farley insists that evidence and meaning are related when it comes to God. 'God comes forth as God into specific designation by way of the redemptive transformations attested to in Christian communities' (Farley 1996: 63). The key is our individual experience of redemption, the breaking out from idolatry into the 'freedoms of redemption' (Farley 1996: 72). Our experience of redemption calls forth a referent—God—but the challenge then is to talk of this God. This leads to a significant discussion of symbolics. God-talk is justified in the following way:

How do we justify using a particular set of symbols, predicates, or metaphors to express the sacred? The task falls within the theology of God and thus does not suspend but takes for granted the facticity of redemption to which the religious community attests. Insofar as redemption takes place in the spheres of individual agency, relation, and the social, a bespeaking of God will arrive in connection with these spheres. In each case, the particular redemption of that sphere engenders a symbolics of the one and only power that could effect that redemption. (Farley 1996: 110)

Farley then sets out a distinctive account of religious language grounded in ciphers and negations of God and, ultimately, linked with redemption. Farley then contrasts his approach to other theological approaches:

I have tried to mark out a pathway from the facticity of redemption to the symbolics of God. To traverse this pathway is neither to speculate nor to appeal to authority. As to the former, I do not begin with an initial philosophical distinction between God and the world nor do I establish the symbolic content of God by citing specific texts. Those who do proceed in these ways may see the path I am traversing as 'anthropological', even 'subjective'. In one sense they would be right. I do attempt to trace the symbolics of God back to discernments, convictions, and beliefs of individuals, to human interrelationality, and sociality. The basis of this procedure is that God comes forth as God in connection with redemptive transformations of the spheres of human reality. (Farley 1996: 123)

For Farley, the approach to theology is much more bottom-up rather than top-down. He takes very seriously those critics of religion who argue that God-talk is illegitimate and irrational. These critics are significant conversation partners. He very much wants to start where we all are, and not from some assumed revelation or privileged community.

The result of all this work is to suggest that the most appropriate metaphor for God's activity is divine empathy.

The rich contents of redemption, the event of Jesus as Christ, and the symbolics of God all point to a single metaphor for God's activity, the metaphor of divine empathy.... The divine activity has all four of these features: participative suffering, self-impartation, perception of our experiencing, and compassion. Divine empathy here will be an inclusive term for this collection of metaphors. (Farley 1996: 295–6)

By stressing divine empathy, Farley takes a metaphor that traditional theology has found problematic. This again is characteristic of revisionism: the resulting theology seeks to correct certain 'errors' in the traditional account of God.

Edward Farley's colleague at Vanderbilt Divinity School was Peter C. Hodgson. And it is to Hodgson that we turn next. In his *Winds of the Spirit: A Constructive Christian Theology* (1994), Hodgson sets out the challenge of 'constructive theology'. The very term constructive theology embodies the revisionist task. Hodgson explains:

> [W]e can get carried away with intellectual systems, forgetting their limited, fragmentary, situation-dependent, heuristic character. This is where the word 'constructive' has certain advantages over 'systematic'.... In order to construct, we must deconstruct. But because of deconstruction, we must construct. Indeed, one of the challenges of a deconstructive age is to take up the constructive task afresh. Because of the destruction, waste, fragmentation, and loss that are all around us, we must engage in constructive acts in order to exist as humans as well as to live as Christians and think theologically.... Finally, constructive activity is interpretative activity.... Constructive theology can also be likened to a work of fiction.... The theologian 'invents' but not simply out of his or her subjective fantasy. Rather the inventions are based on multiple resources ranging from ancient texts to communally shared experiences and they elicit the root, radical dimension of these texts and experiences, namely a revelatory encounter with ultimate reality. Theological fiction has an experimental quality: One is invited to enter into its imaginative world, try out its construals, test and modify them in light of one's own experience. Good theology stands up against such tests; it proves its value, its veracity, in a community of discourse over space and time. (Hodgson 1994: 39–40)

This is a revealing description of the theological task, which is true for many revisionist theologians. First, we are in a context that needs an imaginative theology. Hodgson talks here about our deconstructive age. Elsewhere in *Winds of the Spirit*, he describes the challenge of postmodernism, the emancipatory quest (with our heightened sensitivity to suffering and oppression and our recognition that this can be changed), the ecological quest, and the dialogical quest (the importance of dialogue between religions and beyond). Second, the basis of constructive theology is built on a particular analysis of how the experience of God shapes a community. Hodgson implies here a pre-textual experience 'with ultimate reality' which is the control on his theology. For Hodgson there are 'root experiences or revelatory events that give rise to faith; the expressions of faith in language, texts, traditions; and the interpreters or believers who engage in both faith and practice in specific cultural contexts' (Hodgson 1994: 31). Revisionist theologians bypass the Bible in order to get back to what constitute the authentic control on theology: the initial experiences of the divine that birthed the Bible.

The result of this methodology is a trinitarian theology. With the three cultural quests (the emancipatory, the ecological, and the dialogical), Hodgson argues for a correlation (loosely understood; see Hodgson 1994: 46) between 'these quests and a triadic structure of divine life, namely *freedom*, *love*, and *wholeness*'. Hodgson explains:

> God is the One who creates out of love that which is radically different from yet deeply related to God, namely the world, and who liberates this world from its fallenness, fragmentation, and futility by drawing it into everlasting communion with God and empowering the endless struggle against evil. God is the One Who Loves in Freedom. God is not an isolated supreme being over against the world; rather, embodied by the world, incarnate in the shapes of Christ, God becomes a concrete, living relational God, 'Spirit'. (Hodgson 1994: xi–xii)

The result, then, is that the language of the tradition is used to reconceive our understanding of God in such a way that enables humanity to face the challenges of living in the modern world.

We shall now consider more briefly two further revisionist theologians, Schubert Ogden and Gordon Kaufman. Schubert Ogden is a Methodist who spent much of his career at Southern Methodist University. Ogden shares with Tracy the view that the task of theology involves the work of correlation. For Ogden, Christian witness needs to connect with human existence. However, he insists that this work of correlation is subject to two criteria: the first is appropriateness to the normative Christian witness; and the second is the credibility of the idea as judged by the canons of 'truth universally established with human existence' (Ogden 1992: 3). Ogden works on a similar canvas as Tracy: he shares a commitment to process theology and affirms many of the insights of liberation theologians. And he has proposed what he calls a 'revisionary Christology', in which the task is to determine the meaning of Jesus for us.

The last theologian I wish to consider is the Mennonite theologian Gordon Kaufman. Compared to Tracy, Neville, Farley, and Ogden, Kaufman is the most radical. Kaufman explains that there are four 'fundamental dimensions' of his faith and piety that are assumed in his theological system.

> These are (a) my deep sense of the ultimate mystery of life; (b) my feeling of profound gratitude for the gift of humanness and the great diversity which it manifests; (c) my belief (with this diversity especially in mind) in the continuing importance of the central Christian moral demand that we love and care for not only our neighbors but even our enemies; and (d) my conviction (closely connected with this last point) that the principal Christian symbols continue to provide a significant resource for the orientation of human life. (Kaufman 1993: xii)

Although Kaufman admits that much of his theology is 'agnostic' (Kaufman 1993: xiii), it retains plenty of content. He wants to reinterpret the symbol 'God' so that it is less oppressive (to the poor, the marginalized, women) and yet still places a demand on humanity. So 'God' becomes 'a norm or criterion or reality—what I call an "ultimate point of reference"—in terms of which all else may be assessed and understood' (Kaufman 1993: 28). It is an ultimate point of reference which judges our values, hopes, and aspirations in this life. Kaufman is opposed to any dualism that sets God against this world, life against heaven, or nature against spirit (Kaufman 1993: 326). Given that all language is a human construct, we should not be afraid of reinventing our concept of God so that it more obviously affirms life and justice. The 'God' symbol, explains Kaufman, 'must be understood as a product of the human imagination' (Kaufman 1993: 39). This frees us up to seek an appropriate redefinition of it. Along with God, Christology too is revisited. Kaufman wants a wider Christology in which 'Christ' brings 'a new communal ethos in history' (Kaufman 1993: 396). And on ecclesiology, Kaufman sees the churches as a 'community of reconciliation and humanization' (Kaufman 1993: 442). For Kaufman, the revisions need to be radical and dramatic.

V. The Future of Revisionism

James Buckley writes, 'The key achievement of revisionists and liberals has been to challenge our received practices and teachings about truth, human beings, God, and Christ' (Buckley 2005: 222). Buckley's point stresses two aspects of revisionist theology. The first is that it is heavily shaped by western post-Enlightenment thought. The whole project of modernity is assumed. Although it is true that Tracy recognizes the needs to embrace the insights of postmodernism and criticizes Kaufman for his 'uncritical acceptance of modernity' (Buckley 2005: 221), modernity remains a key defining event for the revisionist theologian. It is an axiom driving revisionist theology that modernity has made much of the traditional package of Christian doctrine problematic. The second aspect is that revisionism shares with modernity a problem with truth. This is a major internal debate, an issue that divides many of those involved. How and in what way can God-talk correspond to reality? And, crucially, how do we know which theological account is more appropriate?

For these two reasons, the momentum behind revisionist theology does partly depend on the project of western modernity. For much of the twentieth century, when the secularization thesis was still in vogue, some form of revisionism seemed both inevitable and essential. Unless Christian theology could find some way of accommodating the insights of science, feminism, the social sciences, and our growing historical sensitivity, then secularization would consign Christianity to the dustbin of history. However, at the start of the twenty-first century, our perceptions of the world are changing. The western mixture of a technological and market-orientated society, coupled with weaker allegiances to religious community, has not been found elsewhere in the world. And even in Europe, some sociologists of religion believe that the secularization thesis was not justified by the evidence (Davie 1994; cf. Bruce 2002). At any rate, although globalization and modernity are touching every part of the world, this is not creating the pressures toward secularization found in Europe. American religious life is as robust as ever. Islamic revivalism is sweeping large parts of the Middle East, Africa, and south-east Asia. And Christianity is growing dramatically in Africa and Latin America. Philip Jenkins makes the point well:

> The denominations that are triumphing all across the global South are stalwartly traditional or even reactionary by the standards of the economically advanced nations. The churches that have made most dramatic progress in the global South have either been Roman Catholic, of a traditional and fideistic kind, or radical Protestant sects, evangelical or Pentecostal.... For over a century, the coming decline or disappearance of religion has been a commonplace assumption of Western thought, and church leaders have sometimes shared this pessimistic view. Every so often, some American or European writer urges the church to adjust itself to present-day realities, to become 'relevant' by abandoning outmoded supernatural doctrines and moral assumptions.... Viewed from Cambridge or Amsterdam, such pleas may make excellent sense, but in the context of global Christianity, this kind of liberalism looks distinctly dated. (Jenkins 2002: 7–9)

This growth in conservative religion is partly a result of globalization. Mobility has made it easy for resources and ideas to reach every part of the world. With the arrival of McDonald's restaurants and western medicine in a city, traditional forms of Christianity and Islam have also come. Market-orientated capitalism and science have made the spread of traditional religions possible.

It is partly this link between revisionism and western modernity that explains the limited impact that revisionism has had on the Christian community. It is most popular with the Protestant mainline in the United States (Episcopal, Methodist, Lutheran, Presbyterian, United Church of Christ) and their European counterparts. As these denominations are relatively small, there is a real risk that revisionism will appear to be a niche theology for the semi-secular Christian minorities in Europe and North America.

One important response to the growth in conservative theologies is to argue that revisionism is itself a traditional theological method. Several English theologians are arguing that a commitment to revisionism is in continuity with the underlying method of much traditional Christian theology. For example, Keith Ward argues for an 'open orthodoxy' which 'will be true to the main orthodox Christian tradition, yet which will be open to a fruitful interaction with other traditions, and with the developing corpus of scientific knowledge' (Ward 1994: 1–2). It is an open orthodoxy because it is both open to being shaped by non-Christian traditions and orthodox in that it shares with the tradition a recognition that all truth belongs to God. It is undoubtedly true that St Augustine of Hippo and St Thomas Aquinas were both committed to developing the tradition in conversation with the insights from non-Christian sources. In the case of Augustine, the key conversation partner was Neoplatonic thought. Aquinas learned from Aristotle through Islamic and Jewish thinkers (Markham 2003; Burrell 1986). Understood in this way, the challenge of shaping the Christian tradition in conversation with non-Christian sources is not a radical innovation but a continuation of the underlying methodology of the tradition. Revisionism, then, is seen less as being in dialogue exclusively with modernity and as open to dialogue with a variety of sources. Following Robert Neville, the theological task must include the conversation with other religious traditions.

On the whole issue of truth, these more traditional revisionist theologians are clear. Although they acknowledge the difficulty of showing how theological assertions correspond to and describe reality, they also maintain that such a task is both possible and important. Keith Ward is an uncomplicated critical realist (Markham 2003: 159–67). He believes that there is a basic theoretical rationality which is universal.

> There are some very basic rational criteria which can be brought to bear upon all claims to truth, in religion as elsewhere. Rationality involves the use of intelligent capacities, including the capacity to register information correctly, to compare similar pieces of information, to deduce and infer in accordance with rules of logic and relate means to ends effectively. A rational person can act on a consciously formulated principle in order to attain an intended goal.... Such simple forms of reasoning are necessary to any form of intelligently ordered social life. They are not, and cannot be, culturally relative. (Ward 1994: 319)

This means in practice that any theological account of God and God's relations with the world must be internally coherent; if it is coherent, then it is a matter of evidence, explanatory power, and plausibility. He is impatient with those who want to describe different and incommensurable traditions with different rationalities.

> If one asks to what 'tradition' these basic criteria of rationality—self-consistency, coherence with other knowledge, and adequacy to available data—belong, the answer must be that they belong to the tradition of being human, as such.... [T]hey are principles of rationality which are built into the necessary structure of human social life, and thus function as desirable ideals for any community that wishes to survive for any length of time. (Ward 1994: 320)

For Ward, the task of revisionism should take seriously the challenge of applying these criteria, but should not endlessly question their validity. It is a fundamental human instinct to make sense of this complex world in the best way possible. This quest for the truth must underpin the revisionist theological project.

With some revisionist theologians making these modifications, it is hoped that the basic impulse of revisionism can reach beyond the elites in North America and Europe. However, even if revisionism remains confined to the progressive and liberal parts of the world, a case can be made that the challenge of revisionism is important for all forms of Christian theology. All forms of theology need to think through their method, and there is a primacy about method in revisionism which is not found elsewhere. James Buckley notes in passing that 'almost all Christian theologians aim to "revise" their Christian heritage in some respects or "liberate it" from its foibles and sin' (Buckley 2005: 213). Buckley's point is that one should be very careful about the use of the label 'revisionist'. However, the opposite point is equally true. If all theologians are in the business of 'revising their Christian heritage', then the appropriate method for such revising is crucial to all theologians. Issues concerning authority, the appropriate symbols, and the plausibility and coherence of beliefs are issues that interest all theologians. Credit should be given for asking the right questions and wrestling with the right issues.

References

Bruce, Steve (2002). *God is Dead: Secularization in the West.* Oxford: Blackwell.

Buckley, James J. (2005). 'Revisionists and Liberals'. In David Ford and Rachel Muers (eds.), *The Modern Theologians*, 3rd edn., Oxford: Blackwell Publishing, 213–28.

Burrell, David (1986). *Knowing the Unknowable God: Ibn Sina, Maimonides, Aquinas.* Notre Dame: University of Notre Dame Press.

Cupitt, Don (1987). *Long-Legged Fly: A Theology of Longing and Desire.* London: SCM.

Davie, Grace (1994). *Religion in Britain since 1945: Believing without Belonging.* Oxford: Blackwell.

Farley, Edward (1996). *Divine Empathy: A Theology of God.* Minneapolis: Augsburg.

Hodgson, Peter C. (1994). *Winds of the Spirit: A Constructive Christian Theology.* Louisville: Westminster John Knox.

Jantzen, Grace (1998). *Becoming Divine: Towards a Feminist Philosophy of Religion.* Manchester: Manchester University Press.

Jenkins, Philip (2002). *The Next Christendom.* Oxford: Oxford University Press.

Kaufman, Gordon D. (1993). *In Face of Mystery: A Constructive Theology.* Cambridge: Harvard University Press.

MacIntyre, Alasdair (1988). *Whose Justice? Which Rationality?* London: Duckworth.

Markham, Ian S. (2003). *A Theology of Engagement.* Oxford: Blackwell.

—— (2004). 'Zins V. Ethisch'. In *Theologische Realenzyklopädie.* Berlin: Walter de Gruyter, 36. 687–91.

Neville, Robert Cummings (1991). *A Theology Primer.* Albany: State University of New York Press.

—— (1996). *The Truth of Broken Symbols.* Albany: State University of New York Press.

—— (2005). 'Critical Study of Ian S. Markham, *A Theology of Engagement*'. *Conversations in Religion and Theology* 3/2: 140–50.

Ogden, Schubert M. (1992). *On Theology.* Dallas: Southern Methodist University Press.

Ruether, Rosemary Radford (1983). *Sexism and God-Talk: Toward a Feminist Theology.* London: SCM.

Schleiermacher, Friedrich (1999). *The Christian Faith.* London: T. & T. Clark.

Swinburne, Richard (1977). *The Coherence of Theism.* Oxford: Oxford University Press.

Tillich, Paul (1953). *Systematic Theology,* i. London: Nisbet.

Tracy, David (1990). *Plurality and Ambiguity: Hermeneutics, Religion, and Hope.* Chicago: University of Chicago Press.

—— (1996). *Blessed Rage for Order: The New Pluralism in Theology.* Chicago: University of Chicago Press.

Ward, Keith (1982). *Rational Theology and the Creativity of God.* Oxford: Blackwell.

—— (1994). *Religion and Revelation.* Oxford: Oxford University Press.

Welch, Sharon (1985). *Communities of Resistance and Solidarity.* Maryknoll: Orbis.

Suggested Reading

Buckley (2005).

Farley (1996).

Gilkey, Langdon (1979). *Message and Existence: An Introduction to Christian Theology.* New York: Seabury.

Hodgson (1994).

Kaufman (1993).

Markham (2003).

Neville (1996).

Ogden (1992).

Ruether (1983).

Tillich (1953).

Tracy, David (1981). *The Analogical Imagination: Christian Theology and the Culture of Pluralism.* New York: Crossroad.

Ward (1994).

CHAPTER 34

POSTMODERN THEOLOGY

WALTER LOWE

THERE is a certain madness in Christianity—in a desert God who is jealous and passionate, in a saviour who speaks in apocalyptic terms, in a life of sacrificial love, in the scandal of particularity. In principle, a confessional theology should bear the mark of this madness, but the mark or wound must constantly be renewed. The resources for such renewal will come from without the Christian community as well as within, if only because 'without' and 'within' are porous. Postmodernism at its best is of interest because it helps theology think hard and self-critically, and because it is itself in touch with a certain madness which may just possibly be constitutive of who or what we are.

I. INTRODUCTION

It is natural to ask whether the notion of God as 'Other' bears any relation to 'the Other' of postmodernism. And what of 'difference'? Let us begin with the early Barth's familiar declaration that, if he has a system, 'it is limited to a recognition of what Kierkegaard called the "infinite qualitative difference between time and eternity"' (Barth 1968: 10). One might think that because of the theological marker 'infinite', Barth's usage is specifically theological and *sui generis*. But how is one to account for what happens when we turn from Barth's preface, where he is quoting Kierkegaard directly, to the commentary itself? Here the term 'infinite' disappears: Barth speaks quite simply of 'qualitative difference between God' and the human being (Barth 1968: 39, cf. 50). The effect is, to all appearances, a retreat from radicality to truism. That there might be a 'qualitative difference' between time and eternity seems altogether obvious. Either this is a lapse on Barth's part, or he sees in qualitative difference some unappreciated significance.

The explanation lies with what Barth takes to be a pervasive, intransigent tendency in human language and thought. 'We assign [God] the highest place in our world; and in so doing we place him fundamentally on one line with ourselves and with things' (Barth 1968: 44). So entrenched is the tendency Barth postulates that even the term 'infinite' leads us to imagine a (limitless) extension of the finite. Undisturbed is the assumption that somehow, in some fashion, God and 'ourselves and... things' all exist 'on one line'. To draw a term from the postmodernist thinker Emmanuel Levinas, the qualifier 'infinite' does not assure exemption from the hegemony of 'the Same'. As we shall see, Barth, Levinas, and Derrida do share at least a negative point of reference in their resistance to our thinking's entropy toward 'the Same'. Thought is often conceived as an ascent toward the One, but in the present critical context it is rather a decline. The determination to swim against the current is a thread running through postmodernism and its most interesting antecedents. It also suggests some tentative affinity between postmodernism and the task of systematic theology (Lowe 1993: 33–5).

Kierkegaard was acutely aware of how the understanding of Christianity is affected by an assumption of sameness. In the *Journals and Papers* he observes:

> The greater honesty in even the most bitter attacks of an earlier age upon Christianity was that the essentially Christian was fairly well allowed to remain intact. The danger in Hegel was that he altered Christianity—and thereby achieved agreement with his philosophy. In general it is characteristic of an age of reason not to let the task remain intact and say: No—but to alter the task and then say: Yes, of course, we are agreed. (Kierkegaard 1970: ii. 226)

Where reason, common sense, and Christianity concur, there offence, shock, and otherness are lost. Christianity ceases to be a calling, becoming a mere adornment.

In this light it would be a disservice if the present chapter were to suggest that theology and postmodernism can simply coalesce. Yet it would be helpful if the two were found to share something more than a negative orientation. We need a positive point of reference, but not too positive. Let us consider another example from Barth. In his exegesis of Romans 1: 20, 'the invisible things of God are clearly seen', Barth confronts an awkward situation. It sounds like natural theology. One expects him to draw back, but he does not. Rather he interprets 'the invisible things of God' as 'the insecurity of our whole existence, the vanity and utter questionableness of all that is and of what we are'. It is this insecurity and questionableness which, Barth asserts, lie 'as in a text-book open before us' (Barth 1968: 46). The universal availability of this awareness is not an incidental matter; it is essential to the universality of responsibility and sin that Barth, following Paul, affirms.

Questionability and its universality may be crucial to the encounter between theology and postmodernism. Questionability provides a point of orientation that is not simply negative, yet neither is it simply positive; in effect it opens a liminal space that eludes dogmatism altogether. This in turn raises the question of whether the questionability that lies 'as in a text-book open before us' is a merely provisional, transitional matter. Is questionability a puzzle that Christianity proceeds to solve? Or is it not so easily dispatched?

II. The Dispute over Humanism

Critics charge that postmodernism is antithetical to basic human values. Postmodernists reply that humanism itself is more of a construct than its advocates admit. The matter cannot be settled here, but some historical reminders are pertinent.

Historically, theology has been less than constant in awareness of its questionability. When the Enlightenment called Christian triumphalism to account, theology could no longer regard itself as the uncontested custodian of eternal benefit and found itself assailed as an agent of oppression, the enemy of humanity's newborn self-awareness. Theologians unwilling to trade down to deism were on the defensive. To those struggling against the cultured despisers of religion, the emergence of Romanticism (an insurgency internal to modernity itself) seemed providential. For in Romanticism religion (properly understood) is not the enemy but the very heart of human aspiration, the voice of yearning for 'something more' than the material benefits and quantified universe of a positivistic world view. Abruptly the tables were turned: science itself (or scientism) was seen as that which barred the way to the fully human. Science was now the enemy of human flourishing, what William Blake decried as the 'single vision' of 'Newton's sleep' (Blake 1970: 62).

From this stemmed Romantic theology. No longer an abstraction, the notion of God was knit to human experience by a number of mediating terms. 'Transcendence' is a prominent example. The longing for something more was understood to be, at one and the same time, an expression of human transcendence and a search for—and thus an implicit linkage with—the transcendent itself. Ultimately, human transcendence and the transcendent itself were of a piece. Similarly, the terms 'spiritual' and 'divine' served as welding points for the exuberant new theology. But although the Romantic gambit produced a powerful apologetic, it did so at a price. For notwithstanding its tireless celebration of richness and diversity, Romanticism required an *Anknüpfungspunkt*, a point of contact. The logic of

Romanticism required some point of aspiration, be it *telos* or origin, be it high or deep, where creature and creator were at one. It required a point where transcendence communed with the transcendent, like with like, and thus of necessity a point of sameness. Beyond appearances and protestations, religious Romanticism actually concurred with what it opposed; it drew its very hope and confidence from an inward dominion of 'the Same'. In Kierkegaard's phrase, it was Romanticism far more than the Enlightenment that murmured the soporific words, 'Yes, of course, we are agreed' (Lowe 2006).

The point of these loosely historical ruminations is to suggest that there can be such a thing as an ideology of transcendence, and that any humanist who dismisses postmodernism needs to ask whether she or he may not be tacitly wedded to something of this sort. And, I hasten to add, a similar misgiving must be registered against a certain *prima facie* postmodernism. For there is on the market a putative postmodernism that seeks transcendence, repackaged perhaps as transgression, on the cheap. Its characteristic gambit is to collapse modernity into the Enlightenment, and the Enlightenment into the Newtonian world view, all the while professing sensitivity to difference. Such self-serving reductionism is disingenuous at best; for while it is easy to argue that any sort of postmodernism represents a break from Newton, it is much more difficult to show that those who have so narrowed their target represent a break, much less an epochal shift, from Romanticism (Ward 1997: xl–xli). In short, humanistic values are not a simple given, and neither is the touted arrival of a new, postmodern epoch.

III. Hegel and Heidegger

Hegel saw more clearly than others of his time that Romanticism alone could not furnish the solution. Its pillorying of the Enlightenment was more symptom than remedy. If it fiercely opposed an objectifying rationality, was it thereby unaccountable to reason? If not, then it must imply a further, perhaps higher form of reason. But that was something that Romanticism could not bring forth on its own. In Hegel's terms, Romanticism gave voice to the 'unhappy consciousness' of the modern age. For a more comprehensive perspective, Hegel reached back to Aristotle's vision of a world in which each being has as its very essence an inherent potential, a drive toward self-realization. The acorn bears the oak within it. But Hegel transformed Aristotle's harmonious, circumscribed classicism in light of Romanticism's limitless aspiration. Romanticism's peculiar drive is not just to realize itself but to transcend itself, and in the very act of transcending, to realize its truer self. Through Hegel Romanticism could know its inner truth as being the demand for transcendence as endless self-transcending. If Hegel's thought was ambitious, it was perhaps because he believed that modernity's unhappy consciousness was a stifled cry for liberation, the need for a context of constant self-transcendence, which is what Hegel means by Spirit.

All this is said to prevent us from simply dismissing Hegel, who may be our modern Aristotle, unveiling the hidden logic of the age (Marcuse 1960; Badiou 1999). His recognition that at the heart of modernity is the overcoming of purported essence has given us categories of thought by which we continue to live. The 'human potential' movement, for example, is shot through with Hegelian concepts, albeit at third or fourth remove. In an epoch of virtual reality, image management, and economics as shared delusion, the spectral coalescence of 'system' and 'spirit' seems to be happening before our eyes. Two features of this inheritance are important for our reflections: an impatience with determinacy, which is readily associated with confinement and limitation; and a Faustian fascination with negativity, which as the power of freedom dissolves the dumb givenness of the 'in-itself' and propels being into becoming (Nancy 2002). Of this restless Hegelian inheritance, postmodernism is both critic and symptom.

Kierkegaard knew unhappy consciousness, but unlike Hegel he did not believe in immanence. That is, he did not believe that the task of being human bore its solution within itself, as a tacit power or potentiality. It is the thrust of Kierkegaard's entire dialectic that, contrary to Romanticism, contrary to Hegel, and contrary to much of the modern age, the human individual's true *telos* is not a point of transcendent contact. It is not a knowing of like to like (hence the pivotal importance of the difference between time and eternity) (Hannay 1982: 19–53). If postmodernism is pertinent to theology, it is in helping theology see this.

Like Kierkegaard, Martin Heidegger takes the difficult path of seeking truth not in the resolution of unhappy consciousness, but by its actual or imaginative intensification (Caputo 1987). But for Heidegger the crucial distinction was the 'ontological difference' between being and particular 'ontic' beings. No event in European philosophy of the last century had greater impact than Heidegger's relentless insistence that reclaiming the ontological difference required an uncharted transformation of thought. Specifically, he charged that, throughout its entire history since the Presocratics, western philosophy had largely forgotten this generative distinction that had been its first inspiration, so that the very doing of philosophy covered the difference over. Thus philosophy, like human existence itself, had to be excavated, as it were, to expose its suppressed awareness. For while the difference is primordial, it cannot be known directly: truth hides itself. Thus the thinker must proceed indirectly, by a careful dismantling of inherited modes of thought. And the process cannot be accomplished, as Nietzsche would have it, with a hammer. It must be attentive, supple, and self-critical, else it will helplessly repeat received patterns of thought. For Heidegger, real thinking means confronting (in Barth's terms) our 'questionability'. But the questionability is not simply negative: this is no thoughtless nihilism. For that which denies and disguises can be shown, with sufficient attention, to offer clues to that which is hidden. The elusive difference still permits certain events of meaning, as in poetry, in which truth glimmers forth.

The forgetfulness of being does not imply that the actual word 'being' had been forgotten. Far from it. But being is regarded in much of western thought as itself a sort of object, a being or, in Heidegger's term, 'ontic'. That is the fallacy or forgetfulness that constitutes ontotheology, which Heidegger regarded as the fall of western thought. The place of being is given over to God or some absolute stand-in, which is assigned the highest place among other places, and thus becomes a being among beings. The product of such laxity is what Heidegger castigates as ontotheology, in which the 'ontic' and the 'theology' together suppress real thinking under a hegemony of 'the Same'. What Derrida saw was that countering this entropy of culture and thought required that 'difference' be honoured in its own right.

IV. Derrida and *Différance*

Deconstruction does have a certain logic (Derrida 1988; 1995; Bennington and Derrida 1993; Lucy 2004). Suppose we begin with the structuralist observation that our thought and language are shaped by basic categories which are often contrasts, such as night and day, male and female, black and white. In many cases, one member of a dyad will gain preference, generating an explicit or implicit hierarchy. If hierarchy is exacerbated to the point of polarization (if 'spiritual meaning' is pitted against 'literal meaning', for example), there will be an effort to expel the allegedly lower, negative element, which by now is viewed as impurity.

In the ontological hierarchy, the highest, normative realm is exempt from dependence upon the lesser orders of being by the assumption that it carries within itself a self-evident authority. This self-authenticating immediacy may be that of simple sense perception ('red here now'), for example; or it may be Hegel's self-transparency of Spirit, as Spirit becomes more fully self-aware. Whatever the particulars, the supposedly self-authenticating reality is what Derrida means by 'presence'. Presence is, in short, what is taken to be unquestionable, and that is what gets the deconstructionist's excavation of questionability going.

It is important to note that Derrida's scepticism about claims of presence is no arbitrary nihilism, but an inductive generalization based on the close examination of a variety of cases and texts. What Derrida seeks to demonstrate is that in actual textual practice the effort to establish a realm of pure self-evidence by exiling recalcitrant elements does not in fact succeed. Rather, the abolished element reappears and does so, not at the periphery, but at the very centre—within the holy of holies, as it were. Further still, where the disavowed element reappears, it turns out that it is performing a function that is in practice indispensable to the supposedly self-sustaining presence! If I may offer a somewhat artificial example: we are often informed that the (supposedly) static, changeless God of classical tradition is no longer viable; what we need instead is a thoroughly (purely) dynamic conception of God in keeping with the present modern or postmodern epoch. Imagine then that one were to respond somewhat playfully, 'Tell me more about this dynamic character of God. Is it something that comes upon God in fits and starts like a seizure?' The response might be, 'Obviously you have understood nothing. God's creativity is endless, it is constant.' In effect, God is unchangingly dynamic. Thus may terms expelled reappear at the centre, in a manner that seems to have a logic of its own.

Elementary as it is, the example gives a sense of what Derrida is up to in even his densest writings. Specifically, Derrida charges that western philosophy has been 'logocentric' in its elevation of the personal spoken 'word' over the 'dead letter' of writing. Nor is this seemingly innocent act of preferment confined to philosophy. It may be observed full-blown in the Christian triumphalism that exalts a God-Logos by condemning the putative 'dead letter' of Jewish tradition. In such cases deconstruction proceeds by a sort of textual ju-jitsu. If one asks, for example, what makes exposure to the spoken word so important, one may find, in the actual text that declares the spoken word superior to the written, that it is because the experience of hearing the spoken word is so vivid that it indelibly 'imprints' the event upon one's memory (Derrida 1974). But note that, however vigorous the counter-case that writing may in some sense have precedence over speaking, the purpose is strictly tactical. That is to say, the aim is not to replace one presence with another, but to exhibit through counter-example the questionability of the initial claim. Similarly, when Derrida resorts to the esoteric term *différance*, it is a way of signalling that he intends something more penetrating than simply replacing sameness with difference, as the term is commonly understood.

This relates to Derrida's critique of Heidegger. Within Heidegger's ontological difference, one member (being) enjoys a certain primacy over the other. One evidence of this is the air of nostalgia that envelops being in Heidegger's late, quasi-mystical writings. Being (or some related term) assumes a sort of ontotheological role as original source and home. One might say that, within the ontological difference, Heidegger gives primacy to ontology, whereas Derrida will argue that Heidegger's own best insight lay rather with an event of differing/deferring that displaces the very notion of origin.

V. Derrida and Undecidability

Derrida does not deny the actuality of meaning; neither does he counter presence with 'pure absence'. Moreover, he shuns the Hegelian tradition of seeking transcendence through negation. Derrida's characteristic move is rather to associate meaning with excess. An early, formative event was Derrida's discovery of an excess of meaning that Edmund Husserl's phenomenology could not explain. A square circle is not an object that can appear unambiguously, as a full presence, in one's imaginative experience. Thus, according to Husserl's philosophy, it can have no meaning. Yet the phrase 'square circle' does have some sort of meaning. It might work well in a poem, for example; or, for that matter, in the previous sentence. If deconstruction has a founding moment, this is it. In some unaccountable fashion, to some undefined extent, language does exhibit a capacity to mean on its own, in its own right, as it were, with no need of an authorizing presence.

In the remarkable book *Jacques Derrida*, Geoffrey Bennington recalls the three classic elements of language: the sign (the mark or the sound 'tree'), the referent (a physical tree), and the sense (the concept of tree). He then proceeds to show that in point of fact Derrida does not deny any one of these (Bennington and Derrida 1993: 23–42). (One might indeed say that, consistent with his respect for the tradition he critiques, Derrida is something of a Platonist. Of course, concepts are not available to the mind as presences, as the idealist might wish, but they do have a certain objectivity that must be respected and assiduously traced. Certainly for Derrida there is no such thing as a 'free play' in which concepts can be tossed about at will.) Bennington's point is that deconstruction does not deny any of the linguistic triad; it only denies that we ever have any one in isolation from the others. Each bleeds into the other. Is it, for example, of no significance or meaning whatsoever that the mark for the first person singular in English is uniquely a capital letter? Or that the letter happens, in this patriarchal culture, to stand erect? Or that there is a material, phonic link to 'eye' in a culture that tends to regard the subject as an observer—the high-eye I?

This brings us to 'undecidability'. When we have to make a decision, we naturally look for something—a conviction, a fact, a feeling, perhaps a well-established custom—upon which the decision may be based. But none of these has a power, authority, or presence sufficient in and of itself to determine the decision. In this sense, the situation is one of 'undecidability', like 'ambiguity' in existentialism. By no means does such undecidability imply that no decision can be made. It simply means that the decision does need to be *made*. An authentic decision is not just read off the givens of the situation. Undecidability does not cancel the ability to decide, but rather provides the very ground for the possibility (a phrase we will return to later) of a decision that is not mimicry. The concluding sections of this chapter will consider how undecidability may relate to religious understandings of faith.

VI. Levinas: The Ethical as Excess

For Levinas (Davis 1996; Critchley 1999; Smith 1983), the burning question is whether we are 'duped by morality', whether warfare and torture are the underlying truth of our existence—as is implied when national leaders speak of 'taking off the gloves' (Greenberg 2006). Levinas like Kierkegaard opposes system or, in the phrase we have borrowed from him, the hegemony of 'the Same'. But his resistance is born of the twentieth-century invention of all-encompassing militarization in which a 'state of emergency' becomes the norm and respect for persons is indefinitely suspended. Levinas is witness that awareness of totalization is not the same as a stupefied submission to it. 'Freedom', he writes, 'consists in knowing that freedom is in peril. But to know or be conscious is to have time to avoid and forestall the instant of inhumanity' (Levinas 1969: 35). For our very being-conscious arises from a primordial awareness of the reality, the face, of the other. Like Kierkegaard he breaks system open with the ethical, but in a manner that regards the ethical as inherently insurmountable.

The subheadings of the first chapter in Levinas's *Totality and Infinity* (1969) offer a sort of synopsis. Let us consider them seriatim. *Desire for the Invisible*: desire is a theme drawn from Romanticism, but now the reliance on sameness is severed. 'The metaphysical desire does not rest upon any prior kinship' (Levinas 1969: 34). *The Breach of Totality* (Levinas 1969: 35) occurs only when we realize that totality is not just an external system 'out there', against which I stand as heroic individual. For the 'I', understood in western thought as a continual process of growth through assimilation, is itself a making-same. It is for this reason that the irruption of the ethical, in the form of the face of the other person, is experienced as an invasion. *Transcendence Is Not Negativity*: Levinas refuses to conceive spirit as in any sense a negation of the finite. *Metaphysics Precedes Ontology*: *contra* Heidegger, our relation to the other as being (the other person, 'the face') precedes the question of being. *Contra* ontotheology, the pre-eminent other is not God. Questionability, we have seen, eludes the categories of negative and positive. But this does not prepare us for Levinas's assertion that the face of the other 'is imposed upon the I beyond all violence by a violence that calls it entirely into question' (Levinas 1969: 47). What can this mean?

Transcendence as the Idea of Infinity (Levinas 1969: 48): Levinas's notion of the face has perplexed many of his readers. He consistently declines to give a concrete description. Some of the enigma arises from his depiction of the face as being 'before' me in two distinct senses of the word. The face is before me in a spatial sense in that I encounter it, I am accountable to it. It says, 'Do not kill me.' Yet at the same time it precedes me, or precedes my 'I', in a quasi-temporal, genetic manner.

It may be said to *produce* my capacity for accountability, my vulnerability to that which is other than myself and, in this primordial sense, my very self.

A key to this enigma of the twofold 'before' may be found in what might seem a philosophical technicality. This is the distinction between 'transcendence' and the 'transcendental'. Transcendental reflection is Kant's term for a distinctive mode of thought that reasons back from a given actuality (e.g., the achievements of science) to the 'conditions of the possibility' of that actuality (Allison 1983: 3–34). This naturally sounds quite abstract, but upon examination one finds that its function in Kant's thought is to get leverage on the pre-critical naivety of metaphysical ontotheology. Specifically, it enables us to escape imprisonment within our common habit of thinking in terms of cause and effect. 'Imprisonment' is not too strong a word, for the language of cause and effect necessarily posits an underlying sameness, without which cause and effect would not connect. In contrast, the abstract notion of a 'condition of possibility' demands no assumption of sameness between the 'condition' and the corresponding actuality. Thus, to take a crucial example, one can reflect on the notion of God without assuming that God functions as a being among other beings.

Transcendental reflection opens a space for irreducible difference, as in Kant's firm distinction between ethics properly understood and self-interested calculation, which bears directly on Levinas's portrayal of the ethical as irreducibly other (Wyschogrod 2000: 102). When Derrida calls *différance* a 'quasi-transcendental' (Derrida 1988: 127), he offers insight into Levinas as well. Levinas's account of the face of the other invading the very being of the self is anything but abstract. Yet the effect of this primal trauma, occurring in a quasi-time before time, is to render me questionable, 'response-able', accessible to the world. And in this sense it is the condition of the possibility of my being human.

VII. Deconstruction and Faith

A longing for 'something more', some greater meaning, is central to contemporary religious discourse. But we are understandably uneasy with the deconstructionist proposal that somehow, to some extent, language might 'mean' without us. We are understandably unsettled by the notion that the linguistic event of meaning might become errant; that it might not be defined and delimited by our originating intention. Surely, one wants to say, questionability can go only so far. Surely there is an originative moment when my meaning is 'present' to my inner awareness in a mental act of meaning or intending. Surely meaning is meaningless if there is not some such origin to which one can return, a stabilizing point of reference. In short, we want 'something more' (transcendence, etc.), but we want it to stand still!

Both are natural: the longing for meaning as transcendence, a going-beyond, and the desire for meaning as stability, lest there be chaos. Yet the mere coexistence of these natural impulses is enough to ensure that we will remain invested in the truly cockeyed notion of a stabilized transcendence. Yet is not a 'stabilized transcendence'—a constant going-beyond that is simultaneously an untroubled foundation—what is often meant by 'God'? All the ingenuity of ontotheology can scarcely disguise the fact that such a notion bears no discernible relation to the God of Hebrew scripture. Yet the notion of a stabilized transcendence may seem unfazed, the purest instance of self-evident presence. Ontotheology, then, is not a distant system; it lies very close to hand. This being so, it may be ill-advised to set any predetermined limit to theology's need for a Kierkegaardian vigilance. And while deconstruction is not identical to such vigilance, it can ably assist it.

In a lecture given shortly before his death, Derrida spoke about the relationship between deconstruction and faith. For our purposes, three points are crucial. First, he acknowledged that there are certain limits to what deconstruction can do. He affirmed that on the subject of "grace given by God," deconstruction, as such, has nothing to say or to do. If it's given, let's say, to someone in a way that is absolutely improbable, that is, exceeding any proof, in a unique experience, then deconstruction has no lever on this' (Sherwood and Hart 2005: 39; Derrida 2002). Developing the theme, he declared that '[t]he possibility of this grace is not publicly accessible. And from that point of view, I am really Kierkegaardian: the experience of faith is something that exceeds language in a certain way, it exceeds ethics, politics, and society' (Sherwood and Hart 2005: 39). Before the improbable possibility of such experience, deconstruction stands silent.

But this exemption obtains only insofar as the gift is given 'in a way that is absolutely improbable, that is, exceeding any proof'. It therefore follows that, second, when and if the gift is in fact set within any kind of supportive, explanatory framework, as it is whenever one ventures to write or speak about it, then deconstruction has something to take hold of. The instant it becomes anything less than absolutely improbable, it is no longer exempt. In Derrida's words, 'once this grace, this given grace, is embodied in a discourse, in a community, in a church, in a religion, in a theology'—all of which are by their very nature structural and systemic—'then deconstruction... may have something to say' (Sherwood and Hart 2005: 39).

Derrida appends a third reflection. He suggests that deconstruction's self-limitation regarding the improbable possibility (in other deconstructionist contexts, the 'impossible possibility') may not be a simple function of ignorance, of deconstruction's acknowledging that there may be something entirely beyond its ken. Perhaps it 'is not simply a weakness of deconstruction'. Perhaps it is because deconstruction itself 'starts from the possibility of, if not grace, then certainly a secret, an absolutely secret experience, which I would compare with that of grace. That's perhaps the starting point for any deconstruction' (Sherwood and Hart 2005: 39). This third point occurs between references to deconstruction's being 'totally disarmed', but it nevertheless suggests that deconstruction may have its own acquaintance with the improbable possibility which the religious believer construes as grace.

The first point affirms that, in a certain specific regard, faith and grace escape questioning; and the third point backs this up by adding that deconstruction, in its own right, posits something analogous. The implication would be that, because deconstruction knows of itself that such a secret can occur, it respects the secret or its counterpart when it occurs as religious faith. But in another sense deconstruction may take back with this third point what it offers with the first. For if deconstruction does know something of such a secret, might it not also be the case that deconstruction actually knows it better, for example, in a less biased, less parochial manner? Might it not be that the various determinate religions are best understood as imperfect instantiations of an elusive something that deconstruction evokes with less need to control or nail down?

John D. Caputo's masterful *The Prayers and Tears of Jacques Derrida* (1997), which makes the case for a prophetic dimension in deconstruction so well that one can forget the case ever had to be made, tends in this direction, even if only as a tactical manoeuvre. The book pursues deconstruction's relations with religion across several domains—the apophatic, the apocalyptic, the messianic, gift, circumcision, and confession. Derrida's own phrase, which appears as subtitle, 'religion without religion', may itself suggest a certain ordering. Certainly, Derrida's *sans*, translated 'without', is not a simple negation. Nevertheless, the phrase anticipates a series of distinctions that, in Caputo's account, incline toward prioritization. Examples include a distinction between 'the apocalyptic' and specific apocalyptics, and between 'the messianic' and specific messianisms, such as Christianity. Of the messianic, Caputo, expounding Derrida, writes, 'Once the messianic is given determinate content, it is restricted within a determinable and determining horizon, but the very idea of the messianic, of messianicity, is to shatter horizons' (Caputo 1997: 118). Deconstruction's wariness about the determinate religions can be explained in the time it takes to say 'Inquisition'. The theologian, however, must add—with head bowed in repentance, one would hope, and yet stubbornly—that warranted wariness cannot preclude the possibility that God has chosen to wade into the realm of human perversion, and has opted *in actu*— in point of fact—for determinacy.

VIII. Conclusion

It would not be wrong to say that the relationship between postmodernism and Christian theology is undecidable, requiring a decision. But it would be trite. And actual texts, including those criticized in this chapter, are seldom trite.

On Behalf of Christian Theology

Christian theology testifies to the decisive significance of the life, death, and resurrection of Jesus of Nazareth. To ascribe such significance not just to particularity but to one particular particularity constitutes 'the scandal of particularity', which is 'foolishness' to a universalizing philosophy (1 Cor. 1: 23). An early product of Heidegger's distrust of the ontic was Bultmann's program of demythologizing, which reflected an all too modern conviction than the particulars of history could not bear the truth of revelation. Alain Badiou has written brilliantly on St Paul, but when he declares emphatically, 'Paul's thought dissolves incarnation in resurrection', one worries that the crucifixion itself is being sloughed off as merely ontic (Badiou 2003: 74). In such cases, the theologian must speak forthrightly of the possibility of a philosophic dogmatism.

Once aroused, confessional theology may take a deconstructive turn on deconstruction itself. Is it perhaps the case that deconstruction subtly moves from distinguishing between faith as improbable possibility and the determinate faiths, to insinuating a hierarchical priority and/or preference of the former above the latter? And might not such a preference then drift into an arbitrary exclusion of the confessional alternative? It is not without reason that Barth and Bonhoeffer are adamant that Christian theology must begin not with possibility (or with 'conditions of possibility') but with actuality, the actuality of the Christ event (Bonhoeffer 1996). A theology that gets this fundamental warrant or starting point right can then proceed at leisure to engage the philosophers on speculative issues of possibility. But it will talk about the possibility of 'gift', for example, in light of God's actual self-giving through God's incarnational identification with finite, fleshly determinacy.

Pressing further still, theology might 'enframe' and assess postmodernism through, say, Kierkegaardian categories. On such an account, much of postmodernism might be seen as an ingenious variant of Kierkegaard's aesthetic mode, as in Mark C. Taylor's *Erring: A Postmodern A/theology* (1984), which advocates linguistic 'free play'—a notion which Derrida for his part disavows (Derrida 1988: 115). To that form of postmodernism one can then contrast other forms that proactively engage in ethical issues, attesting in one fashion or another to the call of the ethical. And in signal cases such as Levinas and Derrida that call leads beyond ethics as conventionally conceived to what can fairly be called a rigorous form of 'Religiousness A'. This is high praise indeed, recalling Climacus' depiction of Socrates as the further reach of human possibility. But then there still does remain one further possibility (for Kierkegaard is here speaking in the language of possibility), namely 'Religiousness B', the Christian message that eternity has entered time. By contextualizing postmodernism in this manner, the theologian might locate, affirm, and critique the several forms of postmodernism while yet reserving the most crucial role for Christian testimony.

On Behalf of Postmodernism

In the vying of theology and deconstruction we witness what might be called the dance of exemplarity (Sherwood and Hart 2005: 43–4). Each is construed as an example of something, such as forms of messianicity or spheres of existence, which the other understands more comprehensively. But as long as the participant parties remain committed to reading one another's texts attentively and openly, observing what Derrida calls the ethics of discussion, the result will be not a clash of ideologies but sharpened insight into where 'we', the tremulous we of the conversation, are now, in the ever shifting moment of culture and history. If people are to live together, such conversation needs to happen. In this conviction, deconstruction is true to its Enlightenment roots.

On behalf of deconstruction, we may note in the present instance that Kierkegaard's spheres of existence, however delicately handled, are a sort of explanatory framework. Such frameworks, moreover, characteristically have trouble appreciating their constituent elements in their own right, apart from their function within the envisioned 'totality' or whole. Yet Levinas's radicality springs from his unfailing awareness of the irreducibility of the ethical. To know the ethical at all is to know it not as example but as command; to know it in its own right. Levinas is in fact quite reserved in talking about God, but the reserve is entirely misconstrued if it is read as negative, as a refusal or inability to take a logical step. Rather, the reserve bespeaks awareness that the ethical constitutes the one non-negotiable test of any putative theology. A theology that does not constantly confront the face, the ethical in its own right, demonstrates thereby that, in Kierkegaardian terms, it is spiritlessly aesthetic.

Finally on behalf of postmodernism, we may observe how it may redeem the concept of the infinite from ontotheology's placement of it on a line with the finite. For Levinas, the occurrence of some notion of the infinite in our minds, despite its uncontainability within the constructs of our minds, alerts us to our own questionability (Levinas 1989: 76). The infinite so conceived does not represent 'the immanence' of some 'state of the soul' (Levinas 1989: 76). It is not a point of contact. It arouses a desire that is in no way self-referencing, but turns entirely toward the desired. 'This endless desire for what is beyond being is dis-interestedness, transcendence—desire for the Good' (Levinas 1989: 177). The infinite arises in its own right—and as such it contests the canker of self-interestedness that may lodge within religious proclamations of 'salvation'.

Ad Hoc Alliances

Between theology and postmodernism there can occur occasional *ad hoc* alliances. We have seen that a certain appropriation of Kierkegaard can offset an *a priori* bias against determinacy, but such efforts are always at risk of succeeding too well. The very argument for the possible necessity of a leap of faith may render the leap more plausible, thus less of a leap, and the theology less confessional. In such a situation, a tactical alliance with deconstruction might actually make a confessional theology more confessional.

I close with one specific invitation to such alliance, an obstacle to hearing the Christian message found within the church as well as without. When a person ventures to proclaim Christ in the present culture, it is commonly assumed that one is attesting to some 'experience' of God (for without the warrant of experience, the testimony is instantly deemed inauthentic)—and thus to some 'contact' with God. Claiming some *Anknüpfungspunkt* is virtually required just to get a hearing. Moreover, the contact is assumed to be a matter of like-to-like; and since God must be understood as spiritual reality, the speaker must be attesting, *ipso facto*, to her own effective spirituality. Thus an effort to point away from oneself to Christ is received as being self-referential. To use Paul's term, it is heard as boasting—indeed, boasting of one's own salvation. For to have an inner affinity to God, a relation of like to like, and to have that affinity brought to life by actual contact—is that not to be saved (Lowe 2003)?

In its very effort to be confessional, theology is at grips with the hegemony of 'the Same', the fatal assumption of like to like. Ontotheology is not a system remote from us but very near to hand; and nearest of all, perhaps, in our 'humanism', our anthropology. Theology's alliances may be *ad hoc* and tactical. But that does not make them any less essential.

References

Allison, Henry E. (1983). *Kant's Transcendental Idealism: An Interpretation and Defense.* New Haven: Yale University Press.

Badiou, Alain (1999). *Manifesto for Philosophy.* Albany: SUNY Press.

—— (2003). *Saint Paul: The Foundation of Universalism.* Stanford: Stanford University Press.

Barth, Karl (1968). *The Epistle to the Romans.* London: Oxford University Press.

Bennington, Geoffrey, and Derrida, Jacques (1993). *Jacques Derrida.* Chicago: University of Chicago Press.

Blake, William (1970). *The Letters of William Blake.* Cambridge: Harvard University Press.

Bonhoeffer, Dietrich (1996). *Act and Being: Transcendental Philosophy and Ontology in Systematic Theology.* Minneapolis: Fortress.

Caputo, John D. (1987). *Radical Hermeneutics: Repetition, Deconstruction and the Hermeneutic Project.* Bloomington: Indiana University Press.

Caputo, John D. (1997). *The Prayers and Tears of Jacques Derrida: Religion without Religion.* Bloomington: Indiana University Press.

Critchley, Simon (1999). *The Ethics of Deconstruction: Derrida and Levinas.* Edinburgh: Edinburgh University Press.

Davis, Colin (1996). *Levinas: An Introduction.* Notre Dame: University of Notre Dame Press.

Derrida, Jacques (1974). *Of Grammatology.* Baltimore: Johns Hopkins University Press.

—— (1981). 'Plato's Pharmacy'. In id., *Dissemination*, Chicago: University of Chicago Press, 61–171.

—— (1982). 'Différance', In id., *Margins of Philosophy*, Chicago: University of Chicago Press, 1–27.

—— (1988) 'Afterword: Toward An Ethic of Discussion'. In id., *Limited Inc.*, Evanston: Northwestern University Press, 111–60.

—— (1995). *Points . . . : Interviews, 1974–1994.* Stanford: Stanford University Press.

—— (2002). *Acts of Religion.* New York: Routledge.

Greenberg, Karen J. (ed.) (2006). *The Torture Debate in America.* Cambridge: Cambridge University Press.

Hannay, Alastair (1982). 'Turning Hegel Outside-In'. In id., *Kierkegaard*, London: Routledge, 19–53.

Kierkegaard, Søren (1970). *Søren Kierkegaard's Journals and Papers.* Bloomington: Indiana University Press.

Levinas, Emmanuel (1969). *Totality and Infinity: An Essay on Exteriority.* Pittsburgh: Duquesne University Press.

—— (1989). *The Levinas Reader.* Oxford: Basil Blackwell.

Lowe, Walter J. (1993). *Theology and Difference: The Wound of Reason.* Bloomington: Indiana University Press.

—— (2003). 'Christ and Salvation'. In Kevin J. Vanhoozer (ed.), *The Cambridge Companion to Postmodern Theology*, Cambridge: Cambridge University Press, 235–51.

—— (2006). 'On the Tenacity of Christian Anti-Judaism'. *Modern Theology* 22/2: 277–94.

Lucy, Niall (2004). *A Derrida Dictionary.* Oxford: Blackwell.

Marcuse, Herbert (1960). *Reason and Revolution: Hegel and the Rise of Social Theory.* Boston: Beacon.

Nancy, Jean-Luc (2002). *Hegel: The Restlessness of the Negative.* Minneapolis: University of Minnesota Press.

Sherwood, Yvonne, and Hart, Kevin (eds.) (2005). *Derrida and Religion: Other Testaments.* New York: Routledge.

Smith, Steven G. (1983). *The Argument to the Other: Reason beyond Reason in the Thought of Karl Barth and Emmanuel Levinas.* Chico: Scholars.

Taylor, Mark C. (1984). *Erring: A Postmodern A/theology.* Chicago: University of Chicago Press.

Ward, Graham (ed.) (1997). *The Postmodern God: A Theological Reader.* Oxford: Blackwell.

Wyschogrod, Edith (2000). *Emmanuel Levinas: The Problem of Ethical Metaphysics.* New York: Fordham University Press.

Suggested Reading

Bennington and Derrida (1993).
Bewes, Timothy (200). *Reification, or The Anxiety of Late Capitalism.* London: Verso.
Bowie, Andrew (2003). *An Introduction to German Philosophy:* From Kant to Habermas. Cambridge: Polity.
Caputo (1997).
Derrida (1998) and (2002).
Hart, Kevin (2004). *Postmodernism: A Beginner's Guide.* Oxford: Oneworld.
Lakeland, Paul (1997). *Postmodernity: Christian Identity in a Fragmented Age.* Minneapolis: Augsburg Fortress.
Levinas (1989).
Vanhoozer, Kevin J. (ed.) (2003). *The Cambridge Companion to Postmodern Theology.* Cambridge: Cambridge University Press.
Ward, Graham (ed.) (2001). *The Blackwell Companion to Postmodern Theology.* Oxford: Blackwell.
Ward, Graham (2003). *True Religion.* Oxford: Blackwell.

CHAPTER 35

LIBERATION THEOLOGY

CHRISTOPHER ROWLAND

I. Liberation Theology and Contextual Theology

Liberation theology is a form of contextual theology, in which the experience and circumstances of the interpreters are given a prime importance as the first step in seeking to be a disciple of Jesus. It is aptly summarized in the popular education material familiar in Latin American churches, where priority is given to the 'text of life' as the key to the approach to the biblical text.

Properly speaking, liberation theology refers to that way of engaging in theological reflection pioneered in Latin America and associated with the work of Gustavo Gutiérrez. It has also come to be linked with other forms of theology with which it is closely related methodologically, namely, feminist theology, black theology, and various other kinds of contextual theology (though from the point of view of historical theology there is no form of theology which is context-less, even the supremely abstract theologizing of the medieval scholastic theological tradition). Feminist theology is much more critical in its use of the Bible, and issues of gender and race were not really part of the political profile of the earliest forms of liberation theology. Nevertheless all these ways of doing theology are characterized by an embracing of experience, broadly defined, as the necessary context and basis for theology.

The theology of liberation arises out of the specific needs and concerns of the poor. For example, in a country like Brazil, where the struggle for access to land is such a potent political issue, especially in rural areas, the story of the Exodus and the promised land has enabled the perception of a direct link between the present circumstances of many peasants and the biblical narrative (Barros Souza 1983). In such a correlation, however, there is no expectation of a blueprint from the Bible, the tradition, or contemporary theologians or bishops, which will offer unambiguous guidance, independent of the circumstances in which the people of God find themselves. The basic theological assumption undergirding this approach is that God does not come from outside such a situation but is to be found there, just as much as in the Bible, church, and tradition. The theology of liberation seeks to understand faith from within particular historical contexts. The fundamental hermeneutic starts from humanity, moves thence to God, and then from God back to humanity. Liberation theology is an understanding of the faith from a commitment to the poor and the marginalized, an understanding of the faith from a point of departure in real, effective solidarity with the exploited and the vulnerable.

The first step of the theology of liberation is to grasp the reality of the context in which one finds oneself, assisted by a variety of interpretative tools chosen by the theologian to enable the understanding of injustice. A parallel step is theological in something approaching a traditional sense of theology: it consists in confronting the reality of suffering, which is analysed and better understood in the light of the revelation learnt in the heart of the church community. Finally, there is a stage of reflection concerning orientation towards more insightful action. It is important to note, as we shall see below, that the initial step is not reflective but committed and active. The theology of liberation is done by those either directly involved in liberating action or linked with it in some way.

For this volume to contain an essay on liberation theology seems natural, given its extraordinary influence on theology in the late twentieth century. Nevertheless the propriety of its inclusion deserves some consideration. The *content* of liberation theology is indistinguishable from a variety of types of theological reflection, both ancient and modern, with a political hue. Its contemporary parallels include the writings of Moltmann (1977) and Metz (1969; 1980), both of whom are often linked to liberation theology. The crucial difference which separates liberation theology, in all its various guises, is its method. Of course, all systematic theology worthy of the name is methodologically self-aware, carefully constructed, and hermeneutically precise. Liberation theology is no exception; but the peculiar form of its theoretical engagement and reflection is what distinguishes it from much modern theology. The latter, situated as it is in the modern academy, which prizes detachment and the quest for objectivity, is very much at odds with a theology whose very practice demands commitment and involvement, the very opposite from detachment. Both supporters and detractors of liberation theology can give the impression of homogeneity in the outline of its theology, when in fact its genius lies in its very diversity and contingency. Thus, the authors of the collection *Mysterium Liberationis* offer a presentation of the traditional components of systematic theology from a liberation theology perspective (Ellacuría and Sobrino 1993). And from opponents, the various statements which emerged from the Vatican during the papacy of John Paul II treat liberation theology as a homogeneous entity. This is misleading. Not only are there a variety of contexts, but many different approaches to them, and very different relationships with the popular movements in church and society which have spawned liberation theology. To lump together the work of Segundo from Uruguay with that of the Boff brothers from Brazil, Gustavo Gutiérrez from Peru, and Jon Sobrino from El Salvador is to create a spurious entity which never exists in quite that 'pure' form. Liberation theology is, rather, determined, as its exponents believe it to be, by the very contexts in which they work, and their writings cannot therefore be easily reduced to a single system. There are important distinctions to be made between the various theologians of liberation writing in different contexts, politically and ecclesiastically.

Liberation theology has, then, been a protest at the way theology can be abstracted from ordinary life. Its starting place was not detached reflection on scripture and tradition but the life of the shanty towns and land struggles: the lack of basic amenities, the carelessness about the welfare of human persons, the death squads, and the shattered lives of refugees in a continent which at the time of its genesis was dominated by military dictatorships and vast discrepancies of wealth and opportunity. It is here in particular that its distinctiveness as compared with the theology of North American and European academies is most marked. Gustavo Gutiérrez characterizes it thus:

> the question in Latin America will not be how to speak of God in a world come of age, but rather how to proclaim God as Father in a world that is inhumane. What can it mean to tell a non-person that he or she is God's child? (Gutiérrez 1983: 57)

II. The Historical Context of the Theology of Liberation I: The Second Vatican Council and the Emergence of the CEBs

Liberation theology emerged within the wider context of Catholic social teaching and, in particular, the significant development of Roman Catholic theology based on the

Second Vatican Council and the encyclicals associated with it (Hebblethwaite and Dawson, in Rowland 2008). The decisions taken by the Latin American bishops at their epoch-making meeting at Medellín and reaffirmed at Puebla, with the explicit commitment to take a 'preferential option for the poor' (Hennelly 1990; Walsh and Davies 1984; Gutiérrez 1993), were, in addition, crucial in its development.

Despite Latin America having a reputation for a progressive theological tradition, the influence of the theology of liberation is actually quite small. Countries like Mexico, Argentina, and Colombia, which have conservative church hierarchies, show little evidence of the grass-roots theology and episcopal support for liberation theology which are evident in Brazil, Peru, and, to a lesser extent, Nicaragua. The power of diocesan bishops is such that attempts to develop grassroots movements without episcopal support find the going very tough indeed, despite the fact that for large numbers of people the social conditions are equally bad as those in dioceses where the theology has taken root. Similarly, in those dioceses where the diocesan bishop is supportive, that power can be used to push a diocese in a progressive direction far more rapidly than would be possible in a more Protestant area. The importance of what has happened in Brazil over the last thirty years makes it the obvious country to focus on to understand further the theology of liberation.

The promotion of 'basic ecclesial communities' in encyclicals like *Evangelii Nuntiandi* is one way that liberation theology has come to be rooted in the 'basic christian communities' (the CEBs). The basic communities are a significant component of both the contemporary political and ecclesiastical scene, especially in Brazil, where, particularly in the 1970s and 1980s, such communities became the typical mode of evangelization. A constant refrain of all the different liberationist approaches is that the perspective of the poor and the marginalized offers another story, an alternative to that told by the wielders of economic power whose story is privileged as the 'normal' account. In the CEBs, hitherto oppressed persons have become the particular means whereby the divine perspective on human existence is offered. They are the 'little ones' who are vouchsafed a peculiar insight into the identity of the divine wisdom (Matt. 11: 25). The vantage point of the poor is particularly and especially the vantage point of the crucified God, and may act as a criterion for theological reflection, biblical exegesis, and the life of the church. The poor are the means by which the church can learn to discern the truth, direction, and content of its mission, and can assure the church of being the place where the Lord is to be found.

Few exponents of the theology of liberation would want a consideration of this distinctive theological approach to start with a story of episcopal decisions or professorial disquisitions. Rather, it is with the 'reality' which confronts millions in the continent that it should begin. The contrast between the gross affluence of the tiny minority and the squalor and poverty of the majority has prompted priests and religious to think again about their apostolic task and, in so doing, to learn the importance of living and working with and learning from the poor. The theology of liberation has taken root outside the walls of the seminaries and basilicas, often far away from the nearest priest.

It is the richness of human experience which has helped to promote the theology of liberation in many parts of Latin America. The story of the Roman Catholic Church in São Paulo in the final decades of the twentieth century has revolved around issues linked with the mushrooming of migration within Brazil, particularly from the impoverished north-east to the cities. Conditions in rural Brazil are appalling. As the economy has expanded, those desperate to keep body and soul together have drifted to the big cities, particularly those of the more economically prosperous south-east, drawn by the promise of a better life. As migrants arrived in the city, many with only the possessions they could bring with them, they resorted to making makeshift homes on any piece of spare land available, even under motorway arches. It was this desperation which led to the massive spread of shanty towns where the majority of São Paulo's population lives. Squatters who occupy land and build their rudimentary dwellings are harassed by the police, often provoking violence, while those who have gained title to their land may be evicted by private security firms hired by land speculators. Deaths are all too frequent an occurrence in some areas. Recourse to the courts is often difficult, despite the growth of law surgeries and human rights work. Even with the return to democracy in Brazil, the plight of the urban homeless continues to deteriorate. During the time of the economic boom there was work: men could participate as labourers in building projects—luxury homes for São Paulo's elite, for example; and women could get work as maids for that same group. In times of economic recession, however, work is not so plentiful. Such conditions have made women's work essential for existence. In situations where it is not possible for friends or relatives to look after them, children are left to join the very large number of others in São Paulo who roam the streets, increasing the already alarming problem of 'street children'.

During the period of military dictatorship in Brazil in the late 1960s and 1970s, close links were forged between the churches and other groups struggling for human rights. This time saw a development of popular movements of which the CEBs are a tangible expression. Grass-roots participation during the military dictatorship was focused on church-based bodies, providing an umbrella for individuals from different backgrounds to meet and work for common goals. It was perhaps this experience above all which laid the foundations for the fruitful dialogue and cooperation between the churches and various groups struggling for justice for the majority of São Paulo's population. The community of interest among a wide range of people, many hitherto disenchanted with religion, was galvanized by the shared experience of persecution. This led to a 'rainbow alliance' of Christians and trade unionists and politicians on the left for securing a more humane environment for ordinary people. Throughout the period of the military dictatorship, the church in São Paulo was tireless in its defence of human rights; Christians and non-Christians alike suffered torture and even death. There followed a long official campaign of vilification of the leaders of the CEBs, who were indicted as crypto-communist. During the massive influx of migrants into the *favelas* which grew up on the periphery of the city, the archdiocese of São Paulo, in response to Medellin's 'preferential option for the poor', devoted significant resources, both human and financial, to support such people. Gradually, a pastoral plan emerged with the following priorities for mission: the defence of human rights; the defence of the right to work and the rights of workers; the defence of the poor on the outskirts of the city; and the organization of the people of God into CEBs.

III. Historical Context II: Since 1989, the Vatican Reaction, the Collapse of Communism, and the Future of Liberation Theology

A number of factors have influenced the development of liberation theology since the 1980s (Hebblethwaite, in Rowland 2008; Petrella 2004 and 2005; Althaus-Reid 2000; Batsone et al. 1997; Bell 2001). Two 'instructions' regarding liberation theology were issued by the Congregation for the Doctrine of Faith in the 1980s: a 'more negative' one in 1984, and a 'less negative' one in 1986. While the Congregation for the Doctrine of the Faith's earlier instruction contained statements which echo liberation theology, the document's purpose was 'to draw... attention... to the deviations, and risks of deviations, damaging to the faith and to Christian living, that are brought about by certain forms of liberation theology which use, in an insufficiently critical manner, concepts borrowed from various currents of Marxist thought' (introduction, in Sacred Congregation 1984). This instruction sets out a critique of what are seen as some of liberation theology's Marxist assumptions. The first concerns the relationship between sin and social structures. The instruction simply denies the possibility of making any such distinctions within Marxism. There is a denial that the 'analysis' can be separated from the world view. It rejects the way that God and history are identified and the confusion between the poor of the scripture and the proletariat of Marx. The chief difference between John Paul II and liberation theologians was the systematic 'spiritualizing' of the theme of poverty. For example, the Exodus experience, so central to liberation theology, was reinterpreted; the political aspect was subordinated to a spiritual purpose. The second instruction declared, 'The Exodus... has a meaning which is both religious and political. God sets his people free and gives them descendants, a land and a law, but within a covenant and for a covenant' (Sacred Congregation 1986: §44). There is acceptance of the basic assumption of liberation theology—God's preferential option for the poor—but this is subtly interpreted as 'God's preferential *love* for the poor'. Whatever the negative tone of both documents, it was evident that some of the language and commitment at the heart of liberation theology had seeped into the Vatican rhetoric and thence into the theological mainstream of the church.

The fall of the Berlin Wall in 1989 was seen by some as the death knell of liberation theology. This would only have been true if liberation theology were indissolubly linked with the kind of socialist project which had typified the Marxist-Leninist regimes of Eastern Europe. It is true that there have been cordial links with Castro's Cuba, and during the period of the Sandinista regime there was a regular flow of visitors from different parts of the progressive Catholic church in South America to Nicaragua to offer support to the regime and its Christian supporters, especially at the height of the war with the US-backed Contras in the 1980s. As such, Nicaragua was a kind of beacon of hope, as Cuba had been for the left a decade or two earlier. The upheavals in Eastern Europe could not fail to have their effects, however, in an era characterized by globalization and the hegemony of US culture, alongside a vibrantly reactionary Roman Catholic Church which sought to check progressive interpretations of the Second Vatican Council. Progressives were replaced in dioceses in Brazil, and the broadening influence of liberation theology was slowly checked. In a memorable phrase, Clodovis Boff compared the situation of the Roman Catholic Church and the CEBs in Brazil with toothpaste which has been squeezed out of a tube and which can never be put back again. At the grass roots, the liberationist perspective still has its effect, less often heard of, but still pervasive. Elsewhere there has been a subtle change in the emphases of those engaging with liberation theology: cultural criticism, ecological issues, compromise with the perspective of radical orthodoxy, and gender politics have become more prominent. Yet the main strands which gave liberation theology its distinctive role have never been completely lost, even if there has been some evidence of a drop in confidence in the particular political project which gave liberation theology its peculiar hue in the last two decades of the twentieth century.

Liberation theology's genius, and the key to its re-emergence, is its commitment to specific contextual projects—not the various theoretical and culturally aware developments that have emerged in the last decade. There is evidence that some regard the post-1989 situation as an opportunity rather than a threat. The old socialism-capitalism dualism has been replaced by a recognition that the all-pervasiveness of capitalism needs to be challenged by an acknowledgement of the complexity of that phenomenon and the myriad opportunities it now offers for social change. When liberation theology loses its commitment to engagement in historical projects to bring life where there is death, it will have lost its soul. Liberation theology put its finger on the pulse of the historical change which is fundamental to the work of the Holy Spirit who makes all things new. Its practitioners have achieved this by realizing that theological understanding comes through commitment to action—and discernment as a complement to that—a commitment to the reading of 'the signs of the times' and the changes which they demand in the service of the vulnerable (Petrella 2004).

IV. Praxis and Theory: Epistemology and the Method of Liberation Theology

In liberation theology, faith, reflection, and real life are in dialectical relationship with each other. It is above all a new way of *doing* theology, in that action, rather than detachment and silent reflection by themselves, is deemed to be adequate. It is new in the sense that it contrasts with much of the university or seminary theology of the last two centuries, which prioritizes intellectual discourse and esteems detachment from life and, increasingly, from the practices of prayer and charity. In some ways, liberation theology echoes the theological method of an earlier age when worship, service to humanity, openness to God, and theological reflection were more closely integrated and when the conduct of the Christian life was an indispensable context for theology. What has been rediscovered in liberation theology in particular is the commitment to the poor and marginalized as fundamental for meeting with God. Commitment to, and solidarity with, the poor and vulnerable are therefore the necessary basis for theological activity. So, one first of all *does* liberation theology before learning about it. Or, to put it another way, one can only learn about it by embarking on active solidarity with and concern for the amelioration of the suffering of the poor and marginalized. Liberation theology cannot adequately be understood except by commitment in solidarity and action. Because of the deep-rooted connection of this theology with particular contexts and experiences, liberation theology presents peculiar problems for those who seek to write *about* it. A proper understanding of it demands something more than an intellectual appreciation alone. Understanding involves the move from a previous position of detachment, to be open to that transformation of perspective which comes either at the margins of society or in social estrangement. To paraphrase the dialogue of Jesus with Nicodemus in John 3, it is only by changing sides and identifying with the Christ who meets and challenges men and women in the persons of the poor, the hungry, and the naked that one may 'see the kingdom of God' (John 3: 3; cf. Boff, in Ellacuría and Sobrino 1993: 57–84; Graham 1996).

The basic method of liberation theology has its analogy with Marxist epistemology. The fundamental Marxist insight that consciousness is determined by one's historical context and activity in that context has its echo in liberation theology's method. It is important to see liberation theology as a parallel development to Marxism rather than as a deliberate attempt to insert Marxism into Christian theology. At most, Marxism provided a language for the experience of solidarity with the poor. 'Praxis', for Marx, is both a tool for changing the course of history and a critical tool. Praxis arises out of, and is determined by, the consciousness-shaping activity undertaken in historical contingencies. Consequently, praxis changes, perhaps even revolutionizes, the understanding of reality through human action. In one of his most famous sentiments, expressed in *The German Ideology*, Marx criticized Ludwig Feuerbach for supposing that all that was needed was a better consciousness of the world when what was actually needed was a comprehension of reality through the activity of changing it. Marx considered the lack of any activist, committed element an Achilles heel in what considered itself a critical philosophy. This is also at the heart of liberation theology's critique of much theology, ancient or modern.

The centrality of a praxis-based epistemology in liberation theology might appear to give weight to the critique of the Vatican, for example, that it is too wedded to an atheistic philosophy. This would be a mistake, however. A glance at Gutiérrez's classic *A Theology of Liberation* will reveal how marginal Marxism is to its theological fabric, even if its sentiments, critical perspective, and focus on the poor are superficially similar. At most we may regard this similarity as evidence of the importance of Marxist hermeneutics as a heuristic device for liberation theology, opening a pathway to the Christian tradition, viewed in its broadest sense. Furthermore, it enables an appreciation of the centrality of praxis as a major determinant of theological reflection. Like Marxism, liberation theology rejects the priority of detached thought in determining the understanding of God, instead prioritizing both the historical activity and the identification of the poor with their privileged position as objects of divine mercy and vehicles of insight into the divine will. The question of God cannot therefore be divorced from questions which arise from practice. Hegel already recognized this, and his criticism of aspects of contemporary theology could well apply:

> It is to be noted that there is a type of theology that wants to adopt *only a historical attitude* towards religion; it even has an abundance of cognition, though only of a historical kind. This cognition is no concern of ours, for if the cognition of religion were merely historical, we would have to compare such theologians with counting-house clerks, who keep the ledgers and accounts of other people's wealth, a wealth that passes through their hands without their retaining any of it, clerks who act only for others without acquiring any assets of their own. They do of course receive a salary, but their merit lies only in keeping records of the assets of other people. In philosophy and religion, however, the essential thing is that one's own spirit itself should recognise a possession and content, deem itself worthy of cognition, and not keep itself humbly outside. (Hegel 1984: 128)

The indissolubility of knowledge and action is the basis for a concept of education at the heart of liberation theology. Paulo Freire, a crucial figure in the emergence of popular education linked with liberation theology in Brazil, emphasizes the link between knowing and doing. For Freire, the human being should be engaged in active inquiry 'with the world, and with each other'—inquiry leading to liberation and transformation, to 'mutual humanization' (Freire 1972: 46–9). 'In Freire's analysis, not only is knowing intimately associated with doing, right education with transformation, but the place where the transformation must first take place is in *the very act of education itself.* The "how" of education is inseparable from questions of epistemology, ethics, politics, and also theology.' Thus the transformation of the learning process into a student-centred or genuinely 'humanist' education is not merely a fashion or a learning technique; it is transformative action with the goal of far wider-ranging societal transformation (Bennett-Moore 1997: 36–8).

Such theological presuppositions reflect crucial issues in the Bible. An oft-quoted passage is Jeremiah 22: 15–16 where the prophet asserts that knowing God is doing justice (Miranda 1977: 47–50). Even more importantly, the fundamental learning experience in the Gospels is not the teaching Jesus gave his disciples but their activity in walking with Jesus on the way to Jerusalem. To learn what it means that the Son of Man must suffer means taking up the cross (Mark 8: 38) and following Jesus by going up to Jerusalem. The reported prophecies of the Passion (e.g., Mark 8, 9, 10) are incomprehensible without the learning experience of accompanying Jesus to Jerusalem. This is not just a spiritual journey but, as all the Gospels indicate, a journey to the very teeth of the centre of power in Judean society: Jesus becomes the victim of the high priest's decision that 'it is better... to have one man die for the people' (John 11: 50).

The importance of the theme of 'the way' is now widely recognized in discussions of the Gospel of Mark, for example (Marcus 1993). Nowhere is it better demonstrated that the contingent basis of theological understanding is in action, rather than contemplation and detachment, than in Matthew 10: 20–2. Here the situation is one in which a particular form of demonstration of commitment results in the inspired word of the Spirit in the one bearing witness. Similarly, in Matthew 18, the *practice* of reconciliation is the prerequisite of the presence of the living Christ. 'For where two or three are gathered in my name, I am there among them' (Matt. 18: 20). Christ's presence turns out to be the consequence of reconciling action. The divine presence, therefore, is to be found in contexts of practical demonstration of forgiveness, just as the meeting with the eschatological judge in this age turns out to be service to 'the least of these who are members of my family' (Matt. 25: 40). What happens in this world, most especially to 'the least of these', is theologically fundamental. The understanding of the Christian scriptures in particular is an activity and a discipline inseparable from that action which is epistemologically fundamental. Such fundamental praxis-orientated epistemology is the foundation for all critical reflection. As in Marxism, it is not one's left-leaning preferences or opinions which lead to a particular perspective, but the commitment to and active involvement with the poor as participants with them in their peculiar role in the divine economy that is the basis of criticism. Liberation theology, therefore, is not to be confused with some kind of armchair radicalism in which the thoughts of a liberal intelligentsia offers an Olympian perspective on the doings of fellow men and women. Indeed, it is precisely those doings, especially of the most vulnerable and the weakest of the earth, which grant a different, critical perspective.

V. The Bible: The Written Text and the Text of Life

Among the CEBs, the Bible has become a catalyst for the exploration of pressing contemporary issues relevant to the community, offering a language so that the voice of the voiceless may be heard (Gorgulho, in Ellacuría and Sobrino 1993: 123–49; Croatto 1987). In the CEBs' engagement with the Bible, there is an immediacy about the way the text is used because resonances are found with the experience set out in the stories of biblical characters. Thus, the Bible offers a means by which the present difficulties can be shown to be surmountable in the life of faith and community commitment. To enable the poor to read the Bible has involved a programme of education on the contents of the biblical material, so that it can be a resource for thousands who are illiterate. In such popular education programmes, full recognition is taken of the value of the experience of life. (Examples of material produced by the archdiocese of São Paulo may be found in Rowland and Corner 1990: 7–20.) The community setting means an avoidance of a narrowly individualist 'religious' reading. The experience of poverty and oppression (often termed 'life' or 'reality') is as important a text as the text of scripture itself. It represents another text to be studied alongside that contained between the covers of the Bible. God's word is to be found in the dialectic between the memory of the people of God in the Bible and the continuing story to be discerned in the contemporary world, particularly among the people with whom God has chosen to be identified. This twofold aspect is brought out clearly by Carlos Mesters:

> the emphasis is not placed on the text's meaning in itself but rather on the meaning the text has for the people reading it. At the start the people tend to draw any and every sort of meaning, however well or ill founded, from the text .... the common people are also eliminating the alleged 'neutrality' of scholarly exegesis .... the common people are putting the Bible in its proper place, the place where God intended it to be. They are putting it in second place. Life takes first place! In so doing, the people are showing us the enormous

importance of the Bible, and at the same time, its relative value—relative to life. (Mesters 1993: 14–15; cf. 1989)

Latin American liberationist hermeneutics is succinctly set out by Clodovis Boff (C. Boff 1987; Sugirtharajah 1991: 9–35). Boff describes two different kinds of approach to the Bible. One is more immediate, in which the biblical story becomes a type for the people of God in the modern world. In the other approach, what Boff describes as a 'correspondence of relationships' method, the Bible is read through the lens of the experience of the present, thereby enabling it to become a key to understanding that to which the scriptural text bears witness—the life and struggles of the ancestors in the faith. This exploration of scripture in turn casts light on the present. What is important about Boff's model is that it is not a quest for formulas to copy or techniques to apply from scripture. Scripture offers orientations, models, types, directives, principles, and inspirations—elements permitting us to acquire, on our own initiative, a 'hermeneutic competency'. This then offers the capacity to judge, on our own initiative and in our own right, 'according to the mind of Christ', or 'according to the Spirit', the new, unpredictable situations with which we are continually confronted. The Christian writings offer us not a *what*, but a *how*—a manner, a style, a spirit (Sugirtharajah 1991: 30).

In all of this there is an assumption that the poor are not just objects of pity but subjects in their own right, with a peculiar capacity to understand the ways of God. The poor are blessed because they can read scripture from a perspective different from that of most of the rich; they find in it a message which can easily elude those who are not poor. The poor are privileged in the eyes of God and should be the particular concern of all of those who claim to be concerned with the ways of God. Poverty is not glamorized, however. The beatitudes reveal the character of a God who identifies with the poor and marginalized: 'the kingdom of God comes first and foremost for those who by virtue of their situation have most need of it: the poor, the afflicted, the hungry of the world' (Segundo 1985: 62). The kingdom is coming because God is humane, because God cannot tolerate the situation of the poor and is coming to make sure that the divine will is done on earth. Jesus' identification with the wretched of the earth, whether in his divine self-emptying (Phil. 2: 6–11) or in the character of the relationships he established during his mission, demonstrates solidarity with those on the margins.

Liberation theologians would accept Jürgen Moltmann's assertion (on the basis of Matt. 25: 31–46) that the wretched 'are the latent presence of the coming Saviour and Judge in the world, the touchstone which determines salvation and damnation' (Moltmann 1977: 127). That is a significant role. Because the poor are particularly close to God and the place where one can meet the risen Christ, they constitute the place from which to view the way the world and the tradition are being used. Oppressed persons mediate God because they break down the normal egotism with which human beings approach other human beings. Through them we can begin to engage the question of what 'being God' means. Those who deal with the oppressed discern that it is they who are being spoken to, indeed evangelized, not those whom they set out to help. So, to search for God means searching for the poor (Sobrino 1984: 222). This has ecclesiological implications, for the poor become channels for discerning the identity of the church and the direction and content of its mission. It is not the case, as Jon Sobrino has put it, that the church of the poor is 'automatically the agent of truth and grace because the poor are in it; rather the poor in the church are the structural source that assures the church of being the real agent of truth and justice' (Sobrino 1984: 93, 95). So the church of the poor is not simply a reality alongside mainstream Christianity; rather, the mark of the true church is its acceptance of the perspective of the poor.

Theologians like Leonardo Boff have been at pains to stress the deep roots of the 'basic ecclesial communities' in the life of the Catholic church. Certainly the communities may offer a new perspective and are a sign of hope for the renewal of the church; but Boff makes it quite plain that he does not conceive of them as an embryonic sect, though some critics portray them as such. Rather, Boff argues that they are the leaven in the lump, a remnant within the people of God (L. Boff 1986: 63).

In the writings of liberation theologians the repeated emphasis on Jesus and the Gospels is the central criterion of obedience. Like their European contemporaries, the theologians of liberation have taken up the quest for the historical Jesus as a means of criticizing a preoccupation with the superhuman, remote Christ of ecclesiastical confession. Liberation theologians believe that the historical Jesus was situated, personally involved in a situation that displays structural similarities to that of present-day Latin America (Sobrino 1978: 351–3). In the Christologies of Sobrino and Boff, for example, there is a stress on the importance of the historical Jesus as a central criterion by which the theology of the church, particularly its dogmatic explication of Jesus' significance, may be judged (Sobrino 1978; L. Boff 1979). A historical person wrestling with the specific social and political problems posed by his context offers liberation theologians a direct analogy to struggles in their own specific contexts. The various interpretations of liberation theology in Latin America seem to echo the theme: if a Christology disregards the historical Jesus, it turns into an abstract Christology, one that avoids the responsibility to engage with history in all its particularities, one that is alienating and liable to escapism.

VI. Liberation Theology and Ideological Criticism

One of liberation theology's challenges to theology has come from the recognition of the 'ideological' character of all theology and its role within a complex political struggle within the churches of maintaining the ascendancy of certain positions

(Segundo 1976). The emphasis on the contextual nature of all theology has led liberation theologians to question the absolute character of theological pronouncements from the past as well as the present, and to attempt a theological unmasking of reality. Leonardo Boff, for example, challenges theologians to be aware of the socio-economic context in which they practise their theology:

> Theologians do not live in clouds. They are social actors with a particular place in society. They produce knowledge, data, and meanings by using instruments that the situation offers them and permits them to utilize.... The themes and emphases of a given Christology flow from what seems relevant to the theologian on the basis of his or her social standpoint.... In that sense we must maintain that no Christology is or can be neutral.... Willingly or unwillingly Christological discourse is voiced in a given social setting with all the conflicting interests that pervade it. That holds true as well for theological discourse that claims to be a 'purely' theological, historical, traditional, ecclesial and apolitical. Normally such discourse adopts the position of those who hold power in the existing system. If a different kind of Christology with its own commitments appears on the scene and confronts the older 'apolitical' Christology, the latter will soon discover its social locale, forget its 'apolitical' nature, and reveal itself as a religious reinforcement of the existing status quo. (L. Boff 1979: 265–6; cf. Avineri 1968: 135).

To view liberation theology as merely a species of the ideological criticism widespread in politically left-leaning academia would be a misjudgement, whatever the similarities or apparent indebtedness to Marxist ideological critique. Use of ideological criticism is the consequence of pre-existing commitments to the poor and the disadvantaged on the part of the writers concerned. Indeed, the social engagement of those involved in higher education has become a widespread feature of Brazilian intellectual life, with many university institutions requiring that a significant part of the syllabus in which their students engage and the research their staff undertake should involve social engagement and have relevance to the lives of the communities in which the universities are located. This is a version of the vision of the 'organic intellectual' suggested by Antonio Gramsci and often alluded to by liberation theologians who spend a significant part of their working lives oscillating between study, teaching, and engagement with local communities (Hoare and Smith 1971: 10 ff., 60, 330; West 1999).

VII. Liberation's Contribution to Systematic Theology

Doctrinally, liberation theology departs little from the theological mainstream. Indeed, the claim of its exponents that it is a new way of doing theology indicates that its novelty lies in its method rather than its content. Its character, particularly its situatedness, its concern for improving the lot of the poor, and its emphasis upon protesting on behalf of the vulnerable, makes it particularly important for ecclesiology, pneumatology, and eschatology (the connection with Joachite pneumatology is made explicitly by Comblin in Ellacuría and Sobrino 1993: 474–5). The implicit pneumatology of liberation theology stresses the activity of the divine Spirit in the world which does not confine the Spirit's activity either to the church or to its official representatives. The Pauline vision of the body of Christ in which all have their role to play challenges simple hierarchical, ecclesial models. It is that aspect of the theology of liberation which led to the criticism by the Vatican of Leonardo Boff's *Church: Charism and Power*, in which an egalitarian church polity was outlined (L. Boff 1985). Prophecy and reading the signs of the times become key elements in the life of a church committed to the poor and the marginalized through understanding God's will in history (Ellacuría and Sobrino 1993: 289–327, 328–49). The theological anthropology which is informed by pneumatology questions the fatalism of a view of human sinfulness which despairs of the possibility of change. Not that there is any lack of recognition of the pervasiveness of sin, but, following the emphasis of Catholic social teaching on structural sin, this is not confined to the individual but also involves the critique of the exercise of power in institutions which are themselves pervaded by that which leads to oppression.

Liberation theology has thus given prominence to themes neglected in the mainstream Christian tradition. It has been important to retrieve 'alternative stories', whether neglected or buried. This has been a significant component of feminist biblical interpretation (Grey, in Rowland 2008; Keller and Radford Ruether 1995; Selvidge 1996; Althaus-Reid 2000). The remarkable 'hinterland' of radical themes in the Christian tradition has gradually been accessed (Bradstock and Rowland 2002), following in the footsteps of an approach to Christian tradition famously pioneered by Ernst Bloch's *The Principle of Hope* (1986). It is its hope for a better world which links liberation theology in general terms with the chiliastic tradition down the centuries (Ellacuría, in Ellacuría and Sobrino 1993: 251–88). The legacy of Augustine's *City of God* had been so pervasive in Christian doctrine that the view of a this-worldly hope has either been interpreted in other-worldly terms or simply pushed to the margins of the Christian tradition. Joachim of Fiore's interpretation of the Book of Revelation and his trinitarian historicism provoked a very different attitude to eschatology (Reeves 1969). In it there is a decisive break with Augustinian eschatology, in that the task of the church is not to prepare people for the world beyond but to be co-workers of God in bringing in the kingdom. This has two aspects: a hope for the coming kingdom in this world (about which utopian language can sometimes be used; see Libânio, in Ellacuría and Sobrino 1993: 716–28), and the conviction that human agency is an important component relating to the establishment of the coming kingdom. Eschatological events ceased to be mysterious, transcendent entities; they became present, historical possibilities. Indeed, in the hands of Joachim's followers their own contemporary history and their own part in it became the arena for the fulfilment of the eschatological promises.

Both the Joachite tradition and liberation theology echo New Testament texts, and in this very important respect differ markedly from other areas of the Christian tradition. Theirs is a hope for this world rather than for some transcendent realm. The future does not function solely as a regulative ideal which acts as a stimulus to action, for it is also an inner dynamism which acts as a driving force to bring about radical change and to fulfil the hope for a new order in the present. Joachim's strong sense of his own time as of great significance in human history not only reflects New Testament eschatology but also led to an appreciation of the present moment (*kairos*) in human history as an opportunity for historical action of eschatological significance. Indeed, a major contribution of the churches in South Africa, the *Kairos Document*, picked up this language of timely theological and ethical engagement in politics (Kairos Group 1986). It would be wrong to see this kind of theology, whether in Joachite tradition or in liberation theology, as a mere by-product of modern Christian activism, for the implicit pneumatology in both presupposes that human actors have their part to play in preparation for the dawning age.

The influence of liberation theology on systematic theology in general terms reflects its character. The dialectic between social context and theology has become widely acknowledged even if the effects of this acknowledgement have not always led to any significant change in the way systematic theologians have done their work. Nevertheless there has been divergence between North America and Europe in this respect. In the former, contextual theology is a cornerstone of much theological work, and there is a wider recognition of the social context of all theology. The situation is rather different in Europe, where the influence of liberation theology has tended to be more on the fringes of higher education institutions; on the practice of adult theological education, however, its impact has been enormous. Theology is not just a matter of abstract theorizing, but of reflection on an active faith. The meaning of scripture and tradition is subordinated to experience as the primary datum; the text of everyday life is given priority over the text of the Bible. Patterns of biblical exegesis which have emerged in parts of Latin America over the last decades offer the most recent example of the way the practical faith of the non-professional reader can be resourced by a mode of reading of the scriptures which does not need—even if it was often supported by—sympathetic intellectuals (West 1999).

The dominance of the Roman Catholic Church in Latin America has meant that the character and theological context has been conditioned by the Catholic theological agenda. Nevertheless some mainline churches in Latin America have supported the outlines of liberation theology. In countries like South Africa, experience of oppression of the majority in the period of the apartheid regime led Protestants to a similar kind of theological method to that which emerged in Latin America. There is an affinity with both the political theology of Europe and North America and the important emphasis on history which emerges in both the work of Pannenberg and Moltmann, both of whom, arguably, reflect a greater distance from the dominance of an Augustinian eschatology in the light of an engagement with the biblical view of history (Gilbertson 2003).

Liberation theology forcibly reminds us that the contemporary theological enterprise cannot escape critical reflection on its assumptions and preferences. The preference in liberation exegesis for the teaching of Jesus on the reign of God, rather than the Pauline or Johannine theologies, manifests its own wish to identify the gospel as good news for the poor and as the quest for social justice. The Synoptic Gospels and the Book of Revelation have formed the most important part of the liberation process in certain sections of the church in Latin America. Liberation theology has reminded us, if nothing else, that when viewed from the underside of history, from the poor and the marginalized, the message of the kingdom looks rather different from the way in which it has been portrayed by those who have had the power to write the story of the church and formulate its dogmas and its social concerns.

References

Althaus-Reid, M. (2000). *Indecent Theology: Theological Perversions in Sex, Gender and Politics.* London: Routledge.

Avineri, S. (1968). *The Social and Political Thought of Karl Marx.* Cambridge: Cambridge University Press.

Barros Souza, M. de (1983). *A Biblia e a Luta pela Terra.* Petropolis: Commissão Pastoral da Terra.

Batsone, D., Mendieta, E., Lorentzen, L., and Hopkins, D. N. (1997). *Liberation Theologies, Postmodernity and the Americas.* London: Routledge.

Bell, D. M. (2001). *Liberation Theology after the End of History: The Refusal to Cease Suffering.* London: Routledge.

Bennett-Moore, Zoë (1997). 'On Copy Clerks, Transformers and Spiders: Teachers and Learners in Adult Theological Education'. *British Journal of Theological Education* 9/3: 36–44.

Bloch, E. (1986). *The Principle of Hope.* Oxford: Blackwell.

Boff, C. (1987). *Theology and Praxis.* Maryknoll: Orbis.

Boff, L. (1979). *Jesus Christ Liberator: A Critical Christology for our Time.* London: SPCK.

—— (1985). *Church: Charism and Power: Liberation Theology and the Institutional Church.* London: SCM.

—— (1986). *Ecclesiogenesis: The Base Communities Reinvent the Church.* Maryknoll: Orbis.

Bradstock, A., and Rowland, C. (2002). *Radical Christian Writings: A Reader.* Oxford: Blackwell.

Croatto, S. (1987). *Biblical Hermeneutics: Toward a Theory of Reading as the Production of Meaning*. Maryknoll: Orbis.

Ellacuría, I., and Sobrino, J. (1993). *Mysterium Liberationis: Fundamental Concepts of Liberation Theology*. Maryknoll: Orbis.

Freire, P. (1972). *Pedagogy of the Oppressed*. London: Penguin.

Gilbertson, Michael (2003). *God and History in the Book of Revelation: New Testament Studies in Dialogue with Pannenberg and Moltmann*. Society for New Testament Studies Monograph Series 124. Cambridge: Cambridge University Press.

Graham, E. (1996). *Transforming Practice: Pastoral Theology in an Age of Uncertainty*. London: Mowbray.

Gutiérrez, G. (1983). *The Power of the Poor in History*. London: SCM.

—— (1988). *A Theology of Liberation*. London: SCM

—— (1993). *Santo Domingo and After: The Challenge for the Latin American Church*. London: Catholic Institute for International Relations.

Hegel, G. W. F. (1984). *Introduction to Lectures on the Philosophy of Religion of 1824*, i. *Introduction and Concept*. Berkeley and Los Angeles: University of California Press.

Hennelly, A. T. (ed.) (1990). *Liberation Theology: A Documentary History*. Maryknoll: Orbis.

Hoare, Q., and Smith, G. N. (eds.) (1971). *Selections from the Prison Notebooks*. London: Lawrence and Wishart.

Kairos Group (1986). *The Kairos Document: Challenge to the Church: A Theological Comment on the Political Crisis in South Africa*. Grand Rapids: Eerdmans.

Keller, R. S., and Radford Ruether, R. (eds.) (1995). *In Our Own Voices: Four Centuries of American Women's Religious Writing*. San Francisco: Harper.

Marcus, J. (1993). *The Way of the Lord: Christological Exegesis in the Gospel of Mark*. Edinburgh: T. & T. Clark.

Mesters, C. (1989). *Defenseless Flower*. London: Catholic Institute for International Relations.

—— (1993). 'The Use of the Bible in Christian Communities of the Common People', In Norman K. Gottwald and Richard A. Horsley (eds.), *The Bible and Liberation: Political and Social Hermeneutics*, Maryknoll: Orbis, 3–16.

Metz, J. B. (1969). *Theology of the World*. New York: Herder and Herder.

—— (1980). *Faith in History and Society: Towards a Practical Fundamental Theology*. New York: Seabury.

Miranda, J. P. (1977). *Marx and the Bible*. London: SCM.

Moltmann, J. (1977). *The Church in the Power of the Spirit: Towards a Messianic Ecclesiology*. London: SCM.

Petrella, I. (2004). *The Future of Liberation Theology: An Argument and a Manifesto*. Aldershot: Ashgate.

—— (ed.) (2005). *Latin American Liberation Theology: The Next Generation*. Maryknoll: Orbis.

Reeves, M. (1969). *The Influence of Prophecy in the Later Middle Ages*. Oxford: Oxford University Press.

Rowland, C., and Corner, M. (1990). *Liberating Exegesis: The Challenge of Liberation Theology to Biblical Studies*. London: SPCK.

—— (ed.) (2008). *The Cambridge Companion to Liberation Theology*. 2nd edn. Cambridge: Cambridge University Press.

Sacred Congregation for the Doctrine of the Faith (1984). *Instruction on Certain Aspects of the 'Theology of Liberation'.* London: Catholic Truth Society.

Sacred Congregation for the Doctrine of the Faith (1986). *Instruction on Christian Freedom and Liberation.* Vatican City: Incorporated Catholic Truth Society.

Segundo, J. L. (1976). *The Liberation of Theology.* Maryknoll: Orbis.

—— (1985). *Jesus of Nazareth Yesterday and Today*, ii. *The Historical Jesus of the Synoptic Gospels.* London: Sheed and Ward.

Selvidge, M. J. (1996). *Notorious Voices: Feminist Biblical Interpretation, 1500–1920.* London: SCM.

Sobrino, J. (1978). *Christology at the Crossroads: A Latin American Approach.* London: SCM.

—— (1984). *The True Church and the Church of the Poor.* London: SCM.

Sugirtharajah, R. S. (1991). *Voices from the Margins.* London: SPCK.

Tombs, D. (2002). *Latin American Liberation Theology.* Boston: Brill.

Walsh, M., and Davies, B. (eds.) (1984). *Proclaiming Justice and Peace.* London: CIIR and CAFOD.

West, G. (1999). *The Academy of the Poor: Towards a Dialogical Reading of the Bible.* Sheffield: Sheffield Academic.

Suggested Reading

Bell (2001).

Boff, C. (1987).

Boff, L. (1985).

Bradstock and Rowland (2002).

Ellacuría and Sobrino (1993).

Freire (1972).

Gutiérrez (1988).

Hennelly (1990).

Mesters (1989).

Petrella (2004).

Rowland (2008).

Segundo (1976).

Sobrino (1978).

CHAPTER 36

COMPARATIVE THEOLOGY

FRANCIS X. CLOONEY, SJ

Reflection on other religious traditions, though articulated in myriad ways, has of course occurred in religious traditions from their very beginning. So too theologies, obligated to some norms of reason and to the quest to understand and (to some extent) explain what is believed, have of necessity had to engage the thought and practice of the other traditions which helped shape the context for intelligibility in any given era. The Christian tradition (which remains the primary though not exclusive focus of this essay) is no exception, and even before Christianity, the Jewish people already shaped their language about God with an awareness of how their neighbours were speaking; they likewise articulated their own identities in comparison and contrast with those of their diverse neighbours. Other religious traditions too have had to keep reshaping their self-understanding in light of their religious 'others'. Moreover, despite numerous misunderstandings and tragic, shameful moments of hostility and violence, throughout history religious cultures have nonetheless often related to one another with subtlety, sophistication, and boldness. Intentionally or not, interreligious exchange seems on the whole to have been a positive rather than negative phenomenon.

As but one dimension of this larger, ongoing exchange, comparative theology is not an entirely new beginning. Today, however, the proximity of religions to one another is greater than ever and the resources for understanding religions other than one's own are unprecedented; accordingly, the opportunities are greater and responsibility more acute, and so it has become nearly impossible to justify not studying other traditions and taking their theologies into account in light of contemporary canons of learning. While theology can never be reduced to a single task, theological reflection in its mature form always stands in a dialogical relationship to the theologies of other religions, both in general and with respect to (nearly) every topic. This commits the theological community to the practice of what will here be termed 'comparative theology', the practice of rethinking aspects of one's own faith tradition through the study of aspects of another faith tradition. Other dimensions and the implications of this very brief definition will become clearer as we proceed.

As a form of theological exchange, comparative theology is particularly interested in highlighting the nature, dynamics, and use of doctrines and their referents within traditions but also across boundaries. Thus, for example, candidates for analysis will include faith, truth, sin, grace, salvation, community, and worship, both in general and in more specific doctrinal forms, plus an even wider range of vaguer but still fruitful terms such as union or communion, delusion, liberation, humility, devotion, spiritual knowledge, compassion, and healing. And there are still other terms and areas of study to be identified through learning from traditions whose concepts have until now been either ignored or poorly translated into English or borrowed without much theological sophistication; for the theologians of other traditions were not merely saying 'in their own words and concepts' what 'we' have already been meaning and saying. So too, like other forms of theology, comparative theology is to some extent interested in how religious traditions explain their own views of common human realities, ranging from birth and death to sex and love, eating and marriage, money and power. Since comparative theology is liable to the same range of meanings and perspectives as theology in general, it cannot be definitively identified in a single or univocal way; since in its current formulation it is new, it is not ready for sure and settled definitions. The following description therefore seeks only to highlight some key features and problems of a vital yet still developing discipline.

I. Detecting the Origins of Comparative Theology

The term 'comparative theology' has a long history that requires further research, even if we are unlikely to discover any definitive and single meaning for it. The term has been in use at least since 1700 when James Garden published his *Comparative Theology; or The True and Solid Grounds of Pure and Peaceable Theology: A Subject very Necessary, tho hitherto almost wholly neglected.* Garden, possibly inspired by the controversial Dutch mystic Antoinette Bourignon, contrasts 'absolute theology', 'that knowledge of religion [which] considers its Object only as revealed and enjoined, or instituted, by God, and its business is to find out those things which are proposed to us in the Scriptures to be believ'd or practis'd, and to discern and distinguish them from all others', with a 'comparative theology' wherein 'the respective Knowledge of Religion ponders the weight or importance, and observes the Order, Respect and Relation of things belonging to Religion; whether they be points of Doctrine, or Precepts, or sacred Rites, and teaches to distinguish and put a difference between the Accessories of Religion, and the Principles; the Circumstantials and Substantials; the Means and their Ends' (Garden 1700: 3–4). Garden is speaking of intra-Christian and not interreligious differences, but his principles—a focus on common rather than dividing elements, and a determination to minimize the realm of exclusive, absolute features of Christianity—are in spirit akin to some of the best comparative work in following centuries. Where else and how else the term was used during the eighteenth century, however, remains an object of research.

In the nineteenth century, as comparison gained respect as a scientific method, comparative theology was used more often, even if not frequently. In works such as *Natural Religion* (1898) and *Introduction to the Science of Religion* (1899), F. Max Müller speaks occasionally of 'comparative theology'. Religions can be compared, but not in a 'comparative religion' discipline; 'religion' cannot of itself generate that kind of second-order reflection. Rather, comparative theology is the reflective discipline in which religions are compared (Müller 1898: 47). In a comparative theology the comparativist does not privilege his own religion as exceptional, but treats all religions as natural and historical (Müller 1898: 52). Unlike general or natural theology, comparative theology is a study of religions in their particularity, aimed at noticing both what is unique and what is shared with other religions (Müller 1898: 53). Just as comparative philology transformed the philosophy of language, so too comparative theology will transform 'theoretic' theology (Müller 1899: 146). We can also note that Müller links theoretic theology with the philosophy of religion and explanations of natural religion; with respect to religions other than the Christian, today's theology of religions is a descendant of theoretic theology.

William Warren, president of Boston University for much of the second half of the nineteenth century, promoted the study of religions at the university. In an 1887 commencement address, 'The Quest of the Perfect Religion', he 'dreams' a universal deliberation on religions, which concludes in determining that the Christian religion is indeed perfect (Warren 1887). He also taught a course entitled 'Comparative Theology and Philosophy of Religion', and perhaps all his reflections may be grouped under that rubric. James Freeman Clarke's *Ten Great Religions: An Essay in Comparative Theology* (1892) offers a wide study of the doctrines of different traditions, aiming to show their truths' inclusion in the larger truth of Christianity, the full and perfect religion (cf. Clarke 1896). At the turn of the century, J. A. MacCulloch wrote a *Comparative Theology* (1902), dedicated to facilitating comparisons on particular themes between Christianity, the absolute religion, and other religions, all for the purpose of an informed proof that Christianity alone is the perfect religion, but also the religion that includes all that is best in other religions, thus fulfilling them. Despite what today might be considered evident flaws of their approach—research at the service of already settled conclusions—comparative theology as practised by Warren, MacCulloch, and Clarke seems nonetheless to have advanced understanding of and appreciation for religions.

As for its more substantive history as a primarily Christian enterprise rooted in particular interreligious encounters, comparative theology lies in closest continuity with the theological reflection on other religions in the patristic era and, more fully, in the missionary period of the sixteenth century and thereafter. Spanish and Portuguese missionary scholars, as well as Italian, French, and later British, all reflected on their religious 'others'. Even if the conversations between missionaries and 'natives' were neither neutral nor entirely open-minded, such reflections were often worked out in great detail and in close conversation with intellectual representatives of various religions, strengthened in some cases by careful attention to particular texts which were often first studied and translated by missionary scholars. Comparative theology shares this attentiveness to the particularities of other religious traditions and their concern for specific ways in which the Christian faith interacts with different faiths.

One may therefore profitably seek in missionary writings a glimpse of the prehistory of comparative theology. To take some examples from India, the writings of Roberto de Nobili and Jean V. Bouchet, both Jesuit missionaries in south India at the beginning of the seventeenth and eighteenth centuries respectively, show how Christian theological suppositions, guided by a care for the particularities of the Hindu traditions, support and prompt strikingly engaged works of scholarship. De Nobili seems to have read carefully the famous *Laws of Manu* in attempting to decipher the religious meaning and structure of Indian society, while, in his letters (collected among the famous *Lettres Édifiantes et Curieuses*), Bouchet rather elaborately compares the mythologies of the Indian and Greek gods, the Indian and Greek understandings of reincarnation, and even the legal systems of India and the West. Both missionaries drew the study of India into their consideration of Christian theological themes in a serious way, even if we can today wish that they had been more explicit regarding how they actually benefited from their study. In the Protestant context, we may point to Bartholomeo Ziegenbalg's *Genealogy of the Malabarian Gods* as a remarkable eighteenth-century work of scholarship wherein theological interests are fruitfully merged with detailed knowledge of another tradition. Even in the twentieth century, we still find works such as Pierre Johanns's *To Christ through the Vedanta* (published serially during 1922–34), a learned and detailed analysis of Vedanta religious and philosophical ideas with an eye toward identifying their enduring meaning and value.

Although Johanns's Thomistic frame would today not be taken as the unexceptionable standard by which to judge other intellectual systems, but would rather be submitted to same critique as the Indian materials, within the bounds of his framework Johanns proceeds as an exemplary comparativist, well versed in both sides of his scholarly comparison, and persisting throughout in his determination to uncover theological meanings and to leave as much space as he thought possible for a generous reading of India.

Comparative theology as the theologically conscious study of religions other than one's own may today be exemplified by a wide range of works, including many which do not use the term 'comparative theology'. Thus, in *Knowing the Unknowable God* (1986) and *Freedom and Creation in Three Traditions* (1993), David Burrell has explored how Aquinas interacted with thinkers such Maimonides and Ibn Sina in crafting respectively his understanding of God and of creation. In *The Gospel of Mark: A Mahayana Reading* (1995), John Keenan reads the Gospel of Mark in light of Buddhist theology, while in *The Wisdom of James: Parallels with Mahayana Buddhism* (2005), he extends this project to another New Testament book. James Fredericks brings Buddhist and Christian insights into conversation in his *Buddhists and Christians: Through Comparative Theology to Solidarity* (2004). In a more extended project, Keith Ward wrote a series of four volumes in comparative theology: *Religion and Revelation* (1994), *Religion and Creation* (1996), *Religion and Human Nature* (1998), and *Religion and Community* (2000). During the same decade Robert Neville directed an ambitious project bringing together philosophical theologians and area experts for an extended conversation that resulted in three edited volumes, *The Human Condition, Ultimate Realities,* and *Religious Truth* (2000). Michael Myers's *Brahman: A Comparative Theology* (2001) attempts 'a critique of systematic theology from the comparative perspective', making use of insights gleaned in India to rethink issues in Christian theology. (My own works, such as *Theology after Vedanta* (1993), *Hindu God, Christian God* (2001), and *Divine Mother, Blessed Mother* (2004), may be included in the category of 'comparative theology'.)

In light of the preceding history and examples, it is useful to distinguish two underlying motives that nourish comparative theology. Beginning with James Garden (or before), there is the determination to discern and stress what religious people have in common, for the sake of mutual understanding and peace. With Müller and thereafter, we find the goal of an objective study of religions furthered by the use of the methods of scientific comparison. The former is allied with what today we might term ecumenical or interreligious dialogue, while the latter most naturally merges with the scientific and historical study of religion and more analytic disciplines. In both, the particular details of religions are privileged over against merely theoretical and *a priori* conceptions. In *The Invention of Religion* (2005), Tomoko Masuzawa examines the influence of comparative theology in the nineteenth century in relation to the emerging discipline of the study of religion, concluding that comparative theology may well have had a greater legacy than its more ambitiously scientific and ostensibly more neutral counterparts.

For a more formal contemporary understanding of comparative theology, we turn first to David Tracy's essay in *The Encyclopedia of Religion* (1987). Tracy argues that the fact that 'theology itself is now widely considered one discipline within the multidisciplinary field of religious studies impels contemporary theology, in whatever tradition, to become a comparative theology .... On strictly theological grounds, the fact of religious pluralism should enter all theological assessment and self-analysis in any tradition at the very beginning of its task' (Tracy 1987: 446). He notes two pertinent understandings of comparative theology: first, as a discipline within the history of religions, in which theologies from different traditions are compared; second, as 'a more strictly theological enterprise ... which ordinarily studies not one tradition alone but two or more, compared on theological grounds' (Tracy 1987: 446). He goes on to highlight four major moments in a comparative theology: reinterpreting central religious symbols in a religiously pluralistic world; providing theological interpretation with new foundations comprised of both tradition and contemporary pluralism; addressing questions of religious pluralism on explicitly theological grounds; and finally, in light of these, reviewing tradition by a hermeneutics of suspicion and critique and by a hermeneutics of retrieval.

Keith Ward too has stressed the necessarily interreligious nature of theologizing as it is being reconceived today, indicating 'that theology is the discipline of reflection upon ideas of the ultimate reality and goal of human life, of God, and of revelation. People of many diverse beliefs can undertake it. It is better undertaken in knowledge of and in conversation with those of beliefs other than one's own' (Ward 1994: 46). Consequently, theologians properly explore given theological topics such as creation or revelation in several traditions and then articulate positions in light of common features that have been discovered. Such scholars deserve to be recognized as 'full and proper theologians'. Ward distinguishes between confessional theology, 'the exploration of a given revelation by one who wholly accepts the revelation and lives by it', and comparative theology, 'an intellectual discipline which enquires into ideas of the ultimate value and goal of human life, as they have been perceived and expressed in a variety of religious traditions' (Ward 1994: 40). The former is focused on revelation, the latter on God's wider work in the world. Ward locates his four-volume work in the latter category as primarily comparative and not confessional in nature, even if it quite evidently also sheds light on the doctrines and values treated in a confessional theology.

While it may be useful to distinguish between comparative and confessional theologies, these need not be formally divided as disciplines between which a theologian must choose. Rather, we have entered an era where constructive, confessional theology will ordinarily be comparative in its practice. Comparative theology can also be, and normally is, a theology that remains primarily constructive in a more narrow sense. As such, its deliberations are rooted in multiple traditions, even if the comparativist normally, perhaps necessarily, remains a member of just one community. One reads another tradition while remaining mindful of one's own; one brings to bear all the expectations and skills one has developed in one's home tradition, while keeping mindful of the ways in which this approach is necessarily different from and even inadequate to the tradition one is studying. Then, after a close reading and appropriation of the other, one reads again one's own, this time in accord with the affect generated out of one's study of the other.

This dialectical process leads to a certain kind of change in one's own theology—having less to do with content and more to do with approach, how one reads familiar documents, for example. Traditional and newer themes are rethought in light of comparative study for the sake of knowledge of God and also with respect to theological concepts related to one's knowledge of God. This is undertaken also for the sake of a more intense confessional conversation within the comparativist's home tradition, for comparative theology, like other theological disciplines, is always primarily for one's own community. These key activities are accompanied by all the smaller choices that theologians make when seeking to render their work meaningful and useful for their faith community. All this is a reading practice that attends to the smallest of differences, while yet changing the entire context for theological reflection. Even if the specific content of one's theology may have changed only minimally or not at all, on a quieter level context and nuance will have shifted rather deeply.

II. The Multiple Dimensions of a Comparative Theology

Although comparative theology is a specialist discourse deeply informed by attention to the details of multiple religious and theological traditions, like other modes of Christian theology it can be specified according to a variety of possibilities and purposes. It is no more likely to be successfully narrowed to a single method or purpose than are other modes of theology. Comparative theology's engagement with other theologies is a complex enterprise, usefully understood within a fuller set of moments of which the comparative is only one. Around comparison, before and after it, we can highlight its interreligious, dialogical, and confessional (or apologetic) dimensions.

First, if theology is to be comparative, we must first of all concede the interreligious nature of theology itself. Theologizing, defined as faith seeking understanding or in some analogous way, is a religious thinking that is undertaken by people in different religious traditions. Theologies occur within the bounds of specific religious traditions, but such thinking occurs in ways that are broadly and commonly human, cultural and linguistic differences notwithstanding. Faith may be a gift that neither originates in nor is quantitatively improved by ratiocination about that gift; but theological reflection occurs when believers begin to think through, probe, and explain what they believe, in a process that seems necessary whenever faith is more than a finished artefact simply transmitted from one generation to the next.

Although 'theology' is a term which, judging from its history in the Christian West, possesses a range of specific meanings, to claim that it is interreligious means that it is not wise to reserve the term entirely for the Christian context. Thus, for example, we can refer not only to Christian theology but also to Hindu theology, whether we use a definition as basic as 'faith seeking understanding', or more expansively refer to reflection on revealed truths preserved in a canon of texts and handed down in a tradition, etc. For we can notice that the Hindu traditions of India are sensitive to the differentiations that make room for the 'theological' (Clooney 2002). Thus, in traditional India, reasoning carried forward without an immediate appeal to authoritative religious sources is distinguished from reasoning marked by early attention to scripture and other religious authorities; the latter is valued highly, and is to a large extent what we call theological reasoning. Some Hindu reasoning is only very indirectly allied with religious truth claims or religious practices. For example, some Hindu piety is deeply religious and is presented as immune to critical examination. But reasoning and piety often cooperate to distinguish a faith that is received and reviewed in a critical fashion. Since modern India has in fact been influenced by many ideas that originated in the West, and since the designation 'theology' need not be pejorative, there is no *a priori* reason to avoid talking about 'Hindu theology' as a properly Hindu mode of thought that can be usefully distinguished from 'Hindu philosophy' and 'Hindu religiosity'. Similarly, one might argue for Islamic and Jewish theologies, with specific differences noted, but also, though in light of greater differences requiring further explanation, for 'Buddhist theology' or 'Taoist theology' and even for theologies orally transmitted in Native American or African traditions.

Such uses of the term 'theology' can be valuable even when we still do not pretend that all such traditions are theological in exactly the same way. The point is rather to insist that very little of importance in method or content belongs exclusively to one theological tradition or one religion, even when concepts and themes are indeed properly located in specific contexts and remain rooted in the particularities of specific faith traditions. As an intellectual project, theology is composed of intellectual practices that can be recognized by intelligent believers in multiple traditions and are not likely to be unique to any particular tradition. But again, this is not to deny that for the most part theology can and should still be undertaken in accord with particular traditions' beliefs, doctrines, and practices.

'Theology' and 'comparative' will still have their strongest resonances in the Christian tradition.

Second, if theology is an intellectual religious activity practised in various cultural settings, and if theologians can profitably notice similarities and differences in method and content across religious boundaries, then it is in keeping with its own integrity that this interreligious and comparative theology can and ought to be conceived and practised as a properly dialogical activity. What is learned from interreligious and comparative perspectives must be tested and extended in a richer interactive encounter among the two or more traditions being compared, as believers learn to think together across religious boundaries. The theologian owes it to members of the tradition she or he studies to understand and appreciate what they say and mean, whether or not she or he agrees with it. Those whose texts are studied must be able at least to recognize what is being said about them.

It is also important to note that the theologian who ventures into contact with another religious tradition is faced with the prospect of becoming an object of study as well, as her or his theologizing is assessed according to the expectations of the other tradition. Once theology is practised with attentiveness to the interreligious context, theologians are doubly accountable. Giving reasons for their faith, they become accountable to their religious others for interreligious accuracy and theological sensitivity and acumen in what they write about the other religions. For the sake of mutual understanding, they are likewise called to give an account of themselves and their tradition in light of what believers in other traditions are saying about the specific theological positions in question.

While 'comparison' and 'dialogical accountability' can mark much the same terrain, the two terms can be usefully conceived as consecutive: comparative attentiveness leads to dialogical accountability, to mutual learning, and thus to the constitution of a wider community of conversation and learning. The task of theologians on both sides is, ideally, to choose to enter upon a conversation that flows from mutual study, and thereafter upon an ongoing theological practice deepened in light of that conversation. In this new dynamic, no one partner gets to determine finally what the conversation means. If theology is interreligiously dialogical, theologians must work with an awareness that others' positions are already multi-dimensional, reflective, and theological in ways analogous to those held by the Christian theologian. It will no longer be acceptable to survey other traditions as if from a higher position or as if other traditions are simply raw materials for interpretation.

Like Christian theologians, the theologians of other traditions have their own personal and communal agenda, their own hierarchy of sub-disciplines, their own expectations about the qualifications of an audience, and their own estimates of outsiders. They may still have strong opinions about 'theology' and 'comparative' and whether these terms usefully apply to their own traditions. On both sides and together, myths are heard and images contemplated, rites observed, divinities described, explained, reverenced. All of this occurs in studies that may begin as 'our' scrutiny of 'their' religious ideas or texts, but that in the longer run also become occasions for reversal, wherein the theologians of the other religion submit the 'visiting' theologian and her or his tradition to a scrutiny appropriate to the visited tradition's own methods of investigation. Accordingly, even the foundations of theology and one's basic motivations become the matter for interreligious conversation. Such is the ideal, even if we must also admit that this mutual accountability is at present only a desideratum only rarely witnessed in practice.

Third, the inevitably and permanently dialogical character of an interreligious and comparative theology does not mean that such a theology always eventuates in mutual agreement and understanding. Such a theology can remain confessional, even apologetic. The dialogue essential to an interreligious theology must be vital enough that it can become an argument in which differences are highlighted, accentuated, and debated. Even after comparison and during the give and take required by dialogical exchange, theologians should remain able to affirm the content of their faith as true, with a deepening sense of its intelligibility for those who believe it already; they should remain able to offer arguments in favour of the truth of their faith and to attempt to persuade their interlocutors. If some comparative theologians choose to be more or less confessional and apologetic than others, here too comparative theology only demonstrates the same range of choices found in theology in general.

However comparative theology proceeds, the theologian can still adhere to the norms of theology as ordinarily practised in her or his own tradition. Doctrines can be received as true and practices taken very seriously as efficacious means of grace. If reading is the primary instrument of one's theology—as is the case for most theologians most of the time—one will be able to continue reading the works of one's own great theologians, even if one also reads theologians from other traditions. Comparative study need not obviate doctrine, truth, or value; conversely, no amount of reflection on the presuppositions, methods, or importance of one's own tradition can succeed in obviating the need actually to read and learn from other traditions. Insofar as possible, then, this textual scholarship should be filled out in interreligious theological conversation. One talks and interacts with theologians from the other tradition, explains one's beliefs and writings, and asks questions about their beliefs and writings, showing a willingness to learn from those theologians of other faiths. In ideal circumstances, one also sees, hears, tastes, smells, and touches the 'reality' of the other tradition. While it is proper and necessary to study the classic texts of other traditions—from its oldest scriptures to its medieval treatises and modern monographs—one must also be alert to still more recent developments, as each tradition stakes out its contemporary meanings in new situations which will, one presumes, be substantially but not entirely predictably conformed to older texts and doctrines or to any single notion of religious reflection or theology.

Finally, to state a point that by its very nature cannot really be illustrated here, it is crucial that comparative theology be practised, and not merely described in theory or with respect to method. This is in part because the field is a new one and in need of a richer store of examples before definition can be satisfactory; in part because a merely theoretical representation of comparative theology will be likely to remain the property of only one of the traditions involved; and in part because comparative theology, as comparative, is essentially reflection on practice, subsisting in its practice. Accordingly, it is at this point that we might well take up a series of examples by which to make the preceding points more specific. Thus, again staying with India, we might study a passage from chapter 6 of the Chandogya Upanisad, with special attention to its account of the origins of the world and of the nature of the self; we might then examine its interpretation according to the Brahma Sutras, the commentaries of Sankaracarya (in the non-dualist school of Vedanta) and Rangaramanujamuni (in the qualified, theistic Vedanta tradition); finally, we might turn to analogous texts, interpretations, and themes in the biblical and Christian traditions. Or we might take up a devotional text composed in Tamil or Bengali and, with attention to its differences from the texts of the Sanskrit tradition, explore more deeply the images and expressions of love and religious love in such a text, and then, again reflectively, trace and be touched by similar images in the texts of the Jewish and Christian spiritual traditions. Or, more to the point of this essay, we might explore some classical *loci* in Sanskrit and Tamil with an eye toward understanding what might count as a Hindu or Vaisnava or Saiva theology, so as further to assess how such a theology would be similar to and different from the content and methods of a Christian theology. Specific studies like these three examples from the Indian context as read by a Christian theologian provide the necessary basis for observing comparative theology in the act, and a descriptive essay such as this present piece ought not be taken as replacing this more primary work.

III. Some Problems

Multidimensional and complex, comparative theology is a practice deeply rooted in particular faith communities; yet it is also generative of new configurations that challenge theologies and their established faith communities, and possibly move beyond them, too. Comparative study is always, of course, complicated in ordinary ways, because it is hard to make good comparisons and because its intellectual production is to be analysed in the harsher light of wider debates pertaining to culture, society, the arts and sciences broadly imagined, and a host of local and global political concerns. As a relatively new discipline, it is perhaps all the more vulnerable to the shifting moods and boundaries of a modern scholarship distinguished by cultural and religious pluralization (even as the world becomes more uniform in some ways); by the growing availability of detailed information about traditions, making stereotypes, reductions, and ignorance ever more inexcusable; by a more vulnerable and acute global consciousness in a post-colonial, post-missionary context; by scepticism about the possibility of neutral or detached scholarship syntheses; and by the (re)insertion of the author's own self in her or his study, so that all scholarship is essentially and even explicitly autobiographical. But within this broad complex of problems, six can be noted as of particular importance.

A first problem, already alluded to, arises in light of the current turn to popular religion, particularly with respect to religions in actual practice. In this context, one may object that a comparative theology defined in terms of texts and reading becomes a narrow and elitist discipline, possibly an obstacle to a more ample interchange among religious people today. Surely, though, most theology by most theologians is textual. It has always been, materially at least, a matter of reading texts that have stood the test of time, and there is no reason to expect a so very different approach from comparative theologians. Moreover, texts are often the easiest way to access another religious tradition, particularly in its articulate classical forms. But even if reading is the most practical and solid means of theological learning, there is no reason why some comparative theologians cannot choose to proceed by way of attention to art, music, ritual, and the various modalities of popular religion; they will still, however, turn the fruits of that attention into writing, and thus return to the conversation of those who write and read.

Second, it may seem likely that comparative theology, even if named a Christian (or Hindu or Muslim, etc.) theological enterprise, will after some time smoothly transmute into comparative religion or a similar discipline, thus becoming a mode of comparison linked to a theological frame by way of ancestry but lacking a specifically religious commitment or finality. What begins as theological may end as a simpler and flatter comparison of religious ideas on neutral grounds, without theological identity and grounding in a faith community; the theological frame becomes thinner and thinner even as comparative detail accumulates. Judgements may be postponed or entirely ruled out, while even a commitment to objectivity and impartiality in a pluralistic society may seem to push communal and theological perspectives decisively to the side.

But there is no reason why the dynamic of comparative theology must be assessed in terms of this rather extreme eventuality. Comparative theology engages a wide array of issues and draws upon varied disciplines, but still in a way similar to that employed by theologians who do not do comparative study. If a theologian or ethicist can delve deeply into the world of science or literature or psychoanalysis without losing her or his faith bearings, so too the comparativist can study another tradition deeply without ceasing to be a believing theologian or without ceasing to contribute to her or his own religious tradition as an enterprise nourished by many inquiries that reach beyond the context of theology narrowly defined. The attention to the dynamic described above—the comparative theologian engages in a study that affects and is affected by the theologian's own person and personality—should help prevent immediate or gradual detachment from the intensity of the faith perspective and theological inquiry, just as theological commitments are not entirely marginalized by philological or historical questions. If comparative study is consciously reflective, it should intensify rather than relativize religious and theological commitments.

Third, and from the opposite direction, one may insist that comparative theology, however neutrally or pluralistically described, remains a rather deeply, even narrowly, Christian enterprise. Despite all the nuances and cautions stated above, 'theology' is still a Christian construction with roots and a history distinctive to the Christian tradition. Comparative theology, deeply implicated in a Christian context, may then appear to remain a mode of discourse that other traditions cannot adopt without contortion. It may in effect be a largely one-sided conversation among Christians shared with just a few others willing to adopt a Christian mode of religious reflection. Certainly, it remains necessary to remember that comparative study has a largely European and Christian history, and that 'theology' is a mode of religious intellectual discourse defined and practiced most comfortably in the Christian tradition. Even in this essay, comparative theology has been presented largely as a Christian production in terms of its history and features. It is also true that if we consider the multitude of religious languages proper to different traditions, 'theology' remains at best an analogous term that will not be exactly applicable in traditions other than the Christian. But as has been stated above, one need not conclude that theology and comparative theology have been or will have to remain only Christian productions. Believers in every tradition have 'faith', they need to think about what they have faith in, and they live in a world that is increasingly pluralistic. We can still insist that inquiry into one's faith, so as to understand and make sense of it, surely occurs in other religious traditions, and that such thinking is best named 'theology'. Jews and Muslims, Hindus and Buddhists, and people of other traditions all do theologize and cannot but enter into conversation with theologians of many other traditions. Thus they too have to become comparative theologians: these are legitimate claims, even if claims rooted in Christian intuitions and analogies that can never become entirely or simply matters of fact. 'Comparative theology' is still a better name for faithful religious reflection in this context—preferable to other terms that one might use in naming the kind of interreligious reflection sketched in this essay. In any case, 'theology' has a future as well as a past, and its meanings will continue to change during the ongoing conversation among believers.

Fourth, even if attention to detail, close reading, etc., are important, one might still object that in the end the real goal of comparative theology is to discern some truth parsed according to the norms of Christian theology—a truth which can only be articulated after and apart from comparative practice in a theology of religions, and even then according to more systematic judgements about the uniqueness of Christ and of Christianity among world religions. In this light, comparative theology cannot answer the questions it raises, but stands only as a propaedeutic exercise that may usefully provide resources for more explicit and traditional Christian theological reflection. Comparative theology may even be charged with concealing the assumptions of the theology of religions according to which comparative work gains theological significance. Certainly, we need to acknowledge the necessarily broader context in which comparative theology is possible—its interreligious, dialogical, and confessional frame—and the related scrutiny of Christian sources that occupies the theologian of religions. But the theology of religions, which is primarily Christian reflection on Christian resources, remains distinct from comparative study and by itself always falls short of those practices and purposes that are inherent in comparative study and evident only in its actual practice. Comparative theology remains substantively theological on its own, even if it does stand in a fruitful relationship with a subsequent theology of religions.

Fifth, close attention to another tradition's theology may in fact lead to a basic scepticism about the viability of concepts and words across theological boundaries. Different languages and theological traditions, the danger of identifying similarities which are only apparent, and innumerable distinctions and subtle differences may make it almost impossible to speak theologically across boundaries. So too, the sheer amount of data may become overwhelming. The meaning of other religions endlessly subdivides, from a simple question about 'the religions', to a nearly infinite series of complex choices and smaller questions about particular theological topics. Progress on the largest questions—Which religion is the truest or best? How does God save the world?—slows down to the point that one realizes that one will never know enough to draw conclusions. Comparative study might then seem merely a ploy for permanently postponing difficult theological judgements about other religions.

It is simply true that comparative study makes the project of posing and answering large questions more difficult, even as swifter progress is being made in clarifying many smaller theological topics. We may thus determine that different traditions do not mean the same thing by words appearing in English as 'God', 'sin', 'grace', etc., and we may learn very much from each tradition on how to nuance such words, even in English. It is also true that, once traditions are recognized as theological, they are less easily categorized, and they become resistant to the efforts of other traditions to determine 'the' theological meaning to be assigned to them. Facts can be annoyingly stubborn resisters to theory. A key question then is whether one can really state a meaning for the ongoing theological conversations that occur among religious intellectuals who have something in common but still differ from one another, who share the task of a dialogical accountability, and who have both to listen and yet still to confess and argue for their faith. It is not that conclusions become impossible or are ruled out, but only that the skills required for drawing conclusions become greater and more demanding. The future of theology may in part lie in this comparative project, but for now a trade-off may be inevitable: vastly more and more sophisticated knowledge on each theological topic, but also a postponement of answers to the great questions. Yet it is not necessary to conclude that the situation will forever remain this way. Perhaps we must simply be patient for a century or two, until the implications of comparison become more familiar and coherent.

Finally, and to head in yet another direction, the preceding pages may seem to suggest that comparative theology implies and even calls into existence a new religious community with a new 'interreligious faith' explored in 'comparative theology' and no longer viably traced back to a particular faith community and its theological discourse. Understanding will not be able to stop neatly at the edge of experience, and believers who share new experiences may in fact bring new spiritual insights to new communities, with new questions, new ways of responding to them, and new answers with their own additional implications. If theology is faith seeking understanding within a community context, then this new faithful search and gradually dawning understanding may seem to transform basic religious understanding, pushing it beyond a community's boundaries, and possibly convening a new community of comparativists. A Christian comparative theology, or a Buddhist one, might then conceivably cease to be exclusively Christian or exclusively Buddhist.

Comparative theology may, in this way, be seen as a rather dangerous enterprise. The emerging of a new community may occur not because of explicit contradictions to or breaks with Christian or Buddhist doctrine, nor because specific novel teachings are added to a given tradition, nor merely because many comparativists are liberals, but rather because comparative theological practice is increasingly comprised of questions, investigations, and research that fit within the confines of no single religious community. If we think differently, this affects how we live and, in some way, how we believe. A new theology may indicate a new theological community, comprised of believers, many of them theologians, who are committed to thinking across religious boundaries, balancing the questions of their own home tradition with attention to the questions of other traditions as well, and drawing on norms and authorities traceable to multiple traditions. Still, such intellectuals will ordinarily and for the most part remain members of more traditional religious communities, intent upon introducing the comparative questions back into that community. Faith will normally be deepened, not altered or redirected. Further speculation is needed on where comparative work actually leads, sociologically and theologically, perhaps in the theology of religions discipline that follows upon comparative theology. Again, patience is required given the novelty of the situation created by comparative theology.

Comparative theology is a constructive and reflective theological discipline that is not yet mature in either its theoretical or its practical dimensions. It must be practised at greater length, in still more particular instances, by theologians from outside the Christian tradition, and thereafter analysed and explained with attention to other emerging and fresh ways of doing theology. Only then can we imagine making a more settled assessment of the field, its major themes, its impact, and where it leads. For now, we must keep paying attention to what actually happens when one attends to traditions other than one's own, drawing comparisons on a small scale and prizing both similarities and differences, and for a time sacrificing the clarity to which we may feel accustomed in more well-established areas of theology.

References

Burrell, David, CSC (1986). *Knowing the Unknowable God: Ibn Sina, Maimonides, Aquinas.* Notre Dame: University of Notre Dame Press.

—— (1993). *Freedom and Creation in Three Traditions.* Notre Dame: University of Notre Dame Press.

Clarke, James F. (1892). *Ten Great Religions: An Essay in Comparative Theology.* Boston and New York: Houghton, Mifflin and Co.

—— (1896). *A Comparison of All Religions.* Boston and New York: Houghton, Mifflin and Co.

Clooney, Francis X. (2002), 'Restoring "Hindu Theology" as a Category in Indian Intellectual Discourse'. In Gavin Flood (ed.), *The Blackwell Companion to Hinduism*, London: Blackwell, 447–77.

—— (2004). *Divine Mother, Blessed Mother: Hindu Goddesses and the Virgin Mary.* New York: Oxford University Press.

Fredericks, James L. (2004). *Buddhists and Christians: Through Comparative Theology to Solidarity.* Maryknoll: Orbis.

Garden, James (1700). *Comparative Theology; or The True and Solid Grounds of Pure and Peaceable Theology: A Subject very Necessary, tho hitherto almost wholly neglected.* 'Printed and Sold by the Booksellers of London, and Westminster'.

Johanns, Pierre (1996 [1922–34]). *To Christ through the Vedanta.* Bangalore: United Theological College.

Keenan, John P. (1995). *The Gospel of Mark: A Mahayana Reading.* Maryknoll: Orbis.

—— (2005). *The Wisdom of James: Parallels with Mahayana Buddhism.* Mahwah: Newman.

Müller, F. Max (1898). *Natural Religion: The Gifford Lectures Delivered before the University of Glasgow in 1888.* London: Longmans, Green, and Co.

—— (1899). *Introduction to the Science of Religion: Four Lectures Delivered at the Royal Institution in February and May 1870.* London: Longmans, Green, and Co.

Myers, Michael W. (2001). *Brahman: A Comparative Theology.* Richmond: Curzon.

Tracy, David (1987). 'Comparative Theology'. In *The Encyclopedia of Religion*, New York: Macmillan, 14: 446–55.
Ward, Keith (1994). *Religion and Revelation.* Oxford: Oxford University Press.
Warren, William F. (1887). *The Quest of the Perfect Religion.* Boston: Rand Avery.

Suggested Reading

Clarke (1892).
—— (1896).
Clooney, Francis X. (1989). 'Christianity and World Religions: Religion, Reason and Pluralism'. *Religious Studies Review* 15/3: 197–204.
—— (1993). *Theology after Vedanta: An Experiment in Comparative Theology.* New York: State University of New York Press.
—— (1995). 'The Emerging Field of Comparative Theology: A Bibliographical Review (1989–95)'. *Theological Studies* 56/3: 521–50.
—— (2001). *Hindu God, Christian God: How Reason Helps Break Down the Barriers Between Religions.* Oxford: Oxford University Press.
—— (2003). 'Theology, Dialogue, and Religious Others: Some Recent Books in the Theology of Religions and Related Fields'. *Religious Studies Review* 29/4: 319–27.
Kitagawa, Joseph M. (1959). 'The History of Religions in America'. In id., *The History of Religions: Essays in Methodology*, Chicago: University of Chicago Press.
MacCulloch, J. A. (1902). *Comparative Theology.* London: Methuen.
Masuzawa, Tomoko (2005). *The Invention of World Religions: Or, How European Universalism Was Preserved in the Language of Pluralism.* Chicago: University of Chicago Press.
Neville, Robert (ed.) (2000*a*). *The Human Condition.* New York: State University of New York Press.
—— (2000*b*). *Ultimate Realities.* New York: State University of New York Press.
—— (2000*c*). *Religious Truth.* New York: State University of New York Press.
Sharpe, Eric J. (1986). *Comparative Religion: A History.* Peru: Open Court.
Ward, Keith (1996). *Religion and Creation.* Oxford: Oxford University Press.
—— (1998). *Religion and Human Nature.* Oxford: Oxford University Press.
—— (2000). *Religion and Community.* Oxford: Oxford University Press.

CHAPTER 37

FEMINIST THEOLOGY

JOY ANN MCDOUGALL

AT a time of increasingly local theologies, feminist theology offers one of the few genuinely global theological movements today. With its roots in North American and European soil, feminist theology has swept rapidly across the globe, inspiring women's liberation movements in disparate confessional and cultural traditions. Today one finds lively feminist conversations among Roman Catholic, Protestant, and Orthodox women theologians in North American, Latin American, European, African, and Asian contexts (Ruether 2002). While definitions of feminist theology are to some degree culture-specific, certain features unite the movement: defending the equal status of women as created in the image of God; supporting women's flourishing through improved education, health care, and leadership opportunities in the public sphere; and giving special attention to women's experiences of God, the self, and the world. Feminist theologians worldwide seek to expose the institutional and ideational structures that deprive women of their dignity as God's beloved creatures, and to transform situations of gender oppression so as to support the full flourishing of the whole community of God's creation. Here feminist theology aims at something more than a women's-only discourse. To borrow a phrase from theologian Rebecca Chopp, feminist theology seeks to accomplish 'saving work': offering bold interpretations of Christianity that seek to renew the life of the church and its witness to the world (Chopp 1995).

Beyond the fact of its global reach, one of the most telling signs of the feminist theological movement's significance is its current diversity in terms of scriptural hermeneutics, doctrinal issues, and methodologies. While Christian feminists may speak in unison about defending the equality of male and female as created in the *imago Dei*, they often disagree in the next breath on the nature of God-talk, atonement, and ecclesiology. Similarly, important disagreements exist among feminists about which critical theories, from post-structuralism to post-colonialism, psychoanalysis to cultural studies, are most useful for supporting a feminist theological agenda.

Given these widening debates, mapping the contemporary scene of feminist theology has become a precarious enterprise. As a first step one can distinguish three major waves in the development of feminist theology. The so-called 'first wave' includes the earliest defences of women's access to the preaching and teaching offices in the church and greater participation in the political sphere (1840–1920s). The 'second wave' begins with the first in-depth analyses of patriarchy and sexism in the Christian traditions and the rise of feminist biblical hermeneutics in the US and Europe (1960s–80s). The 'third wave' comes with the emergence of womanist, *mujerista*, and non-western feminist theological movements, all of which bring distinctive cultural experiences to the gender debate. In response, third-wave feminism has become cognizant of its own 'false universalisms', and of the need to situate its gender discourse within interlocking analyses of race, economic status, and sexual orientation (Pauw and Jones 2006: xii). At the same time third-wave feminists have become increasingly sophisticated in their use of secular gender theories and postmodern philosophical frameworks for doing their theological work (Chopp and Davaney 1997).

While these three waves trace feminist theology's development, they prove less helpful in mapping its contemporary geography. Other commonly used typologies, such as the juxtaposition of radical and reform feminisms, distinguishing those who abandon their confessional traditions from those who wish to reform these traditions, also prove rather blunt cartographical instruments. Among contemporary feminist theologians, the priority and possibilities of allegiance between feminism and ecclesial traditions have grown more complex and contested than ever. The radical-v.-reformist map lacks a sufficiently fine grain to describe with precision how particular feminist projects relate to their traditions' pasts or strive to transform their futures.

In order to gain a better angle of vision on feminist theology today, a different tack altogether may be helpful: that of peering through the lens of a particular doctrine—namely, the doctrine of sin. Hamartiology offers a unique vantage point on the feminist debate, especially since this issue ignited debate in the early seventies as a rising generation of second-wave feminist theologians found modern analyses of sin woefully inadequate to address women's lived experiences. From that point on, the doctrine of sin has been the cornerstone of feminist theological analysis. As Rebecca Chopp points out, feminist theology depends on an 'implicit doctrine of sin': 'Feminist theology is predicated upon the assumption that something is drastically wrong. Most specifically, sin is identified with patriarchy' (Chopp 1993: 12).

In simplest terms, patriarchy describes a social organization in which power lies in the hands of the dominant man or men over against ranks of others, especially women, who are subordinated to men's authority in the home, the church, and the public sphere. The sin of patriarchy brings with it its most faithful companion—sexism, the belief that persons of the male sex are by nature superior to those of the female (Johnson 1992: 23). While feminist theologians may disagree on the roots and remedies for these twin evils, they all aim to identify and rectify the patriarchal distortions in the symbolic order, in human relationships, and in institutional structures which deprive women of their full flourishing.

One can analyse what has happened in feminist theologies of sin to date by observing how the doctrine of sin has migrated from modern theological anthropology to other doctrinal locations (cf. Kelsey 1993). This will allow not only investigation of the major feminist reconstructions of the doctrine of sin, but also the detection of their ripple effects within the whole enterprise of feminist theology. This chapter will describe three such migrations of feminist sin-talk: first, a migration to the doctrine of redemption or liberation; second, to that of creation; and third, within the realm of theological anthropology itself. Each of these migrations has contributed important critiques of the classical western doctrine of sin. Even more, they have set a formidable agenda for future feminist theological work. Before looking at these different strands in the contemporary debate, however, let us first glance back at the origins of the feminist critique of sin in modern theology.

I. Overturning the Promethean Paradigm of Sin as Pride

In the late seventies and early eighties, Valerie Saiving, Judith Plaskow, and Rosemary Radford Ruether touched off an initial feminist protest against the doctrine of sin by challenging the analysis of sin in the works of Reinhold Niebuhr, Anders Nygren, and Paul Tillich. They argued that these modern theologians' root paradigm of sin as pride—what feminist Mary Grey later dubbed 'the Promethean paradigm of sin'—hardly fits the lived experience of women (Grey 1994: 234). Rather than falling into boastful arrogance and self-exaltation, women often struggle with exaggerated humility, permeable ego boundaries, and the 'failure to become a self at all' (Grey 1994: 234). Locating sin in an individual's rebellious will (or in modern terms, the self-inflated ego) presumes a possession of agency and autonomy that most women do not enjoy.

Not only does the category of pride miss the mark in identifying the source of women's alienation, but Christian sin-talk itself has been complicit in women's gender captivity. Since the earliest beginnings of Christianity, theologians have explained the presence of sin in the world in terms of Eve's original disobedience and seduction by the serpent in the Garden of Eden. The history of Christian thought thereafter gives ample evidence of how the tradition has held women disproportionately responsible for sin's damning history of effects and also treated their bodies as suspect as a source of sexual temptation (Kvam, Shearing, and Ziegler 1999). Due to their supposed susceptibility to sin, women have been systematically subordinated to male authority in the family, the church, and the public square. Given this aetiology of sin, it is no wonder that Christian sin-talk conjures up in women false guilt and self-blame, thus cementing them ever deeper into unhealthy patterns of subordination and self-sacrifice.

With the advent of womanist, *mujerista*, and Asian feminist theologies over the past two decades, this early feminist critique of the sin of pride has rightly received critical scrutiny. To take one powerful example, womanist theologians have challenged that white feminists are hardly exempt from their own 'will to power' when it comes to participating in racist structures of society, or even in making universal claims about the nature of women's experience. Feminist theologians had privileged the issue of gender over that of race or class, and in so doing had overlooked their own complicity in black women's oppression. In response, womanists focused on providing more holistic analyses of discrimination and improving the quality of life of the entire African-American community (Townes 1993).

Despite such significant points of contention, the basic outline of the early feminist critique of Christian sin-talk stands today. Feminists had exposed the long-standing androcentrism that infected Christian discourse about sin in the West. Not only did much of the classical language about sin assign disproportionate blame to women, but it also hid from sight the gendered dimensions of sin's bondage. Once feminists had demonstrated how deeply sin-talk was enmeshed in oppressive gender dynamics in society, it became evident that Christianity needed a different theological vocabulary if it were to speak in a life-giving way about sin.

II. The First Migration: The Original Sin of Sexism

Many of the pioneering second-wave feminist theologians addressed the androcentrism of Christian sin-talk by shifting the focus of the doctrine away from personal sin to the structural sin of gender oppression. Appropriating the classical story of the fall, these feminists identified sexism as the original sin from which both women and men need liberation. For example, Rosemary Radford Ruether, in her influential work *Sexism and God-Talk: Toward a Feminist Theology* (1983), diagnoses the sin of sexism as a distortion of the most basic form of human community, the 'I–Thou relationship' between man and woman. Instead of being a relationship of freedom and mutual recognition, the relationship becomes one of tyranny and victimization, a structure of domination which gives rise to other forms of alienation: 'from one's self as body, from the other as different from oneself, from nonhuman nature, and from God/ess' (Ruether 1983: 161). Ruether catalogues many of sexism's actual sins, for example, the violence against and the commodification of women's bodies, a sex-segregated labour force where women receive lower pay and prestige, and women's exclusion from leadership roles in church and society.

Like many in her generation, Ruether traces the sin of sexism to a fall into dualism, a 'self–other dichotomy' that treats women as the other and then subjects them to 'false-naming, projection, and exploitation' (Ruether 1983: 162). Although Ruether appeals to a modern dialectical analysis of the human condition to explain the dynamics of sexism, she does not locate sin, as modern theological anthropology does, in the individual ego. Sexism is first and foremost a structural sin, 'a systemic social evil' based on a 'pre-existing system of male privilege and female subordination', which shapes all of us from birth (Ruether 1983: 182). Therefore, while persons bear personal responsibility for perpetuating this patriarchal order, they also inherit its distorted patterns of gender relations. In quite classical terms, Ruether argues that the original sin of sexism is both radical in nature and universal in scope; it is inescapable and all-encompassing in its distorting power.

For those feminists who anchor the problem of sin in sexism, redemption lies in liberating humankind from unjust patterns of gender relations. The first step in that process comes with the recognition of the violence and violation that sexism causes. Feminist theologian Rebecca Chopp speaks here of exposing sexism's 'depravation' and 'deprivation', that is, how it 'destroys the very conditions of survival' and 'deprives personal and social (and natural) flourishing in that created potentials go unrealized' (Chopp 1993: 13). With the identification of concrete forms of gender injustice arises the recognition that patriarchy is not a natural order but rather a cultural production; it is a man-made reality that can be overturned. Herein lies the possibility for a feminist 'conversion', a turning around in which women 'discover themselves as persons' and experience liberating grace as the anger to 'break the chains of sexist socialization' (Ruether 1983: 186). For women and men alike liberation comes with the formation of relationships of mutual interdependence and a renewed sense of the community of all creation.

For this first strand in the feminist debate, the key to liberating society from sexism ultimately turns on establishing different models of gender relations built on equality, mutuality, and friendship. These proposals entail much more, however, than socio-ethical programmes of liberation; they offer full-scale agendas for reforming the Christian tradition's vision of the self, the world, and God. To take a well-known example, Sallie McFague, in her *Models of God: Theology for an*

Ecological, Nuclear Age (1987), calls for an end to the monarchical model of God, which in her view has sanctioned hierarchalism and structures of domination in Christianity. McFague proposes instead a threefold model of God as Mother, Friend, and Lover. These three metaphors for God express 'forms of fundamental intimacy, mutuality and relatedness' that highlight the interdependence of all life (McFague 1987: 85). Such revised God-language, McFague contends, will not only transform gender relations but also foster a different sensibility—an ethic of care, healing, and companionship among all of creation (McFague 1987: 92).

III. The Second Migration: The Tragic Suffering of Creation

Building on these initial feminist analyses of sexism, a second group of feminist theologians took a different path to redressing the gender trouble with sin. Feminist process theologians such as Catherine Keller, Mary Grey, and Marjorie Suchocki and ethicists such as Wendy Farley and Kathleen Sands challenged the Christian West's preoccupation with sin, and particularly its explanation of evil as the fallout from human action and, therefore, as humankind's rightful punishment. These feminists questioned whether such a version of the Christian narrative leads to needless self-blame and guilt for unjust suffering: 'Christianity', challenges Farley in her most recent work, 'has taught us we suffer because we have fallen into sin, and that at some level, our sufferings are justified. Like the abused and traumatized, we feel guilty for suffering inflicted upon us' (Farley 2005: 20). Furthermore, Farley among others criticizes the notion of original sin for involving a logic of divine retribution that defies the depths of divine love and leads to condemnation of, rather than compassion for, one's neighbour and oneself.

This second group of feminist theologians prescribes a radical cure: abandon the Augustinian interpretation of the fall narrative and with it the whole notion of original sin. They advocate instead either a process or a tragic view of creation, both of which see the world as tainted with violence and vulnerable to the wound of suffering from the very beginning. To take Farley's work again as our example, she presents a tragic vision of the human predicament. 'Finitude itself', she observes, 'seems to be tragically structured: the conditions of finite existence include conflict and fragility. This tragic structure is not evil, but it makes suffering both possible and inevitable prior to any human action' (Farley 1990: 31–2). In other words, radical suffering is woven into the fabric of creation as the price that human beings pay for their exercise of freedom.

In keeping with her tragic vision, Farley replaces the notion of a 'bondage to sin' with that of a 'bondage to suffering'. She offers a realistic picture of the deep woundedness that afflicts human beings without incurring the shame and guilt that accompanies sin-talk. Speaking of a 'bondage to suffering' has the specific feminist advantage of uncovering types of anguish in women's lives that are poorly diagnosed under the rubric of sin. For example, Farley points to the way in which common descriptions of sin as selfishness, with their prescribed remedy of self-sacrifice, either obscure or, worse, valorize women's 'addiction to care-giving' (Farley 2005: 24). Such traditional sin-talk leaves women ignorant of the true source of their spiritual discontent and deceived about their souls' deepest longings for love and delight.

As we saw with the first migration, this feminist reconstruction of sin-talk also has significant repercussions for the doctrine of God. Here, too, feminists roundly criticize the patriarchal concept of God as omnipotent and impassible. Such a picture of divine power jeopardizes both finite freedom and the integrity of divine goodness. Many of these feminist theologians prefer to describe God's power instead in terms of compassion, as a divine eros that desires relationship rather than possession, reciprocity rather than domination. Divine compassion involves more than solidarity and grieving with human suffering. It brings solace, healing, and strength to human beings in situations of inexplicable suffering. In Farley's words, divine compassion is an 'empowering power' that 'mediates the courage to resist suffering' (Farley 2005: 86).

Redefining God's power in terms of compassion lends a distinctive feminist ethos to the Christian life. For Farley, Grey, and others, this understanding of God calls human beings, too, to practise compassion as the only ethical response to humanity's radical suffering. As Farley describes it, compassion is an 'enduring disposition' that rests on our capacity to recognize the humanity of another and to desire his or her wellbeing (Farley 1990: 73). Within a feminist framework the practice of compassion does the saving work of restoring women's dignity and bringing renewed hope into situations of deprivation and despair.

IV. The Third Migration: Reforming Theological Anthropology

A third strand of feminist theology took the doctrine in yet another direction: reforming the notion of sin within theological anthropology itself. Feminist practical theologians and ethicists such as Mary Potter Engel (1990), Daphne Hampson (1996), Carol Hess (1997), and Linda Mercadante (2000) took the modern paradigm of sin as distorted self-relation and reconfigured it in feminist terms. Instead of situating women's sin on the underside of modernity's self-exalted ego, this third group of feminists strives to break free of the paradigm of the modern ego altogether. They propose an alternative model of selfhood constituted through mutually caring relationships with others. As Daphne Hampson describes this feminist self, she is 'centered in relation': 'a self which, having a certain integrity and agency, finds itself through deep connections with others' (Hampson 1996: 106). This self does not oppose the other in order to secure its identity; nor is the self defined strictly in terms of its relationships with others. Rather, in relationships of mutual recognition and affirmation, each person establishes her or his integrity and agency in proportion to and relationship with the other. In this feminist economy of relations, the values of equality, reciprocity, and friendship prevail.

With the help of feminist psychological analysis, moral development analysis, and sociological analysis, the theologians propounding this model of selfhood exposed the unhealthy forms of self-denial and damaging forms of interpersonal relationship which thwart women's selfhood and thus undermine their agency and full flourishing. By attending to the narratives of women's lives, these theologians began to speak about the dynamics of sin using new categories such as 'triviality', 'hiding', 'anguish', and 'sloth', as well as 'violence' and 'abuse of the vulnerable' (Jones 2000: 111). Such new categories not only give voice to women's lived realities, but also show how classical language about sin can collude with unjust gender relations.

For example, Mary Potter Engel demonstrates how the Protestant rubric of sin as lack of trust in God proves deeply problematic for victims of sexual and domestic abuse. Abuse victims, having been so violated by the abuser that they trust no one, often live lives governed by fear. Engel suggests that in such situations we can best interpret sin not in terms of the victims' lack of trust in God, but rather as the perpetrators' 'betrayal of trust' in violating the most sacred bonds of trust that exist between human beings (Engel 1990: 158). Abuse victims often deepen their suffering from this sin by exhibiting its underside: 'self-blame' and a 'lack of care' for themselves as they search for redemption from their perceived unworthiness (Engel 1990: 160). Blaming survivors of abuse for a sinful lack of trust in God only exacerbates this sense of unworthiness; they need first to regain self-respect and self-trust before they can lend such trust to others, including God.

To take a more mundane example, Carol Lakey Hess analyses how our culture prescribes to women a nurturing imperative by socializing them from childhood on to become the primary caregivers in their families. As a result, many women become stuck in the interpersonal phase of human development, in which a person defines herself in terms of the expectations of others or the larger group; such a one-sided focus on the wishes of others makes it difficult for women to claim self-ownership and responsibility (Hess 1997: 68). Hess concentrates in particular on the way in which religious education contributes to this 'girl-denying culture' by cultivating the virtues of humility, obedience, and submission among the faithful, thus reinforcing the message that girls and women might fall into sin by claiming their agency. She describes the spiritual effects of this gender socialization as 'prophetic torpor', a form of *acedia* that results in 'the diminished capacity to care about and respond to injustice' (Hess 1997: 44). To this spiritual sickness, Hess offers a broad-based pedagogical remedy: expand our understanding of caretaking in our churches not only by cultivating empathy with others but also by supporting vigorous dialogue based on respect for others' differences as well as encouraging the confrontation of injustice.

V. What's Happened to the Feminist Doctrine of Sin?

Before identifying some challenges which face feminist theologies of sin today, three key contributions which they have made to the discussion thus far should be highlighted. First, feminist theologians have uncovered significant hidden forms of sin. They have exposed forms of personal anguish, physical suffering, and institutional injustice that were obscured or at times falsified by classical sin-talk. By giving testimony to women's struggles with sin, feminists do more than simply add to the lengthy history of humankind's sins. They perform acts of lamentation and truth-telling that expose the deceptions involved in such situations (Chopp 1993: 13–14). Such lamentation helps individuals to acknowledge the wounds of the past and summon the strength to combat sin's ongoing force in their lives.

Second, feminist theologies of sin propose powerful strategies for restoring women's dignity, improving their self-esteem, and lending them courage to resist gender oppression. Whether couched as liberation from unjust structures, as practices of compassion, or as psychological healing, feminist remedies for sin remind us that the point of Christian sin-talk is not to assign blame or to tear persons down, but to nurture persons and communities of faith. Above all, feminist sin-talk seeks to empower women's agency and inflame their hearts with a deep passion for justice. At the same time, feminist theologies offer broad-based ethical proposals for communities of faith. As we saw above, feminist theology seeks to cultivate the values of empathy, reciprocity or mutual recognition, and care for all of creation. It seeks a 'conversion of consciousness' that will affect not only the economy of gender relations but also unjust attitudes toward the earth, the global economy, and other marginalized groups in society (McFague 1987: 119).

Third and finally, feminist theologies of sin have recovered dimensions of divine love largely lost from sight in modern theology. Most feminists express dissatisfaction with concepts of God that emphasize God's distance from creation, lack of real relationality, and impassibility in the face of radical human suffering. Instead, feminists affirm a God who is intimately involved in the world's wellbeing. Theologians such as Elizabeth Johnson or Sallie McFague do so by appealing to female imagery for God, which depicts God as, for example, a mother giving birth to and nurturing her children (Johnson 1992: 170–87; McFague 1987: 97–123). They use such metaphors not to project female gender onto God or to identify women essentially with motherhood, but rather to claim women's symbolic world as equally capable of mediating the divine. Other feminist theologians such as Ruether prefer gender-neutral language for God but still highlight God's intimate and passionate desire for relationship with God's beloved creation. Either way, feminist theologies stress the inclusiveness of divine compassion, which works tirelessly for the redemption of all things.

Without denying the fruits of the feminist debate thus far, let me offer two major challenges for feminist theologies of sin today. First, can feminist theologians develop a rubric for describing humankind's common predicament of sin? This is not to suggest that contemporary theology is ready to leave behind gendered discourse about sin. Not in the least! Given the many faces of gender oppression that feminist theologians have uncovered, Christian theology today surely needs a pluriform language and multifaceted analysis in order to describe how the gender dynamics of sin work. Furthermore, as recent debates among feminists, womanists, and post-colonial feminists demonstrate, localized discourses about sin are critical if we are not to overlook the particular afflictions besetting different communities of faith.

Even with the ongoing need for gendered discourse about sin, however, the development of a common root paradigm for sin holds out significant advantages for feminist theologies. For one, such a root paradigm affirms humankind's solidarity in sin. It reminds us that sin is an all-encompassing condition; none of us are immune to its deceptions or escape its destructive power. In other words, by anchoring gender analysis in such a root paradigm of sin, feminists underscore that patriarchy and sexism are neither just a woman's problem nor a merely passing phenomenon. A common paradigm for sin reminds us that all human beings participate in gender constructions not of their own making and therefore need to be vigilant about unmasking the injustice that such constructions may do unto others and themselves. Moreover, an inclusive definition of sin lends feminist theology a self-critical moment, so that it does not pretend any false innocence about the ways in which the victims of patriarchy also perpetrate sin against others.

But feminist theology finds itself in a tricky situation in developing such a root definition of sin. On the one hand, feminists must speak powerfully about the systemic gender oppression that pervades corporate life and cultural institutions; on the other, they must describe the distortions in personal relationships that are equally pernicious forms of sin. Certainly all theologies of sin struggle with how to adjudicate the social and the individual dimensions of sin without reducing one to the other. But this becomes a particularly delicate balancing act for feminist theology, which must do justice to the depth dimensions of gender oppression, be it in the social, linguistic, or psychological order, without portraying women as helpless in patriarchy's grip. To do so would undermine feminist theologies' ultimate aim of empowering women as agents in transforming their circumstances. While feminist theologians must encourage personal responsibility, they must also avoid the trap of blaming the victim for her plight. They should convey to women the power to resist their gendered bondage to sin without overburdening them with the charge of accomplishing their own salvation.

This first challenge of developing a root paradigm for sin bears on a second challenge for feminist theologies of sin today: Can feminist theologians develop a robust *theological* concept of sin, that is, a concept defined in terms of human beings' relationship to a transcendent God with a beneficent will for humankind? Feminist theologies of sin have largely stopped speaking of sin as either a ruptured relationship to God or a refusal of God's will for humankind. Feminist theologians steer clear of appeals to a transcendent God on the assumption that such a move would reintroduce hierarchical notions of the God–human relationship and inscribe women back into a dangerous economy of relations built on domination and dependency. As a result, feminist theologies of sin embrace a radical immanentalism that focuses exclusively on harmful realities within the created realm. They define sin either as wrong relations in human society and its institutions (the first migration), as flaws and vulnerabilities endemic to the fabric of creation (the second migration), or else as distortions in the human being's psychological and moral development and gender socialization (the third migration).

Such immanent analyses of sin clearly provide a welcome corrective to the highly individualistic and spiritualized notions of sin in much early twentieth-century theology. Nonetheless, it appears that a certain 'pragmatic atheism' (McFadyen 2000: 10) has seized hold of feminist discourse about sin. Invoking such a term is not intended to suggest that feminist theologians have given up entirely on the concept of God. As we have seen above, most have not. Rather, it is to contend more pointedly that the providential agency of a transcendent God has become superfluous to most feminist analyses of sin. Either the notion of the human being's dependence on a radically transcendent God disappears altogether from feminist theologies (e.g., Sands 1994), or, if it does appear, this relationship does not actually bear on the interpreter's analysis of sin (e.g., McFague 1987). If the charge of 'pragmatic atheism' is correct, then feminist theology has forfeited its distinctive power, beyond that of other feminist disciplines (such as psychology, philosophy, and sociology), to diagnose and denounce gender oppression in the human condition. Feminist sin-talk as it stands now may lend moral urgency or personal piety to secular critiques of women's oppression, but it has ceded the theological grounds on which it can critique the idolatry of the patriarchal order.

VI. Re-Envisioning a Feminist Theology of Sin

What might a theological concept of sin that would support the feminist theological agenda look like? Can such a concept be both capacious enough to describe human beings' solidarity in sin and still incisive enough to illuminate sin's specific gendered expressions? In the remainder of this chapter, let me sketch one way in which feminists might begin to meet these twin challenges.

A solid starting point can be found in the vision of a radically transcendent God proposed by Kathryn Tanner in her work *Jesus, Humanity and the Trinity* (2001). Tanner describes God as 'the giver of all good gifts, their fount, luminous source, fecund treasury and store house' (Tanner 2001: 1). Like many in the feminist debate, she emphasizes how God takes delight in creation and works tirelessly for its full flourishing. In the communication of divine goodness, God expresses and fulfils the providential purpose for which God created the world and, in particular, humankind.

Especially instructive in Tanner's vision of God is that she cuts the knot that feminists usually tie between a radically transcendent God and a divine economy of domination. Since God's agency operates on a different plane of causality than that of humankind, dependence on this transcendent God does not undermine the creature's agency; rather, in the divine economy of grace, the more the creature depends on God, the more empowerment she receives for her good (Tanner 2001: 3). While this divine–human relationship certainly has a hierarchical structure, it is one founded entirely on God's gracious and ceaseless self-giving, so that dependence on God becomes a source of abundant life.

Tanner also sketches a theological concept of sin that a feminist vision can turn to advantage. She defines sin in the simplest terms as a denial of or opposition to God's gift-giving nature. 'Human beings', explains Tanner, 'in this way sin, by closing their eyes to and blocking the reception of God's gifts to themselves or others' (Tanner 2001: 46). To describe this reality of sin, Tanner invokes two major metaphors, the primary one being that of blockage. In an enactment of the very opposite of the divine communication of goodness, human beings block divine gift-giving by refusing to receive the gifts, by separating themselves or others from the gifts, or else by refusing to share God's good gifts with others. In all these ways, human beings stop the free flow of God's plenitude.

Tanner takes as her second metaphor the image of blindness or closing one's eyes to the reality of God's good gifts. Here sin assumes the form of a profound mistake or self-deception about our graced identity. In sin, human beings blind themselves (or are blinded) to the boundless possibilities of receiving God's good gifts and to the human vocation of distributing these good gifts to others. With this second metaphor, Tanner reminds us that sin is at its root a lie or delusion about our true condition. Of course, our failure of vision does not mean that God halts the flow of good gifts. God continues to shower us with good gifts regardless of whether we deserve them or receive them with gladness of heart.

There are at least three ways in which this understanding of sin might meet the twin challenges posed to contemporary feminist theology of sin. First and foremost, this notion of sin weds the divine and the human, the transcendent and the immanent dimensions of sin without sacrificing one to the other. On the one hand, when we sin, we sin against God, for sin violates God's deepest desire for sharing good gifts with creation. On the other hand, sin disrupts the economy of right relations in the created realm; it manifests itself in distorted relations among individuals, societies, and the nature world. Furthermore, this notion of sin aptly describes both personal and structural sins. Although a refusal or obstruction of God's good gifts might very well name the problem of an individual human heart, it could just as well describe institutional discrimination or cultural prejudices against women. Indeed, if one recalls some of the expressions of gender oppression that feminists have identified—lack of self-care, betrayal of trust, lack of public recognition for one's work—this rubric for sin identifies their theological injustice. Such sins block women from claiming their God-given gifts and in so doing diminish their full flourishing.

Second and just as importantly, this concept of sin admits of both active and passive interpretations, which allows it to address sin as a common condition. One can speak of 'refusing' and 'being refused', of 'blocking' and 'being blocked from' the flow of God's good gifts. Such active and passive descriptions of human sin serve as more than a rhetorical flourish in a feminist theology. They permit the theologian to address the complex interplay of gender constructions and social structures in a given situation, in which it is often difficult to determine individual agency and thereby to assign singular personal responsibility. In particular, the language of 'blockage' or 'blindness' highlights the common predicament of patriarchy; both perpetrators and victims, sinner and sinned-against, possess distorted visions of the proper economy of gender relations, and therefore share in the act of sinning.

Third and finally, this rubric for sin overcomes the logic of divine retribution that many feminists rightly criticize in other classical paradigms of sin. Tanner overturns this logic primarily by using root metaphors for sin that do not rely on a forensic model of sin and justification. Her proposal does not define sin as disobedience to a moral law; nor does she uphold the notion that sin incurs judgement and punishment by a divine lawgiver. This is not to say that sin does not have deadly serious consequences; as Tanner describes them, 'our sins interrupt the reception and distribution of the free flow of divine gifts, bringing suffering and death in our train' (Tanner 2001: 86). Such sufferings do not represent, however, a divine punishment for our actions, but are the natural consequence of having disrupted the divine economy of grace. We bring suffering on ourselves and on others by blocking the reception of God's beneficence. In response to our sinful realities, God does not ruthlessly punish, but instead demonstrates the inclusiveness and depths of divine compassion: God showers victims and perpetrators alike with the good gifts needed to heal their wounds and restore their souls and bodies to abundant life.

VII. The Bondage of the Eye/I: The Gendered Condition of Sin

While this notion of sin as opposition to God's gift-giving offers us a paradigm that can both acknowledge humanity's common predicament of sin and speak of it in theological terms, this model can only take us so far in re-envisioning a feminist theology of sin. As suggested above, specific gendered discourse about sin remains essential to analysing those varied forms of oppression that women experience and to which they become captive. One way of retaining such gendered discourse would be to reform the classical metaphor for sin, 'the bondage of the will', to that of the 'bondage of the eye/I'.

This double-edged metaphor is intended to unseat the will as the privileged site for diagnosing the problem of sin. The dynamics of the will are particularly ill-suited for identifying the social or structural dimensions of sin, which resist the assignment of individual agency and therefore of culpability. Moreover, describing women's condition as the 'bondage of the will' risks reinforcing the double bind alluded to earlier, namely, of either blaming women for their own victimization or else sapping them of the personal agency necessary to resist patriarchy's force. By shifting the description of bondage to the visual sphere, gender oppression can be understood as a profound blindness or distortion in one's sight. The metaphor of 'the bondage of the eye' better describes how personal agency, gender constructions, and social structures often collude together in order to deceive women concerning their grace-filled identities. Meanwhile, the other side of this metaphor, 'the bondage of the I', draws into clear sight the fallout of gender oppression—the captivity of one's self to the desires, expectations, and needs of others.

One might well ask why the language of 'bondage' should be retained at all. Why try to wrestle a blessing from an aspect of the Christian tradition that has so plagued women's lives with guilt and paralysing self-doubt? Why not instead follow the path taken by other feminist theologians and abandon altogether the analysis of the human condition as ensnarement in sin? One critical reason for retaining the notion of the 'bondage of sin' is that this language underscores the gravity of gender troubles. The image of being held captive depicts the intractable and insidious hold which gender constructions—that *mélange* of gender expectations, stereotypes, and power relations—have upon women's and men's bodies, minds, and souls. In short, it reminds us that the problem of sexism is not merely a matter of ignorance or a denial of rights (although surely it includes both of these aspects). Sexism is a radical distortion that cuts to the core of individuals' identities and society's perceptions. Feminist theologian Serene Jones is entirely right to argue that gendered forms of oppression can have a 'total hold' on our existence; they go 'all the way down' (Jones 2000: 103).

By reframing the metaphor of bondage in the visual sphere, feminist theology can also address both the individual and the social dimensions of sexism. 'The bondage of the eye' describes most readily the predicament of an individual who fails to see through the androcentrism that distorts his perception of women's desires, needs, and gifts of grace. We can apply this term equally well, however, to institutions that turn a blind eye to their patriarchal structures. One can easily find blatant examples of such distorted vision, such as the significant wage disparities between men and women in most professions; but one might also consider social forces that are harder to spot, for example, the nearly impossible demands placed on working women who must juggle childcare and professional responsibilities, or else the stained-glass ceiling that women in the ministry regularly encounter in their churches. The metaphor of the 'bondage of the eye' seems particularly suited to identifying structural sins such as these—what theologians might call sins of omission, in which persons fail to look at or are unable to recognize gender inequities for what they are.

Beyond describing such failed individual and institutional sight, the 'bondage of the eye/I' metaphor points to the cultural forms of this gendered bondage to sin. To take just one example, this metaphor can be used to describe how women's identities are trapped by the colonizing gaze of the visual media in our culture. Curiously enough, in a 'post-feminist' age we see more examples than ever of the use of videos, television, and billboards to turn women into objects of others' visual pleasure. The power of this colonizing gaze becomes apparent when we consider how women subject themselves to 'body management practices', from workout regimens to fat-reduction programmes, in order to meet our culture's 'tyranny of slenderness' (Kim Chernin, in Bordo 1993: 33). Feminists have pointed out for years that such normalizing practices are not a matter of choice for women, but instead manifest a cultural bondage in which women homogenize their bodies to desires and standards not their own. Speaking of women's predicament as 'bondage of the eye/I' at once highlights the distorted cultural vision that women participate in when they conform their bodies to sexist images, and underscores how such gendered body ideals possess a colonizing power over women, transforming them into shadows of their true identities.

What, in conclusion, might redemption or liberation from this gendered bondage of the eye/I entail? To keep with the ocular metaphor, what might it take to clear women's vision today? Let me suggest first that clearing one's sight requires developing spiritual practices that help strip away false gender identities and distorted self-images while creating space for women's flourishing through strengthening their relationship to the divine. Christian theologians have long held that knowledge of sin requires purging oneself of false views of the self in order to gain insight about one's true identity as *imago Dei.* As feminists have pointed out, those whose selves have already been stripped away by patriarchy have to travel a quite different *via purgativa* (cf. Grey 1989: 86–9). Feminist spiritual practices must offer women positive images and experiences of the self while helping them to identify and to resist destructive ones. Such feminist spiritual practices must also involve women 'coming to their senses', that is, engaging in embodied practices that help women overcome their alienation from and distrust of their bodies. As theologian Stephanie Paulsell reminds us, women today need to rethink even the most ordinary of practices—eating, bathing, and resting—so as to celebrate the body's pleasures and to protect its sacred vulnerabilities (Paulsell 2002). While the Christian tradition may hold precious spiritual resources for the interior journey at hand, it has a terribly long way to go in formulating disciplines that cultivate reverence for women's bodies.

Clearing one's sight also requires a face-to-face confrontation with the political and material sources of women's oppression. In other words, women's redemption from 'the bondage of the eye/I' calls for linking spiritual practices with consciousness-raising and engaged social and political action. To this end feminist theologians need more than the spectacles of faith to clear their sight. They need the help of feminist critical theory—be it post-structuralist, Marxist, or psychoanalytical—to gain the power to see what has been eclipsed in theological discourse. At the same time, feminist theology needs communities of faith to act as a prophetic witness to the world by incarnating new possibilities for just gender relations in the family, the workplace, and the life of the church.

Within this proposed theological framework, Christian feminist theology must view redemption from the gendered bondage to sin as ultimately an eschatological goal; for women and men see their God-given gifts now only in a glass darkly, and await the day when they will delight in them fully. To recall the eschatological dimension of this framework is not to quell feminist passions about the present injustice of gender inequities, but simply to acknowledge feminist theology's finite vision. Feminist theology cannot see sin and redemption once and for all, nor does it possess an innocent eye that does not conceal. To claim such a vantage point would be to fall back into the Promethean sin of pride from which feminist theology seeks to emerge. More importantly, feminist models of redemption are eschatological because they do not seek to restore what once was, but to create what never has been. Therefore, gaining true feminist insight into sin requires ongoing discernment, vigilant critical inquiry, and visionary hope that women and men might one day discover the fullness of their life together.

References

Bordo, Susan (1993). *Unbearable Weight: Feminism, Western Culture, and the Body.* Berkeley and Los Angeles: University of California Press.

Chopp, Rebecca S. (1993). 'Feminism and the Theology of Sin'. *The Ecumenist*: 12–16.

—— (1995). *Saving Work: Feminist Practices of Theological Education.* Louisville: Westminster John Knox.

Chopp, Rebecca S., and Davaney, Sheila (eds.) (1997). *Horizons in Feminist Theology: Identity, Tradition and Norms.* Philadelphia: Fortress.

Engel, Mary Potter (1990). 'Evil, Sin, and Violation of the Vulnerable'. In Susan B. Thistlewaite and Mary Potter Engel (eds.), *Lift Every Voice: Constructing Christian Theologies from the Underside*, San Francisco: Harper & Row, 152–64.

Farley, Wendy (1990). *Tragic Vision and Divine Compassion: A Contemporary Theodicy.* Louisville: Westminster John Knox.

—— (2005). *The Wounding and Healing of Desire: Weaving Heaven and Earth.* Louisville: Westminster John Knox.

Grey, Mary C. (1989). *Redeeming the Dream: Christianity, Feminism and Redemption.* London: SPCK.

—— (1994). 'Falling into Freedom: Searching for a New Interpretations of Sin in Secular Society'. *Scottish Journal of Theology* 47/2: 223–43.

Hampson, Daphne (1996). *After Christianity.* Valley Forge: Trinity Press International.

Hess, Carol Lakey (1997). *Caretakers of Our Common House: Women's Development in Communities of Faith.* Nashville: Abingdon.

Johnson, Elizabeth A. (1992). *She Who Is: The Mystery of God in Feminist Theological Discourse.* New York: Crossroad.

Jones, Serene (2000). *Feminist Theory and Christian Theology: Cartographies of Grace.* Minneapolis: Fortress.

Kelsey, David (1993). 'Whatever Happened to the Doctrine of Sin?' *Theology Today* 50: 169–78.

Kvam, Kristen E., Shearing, Linda S., and Ziegler, Valerie H. (eds.) (1999). *Eve and Adam: Jewish, Christian, and Muslim Readings on Genesis and Gender.* Bloomington: Indiana University Press.

McFadyen, Alistair (2000). *Bound to Sin: Abuse, Holocaust, and the Christian Doctrine of Sin.* Cambridge: Cambridge University Press.

McFague, Sallie (1987). *Models of God: Theology for an Ecological, Nuclear Age.* Philadelphia: Fortress.

Mercadante, Linda (2000). 'Anguish: Unraveling Sin and Victimization'. *Anglican Theological Review* 82/2: 283–302.

Parsons, Susan Frank (2002). *The Cambridge Companion to Feminist Theology.* Cambridge: Cambridge University Press.

Paulsell, Stephanie (2002). *Honoring the Body: Meditations on Christian Practice.* San Francisco: Jossey-Bass.

Pauw, Amy Plantinga, and Jones, Serene (eds.) (2006). *Feminist and Womanist Essays in Reformed Dogmatics.* Louisville: Westminster John Knox.

Plaskow, Judith (1980). *Sex, Sin and Grace: Women's Experience and the Theologies of Reinhold Niebuhr and Paul Tillich.* Lanham: University Press of America.

Ruether, Rosemary Radford (1983). *Sexism and God-talk: Toward a Feminist Theology.* Boston: Beacon Press.
—— (2002). 'The Emergence of Christian Feminist Theology'. In Parsons (2002: 3–22).
Sands, Kathleen (1994). *Escape from Paradise: Evil and Tragedy in Feminist Theology.* Minneapolis: Fortress.
Tanner, Kathryn (2001). *Jesus, Humanity, and the Trinity.* Philadelphia: Fortress.
Townes, Emilie M. (ed.) (1993). *A Troubling in My Soul: Womanist Perspectives on Evil and Suffering.* Maryknoll: Orbis.

Suggested Reading

Farley (2005).
Gebara, Ivone (2002). *Out of the Depths: Women's Experience of Evil and Salvation.* Minneapolis: Fortress.
Grey (1989).
Hampson (1996).
Hess (1997).
Isasi-Diaz, Ada Maria (1993). *En la Lucha: A Hispanic Women's Liberation Theology.* Minneapolis: Fortress.
Johnson (1992).
Jones (2000).
Keller, Catherine (1986). *From a Broken Web: Separation, Sexism, and Self.* Boston: Beacon.
McFague (1987).
Pauw and Jones (2006).
Plaskow (1980).
Ruether (1983).
Sands (1994).
Townes (1993).

Index

Lightning Source UK Ltd.
Milton Keynes UK
UKOW07f0052020517
300305UK00002B/2/P

9 780199 569649